SOMETHING TO DECLARE

ALSO BY JOHN SIMON

John Simon

SOMETHING TO DECLARE

Twelve Years of Films from Abroad

 Clarkson N. Potter, Inc. / Publishers
Distributed by Crown Publishers, Inc.   *New York*

To my mother and to the memory of my father

We gratefully acknowledge the permission to reprint articles which originally appeared in *Esquire; Evergreen Review* published by Grove Press; *Maclean's Magazine; National Review; The New Leader,* copyright © 1970–73; The American Labor Conference on International Affairs, Inc.; *New York,* copyright © 1975–77 by News Group Publications, Inc; *The New York Times* © 1971–74 by The New York Times Company.

Published by Clarkson N. Potter, Inc., One Park Avenue, New York, New York 10016, and simultaneously in Canada by General Publishing Company Limited

Manufactured in the United States of America

Library of Congress Cataloging in Publication Data

Simon, John Ivan.
   Something to declare.

   Includes index.
   1. Moving-pictures—Reviews.   I. Title.
PN1995.S497 1983   791.43'75   82-16534
ISBN 0-517-549034

10 9 8 7 6 5 4 3 2 1

First Edition

*My deepest gratitude, once again, to Nancy
Novogrod. Though technically my editor, she
ended up, owing to my inefficiency, as more than
a collaborator and scarcely less than a coauthor.
And thanks also to Ellen Tarlow for her assistance.*

Contents

Preface

IT SEEMS TO ME that the title *Something to Declare* encapsulates the tragedy of foreign films in America. Though many foreign films don't make it over here, those that do are not necessarily the best. Popular success, sensationalism, or the mere fact of coming from some major film industry—French, German, Italian—may be more important than quality. But if a good foreign film does make it to America—if distributors and exhibitors do not deem it uncommercial—all kinds of duties are levied on it because it has "something to declare."

By being foreign, which usually means in a foreign language, the film automatically gets more limited distribution; plays only in special theaters, unless it happens to be something as foolish as *Diva* or *La Cage aux Folles*. A plurality of American moviegoers cannot be bothered with reading subtitles, or grapples with them only reluctantly, unenthusiastically. As a result, in many an American city (unless it happens to be a college town), foreign films can be seen either not at all or only very briefly, and then often in uncomfortable, inaccessible theaters. Exhibitors, rightly or wrongly, don't want to take chances.

Sometimes the alleged solution is to dub a film into English, just as American pictures are frequently dubbed into the language of the country in which they are being shown. But that too is slapping a heavy duty on a film: a dubbed version is never the real thing, especially if, as in this country, the dubbing is often done ineptly, indeed crudely. But it does not pay to dub most foreign films, which means that they don't get shown on television (who'd want to read those tiny subtitles, it is argued), and yet another important outlet is lost. All these penalties are, I hope, implied by the title *Something to Declare;* it is as if a cultural customs office exacted a heavy toll on a foreign film just because it is foreign. A protective tariff, as it were.

But there is something even more drastic. The problem with the better foreign films is that—unlike the majority of American movies, even the superior ones—they have something to declare, something to say. They are not just devices for killing a couple of hours, not just movie-movies. They do not merely entertain but also, by provoking thought, sustain. And for this, they incur the heavy duty of disregard. A public afraid of having to confront a little reality, to feel more strenuously committed—to think—simply stays away. Such films have something to declare, but virtually no one to declare it to.

Some people, even some persons close to me, contend that I am better on foreign movies than on American ones because of my European origins. I doubt whether this is true. But if it is, it is more likely because I am better on films that have something to say, that approach or attain the condition of art. Such films—for social, cultural, economic reasons—occur more frequently abroad. If my discussions of them generate greater interest in and appreciation for the good ones, while also demonstrating the badness of the others (which, with their artiness, pseudo-intellectualism, or mere foreignness often possess snob appeal), this book will have served its purpose.

FILMS

French Ups and Downs

HERE ARE TWO attempts by the French cinema to shake off its current torpor. The first is *Borsalino,* a gangster film by Jacques Deray. Deray is known to me only for having been, back in 1955, one of two assistant directors to Buñuel on *Celà s'appelle l'Aurore* (the other was Marcel Camus, who made the vastly overrated *Black Orpheus,* and sank back into oblivion). I don't know what he has done in the intervening fifteen years, but judging from *Borsalino,* Deray may have been constantly watching Hollywood gangster films of the Cagney-Bogart-Raft-Robinson variety, a composite of which he re-creates in a more lavish, up-to-date fashion.

Borsalino has been pounced on by American auteur critics, presumably because it poaches on preserves their memories like to haunt undisturbed. It reminds us indeed of something Raoul Walsh or Douglas Sirk might have directed for the delight of yesterday's unwashed and today's auteurists, and, being epigonous, may seem inferior. But the fact that it re-creates the Marseilles of 1930 impeccably while slightly kidding its generic models adds a certain spice to it. The script has four coauthors: Jean-Claude Carrière, novelist, playwright, and Buñuel's scenarist; Jean Cau, best known for his first novel, *The Mercy of God;* Claude Sautet, a director in his own right about whom more anon; and Deray himself. Its philosophical overtones are insufficient or excessive, and there are improbabilities such as people with reasons to believe themselves targets for gunmen not taking the least precautions; otherwise, it is a script that flows along nicely without ever soaring.

What makes *Borsalino* good fun to watch is the mood it generates and sustains: a cannily doled out mixture of meaning it and not meaning it, of nastiness and nostalgia, of ferocity and charm. The two brawling, competitive, mutually admiring and mistrustful brothers-in-mayhem, played by Jean-Paul Belmondo and Alain Delon, are commonplaces of both the American and the European film, but Belmondo's rambunctious bonhomie and Delon's waxen suavity complement each other as neatly as heads and tales—as a matter of fact, one of the running gags of the film involves a couple of rigged coins: one all heads, one all tales, side by side in Belmondo's pocket.

But the mood is sustained even more by a long succession of locations, sets, costumes, sinister or sleazy faces that evokes both a bygone era and a seemingly never-to-be-exhausted theme in consummate detail. The hierarchy of the underworld as it shades into superrespectability is perfectly captured in Francis de Lamothe's décor and Jacques Fonterey's costumes, which include the famous brand of men's hats that gives the film its title. The abundance of vintage cars, period furniture, authentically costumed extras is inexhaustible yet not, to my eye, ostentatious. Add to this a supporting cast that looks like real people, a background score by Claude Bolling that is extremely catchy (though the main theme is reprised to a fare-theewell), highly competent color photography by Jean-Jacques Tarbes, and 3 straightforward direction, and you have the stuff of sound entertainment.

Beyond that, there are Belmondo's always nimble, always vital performing and Delon's satanic good looks, although his face has become a trifle chubby of late. The reason may be inaction: in an interview, Delon spoke of his regard for Montgomery Clift, who "never moved a muscle unnecessarily," something Delon improves on by never moving a facial muscle even necessarily. But he does have those looks, and he wears fancy clothes with the ultimate of conviction. Considering that the two real-life gangsters who inspired the story ended up as Nazi collaborators, it is too bad that the film opts for a more romantic ending, yet that may be legitimate for a movie that does not aspire to the condition of art.

A film that does so aspire, however, is *The Things of Life*, by Claude Sautet, one of *Borsalino*'s coscenarists. Sautet's film—with *Borsalino*, one of the two overwhelming hits of Paris—emerges more pretentious and less remarkable. It concerns the last day in the life of a successful middle-aged architect before he dies in a car accident. Pierre, divorced from his wife, Catherine, now lives with a much younger girl, Hélène; is still torn between his old love and his new; and, in another sense, is bored and exasperated by both. With numerous flashbacks and flash-forwards, as well as generally rapid-fire editing, the film presents snippets of Pierre's memories, expectations, and quandary. There are the happy times on the Ile de Ré off La Rochelle where his wife continues to maintain their summer house; the somewhat strained relations with his son, who invents silly but lucrative electronic gadgets (e.g., a bird machine that can twitter with adjustable gaiety and requires no feeding or cage-cleaning); his friendship with François, a rather demanding companion; and his ambivalent tolerance of a cadging father.

When Pierre, after a tiff with his mistress, drives off on a rainy night to a business meeting in Rennes, these "things" of his life impinge on his consciousness until he gets involved in a freak accident that leaves him hovering between life and death. His kinfolk and friends converge on the hospital at Le Mans, where he dies on the operating table, while envisioning himself as drowning to the accompaniment of imaginary organ music that slows down (actually *se détraque:* gets out of whack) because a musician is missing. The wife takes it stoically; the mistress is shattered. *Finis.*

It is far from clear what Sautet thought he was saying with this film, which he coadapted from a novel. Perhaps the idea was to show that famous business of an entire life flashing past the eyes of a drowning man: in the film, the pieces of Pierre's life are neatly mosaicized and accounted for. But, as mosaics will, it all remains two-dimensional. Relationships are not revealed to us beyond the *données,* and we haven't the faintest idea, for example, why Hélène should be that painfully, irrevocably in love with the rather ordinary, absent-minded, even cold Pierre; what the friendship between François (dully played by Jean Bouise) and Pierre is really about; whether Pierre is in fact a dedicated architect and a genuine artist (there are brief indications pointing in contradictory directions).

4

Or Sautet may want to tell us more about dying than about life. The carefully choreographed collision, involving two trucks, shows Pierre's gun-metal Alfa Romeo performing an elaborate ballet—skidding, hurtling into a ditch, tumbling, tossing out its driver, crashing into a tree, and, finally, bursting into flames. This is shown first in slow motion, then repeated at natural speed. It also appeared behind the opening credits, and fragments of it are embedded in the body of the film. It is hard to say what Sautet is obsessed with most: the violence of the accident, death (though it proves not gloriously instantaneous but, rather as in Céline, on the installment plan), or the immolation of an expensive sports car? But obsession there is. In fact, the whole last part of the film is an almost fanatical documentary about what it is like to be involved in a fatal accident on a French highway.

There is one flaw: in one shot of the accident, the stunt driver in his crash helmet is plainly visible. Everything else is portrayed with scrupulous, documentary attention to detail. The ensuing traffic bottleneck; every type of reaction from the crowd; each thought of the dying man; all the ministrations of the police, priest, doctor, ambulance drivers, and hospital staff is minutely recorded. But it adds up to little insight, drama, or poetry. It chiefly provides the truly brilliant cinematographer, Jean Boffety, with opportunities to display his artistry—as in an extreme closeup of a bystander's boot smack in front of Pierre's eyes as he lies crumpled in the grass: alongside the boot, swaying cornflowers and poppies; on its vamp, a fat bee disporting itself. Is the message Keats's "I have been half in love with easeful Death"?

I think not. The point seems to be that dreary *chosisme* that has taken over so much of recent French thought and art: the worshipful scanning of *choses*, things. The title is a clue: *Les Choses de la vie*. Throughout, people are obsessed with objects: Pierre's son with his *trucs* (gizmos), Hélène's father with rare first editions, François with a special wine he gushes about, and so on. Dying, Pierre thinks less of his wife or mistress than of the shutter on the Ile de Ré house that needs fixing, the oval table that has been damaged, the beloved sailboat that requires some repairs. Objects are the carriers of one's history: wallpaper, a quilt, cigar stubs seen in Catherine's apartment spell out for Pierre her past and present; the auctioning off of a Renaissance commode brings together Pierre and his future mistress; a lovers' quarrel is summed up in the violent overturning of a glass of red wine. The lighting of cigarettes and the smoke oozing from them ritualistically punctuates every utterance, envelops every step of the action, and would drive the American Cancer Society insane. And there are multitudes of other objects, from shirts to oxygen masks, that the camera caresses, hovers over, burrows into.

Yet this is as superficial as the treatment of people—unlike Rilke's *Dinggedichte,* where things are explored, interpreted, made to yield up their secret inner life. Though Boffety's camera works wonders, Sautet's film merely flits from one kind of surface to another. Michel Piccoli, Romy Schneider, and the admirable Lea Massari are flattened by the film into façades.

Propaganda and Pretension

THE EIGHTH New York Film Festival brings to fruition the tendencies inherent in the undertaking from its inception. For this Eighth Festival is a scandal and those primarily responsible for it are Richard Roud, the festival director, and the Film Society of Lincoln Center, which tolerates the kind of direction Roud provides. Most of this year's festival films were not merely awful; they were so maniacally tendentious that the average liberal who sat through the lot of them—assuming that anyone but a critic or madman could have lasted the course—had to emerge as a Spiro Agnew.

The films were, with a very few exceptions, either leftist or homosexual propaganda, and, in especially felicitous cases, both. Now I have no grave objections to such slanting as long as it does not exclude artistic merit and does not come at me in long, unrelieved succession. But that is what I got, punctuated with press conferences where the directors, abetted by those who tend to constitute the audience for the press screenings and conferences, vied with one another as to who could spread the gospel of Marx and revolution most blatantly.

I realize that film is a young art, appealing especially to youth, and youth understandably gravitates to the Left and toward rebellion. I realize also that conservatism is less of a stimulant to creation than is the fiery craving for change, which seizes on any art, and film in particular, as a political weapon. Furthermore, there is something very attractive about commitment to the poor, the oppressed, the toilers, the radical idealists—at least as such commitment looks on film. Who would not espouse the ideals of the Left, without its bureaucratic despotism, its repression, its anti-individualism? Certainly a film advocating the rule of the people is more appetizing than one advocating Doris Day or America *über alles;* but when the vision becomes reality, the commissar and the prison camps prove rather less desirable than the superstar and the chain stores. It could be argued that a film is not necessarily responsible for its possible political consequences if it is a valid work of art; most of the films at the Eighth Festival, however, were unmitigated trash.

Not just ordinary trash. Stupid, pretentious, inept, aggressively boring pieces of militant anti-art, selected and fulsomely advocated by Roud and his program committee of four. Roud seems to be waging a war on bourgeois-heterosexual society. When several people asked me whether he was doing this consciously or unconsciously, I answered that I neither knew nor cared, the results, in either case, being the same. And sharing the blame for Roud's appalling selections are the Lincoln Center Film Society, the critics who review them rapturously, and that part of the audience that does not hiss and walk out on the films—as a good many people do.

Let me briefly describe some of the typical horrors. There was *Othon,* by the supremely perverse and incompetent Alsatian filmmaker, Jean-Marie Straub, whose two earlier monstrosities, *Unreconciled* and *The Chronicle of Anna*

Magdalena Bach, were the nadirs of previous New York Film Festivals. *Othon* is one of Corneille's later and weaker tragedies, dealing with a bloody power struggle in ancient Rome. It is Straub's conceit to have actors in costume play the tragedy against old Roman backgrounds. Yet the soundtrack hums with contemporary Roman traffic, and there are a few panoramic shots of the modern city. To top it off, ancient Rome is seen as ruins or restorations, and the play itself is a product of seventeenth-century France, one of the last great ages of European autocracy. So there are ironies within ironies at work here, which, on paper, might seem fairly interesting. But this intrinsically mediocre play is further undermined by Straub's production.

Some of the actors are French, but have been instructed to read their lines as fast and uninflectedly as possible, making nothing of the rhetoric that is the dubious mainstay of Corneille's later works. Just as these actors are allowed no emotion in their speech, they are not permitted to register the least facial expression. The rest of the cast are Italians, and the younger ones among them add to the other alienation effects their ghastly pronunciation of French. The older Italians, of course, cannot be kept from emoting; but what with their thick accents and the lifeless zombies around them, they end up even more absurd than the others. Furthermore, both actors and camera are held down to minimal movement; speakers are often shown only from the back, and sometimes not at all, during an entire scene. As for the anachronistic sights and sounds, even when they don't actually detract, they add nothing.

It must be remembered that the most ingenious transferrals of plays to the screen are not truly satisfactory; classic plays work even less well; and feeble classic plays, literal-mindedly transferred, rattled off by human metronomes, badly if at all directed, are intolerable. At the critics' screening of *Othon*, well over half the unusually small audience walked out, but the few dozens of fanatics who remained, applauded with that special frenzied defiance that turns critics' screenings and public showings at the festival into social or political demonstrations. *Othon* is a play in which women are reduced to preposterous pawns, though whether sexual as well as political implications induced Straub to pick it, I could not say. Certainly power looks bad in this film. But filmmaking looks much worse yet.

Another atrocity was Marguerite Duras's *La Musica*, easily as bad as, though made before, *Destroy, She Said*, one of the horrors of last year's festival. Two unutterably dreary characters, a just divorced husband and wife, mope about a nearly empty provincial hotel and speculate about their past and future. They do this in the standard Duras language, which sounds like a semidemented phrase book, or an ultra-long-playing Linguaphone record teaching zonked French to the mentally retarded.

Yet another film, *Even Dwarfs Started Small*, by a German filmmaker of less than no talent, Werner Herzog, has a cast of some twenty-six or twenty-seven dwarfs and midgets, who, ostensibly because they are condemned to live in a normal-size world, perform one outrage after another. Not only small but also misshapen, perverted, and often cretinous, these creatures, confined to an institution, are shown tormenting chickens, killing a sow, 7 parading about with a crucified monkey, breaking a camel's legs, destroying a car, climbing up on a banquet table and hurling the food at one another and all over the place, getting two blind midgets to fight each other with sticks, trying to induce two of the most imbecile among them to fornicate, eating each other's scabs, slobbering over campy thirties pinups, cutting down the one fine palm tree around, and burning the director's potted plants.

The scene is the institution's courtyard in an unspecified Mediterranean country, and the soundtrack, for no good reason, periodically erupts into the shrillest and most garish flamenco singing, often to the visual accompaniment of a one-legged hen being pecked to death by "normal" fowls. Herzog doubtless thinks that he has made a profound symbolic indictment of our society, though he cannot pick up a camera without deeply incriminating himself. But, then, the camera is rapidly becoming as associated with the hands of mental invalids as the rattle used to be with the hands of medieval sufferers from the plague.

The festival also had its obligatory Godard film, *Wind From the East,* a piece of infantile Maoist propaganda, so boring, antifilmic, sloppily made, and, yes, insane, that I can see no point in a detailed description of it. Mostly, it shows a bunch of kids acting out a mirthless parody of an American western, which is supposed to exemplify the exploitation of the Third World; in between there are the usual Godard intertitles and narration as hollowly grandiloquent as it is inflammatory, this time dubbed into English by lowbrow voices mispronouncing every conceivable word. (I particularly liked something about the lip-sick correspondent for human night—the Leipzig correspondent for *L'Humanité!*) A disciple of Godard's, a certain Marin Karmitz (the son of a millionaire businessman protégé of King Karol of Rumania), was represented by a piece of inept agit-prop called *Comrades,* teaching the workers how *not* to try to reason with management but simply take over the factories.

Agit-prop, poster art, and corny grand opera combined into a trite pageant, *The Inheritors,* by the Brazilian Carlos Diegues. Forty years of Brazilian history were compressed into two hours of politcal platitudes, high-flown revolutionary and counterrevolutionary rhetoric, and predominantly static visual non sequiturs. There were two films by Italy's most pretentious young director, Bernardo Bertolucci, who derives from both Visconti and Pasolini, while adding showiness and pseudoprofundities all his own. *The Conformist* was a piece of viscous Visconti, *The Spider's Stratagem* an exercise in combining the symbolic naturalism of *Teorema* with the mock-thriller elements of Godard's *Made in U.S.A.* Bertolucci's snide answers were a perfect match for the idiotic questions of the festival press-screening audience, and I especially cherished his comment that bourgeois anti-Fascism during World War II had nowhere near the value of Communist anti-Fascism.

Then there was *The Cannibals* by Liliana Cavani, a retelling of the Antigone story, but with Tiresias as a Christ figure—perhaps so that the odious Pierre Clémenti could be worked in (in *The Conformist,* more appropriately,

8

he played a homosexual seducer). The film is unable to update the story without making it both ludicrous and unbelievable, and the dialogue does not even pass muster as Communist propaganda. Miss Cavani, the least feminine directress seen hereabouts since Marguerite Duras, informed us during the press conference that the only attacks on her film came from the Vatican and the extreme Right, thus deftly disposing of her potential critics. She also explained that the title referred both to what the American Establishment called the blacks, and to that Establishment itself.

And so it went, which makes me want to put a question to the Film Society of Lincoln Center. Its president is an investment banker; its chairman is president and chairman of American Can and, among other things, president of Keep America Beautiful, Inc., and national chairman of Religion in American Life. He once upbraided a festival official for not showing films like *The Sound of Music.* I can understand these gentlemen's not knowing anything about film and being unable to tell a work of art from a pile of Straub, or a festival director with taste and discernment from a Richard Roud. But why, I ask, would capitalists want to sponsor a festival relentlessly dedicated to the overthrow of the values they themselves embody?

The Film Festival included an unusually large number of "Special Events," some from the French Cinémathèque, some from the American Film Institute, some from the Museum of Modern Art, which looked provocative in the program, but which a single human being, assuming he could fit them into his schedule, could not digest on top of the festival's main attractions.

Mistreatment is the first feature by Lasse Forsberg, a thirty-seven-year-old Swedish television documentarist. One problem with the film is that it is subprofessionally directed, photographed, and edited by Forsberg himself; another is that much of it was improvised by the cast and, as usual with extensive improvisation, does not work. But the worst problem is the concept underlying it. Knut, a sporadically employed stevedore (played by Knut Pettersen, who is that in real life), has a grudge against the welfare state, and steadily fulminates against it. He starts haranguing a young man who gets out of a Jaguar with a girl to the effect that he, Knut, really owns the car, seeing that he is a member of the working class that made it. When the young man tries to argue the point, Knut knocks him down.

After his arrest on an assault charge, Knut becomes the subject of various social workers' and psychologists' attention. He is invariably rude and pugnacious, and his defense is always a diatribe, sometimes neither unclever nor wholly unjustified, against bourgeois society. As he grows more and more violent, he ends up in a hospital. After a particularly savage, though again not wholly unfounded, outburst, he has to be strapped down to his bed. The film, naturally, does not begin to resolve the questions it raises. But it is clear enough that Forsberg's sympathies are with Knut, that this intelligent albeit neurotic plebeian malcontent is perceived as superior to a tolerant but conventional society that finally can do no better than straitjacket him.

9

The answer to this indictment is obvious. In a Communist society, Knut would be just as much of a misfit, for his difficulties are not social but emotional. He is fundamentally unable to accept discipline, rather more exacting in a Communist state than in Sweden. He would clearly not be driving around in a Jaguar even in the most Marxist of societies, and his loafing, recalcitrance, and hostile tirades would have calamitous consequences. Actually, the treatment accorded Knut is essentially clement and patient, and relatively individualized. And it is just this sort of fuzzy thinking and misguided sympathy that Forsberg indulges himself in that undermine a viable but imperfect democracy and send it hurtling into a so-called people's republic, which invariably turns out much worse.

A curious little English film, the first feature by Maurice Hatton, another TV documentarist, was called *Praise Marx and Pass the Ammunition*—which might have served as overall title for the festival. The movie is a handsomely photographed trifle, an affectionately mocking tribute to a clandestine revolutionary cell, showing it as both dedicated and absurd. The hero spends his days persuading workers to take over factories, and his nights revolutionizing middle-class girls in bed, his goodly repertoire of Marxist quotations proving seemingly equally efficacious for both purposes. And, of course, there are the standard squabbles between orthodox party-liners and alleged or real revisionists. It is a tepid, paltry film, but it has some sense of humor, rare in a Marxist context.

The festival also dredged up *Une simple Histoire*, by the French-Tunisian director Marcel Hanoun, who has an underground reputation as a director's director and as the secret essence of what the New Wave was really about. What we saw was a 1958 television film, with all the constricting characteristics of the genre. It is the story, based on fact, of a woman from Lille who comes to Paris looking for work and brings along a small daughter. Things go from bad to worse as no work can be found, society is harsh and unconcerned, and the woman's small stock of money rapidly dwindles. On the verge of starvation, mother and daughter are rescued by good Samaritans.

If the woman had had any sense, she would have stayed in Lille, where she had family and friends, and looked for work there. Later, with somewhat greater savings, she could have come to Paris. In any case, the Zolaesque catalogue of her misfortunes and mistreatments is presented without artistry or depth, simply as a condemnation of capitalist society, and ignores the woman's own rashness. Hanoun's two innovations are that the soundtrack superimposes the woman's first-person narrative on snatches of the actual dialogue, and that a mundane statement like "I opened the door and went out" is accompanied by its equally matter-of-fact visual equivalent. The latter device, to be sure, conveys humdrum dreariness, but in a way that is the exact opposite of art; as for the former, since there are no significant discrepancies between the dialogue and the narration, the effect is the aural counterpart of a blurred snapshot in which a face has two noses and four eyes.

Even the less manifestly leftist or anti-Establishment films of the festival tended to have at least implicitly disestablishmentarian tendencies. Alain

Resnais's elaborately trivial, grandiloquently vacuous *Je t'aime, je t'aime* contains a critique of science without conscience, i.e., in capitalist hands. A better but ultimately incoherent film, Kjell Grede's *Harry Munter,* was probably picked for the festival because of an anti-American subplot (American big-business interests wooing an independent-spirited young Swedish inventor to come to work for them in the U.S.—and in the process seducing his mother away from his father). The film, despite lovely touches, falls below Grede's earlier *Hugo and Josephine,* which Warner Brothers has yet to release.

Other films were shown, presumably, because they are the works of well-known directors: thus Satyajit Ray's primitively made, visually barren, simple-minded and sophomoric-humored *Nights and Days in the Country,* or Claude Chabrol's slickly efficient but hollow and specious *The Butcher.* Most disappointing among these was *Scavengers,* by the marvelous Ermanno Olmi, who this time came a cropper with an old-hat subject, indifferently put together for television, and containing little of that carefully and poetically articulated detail that gave his earlier works such simple nobility. (Janus Films, which bought his preceding and excellent *One Fine Day,* has been sitting on it this many a fine day.) Olmi's new film, a celebration of the scavenger as an anti-Establishment loner, fitted into the festival pattern, but did not get across even its elementary point with noteworthy forcefulness.

Before I discuss the other main features of the festival—all except the best one of them already in general distribution and, therefore, dubious choices (why should anyone bother with a single performance at Lincoln Center if, the following week, he can have the film in continual showing for fifty cents less?)—a few more general observations are in order. Two retrospectives were part of the main festival fare. One was an anthology from the films of the French Cinémathèque, entitled *From Lumière to Langlois,* accompanied by a 52-minute tribute to the Cinémathèque's director, entitled *Langlois.* Since Henri Langlois is the member in charge of retrospectives on the Festival Director Richard Roud's four-man Program Committee, this tribute to himself seemed a bit revisionist in the current context.

That program was not screened for critics, but I managed to catch the second retrospective offering, Mizoguchi's *Chikamatzu Monogatari* (1954). While I have respect for the late Kenji Mizoguchi, I find him less compelling than some three or four other Japanese directors, and this particular film (though vastly superior to the wooden *Princess Yang Kwei-Fei,* chosen by Langlois for one of the Special Events series) represents him at less than his best. But Mizoguchi has become a cult director among buffs and auteurists, and he is rapidly acquiring the kind of sacredness enjoyed by a Fritz Lang or Busby Berkeley.

Remarkably poor, and generally pretentious and arrogant as well, were this year's shorts. I will not bore you with an account of them, but will mention only that even among hardened festival fans and dedicated omnivores, walking out on the shorts reached new heights. There was one big disappointment in this category: Kon Ichikawa's documentary, *Kyoto,* which, despite a good touch or two, showed little of that director's usual mastery.

So that is what we got, thanks to Richard Roud and his committee, 11 consisting of Andrew Sarris, Arthur Knight, Susan Sontag, and Henri Langlois. Exactly how the committee functions is unknown: Roud refused to answer questions on this subject. Two facts are apparent: (1) Roud picked its members because their tastes do not significantly differ from his; and (2) in any normally managed operation, such a committee would not remain the same from year to year. I have often enough expressed my opinions of Sarris and Sontag, and see no need to repeat myself here. About Knight I concern myself as little as about the movie reviews in the *Los Angeles Times,* from which his are indistinguishable. Roud's own criticism can best be gauged from the blurbs for the festival program, mostly the product of his leaky pen. Concerning *The Inheritors,* he writes: "The surrealist succession of betrayal and compromise is rendered beautifully by the constant shifting of the camera angle, the vertiginous spatial ambiguity and total meta-theatricality."

If you think that preposterous, consider Roger Greenspun's review *(New York Times,* September 14) of the festival's most brazenly uncinematic film, Jean-Marie Straub's *Othon,* discussed on a preceding page. Greenspun's critique contains gems of metacriticism that even Roud would find hard to match—gems, in fact, worthy of Greenspun's mentor, Sarris. We read: *"Othon* is magnificently performed by its almost expressionless cast," and, better yet, "This year, as in the past, the festival paid Straub its greatest tribute (the only valuable, though not infallible, objective test of a film's importance I know of) when at the press screening of *Othon* half the audience got up and walked out." Poor Greenspun! The number of his favorites that must have flunked his "objective test" can be equaled only by that of his pet peeves that triumphantly passed it, but I do hope he gets to see many more films by this master in an emptied hall. Goethe's Mephistopheles said it (more or less): *"Straub soll er fressen, und mit Lust."* As for Roud, he has already been fired from his two other jobs, as director of the London Film Festival and film critic of the *Guardian.* Patience may wear out in New York too.

October 5–19, 1970

A Garden of One Delight

THE ONE thoroughly fine film of the festival was the Spaniard Carlos Saura's *The Garden of Delights,* which may also have been picked for its veiled anti-Fascism rather than for its shining excellence. It tells of a great Spanish industrial family whose fortune is declining, and its desperate machinations to rekindle the memory of the eldest son, now fiftyish, left partly crippled and amnesiac by an auto accident. This Antonio is being manipulated in elaborate and frantic ways by his father, wife, and grown children into remembering the number of one of those anonymous Swiss bank accounts where he secreted large sums that both the family and the factories could now use. As mnemonic jolts, various traumatic scenes from Antonio's child-

12

hood and young manhood are reenacted for him (an actress has been engaged to play his dead mother), but the reenactments now take on both farcical and sinister coloration.

The film proceeds parallelly on four levels: the reenactments; Antonio's independent memories of the past, often pertaining to a lusty aunt with whom he had a protosexual relationship; the events in the present, in which he struggles to relearn speech, writing, and thinking, and suffers several pathetic setbacks; and, finally, events in a limbo or dreamworld where certain visions, usually painful or frightening, torment Antonio. There are bits here that do not work—notably a walk through a ruinous machine shop, and a longish flashback showing Antonio persuading his father to expand the family business into big business. Almost everything else, however, adds up cogently to a hallucinatory vision of personal and familial greed emblematic of a nation's decay.

Consider, to begin with, one of the less predigious scenes. Antonio, sitting in his wheelchair in the garden, has wearied of practicing to re-create his signature with his semiparalyzed right hand. He listens to the birds singing in that huge park of a garden. They are delicious songsters trilling away at leisure, but every once in a while a crow or raven intrudes on the concert. Suddenly, as Antonio listens with befuddled intensity, the raven's croak changes into something darker still, the neighing of a horse. And presently, among the tall bushes, we begin to catch glimpses of a knight in armor—three of them, in fact. We even see bits of physiognomy behind a not entirely close-fitting visor—could these be rustics hired by the family? But no; the knights prepare to charge. They gallop, lances lowered, across the broad lawn where most of Antonio's visions crop up. (The film is named after the Bosch painting at the Prado, *The Garden of Earthly Delights,* showing monsters of sensuality disporting themselves.)

Antonio rises from his wheelchair and manages to stagger into his wife's room. She primps in front of her mirror and complains about their children to her uncomprehending husband. Next, she tries to get him to reveal the combination to his wall safe hidden—the camera captures this fact with rapid casualness—behind an engraving of three mounted knights in battle array. By showing the effect before the cause, Saura re-creates in us his hero's puzzlement.

The scenes in which the greedy family tries to jog, jolt, or needle Antonio's memory back into functioning are all perfect blends of the hilarious and gruesome, and at the same time comment wryly on present-day Spanish society. For example, when Antonio's father has a documentary of the Civil War screened for his amnesiac son, we are drawn into Antonio's bewilderment as bedraggled troops hurtle on while a female voice recites verses from Rubén Darío. With sudden, cruel comedy, the father bursts through the screen in Phalangist uniform, back from the wars and trumpeting the victory. "The film . . . the film . . ." the son keeps muttering, and indeed, as the woman's voice sobbingly declaims on, the film continues to lurch across the shattered screen, looking as unvictoriously frazzled as Antonio, whom his father is already dragging toward a new ordeal. The Civil War emerges as a   13 tasteless joke here, a cheap trick to bring back a misplaced memory, and even that only to recoup the money locked up in that memory.

Or take the opening scene in which Antonio, in his wheelchair, is forced into a room of the sumptuous family house with a large, stentorian pig, to re-create the occasion when, as a five-year-old, he was locked into the pigsty as punishment for some petty offense. The pig hustled through the living room, an actress being made up to look like Antonio's dead mother, the father wearing a ludicrous toupee to become his former self, the house being refurbished to appear as it did decades ago, the phonograph playing a dripping popular song of the time crooned by Imperio Argentina and bearing the ironic title "Recollection," a helpless grown man mumbling "No! No!" as a nurse wheels him toward a carved oaken door from behind which malevolent oinks are hitting him in the face, a whole family in a hubbub to make the wretched reenactment come off—all this gains immeasurably in effectiveness by Saura's dumping it in our laps without explanation. That we have to unscramble it gradually, makes the weirdness more dizzyingly alive.

Within this appalling, brilliant context even individual lines assume ominous intensity. Thus, while removing his toupee, the father assures the family that he pitied his son even when he was first obliged so to punish him: "For years the poor boy would see himself surrounded by pigs." Throughout the film, dialogue has this kind of savage resonance. When the auto accident responsible for his amnesia is conjured up by Antonio as happening on the spacious lawn that sprouts memories and daymares, we hear him moan out a line he has spoken before, but taking on full significance as he slumps, bloodied, behind the wheel, and once we have seen sequence after sequence of familial brainwashing: "Do what you like with my body," he groans, "but do not touch my head!" We grasp that this is what the family has been doing to him, from infancy to amnesia: messing with his head.

As penetratingly as it uses images, sounds, dialogue, even single lines, the film uses music, too. When Antonio envisions the Civil War as a pitched battle between two gangs of children hurling stones at one another from behind wooden shields—again on that lawn of the garden of delights—the soundtrack gives out with Prokofiev's battle music from *Alexander Nevsky*. There is a magnificent contradiction between that noble, patriotic music and these nasty, senseless little games, that become earnest and horrible as the shields and the foreheads behind them begin to crack open.

Then there is the scene where Antonio's wife drives him back to a park and fountain in Aranjuez that have romantic associations for them; just before they get out of the car, she starts the lovely slow movement of Rodrigo's "Concierto de Aranjuez" on the car cassette-player. The evocative music clings to the pair on their sentimental walk through the park; but the quick preceding shot of a gloved hand locking the cassette into place and calculatingly starting up the mechanism with that insinuating adagio movement, undermines, even cancels, the music's tenderness.

The Garden of Delights is full of bizarre felicities, not the least being the casting of the noted comic actor, José Luis López Vázquez, in the serious yet also somewhat absurd part of Antonio. Since it is a near-nonspeaking role, much of it done wedged into a wheelchair, everything depends on facial play. Vázquez's expressions—the way he wiggles his eyes, the ruffling and unruffling of his brow—are unsurpassable in their bedeviled, funny-sad grotesquerie. Saura helps with camera angles that are just a little odd, and timing full of creative dawdling.

Incisively photographed by Luis Quadrado, the film is directed with the unassuming smoothness that Saura must have learned from his master, Buñuel, at his best. The concluding scene, Antonio's abdication, his opting out, is conveyed by a visual metaphor that is strikingly simple yet rich in overtones, and a fitting climax for this adult and intelligent film. Shockingly, *The Garden of Delights* has not acquired an American distributor; unless it does, we'll be deprived of what I consider, after Bergman's *A Passion,* the best film of the year.

The remaining festival films were promptly available in general showings, and one, *Kes,* has already bit the dust. Ken Loach's film is the story of Billy, a small squelched boy in a shabby Yorkshire mining town, who has a bullying wretch of an elder brother and an absentee mother. Billy steals a kestrel chick from its nest, and, with a likewise stolen book on falconry, proceeds to tame and train the bird. The relationship between hawk and boy contrasts with the child's unhappy school and home drudgery; similarly, the luminously soaring bird is the opposite of the grimy descent into the coal pits, which Billy will not tolerate.

But despite increased naturalism, neither the screenplay nor the direction manages to soar above the usual boy-and-his-(you fill in the name of the creature) story. The Yorkshire accents are genuine to the point of impenetrability, the photography is routine, and Loach lacks a sense of rhythm and proportion. Thus the boy-bird scenes are relatively sparse and underdone, whereas a comic soccer game and other school disasters are overextended, funny though they be. Young David Bradley plays Billy with an authenticity that is rather too literal, and for all its honestly bitter taste, *Kes* is a bit like a tall glass of warm, flat porter.

Another film with a juvenile protagonist, Truffaut's *The Wild Child,* was the festival opener and arrived with considerable advance fanfare. It is the late-eighteenth-century true story of a wild boy, aged twelve or thirteen, who was discovered running about naked and on all fours in the woods of Aveyron, France, and was presumed to have been brought up by wolves. When the boy was captured and transported to Paris, experts were all set to condemn him to an institution for the hopelessly retarded; but Dr. Jean Itard, a specialist in the training of the deaf, convinces colleagues and authorities that he can redeem this child for human society. He takes the boy to his suburban house, complete with a large, kindly housekeeper, Mme Guérin, and proceeds to civilize him patiently, strenuously, and with a nice blend of sternness and humanity.

The film follows Dr. Itard's diary fairly closely, I gather, in retracing the difficult, tentative steps of the boy's progress: the ingenious yet simple experiments; the occasional triumphant leaps ahead often followed by retrogression; the almost disheartening slowness of it all brightened by modest advances. Truffaut uses a deliberately old-fashioned technique: simple décor, stiff camera setups and less than fluid movements, much irising in and out of scenes, and a patchwork of brief sequences that is suggestive of the one- and two-reelers of yesteryear. The elaborate narration from Itard's journal (delivered by Truffaut himself in rather awkward English) and the severe black-and-white cinematography of Nestor Almendros bespeak a bygone era while also contributing Brechtian *Verfremdung*. The fact that Truffaut himself plays Itard rather inflexibly and self-consciously, as directors often will, increases the alienation effect.

In a sense, the tight, geometrical, syllogistic movement of the film conveys the mechanistic, rationalistic, positivist concepts of life and society in the eighteenth century. The boy suffers a relapse, returns to nature, finds that he is no longer equipped for the wild life, distressedly comes back to the doctor who happily continues his education. After he makes some further progress, the uncomprehending boy is told by Itard that he is no longer a beast though not quite yet a man. And the film ends on the hopeful note of Victor, as Mme Guérin named the child, learning and developing.

The facts of the case are that the real-life Victor never properly learned to talk, remained incapable of all but menial tasks, stayed under Mme Guérin's care, and died in his early forties. Not exactly a splendid success for culture and medical science. But Truffaut apparently wants to tell us that, however exhilarating the freedom of the forest animals may be, becoming a social animal is better. In order to make that point, he has to cut off his story early, and that makes for an undramatic and dishonest ending.

There is ambivalence here. Itard is not without wistfulness about the natural existence from which Victor has been wrenched, and Almendros's otherwise chaste cinematography gets almost lush in some of the forest scenes. It is as if the doctor—or Truffaut—had to prove to himself as well that the civilized state is superior, so that the zeal and effort were expended not only in behalf of science and the child. But such complexity, if it was intentional, would require a richer script and a better actor than Truffaut to bring it out. Jean-Pierre Cargol, the gypsy boy whom Truffaut dug up to play Victor, is very good. Not adorable, yet fetching; neither handsome nor plain, he is actually, or artistically, all spontaneous naturalness. The impact of the film is due in large measure to him, and I can only hope that he will evolve more pleasantly than that other Truffaldian Jean-Pierre, the by now insufferable Léaud, to whom the film is dedicated.

As long as Truffaut was going to make a film about a wild child (and there were several cases of unwanted and abandoned children surviving in the woods), I wish he had picked the much more interesting case of Kaspar Hauser. This boy, found in a hollow tree near Nuremberg in 1828, proved eminently intelligent, and was mysteriously killed five years later. Both the facts and the legends attached to the case are absorbing, and Kaspar Hauser has been the subject of many works of prose and verse, among which Jakob Wasserman's novel is the most important. Still, *L'Enfant sauvage* is a nice enough minor film, and worthier of Truffaut's talents than the brides and mermaids he has been dabbling with of late.

The Old Masters were represented at the festival by Buñuel's *Tristana*. A tidily directed film, it is based on a novel by the Spanish Balzac, Pérez Galdós, from whom Buñuel previously derived his *Nazarín*. I have not read the novel, but would wager that it makes more sense than the film does, with its Gothic excrescences and nonsensical central figure. This Tristana is an innocent young orphan girl in Toledo circa 1920 (updated from the novel), who becomes the ward of Don Lope, a former admirer of her mother's. A charming, impoverished elderly roué, he still cannot resist a pretty girl and lives by a chivalric code of genteel poverty and fierce anticlericalism. With his faithful servant Saturna, they subsist on whatever he can get from hocking family heirlooms. When Don Lope can no longer resist Tristana, whom he asked to regard him as a father, he persuades her to regard him as a husband as well. Though unenthusiastic, the girl becomes his mistress without demur, in an almost uncannily matter-of-fact way.

Her heart, to be sure, is not in it, especially since he is a jealous old goat. She meets a handsome young painter, Horacio, practically flings herself at his feet, conveys to him her intense hatred for Don Lope, and after he has buffeted her about a little for no longer being a virgin, and has likewise punched Don Lope in the nose for being an old goat and having conceived the ridiculous notion of challenging him to a duel, Tristana gets Horacio to elope with her. We learn that they have been living together quite well, comfortably but not luxuriously—whereas Lope has inherited a fortune from his devout sister who did not talk to him during her lifetime. Tristana develops a tumor in one leg, thinks she will die, insists that she be taken back to Lope, which Horacio obligingly does.

The result is that Horacio is forthwith despised by Tristana as a weakling, Lope resolves never to let the girl go again and takes care of her in grand and loving style. Tristana's leg is amputated, Horacio is sent packing. The girl, though somewhat embittered, manages well enough with her artificial limb (on which Buñuel dwells with his customary fetishism); she even plays the piano quite nicely, but is full of contempt for Lope's doting love.

Nevertheless, she marries him, and treats him as shrewishly as possible, denying herself to him sexually both before and after the wedding. She now gets her kicks from playing strange games with Saturna's deaf-mute son. Back when he was a problem child, the young Tristana already felt a queer kinship for him; now that he is a rather sullen servant to Don Lope, she resists his advances but shows her naked breasts to him from the balcony while he gapes upward in mute torment. Don Lope sinks into senility and becomes quite friendly with the clergy who come around to sponge a little; Tristana grows bitterer and meaner, does not call the doctor when the old man lies abed in chills and fever, indeed opens the window at dawn, so that he is sure to catch his death, and she to inherit his wealth.

Even if Buñuel had not worked in some of his usual tricks, such as Tristana's recurrent nightmare in which Don Lope's severed head appears to her 17 as the clapper in a giant bell, the film still would not make sense because the heroine's eccentricities and turnabouts remain as unsounded as they are unsound. Nothing is motivated or analyzed; every weird switch has to be taken on faith. Don Lope's character is more real—though even here there are some disturbingly unanswered questions—and he is thoroughly humanized by Fernando Rey's warm portrayal, a further refinement of a role Rey created in *Viridiana.*

In the part of Saturna, Lola Gaos oozes decency and dignity, and there is much to be said for the somber, burnished look with which José Aguayo's camera endows the remoter byways of Toledo. But neither Catherine Deneuve nor Franco Nero can act beyond a pout or grimace (one almost feels that the dubbing into Spanish helps their performances—though, alas, not enough), and *Tristana* leaves one with a sense of forced oddity, willful distortion, and wasted directorial skill.

October 19–November 2, 1970

Firebrands

Cromwell, a film written and directed by Ken Hughes, defies assessment. One learns that Hughes's version is at least forty-five minutes longer than the print Columbia has seen fit to release, and that the director is thoroughly unhappy about it. Certainly what we are seeing is inconsistent with any logical presentation of the story. Characters whose importance we know from history—or, failing that, from the billing they get on screen and in the program—are reduced to walk-ons or bit players in the released version. The years of Cromwell's protectorship are summarized in a few sentences of narration as the image switches from the troubled living man to his catafalquelike cenotaph.

There is no getting around the feeling that in this *Cromwell* we behold a historic tapestry on which multitudes of exceptionally hungry moths have been feasting away. What remains, despite its historical inaccuracies, is often impressive though rarely affecting. The question of faithfulness to historical data is a tricky one. I would say that where the historical fiction merely incorporates facts in a magnificent imaginative construct, a certain amount of poetic license can be forgiven. But where the mind at work is not that of a true creative artist, only that of a competent literary or filmic journalist, observance of historical facts becomes, if not a necessity, at least a useful compensation for what is lacking in genius. What is bothersome about this film is its unsubtle idealization of Cromwell; although Charles I is presented in an essentially balanced manner, Cromwell is made more pure than puritanic, more profoundly right than priggishly righteous. The film tries to show us the man, warts and all, yet it minimizes the outer and inner warts into mere beauty or blind spots.

18

Nevertheless, the battle sequences are among the very best I have ever seen, striking a nice equilibrium between detail and overview, between dizzying turmoil and clear perspective. They remind me, *mutatis mutandis,* of those in *Henry V,* and for battle sequences that is high praise indeed. Then there are some extremely fine performances. Richard Harris's Cromwell, to be sure, is rather uneven—largely because his vocal quality fluctuates between fascinating roughness and a constrained squeakiness that left me in doubt as to which would break first: Harris's vocal cords or my eardrums. There are times, also, when the actor strikes poses more suited to pageants on the village green than to film, but this may be the director's dark doing. Otherwise, Harris does a very creditable, occasionally even stirring, job; above all, he succeeds in keeping his rampaging intensity suitably leashed.

Even if Alec Guinness looks and acts a slightly older and more threadbare Charles than history indicates, he gives a dignifiedly worldly, quietly felt performance, unmarred by that irritating self-indulgence, or self-parody, he has often fallen into in recent years. Here his modulations are almost microscopically subtle, his effects never easy, and the very pathos sternly soft-pedaled. He may look less like a grandiose Van Dyck than a modest Ter Borch, but he still looks quite splendid. As his queen, Dorothy Tutin may be a mite more shrewish than necessary, but she strongly resembles Henrietta Maria and is a good enough actress to make even a simplistic interpretation come bitingly alive.

No less important are the performances by a number of excellent British character actors. Frank Finlay's John Carter and Patrick Magee's Hugh Peters have been chopped down to a few shreds, as has Zena Walker's Mrs. Cromwell (adding insult to injury, the American gala program misidentifies the distinguished Miss Walker as "Josephine Gillick"). But others come through handsomely. Douglas Wilmer is wonderfully dour, decent, brave, and scrupulous as that Fairfax whose name, Milton tells us, "fills all Mouths with Envy or with Praise"; Nigel Stock is a tower of tormented strength as Hyde, the future Earl of Clarendon; Michael Jayston is a grimly headlong Ireton; Geoffrey Keen is a robustly upright John Pym (whom the program does not even bother to list). And though Robert Morley overdoes the Earl of Manchester, Charles Gray is a superbly contemptuous, glacial Essex. Timothy Dalton is a dapper Prince Rupert, but the script or the cutting turns him into a stereotype, and there is little justification for the scenario's fusing Bishops Judson and Laud.

Still, the film holds one's interest, not least because of Geoffrey Unsworth's intelligent color photography. Unsworth (best remembered for *Becket* and *2001*) uses color vividly, not lushly; he strives for faithfulness rather than bravura, but can, in the right places, produce spectacular effects. These include the nightfall when Pym and Ireton, at the beginning of the film, ride out to seek Cromwell, and, later, that strange, almost more steely than somber dusk in which Cromwell confronts the body of his fallen son. What remains of *Cromwell* is less than memorable, but Ken Hughes (whose *Trials of Oscar Wilde* is an unjustly neglected movie) provides us with some lively watching all the same.

Some cutting has also been done—in this case by United Artists—on Gillo Pontecorvo's third film, now entitled *Burn!* and twenty-five minutes shorter than the director intended. But here the cuts, while very likely inept and damaging, at least do not interfere with and obscure history. It is sad to think that this high-sounding and essentially hollow film is the work of the man who in *Battle of Algiers* made one of the most restrained yet shattering films of recent times, so real that most people mistook large chunks of it for newsreel footage. Of course, there was Pontecorvo's melodramatic and cliché-ridden first film, *Kapo,* to which *Burn!* bears a greater resemblance.

The new film is the story of Sir William Walker, a British secret agent sent to Queimada, a Portuguese colony in the Caribbean. Both the island and the agent are, often painfully, imaginary. "Queimada" means "burned," because the island was razed by fire in the sixteenth century and repopulated with African slaves. They are now beginning to revolt, and Walker is here to stir up trouble for Portugal to the benefit of England. (There were actually no such hostilities between England and Portugal in the mid-nineteenth century, but I shall explain that later.) Walker finds that the powerfully built black who carries his bags is material from which a native leader could be forged. So he trains this José Dolores and his followers in guerrilla warfare, gets them to rob a bank, then denounces them to the Portuguese authorities. Now they are outlaws and the rebellion is on.

Walker's next step, taken with the assistance of a friend, the mulatto clerk Sanchez, is to persuade the colonists to join the blacks in a revolution against Portugal. This comes to pass. Walker helps Sanchez kill the governor, and when José Dolores, though a most able general, discovers that he and his blacks cannot govern the island, Sanchez is appointed president. José and the freed slaves withdraw to the mountains of the interior, and the settlers and mulattoes rule the island with the help of the British sugar company. As Walker returns to England, he mentions another assignment in Indochina. Here an important clue is let out of the bag, or, more precisely, hurled at us, bag and all.

Ten years later, Walker is summoned back to Queimada. The colonist regime, puppet of the British sugar company, has proved only slightly preferable to that of the Portuguese. José Dolores and his men have started a new revolution. Things are bloodier than ever, but when Sanchez finally makes a weak effort at doing right, Walker, with colonial and British support, gets him executed. Now it is Walker and several regiments of British redcoats against his former disciple and protégé, once almost his friend. José is finally captured and, firmly resisting Walker's attempts to save him, chooses martyrdom for the cause. A defeated victor, Walker is about to re-embark for England when a voice, reminiscent of José's years ago, offers to carry his bags. As he holds them out to the supposititious porter, he is stabbed to death by him: Walker's lessons and José Dolores's example live on and bear fruit.

Some of the film's inconsistencies are caused by the fact that it was first laid and shot in the Spanish colonies, where it would have made more sense. But the Franco government stopped cooperating and threatened a boycott.

So the oppressors had to become the Portuguese and the shooting was transferred to Colombia, the Caribbean, and North Africa. Some cuts and changes were necessitated by this; other bits were hacked out later in New York. But *Burn!* is basically uneditable; it is full of ideological rhetoric, pregnant with heavy political innuendo, virtually predestined for a primer of black revolution.

The characters are rudimentary, like Sanchez, or do not make sense, like Walker. Who is this Sir William? What sort of private life does he have? Why do his words make sense (let's not turn these blacks into martyrs) and his actions not? For he seems to have nothing but contempt for the British, yet serves them all too well; he appears to be full of admiration for José Dolores and his cause, yet he destroys them, or tries to. Such contradictions can be resolved; their examination might, in fact, be most rewarding. But the film prefers just to make pronunciamentos or shoot action sequences that can get along very well without involvement from us.

Despite this, Pontecorvo shows ability. The beginning of the film is quite gripping, and there are good crowd scenes. With the help of his cinematographer, Marcello Gatti, he captures colored skins and colorful costumes against white buildings with a pastel lyricism. Jungle warfare, guerrillas being burned out of their hideouts and cozily mowed down as they come running through the flames, mass executions—many such grim incidents and details are well managed, though one misses the absolute lifelikeness of *Battle of Algiers.*

Moreover, though Renato Salvatori's performance as Sanchez does not amount to much (he may have been cut too severely, his English is poor and his make-up wretched), Evaristo Marquez, an illiterate Colombian peasant, is marvelous as José Dolores: handsome, masterful, exuding both strength and strength of purpose, and surprisingly convincing as an actor. But the score by that most fascinating composer, Ennio Morricone, miscarries, and Marlon Brando gives his by now customary affected performance as Walker. His English accent, though not bad, sounds rather like an impersonation of Queen Elizabeth II, and I expected him to break into that notorious "My husband and I . . ." any moment. He may have sunk more effort into his accent than into his acting.

A curiously unmoving film, this, in which even José Dolores, finally, makes no sense: his transition from illiterate slave to quite well-informed, worldly-wise, and profoundly philosophical leader is too swift, easy, and unconvincing in the script or editing. Like Walker, he is denied a private life, or any bit of personality unrelated to his function as a revolutionary general. Pontecorvo and his scenarists, Franco Solinas and Giorgio Arlorio, have proceeded too schematically, and produced a poster, a poster already frayed and half torn off its wall.

Claude Chabrol's *This Man Must Die* is a film coated with surface glitter. A recent Chabrol retrospective at the Museum of Modern Art, though incomplete, sufficed to confirm me in my opinion that Chabrol possesses a mixture of slick technical facility and a mind preoccupied with human stupidity, perversion, and madness. This makes him pass for an artist among 21 those who read the mixture as cinematic art combined with psychological profundity. But let me grant Chabrol the unpredictability of unevenness, enabling him to make movies as awful and imbecile as, for instance, *Ophelia, Leda,* and *The Third Lover,* and also, at least once by some lucky accident, *La Femme infidèle.*

There is, of course, a middle ground to which *This Man Must Die* belongs. It is the story of a man tracking down the hit-and-run driver who killed his son. He gets involved with the beastly culprit and various members of his family, has an affair with the beast's sister-in-law and becomes a father-surrogate to the beast's son, and—well, I suppose I must not reveal the tricky ending. Typically, the plot (derived from a novel by Nicholas Blake, a pen name of the present Poet Laureate) keeps uneasily shifting between contrivance for purposes of suspense that is never very suspenseful, and attempts at high seriousness, social commentary, and art that are mostly showy posturings.

Once more Chabrol trots out his stable of trusted undependables. Jean Rabier comes up with the usual misty proto-pastel effects, and a limited palette that wants to look subtle but ends up looking washed-out. The screenplay, as so often, is a collaboration between Chabrol and Paul Gégauff, who again parades his feeble literary jokes. Thus when a provincial housewife tries to impress a visiting minor writer with her literary erudition, her benightedness and clumsiness are laid on with a trowel that might have been borrowed from Bob Rafelson. (Chabrol sticks in a cute in-joke when, after listing her preferred *nouveau-roman* writers, the woman hesitantly adds, "Even Gégauff . . .") Helping a young student with his homework on the *Iliad,* the hero pontificates: "Kafka is, in a way, the same thing, but Homer is more beautiful." Yet this novelist-hero and champion of high art (Chabrol is the same thing, but less beautiful) will say: *"Tu réalises ce que tu dis?"*—where *réalises* is a thoroughly nasty bit of Franglais. Even the score by the faithful Pierre Jansen is back to that erratic music-making that was his before he hit on the felicities of *La Femme infidèle.*

November 16–30, 1970

Lean Years

MOST FATUOUS of the current blockbusters is David Lean's *Ryan's Daughter.* In well over three hours of Super Panavision, with what seems like the entire West Irish coast getting into the act, with a whole elaborate stone village built for the film, and at a cost of $13.6 million, Lean and his scenarist Robert Bolt have told a simple-minded story. It concerns a young publican's daughter in a tiny coastal village of Ireland who gets a widowed school-teacher to marry her, only to find him not the romantic hero of her dreams. The time is 1916, and a new British commander is appointed to the small local garrison. He is a shell-shocked major with a leg wound that gives him a Byronic limp, but also likens him to the misshapen and hobbling village idiot.

Our heroine, Rosy Ryan, and this young, unhappy, dashing aristocrat fall instantaneously and madly in love. Charles, the patient and kindly husband, waits for the passion to burn itself out and says nothing. An IRA commander comes to the village with his men during a violent storm to pick up guns and ammunition the Germans are floating over to him from a boat. Rosy's father, the publican, betrays them to the British, for whom he has been informing all along. The villagers, who have always hated Rosy for being a "Princess," and now for carrying on with a British major, assume that she betrayed the Irish heroes and publicly strip her and shave her head.

The major, with whom Rosy had already broken off her affair, commits suicide by blowing himself up with some of the German dynamite. The wise, hard-drinking, tough but kindly village priest—who, like the village idiot, keeps weaving in and out of the action rather arbitrarily—now helps Charles and Rosy leave the village for Dublin. They are jeered by the crowd, but Father Hugh suggests to Charles that the profoundly chastened couple should not separate as they plan to upon reaching the city. On this note of tantalizing uncertainty the film ends, leaving me as unconcerned with its outcome as with its 189 minutes of preceding hokum.

Lean has got the usual eloquent imagery from his immaculate cinematographer, Freddie Young. The astutely chosen locations, the marvels of nature are shot with a scope and definition and technique that would have made James Fitzpatrick of the travelogues slobber with envy. But who needs the puny people and trite plot, not to mention the dialogue straining to be understated and significant, to clutter up the Panavision? The villagers are shadowy, the minor characters dimensionless, and the principals seem to be carved from used celluloid (B-movie variety). This is the sort of film in which the lover appears on the scene with an immense sunset haloing him from head to dragging foot, seduces the heroine under orgies of sunlight in the overhanging leaves (and a forest of symbols all around), haunts his mistress as a mighty apparition silhouetted on a hillside against the night sky, and blows himself up only after watching the fieriest of suns sink into the sea.

But I could even believe in this dime fiction more than in Robert Mitchum as a shy, sensitive, somewhat repressed, Beethoven-loving Irish schoolmaster; and much more than in Christopher Jones as a darkly brooding, psychically and physically damaged, equally sensitive (though less repressed) British major. The one thing authentic about Jones is his accent, and that was dubbed in by someone else; about Mitchum, undubbed, nothing is genuine. Sarah Miles is a sexy and charming Rosy, but not the actress who could carry this Leviathan on her back. Only Trevor Howard, as the priest, and John Mills, as the idiot, score Pyrrhic victories.

David Lean is altogether a strange case: a man afflicted with gigantism, who wants to make bigger and bigger movies even though his small and medium-sized ones are often very good, and his big ones tend to be disappointing. *Hobson's Choice,* a small family comedy with social overtones, based   23 on a play and set in a small town, is one of the finest comedies the English film—rich as it is in savory comedies—ever produced. With the collaboration of Noël Coward, Lean made those two somewhat sentimental yet enormously affecting films, *In Which We Serve* and *Brief Encounter,* still modest in size, though the British Navy played a goodly part in the former—but nothing like the starring role Darryl F. Zanuck would have given it. Even here it was perceptible, however, that while Lean was a very fine craftsman indeed, he ultimately lacked the intense imagination, the vision of the artist.

Notable, too, were Lean's two medium-large, fetching adaptations from Dickens, *Oliver Twist* (mutilated in America at the insistence of Jewish pressure groups) and *Great Expectations,* the latter flawed only by the unappealing Valerie Hobson, the producer's wife, as the grown-up Estella (the adolescent one was ably and alluringly embodied by Jean Simmons). Then came Hollywood and the big films, beginning with *The Bridge on the River Kwai,* a solid entertainment based on a bestseller, beautifully acted, photographed, and directed, as Lean's films generally are; but, typically, Lean changed the movie's ending to something more upbeat than Pierre Boulle, hardly a profound novelist, had provided. Now Lean discovered his favorite screenwriter, the respectable upper-middlebrow playwright Robert Bolt, author of one good play, *A Man for All Seasons,* and several poor ones.

The first Lean-Bolt collaboration was *Lawrence of Arabia,* which also marked the arrival of another partner of almost equal importance, the superb cinematographer Freddie Young (sometimes billed as Frederick, sometimes as Fred A., but by any name inspired). *Lawrence* was an important film because it proved that a huge spectacular could be made intelligently and artistically, large production values not excluding literacy—something never fully achieved before or since. To be sure, history was tampered with, often without compensatory gains in artistry, and a certain lack of depth was frequently felt. Matters were worsened by considerable snipping of the film by Columbia very soon after its release and without Lean's permission; it is now to be re-released with additional cuts made by Lean himself, a concession I find disappointing, especially from a conscientious craftsman, let alone an artist.

The next superproduction was *Doctor Zhivago,* in which Bolt made a balls of Pasternak's already uneven novel, and for which Maurice Jarre wrote an even soupier (but catchy, oh so catchy!) score than he did for *Lawrence.* Artistically, almost nothing was right about the film except, once again, Young's color photography; and there were, scattered throughout, some of those nice workmanlike details in the sheer crafting of the film, its *facture,* as French can felicitously express it. Sadly, though expectably in our age, *Zhivago* proved a great popular success, whereas *Lawrence* has yet to recoup its outlay. Still, the ambitiousness and scope of *Zhivago* were at least justified by the magnitude of its subject.

Ryan's Daughter is the first time Bolt, and one of the rare times Lean, opted for an original screenplay. Yet again Young's camera performs miracles, but some of these miracles—no fault of Young's—are in highly questionable taste.

24 Thus when Rosy (get the symbolism of the name?) is finally gorgeously

made love to deep in the woods, a flaming cross of sunlight appears in the overhanging foliage—of the sort that the heavens formerly lavished only on Roman emperors they wanted to convert to the true faith; two dandelions (two, you see?), loose their seeds; and a moss-covered, horizontal log at the scene of the fulfillment performs double duty as a sort of joint G-string covering the operative parts of the lovers, and as a symbol for one of those parts. That entire ride into the forest and subsequent lovemaking should be analyzed shot by shot, it is so clever and horrible—with details like bits of plant life bending under the horses' hooves in extreme closeup.

If someone now told me that there was even a shot of two hares or squirrels in amorous pursuit, I would believe that too. As it is, I can neither affirm nor deny it, for my memory is just as capable of playing tricks on me as is Lean's latter-day filmmaking. It would be interesting to compare Rosy's seduction with the rape of the wife in *Rashomon*. There Kurosawa, too, shoots up into the trees to show the sunlight beating down through the leaves, but the effect is used with admirable restraint. There is very little restraint of any kind in *Ryan's Daughter*, and what there is actually is damaging. The film lacks the courage of its own low romanticism and omits any number of *scènes à faire:* the flashback to the major's unhappy return to his wife; Rosy and the major's last night out on the heath together (Rosy's leaving her sleeping husband's bed and running out into the chilly Irish night barefoot and in a filmy nightgown is, distinctly, a scene that should have been thought obligatory to avoid); the major's suicide; the final happy ending.

Let me explain. It is subtle of the film to eschew these obligatory scenes—just as it is subtle for it to allow Ryan's treachery to go unrecognized and, except by his conscience, unpunished. But subtlety is a mistake in a film whose blatant ambition it is to give cosmic importance to a trivial story of a young wife's coming of age through an unhappy episode of storybook adultery. This by bringing in World War I, the IRA, a spectacular storm that threatens to submerge the entire western coast of Ireland in the Atlantic, and 192 minutes of Super Panavision 70 including sea, sand, rocks, woods, and a specially built village of solid stone. Solid workmanship is the Lean hallmark (and, hereafter, a landmark as well): on this film, too, the director spent two or three years planning and shooting. But the vast edifice of the film only dwarfs its already pint-sized characters into Lilliputians. The effect is one of dormice inhabiting the Temple of Karnak.

Now add to all this the gushy score of Maurice Jarre. For *Lawrence,* Jarre had donned the mantle of Tchaikovsky; for *Zhivago,* he picked up the pen of Rachmaninoff. Here he tries to make like a bigger and splashier Nino Rota, and comes off worse yet, because you can be sweeping in the manner of those Russians and at least capture their grand scale, but how will loudness and busyness render the delicacy of Rota's scores for the earlier Fellini films? (The fact that even Rota can no longer write a good Rota score is beside the point.) Pretentiousness and banality are the salient features of this music and, to only a slightly lesser degree, of the movie as a whole. The excuse Bolt and Lean give for all their shallow romanticizing is that the film is to be understood as representing Rosy's point of view, the way a girl who reads a 25 piece of Georgian dime fiction, *The King's Mistress,* imagines or rearranges the world around her.

But superficiality, overblownness, a prodigality of extreme long shots, fantastic bird's- or worm's-eye views dominate the film. Even the scenes in which Rosy is not present are shot in this manner: grand images, hollow gestures, and rather-too-homespun bits of wisdom from the priest or schoolmaster—themselves naïve romanticizations of good, simple men—all contribute to making what should comment on Rosy scarcely different from what Rosy sees. The sensibility that produces *The King's Mistress* is painfully close to the one that produces *Ryan's Daughter.* Lean's best friend was the limited budget; he tried to escape it from the very beginning, and finally did. Alas, the best years of Lean were his lean years.

November 30–December 14, 1970

But Who'll Police the Policemen?

How DISAPPOINTING a follow-up to *Z,* that fine piece of commercial filmmaking, is Costa-Gavras's new movie, *The Confession.* Based on an account by Artur and Lise London, it has a screenplay by Jorge Semprun *(Z, La Guerre Est Finie),* and absolutely solid color photography by the wonderful Raoul Coutard. This is the autobiographical story of what Stalinist Communism, in this case in Czechoslovakia, could do to its victims. Based on the infamous Slánsky trial, as related by one of the three surviving defendants (the rest were executed), it is a thoroughly detailed account of how physical and psychological torture unmans people and breaks up long, happy marriages; of how the most self-incriminating confessions can be extracted from innocent people; and of how hard it is to shake a true Communist's faith in his party, even when that party is slowly and brutally killing him.

I have not read the Londons' book, and cannot say whether it adds to our knowledge of what previous books, journalistic accounts, plays, and films have already told us. The film version certainly does not. It is all there in minute, agonizing particulars, but, barring some unvital details, we knew from earlier sources about these monstrous cruelties, subtle undermining techniques, and purblind belief in the party. There must exist by now a vast enough library on the subject to furbish a thriving doctoral program.

The Confession, besides being harrowingly accurate, does nothing; it refuses to extend its indictment to Communism in general, or, more appropriately, to human nature itself. It does not even answer the obvious questions of why London in particular should have been spared the death penalty, or how he and his wife became reconciled, or what the children made of all this, or why he continues to be a Communist. To London, this entire grisly chapter of history that nearly killed him proves only that Stalinism was bad.

To put it another way, the unjust suffering of the inarticulate is as sad as that of a poet; but the inarticulate cannot shed light beyond narrating the facts more or less well, while a poet pushes through to greater understanding of the underlying truths. Yves Montand as London, and a large and unexceptionable cast, do everything they can, but an unrelieved chain of horrors, even though tactfully and artfully rendered, does not yield more than some sympathetic pain—and that, too, gradually fades into apathy over the film's very considerable stretch. Moreover, the film will not convert anyone to anything: our youth who worship Ho and Mao as shining saviors will not be swayed by some grubby Slánsky Affair in Stalinist Prague two decades ago.

Elio Petri is one of the strangest film directors around. This strangeness does not lie in his predilection for films about high society and opulent living, even though he is an avowed Communist; he may, after all, be helping to undermine what he depicts and deprecates. The truly peculiar thing is the qualitative difference—indeed, chasm—between such strident claptrap as *The Tenth Victim* and, much worse yet, *A Quiet Place in the Country*, and such very honorable films as *We Still Kill the Old Way* and, even better, *Investigation of a Citizen Above Suspicion*. Somewhere in between falls Petri's episode for the film *High Infidelity*.

Investigation, which Petri scripted with Ugo Pirro, a writer of talent, is not without its flaws; but it is a work of considerable intelligence, wit, and style. Though its impact is smaller than that of Rosi's similarly activist *Hands on the City*, it is a more complex and ingenious achievement, more fertile in its cinematic invention and more lasting in the memory.

The film concerns the Chief of Rome's Homicide Squad, who, on the day of his promotion to Chief of Political Investigations, kills his mistress. The woman, Augusta Terzi, is a sadomasochist thrill-seeker, married to a homosexual and implacably promiscuous. She plays little games with the Chief: re-creating notorious sex murders, photographing them, enacting the suspect and the investigator in a brutal police grilling, and so, unwholesomely, forth. The atmosphere is that of heterosexual Genet or Albee, and not even all that heterosexual: the Chief's laying of hands on subordinates or accused men may be an expression of authority—or something quite different.

Anyhow, on the day in question, the Chief arrives at Augusta's elaborately overfurnished art-nouveau apartment, and answers her excited question about how he will kill her *this* time by saying he will slit her throat. After they make love (or hate) under her black sheets, he does in fact casually slit her throat with what seems to be a Gillette razor blade. The ease with which he does it is, of course, a great tribute to Gillette, though not physiologically convincing; but let that pass. The Chief proceeds to leave every kind of fingerprint, bloody footprint, and other telltale evidence, reports the murder telephonically to the police, and takes a couple of bottles of champagne from the refrigerator for the office party celebrating his promotion. He wants to prove that, despite all the signs pointing toward him, he will not be apprehended because of his state of being divinely above suspicion. *Insospettabilità,* 27 as the Italian has it, in seven resounding syllables that he spouts with relish.

From this point on, the Chief plays a queasy double game illustrative of his split personality: he keeps giving the police clues that will condemn him, but he also throws dust in the investigators' eyes, either by making others look, at least temporarily, suspect, or by destroying some of the most incriminating evidence against himself. He is equally double in his relationship with Augusta. She is generally his victim, kneeling and trembling before his paternal authority; yet she can also swing over into becoming his tormentor, jeering at him for his infantilism, sexual inadequacy, and alleged policemanish odor. At such times it is he who crawls to her, and his boasts and threats and imprecations against being called a child sound more like sorry wheedling.

The relationship with the woman he murdered is told in flashbacks interspersed with the investigation and the Chief's assumption of his new job; as we find out more about the Chief's political personality, we learn more about his sexual problems as well. The Chief (he remains unnamed) is, to be sure, a character derived from the Police Chief in Genet's *The Balcony,* and it is from there that the relation between oppressive political power and sexual impotence is taken. The equation is rather glib, and probably just a fantasy on the part of those who justly but impotently oppose excessive police power; but it is worth speculating about, and it does give that dazzling actor, Gian Maria Volontè, a chance to display his many-sided talent.

The effortlessness with which Volontè slips from one aspect of the Chief into the other is thrilling to watch. His looks are a cross between those of Laurence Olivier and François Périer, and he can at will become intense, brooding, dashing—like Olivier, or bring forward his Périer side, and appear sneaky, measly, ridiculous. His Chief is a performance as full of stops as the organ at Notre Dame, and though he plays splashily, he is not hammy. Even in the madness of this man there remains some vestigial self-control. Whether he is manipulating people by their ears, jowls, or scruffs of the neck, as if heartily patting so many sheep toward slaughter or a brief stay of execution (for, to him, all are guilty), or whether he is himself groveling before authority, a mistress, or a Communist student he would like to get to accuse him of murder, Volontè keeps the character odious and frightening, but credible and, at times, almost pitiable.

Scarcely less accomplished is Elio Petri's direction. None of the excesses that made *A Quiet Place in the Country* one of the year's most jarring and pretentious films is to be found here. While the cutting is fast (the editor was the brilliant Ruggero Mastroianni), this is not meant simply to dazzle us, but to accentuate the nervousness of the people and, as it were, the situation. It is never so fast that you cannot follow it, and there are adequate establishing shots as well as a minimum of tricky camera angles. Even the extreme closeups are much more sparing than in *We Still Kill the Old Way,* and there is an excellent sense of the *genius loci* in such places as the police files or wiretap listening room; Augusta's swooningly oppressive love den contrasts tellingly with the airy, sparsely furnished, sterile apartment of the Chief.

Petri, I repeat, collaborated on the screenplay with Ugo Pirro, and the dialogue is not only urbane and sardonic, it can also exude a sinister spell, as in the Chief's inaugural address as head of the political police, when he exalts repression as a vaccine. "Repression is civilization," he proclaims in messianic tones; and "we must keep this Law immutable, sculptured in time." The speech is full of statistical data used to subserve fanatical conclusions, and manages to make totalitarianism sound almost rational. No less coruscating are such humorous tidbits as a disquisition on Rome's graffiti, whose nature and number mirror both the changing tides of politics and the changeless ocean of human absurdity. Among others, there were in the course of the past year, we are told, eleven graffiti for Herbert Marcuse and one against, as well as two for "a certain Sade," as a mystified policeman reports.

Toward the end, the script gets a trifle unsure of itself. Some episodes are unduly dragged out, and one or two are rushed over. But I like the ending, left open as befits a film that invites reflection rather than glib assent (even if, in its secret heart, it may yearn for easy assent as well). The Chief imagines himself exculpated despite his obvious culpability—a kind of fascist farce that is the counterpart of communist farces (as chronicled in *The Confession;* Pirro and Petri, please note!), where men are condemned and executed despite their obvious innocence. Then, as the film ends, the scene the Chief has been imagining begins to take place in actuality, but stops before we can find out whether life will corroborate criminal fantasy.

Investigation can boast further virtues. There are marvelous supporting performances, notably from the voluptuous Florinda Bolkan (who, if she weren't a Brazilian bombshell could easily be a Bolkan tinderbox), beautifully conveying the pathetic childishness at the core of Augusta's sophisticated perversion. I greatly admired also Gianni Santuccio as the police commissioner, the suave embodiment of sane, respectable corruption—as opposed to the Chief's insanely fanatical one—enthroned in his office among Etruscan art treasures subverted from the nation's museums.

Luigi Kuveiller's color cinematography is competent without being outstanding, but it does achieve the desired moody, indeed morose, atmosphere. Particularly effective is the use of the garish orange glass that serves as partition for the police computer rooms, and that makes the people inside them look like sufferers from jaundice basking in a particularly fruity sunset. One of the very best things about the film is the music by Ennio Morricone, who, when he does not go wildly electronic, is by far the most interesting composer now working in films. The score consists chiefly of one haunting theme, with overtones of Weill and Nino Rota, but basically Morricone: sweet-and-sour, now jaunty or jeering, now sensual and insinuating, it is run through a number of variations and suggestive orchestrations, one of them sounding like a jew's-harp electronically amplified into a superdouble bass. If nothing else, the film is a splendid study of madness at work, in an individual and in a society, the two forming a hallucinatory symbiosis.

Artists As They Aren't

MANY IS the unsavory film I've had inflicted on me. There have been underground obscenities and aboveground monstrosities galore, but none succeeded in making me actually physically sick. This honor was to be reserved for Ken Russell's *The Music Lovers*, a movie that, during three separate sequences, had my stomach turning in unison with Tchaikovsky's body in the grave. For the film purports to be a biography of the famous Russian composer, and is so bad and distasteful that, besides ruining whatever reputation Russell may have, it puts a serious dent in Tchaikovsky's.

Readers will remember that I was not much impressed by Russell's *Women in Love*. Unfortunately, I have not seen Russell's BBC documentaries on, among others, Delius, Richard Strauss, and Isadora Duncan. The last of these is said to be very fine; the first charming, although exaggerating Delius's importance as a composer. The Strauss TV film, however, is, apparently, hateful: it makes Strauss out to have been a dyed-in-the-wool Nazi and, consequently, a worthless composer. The first assertion is vastly exaggerated, and the second would not follow even if the first were true. But Russell is an oversimplifier, a vulgarizer—not, in itself, an unuseful thing to be, in a middlebrow-oriented society that needs its Will Durants and John Gunthers. But a vulgarizer who is himself preeminently vulgar and egregiously uninterested in truth is a reprehensible figure.

In the case of *The Music Lovers*, originally entitled *Tchaikovsky*, Russell has indulged himself in a freewheeling fantasy about the composer's life, using a few facts (and disregarding a great many more), a handful of rather debatable surmises, and a prodigality of out-and-out fabrications. Now this is not to be confused with your average "fictionalized biography," where the author makes use of all available biographical data and fills in the story with his own interpretations and speculations, including imaginary but plausible dialogue. Even that has always seemed to me, except in the case of masterpieces like Graves's *I, Claudius*, a not quite reputable genre. Russell (on film rather than paper, but the principle is the same) does something else: he wallows in his melodramatic, scabrous, sensationalistic fantasies, and attempts to elevate and legitimize them by draping them around the defenseless figure of a dead genius. Though I am not a great admirer of most of Tchaikovsky's music, seeing the man and his work thus insulted and degraded obliges me to hasten to his defense.

I wonder what Russell is trying to say with this film, even on his own shoddy level. Tchaikovsky was a homosexual in a society that viewed inversion intolerantly and repressively—as, to a lesser extent, our society still does; if that theme moved Russell, it could have yielded, even at this late date, a film of interest and humanitarian impact. But although Tchaikovsky's homosexuality is very nearly the center of the movie, not only is the problem denied an iota of serious examination, the very word is never pronounced in this film that dares not speak its theme. The one time it is, presumably, spoken—into the ear of Tchaikovsky's good angel, Mme von Meck, by his evil demon, Count Chiluvsky—it is deliberately drowned out by the explosions of fireworks. The only levels on which the composer's inversion seems to concern Russell are (1) amateurish Freudianizing about how his hero got to be that way, and (2) cheap exploitation of this aberration by confronting it with the supposititious oversexedness of Nina, the girl Tchaikovsky married and separated from eleven weeks later.

The inept psychiatricizing consists of making Tchaikovsky excessively involved with his mother and, especially, his sister—then, without examining either of these propositions more than cursorily, embroidering heavenly and hellish visions around them. Thus we get a typical cigarette-commercial fantasy of the composer and his sister cavorting through every kind of landscape and clime—worsened by the fact that it goes on immeasurably longer than the late cigarette commercials. It may not give you lung cancer, but it shrouds human truths in a smokescreen that gets in your eyes.

Mamma, who died of the cholera and the monstrous scalding baths that were considered an effective remedy for it, is portrayed as an aging nude woman being parboiled alive. Added to the awkwardnesses of a distinctly flaccid body are the horrors of the torture and the hideousness of cankers disfiguring both body and face. Cholera does not cause these festering sores, but they may occur as a side effect; Russell, characteristically, leaps at any ugliness he can drag in.

Later we see Tchaikovsky wooing his mother's kind of death by drinking a glass of unboiled water during a cholera epidemic. It is possible that he actually did do something like this deliberately, but the film does not examine his motivation leading up to such an act beyond showing us yet another fantasy in which everyone he ever knew seems to be chasing after him, grabbing at him (to the tune of the *1812 Overture*), and making him comment wryly on his sister's not having left him even the least memento in her will. We do, however, get another revolting hot-bath routine, now with Piotr Ilyich as the agonizing victim.

Russell does not want to get involved in any honest analysis: dishonest tamperings with fact seem to suit him much better. Thus he makes the composer's brother, Modeste, not a solicitous helper and fellow homosexual, but a callow, exploiting heterosexual. Why? Because if both brothers were pederasts, we would not, I dare say, have the cozy distinction between the sensitive but sick artist and the crass but healthy philistine, which best serves Russell's simplistic and flashy taste. Moreover, there might be something less romantic about a mamma who turns all her sons into inverts. And there would then be no crude and convenient butt for Piotr Ilyich's superior, artistic witticisms. When the unsympathetic Modeste, after a long session of searching for a title for the Sixth Symphony, sneeringly calls his brother pathetic, Piotr can with ironic superiority thank him for his precious help and actually name the work *Symphonie pathétique*.

There are quite a few of the old Hollywood lives-of-famous-men clichés in   31 the film. There is the obligatory scene where "Rubinstein" (Anton and Nicholas fused!) tells off Tchaikovsky after the (fictitious) première of the First Piano Concerto, insisting that except for a bit here and there, it is no good and needs a lot of reworking. There is, I think, not a little truth in that, even if nary a Rubinstein ever uttered it, and Russell and his scenarist might have stopped to consider how informed musical opinion rates the piece. But they are only after the cheap hindsight-irony the scene contains: something for the unwashed to laugh at, even though they are the very ones who would have had no use for Tchaikovsky then, and doubtless still prefer Richard Rodgers or Janis Joplin to the likes of him. The exact counterpart of this scene, by the way, can be found in *Song of Norway,* the current trashy mass-consumption musical about Grieg; yet I am sure Russell would have a fit if his "work of art" were likened to this banal family entertainment.

What seems to fascinate Russell and his scenarist (the same Melvyn Bragg who collaborated on the poor screenplay of *The Loves of Isadora*) even more than their ex-eponymous hero, are the two women in his life other than his mother and sister. These women—Nina, the wife, and Madame von Meck, the patroness—were undoubtedly interesting figures, but hardly, I dare say, the outrageous grotesques that the film turns them into. Nina is made into a romantic schoolgirl writing swooning fan letters to famous or dashing strangers, a crazy and destructive nymphomaniac and sadomasochist, and a touching little woman heartbreakingly in love with a husband who cannot requite her ardor. This last finally drives the poor thing utterly mad. Nadezhda von Meck, on the other hand, is presented as a painfully plain, hyper-emotional pseudo-esthete, who, though never meeting him (which is, historically, more or less true), passionately licks a peach Tchaikovsky has bitten into and abandoned, or sneaks into his room and lies down beside him while he sleeps and has a kind of platonic orgasm induced by sheer parallelism.

Stefan Kanfer of *Time* is right to point out that Russell is heavily influenced by Peter Brook's theatrical productions. Mme von Meck, for example, is supplied with two creepy sons, a blond Tweedledee and his black-haired Tweedledum twin, derived from the two eunuchs as visualized by Brook in his production of Dürrenmatt's *The Visit.* And the asylum scene, showing Nina in her ultimate decline into insanity, is an obvious bid to outdo Brook's madhouse *mise en scène* for *Marat/Sade.* In this thoroughly offensive sequence, Nina squats on the grating of an underground dungeon enclosing the most raving and malformed lunatics. As she defiantly sniggers at her appalled visiting mother, the madmen's hands reach up under Nina's skirt to indulge in a gang-diddling. This is supposed to be her revenge on her venal, unscrupulous parent who pushed her into prostitution, but the true victim is the viewer's stomach.

Scene after scene flaunts Russell's exhibitionism, his overloading every shot with stifling excess. When Tchaikovsky performs at the Moscow Conservatory, we keep crosscutting from him to the film's principal characters conveniently foregathered in the audience, and to their concurrent daydreams. Not only is each of these sequences like a collection of tawdry picture postcards, they all have a way of looking ultimately alike. And we realize finally that the whole thing is Ken Russell's daydream: life, art, history as seen through the eye of a megalomaniacal interior, or, more exactly, exterior decorator.

But Russell could not have concocted this much gook without accomplices. Chief among them, besides his scenarist, is Glenda Jackson, an actress of some talent, whose entire persona, however, is made up of contempt and even hatred for the audience. In almost every play or film she inflicts her naked body on us, which, considering its quality, is the supreme insult flung at the spectators.

In the film's most nauseating scene, Piotr and Nina get drunk on the train carrying them back from their unsuccessful honeymoon. The compartment is luridly lit, the train bounces around like a billygoat, the handheld camera practically turns somersaults. Richard Chamberlain tries (as he does throughout) to look sensitive and suffering, and Miss Jackson proceeds to strip to the buff in order to seduce him. She allows the camera to photograph her from the most prying angles, including one shot up her anus and vagina, which, combining with the frenzy of the montage—the food and drink (the couple have just eaten) spilling and scattering, a rapid-fire catalogue of Miss Jackson's physical uglinesses from face to feet—makes for some of the most hateful viewing in all my filmgoing experience.

A considerably better film, yet also a considerably bigger disappointment, is the latest and supposedly last installment in Truffaut's semifictional screen autobiography, *Bed and Board.* The films about Antoine Doinel (Truffaut's name for his amiably altered ego) have steadily decreased in quality since *The 400 Blows,* and in this one pussyfooting cuteness preponderates. Antoine is married to Christine, whom he was courting in *Stolen Kisses,* and they lead a hectic newlyweds' life. Once again Antoine goes from peculiar job to peculiar job (here from live flower-dyer to radio manipulator of toy boats in a display pool of an American shipping firm), once again he dallies with a woman other than his true love (here a charming but wholly improbable Japanese girl), once again everything works out happily in the end.

The main trouble is that Truffaut's comic vein runs thinner and thinner. Actually, Truffaut is not a comic filmmaker at all: his best efforts are, always, serious films laced with comic touches. When there are too few comic overtones, or too many, or when he tries for straight comedy, things have a way of going wrong. Now, for example, he introduces such running gags as a chap who keeps borrowing more and more money from Antoine, and a mysterious stranger who turns out to be something quite different from what he is taken for (a device used much better, because in a less pat way, in *Stolen Kisses*). The jokes are not funny, because they are dragged in arbitrarily and irrelevantly, and their spacing and timing are sloppy.

Antoine's job-bungling becomes tiresome from sheer predictability and from a kind of impatience with detail Truffaut here alarmingly exhibits. In addition, one is forced to wonder why anyone hires this inveterate incompetent, both accident-prone and supine, and what on earth the piquant and spunkily crackling Christine (*pétillante* is the *mot juste,* but missing in English) and the lovely and patient Kyoko could possibly find lovable about him. Truffaut is further hampered here by the unhappy way his fictional stand-in has developed. Jean-Pierre Léaud, so moving as an adolescent, has grown into an unprepossessing young man. Or, rather, *not* grown—in height, artistic stature, and the ability to convey an inner life of any but the most trivial kind. Truffaut picked Léaud for *The 400 Blows* because the boy rather resembled him in appearance and had a similar dropout and reform-school background. But even though the physical similarity between the filmmaker and the performer continues, Léaud has become one of the emptiest, most deadpan, least suggestive actors around. He looks like a typical young Parisian hoodlum, has the facial expressions of a sleepwalking gutter rat, only one notable gesture (smoothing back his hair), and a voice that sounds like sand squeezing through a sieve. Having played in so many Godard and quasi-Godardian films has dehumanized Léaud even further.

But what, finally, is Truffaut trying to say with *Bed and Board?* He is, apparently, hinting at some sort of description of how a young artist is formed: very unconvincingly Léaud-Doinel is beginning to write a novel in this film. Regrettably, Truffaut tells us as little about how one becomes, or is, an artist as Ken Russell does in his Tchaikovsky film. Not that there is anything tasteless here—if anything, the film is prudishly overdecorous—yet neither is there anything incisive, illuminating, new. Claude Jade is a likable Christine, Hiroko Berghauer an exquisite Kyoko. Nestor Almendros's color cinematography is getting better, though it has quite a way to go yet to catch up with Raoul Coutard's, and there are a few droll moments in the story and staging. The film gives no offense, and no enlightenment. From a major filmmaker, that is a minor but distinct sin.

March 8, 1971

Knee-Deep in Profundities

PRECONIZED by our most powerful auteurist publication, the *New York Times,* Eric Rohmer's *Claire's Knee* is enjoying an improbable popularity. Some of the box-office onslaught can be explained by the success of Rohmer's previous film, *My Night at Maud's,* likewise puffed way beyond its slender deserts by the two resident auteur critics of the *Times. Ma Nuit chez Maud* was a well-meaning, amateurish film with painfully foursquare camera placements and movements, literal-minded throughout, and with certain intellectual aspirations in the dialogue meant to compensate for the meager, contrived plot and the lack of development in the characters.

Yet *Maud* did at least have one devastating performance by Françoise Fabian, and there was a measure of reality in the hero's basic problem, even if the sophomoric philosophizing on the soundtrack served only *pour épater les bourgeois*. In *Claire's Knee,* however, the central theme is quirky, elusive, and finally quite trivial. This is still another of Rohmer's "Six Moral Tales," in each of which a man seemingly slated for one woman flirts or dallies with another, only to end up with the first. I am not sure that the subject, including its permutations, is worthy of a hexameron; in Rohmer's hands it achieves a lack of urgency comparable only to the question of whether a fly will succumb to the flypaper or the fly swatter.

Jérôme, the thirty-fivish French consul to Stockholm, is spending a summer month at Lac d'Annecy in Haute-Savoie near the Swiss border, an Alpine paradise for the leisured and sometimes bored. He is selling his delicious villa and, next month, will go back to Sweden to marry Lucinde, a woman journalist he has been living with happily for some time. He discovers that Aurora, a Rumanian novelist and old friend of his, is vacationing at a neighboring villa, where the proprietress, Mme Walter, lives with her sixteen-year-old daughter, Laura. Aurora has an unfinished short story about an older man and a very young girl; to provide it with an ending, she encourages Jérôme to get involved with Laura, who, it would appear, has a crush on him.

There are numerous conversations among Aurora, Mme Walter, Laura, and Jérôme about love and marriage and family relations. Aurora and Jérôme, in particular, chatter endlessly about love, and conduct a kind of platonic *amitié amoureuse*. Laura is allowed to go on a two-day excursion into the mountains with Jérôme; when, finally aroused, he kisses her, her infatuation has already waned, and there are no further developments. There is more quasi-profound chitchat with Aurora about indulgence and abstinence. Finally, Claire, Laura's somewhat older half sister, arrives.

Claire is an extrovert and happily in love with Gilles, another extrovert roughly her age. Jérôme now has further talks with Vincent, a somewhat girlish classmate of Laura's, who seems to nurture an unrequited love for her. Laura goes off to England on a vacation, and Jérôme gets more and more excited by Claire—particularly, as he confides in Aurora, Claire's knee, which he must fondle. Caught in a storm with Claire (who, generally, ignores him), he tells her about a peccadillo of Gilles's with another girl, rather exaggerating it. He makes the girl weep and, by way of consolation, is able to caress her knee. (Why she lets him do it is not made clear, but otherwise there wouldn't be even this much of a story.) His summer holiday ending, and with Claire and Gilles reconciled, Jérôme feels his craving allayed. He bids adieu to Aurora, who, it emerges, is engaged to a man in Geneva. Jérôme leaves for Sweden and the somewhat ambiguous prospect of marriage to Lucinde.

If this synopsis suggests the heights of inconsequence, it is nothing compared to the same material strung out to feature length. But Rohmer's triviality is unlike anyone else's: on the one hand, it is shot through with unprepossessing little kinkinesses; on the other, it demands to be taken seriously, as though it were full of subtle perceptions and grave pronouncements. Not only is that whole knee business presented as if fraught with existential significance, but the very details of dialogue attitudinize themselves into a sort of hysterical pregnancy.

Take Aurora's reply to Jérôme's concern over her "zero" love life: "I'm like you, *mon cher*. Chance offers you a woman, so you take her. Chance offers me nothing, so I take nothing. Why try to fight destiny?" The fact that Aurora has a man stashed away in Geneva would seem to give the lie to the remark, but let that pass. More to the point, to take someone and to take nothing are not at all the same thing. And why would chance make such distinctions between two worldly persons? Or is Aurora foolishly blaming on chance a matter of temperament? Yet Aurora is presented as wise. And how do we get from chance to destiny, as if the two were really identical? The film is full of such pseudophilosophical nonaphorisms, but people are so impressed with anything that pretends to be Thought coming at them from the screen that they fall over backward in wonderment.

Undeniably, the film has minor assets. The Savoyard landscape is sumptuous, the living in it gracious, and even nugatory wordmongering can garner some prestige from such elegant settings. Nestor Almendros's color cinematography is accomplished and provides Rohmer with the flattened-out backgrounds he wanted, presumably to suggest theatrical backdrops. Theatrical, in fact, is what Rohmer's films usually are; but in an age that wants its films as "filmic" as possible, you can always count on a certain *éclat* by going squarely against the current. Béatrice Romand, as Laura, conveys the Gallic *gamine* to perfection, down to the smugness that gives the charm a bitter aftertaste. As her mother, Michèle Montel exudes mellow womanly understanding.

The rest are less convincing. While Jean-Claude Brialy makes Jérôme engaging, he fails to suggest any depth in the man. As Claire, Laurence de Monaghan contributes a trim little figure and not much else—even her knee seems hardly worth genuflecting to. Worse yet is Aurora Cornu, as the novelist. A real-life Rumanian poet-novelist, she speaks with an accent that is an insult to French, although Rumanians used to be famous for speaking it almost better than the natives! She looks frowzy and bovine, and cannot act at all: repeatedly her eyes emit SOS signals in the direction of the cue cards. This is too bad because Aurora and Jérôme are meant to embody that sophisticated, playful, satisfied but not satiated relationship between cultivated ex-lovers—an easy affection that can go toward intimate friendship or fleshly intimacy with equal unconstraint. Miss Cornu is a total loss where Annie Girardot or Françoise Fabian would have made luminous sense.

Still, if anything can genuinely attract American audiences to this flimsy film, it is that relationship, as well as the faintly perverse one with Laura, who discusses her "love life" with a kind of Simone de Beauvoirishness no American girl her age could approach. For the cultists, to be sure, there are all kinds of idiot's delights, ranging from the film's unfolding as pages from the hero's diary—with a handwritten date preceding each uneventful episode—all the way to that photograph of Lucinde that Jérôme shows his friends: a picture of Jeanne Moreau. But for all its philosophizing, *Claire's Knee* remains dullish: not much patina on that patella.

March 22, 1971

Hoarse Operetta

BERNARDO BERTOLUCCI must be one of the world's most overrated film-makers, and in few professions does overrating race ahead as unchecked as in film. His first picture, *La commare secca,* was pure trash; his second, *Before the Revolution,* much admired by the critics, was murky, pretentious, and juvenile, and fed parasitically on *The Charterhouse of Parma,* to which it was an extended allusion. I never saw *Partner,* but even Bertolucci's partisans deplore that one. *The Spider's Stratagem* was a baroque phantasmagoria, its meaning virtually inscrutable, its pretentiousness insufferable. Now along comes *The Conformist,* based on Alberto Moravia's novel—Bertolucci's first film, we are informed, aimed at a broader audience: more accessible, but no less fine.

I wish I could bring myself to read another Moravia novel so as to determine where the book's flaws end and those of Bertolucci's screenplay and direction begin. But this much is clear: Moravia's and Bertolucci's modes are, except for a shared fascination with sexual aberrancies, antipodal, and can yield only a Punch-and-Judy mismating.

Moravia tends to give us narratives in which a rather commonplace but dryly ironic view of political and sexual shadiness is supposed to take the place of texture, depth perception, life; the manner, until recently, has been predominantly psychological realism. Bertolucci, on the other hand, with a sensibility that derives from Visconti, Zeffirelli, and Pasolini (whose assistant he once was), strives for lavishness: opulent, indeed suffocating, atmosphere; bizarre, even surreal, effects; wallowing in private fantasies. Put these two modes together, and you may easily get ambiguity, but of the most fortuitous and barren sort, for which a phrase from a poem by Jorge Guillén seems the perfect epitaph: *desierta refulgencia*—arid brilliance, a desert of refulgency.

The story concerns Marcello Clerici, a young middle-class intellectual from a messy family who so craves respectable comformity that, in 1938, he joins the Fascist party, marries an utterly conventional and silly petit-bourgeois girl, Giulia (Stefania Sandrelli), and agrees to turn his Parisian honeymoon into profit as well as pleasure by undertaking to assassinate his formerly beloved professor of philosophy now a prominent anti-Fascist in exile. Achieving acceptance entails certain costs for this intellectual: betrayals wreaked on his parents, partial acceptance of the Catholicism he abhors, putting up with the crudities of his wife and her world.

But Marcello is trying to shake off the memories of a traumatic act of violence when, aged thirteen, he was picked up by a strange chauffeur and, apparently, sexually molested. So eager is he to escape from his sense of uncleanness that he does not balk at self-purgation through politically approved murder—the psychologizing seems rather facile here, but let that pass. Moravia was, presumably, most concerned with *la trahison des clercs,* which the hero's name, Clerici, points to; Bertolucci is much more interested in the sexual twilight (fancied also by Moravia) and in surreal imagery.

Thus when Marcello has just betrayed his mother's Chinese chauffeur (all these evil chauffeurs!), dope purveyor, and lover to the authorities, we see him jesuitically escorting her across the untended autumnal front lawn. Given the low-angle shot, most of the screen becomes inundated with sere leaves a wind blows across the lawn to the accompaniment of a lushly melancholy crackling. So a cowardly and finally impious act is suddenly drenched in extraneous, meaningless beauty. Or take the honeymoon trip. In a private compartment of the Paris-bound train, Giulia confesses to Marcello that she is no virgin; she has had, as a very young girl, a long and grubby affair with the elderly and unprepossessing family lawyer. She communicates this hesitantly, but Marcello, who is marrying her only for her body and the *embourgeoisement* she offers, merely laughs. Giulia takes this as a sign of great generosity, and as she tells how the lawyer undressed her bit by bit, Marcello reenacts the seduction.

This must be meant in Moravia as a sardonic-moralistic comment on middle-class mores, and Bertolucci, I dare say, sees it that way, too. But he cannot refrain from gorgeously gimmicking up the scene: much of the time, the couple is shot as a reflection in the train window, superimposed on the sumptuous marine landscape beyond. And as the giggling, mean wedding night progresses, we keep seeing in the windows bits of loveliness flitting by, and the colors of day exquisitely modulating into those of night.

Now what does this juxtaposition accomplish? Is it meant to stress the contrast between natural beauty and human sordidness? But that is quite irrelevant to the work as a whole: the good natural life does not enter into it at all. Is the beauty of the backgrounds meant to give glamour to evil? That cannot be the point either: Fascism is meant to be seen as a niggling nastiness, an extension of bourgeois pettiness to the ultimate ugliness of treachery and murder. In the film, however, vice is superb, larger-than-life-size (certainly larger than virtue-size) and, as it were, heroic. This is an expression of Bertolucci's love of décor for décor's sake and, very possibly, of a worse love yet.

We get Fascist office buildings that are majestic marble mausoleums in which sparse but enormous furniture looms in the middle of vast travertine expanses, and footsteps and voices echo like distant waterfalls in mountain landscapes. An insane asylum is a giant sports amphitheater, all marmoreal whiteness, where inmates and guards seem about to compete in some nightmarish Olympic games. Similarly, in Paris, a working-class *bal musette* looks like a gala affair, parquet and plate glass; the seedy apartment of the exiled Professor Quadri turns into an art déco show at the Orangerie.

People are often made to appear just as bizarre and baroque as their surroundings. When the Clericis call on the Quadris—he is married to Anna, a young and sexy blonde (Dominique Sanda)—Anna is promptly having intercourse with Marcello while really trying to seduce Giulia; Marcello is fascinatedly watching Anna making sexual advances to his wife, while the seductress also watches the husband watching; the good Professor Quadri is soon propositioning Giulia. All this could perhaps be made believable—Moravia may even carry it off; Bertolucci, however, prefers to make it into a madcap operetta. *"The Damned,"* Bertolucci has quipped, "is opera; *The Conformist* is operetta." Even this witticism was a steal from Visconti, who had said that Hitler and the Nazis were operatic, whereas Mussolini and the Fascists were operettic. But *The Conformist* shouts too much: it ends up as a hoarse operetta.

Perhaps the most blatantly pretentious scene has Marcello, on the way to Paris, stopping off to see a Fascist functionary at Ventimiglia. The set is first a huge Chiricoish painting of a seascape, then the painting dissolves and we see the same panorama as reality. Next, Marcello enters the indicated building, which looks like a fancy art gallery but proves to be a brothel that, in turn, houses the Fascist's office. Marcello first sees a whore improbably dressed in a blackshirt's uniform, a whore who is a prefiguration of Anna, and played by the same actress. Presently a horrible hag ushers him into the Fascist's office, where everything from the lintels to the desk is covered with closely stacked walnuts. After this unexplained incursion of the surreal, reality swiftly returns.

Except, of course, that reality almost always looks expressionistic in Bertolucci. Thus Marcello and his sidekick, the triggerman Manganiello, drive in pursuit of the Quadri car through snowy landscapes of gossamer, fairytale stuff. They catch up with the Quadris—Anna was not supposed to go along, but did and must now also be wiped out—exactly in the woods where the ambush is laid. The tall, fantastic trees are photographed as a mighty cathedral with shafts of light slanting in through rose windows just out of sight. While Marcello watches, frozen in his impotence, the professor is murdered in unlikely fashion by a crowd of men with knives, striking again and again—shades of *Rocco* and Julius Caesar. Anna manages to run up to Marcello's locked car; he sits impassive while she bangs at the window screaming for help. *In extremis,* she runs into the woods; the pursuers' knives have miraculously changed into guns, and she is, after an unconscionably long chase, gunned down from behind. Yet there is no wound on the back of her head or body; her entire face, though, is covered with blood!

The film's last scene, added by Bertolucci, tops even this in improbability and portentousness. It shows Marcello ambiguously ogling a naked young homosexual under the most preposterous circumstances. The film's attitude toward homosexuality, too, is wholly and clumsily ambivalent. Though the oafish Manganiello speaks with loathing of "cowards, pederasts, Jews," Bertolucci portrays homosexuals with an almost equal lack of understanding and sympathy, yet he seems fascinated by the subject. Unless, of course, it is his mannerist exaggeration taking over again.

The acting in such a film must needs be minimal. Jean-Louis Trintignant as Marcello confines himself to making a few nasty faces and striking a few fawning postures. All the women in the film—whether mothers, wives, or maids—are stupid, spiteful, or weird and get to do even less acting. *The Conformist* is a sweltering desert crisscrossed by mirages that, being someone else's figments, make no sense even as mirages.

April 19, 1971

From St. Tropez to Siberia

ERIC ROHMER is at it again. This time it is *La Collectionneuse*, the fourth of his "Six Moral Tales," fitting into the grand scheme between *My Night at Maud's* (#3) and *Claire's Knee* (#5). Why Rohmer should think the subject of a man drawn from one woman to another and finally drifting back to the first so endlessly fascinating as to deserve six full-scale treatments I am at a loss to say. But if Giorgio Morandi could paint nothing but bottles all his life and make art out of them, Rohmer may be allowed his particular emotional bottleneck.

Adrien, an art dealer and playboy, has parted somewhat sourly from his mistress Carole, who has gone to London for the summer. He and a pop-artist pal, Daniel, share an absent friend's St. Tropez villa for the summer with a girl they have not previously met, Haydée, on whom Adrien once walked in when she was having sexual intercourse. Haydée sleeps around assiduously and is dubbed by the young men *la collectionneuse*, the collectress of men. They bait and insult her, which she takes mostly with a kind of provocative indifference. She finally drops her various swains, considers Adrien briefly, and settles on Daniel. Adrien, fascinated by the girl in spite of himself, plays an elaborate game of self-delusion. And when Daniel walks out on Haydée, Adrien palms her off on a rich and richly repulsive American client.

At last, Adrien and Haydée are driving back to the villa and the much-postponed consummation. She gets out of the car to talk to some boys who want her to drive to Rome with them; Adrien is blocking the traffic and is told to move on a little. Once the car is rolling, however, he no longers wishes to stop. He lets chance or a whim deprive him of Haydée. Alone and morose at the villa, he finally picks up the telephone to inquire when the next plane leaves for London. *Voilà.* Slight as the story is, it is told with many a halt and lurch, inconclusive little episodes that have no shape or special significance, details that seem to await some ingenious exegete to find a meaning for them.

Rohmer is the master of the well-turned epigram that only lacks wit, the apothegm through whose loose bottom the significance has dropped out. 40 "Polarization is like extrapolation, a completely obsolete theory." "What fascinated me in you was your insignificance." "My fortress of morality was yielding: Why not one brief liaison clearly defined in space and time?" "My life was always my profession: I decided to do nothing well." That, though in a different sense, is what Rohmer does, too. The witticisms, the insights, the character study—none of them works.

The whole thing smacks of improvisation, and the three principals are, in fact, credited with help on the dialogue. This is a dubious method at best; when the actors are clods even at acting, it is positively disastrous. Patrick Bauchan is a perpetually snide but otherwise expressionless Adrien, Daniel Pommereulle is sulky and vaguely effeminate as Daniel, and, as Haydée, Haydée Politoff has a nice figure but a face that could take best of breed in the Pekinese division of any dog show, and gives no evidence of histrionic or even obedience training. I tend, on principle, to mistrust films in which the author's invention is so sluggish that it cannot even create fictitious names for the characters.

Near the beginning of the film a young woman says that she can only be friends with beautiful people. As she develops her theory, she comes up with some mildly interesting paradoxes. Had the film proceeded to develop and dramatize this theme, it might just barely have made a contribution to our understanding of the erotics of social intercourse. Instead, it follows the maunderings of three insignificant and pretentious people in so soggy, faltering a fashion that it should set admirers of Rohmer's other films to reexamining them. They might find that these films, too, though less clumsily than *La Collectionneuse,* are cast in the unsatisfactory mold of the O. Henryish or Maupassantian anecdote, stretched out beyond endurance, and decked out with quasi-literate, shallow or hollow badinage. In the present case, neither Nestor Almendros's color cinematography nor Rohmer's handling of the camera can do so much as squeeze a little atmosphere out of St. Tropez, which constitutes an overwhelming underachievement in itself.

"That emptiness around the human figure that you create by means of objects!" a fawning critic gushes to Daniel in one of the film's several prologues. Rohmer goes Daniel one better and extends the emptiness right into the figures.

Casper Wrede's movie version of Aleksandr Solzhenitsyn's *One Day in the Life of Ivan Denisovich* is a film that plainly demonstrates the possibilities and limitations of the medium. It is a responsible, conscientious transposition of the short novel to the screen, yet, despite incidental felicities, it does not truly come off. Why?

The novella is told from Ivan's point of view: we get the bare, dismal facts of a day in a Siberian "special" camp of the Stalin (and, presumably, Brezhnev) era as filtered through the consciousness of a simple carpenter, a man of courage, cunning, pawky common sense, and also decency. He has been condemned to ten years' imprisonment merely because his speedy escape from Nazi captivity in 1941 looked suspicious to the Russians. He has outlasted eight years of subhuman forced labor in subzero colds, and will maintain a sizable part of his dignity through the remaining years, thanks to   41 resiliency, resourcefulness, and a sense of humor. But the way he looks at his life simply is not the way the camera sees it. Ivan, down-to-earth though he be, is reflective: and the camera does not reflect.

Take the incident involving another inmate, a former navy captain who is led off to "the cells": for a petty protest, he is given ten days in a cell that is a barely heated icebox. There the cold penetrates deeper than the lashes of the knout, one sleeps on the wooden floor, rations are minimal. In the book, Ivan thinks: "Ten days! If you had ten days in the cells and sat them out to the end, it meant you'd be a wreck for the rest of your life. You got TB and you'd never be out of hospitals long as you lived. And the fellows who did fifteen days were dead and buried." The film briefly shows the captain hunched up helplessly in his cell. But it does not and perhaps cannot give you the vital information of Ivan's interior monologue.

To be sure, the film uses voice-over narration where it considers it proper and necessary. This sparing use is absolutely judicious, but it manages to become obtrusive, even though the voice is, correctly and unmelodramatically, Ivan's own. The problem is that narration is the novel's medium; on film, it tends ever so slightly to clash with, or needlessly duplicate, the images we see. In the present case, because Ivan's reflection is a sort of parenthesis, the film had to omit it and we do not learn the full horror of the captain's ordeal. But something still more important gets lost: the offhand, almost humorous tone of Ivan's comments that, paradoxically, makes the dreadfulness even greater by showing how accepted, banal a part of existence it has become.

And something else. The brief comment, which in Solzhenitsyn often pierces the heart, cannot be rendered by any medium but print—especially if it is followed by some white space, inviting a pause for meditation. When the captain is led away, the others shout after him, "Keep your chin up!" and "Don't let 'em get you down!" This the film reproduces. But then the text reads: "What could you say?"—end of paragraph, blank space. What can the film do to equal these few plain, helpless, undramatic but shattering words? A great director, which Wrede is not, might have found a solution; but even the greatest could not find cinematic equivalents for every one of literature's major and minor triumphs.

The matter of parentheses is particularly important here: "and death i think is no parenthesis," ends one of E. E. Cummings's finest lyrics; but living death, life in a prison camp, is precisely a parenthesis. The body is confined in space and, even more, in a daily round of dreary and dehumanizing activities or brutish exhaustion. That leaves the mind free, indeed forces it, to roam obsessively in the backward, the forward, the sideways. What the body does is piddling and linear, although the line may be a frantic zigzag. But the mind, the mind creates desperate, speculative, life-giving parentheses of its own, where the abject prisoner lives suprareally. And the camera is, for the most part, denied access to these.

Yet just as the camera underachieves in some areas, it accomplishes too much in others, with equally untoward results. The color photography here is by Sven Nykvist, Ingmar Bergman's superlative cinematographer. For the prison barracks scenes, Nykvist gives us exactly the right hues: soiled blues and lackluster browns, colors that do not improve on the situation. But when the prisoners are marched out to their terrible labor as the icy dawn is about to break, the screen becomes overwhelmingly beautiful. Strange, unsuspected colors appear in the northern sky: nacreous, opalescent, boreally understated. As the camera comes in on or withdraws from the trudgers, we see less or more sky around them; and each time we see more, the color has subtly, insinuatingly modified.

No less lovely is the sky-show at evening, when the prisoners return. In both instances the snow on the ground provides an obbligato to the celestial color organ, a neutral, blue white bass that modulates into white or black to stay in harmony. It is too beautiful, and it is no use saying that's how it is in Siberia or in northernmost Norway, where the film was shot. That is not the way Ivan Denisovich, or any of the other unfortunates, would have seen it. It is too ennobling.

Otherwise, the film has merits. It is faithful to the book; it is at least adequately directed; and it contains sober, apt performances. If *One Day* is sometimes hard to follow, that is in the nature of the material: the weird regulations and circuitous machinations of the camp. Regrettably, too, half the cast speaks with a Norwegian accent, and the other half with British ones, mostly Cockney or Yorkshire, to indicate humble origins. The result, to my ear, is less than convincing. But Tom Courtenay is a believable and likable protagonist who does not become overingratiating; and the various British and Norwegian characters make much out of their generally small parts.

The centerpiece of the film is a hefty chunk of toil, the building of a house with the most primitive means in far-below-zero weather. Both the biting cold and the hard-bitten methods of scrounging for illegal heat are well conveyed. Moreover, film has seldom communicated so palpably the hardness, roughness, exhaustingness—the very feel—of labor; and also its minuscule, sneaky exultations when whatever shifty stratagem yields badly needed results.

Like the novel—and here it is a match—the film shows persuasively how much under the most bestial circumstances men can hold on to their humanity, can find crevices in the rock of inhuman discipline from which kindness sprouts. Now it is the saxifrage of a smile, now the hardy lichen of intellectual debate about the artistic merits of Eisenstein's films. In fact, such things as prisoners discussing *Potemkin* or avidly reading a newspaper account of Zavadsky's latest production are among the sunniest occurrences in this icy inferno.

It is to Solzhenitsyn's credit that he does not show extraordinary brutalities where the ordinary ones will do nicely. And, again like the book, the film records a *good* day in Ivan's life—which is the loveliest and saddest thing about it. There are some obviousnesses: I wish, for instance, that a debate about God did not take place between prisoners Karamazovishly named Ivan and Alyosha. Still, it is finally a life-enhancing movie, deserving a place somewhat higher than that of a mere respectable failure.

The film adaptation, however, cannot do for this book what Leoš Janáček's musical genius did for a very similar work, Dostoevsky's *From the House of the Dead,* turned by Janáček into an opera as great, if not greater than, the original. It is because music is farther than film from literature, because it does not invite close comparisons, that an autonomous success can result in it even from an adaptation.

May 17–June 14, 1971

Deadly Clowning

THE OLD MASTERS continue to strike out. Federico Fellini's *The Clowns* was made for television, but even that cannot excuse it. It is meant to be part documentary about the lives of the clowns; part history of the clown's provenance, evolution into types, and present decline; part autobiography, showing Fellini's early-acquired and enduring love for the circus; part exploits of Fellini and his crew tracking down famous old clowns or the scarce records they left behind; and part philosophizing about parallels between clowns and humankind, and the relations of the clowns to Fellini characters. On all these counts, the film relentlessly fails.

As a documentary, it is defiantly antitruth. We are allowed to guess right away that Fellini's "crew" are in fact clowns, something that is later grandly, and rather unfunnily, revealed. Cute incidents keep unspontaneously cropping up. Pierre Etaix, the film comedian, takes Fellini and crew to his place to screen a unique film about the great Fratellinis, those legendary clowns to one of whose granddaughters he is married. But the film promptly catches fire in the projector, and we are left darkling. Fellini and crew go to the immense skyscraper of the French National Radio and TV to dig up the only existing film record of another famed clown, only to find it so short and slight as to be useless. The harridan in charge inquires of our celebrated director whether he is Monsieur Bellini! How perishable a thing is fame, we are to note with melancholy—a great clown's or great filmmaker's.

The interviews with stellar clowns are postsynched by God knows whom. A renowed clown said to be Spanish in the film is listed in the credits as French, and speaks with an accent that is neither. As in all Fellini films, foreign accents almost invariably come out German, either because they elicit the biggest yuks in Italy, or because of some special Fellini grudge. In any case, most of this dubious dubbing quickly yields to voice-over summaries of a particularly highfalutin and heart-tugging sort, presumably because what was actually said did not falute sufficiently high or tug heartily enough. If the point is not cinéma-vérité but a piece of lively pseudohistory, a story film about a clown, a true fiction film, would serve artistic truth far better than this fictionalized historicism.

44

Even worse are the staged set pieces. The Fratellinis entertain at a madhouse, with such throat-catching details as one patient staring away from the performance and grimly into the camera. The Fratellinis clown at a field hospital while (again!) one of the shell-shocked wounded fixedly gazes ahead of him into space. A celebrated French clown lies dying in a hospital, but sneaks out to the circus to catch the act of the two new favorite clowns. He applauds them generously; at dawn, he is found there in the bleachers, dead. These vignettes are coy to the point of odiousness, but Fellini has to add insult to injury: a dozing nun near the sickbed from which the clown steals away is revealed as—a man in nunnish drag. By such desperate stratagems Fellini tries to drag humor into this farrago.

The obverse of Fellini's sentimentality is his crudeness. So we get all kinds of freaks and brutes performing garish feats gratuitously mixed in with clowning. Typical example: two enormous women slugging it out for the presumptive title of Most Monstrous Womanoid Grotesque. More offensive yet is a series of closeups of Anita Ekberg. The camera zooms in on her again and again as she laughs maniacally in front of the leopards' cage. The woman-mountain Ekberg shakes her platinum mane at us and bares massively sculptured rows of teeth in a carnivorous leer as the camera lands reiterated haymakers on her puss. The narration spouts equivalent vulgarities about the most savage beast of all. No more than the leopard, alas, can Fellini change his spots.

The gratuitous presence of Ekberg is only one of numerous *hommages* Fellini pays to his earlier films. Thus, for instance, several staged sequences about odd characters Fellini compares to clowns reintroduce personages we remember from *Variety Lights, The White Sheik,* and, especially, *I Vitelloni,* whole episodes of which are here grotesquely reenacted. The little Federico at the beginning of *The Clowns* who gazes rapturously at the arriving clowns is, once again, the young boy from *8½* who feasted his eyes on the seaside dance of the huge, clownish Saraghina. The parallels are less between circus and life than between *The Clowns* and Fellini's filmography; and what makes these self-tributes particularly unfortunate is that the scenes worked so much better in the films where they originally appeared.

No clear history of the clown emerges, no panorama, no perspective. But there is the implicit philosophizing or allegorizing. The clown "crew" Fellini drags around with him symbolizes the oneness of the clown show and the cinema; the end of *The Clowns* with its grandiose mock funeral of an imaginary superclown, a funeral that turns into a fiesta, symbolizes the immortality of clowning—including, of course, Fellini's. As if this weren't enough, there is an epilogue: a living clown and his beloved, dead colleague play a trumpet duet of "Ebb Tide" to each other across the cavernous space of an empty circus. The immortality of the soul is presumably demonstrated by this maudlin duet. Immortality of the clown, of the soul, of Fellini—how beautifully they blend together in this fake of a film.

Consider one much admired scene. The small, silly, irascible stationmaster of a two-lira railway station (out of *I Vitelloni*) is mocked by a passing train-   45 load of raffish schoolboys. He promptly summons a pasty-faced comic giant of a Fascist official, and the louts are forthwith deferentially offering the Fascist salute as the tiny stationmaster beams in ecstasy. As political satire, compare this with any scene from Luciano Salce's *Il Federale,* and it is immediately shown up as impotent posturing. There is supposed to be a parallel between the pedantic domineering white clown, or Pierrot, and the Fascist official; and also between the slovenly, furibund, often pathetic Auguste (the other principal clown type) and the stationmaster. But when you have likened two supposedly typical figures from life to a pair of allegedly major types of clowns, what have you really said? That there is a parallel between the circus and life? That the horrors of history have their grotesque aspects? *The Clowns* is not even staged cinéma-vérité; it is *cinéma-vérité de La Palice:* not cinema-truth but cinema-truism.

Luchino Visconti is not really an Old Master, rather a master forger, but he too strikes out dismally with *Death in Venice.* In a letter of 1910 to Samuel Lublinski, Thomas Mann wrote: "What is art? What is the artist? This mixture of Lucifer and Clown." Later that year, after a meeting with Gustav Mahler, Mann said to his wife that for the first time he had the feeling of having met a truly great man. Next year, Mahler died prematurely, not yet fifty-one. Shaken by the news, Mann wrote the novella *Death in Venice,* about the dying of a great writer, to whom he gave Mahler's first name and age, and a few of his external features. What Mann wrote in his one letter to Mahler, about recognizing in him "the gravest and holiest artistic will of our time," applies equally to the novella's protagonist, Aschenbach.

Gustav von Aschenbach resembles Mann much more than Mahler, though even that is not particularly important; the novella is really, as we are told in it, about "the questionable nature of art, of artisthood itself." Indeed, Mann's writing is a continuous inquiry into the dual nature of art, its delightful playfulness and its Luciferian disregard for ordinary proprieties. Even while being a denial of life in its cruder, and perhaps happier, aspects, the pursuit of beauty and art dooms its adepts to spiritual and imaginative excesses far more depleting than any toll that mere living could exact. Art, in its very purity and demandingness, becomes a kind of decadence (or so, at least, the somewhat strait-laced Mann saw it), and *Death in Venice,* with subtle ironies within ironies, probes the doubleness of Aschenbach: strict classicist in his writing, repressed sensualist in his innermost being. Erich Heller aptly refers us, in connection with the novella, to the finest verses of August von Platen, a poet Mann admired: *"Wer die Schönheit angeschaut mit Augen, / Ist dem Tode schon anheimgegeben"*—whoever has beheld beauty with his eyes is already delivered into the hands of death.

Aschenbach, as will be recalled, goes to Venice on a whim, feels himself dissolve under the oppressive sun lurking behind cloudy skies and the incessant blowing of the enervating sirocco. At his luxury hotel on the Lido, he espies a beautiful fourteen-year-old Polish boy, Tadzio, whom he wordlessly adores from a distance. Cholera breaks out in Venice, and though its raging is mercenarily hidden from the tourists, Aschenbach learns the truth. Yet he neither warns Tadzio's elegant mother, nor removes himself (despite one feeble attempt) from the pestilential city and the boy who fills him with love. He silently follows the child around and slowly lets himself go in every way—even to the point of allowing the hotel barber to rejuvenate him vulgarly with cosmetics—and eventually dies in his beach chair while watching Tadzio walking on a sandbank in the water. The boy now subsumes Hermes and the angel of death, Eros and Thanatos.

Aschenbach dies of cholera. But, more truly, of yielding to a beauty he has for decades pursued as well as held in check. The novella is not homosexual, or, at least, not overtly so.* The little Pole—of the wrong sex and age, speaking a deliquescent language Aschenbach cannot understand, and deigning to notice the aging writer only now and then with a look of curiosity and mild sympathy—represents the Ineffable, the Unattainable, the Impossible that the true artist spends his life straining after. This desperate flirtation is, finally, a romance with death, and it is giving in to dissolution and death, not to dissoluteness and guilty passions, that Mann's story is mainly about. Mann's Aschenbach permits himself to be shamefully made up once; he does not, like Visconti's, repeatedly wear clownish-looking make-up, and die with it running, mingled with sweat, all over his face, panama hat, and white summer suit. In Mann, it is art and beauty that are suspect and deadly; in Visconti, it is the protagonist who is dirty.

Visconti has turned the hero from a novelist into a composer-conductor modeled on Gustav Mahler. He did this, presumably, because his showy, unintellectual nature—despite intellectual pretensions—is more at ease with music and the gesticulation of the conductor than with cerebration and the tiny wrist movements of the writer. But the novella is intimately involved with the writer's world, his mental processes and analyses—including even mock-Platonic dialogues—that have nothing to do with the musician's sphere. Visconti is a liar when he says Mann wrote the story about Mahler, and a double liar in his representation of that composer's nature. Not only was Mahler not a homosexual like this Aschenbach ("to live for you, to die for you," he wrote, among other endearments, to his beloved wife, Alma, on the manuscript of his last, unfinished symphony), he was the very opposite of the emotionally constipated formalist that a young disciple, Alfred, here accuses him of being.

Alfred is the worst of the many bad inventions of the screenplay by Visconti and Nicola Badalucco, who also collaborated on the abysmal *The Damned*. Back and forth fly platitudes between the master and his demonic pupil, apparently "modeled" on Arnold Schönberg: Visconti must have heard that Mann wrote something called *Doctor Faustus*, whose composer protagonist, loosely based on Schönberg, sells his soul to the devil. The film's pseudo-Schönberg drivels on about "Evil is a necessity, it is the food of genius," and "Do you know what lies at the bottom of the mainstream? Mediocrity!" and "Your music is stillborn!" The real Schönberg once wrote

---

*Postscript 1982. We now know from published diaries that Mann had repressed homosexual tendencies.

Mahler humbly asking him for help with his rent bill, and once more to thank him profusely for sending a larger sum than was needed. That was all.

Not only are these dialogues about music and art of the utmost banality and pretentiousness, they also falsify both Mahler's and Schönberg's ideas about music and belie the nature of the composers' works. Worse, Aschenbach-Mahler is made into a now simpering, now petulant, now blustering fool, who listens to Tadzio badly playing "Für Elise" only to be reminded (flashback) of a favorite whore in a most improbable bordello playing "Für Elise" almost equally badly. The implication of this scene is that Aschenbach could not find fulfillment with his pretty wife, sought out whores, and, as the parting expressions on his and the girl's faces would indicate, failed as much with the profane love as with the sacredly conjugal. Homosexuality, clearly, was the only possible answer!

What Visconti and Badalucco have concocted is worsened by Dirk Bogarde's performance as Aschenbach. Though meant to be only fifty, Bogarde tends to effect an eightyish dodder. Meant to look cold and intellectual, Bogarde's face is pouty, pettish, and rather vapid. After pretending to be infuriated by a hotel error obliging him to stay on in Venice—which he wanted to do all along—he gives a prolonged little smile of secret self-satisfaction that must be the coyest, smuggest, most obvious bit of facial play this worthy actor has ever permitted himself. Shambling along the hotel beach, officiously ordering about the beach attendant (one of numerous twentyish, corrupt-looking youths with whom Visconti populates his movie), eating a strawberry with exaggeratedly fussy gusto, or merely ogling Tadzio with a sheepishness that keeps spilling over into bovineness, Bogarde, in his white togs and funny hat, looks less like *Death in Venice* than like *Monsieur Hulot's Holiday.*

And Tadzio? Instead of a fourteen-year-old ephebe, Björn Andresen is a sixteenish androgyne, looking like a semidepraved version of a figure from Botticelli's *Primavera*. Instead of exchanging a few glances and a smile or two with Aschenbach, he is made to go through a variety of *oeillades,* mysterious little grins, near-contacts. Mann's Tadzio once stands with one hand on his hip; this one nearly always with one, sometimes with both. Mann's Tadzio has two suits and one swimsuit; Visconti's three swimsuits, six or seven more or less provocative street outfits, and a couple of hats to match. Tadzio's playmate, rather than being in every way like him only less attractive, is here about twenty, and as darkly loutish as any male whore you can find on the Via Veneto.

Badalucco and Visconti have not even perceived the figure of Death that appears throughout the story in several strange characters, all vaguely similar. Some of these figures they omit, others they retain: sinister, but without the family resemblance and the deathlike traits. And what of the shabby way Mahler's music is used on the soundtrack? And of the flaccid color photography—sometimes pretty, more often undistinguished—of Pasquale de Santis? True, the lavish costumes of Piero Tosi and opulent décor of Ferdinando Scarfiotti work handsomely; but here, too, the lip-syncing of the Polish dialogue is the worst I have ever seen. Worst of all, though, is the dubbing of Visconti's flashy, blatant sensibility into Mann's thoughtful, ironic novella.

July 26, 1971

Losing Touch

BIBI ANDERSSON is in trouble; so is Max von Sydow and so, worst of all, is Ingmar Bergman, with the Swedish master's first mainly English-language film, *The Touch*. It has only two good scenes, the opening and one where Miss Andersson tries on various outfits before her mirror. Otherwise, it perilously approaches the work of such masters of the bathetic as Pasolini and Chabrol. Andersson and Von Sydow act, even in English, with unabated excellence. Sven Nykvist's color photography is as juicy, succulently ripe as it remained intentionally sparse and austere in *A Passion*. Bergman moves his camera around with superb strategy, especially in those cramped spaces that some frenzied character crisscrosses like a panicky butterfly in a net. But what is it all about?

It chronicles, I guess, the rise and fall of an affair between a Swedish housewife in her early thirties and a German-American-English, Sweden-exploring (i.e., Wandering) Jew, who is an archaeologist. Under the complacent, seemingly content life of the woman, there lurks, we gather, sterility and frustration; but the causes, like those of the woman's alleged immaturity, are just barely adumbrated, certainly not examined. The lover, we learn, is far from being the open, outgoing carnal creature whose intensely dark hairiness contrasts so vitally with the Swedish blondness and blandness. He is, in fact, consumed by a welter of neuroses or worse; but here, again, the causes and consequences are dealt with in an infuriatingly illegible shorthand, or with maddeningly facile symbolism.

Bergman, with the English soundtrack and a sure-fire American box-office star (as Elliott Gould looked then), was out to make a woman's picture, a heart-rending love story, guaranteed to sweep the U.S. market. But he has no feeling for that wretched genre; any Hollywood hack can do immeasurably more with it, precisely because he does not let larger implications seep in. Bergman also lacks language here. The film is in insipid, sometimes slightly stilted, English (no credit is given to whoever helped, or hampered, Bergman with the language), although in any tongue, it would sound slipshod and banal. Gould is beneath contempt: his catfish mouth emits a cutesy baby talk; he has only three expressions—childish eagerness, childish fury, childish hurt—and he uses them as glaring primary colors. His voice is monotonous, his accent much too crude for that of an archaeologist—in fact, one doubts that he could dig up a telephone cable. All this might not be so apparent to   49 a Swede. What should be apparent is the film's triviality and threadbareness, and the sadness of several great artists slushing about in this puddle.

Unlike Bergman, Nicolas Roeg, who made the horrible *Performance*, does not arouse expectations. His current *Walkabout* is the tragicomic story of two young English kids abandoned in the Australian outback and guided back to civilization by an aborigine boy on his solitary "walkabout" (rite of passage). It is based, apparently, on a nice, straightforward novel. Roeg has gimmicked it up with every kind of photographic and scenaristic pretentiousness, irrelevance, and puzzling opacity. Still, the land is fascinating; the kids, black and white, delightful; and you do see, even if dragged in by their tails, a lot of interesting animals.

August 9, 1971

Children in War

IF THERE IS such a thing as a film that makes its viewer a better human being—and I dearly hope there is—*Hoa Binh* is it. It is the story, essentially, of two Vietnamese children: a boy, Hung, aged eleven, and his sister, Xuan, one and a half. The time is not now or last year or tomorrow; the time is, simply and dreadfully, war. The action takes place between Hung's father's departure to join the Vietcong and his return to Saigon, months later, on a secret mission.

He leaves behind his lovely young wife, ill with cancer, who resells food she buys in the market to make a precarious living for herself and their children. Their home is destroyed by bombardment, forcing the family to move in with grudging, surly relatives. Despite her cancer, the mother keeps trudging vast distances on foot; finally, she can no longer refuse hospitalization. She is taken off to die; the relatives make life impossible for the children. Now starts a long odyssey in which Hung, always taking care of little Xuan as his mother instructed him to do, and holding on to the hat his father left behind, wanders around Saigon. He does odd jobs, sometimes successfully, sometimes exploited by greedy older people, sometimes bested by kids more ruthless than he is; somehow, almost miraculously, he and Xuan manage to survive.

The plot is minimal, at times awkward, and barely sufficient to give us the sustained sense of a developing action. There are episodes that do not have the roundedness of a neatly made point; rather, they have jagged edges that do not join smoothly as an indenture with the next incident. There is the shot of Hung walking through the Saigon market gazing in wonder, a shot repeatedly crosscut with stacks of victuals displayed in symmetrical arrangements; this sequence reminds me uncomfortably of an industrial film of some sort, or even a commercial. And there is the scene in the hospital when the returning father is told how and why his wife died; this once, the film lapses into pathos through rapid closeup, crosscutting among father, doctor, and nurse; and echo-chamber effects on the soundtrack.

Otherwise, the film is understated, refined, thoughtful, visually eventful, and of a modesty and simplicity that, given the opportunities for their opposites, are tantamount to saintliness. The understatement is not as in, say, a Pinter-Losey film, fraught with pretentious hinting; it is simply the expression of an ancient, stoic culture caught in an endurance test that keeps going on almost beyond endurance, and that can be combatted only with even more unflinching acceptance.

The film was made by Raoul Coutard, a Parisian who spent eleven years of his youth as a war photographer in Vietnam, married a Vietnamese, worked on some documentary films, and returned to Paris to become one of the finest cinematographers of our time. From *Breathless* to *Weekend,* he shot all of Godard's films, four of Truffaut's, and has worked for other directors as well—recently for Costa-Gavras in *Z* and *The Confession.* This is the first feature film he directed and, though based on Françoise Lorrain's novel, *Column of Ashes,* the script, too, is his. It establishes him as a filmmaker of deep-rooted artistry; in my opinion, it should also earn him the Nobel Peace Prize.

Hoa Bình means, in fact, "peace" in Vietnamese, and the film begins by zeroing in on a map of Vietnam as we hear the voice of an unseen Vietnamese child speaking—in French, this time. Later, everyone speaks his own language. "Do you know what that is, 'peace'?" the voice asks. And adds, "Daddy says, 'When you grow up, you'll know it.' But for thirty years in Vietnam there is war." It is a downy, unfledged voice; it is also a bit stunned, a trifle numb. It is the voice of a child cheated of its childhood.

The film is a little about all sorts of things that happen in a war; but, mostly, it is about what happens to children. It is a film with a master image that, once it falls across your eyes, cannot be unseen or unremembered: an eleven-year-old boy leading, carrying, washing, feeding his tiny, rag-doll-like sister through a city that is both ravaged and thriving, both sorrowing and indifferent to sorrow, both reduced to tatters and bestiality and also making money, resilient, even gallant. Those two diminutive plodders-on detach themselves from the background, assume a life in our minds independent from the story that surrounds them, as do young Thomas de Quincey and the waif Ann from *The Confessions of an English Opium Eater,* or the two children burying dead animals from the other cinematic masterpiece about kids in war, René Clément's *Forbidden Games.* What makes the film deeply moving is the understatement, the calm, the matter-of-factness with which it goes about its task.

It is night in the house of the unsympathetic Cousin Nam, whose earlier hateful glances watched the mother smearing her knee with an ointment that, next to chicken soup, must be the least effective antidote for cancer. Hung has remained awake, in an anxious vigil. The mother, too, is awake with pain, and she tells the boy that this time she will just have to go to the hospital. "But you will be back?" Hung asks. "I don't think so." "But Daddy   51 will be back?" "Maybe, but I'm not sure. You stay here and take care of little Xuan. I'm counting on you." That is all there is to that scene, played in relative darkness, low-keyed in every way, except in the scarablike brilliance of those large dark Vietnamese eyes. Or take the succeeding scene in which the young woman on the stretcher already half swallowed by the ambulance says to her son: "Child, you are going to meet the bitterness of life, but remember the joy and sweetness of childhood and try to give them to little Xuan. . . . Remember joy and hope." And the ambulance drives off into the lush yet somehow damaged-looking landscape along a dirt road as the small boy and miniature girl stand in the lower left corner of the frame. The dust has already settled, but a wind continues to agitate the grasses, the grasses that are taller than the children. The voices are gentle and unportentous, the mother's face composed except for a very slight dent made in it by the pain. Yet these tiny scenes say more against war than does all of a film like *Johnny Got His Gun.*

Coutard works by effects so subtle that one virtually cannot use the ambiguous word "effects" to describe them. From the dark brown hut interior of the first scene just described, he cuts to a dazzlingly hopeful whiteness, on which we then detect the red cross of the ambulance in the second scene. It looks clean and much nicer than Cousin Nam's place, and it means death. That is all. Or take the scene where the father comes out of the nursery caring for little Xuan. The small child starts crying when this by now unknown man tries to fondle her. He steps out into the street, his face almost impassive, and a G.I. in fatigues walks past him. You might not even catch this quickly passing figure as you concentrate on the father; but if you do, you will notice that he is some two feet taller than the Vietnamese man. Although it is almost the very end of the film, it is the first time you see a Vietnamese placed next to an American. And something clutches at your throat: What is this race of maladroit, lumbering giants doing here among these small, neat, graceful people? They simply do not belong.

The chief device, besides restraint, that prevents the film from becoming unilateral and cloying is irony. It appears in various forms. Tragic: the people are made to fight one war by day and another by night; the Cong comes and makes them dig up the roads they had to help build for the Americans and government troops. And each army, in identical fashion, takes away a man or two for execution. Tragicomic: every group proffers the same grand phrases. An American sergeant, an infiltrating North Vietnamese political commissar, and a Vietcong officer all say that they did not want the war, but will fight for twenty years if necessary, etc, etc, with the same pious conviction. Wry: when Hung briefly lands a job as a shoeshine boy, he does poorly because he has to lug Xuan along.

This last scene is shot mostly below the knee—a bootblack's view of the world. The little girl thinks her brother's struggles to get a pair of shoes to hold still, rather than kick him away, a delicious game. While Hung is shining a pair of French shoes, two American boots alongside them orate about the American involvement in the war; the pronouncements are so magisterial, they must come from a top-ranking officer. Then Hung finishes shining, gets up from his knees, and we catch a glimpse of a cap with three noncom's stripes on it.

And there is also purely jocular irony, as when the young people in a South Vietnamese underground Communist cell are shown to be all rich kids in nice clothes, with expensive bicycles. You see them polishing their elegant spectacles while listening to the most high-minded political platitudes.

But what makes the film a work of enduring art is the enormous, nonpartisan sympathy with which it envelops all. There is no political side-taking: the South and North Vietnamese, the Cong, the Americans—all are portrayed as equally right and wrong. Right because they are human beings with the right to a decent life, wrong because they are combatants, whoever started it, whoever forces them to kill. Good men all—except those who are bad: who profiteer, who exploit children, make them toil for them without even paying them properly for it. But such evil people alternate with kindly, generous souls; uncomprehending Xuan and half-comprehending Hung meet with benefactors as well as with brutes. And even the brutes provide some pleasure: a fat woman profiteer has a fat American car; the boys whom she grossly underpays use its grille as their bathroom. They urinate on it, laugh, and are, for the moment, children and happy.

Like the great poet Guillaume Apollinaire, who died of a war and was yet able to see and celebrate its beauties, so Coutard, the poet of film images, also perceives the beauties of this war he detests. There is a brief, piercing scene where Hung watches flares in the night sky above his village. They are among the few beauties the child has been vouchsafed, and his mother steps behind him at the window to lay her hands on his shoulders in confirmation and approbation of his joy. But the smile that bends toward him is overflowing with pity and sadness. Beautiful, too, is the opening scene, in which American helicopters perform a sinister sky ballet. From below rise orange and lavender smoke signals like colored spotlights, and men wear the grotesquely theatrical masks and costumes of war. But the dance is up there above them, danced by gigantic insects that are both elegant dragonflies and devouring locusts—some terrible and enchanting cross between *Fantasia* and *The Hellstrom Chronicle*. It is deadly but also beautiful, and, like an audience bowled over by sheer ecstasy, the vegetation falls over backward underneath the huge helicopters pirouetting down to earth. And the horror and the beauty of it is that one learns to live with the war. With the disappearance of one's father and the death of one's mother. With cruelty, hunger, sickness yapping at one's heels. How dreadful that, when aerial fire reaches the family hut, a child should know exactly, efficiently, how to pack up what is essential for survival, and do it without batting an eyelash. There is one emblematic scene here, in which Hung, Xuan, and several other children spend some of their hard-scrounged coins to look at a movie on a street nickelodeon. We watch their faces glued to the peepholes while their bare feet rub against one another in voluptuous bliss. What *they* are watching   53 turns out to be an old Fernandel flick in which the comedian, in Wild West regalia, farcically shoots it out with an adversary, played also by himself. A grimly comic symbol, this, of the civil war raging around them, complete with American trappings; but the children are beguiled down to their wiggling toes. It is beautiful, and the beauty merely adds to the horror.

The color cinematography of Coutard's long-time assistant, Georges Liron, is decently subdued. This is not at all the kind of photographic razzle-dazzle that famous cinematographers put into their films when they become directors—one thinks of such men as Jack Cardiff, Nicolas Roeg, Freddie Francis, Claude Lelouch, among others. An effect like the yellow-outs, green-outs, and other color fadeouts, for example, derives its authority from the brightly colored smoke signals to the helicopter at the very beginning of the film. These helicopters, planes, and large supply ships (the last sailing down canals so narrow that, from a distance they appear to be moving across dry land) are photographed in all the stateliness, acrobatic bravura, darting energy of a dance of death that seems more choreographed than fought.

Coutard's scenario is as laconic and unassertive as the eloquently subdued performances. Even tiny Huynh Cazenas contributes an utterly charming presence as the baby sister. The entire Vietnamese cast seems possessed of a physical grace that cannot but derive from some ancient, communal, spiritual refinement. But Xuan Ha as the mother and Phi Lan as the boy are—if I may permit myself the kind of word Coutard would never allow in his script—unforgettable. She is a part-time television announcer, whose face is such a blend of wisdom, dignity, and sheer beauty of feature as to produce an overwhelming elation in the beholder. He is the nonprofessional son of lowly workers; a child of exquisite lineaments and with a skater's poise, his expressions are often prematurely at home with grief. But Phi Lan has a smile that is equally ready to backtrack into heartbreak or lunge forward into radiant confidence, a smile that could stop a tank in its tracks or draw tears from a glass eye. Both actors achieve things on screen that would do credit to some of our greatest performers. They accomplish this almost exclusively with a look, a smile, or a little inflection in that strange, gentle, sing-song they speak, a language not of coarse human beings but of flutes, temple bells, and very dainty cats.

Yet *Hoa Binh* is not a disheartening film. It takes the side of all humanity, and particularly of children, with a sweet unself-conscious naturalness that has seldom been equaled where the subject was children in war. There are almost no false moves, and the humblest incidents can effortlessly carry the burden of large statements that remain rigorously enclosed in implication. Just like the one-or-two-line connective narration in French between scenes, which has the sound of haikus or some other delicately understated Oriental poems, the entire film operates with compelling modesty, with a sedulous soft pedal applied to all the sadness, horror, and occasional joy. It is language reduced to susurration, but a susurration that can uplift as well as break the heart with the force of unobstreperous truth.

August 29–September 20, 1971

Middling to Maddening

WALTER ALLEN quotes an unnamed critic's description of L. P. Hartley's work: "comic in manner but full of terror in its implications." Small wonder then that it should have attracted the director-scenarist team of Joseph Losey and Harold Pinter, who have now made a film of Hartley's 1950 novel, *The Go-Between.* Their two previous, not uninteresting yet vastly overrated collaborations, *The Servant* and *Accident,* tried to be comic but full of terrible implications. The not uninteresting and also much overrated *The Go-Between* continues the tradition. It concerns the thirteenth summer of Leo, a poor but genteel boy, spent at the large Norfolk estate belonging to the Maudsleys, the wealthy family of a schoolmate. Here, at the crucial stage of puberty, among the idly and idyllically rich, Leo loses his heart, his innocence, and his future happiness.

The time is 1900, and the film catches the period well enough. But Pinter and Losey must gum up the works with gimmickry. Scenes are ruthlessly foreshortened so that the action lurches ahead jerkily. Various ominousness-increasing devices are dragged in, the worst among them the flash-forwards, whereby we see an episode from the future encroaching, bit by bigger bit, upon the past, needlessly puzzling and unnerving us. If the point is that, as the narrator says at the outset, "the past is a foreign country—they do things differently there," then the past must be unsettling enough by being the past; no need to smuggle the future into it.

Leo, who thinks himself gifted with magical powers, is really a poor minnow out of water in these posh surroundings. He falls in deep, boyish love with Marian, the lovely daughter of the house, engaged to a viscount. Marian toys with Leo's feelings, flirting with him, bullying him, and ignoring him by turns. Gradually she enlists him as a go-between carrying notes to and from Ted Burgess, a tenant farmer with whom she is having an affair. The boy likes Ted and has no idea that the notes refer to assignations; he does not even know about sex yet, and his questions are met with evasions. An interesting network of relationships evolves among Leo and the various Maudsleys, older or younger, and the two men in Marian's life; the film does convey the amusingly quaint and rigid social conventions, condescensions, and contests that form this social fabric whose first unravelings we are allowed to witness.

But other things are muffed. The fun and games, the little fights between Leo and his classmate and host—sometimes playful, sometimes deeply although obscurely hostile—are staged with unconvincing stiffness. Losey has little feeling for the rhythms and choreography of these capers, and they have a leaden arbitrariness about them. Once again, as in *The Servant* and *Accident,* he exhibits a staircase fixation that is positively maniacal. The massive oaken staircase at Brandham Hall is manorial enough, God knows, but Losey dwells on it obsessively, with great thumpings of boots up and down it   55 as well as occasional fisticuffs, as if it were, at the very least, a cross between Jacob's Ladder and the Tower of Babel.

Other Losey fixations are in evidence, too. Almost every time Leo carries a letter between the lovers, we zoom into or out of long shots with a regularity that quickly moves from grandioseness to dreariness. The magic experiments are slurred over and turned into deliberately murky Pinterian hocus-pocus. The crucial cricket match is reasonably well done, though the scene does not quite succeed in emblematizing the different class mentalities involved; the entertainment that follows it permits the humor to sink lower than genteel comedy can afford to stoop. The older Maudsley boy is a stock character, his snobbish attempts at being democratic made overexplicit and ludicrous. I am doubtful whether the mother, played by Margaret Leighton with that fine madness of hers that gets, with every appearance, a little more mad and a little less fine, needs to be quite so demented, and the discovery of Ted and Marian *in flagrante delicto* seems both too crude and too burlesque.

Nevertheless, there is a good plot going here along with acute observation of sociopsychological detail (mostly Hartley's achievement, but at least preserved by the film), and even in splintered form they hold our attention. The scenes of derogation, humiliation, and castration are effectively managed—Pinter and Losey are past masters at this sort of thing. But they cannot, or will not, tell a story cleanly. Burgess's suicide, for instance, and the epilogue with Marian, an old woman sending the lonely, neurotic, middle-aged Leo on a last errand, are clouded almost to the point of incomprehensibility. O art, what botches are committed in thy name!

In the central role of Leo, Dominic Guard is splendidly chubby, forthright, ordinary, and likable—quite unprecious and unactorish—and he holds the picture together. Julie Christie is just adequate as Marian; Alan Bates, as Ted, is beginning to look and act like Hugh Griffith, a frightening case of premature senility. As the grown-up Leo, Michael Redgrave gives the impression of having just come out of a two-hour hiccupping spell and being afraid the fit might start again. Edward Fox's viscount is properly balanced between fumbling friendliness and contumelious remoteness; he exudes that upper-class vagueness of which it is hard to say whether it is shrewd, obtuse, or both in one. Michael Gough makes a nicely abstracted father. Gerry Fisher's color cinematography is delicately inviting; Michel Legrand's music is, as this antimusician's work always is, crassly assertive.

Despite its mediocrity, *The Go-Between* is superior to most of what is playing around. There is, for example, Jerzy Skolimowski's *Deep End,* a film of modish, slick pseudoprofundities, that tries to be everything, but everything on a low financial and intellectual budget. *Deep End* tells a simple little horror story (an older girl toying with a young boy's love, only to find that the game has serious, indeed murderous, consequences); but Skolimowski is hell-bent on proving that he has more than one shoestring to his cheap instrument. The insufferably inflated, alienatingly esoteric, and ultimately quite vacuous Polish writer-director has here concocted a parable about a London public bath, where people come in pursuit of sexual fantasies to be gratified by the pretty, scheming girl attendant (Jane Asher), or the innocent young boy attendant (John Moulder-Brown).

Into these dilapidated, physically and morally disintegrating premises, Skolimowski has dragged everything from Kafka to Genet, from Murnau to Truffaut and Godard, from two-pfennig German expressionism to the most arcane surrealism, in a desperate attempt to stir up new waves in an old pool. It is one of those annoyingly studio-made films where four people represent a crowd, and a whole district is reduced to a set that would fit into your garage—which is wonderfully expressionistic, and so economical, too.

Not only is the film a veritable junk pile of styles, but the pile also keeps collapsing, so you never know which piece of detritus is up. Out of nowhere comes a lengthy *hommage* to Tony Richardson's *The Loneliness of the Long-Distance Runner,* to be followed by what may, for all I know, be an in-joke of the Lodz Film School. The episode with Diana Dors is among the more nauseating examples of porcine naturalism in recent film history.

Amid all this pretentious high attitudinizing (shall we call it altitudinizing?), Skolimowski pays no attention to the performances. As the protagonist, the lifeless John Moulder Brown might as well be John Brown's body moldering in the grave. All in all, *Deep End* merely achieves the uninteresting feat of drowning in its own shallowness.

For sheer moral ugliness, psychic sickness, and aesthetic repulsiveness, even *Deep End* is small potatoes compared to Ken Russell's latest, *The Devils.* Based on a section of Aldous Huxley's sober *The Devils of Loudon* and the middling play John Whiting extracted from it, Russell's film takes a quantum leap from his abominable *The Music Lovers* into a dung heap. The film suffers from spiritual coprophilia, actually, which is rather more serious than mere physical perversion. Warner Brothers is supposed to have snipped out some of the horrors, though what they could find more odious than what they left in defies my feeble imagination.

Russell, who strikes me as something much worse than the mad artist—the mad anti-artist—will stop at no outrage in pursuit of effect for effect's sake. For him, the most aggressive blatancy is the exact equal of artistic impact. That there are people who consider the shock tactics of this bashi-bazouk consistent with artistry seems to me proof positive that our culture has reached the stage of paroxysm, after which, I suppose, there remains only rigor mortis.

Russell re-creates an entire medieval city, indoors and out (except for the hero's residence, which is a kind of Guggenheim Museum full of plaster casts), as one huge bathroom. Everything from fortifications to convents is made of white tiles upon tiles, so that *The Devils* can best be described as a progression from bathroom humor to bathroom horror. The notion that this olio of sadistic, fetishistic, voyeuristic, and pederastic fantasies makes any kind of historical, social, or human comment is as grotesque as the claim that a ten-car smash-up is a work of art. Jean-Luc Godard might, of course, argue that; but, then, insane pretentiousness, thy name is Godard.

Bundles From Britain

Sunday, Bloody Sunday has all the surface glitter a film or a candy wrapper could amass. The plot itself seems dazzlingly new: a young career woman has an affair with a very young sculptor who is also having an affair with a middle-aged Jewish doctor. It is all very sophisticated. Alex Greville is an upper-class divorcée working in executive placement, and leads a moderately swinging life among leftist-liberal friends while keeping a superiorly sloppy house for herself. Dr. Daniel Hirsh is a respectable general practitioner from a wealthy Orthodox family who lives neatly, graciously, and with warm appreciation of the arts. As for Bob Elkin, he is upward-mobile, which describes his sculpture almost as well as his psychosocial status, and swings merrily both ways, with latchkeys to both Alex's and Daniel's flats.

So, you see, it is really a trisexual triangle: one heterosexual, one homosexual, one bisexual—something for every taste and every type of self-identification. And whomever you identify yourself with, you can feel smugly superior to your compeers and kinfolk: Daniel is so ahead of his business-and-synagogue-oriented family; Alex is so emancipated from her parents' civil-service background; and Bob, though lower-class, has soared so high above his origins on the wings of his pop art. (Or op, or slop, or whatever art it is.) And everyone is aware of everything: Alex is jealous of Daniel but also respectful of him—for they both frequent that family of jolly radicals where the small children smoke pot and follow their elder's love affairs; Daniel, for his part, is downright concerned with how Bob may be treating her. Alex's parents are on excellent terms with her ex-husband, and Daniel and Alex even share the same telephone answering service, as they discover to their amusement.

In other words, this is updated Noël Coward or, better yet, Freddie Lonsdale, with lots of good furniture, the biggest and most sumptuous bar mitzvah celebration this side of the Queen's Ball, good-looking cars and children, and sorrows, in the main, gallantly stifled. There are bad moments—like the divorcée's concluding that there are times when nothing is better than something, or the doctor's learning that his lover will not accompany him on an Italian vacation. But it all has a way of being absorbed by those multiple layers of civilized amorality, and the bittersweet final encounter between Alex and Daniel, both abandoned by Bob, has such genteel, fastidious solicitude about it as to make upper-middle-class melancholy look like a positive badge of merit.

Surely, you say, there must be more. A bisexual involved with a socially, culturally, and perhaps intellectually superior man and woman, manipulating them both though also having some genuine feeling for them—this must make for a searching character study. Not in a film by John Schlesinger, with a script by Penelope Gilliatt, it doesn't. The young man is the least examined figure of the three, a mere type, used as a counter to elicit reactions from the others. As he is presented by the filmmakers, and nonacted by

Murray Head, nothing inside him is revealed, not even what his lovers could see in him, except perhaps youth, cockiness, and *nostalgie de la boue*. But, then, maybe the feelings of Alex and Daniel are thoroughly scrutinized? No. Incidents are there—Daniel's embarrassment by the inopportune reappearance of one of his former pickups, Alex's willingness to be swept into a one-night stand with one of her unhappy, aging, suddenly jobless executive clients. Yet I never truly had a sense of what Alex wants from life, or of how Daniel got to be what he is. Or why I should care about either of them.

What Schlesinger and Miss Gilliatt are very good at is conveying the outer shapes of existences, the little rugosities and slicknesses of the contours. The dialogue is crisp enough, and the images even crisper in the color cinematography of Billy Williams, who does better, because less flashily, here than in *Women in Love*. Nevertheless, gimmicks are everywhere: I don't believe that on a gloomy night drive through the center of London, Daniel would encounter a swarm of roller skaters racing down Piccadilly, that innocent kids would be regaled by the sight of young hoodlums vandalizing parked cars, that a doctor would be so humiliatingly disbelieved by a clerk in an all-night drugstore. While such miseries do occur in life, in this film they take on a peculiarly smart-aleck, contrived air—perhaps because the whole movie seems to rely on, consist of such footling cleverness.

There are awkwardnesses, too, such as a flashback to Alex's childhood that remains totally unintegrated and unhelpful, or a final soliloquy of Daniel's that is stilted in its efforts to avoid grandiloquence. Or the device of superimposing the days of the week on the image with which each new day begins— it looks portentous but adds nothing. In fact, the Tuesdays are just as bloody as the Sundays; if the point is the very uniformity and barrenness of all the days, that does not come across very compellingly either.

Actually, these lives are rather too glamorous to justify any great sympathy from the viewer. But the acting, except from Mr. Head, is so good as to jerk unearned sympathy. I am always overjoyed to see that wonderfully solid no-nonsense actor, Peter Finch, who imbues whatever he does with exquisite tact and grace. And, in smaller roles, I greatly admired Tony Britton and Peggy Ashcroft, among many fine others. Glenda Jackson is a powerful actress, but everything about her, including her walk, is just a little too ugly for my taste. And is it in her contract that every film she appears in must also feature that wretched bosom of hers? At least Schlesinger gives it mercifully short shrift.

The director, I repeat, is a dextrous, facile proto-artist. I suspect that it is from Elio Petri that he has learned how to make the furnishings of a place literally act, and it is surely from Truffaut's *Stolen Kisses* with its *pneumatique* cables that the idea of giving the telephone wires a juicy cameo role was derived. Let me describe one typical Schlesinger shot: Bob is seen adjusting a wall clock; he is framed by the top fifth of the wide-screen image, the lower four fifths blotted out by what turns out to be the back of a large armchair. Presently the chair swings around, and we see Alex's head in it in large closeup, with Bob hovering up there in the background. Later, the chair swings back again. It is a sequence during which Alex voices her *de profundis,* 59 but we are much more aware of the camera setup and directorial trickiness than of what is said or felt. Still, let us not minimize the film's ingenuity, especially in such scenes as the death of the dog. Only let us not confuse cleverness with depth.

A much more humane and moving film is the unfortunately renamed *Long Ago, Tomorrow*—though the British title, *The Raging Moon,* is scarcely better. Bryan Forbes has an extremely erratic record both as a scenarist and as a director, but this film, based on a novel by Peter Marshall, shows him at his not inconsiderable best in each capacity. The story sounds unpromising on paper. An arrogant young lower-class soccer player loses the use of his legs. Rather than return to his already cheerless home, he goes to a church-run institution for paraplegics. Here he is a misfit first because of his bitterness and hate; later, when he falls happily in love with another inmate, a thirtyish upper-middle-class girl, it is their love that clashes with the narrow regulations and pietistic minds that govern the institution. If I summarized more of the plot, you'd suspect a *Love Story* on wheels, and you'd be dead wrong.

Yes, the film verges on sentimentality, yet its glory is never to lapse into it. Its pathos is mitigated at one end by a hard sense of practical reality; at the other, by a sane sense of humor. Although this humor occasionally gets a trifle heavy-handed, the sentiment never goes sloppy. Indeed, some passages in the film are as quietly humane, enlightenedly observant, and dignifiedly, genuinely, purifyingly sad as any I have seen on film. Even the occasional clichés are handled with a certain wryness that revivifies their familiarity. But the people, even in tiny parts, are people, the dialogue is the speech of men and women, and the story has a clear-eyed intensity that earns every feeling it elicits.

One of the strengths of the film is Forbes's remarkable sense of rhythm. The length of each scene strikes me as absolutely right, its pacing not only true to itself, but finely contrasting with that of the previous or succeeding scene, and always beautifully dovetailing into what follows. The transitions are particularly harmonious, like carpentry that fits so perfectly with joints and dowels as not to require a single nail. No less praiseworthy is Tony Imi's cinematography, mostly pale colors, and washes of thin green, lavender, gray, brown. It is almost always winter or near-winter, yet the outdoors occasionally take on a richness of russets, a burnished fulfillment. An idyllic trip to the wintry seaside is mostly sobering grays and browns; yet the heroine's coat and the lover's happiness burn with scarlet delight.

Forbes has as good an ear as an eye: the sound effects of the film are marvelous, like the heartbreaking clatter of a Ping-Pong ball that hops away beyond the reach of a paraplegic. But the visual details are nothing short of thrilling: whether the way two figures are reflected, with significant shifts, in the unequal panels of a three-way mirror; or the little lurches of wheelchairs crossing an impudent ridge in a terrace floor. In the leads, Malcolm McDowell and Nanette Newman are unimprovable upon, and the supporting cast is first-rate, with especially incisive performances by Barry Jackson, Geoffrey Whitehead, Margery Mason, and Michael Lees.

October 18, 1971

Legalized Murder, Legitimized Incest

Sacco and Vanzetti is an imperfect film, but not an inartistic or insignificant one. It is chiefly the work of Giuliano Montaldo, who directed and, with Fabrizio Onofri, wrote the script. Montaldo was assistant to Gillo Pontecorvo on that remarkable pseudodocumentary, *The Battle of Algiers,* and some of the same techniques, much of the same moral fervor, and a little of the same excellence can be found in this film. It was shot mostly in Ireland, and, as a former improper Bostonian, I could not help marveling at how right the look is—though, admittedly, I was not around at the time of this infamous twenties trial.

There are a few errors in detail: British spellings like "Defence Committee" or "Fruit Centre," and, I am told, a license plate on a car is wrong. Still, the feel of an older Boston and its environs is persuasively present. This is particularly important in a film that appropriates documentary techniques, and generally strives for historical accuracy. Even Stanley Kauffmann, who disliked the movie, conceded that it tended to tally with the facts. That matters, because it would be regrettable if this terrifying case of human injustice and juridical inhumanity were seriously falsified for the sake of anything—even art. Though minor liberties, I dare say, were taken, no substantial prettification was allowed. Even too romantic truths, such as Edna Millay's riding a white horse around Boston Common in behalf of the condemned anarchists, are omitted.

After a slam-bang start, the film dawdles a little; and we are exposed throughout to a garish ballad composed by the brilliant Ennio Morricone (proving that even brilliance is fallible) with ghastly words written and sung by Joan Baez. A press conference with Secretary of State Palmer is suitably sinister, but does not blend stylistically with what precedes and follows, and thus produces a bit of a letdown. The body of a defenestrated anarchist hurtles through the air; the haunting shot is later repeated as a refrain, but only once or twice, and another good thing remains insufficiently exploited.

The director makes some unfortunate moves in the trial scenes, too: Milo O'Shea, as the defense counsel, enacts the flamboyant histrionics that greatly contributed to the defendants' undoing rather more antagonizingly than seems necessary; and the martinetlike judge of Geoffrey Keen is a bit too richly dripping with prejudice. Though it may be that they were in fact so odious, it would have been dramatically more effective to curb them a little. On the other hand, Cyril Cusack makes the district attorney calmly and believably blood-chilling, with only an occasional sneer too many. The trou- 61 ble lies in part in Montaldo's being Italian, and insufficiently at home with English emphases and accents; these actors sound far too British for Boston.

No matter—once Sacco and Vanzetti are on trial for their lives, the movie begins to come into its own. There are some very good touches here; for example, flashbacks to the actual events as related by the witnesses, but shot out of focus, in the hazy way in which they must have registered. Or, again, a sequence showing the whole robbery photographed so that we do not know till the last moment that it is a police reenactment. And what impresses us most from the beginning: the conception and characterization of the two accused. Riccardo Cucciola is a decent, befuddled, sometimes unnerved yet often sublimely dignified Sacco; meek and stubborn by turns, he is quite often heart-rendingly reasonable as well. Occasionally resorting to pathetic lies, he nevertheless damages himself more by his outbursts of heroic anti-Establishment truth. Gian Maria Volontè is even more compelling as the forceful, defiant, self-destructive Vanzetti, but self-destructive with a nobility that is deleterious only among human beings—among animals or angels, it would be magnificently right. I hear that Volontè did not do his own English dubbing; if so, this is the best-matched voice and most adroit lip-syncing I have seen in some time.

As the case becomes weirder and thornier, as its ramifications spread farther and higher, the film becomes more and more absorbing: the script manages to foreshorten the endless convolutions of the case with clarity and good sense. Claude Mann is not particularly notable as a crusading journalist, but William Prince gives a fine, subdued performance as the eminent Boston blueblood attorney who takes over the defense. Silvano Ippoliti's color cinematography wisely remains unglamorous throughout and unobtrusively slips into monochrome at the appropriate moments. Although the inclusion of newsreel footage is not entirely felicitous, by this time the film has such momentum—such genuine, controlled pathos—that an occasional false step is barely noticeable.

Indeed, some details are nothing short of unforgettable: Vanzetti, awaiting his own execution, watches the lights in his cell dim as upstairs the deadly current is being run through the body of his friend. If only that awful Baez ballad did not return at the end, with its ludicrous refrain, "Here's to you, Nick and Bart,/Live forever here in my heart./The last and final moment is yours,/That ago-nee is your tri-humph!" I wonder whether some of the bad reviews were not for the song rather than for the film.

Louis Malle's *Le Souffle au coeur* (heart murmur, not *Murmur of the Heart,* as it has been officially and incorrectly translated) is a film about growing up in the fifties, and thus invites comparison with Peter Bogdanovich's *The Last Picture Show.* Yet how different these kids coming of age in provincial Dijon are from those others in godforsaken Texas; or, if you like, how different Europe still was from middle America a couple of decades ago. For the young boys in what, granted, is a French city rather than a Texan burg (but would Dallas or Houston have been very different?) are concerned with literature, history, art, politics, philosophy, theology—even if only to rebel against much of what they read or are being taught. When an adult asks his nephew what youth thinks about French involvement in Indo-China, the boy replies, "Youth, dear uncle, does not give a shit." The answer is not as apolitical as it might seem.

This quasi-autobiographical film concerns Laurent, the fifteen-year-old, bright, precocious, somewhat academic son of a hard-working, matter-of-fact Dijon gynecologist and his much younger Italian wife, Clara, who, though she loves him, must have romance in her life and so hops into the cars of various ephemeral lovers. Laurent has two older brothers, fine anti-intellectual screw-ups who bully, patronize, envy, and love him. They both guide and impede his sexual development, and their pranks are among the most amusing aspects of this gently entertaining film. The family also includes uncles and aunts and, especially, Clara's faithful old Italian maid, Augusta, a huge bulwark of black starched skirts and moral rectitude. The relationships of all these people are sketched in with economy and warmth, and with sensitivity that sidesteps sentimentality.

Other relations are handled with equal perception and delicacy: the first experiences with girls and prostitutes; incidents verging on homosexuality with Laurent's ironic and droll confessor and teacher, Father Henri, as well as with a cherubic younger fellow boy scout; group and individual masturbation; secret pornographic readings. There are minor political activities, too, and school, and mass, and confession, and sicknesses, and collecting or stealing American jazz records. But mostly there is the loving—ever more loving—relationship with Clara, the mother for whom the boy has a wide range of feelings: admiration, jealousy, protectiveness, misgivings, and, above all, amazement. The one night of incest between Laurent and Clara is cogently and solicitously led up to, and then as adroitly and sagaciously led away from—back to normality and the resumption of a family life full of little stings and a large, laughing contentment.*

Malle's scenario is intelligent, racy, authentic throughout. At the very outset, when Laurent and a chum are returning home after collecting money for the wounded of Dienbienphu, the friend demands that Laurent return his copy of Brasillach's book on Corneille—he needs it for cramming. Laurent says he isn't through with it; why doesn't the friend's father help him with his homework? "My father isn't an intellectual," the boy protests; "he manufactures washbasins." From this moment on, we know that we are in good hands. And how splendidly simple yet rich in overtones is an exchange like this between Laurent and Clara: "Still, it must be mighty queer being married to a gynecologist." "Mmmm. You get used to it." The film has wit and, even more, humor, and a lovely spirit of forgiveness for all human foibles.

The color cinematography by Ricardo Aronovich is only acceptable—the exteriors tend to have a slightly washed-out look, and an unsolicited mauve

---

* Still, incest is incest, I reflect looking back on the film, and I daresay Malle was a bit too cavalier about it—as if it were a case of the measles that, once recovered from, is over and done with.

haze is frequently hanging around—but the set decoration is perfect, and the Bechet-Parker-Gillespie music works tidily on the soundtrack, shading nicely into sportscasts of the Tour de France, when Laurent prefers to follow that on the radio. After he misses the results of one lap of the race because of a necking session, he can be quite appropriately furious.

The acting is fine, especially that of Daniel Gélin as the father, and of Lea Massari, exquisite as the mother. Ever since her disappearance in mid-*Avventura*, I have been searching for Miss Massari, finding her occasionally and too briefly in mediocre films about Naples, Rome, and Paris. How unexpected and delightful to catch her in full histrionic and womanly bloom in Dijon, of all places! I hope that she will stay with us now, that I shall never have to let her go again for very long.

November 29, 1971

Laughing Violence

Dušan Makavejev, the Yugoslav filmmaker, is a curious blend of artist and prankster. The earliest work of his I saw, *Man Is Not a Bird,* was a rather harsh, realistic film, containing some fairly daring sexual interludes for its country and its time. It was with his next film, *Love Affair or The Case of the Missing Telephone Operator,* that Makavejev achieved his international renown. Here the basic pattern of his filmmaking became manifest: the balancing of two related yet contradictory elements so as to yield some tertium quid—a sense of incongruity, puzzlement, perhaps a Socratic aporia. Or you might call it Hegelian filmmaking: a thesis and antithesis yielding a curious synthesis.

In *Love Affair,* the thesis was a series of illustrated lectures on sexuality and crime by a sexologist and a penologist, counterpointed with an antithesis consisting of a love affair ending in jealousy and murder. But already the schema thickens: Was the thesis, in fact, the theoretical matter, presented in documentary or pseudodocumentary form, and the antithesis the story, the plot? Or was the thesis love and sex, and the antithesis crime and death? To complicate matters further, there were political implications and Brechtian alienation effects in the film, which were to prove increasingly important in Makavejev's efforts. Moreover, as the director has said, the point was not only to illuminate one element by another, but also to incriminate or ennoble it, to change values by juxtaposition and mutual irradiation.

This emerged more cleverly in Makavejev's next film, *Innocence Unprotected.* Here the thesis was a pre–World War II picture made by a Yugoslav acrobat and strong man, whose specialty was hanging from a plane by his teeth. Makavejev unearthed this lost film—a true primitive work about the acrobat spectacularly rescuing a maiden from the distressing hands of a villain and winning her for himself—and intercut it with a cinéma-vérité film in which

64

Makavejev, years later, interviews the original actors, all but one of whom survived the war and its aftermath. To this antithesis a third element is now added: newsreel footage of Yugoslavia in the war, mostly German-made, showing what happened in the period between the two intercut films, and showing it from the point of view of a greater villain, the enemy and his quislings.

The movie had a genuinely odd flavor, what with Makavejev hand-tinting the sequences from the athlete's film, until the sincere but awful photography, poorly preserved and eccentrically colored, closely resembled the primitive paintings of a Rousseau or Bombois—or, better yet, the work of Yugoslav primitives like Janko Brašić or Ivan Generalić. The naïve core of *Innocence Unprotected* is then surrounded by such hypocritical self-righteousness as newsreels of a quisling's funeral or the racy naturalism of survivors reminiscing about old-time filmmaking and the dismal war years. The crucial trouble with all this is that the various elements fail to comment on one another in a truly significant way; one is left chiefly with a sense of Makavejev as a jolly *farceur* full of provocative ideas that do not add up to a substantial whole.

The same, regrettably, goes for his new film, *WR—The Mysteries of the Organism*, an even headier mixture of components, yielding more of a jumble than a complexity. The WR of the title refers to Wilhelm Reich, whom Makavejev admires; part of the film is a documentary about the life and ideas of this strange disciple of Freud, to whom the term "mad genius" may genuinely apply—the "mad" certainly. If the film had stuck to reconstructing and memorializing Reich's interesting albeit misguided work, and his spellbinding and ultimately tragic life, it might have been a truly valuable achievement; but that is not the sort of thing that a master juggler, or jumbler, like Makavejev will limit himself to.

The second layer of the film presents views of a neo-Reichian life-style among New York's bohemia. There is Tuli Kupferberg, the Fug "poet," running around New York as a clown version of a U.S. infantryman, in travestied combat dress with toy submachine gun, while the soundtrack features his feebly satirical poems and songs. There is also Jackie Curtis, the notorious transvestite, talking about and living out his transsexual adventures; and one of the editors of *Screw* having a plaster cast made of his erect penis by an apt but unalluring "sculptress." Some erections, like some film-making, seem to come a little too easily.

The heart of the film, however, is a lusty, though rather slapdash and simplistic, tale of two Yugoslav girl-roommates. One spouts Reichian sex-*cum*-socialism homilies at the populace but does not herself indulge very much; the other, without uttering one abstract noun, romps around naked most of the time, sometimes servicing members of the Yugoslav army, sometimes trying to seduce an earnest Russian skating champion, who spouts, alas, Communism-*sans*-sex homilies. It is the two spouters who finally get together, but when the philosophical roommate persuades the Soviet speed-skating champion to copulate with her, she releases all that repressed fear and hate of sex that Reich diagnosed as the root of Fascism and Soviet 65

Communism. The girl is decapitated by her lover with a skate, after he deposits three or four times the normal amount of semen in her vagina (the English subtitles escalate this into "four or five times"!), but there is a posthumous, semihappy ending to this mildly scatological, or skatological, film.

Other curiosities are woven into the fabric, such as bits of old movies, notably passages from Mikhail Chiaureli's *The Vow,* in which Stalin appears even huger than life-size, only to be crosscut by Makavejev with the cast of the *Screw* editor's penis. Similarly, crude treatment of mental cases—including shock therapy and worse, as well as a horrifying shot of a madman banging his head against a wall—is crosscut with lengthy sequences of patients receiving dubious but loving Reichian or neo-Reichian therapy (possibly too heterodox for conservative Reichians who have joined in condemning this film).

All these disparate theses and antitheses that jostle one another in sometimes studied, sometimes slipshod profusion, do not, in the final count, a synthesis make. While the girl's severed head pontificates orphically, and the formerly rectilinear skater meanders along singing a bittersweet complaint of Bulat Okudzhava's, we are left merely with an image of Makavejev as a true erotomaniac—surely much the most likable kind of maniac there is. But whether Makavejev is an artist in an unfree country posing as a *farceur,* or simply a *farceur* pretending to be an artist, remains an unanswered question.

December 13, 1971

The Screen Bestrides the Stage

PLAYS RESIST screen adaptation much more doggedly than novels. Stage works require additions, and these have a way of being easily deadlier than subtractions; novels often lose much in their transfer to the screen, but the openness of the form—its ability to burrow into psyches and expand into landscapes—can be matched by the camera. A play, ensconced in limited stage space no matter what the stage directions call for and the set designer dreams up, contradicts the free-roaming tendencies of the camera. The lens magnifies everything, even a small room it may find itself locked into. That chamber promptly becomes a microcosm full of details: spots on the ceiling, irregularities in the wallpaper, shadows on the floor, not to mention a universe of furniture and bric-a-brac—and all of this constantly changing shape and size as the camera shifts its position.

Even if slide projections change the backdrop, pieces of scenery float or glide on and off, the lighting shifts drastically from *al giorno* to chiaroscuro, at a play we are still face to face with faces of relatively fixed size within the unelastic frame of the stage. The pores or blemishes of a countenance do not suddenly hit us, the intricate work of fingers is not spelled out for us, and we cannot take in exactly the sliding of a coffee cup from a table and its symbolic splintering into irredeemable fragments. We depend on large gestures, generous verbiage, carefully measured silences, and, above all, on simultaneity: our ability to see protagonist and antagonist, or a whole group of interacting people, at once and without interruption—without the camera's selectivity and never quite impersonal mediation.

Consider Michael Cacoyannis's movie version of Euripides' *The Trojan Women*, an earnest effort by a man with ample theatrical and cinematic experience who has repeatedly returned to *The Trojan Women* in different places, languages, and now media. Granted, Euripides' work is not quite a play in the modern sense, rather a sort of tragic cantata. Troy has been conquered and its great women—the heroic Hecuba, the pathetic Cassandra, the profoundly human Andromache, the diabolic Helen—come on to speak their piece before they go off: the good to slavery and death, the evil to further life and lust. All this is framed by a chorus of ordinary women extending the drama downward, and prefaced by a colloquy between the gods Poseidon and Athena, stretching the tragedy upward into cosmic, metaphysical reaches.

What makes *The Trojan Women* a great work is that here in 415 B.C. someone managed to encapsulate in one short play every possible argument against war, which had previously been exalted, except in cases of civil war. The arguments are cogent, pregnant, poetic, and complete, focusing on the defeated but showing, by implication, the toll on the victors as well. Given the originality, depth of insight, and poetic splendor, the essentially schematic, pat, and undramatic form of the presentation becomes relatively unimportant. But here, of course, the very unreality of theater proves handy, indeed necessary: we are psychologically primed for staginess, unreality on the stage; whereas the camera, as every child knows, does not, or is not presumed to, lie.

The problem for the film adapter and director then becomes how to make this highly stylized play even moderately realistic for his much more realistic medium; or, conversely, how to derealize the film medium; or, perhaps, how to work out a fusion of both modes. But Cacoyannis—no more than anyone else, possibly—is unequal to the task. His setting (ably designed by Nicholas Georgiadis), for example, is real enough, though it shows a ravaged and smoldering Troy from the beginning: to have built an undamaged one and then destroyed it would have exceeded the budget. Yet when at the end of the film the "city" goes up in colossal flames, the sequence is a ludicrous anticlimax. Why would the Greeks burn those burnt-out ruins, and how, for that matter, can those remnants of stone walls catch fire?

But it is not really a matter of money; rather, of indecision and wavering. When Astyanax is thrown off the battlements, the camera becomes, most naturalistically, the falling child, whirling and crashing fearsomely. Yet when the corpse is carried on to become the human pulpit from which   67

Hecuba hurls her imprecations, the boy is all in one piece and undented except for a modest bruise on one cheek. Again, the recitations of the chorus are broken up in various photographic as well as choreographic ways to make them less formalized. But for all the distribution of choric speeches among individuals, for all the closeups on one face or part of it, we never gain a sense of these being particular women with personal tragedies, whereas we lose the massive sculptural and terpsichorean image of highly stylized ritual drama.

The toughest conundrum, of course, is what to do with the long speeches, the solo arias in which these noble women lament their falls. Cacoyannis lacks the nerve, the talent, or the actresses of an Ingmar Bergman, who can keep his camera more or less immobile on Ullmann, Thulin, or either Andersson against a blank background and make a vast soliloquy incandesce.

For Geneviève Bujold's appealing but histrionically insufficient Cassandra, Cacoyannis devises an elaborate balletic chase, with the Greek soldiers as supporting male dancers and the Trojan women as corps de ballet. Religious fervor and human pathos fizzle equally among studied compositions and calculated movements, combined with disconcerting jump cuts between medium shots and closeups and extreme closeups. For Vanessa Redgrave's intelligent and interesting Andromache—unfortunately lacking the ultimate warmth and depth—there is much soft-focus hovering over handsome blue-eyed blondness, and picturesque posing of the actress in front of the mounted armor of her slain husband, flapping abjectly in the wind like a martial scarecrow.

Only for Helen, shrewdly and forcefully though not very seductively incarnated by Irene Papas, has the director come up with some good business, and here his additions are effective: Helen's eyes, in extreme closeup peering out from between the logs of her private stockade; other Trojan women parched with thirst while Helen gets a basin of water for mere ablutions. But I am somewhat disturbed by Miss Papas's thick accent, Greek though it be, and her great confrontation scene is weakened by her having as antagonist Katharine Hepburn. Hecuba is the most important character, the only one who remains present throughout, and she who plays the queen must dominate the action and hold its disparate set pieces together. But what is Hepburn to Hecuba? She offers no stronger stuff than brittle querulousness, head-waggling and lip-trembling, so that the Trojan indomitability shining through the uneasy Argive victory is as missing as Poseidon and Athena.

Cutting the gods' opening scene is understandable in 1971, but a strategic error all the same. For it is from the conversation of the deities that we learn of their weakness and fickleness, and of their intention to make the arrogant Greeks, on their journey home, pay dearly for their triumph. This rounds out the tragic image of war, in which even the victor falls victim to a fundamentally untrustworthy, unmanageable cosmos. Moreover, Helen's argument that Aphrodite is to blame for what happened, though meant to be *in part* sophistic, emerges, in the absence of visible gods, as sheer nonsense. Alfio Contini's color cinematography is appropriately muted and desolate, but black-and-white would have done the job better. The music of Mikis Theodorakis is disappointing when not embarrassing, and Edith Hamilton's translation should have been avoided by Cacoyannis, but then it was all English to him.

Dubious an enterprise as *The Trojan Women* is, it is masterly compared to Peter Brook's *King Lear*. Brook's 1963 production of the play was a considerable mutilation of it; never content with a job half done, Brook's 1969 film version murders it altogether. Misled by that arrogantly inept pseudoscholar, Jan Kott, the pretentious Mr. Brook, director of stage and screen, has given us a film version of *King Lear* that is a catastrophe and a scandal. One of the world's greatest plays—perhaps the greatest—is reduced here to a tricky and prosaic little film, whose only and dubious raison d'être is to promote the talent of Brook at the expense of the genius of Shakespeare.

The film's failure is sixfold at least. The thesis of Kott's essay that so befuddled the eagerly befuddlable Brook is that the world of *King Lear* is closely related to that of Beckett's *Endgame* and other absurdist plays. I doubt if much is gained by explicating the greater work in terms of lesser ones, but Brook's endeavor to translate Shakespeare's tragedy into Beckettese spells instant disaster.

It causes the first, or philosophical, downfall of the film. For comedy—even bleak, black, absurdist comedy—operates most comfortably on one level: the steady discharge of humor, wit, or biting irony that keeps a play on its plateau of high or low comedy. But the nature of tragedy is by definition that of a fall: someone who starts on high is brought, sadly and terrifyingly, low. Thus, to speak Aristotelianly, catharsis takes place: we are purged of our most overwhelming emotions, pity and fear.

Shakespeare's Lear starts as a man with a tragic flaw: an imposing but autocratic old monarch whose prideful foolishness causes his fall. But Shakespeare brilliantly elaborates on the pattern: Lear goes from a mighty but narrow-minded king to a broken, maddened beggar only to rise again, this time spiritually, to a pinnacle of humane compassion and wisdom. Redeemed and exalted by suffering and love, the king is, once again, plunged into calamity and death, this time through no fault of his own. A terrible view of a ruthless, utterly amoral universe is scorchingly driven home. But in Paul Scofield, Brook gives us, right off the bat, a paltry and petty Lear who lets his words crawl out of him, slowly and with almost identical lack of emphasis, like a procession of depressed snails. This is not someone who will learn from the kicks of life; rather, he needs a good kick to come alive at all.

With such a Lear, no heights, no depths; merely, as Brook wants it, an absurd, godless, ridiculous universe, mindlessly grinding down motes to yet more insignificant motes. And why not so? Because the text, as written, is a tragedy and, unlike Beckett's gallows humor, contradicts Brook's vision of cosmic puniness. An arid plain may be a spectacle worth a look, but it is not mountains and canyons, nor should these be converted into a plain. Brook, however, proceeds to raze this mountainous work to fit his concept, and so makes the film fail dramatically as well. He cuts any number of important speeches, shortens or omits whole scenes, rearranges the sequence of things until the atmosphere becomes clotted and viscous, traversed by flashes of quick, mean ugliness, and devoid of a trace of dignity or kindness.

Thus in his stage version of the play, Brook omitted the old man who brings whites of eggs to soothe Gloucester's bleeding eye sockets; in the film, both the servant who gives his life to protect Gloucester's eyes and the one who brings the palliative are shown so quickly, near-subliminally, and puzzlingly, that an audience may well miss this presence of loyalty and devotion in the world—exactly what Brook wants it to do. His wish is to make the dramatis personae as nearly equal in abjection as possible.

Accordingly, we get absurd efforts at whitewashing Regan and Goneril, when the text wants them to be female machiavels; while Lear, Kent, and Cordelia are to be incriminated in every conceivable way, and the good Edgar appears piddling next to the malicious Edmund. The measly Oswald looks downright agreeable as Kent berates and challenges him for seemingly no reason, and Lear's knights turn Albany's palace (as Shakespeare calls it—Brook makes it into a godforsaken fort in the tundra) into a gutted pigsty. We get this boisterousness of the king's retinue only on the say of the villains in Shakespeare, and are hardly meant to take it at face value. Cordelia's abstaining from her sisters' braggadocio, and modestly refusing to eulogize her father for gain, is turned by Brook into a display of haughty coldness. As Frank Kermode observed about Brook's stage version, conservative compared to the movie, "the rot of a directional bright idea can spread through the whole play."

The point of Shakespeare's work is not that everyone is equally dreary and culpable but, clearly, that some are deserving and even noble, while others are bad and even vicious, yet in the long run all are crushed or killed, and in the short run the bad may actually have a better time of it. An awe-inspiring vision, startling for its—or any—time, but the greatness of Shakespeare lies in dramatizing it with calm poetic control, whereas Brook's wretchedness lies in filming something small and spiteful with a dispiriting torpor occasionally shot through with sensationalism and hysteria.

Which brings us to the filmic failure of the movie. There is no facile and flashy cinematic or directorial trick that Brook does not resort to or impose on his able black-and-white cinematographer, Henning Kristiansen. Even placing the film in northernmost Denmark's frozen wastes, so that it looks like a cross between *Scott of the Antarctic* and *Ivan Denisovich* (to say nothing of the heavy-handed borrowings from *The Virgin Spring*) serves mostly to broadcast the director's unusual, ingenious individuality. But if the setting is an unpeopled wilderness of snow and ice, what difference can spending one night on a stormy heath make? One or two centigrades, at the utmost. And the purposeful graininess of the photography, over- and underexposure, eccentric framing of shots, convulsive jump cuts punctuating an entire soliloquy, sudden blackings out of the image while voices drone on, not showing the main character in a scene for the longest time, inscrutably elliptic continuity, intrusive intertitles, and similar devices keep hitting you in the face. You are kept continually busy with Brook's clevernesses and have no time

for Shakespeare's insights and poetry.

What Brook has contrived, in fact, is a pogrom on poetry. No actor is allowed to sound touched in the least by divine afflatus, and Lear and Cordelia, above all, must be as gray and listless as fatigued ghosts that have haunted themselves out. Paul Scofield, an often prodigious actor, has never been comfortable with verse, and falls in happily with the prosaicizing conception. His Lear antagonizes us from the beginning—not properly, because of overbearing pomp, but because of his flat, slow-motion, soporific line readings. The entire cast tidily falls in with Brook's depoeticizing process—with only Alan Webb's Gloucester and Irene Worth's Goneril putting up a sporadic resistance. First, there is that brutal cutting, Shakespeare's loveliest lines being to Brook's scissors like flies to wanton boys. But even when the words are retained, and are not even garbled by the delivery or mangled by the editing or camera pyrotechnics (instead of intertitles, we could use subtitles), how deliberately the poetry is thrown away!

Take that almost unbearably affecting line with which the "mad" Lear responds to Gloucester's wishing to kiss his hand: "Let me wipe it first; it smells of mortality." By pausing too long at the semicolon (a comma in the Folio), by gazing at his battered hands in ragged mittens, by a wholly uninflected line reading, Scofield manages to suggest that there is nothing wrong with his hands that a little Ivory soap could not cure.

Again, Gloucester's tremendous realization that the gods "kill us for their sport" is spoken by a disembodied off-screen voice out of context, while the camera roves across the wintry wilderness—we are not even sure who the speaker is. The result is not a magnificently poetic and tragic existential revelation, but a bit of vague, general gloom indiscriminately spread across the already barren snowscape. Or take the conclusion, when Lear appears with the dead Cordelia in his arms; the entire scene is a shambles, but let me pick three particular travesties. Brook begins by shooting Lear in a medium-long shot as he wildly weaves across the snow and utters a strangled, wavering screech. It looks like a man who has placed second in a yodeling competition shaking the rag doll that is the consolation prize. Then take the deliberate absurdity of Lear's holding the feather that is to register whether Cordelia still breathes some four or five feet from her mouth. And when we get to those five consecutive, shattering *nevers* with which Gielgud, even in a concert reading, can move us to the marrow, Scofield breaks them up into three vocal units in high pitch, so that the line emerges in skittering waltz tempo!

The film, then, is a failure even rhythmically, and rhythm is as all-important to film as to music and poetry. To make the world of *Lear* particularly nasty and brutish, Brook removes the medieval pomp and pageantry of such scenes as the chivalric combat between Edgar and Edmund—indeed, keeps all fighting brief and cloddish, more like bored butchery than manly dueling. This makes several scenes so choppy, rushed, and discontinuous as to be almost farcical, and establishes yet another contender for the authorship of Shakespeare's plays: Mack Sennett.

But the final failure is that of simple common sense. So Edgar is shown prancing about the subarctic snowstorms virtually nude, and Kent's bare 71 feet are kept in the stocks through a quasi-polar night; we wait for Edgar to drop dead of pneumonia, and Kent's feet to drop off from frostbite. But Brook will do anything for an effect, however nonsensical. Thus he turns Poor Tom into a Christ figure, complete with loincloth, outspread arms, crown of thorns. Now this is absurd not only because Tom-Edgar is in no way an expiatory sacrifice, but also because the world of the film is pre-Christian, indeed paleolithic, and Brook's whole point is that any reference to divinity is pointless.

Anything goes in this film, however, as long as every frame proclaims Brook's supremacy over Shakespeare, down to that final shot where the last we see of Lear is his slowly sinking hand and finally, his fading paunch! Yet the worst culprit is not even Brook, but a world that has invested this trendy, smart-aleck director with robes and furr'd gowns of theatrical eminence that hide all the holes in his thinking and feeling.

December 19–27, 1971

Bloodlettings

Macbeth, the film Roman Polanski directed from his and Kenneth Tynan's adaptation of the play, is a much worthier experiment than Peter Brook's catastrophic *King Lear,* and though it still ends in failure, it at least holds our interest and juggles with Shakespeare rather than sabotaging him. Polanski, questionable as his taste may be, has a vivid film sense, and his *Macbeth* is eminently cinematic. In fact, it is so filmic that it fails to be poetic and tragic; because it is often, though not always, good cinema, it manages to be generally inferior Shakespeare. True, the Polanski-Tynan view of the world is as dark as the Bard's was in this play, perhaps even darker; but the film provides a horror that is mostly quantitative, fast-moving, and lateral, whereas Shakespeare's horror is qualitative, gradual, and vertical.

By making the thane and his lady attractive, sexy people in their twenties in a world in which only Duncan is old and smarmy—whereas everyone else is young, tough, and potentially treacherous—a curious shift occurs. The work no longer examines how evil enters the soul of a strong and upright man of maturity and stature—how both from without and within, by supernatural and natural agencies, his being is corroded into first causing and then suffering violence and death, until, with all hope gone, a certain nobility ironically reasserts itself at the end. With a young, lightweight, headlong Macbeth and his pretty, demurely sinning, blond wife, we get a medieval Bonnie and Clyde, victims of a brutish society, out on a murderous lark. Duncan, after all, is a pompous old bore, whom his own scowling sons might easily have done in sooner or later. Indeed, as the film ends, a club-footed, surly Donalbain is off to see the Weird Sisters and, presumably, start the wheel of fortune revolving again.

There are many generally demeaning touches in the screenplay. Reviewers have been particularly impressed by a Ross shown as the possibly unjust betrayer of Cawdor, then becoming Macbeth's stooge in the murders of Banquo and Macduff's family, then becoming a turncoat as Malcolm triumphs, and getting himself an earldom for being the first to snatch the crown off Macbeth's severed head and presenting it to the victor. But this "ingenious" notion is not new; it was first advanced by a certain Libby in *Some New Notes on Macbeth* in 1893. Tynan and Polanski have snatched up Libby's folly as eagerly as Ross the crown, thereby, of course, minimizing Macbeth's evil and dislocating the entire work.

Everywhere in the picture they have made brutality, violence, horror so universal as to suggest that Macbeth is a mere victim of social circumstances. Instead of three witches, there is a whole coven of ugly nude bodies decrepitly disporting themselves. The visions of the future conjured up for Macbeth are pure Grand Guignol. In the end, everyone deserts him, and he must defend his castle alone against Malcolm's army. This is a world in which a half-dead soldier, prone on the battlefield, is repeatedly clobbered by another's mace, until we can see the blood oozing out through the victim's coat of mail.

Uglinesses proliferate. Cawdor's execution is horrifying, Lady Macbeth's death, here a suicide, is mean, and her barely covered corpse is left lying about unattended. The dead Macbeth's head, crown and all, rolls ghoulishly across the courtyard. On the night of Duncan's murder, it rains heavily, and the Macbeths and their guests must run barefoot and in nightshirts all over the unpaved, muddy yard. A particularly doddering porter is shown urinating. Lady Macbeth, naked in her sleepwalking scene, is exposed to the eyes of a loathsome doctor. A dart from a crossbow hits Seyton smack in the face in closeup. And so on.

Along with excesses of such superficial, though often brilliantly directed and photographed, *verismo,* making for diminished tragedy, we get the filmic breaking up of long speeches with various business and movement and scene shifts, making for diminished poetry. There is continuous, highly cinematic action, but the pathos, penetrancy, and depth of poetic words is scattered and largely forfeited.

If, for instance, Macbeth delivers his most famous soliloquy as he bounces down a set of stairs from the battlements of his castle, those repeated tomorrows no longer creep at a petty pace but jog along trippingly. If Macduff utters his piercing "He has no children!" against a background of swirling soldiery, armament, and martial panoply, it loses most of its poignantly welling-up grief. If the lines about "our chief guest" at the fateful banquet are transferred from Banquo to a bear about to be baited, you get cinematic excitement and social commentary, but lose the terrible irony of murderers fawning on their next victim.

What, then, is left? A marvelously paced action film that nevertheless preserves most of the original text; camera movements that are often breathtaking; poetic color photography by Gil Taylor, including a dawn view from the ramparts that is almost as beautiful as a Shakespearean meta-   73 phor; a convincingly reconstructed medieval world; some spectacular sword-play, though Macduff is made into an unduly dirty fighter. And there are fine performances within the limiting concept of the work: Jon Finch as Macbeth, Francesca Annis as the Lady, and John Stride as Ross are particularly impressive both in acting and in looks.

A more unfortunate screen adaptation is that of Giorgio Bassani's novel, *The Garden of the Finzi-Continis.* The script is by those old faithfuls, Cesare Zavattini and Ugo Pirro (along with Vittorio Bonicelli) and the direction by that grand old man, Vittorio De Sica. Bassani's novel itself is feeble stuff: juiceless, blunted writing in which neither people nor places come alive for all the accumulation of dry, flat details.

This autobiographical fiction concerns Bassani's youth in Ferrara during the years leading up and into World War II. The recollections focus on a rich, quasi-aristocratic Jewish family, the Finzi-Continis, who, protected by their sumptuous house and huge, leafy estate, seemingly ignore the rise of Fascism and the first anti-Jewish laws. When the tennis club throws out its Jewish members, Giorgio and other youthful sportifs are invited over to play on the Finzi-Continis' private court; what was only a fleeting, somewhat yearning contact with the rich family develops into a friendship with the son, Alberto, and desperate love for Micòl, the spirited, vaguely intellectual daughter.

It is not really a novel at all, but a memoir of the timid, bookish narrator's unrequited longings for Micòl, who may or may not have been the clandestine mistress of Malnate, a serious young Communist engineer and friend of her brother's, with whom Alberto, in turn, may have been secretly, unrequitedly in love. The main body of the book is remarkably lacking in the kind of incidents that make up a narrative; the death of Alberto from lymphogranuloma and the deportation and presumable extermination of the rest of the family are relegated to a brief, equally unnarrative, epilogue. Bassani probably intended the novel as an evocation of *le vert paradis des amours enfantines;* as an exorcism of the ghost of the blond, vivacious Micòl, that beautiful, unattainable girl who died young and horribly; and as a re-creation of the atmosphere of improvident or fatalistic insouciance with which these wealthy Jews drifted into their undoing.

There is, alas, no movie in that. So De Sica and his scenarists jazzed up the nonstory into a conventional, superficial, occasionally sleazy film. First, they made all four of the young principals gorgeous and dashing. Then they threw in all kinds of hints of guilty passions—homosexual, incestuous, voyeuristic. Micòl becomes a faintly sadistic and incestuous *femme fatale,* Giorgio a masochist, Malnate a coldly efficient seducer, Alberto a man haunted and betrayed by both Malnate and his own sister. There is a pathetic death scene for Alberto, and a horrid sex scene where, at night, Giorgio spies through a window on a barely postcoital Malnate and Micòl, and the girl flaunts her nudity at him. Later, there are the standard chases, roundups, hairbreadth escapes, and deportation scenes, in a weak attempt to recapture the style and motifs of the early neorealist films. Equally halfhearted are the tries at evoking Ferrarese Jewish modes of being, the political moods of the times, and the gracious, vanishing life of dilettantism on the Finzi-Continis' ducal domains.

In these evocative sequences, De Sica painfully demonstrates his loss of touch. The best he can do with the great garden is a long, soft-focus dolly shot through the treetops, a cliché if ever there was one. The camera placements, alternation of shots, and editing are consistently uninspired, the color photography undistinguished. The sociopolitical background is dutifully and listlessly sketched in, with even the scenes of Micòl, Alberto, and Giorgio as children (the sort of thing that used to be De Sica's specialty) lacking savor. The political conversations of the novel are severely pared down in the film, and the ardent discussions of literature, one of the leitmotivs, completely left out.

What is left? The glamorous presences of Dominique Sanda and Helmut Berger as the doomed young Finzi-Continis; the dark and ruthless good looks of Fabio Testi as Malnate (in the book, a large, fat, lax, pipe-smoking fellow); and a sincere performance by Lino Capolicchio as the weak, ineffectual would-be lover, Giorgio. As Giorgio's father—a worried, ex-Fascist Jew, now barred from almost everything—Romolo Valli contributes the film's most authentic, flavorous performing. The poorest characterization is Mlle Sanda's; she emerges as a headstrong, cruel flirt rather than the female equivalent of Hanno Buddenbrook that Bassani seems to have had in mind. But here the script and direction are mostly to blame.

In the end, the film does somehow move you. Even the semiperfunctory portrayal of innocent victims on the way to the gas chambers, even the rather routine and somewhat lurid evocation of an aristocratic way of life brutally snuffed out, has an undeniable, though unearned, power to touch us. Yet poor old De Sica is in a sorry state. From the bad to middling entertainments he has been turning out, there seems to be no way back to *Shoeshine, The Bicycle Thief,* and *Umberto D.* He is like a once-famous operatic tenor turned pop singer and grown old, trying to sing one of the arias from his youthful repertoire, and left wrecked and wheezing on the high C's.

January 10–24, 1972

Misses Through Misdirection

MIRACLES will never cease. Just as I am ready to bet my bottom dollar that Ken Russell could not make a film worth a farthing, along comes *The Boy Friend* to prove me wrong. True, with this film Russell deliberately undertook to confute those of us who claimed that he was incapable of turning out anything wholesome, and though he wins more or less, we do not entirely lose. Coming after monstrosities like *The Music Lovers* and *The Devils,* this movie version of Sandy Wilson's amiable little musical may seem tame stuff 75 indeed; but compared to the stage original—a winsome, harmless, affectionate spoof of the thirties—Russell's film reveals a rather more disquieting aspect. I would not go along with the local wag who dubbed it the first horror musical, but I cannot deny that the surface erupts into ripples attesting to a maelstrom beneath.

Unfortunately, James Aubrey, the head of MGM, saw fit to excise some fifteen to thirty-two minutes of the movie (the figure has been variously reported), and Russell was said to be on the point of challenging Aubrey to a duel unto the death. That this never took place is regrettable, for, whatever the outcome, the movies would have become a better place to live in. As things stand, I don't know whether Aubrey cut the film for greater brevity or greater purity. Nor, given London's lagging behind Hollywood when it comes to feminine pulchritude, can I be quite sure whether the prevailing untoothsomeness of the girls in the film was perversely deliberate. But bits of Russellian kinkiness are recognizable even in this anodyne film.

Thus in the midst of demurely covered-up dancing girls there suddenly bobs into sight Barbara Windsor, a grotesque dumpling whose hypertrophic breasts, under a mere wisp of gauze, jiggle away like melting cathedral bells trying to ring out a fire alarm. Or, in one of several Busby Berkeleyish production numbers, the camera tracks under an endless bridge of thighs, gliding circularly from crotch to overarching crotch. Again, when one of the girls is skipping rope in a stage routine, the rope, manipulated by other girls, is repeatedly tautened and pulled up as if to slice the girl in half, with suggestions of some strange new perversion we might call bisectuality. And when a bunch of showgirls discover that a famed Hollywood director has come to see their failing production of *The Boy Friend* (the musical within the frame story, the latter invented by Russell) in a rickety, gaping, provincial music hall, they proceed to turn the stage into a perpendicular casting couch for him, some of them even dancing their way into his proscenium box.

Still, there is some justification for parts of this. It would have been virtually impossible to translate *The Boy Friend* into film literally and faithfully. The Wilson stage piece is so slight and intimate as to work only on a stage, and a small one in a cozy theater, at that. Once you introduce color and wide-screen photography and the camera's insatiable, nearly uncontrolled hunger for devouring more people and things and space, some kind of adaptation becomes mandatory.

Russell, as his own scenarist, has taken what was a gentle send-up of old musicals and added a not so gentle persiflage of theater, movies, movie musicals, and show biz in general. Various kinds of satire jostle one another. There is the typical backstage infighting, and the notorious movie-musical gimmick of the timid assistant stage manager having to go on for the ailing star to save the show; there is the theatrical cliché of the despotic producer-director bullying everyone in sight, and the movie-musical cliché of a small stage expanding, for a superproduction number, into a vast sound stage where the choreography is afflicted with instant elephantiasis.

So Russell's film swells into an anthology of show-biz absurdities, a compendium of stereotypes impudently exaggerated to the point where we are forced both to laugh and squirm at the imbecility of our favorite entertainments. Russell can put a cliché to inventively new uses. Thus the pit orchestra in this large but almost deserted music hall consists of three jaded players, enabling Russell and his composer, Peter Maxwell Davies, to underorchestrate the already sparsely scored Wilson tunes and give them a sound of even tinnier exiguity. Later, when the theatrical manager wants to impress the great DeThrill, the slumming Hollywood director, he sends out for orchestral reinforcements. All that can be obtained is a trio of buskers, musical beggars who butcher the hit tunes in the street outside the theater. Pressed into pit service, they perform equally erratically, permitting Davies to spice up the caressing melodies with some racy dissonance, a musical fretwork of wrong-note *frissons.*

All this, of course, makes hash of the endearing little stage musical—immerses it in a world of bickerings and bitchinesses, fantasies and phantasmagoria in which the original very nearly drowns. But some of its tunefulness proves indestructible, and for almost every loss incurred there is a bit of incremental invention. As usual with Russell, this invention is pushed all the way to remote archness. There is, for instance, a number where the girls, dressed in national costumes, disingenuously commiserate with the heroine. The girl who sings, "What a shame your fellow turned out to be a rotter and a cad," wears a Dutch costume and a windmill for headgear—an audiovisual pun on rotter and Rotterdam.

Still, I repeat, Russell does convey in the film a vision of film and theater as a curious symbiosis of innocence and vice. He gets able assistance from various quarters, most notably from Twiggy, the fashion model turned actress. This transition has seldom been successful; for one Lauren Bacall who bridges the gap, hosts of others vanish into it after the first failed leap. Some, to be sure, drag on from performance to drearier performance (like Lauren Hutton or Jennifer O'Neill), but more of them (like Jean Shrimpton, Twiggy's chief fashion rival) immediately freeze into miniature Mount Rushmores.

Yet Twiggy, I hope, will last. She already can dance and sing tolerably, and she acts with a charming diffidence belied by a natural grace. She has a quality of wide-eyed wonder, of innate modesty, and as Russell photographs her, her eyes almost bleed out of the image. Twiggy is one of your authentic babes in the woods, and, these days, the woods are anything but full of them. She wanders through the thickets of the film like someone who cannot see the genuine paltriness from the imagined enchantment, cannot see the stunted trees from the fairy-tale forest, and her innocence is catching.

The film also has the excellent services of Tony Walton as set designer, David Watkin as cinematographer, and the aforementioned Davies as resident musician; even Mrs. Russell's tawdry costumes fit the bill, perhaps fortuitously but nicely enough. The acting is generally competent, with Max Adrian's and Vladek Sheybal's overblown caricatures handily absorbed by the outlandishness of the context. The one serious flaw is Christopher Gable, 77 the ex-ballet dancer and favored member of Russell's repertory company, in the male lead. Gable is all right for character parts, but cast as a gorgeous dreamboat he founders immediately.

Some films fail from sheer good intentions, which is the case of André Cayatte's *To Die of Love*. It is a partly fictionalized retelling of the story of Gabrielle Russier, a young teacher of French and classics in a Marseilles *lycée*. Gabrielle was divorced, with two small children, when she fell in love with one of her seventeen-year-old students, a boy who looked as old for his age as she looked young for hers, and who loved her manfully. They tried to live together, but the boy's fanatical family, abetted by antiquated laws, managed to have the youth locked up in an institution and Gabrielle in jail. They shuttled in and out of their confinement and each other's arms.

The battle between the lovers and the family was long and complicated, exacerbated by the judicial backlash to the events of May 1968. Gabrielle lost her job and could not get other teaching positions; in the end, with a few rotten breaks wearing her down even more, she gassed herself to death. She did have a posthumous victory, though, as she had foreseen: the stink of the Russier affair brought about a liberalization of the French laws pertaining to the rights of minors.

André Cayatte is a former lawyer, and most of his films concern themselves with forms of judicial injustice. Two of them are distinguished, although perhaps not great, achievements: *We Are All Murderers* and *Justice Is Done;* I also rather like the somewhat different but still profoundly moral *Tomorrow Is My Turn*. Cayatte is capable of signal failures as well, and *Mourir d'aimer* (the French title sounds much better) is one. The trouble with *To Die of Love* is that it makes the teacher and her young lover superhumanly attractive: too pure, too unremittingly compatible, too unswervingly noble. Meanwhile, the rest of the world—parents, educators, judges, lawyers, doctors—is almost without exception mean, narrow-minded, unhinged, and brutal. The result is a color film that is embarrassingly black and white.

Cayatte goes so far as to make the boy, whom he calls Gérard, look and act older than any seventeen-year-old I have ever seen—unlike, for example, the more justly perceived hero of *Devil in the Flesh,* who is allowed some childish characteristics. Danièle (as Gabrielle is called here) is the model mother of two perfect, blond storybook children; she and Gérard kiss occasionally and are even in bed together, but there is not a moment of true carnality, of palpable sexual passion. The emphasis is all on thwarted love; there is no sense of financial issues, of the inability to survive without a job, of the woman's need to do the kind of work she knew and loved.

Probably the greatest lacuna, however, is the absence of that hysteria verging on madness that must have finally possessed this hounded, desperate woman, and that, far from making her less likable, would have made her more human, believable, and worthy of compassion. True, Danièle is allowed an admission of failure; but she remains cool and dignified even in defeat. Oh, what a little uncontrolled rage and uncontrollable despair could have done for this picture! Typically, Cayatte shifts the locale from Marseilles to Rouen, presumably because that is where Joan of Arc was burned alive. And the film is made of so many little scenes of roughly equal length and intensity that it looks as tidy as a game of dominoes laid out before us, each piece neatly dovetailing into the other.

What saves *To Die of Love* from dying of mediocrity is the lovely, warm, intelligent presence and absolutely unmannered, uncluttered performance of Annie Girardot. She is one of those blessed actresses as incapable of making a false move as of making an excessive one. Her Danièle is, of course, directed for maximal underplaying, but even under such enforced austerity she conveys a great feminine lovingness and a strength without edges to cut yourself on. Had she been permitted to do so, she could have, without relaxing her histrionic discipline, made us brim over with pity. Instead, we are limited to a somewhat academic sympathy as we wonder why these people could not have waited a little longer, until the boy turned eighteen and their problems, at least as stated here, were at an end. Despite genuine moral indignation, the film is not allowed to rise above the level of a rather specialized case history.

February 7–March 6, 1972

Simple Greatness

GOODNESS, in a work of art, is almost always highly specialized, boring, or simply unconvincing. In how many films have you seen plain good people—neither saints nor fools nor heroes—effectively portrayed? You can see them now, in *Tokyo Story*, by the Japanese master Yasujiro Ozu (1903–1963).

Ozu was a giant, like Kurosawa, and rather more so than the, to my mind, overrated Mizoguchi. But, unlike those two, he did not go in for exoticism, historicism, the grand or spectacular manner; he preferred instead to work with everyday people in unspectacular, contemporary situations. His theme is almost always the family, and the conflict or occasional harmony between the generations within it. The films, with their titles usually taken modestly from the seasons (*Late Spring, End of Summer, Early Autumn*), tend to revolve around a marriage or a death in the family, around the isolation of individuals even under the warming cloaks of friendship, kinship, cohabitation.

Perhaps the most beautiful and moving of these still, deep works, *Tokyo Story* (1953), has had to wait nineteen years for its first commercial showing in America. Like the rest of Ozu's oeuvre, it is neither comedy nor tragedy; neither drama nor comedy-drama. Its movement, interspersed with flashes of humor, is from joviality to wistfulness, thence to profound melancholy, redeemed by final illumination. I can find no other category for it than "Ozu," which is to say extraordinarily humane, affecting, and unique.

Tokyo Story deals with an elderly couple who leave their young schoolteacher daughter behind in the small town of Onomichi, while they go to visit their married children in Tokyo. One of the older children is a doctor, who turns out less successful and well-off than his parents had assumed. He and his rather colorless wife represent the ordinary person at his most neutral. A married daughter, a beautician, typifies the crass and stingy sides of ordinariness, still short of real badness. Then there is Noriko, widow of a son lost in the war, who, in contrast to the son and daughter and their spouses, does wonders of self-effacing generosity for the old folks. Like them, she is one of the truly good, without seeming idealized or dull.

To get the parents out of the way and cut down on expenses, the son and daughter hustle them off to an inexpensive seaside resort, where rowdy revelers make sleep impossible. They come back to Tokyo early and find themselves without shelter for the night; Noriko sweetly puts up her mother-in-law, but the old man has to go out drinking with two old friends, former Onomichians, who do not have a bed for him either. Full of sake, the old-timers allow some grievances to surface—mostly disgruntlement about children. Our hero is considered lucky; his progeny has turned out at least passable.

The old couple start out for Onomichi, but the woman is taken ill and they have to spend a few days in Osaka with their unmarried son Keizo. One sleepless night they speculate about their children and grandchildren. They do not permit themselves severe censure; in fact, they come up with all sorts of stoic acceptance and parental glossing over, yet we feel their great unstated sadness underneath. Once back in Onomichi, the mother's condition worsens; by the time the sons, daughter, and daughter-in-law arrive, the old woman is in a coma. During the death vigil and funeral a certain mellowing humanizes everyone, but at the postburial dinner people revert to form. The selfish daughter can hardly wait to make her decent young sister, Kyoko, dig up some of mother's valuables, ostensibly as keepsakes.

The father's reactions to his wife's death are quietly heart-rending. But the devastating climaxes of the whole long film are two conversations between the good people. One is between Kyoko and Noriko: the schoolmistress berates her sister and brothers, and wonders why they can't be as good as Noriko. The latter assures her that it is all a question of age; sooner or later, Kyoko will also have to look out for her own interests first. When they review the injustices of life, Noriko speaks gently of harsh things. So, too, the old lady had said of her children, "Let's think that they are better than most," and her husband, with that subtle yet ingenuous smile of his, answered, "They're certainly above average."

But the real heartbreaker is Noriko's affirmation that she herself will soon become self-centered. If this is not true, the self-depreciation of one of the truly just is unbearably sad; if it is true, and even the best may become tarnished with time, that may be sadder yet. The two young women are seen squatting in a lovely, simple but tasteful Japanese interior. Outside the window are the gracefully flared rooftops of Onomichi, and along the waterway ships are gliding past one another like people that pass in the night. "Isn't life disappointing?" Kyoko blurts out without really raising her voice. Noriko smiles her sweeping, absolute smile and says, very softly, "Yes, it is." If you can sit through this unemphatic little scene dry-eyed, not only do you not know about art, you do not even know about life.

The second conversation is between the father and Noriko. He repeats something his late wife had said to the young woman—that someone so young and fine should not remain faithful to a husband eight years dead, especially one who wasn't all that deserving. The father warmly insists that his wife was right, and presents her old-fashioned pocket watch as a memento to the tearful Noriko. The young woman protests that she is unworthy, that her thoughts have often strayed from her dead husband (as if that were a sin), but the old man gently makes her accept the gift and promise to live a little.

The old couple are good but not perfect. The mother is a bit naïve, over-apologetic, too eager to please. Her obesity is excessive, and she is forgetful and not quite efficient. The father is at times withdrawn and uncommunicative, absent. Their unworldliness and willingness to settle for crumbs verges on being irritating. But those are hardly serious flaws; these people are truly good, and not simperers, dullards, or nonentities. Ozu and his coscenarist, Kogo Noda, have worked a modest miracle.

They were, to be sure, helped by their actors. Chishu Ryu, a strikingly handsome and sensitive-looking man, plays the father (as he does in other Ozu films) with a face that can change imperceptibly from an obliging, helpful smile to an expression of slightly ironic resignation that is still a half smile; he registers intensity of thought and feeling with a furrow of the brow and a sort of sunken-in gaze that are acting at its most economic and eloquent. As the mother, Chiyeko Higashimaya superbly balances cheerfulness with befuddlement, and is childlike and dignified and shrewd all at once; her sweetness has a wonderful complexity to it.

Ozu's direction is sheer understatement. Exteriors are reduced to a few basic, sometimes recurrent, establishing or mood shots; comparable to the painter's quick background brushstrokes, in a matter of seconds they evoke the *genius loci*. A few arrogant chimney stacks and a honking auto horn convey the industrial city; the quiet harbor town is captured in some chugging motorboats and neat little houses decorously deployed up and down tree-studed hillocks.

At first the interiors, too, are treated as scenery: a static camera looks into a house through one or more sets of open screen doors and catches the bustle of the inhabitants as they scurry or flounce in and out of the field of vision. The dwelling becomes an inner landscape that, joining with the outer one, prepares us for the personalities of those who live in it. Thus the film begins with a street in Onomichi along which children are walking to school, in single file and at a steady, orderly pace. The doctor's house, on the other hand, is introduced to us as his elder son (circa eleven) rushes in on his return from school, cavalierly throws his things down, and darts hither and yon aggressively and clamorously.

It is in terms of such contrasts or, less frequently, parallels that *Tokyo Story*   81 makes its points. The grandchildren are shown as spoiled brats whose behavior blatantly parallels their parents' failings. But all this falls into place only much later when, after many letdowns at the hands of her children, the old woman remarks to her husband that some grandparents like their grandchildren better than their children. "I don't prefer my grandchildren," the old man replies, weighing his words carefully; then he adds unenthusiastically, "I like my children better." It is a calmly shattering comment on both children and grandchildren.

The impact is always that of well-placed understatement. In the garish hotel at Atami Hot Springs, the old folks are kept awake by the roisterers downstairs. They lie in their beds sleepless but uncomplaining, only their fans swish and swat nervously and snappishly, and the shot is held a little longer than the viewer can comfortably bear.

Details speak clearly but unobtrusively. In Noriko's pitiful one-room apartment, the large package of Rinso testifies to cleanliness; at his mother's funeral, young Keizo may seem to suffer most intensely, yet he alone does not wear the traditional mourning garb. The doors in the Tokyo houses move noisily, have warning bells attached to them; in Onomichi, they slide open to the mere natural sound of wood against wood. When the old man is widowed, Ozu frames his shots of him in such a way that we are always conscious of the empty space just before or behind him, where his wife used to be seated.

We are aware throughout of kind actions rising above the grayness of everyday existence like beautiful dawns; we also realize how transient and doomed these good deeds are, how beleaguered and confounded. But the sadness then spills over into a third stage: we notice that goodness is not wholly ephemeral, for a link is established between good people that will sustain them, however tenuously and intermittently. When the mother spends that night at Noriko's, a great warmth, born earlier, is confirmed between them. She urges her daughter-in-law to come visit them in Onomichi. "I would like to," Noriko says with her eager smile, "if it were a little nearer." We are reminded of how poor she is, and the old woman answers politely, "You are right. It is so far away." The melancholy of this hits us as we recall her innocent glee upon arriving in Tokyo, when she remarked on how near it really is and how they must come up more often. Nevertheless, we know that their thoughts will visit with each other.

Almost always the dialogue functions with this suggestion-laden spareness—imageless prose haikus, as it were, whose few words resonate far and deep. And the supporting cast is as perfect as the principals, with a particularly astonishing performance from Setsuko Hara as Noriko: I cannot remember another instance of homeliness so transformed by inner beauty. If only the print shown at the New Yorker Theater were better, and if the subtitles were not riddled with lacunae. But do not let that deter you from going: if a statue by Praxiteles can be a masterpiece without head and arms, so can this film without an adequate print or subtitles.

March 20, 1972

Kangaroos and Killers

Outback is a film that has a roughly equal amount of right and wrong things about it. This makes it hard to discuss without one's sounding like a *New York Times* reviewer, one of those professional equivocators specializing in double-bottomed paragraphs or sentences, whose ends carefully contradict their beginnings. To be sure, like most things, movies tend to be mixed bags, but that is no reason for reading a review to be like walking on rugs that are continually being pulled out from under you. *Outback,* however, does its own double-dealing. It purports to be a straightforward account of a dreary and harrowing experience, but it spills over into sensationalism and trickiness, which, given the unusual yet universal subject, is a great pity.

A young teacher is languishing at his job in a one-room schoolhouse in the barren Australian outback, a thousand miles from Sydney. For Christmas vacation, he takes a desolate old train to the nearest mining town—a capital of boredom known to its semicretinized residents as the Yabba. From here, next morning, our hero is to catch a plane for Sydney and his sexy girl friend. During the night, however, he falls prey to the Yabba's two chief entertainments: beer-guzzling and penny-pitching for large sums. He loses all his money. The natives, amiable brutes, extend a helpful, beer-can-bearing hand, and he is reluctantly but ineluctably sucked into a mindless, soulless companionship of boozy bravado, boorish conviviality, and grubby sex.

If the transitions were handled less brusquely, if the milieu were examined more thoroughly; if the weaknesses of the hero's supposedly civilized psyche were traced more cogently in their affinity with and surrender to the ambient vulgarity, if a heterosexual encounter did not have the dice loaded against it and a homosexual one were not dragged in too glibly—if all this did not lead up to some rather purple violence, it could have been a devastating indictment of well-meaning meaninglessness. *Outback,* based on a novel unknown to me, could have epitomized the appeal of the mud, the frailty of culture and fastidiousness dumped in a jolly pigpen. It could have compellingly shown bibulous masculine camaraderie as the dehumanizing phenomenon it is for men and, indirectly, women; and revealed aggressive xenophilia as yet another form of xenophobia.

The screenplay by Evan Jones is unfortunately given to oversimplification, even as Ted Kotcheff's direction leans toward overdramatization. Nevertheless, both have underlying merit and moments of real power. The acting is convincing, especially that of the townsfolk played by the citizenry of Broken Hill. Gary Bond is adequate as the teacher; Chips Rafferty, the veteran Australian actor, is properly drab in his very kindness as a local constable; and Donald Pleasance again does one of his strident, nasal grotesques, this time as a cynical alcoholic doctor—by Conrad out of Chekhov— who becomes both the good and evil angel of the schoolteacher.

Much of the amiable bestiality comes across and culminates in two hid- 83 eous, shattering kangaroo hunts, but the subsequent melodramatic twists and the hero's elaborate hallucinations lack conviction or dramatic necessity. Yet *Outback* holds our attention most of the way.

Another film more interesting than truly successful, *Without Apparent Motive,* is the second work of the young French cinéaste, Philippe Labro. This thriller is based on an Ed McBain novel that Labro and his coscenarist, Jacques Lanzmann, have transposed from our West Coast to the Côte d'Azur. The peculiarly American-style violence produces, against the more gracious and relaxed backgrounds of Nice, a piquant sense of *dépaysement.*

Unhappily, the McBain material is deeply improbable and, in some ways, downright preposterous; the dialogue, admittedly sprightly, is not dazzling enough to blind us to logical blemishes. But Labro has assembled some fascinating physiognomies, and he has both a good sense of rhythm (though his crosscutting in the early sequences gets to be a mite ostentatious) and a nice eye for detail. He has also created a humorous atmosphere that is unusual in recent French cinema, precisely because it is humorous rather than witty. There is less clever irony here than good coarse-grained fun, and taste for the absurdities of death and life.

Labro can create memorable images, such as that of the tough, intrepid inspector, whose mistress has just been killed, absent-mindedly fingering a whistle she once playfully gave him ("If you want me, just whistle"). He is standing in his apartment in front of the closed Venetian blinds, yet enough light filters through to reveal his darkened face against a striated background. Abstractedly, he puts the whistle to his mouth, but his concentration is so poor, or his throat so dry, that only two or three wheezing half sounds dribble out. The face shadowed from without and within, the stripes behind it suggesting so many methodically drawn lines to cancel out the world beyond, the daylight nonetheless refusing to be wholly denied, and those pitiful, aborted sounds trailing off into the somber silence—the director who etched this vignette bears watching.

The film is basically an *hommage* to the type of American movie epitomized by *The Big Sleep.* It has a strain of Gallic sensuality running through it, however, as well as a certain innocence—as if it could not quite believe such a series of murderous snipings to be possible in one of the happy cities of the Riviera. And the characters have become very French (whatever they may have been in the McBain original), like the aging playboy who stuffs his bathing briefs with a large handkerchief in lieu of a codpiece.

Jean-Louis Trintignant gives one of his better performances as the detective protagonist; particularly effective is his sudden mirthless smile that bares his teeth as mechanically as if he were a horse offering itself for sale. There is good acting from almost everyone, or, at least, good type-casting: Laura Antonelli is disturbingly winsome as the neurotic woman behind it all, and Erich Segal makes a quack so unctuous and self-righteous that the audience lets out a jubilant whoop at his demise. Only Dominique Sanda continues to be the glaring nonactress she is, though Labro does much to cover up her debility. In the end, the film runs out of steam and the last shred of credibility; but by then we have had our share of fun.

April 3, 1972

A Mirror for Ourselves

IT IS NOT often that I get to write about a great film, and I wish the typography or the color of the printer's ink—or at least my style—could change to mark the solemnity of the occasion. There being little hope for the first two, I shall have to try to make my words convey to you the splendor and the importance of *The Sorrow and the Pity*. Marcel Ophüls's previous full-length film, *Banana Peel*, left me cold, and certainly did not prepare me for the magnificence of this 260-minute documentary about France under the German Occupation. With this film the son of the overrated Max Ophüls becomes a director of note.

The Sorrow and the Pity tackles its immense subject with conspicuous intelligence. It picks Clermont-Ferrand, a typical provincial capital in the heart of France, and limits itself, by and large, to reconstructing what happened there. The birthplace of Pascal and the locale of Rohmer's *My Night at Maud's*, Clermont-Ferrand is Hicksville to the French. In the farces of Feydeau, it is where the oafish cousin invariably comes from, or where an inconvenient husband is packed off to on maneuvers.

Ophüls and his associates interviewed a cross-section of *Clermontois* and foreigners brought to the town by the war: Germans who occupied it, English fliers who were shot down over it, intelligence agents who infiltrated it. Some of the natives were heroes of the Resistance, others were collaborators or accused of collaboration, many were neither: the apothecary who stayed as neutral as possible for the sake of his large family, the lawyer who defended patriots during the Occupation and collaborators after the Liberation, the schoolteachers who watched non-Aryan colleagues being dismissed and did nothing about it.

One of the sons of Clermont-Ferrand was Pierre Mendès-France; unjustly imprisoned in his home town, he escaped to join de Gaulle. He tells about his wartime experiences calmly, wittily, cogently. This humane Jewish statesman becomes the good conscience of France and the film; its bad consciences, in towns not far from Clermont-Ferrand, are Marshal Pétain and his prime minister, Pierre Laval. The film extends to them and to other high-echelon people: Georges Bidault, Jacques Duclos, Anthony Eden, Albert Speer, General Warlimont of the Wehrmacht, the British Major General Sir Edward Spears, the Resistance organizer Emmanuel d'Astier de la Vigerie, and several others in high positions on various sides.

Interviews that shed absorbing new light on the war years are interspersed 85 with generous newsreel clips—French, German, British—that shed absorbing, often untruthful, old light on the same events. The identical incident is seen through the eyes of a German field officer, a high-ranking German staff officer, and a mere German soldier, as well as from various French and English vantage points. The matters raised shimmer before our eyes and keep changing as they are discussed by successive speakers. We see people as they are now and also, in newsreels and old snapshots, as they were then. We even see a representative German propaganda film (the scandalous *Jud Süss*), and hear about the varying reactions of contemporary French audiences.

War and its ambiguous events become, by turns, a detective story to be pieced together from numerous yet still insufficient clues; a set of curious ironies—of fate, of character, of changing historical climate; a Proustian gallery of characters who are good in their own and their friends' eyes, horrible in the eyes of their enemies, and something midway to our gaze. Finally, the whole becomes a mirror for ourselves: What would we have done in these people's shoes? The mirror refuses us easy answers about who was, or would have been, the fairest of all.

France itself is on the witness stand, or in the prisoner's dock. France, the only country that stopped fighting, signed a treaty, collaborated with the Nazi enemy. Yes, there was a Resistance; but it was smaller and suffered more internal discord than official accounts would have it. Yes, there were brave individuals; but what about the majority: indifferent, callous, cowardly, ready to indulge their anti-Semitism openly and legally, and avail themselves of the Germans to eliminate—in the word's most terrible sense— their competitors?

Acts of monstrous, Sadian cruelty were performed by Frenchmen on their fellow Frenchmen. Hypocrisy had a field day. Could the same have happened here? Is there such a thing as a national character? Why were the Danes and the Dutch, for example, so brave and noble, almost to a man? Why were the French and Italians, by and large, so spineless and dishonorable? And what about the Germans themselves? Were these men we see obvious villains, or only dense, unimaginative individuals, unable to draw correct conclusions?

There are some hints, if not answers, in the maze. Some elderly French teachers seem largely unaware of the persecutions that occurred among their colleagues and pupils, and take a memorial plaque in their school yard to be honoring the school's dead in World War I. They are amazed when the interviewers point out to them that it concerns World War II. One good citizen of Clermont-Ferrand denies ever having seen any Germans around: this, after all, was the Free Zone. A local hotelier did not in the least mind billeting German military personnel, except insofar as it cut down on his tourist trade.

The oily international lawyer, Count René de Chambrun, Laval's son-in-law, maintains that his late father-in-law was the canny savior of France, that he shrewdly yielded on some points to prevent worse disasters. Confronted with evidence to the contrary, the count stares blankly and words fail him, but he concedes nothing. A former German captain still proudly wears his Nazi medals—how are they different from any others, he asks. And how can you call those beasts who ambushed and killed German soldiers partisans, he wonders; a real partisan should wear a white or yellow ribbon or cap to identify him as such.

People can be blind or stupid or both. But the answer is not that simple. A beautician who has suffered much and long at the hands of the "good" French after the war, but who may well have been innocent, bravely admits that she continues to believe in Pétain's policies (none of the Germans actually makes such an admission). And we feel that for a provincial, Catholic petit-bourgeois this was a possible belief. We are not convinced, however, that a man like Georges Lamirand, the minister of youth, had a right to his hero worship of the marshal from up close.

Curiously, we find ourselves sympathizing with Christian de la Mazière, an aristocratic Frenchman, the son of a rightist officer, who had gone so far as to join the Charlemagne Division: Frenchmen in SS uniforms fighting on the Russian front. Forthrightly and courageously, this much chastened man analyzes lucidly how he came to do these things, and we cannot deny plausibility to his arguments. A terrible relativity is seen to inhere in human concepts, actions, judgments.

Not quite all of them, though. Anthony Eden's refusal to judge the French is indisputably humane. The behavior and words of two old farmers, the brothers Louis and Alexis Grave, are unshowily heroic and decent. Their unwillingness to exact revenge from those who betrayed them to the Germans and Buchenwald emerges as the film's most luminous passage, along with the sharp but compassionate evaluations uttered by Mendès-France. One is less at ease with Bidault's cynical wit, and still less so with Duclos's smug imperturbability. Most of the Resistance men appear ambiguous: brave but ambitious and factious, noble and petty at the same time. We would like to know more about them than the film has time for.

Several issues may have been deliberately avoided. The equivocal roles of Catholicism and communism under the Occupation, for example, are barely if at all hinted at. Some things may have been omitted through mere oversight: Did that beautician have to serve the fifteen years of jail she was condemned to? Why does Major General Spears speak such absolutely immaculate French? What is the true ancestry of the shopkeeper Marius Klein, who so ardently asserts his Catholicism?

But we do get some precious bits of information. We learn, for instance, how men become heroes. Emile Couladon was so indignant at not being served steak at a restaurant—it was reserved for the Germans—that he joined the Resistance and, under the *nom de guerre* Colonel Gaspard, became the intrepid, intransigent leader of the Auvergne Maquis. At war's end, he becomes a dealer in electronic equipment; for the sake of selling television sets, he prefers to forget who did what.

Emmanuel d'Astier de la Vigerie was the dissipated black sheep of an aristocratic family, a perennial failure. The refusal of the British to evacuate him, the hopelessness of his situation with his back against the Pyrenées, his fear about the future, inspire him to gather others like himself and start the

Resistance. At the end of hostilities, we see him in a newsreel clip fanatically demanding merciless justice for collaborators. During an interview shortly before his death in 1969, he looks comfortable, benign, and sly, and is all for forgiving and forgetting. Is he wise or just back on opium?

The most moving figure of all is Dennis Rake, former member of the British underground in France, whose heroism, as we hear his ex-chief attest, was unsurpassed. He is now a meek little old man, surrounded by bibelots and petting a cat; he says he was a musical-comedy actor and frankly reveals that he is a homosexual; he adds that he wanted to prove to his skeptical friends that he was as much a man as they. When he tells about a friend in the Resistance confiding in an aunt who turned him in and caused his doom, these bare facts, coming from such a gentle, brave man, assume particular horror.

But then Rake tells about a German officer who believed him to be a Belgian, took him in, and became his lover—and of how he finally left this man because of what his fellow Germans would have done to him had they found him harboring an enemy agent. Here the film becomes deeply touching. This unusual relationship described in the most matter-of-fact terms suddenly makes us realize how much greater love is than war, and how, nevertheless, it is defeated by war. As Jacques Prévert said succinctly in one of his finest poems: *"Oh Barbara / Quelle connerie la guerre . . ."*

Sagacious, ingeniously put together, *The Sorrow and the Pity* allows us to hear the real voices of people—the exact words, tonalities, emphases that reveal or withhold so much. The dubbing (by the BBC) is adroit: it leaves the beginnings and ends of speeches uncovered by translation, so that your ears can judge for themselves. In between, the original voice is turned down and a translation is spoken over it. The English voices are fair approximations, but they are British rather than American and, at times, perhaps a little too emotional. Moreover, these voices affect stage French and German accents on a discriminatory basis: upper-class speakers get the best BBC speech, and only lower-class ones are saddled with the phony Gallicizing and Teutonizing. But these are minor cavils.

The admirable thing about *The Sorrow and the Pity* is that, though it clearly has opinions of its own, it does not force them upon you. A slight tendentiousness was, surely, unavoidable; but you are left amazingly free to make your own discoveries and evaluations. And the film even manages to give you a few glimpses of that graciously rolling Auvergne landscape that inspired those haunting folk songs Canteloube arranged into the "Songs of the Auvergne." Finally, it leaves you with the feeling that, more than France, mankind—some basic insufficiency in us—is at fault.

Near the end of this long film that feels, if anything, too short, we are again at the home of the pharmacist Marcel Verdier, who was a neutral but did not lose his humanity, and who is now surrounded by his large, decent family. Verdier, the film's *homme moyen sensuel,* tells how, when the German rout was already total, he got his one chance to shoot an elderly, pathetic, sniveling German soldier. He refrained, because "It would have seemed more like killing a pig, and that wouldn't have been very interesting." A curious choice of word, that "interesting." Could that be the ultimate human motivation: the need to make boring lives more interesting? Is that what finally makes us kill?

The movie does not issue pronouncements on human nature, but I think Ophüls would subscribe to these lines of the English poet A. S. J. Tessimond: "How much simpler if men were not striped like tigers, patched like clowns; / If alternate white and black were not further confused by greys and browns . . ." I take the ultimate implication of this important, stirring film to be the difficulty of being either good or bad: What a precarious, pitiful thing it is to be people! What a precarious, pitiful thing it is to be swine!

May 1, 1972

The Play Was the Thing

CHEKHOV's *Uncle Vanya* is a play so beautiful that it hurts. But, as in the old joke, it only hurts when we laugh. For we find ourselves closeted in the theater with people who are so absurd as to be resoundingly funny, yet even as we respond to this we realize that the boundary between such ridiculousness and ancient tragedy is as tenuous as the one between these characters and us. The subject of *Uncle Vanya* is self-entrapment, and who among us is free of it? The twin vices of these people are acquiescence in the dullness of their milieu and giving in to the force of habit they generate. Together, the horizontal bars of social inertia and the vertical ones of the daily routine form the window of a prison, a grille on which hope plays tic-tac-toe with reality and always loses.

Chekhov makes his people funny: losers drunk with defeat—not exactly as if it were a victory, but as if it were something aristocratic, heroic, or, at least, saintly. Dr. Astrov, the man of experience, talent, and vision, the scientist full of brave foresight, has very little sight left for the here and now, except to denounce or renounce it. He and Yelyena can toy with the idea of love, yet cannot play that happy game itself. Professor Serebryakov acquires and perfects the husk of a thinker and writer, but none of the insides. He can fool some, like Yelyena, briefly; others, like Vanya, for much longer; and fools, like his former mother-in-law, forever. For himself, he has devised the role of the great man tripped up by the inefficiency of others, but patiently forgiving.

Vanya is worst off: he simultaneously believes he is a potential great man, a Schopenhauer or Dostoevsky, and knows he is a failure—even his one grand gesture turns into a ludicrous fiasco. He finally accepts the inevitable, although it may not really be inevitable and the acceptance is not a true one. Only poor, plain little Sonya's resignation has true nobility. She is the play's one exultant loser, but what happiness is there in patiently ebbing away?

The locked-in, ingrown complexities and paradoxes of the play may be 89 impossible to transfer effectively to the screen. The current Russian filmization, however, is thicker in disasters than the unsuitability of the medium and ordinary bungling could explain. I have no notion of who the director, Andrei Mikhalkov-Konchalovsky, is; I have a pretty shrewd idea of what he is. To begin with the most obvious: anyone who would cast the enchanting Irina Kupchenko as Sonya and have the rather horse-faced Irina Miroshnichenko play Yelyena, is blind or stupid or an insensitive clod. There is little reason for Astrov (or Vanya) to hanker after this Yelyena; still less for his spurning such a Sonya; and none whatever for this lovely creature to call it quits after one failure.

I shall pass lightly over the obtrusive propaganda that repeatedly sneaks grim snapshots of life in czarist Russia into the film to explain the frustrations of the characters and imply the need for the cure that was to come. But just consider what the director does with Sonya's magnificently moving final speech. Only briefly does he linger with the aching girl and her miserable uncle, with the gentle proffering of faith in the afterlife and charity through shared burdens—of hope in hopelessness. Instead, he promptly cuts away to the corridor outside the room, then tracks farther back through the house and finishes with a lengthy aerial shot of the mighty Russian land!

All this while Sonya's voice is heard wistfully, compassionately, tiredly evoking the peace of the hereafter. Surely the camera must stay with the desolate Vanya and the girl who, kneeling before him, ignores her own tears and wipes away his. It is into these two beings—damned or saved together—that the camera must try to penetrate, rather than proudly survey the landscape from the air.

The editing is amateurishly jerky throughout; the camera setups are consistently unimaginative; the pace is unendurably slow. The film pointlessly shuttles between color photography so bad that it seems to have been painted in decades ago by hand (perhaps by way of an *ex voto* from some grateful patient whom Dr. Chekhov himself had cured), and monochrome that leaves one unsure of what shade of black, brown, or bilious it might be. In fact, it is sometimes hard to determine whether the images on the screen are in aborted color or mildewed black-and-white.

The director plays havoc with Chekhov's stated intentions. Thus, though Act I is supposed to take place in the garden (a deliberate note of false optimism), he confines it within the house. When Vanya is shooting at the Professor, the latter is supposed to be "staggering and terrified"; in the film, he calmly turns his back on his assailant. The directing of Serebryakov is consistently wrongheaded. Instead of an overbearing phony who fluctuates between pontification and self-pity, we are given an inconspicuous little man—almost self-effacing when not actually whining, and barely pompous now and then. This provides the film with two Uncle Vanyas.

As for Yelyena, she has been made an ordinary, quite unmagnetic woman, and Telyegin is deprived of all significance. Vanya is played acceptably by Russia's sole Method actor, Innokenti Smoktunovsky, who is here much more restrained than in Kozintsev's *Hamlet* or in *Nine Days of One Year*. Indeed, his occasional Method twitches provide a welcome distraction from

the old-fashioned ponderousness of Sergei Bondarchuk's altogether beefy
Astrov. The two old women are handled well, albeit without great distinction.

Irina Kupchenko is not only, as I mentioned, too pretty for Sonya, she is
also too powerful a performer. The result is an *Uncle Vanya* that is Sonya's
tragedy, and not a balanced group portrait as comic as it is sad. More
comedy is what Chekhov kept vainly asking from Stanislavski, and what this
film, like recent Moscow Art Theater productions, continues to deny him.
Chekhov desperately needs to be saved from the Russians—and from reviewers like Vincent Canby, Penelope Gilliatt, and those others who bowed
down in awe before this abortion.

Yet another fine play—no *Vanya*, to be sure, but outstanding by current
standards—Peter Nichols's *A Day in the Death of Joe Egg*, suffers a B+ to
C change in becoming a film. This autobiographical play told of a young
provincial English schoolmaster, Brian or Bri, of his somewhat older earth
mother of a wife, Sheila, and of how their ten-year marriage finally collapsed
because of their daughter, Josephine. For Joe Egg, as Bri has nicknamed her,
is a spastic, a vegetable, a drain on her parents' time, energy, and joy of
living. Rather Chekhovianly, the play traces the dissolution of a dynamic
marriage owing to tragic circumstances in an almost constantly witty, sometimes riotously funny, manner. The humor, blackish rather than black,
never ignores the sadness of the situation; it is a gritty, brilliant, finally
doomed attempt at living with that irrefutable sadness.

The young British playwright gave us an incisive but sympathetic study of
the mercurial, intellectual father who invents clever little parlor games for
himself and his wife to play: satirical skits, either travestying certain episodes
from the couple's life and struggles with their daughter, or actually inventing brand new absurdities. For example, a Viennese specialist who examined
the child and pronounced her incurable, and a swinging, radical Church of
England priest who offered to do some faith-healing, are devastatingly par-
odied by Brian, with Sheila assisting. She goes along with the charades
mainly to humor Bri; as a woman overflowing with maternal love—extending to cats, birds, and goldfish—Sheila can cherish Joe even as a vegetable,
and refuses to farm her out to an institution.

Underneath the hilarious horseplay, the play becomes an impassioned
contest between Bri's growing belief in euthanasia and Sheila's dogged, un-
reasoning love and need to shelter and mother a life, however wretched.
What makes *Joe Egg* remarkable is that the strong and weak points of both
positions are honestly and appealingly stated, and no argument is weighted
unfairly. The consequence, granted, is misery for both parents; but Bri's
escape is made no more attractive than Sheila's persistence. The viewer must
draw his own conclusions.

Peter Medak, the director, made Nichols write the scenario so as to alter
the play in two ways. First, the parlor games were moved to their supposed
locations, e.g., a hospital or a church; second, formerly narrated episodes
were shown, and additional outdoor scenes created. The trouble with the   91

first device is that it makes the fantasies look almost real; desperate, funny play-acting begins to look like not-so-funny actual events. The trouble with the second is that it dissipates the oppressive, claustrophobic atmosphere of the play and, in some cases, spells out certain actions about which the play left us suspensefully guessing.

The casting, too, is unfortunate: Alan Bates tends to go hammy as Bri, and Janet Suzman is both too elegantly upper class and too rational and svelte for the opulent, working-class, somewhat slatternly Sheila. Even from Joan Hickson, who was fine on stage as Bri's hopelessly commonplace mother, Medak elicits an exaggerated, mannered performance; a stuffy married couple, friends of the family, are pushed even further into caricature. The color cinematography by Ken Hodges is, at best, undistinguished, and the recurrent bits of nudity seem needlessly dragged-in.

Still, people who missed the stage play should see the movie. It does occasionally surprise us with subtle touches; it does address itself to a genuine problem intelligently; it remains funny as well as earnest, and holds the interest even if it no longer grips the heart.

June 26, 1972

Doctor Horroris Causa

IN THE interview that serves as the introduction to my book *Ingmar Bergman Directs,* the following exchange takes place:

> S. How about Hitchcock? Is he someone you learned from?
> B. Yes, of course.
> S. Technically, I suppose. But isn't there a great intellectual emptiness in his work?
> B. Completely, but I think he's a very good technician. . . . *Psycho* is one of his most interesting pictures because he had to make [it] very fast, with very primitive means. He had little money, and this picture tells very much about him. Not very good things. He is completely infantile, and I would like to know more—no, I don't want to know—about his behavior with or, rather, against women.

Women may have fared badly in *Psycho,* but in Hitchcock's new film they fare even worse. *Frenzy* is about a psychopathic sex-killer of women; it is brutal, not especially suspenseful, quite neatly made, moderately skillful in its dialogue, and serves absolutely no aesthetic, intellectual, or moral purpose. It is merely entertainment—of the hollowest, cheapest, most meretricious sort. Nevertheless, on the *New York Times* weekly scoreboard, eighteen critics cast favorable votes for this scented trash. There were no "mixed" opinions, and only two unfavorable ones: from the Newhouse papers' Frances Taylor, and from me. Give the Hitch-hawkers their bittersweet pablum of allegedly sophisticated murder, and they'll salivate themselves right into their habitual hurrahs for the work of this polished, unpleasant infant.

Frenzy concerns a former RAF hero, Richard Blaney, who, after failing at various enterprises including marriage, ends up as a bartender involved with Barbara, a good-natured barmaid. He is a hostile fellow whose bitterness and arrogance get him fired again. Proudly spurning financial aid from Robert Rusk, a dapper, friendly fruit wholesaler in the Covent Garden market, Blaney goes to see his ex-wife Brenda, who runs a matrimonial agency. Her secretary notices his intoxication and violent behavior. Later, when Brenda is found raped and strangled with a tie—yet another victim of the Necktie Murderer, London's answer to the Boston Strangler—strong circumstantial evidence points to Blaney. The audience, however, has been shown friendly, psychopathic Rusk raping and murdering Brenda.

The obvious suspect and the faithful Barbara hide out together. They are briefly sheltered by a former RAF mate, Johnny Porter, and his hateful, suspicious wife, Hetty. Meanwhile Rusk, ostensibly offering help to his friend's girl, brings Barbara to his apartment and does her in, too. The investigation is conducted by Chief Inspector Oxford of the Yard, a somewhat comic figure whose wife, a practitioner of gourmet cooking, inflicts fancy, inedible meals on him. The Porters know that Blaney could not have killed Barbara, yet refuse to come forward with an alibi out of fear of becoming implicated. Left in the lurch, Blaney seeks out Rusk. Under the guise of helping him, the fruit man plants fake evidence on his friend and turns him in. Blaney is given a life sentence.

Inspector Oxford, pursuing a hunch that Blaney may be innocent, tracks down the real culprit. Ironically, Blaney escapes from the prison hospital to kill Rusk just as, unbeknown to him, the case is about to be reopened. Blaney clubs a covered figure in Rusk's bed, who turns out to be Rusk's latest, already strangled, victim. Oxford gets there in time and a further fatal slip-up is averted when he and Blaney catch Rusk redhanded. As the Hitch-hypers will no doubt have it, Providence, which works in mysterious ways, stepped in to put things to right, but not before Blaney has been taught some Christian humility.

Well, I don't know about the mysterious ways of Providence, but the tricky ways of Hitchcock are pretty well known to us all. Though we are told early on who the killer is, the film still capitalizes on suspense and sensationalism. The latter lies in the ghoulish sex murders and naked female corpses turning up everywhere; the former in whether the unappealing innocent will be able to clear himself, or whether the appealing psychopath will get away with murder. It is, finally, a game of Sleuth Along With Hitch, in which the audience is invited to test its sharpness against his.

What makes *Frenzy* different from many—though, significantly, not all—Hitchcock films is that the criminal in it is more likable than the hero. One of the few gripping scenes has Rusk discover that Barbara, as she fought for her life, snatched his diamond tiepin; it is now in the cramped hand of a nude corpse stuffed into a potato sack and being trucked north along with a   93 load of potatoes. Rusk's hairbreadth retrieval of and escape with the pin has the audience, as Vincent Canby writes, "identifying with the killer [and in] the position of cheering on (well, almost) the maniac." In pictures like *The Lady Vanishes, Foreign Correspondent, The 39 Steps,* etc., we were on the side of the hero, a decent fellow except for an occasional minor flaw; in movies like *Strangers on a Train, Shadow of a Doubt,* or *Psycho,* the situation was more ambiguous. But not till *Frenzy* were we happily made to identify ourselves and sympathize with so reprehensible a raping and murdering madman.

The film offers no insights; it does not probe psyches, human relations, or social conditions. Rusk seems to adore his fairly repellent mother, but nothing much is made of that. An anonymous doctor and Inspector Oxford pontificate separately about psychopaths, but neither of them says anything novel, penetrating, or integral to the film. Although Rusk is consistently amiable while Blaney is boorish, no metaphysical notion about the charm of evil and the lack of charm of goodness is developed or even, I am sure, intended.

There is, however, one point where Rusk, his face clouding over with what seems to be genuine distaste, says something about certain women asking for the things that befall them. Even if the film's main raison d'être lies in a minor character's remark, "We haven't had a good, fancy sex murder since Christie, and they're so good for the tourist trade"—with only the word "tourist" to be replaced by "film"—Rusk's statement suggests a deeper motive: the filmmaker's intense misogyny.

True, there is Barbara, the one thoroughly nice woman of the film; but in this role Hitchcock has cast the homeliest of actresses, Anna Massey. (In her nude scenes, he uses a double whose fine body and legs make a mockery of Miss Massey's shapeless scrawniness the rest of the time.) And even this worthy woman becomes the butt of nasty posthumous jokes—as when the bare foot of her corpse keeps hitting Rusk in the face; or when her rigid corpse's fingers have to be cracked open one by one to yield the clutched pin, followed soon by a mock-naïve Mrs. Oxford breaking breadsticks with a creepy emphasis.

Brenda Blaney is pleasant enough, but she seems to have divorced her husband in an unsympathetic way, and she is not very bright in her handling of Rusk. She is raped and killed in explicit, lip-smacking detail, and, once dead, is displayed with eyes bulging horribly, tongue ludicrously hanging out. This may be clinically correct, but the only effect is to engender lack of sympathy for the victim.

As the good women are gleefully desecrated in death, the others are reviled in life. There is Mrs. Oxford, exquisitely torturing her husband's stomach while needling him about his work, which she discusses with an infuriating smugness that makes the third degree seem, by comparison, a Socratic dialogue. More repellent is a sneering female hotel clerk, who is stupid to boot; and still worse is Brenda Blaney's secretary, a prim, self-righteous, man-hating old maid, eager to incriminate an innocent man.

Worst of all is Hetty Porter, who has reduced her husband to a spineless nonentity fearful of testifying in behalf of an old friend. Hetty refuses all

proofs of Blaney's innocence, logical and even ocular. But when she is temporarily foiled in her wish to turn Blaney in, or at least out, she soothes her
rage by going shopping. I doubt if much of this comes from Arthur La
Bern's underlying novel; and whatever Anthony Shaffer's screenplay may
have contributed, the final responsibility is Hitchcock's, as his auteurist wor-
shipers will have to be first to admit. The antifeminism appears also in a
number of casual remarks, as when, upon being told that the women are
raped before being strangled, a man observes, "Well, I suppose it's nice to
know that every cloud has a silver lining."

There is no technical innovation, or even noteworthy technique, to compensate for the meanness and vacuity of this film or its whopping improbabilities. The opening helicopter shots closely resemble those in *Psycho;*
the jocular treatment of corpses takes us back to *The Trouble With Harry;*
Rusk's struggle with the tiepin recalls Bruno's efforts to recover the lighter in
Strangers on a Train. Improbabilities in the plot are too numerous to mention
and extend down to such gross absurdities as Blaney's having been married
ten years and divorced for two, and still looking thirtyish; to have been a
World War II ace, he must have been a flying infant prodigy.

But all Hitchcock cares about is making the audience gratuitously proud
of itself when he lets them divine some obvious next move; and making it
abjectly awed by him when, the next time around, he pulls a fast one. At a
showing I attended, the audience formed a constant chorus of Ahs in facile
glee at guessing right, and Oos in reverential wonder at guessing wrong.
Misogyny and infantilism, as Bergman noted, are the two faces of this clever
anti-artist's arrested development.

July 24, 1972

Cut-Rate Alienation

HAD *La Salamandre* received the short critical shrift it deserves, it could have
been dismissed as a not absolutely untalented little film with its head and
heart resolutely in the wrong places. But the praise lavished on it from most
sides makes it a film crying out for critical scrutiny. The work of a relatively
young Swiss director, Alain Tanner, it presents itself as a sharp comment on
life in Switzerland and, by extension, in any capitalistic society; and also as a
piece of filmmaking that takes over where the New Wave left off and continues the work of Godard and Truffaut in interesting newer directions.
Would that it were so!

Pierre, a struggling journalist, and Paul, a less than prosperous writer
doubling as a house painter, undertake to write a TV documentary about
Rosemonde, a girl who recently made the tabloids. One of a large brood of
impoverished country folk, she had gone to work as a maid for an uncle in
Geneva who cared for her subsistence and schooling. One day, his gun went

off and hit him in the shoulder; in court, he claimed his niece tried to kill him, while she maintained it was an accidental, self-inflicted wound. The jury was hung and the case, finally, dropped. Yet there was evidently friction between the solid bourgeois uncle and the girl who had become a dropout, mother of an illegitimate child, and a drifter from job to job.

Pierre tracks down Rosemonde and starts taping interviews with her and those who know her; he believes her to be innocent. Paul, who is married and has a small daughter, prefers not to meet Rosemonde; he bases his script partly on Pierre's researches, but more on his writer's intuition and imagination. He thinks the girl shot her stodgy uncle, although there were many extenuating social circumstances.

Gradually, both men become more implicated with Rosemonde and, eventually, sleep with her. After she quits her job in a sausage factory, they aid her financially. They accompany her on a midwinter visit to her village to get to know her parents and background. When she is in trouble at her new job as a salesgirl in a shoestore, they try to help her keep the position. But they are now really involved with her and, indirectly, with her part-time boy friend who is a petty criminal. They have lost their objectivity. Even when it turns out that Paul was right, that Rosemonde, in exasperation, shot her uncle, the boys cannot come up with a script. Broke, Pierre goes to Paris to try his luck there, and Paul returns to house painting. Rosemonde manages to get herself fired by lewdly caressing the customers' feet and finds herself once again jobless, free, and, for the moment, euphoric. She is the salamander, which, according to legend, lives mischievously in the fire without getting burned.

In true Godardian tradition, Tanner constructs his film out of loose plot elements, simulated cinéma-vérité, and a rather sententious narration between one fairly static scene and the next. He runs into trouble with all three devices. His plot is humdrum and uninvolving: the three principals are as dull and, in the men's case, unattractive as can be. Pierre is accorded a certain cynical wit, but since there is no evidence that he has the slightest skill as a journalist or any cognitive or imaginative faculties worth attending to, the wit comes out as a mere smart-aleckiness. His attitude toward Rosemonde is a mixture of feeble goodwill and ineffectual exploitativeness, and there is nothing like his mental, moral, and even sexual limpness to leave us unsympathetic.

Paul, on the other hand, is supposed to be a real writer, as demonstrated by the fact that he is married to a poetess who, when he tells her he has been unfaithful, gently reads him a Heine text from *Reisebilder* that has nothing whatever to do with unfaithfulness. He sings when he is unhappy (i.e., makes up inane melodies to infantile verbalizings), and loves his craft so deeply that he would rather work as a house painter than as a literary hack. There is, however, no indication that he is a genuine writer, or that he has any talent except for clowning, which he does incessantly.

Pierre and Paul's mock-heroic philosophizings (e.g., "There are too many people to whom the liberty to be in their own skins is systematically refused") are neither funny enough to be taken as jokes, nor significant enough to be considered seriously—yet that, apparently, is what Tanner wants us to do. And since Jean-Luc Bideau and Jacques Denis are such undistinguished and charmless actors, we are not won over by the performances either.

As Rosemonde, Bulle Ogier is a little more interesting. She is a *jolie laide* whose face changes continually from quite appealing to downright homely, making her rather more of a chameleon than a salamander. More important, she can act, and infuses the routine part of the fecklessly footloose girl with a certain piquancy that verges on pathos. But she is not a great actress, and the shallowness of the part finally reduces her to redundancy. How many variations on the lackadaisical, hedonistic kook who says things like "Why can't people accept me as I am?" can we still take? "People call me lazy, wild, hysterical," she says; they should have called her boring. Besides sex, her chief pleasures are floating in a pool and wildly swaying to rock records. Why doesn't she become an underwater go-go dancer, thus solving her problems and letting us go home?

But Tanner and his coscenarist John Berger, the English Communist art critic and novelist, insist on spurious social significance. It is society, Switzerland, bourgeois capitalism that are to blame for this sad state of affairs, they tell us. There are episodes involving a Civil Defense investigator who badgers innocent citizens, a landlord's emissary who threatens foreclosure (after four months of arrears on the rent!), a sanitation workers' strike, passengers on a trolley car who remain stolid in the face of harassment, a sausage-factory foreman who objects to Rosemonde's potentially unhygienic hairstyle, the shoestore owners who are humorless about their salesgirl's pranks, and, above all, that petit-bourgeois uncle with his moralizing. Collectively, they are meant to convey the chicaneries and frustrations inflicted on one by a society unredeemed by Marxism.

Though Tanner is sometimes witty in his lampoons, he fails to make them convincing. The Civil Defense investigator, for instance, is made to pick his nose—a far too facile way of making him repulsive. The shoestore harridan and sausage foreman are, alas, absolutely right in their demands on the irresponsible girl, and do not deserve the caricaturing they get. The landlord's clerk is made gratuitously ludicrous by stepping into something on the sidewalk that he has difficulty scraping off his shoe. The apathy of the streetcar riders is perhaps mere self-control, and their implied xenophobia seems, at worst, minimal. So Tanner's case against Switzerland is as unpersuasive as his case for his trio of principals. One wonders just how these babes in the Alps would make out under a Communist regime.

Least tolerable, though, is the narration. It assumes a tone of arch knowingness that does not work on any level. For example, after the uncle tells about his wound's still hurting him in a strong wind, we hear the following from the smug female voice that speaks the narration: "Unlike Rosemonde's uncle, Paul very much liked the wind." And we see Paul and his little girl standing expectantly at the wood's edge. The voice continues: "Paul waited for two days, but the wind did not come." Is this meant to be taken seriously, as a lyrical hyperbole celebrating Paul's poetic soul? One hopes not. But if it is a joke, it is on Paul, who is supposed to be the finest person in the film. 97

Why undercut him? Again, when the narration comments on the garbage collectors' strike—"nothing less than order and civilization was threatened"—are we to take this at face value, in which case it is grandiloquently melodramatic; or as irony, in which case it is callow and unfunny?

The answer, I think, is that Tanner is a true Godardian, and does not care. If the thing strikes him as amusing or sonorous or just odd enough, in it goes regardless of appropriateness. Not even a Civil Defense inspector would pick his nose with one hand while ringing a doorbell with the other; but it makes the man absurd and unappetizing, and those are good enough grounds. What reason is there for a scene, brought in out of nowhere, showing a villager sexually molesting Rosemonde? Where did he come from? Did she encourage him? But it's effective—the poor, put-upon girl!—so let's have it.

And what of the silly little games with the voice-over narration? "Outside it was pitch dark," the voice will say, whereupon a character will announce, "It's pitch dark outside." After this strategy has been repeated a few times, as the car with our threesome approaches Rosemonde's village, the narration declares: "They arrived in a very lovely valley." Promptly, Rosemonde mutters: "Here we are in this dump of a valley!" What a lot of setting up for a paltry payoff. And smack in the middle of the fanciest writing, Tanner will fall into a piece of Franglais such as *réaliser* for "realize."

"I wish the world would stop bugging me," exclaims Rosemonde, and we are expected to sympathize. But we don't. With very few exceptions, dull incident has been heaped on dull chatter, and when we find out that the girl did shoot her uncle or that the TV script will have to be scrapped, we could not care less. Nor are we in the least convinced that we have been told anything about Switzerland, the evils of our soceity, or anything else. "Rosemonde has engulfed us," Paul pontificates; but all that has engulfed us is two hours of boredom. And the film is shot in that dreary home-movies type of wishy-washy gray and grayer photography that reminds me of Godard's own early and dismal Genevan film, *Une Femme coquette*, photographed by himself on a—no doubt gray—shoestring.

September 4, 1972

Bristling Brits

SELDOM have I had to revise my opinion of a film upward on seeing it a second time only a few days later. But *The Ruling Class*, which is well worth seeing once, seems to me wickedly persuasive the second time around. The jokes, amusing the first time, become more clearly purposive the second; even the seemingly deficient discipline and overabundant length reveal a perverse cogency and insidious logic. That second time, as the lights went up, I looked everywhere for my objections—under my seat and all the neighboring ones—but I could not find them.

Peter Barnes's script, which closely follows the text of his London hit play, concerns Jack Gurney, who, on his father's bizarre death, comes out of a private mental institution, where he has been treated for seven years as a paranoid-schizophrenic, to become the fourteenth earl of Gurney, lord of sprawling Gurney Manor. His family is shocked: Jack believes he is the Holy Trinity all in one, looks like a storybook Christ, rejects the name of Jack and answers to every name from J.C. to Yahwe from Khoda to the Naz and "any of the nine billion names of God."

Though his carryings-on are mostly nonsensical, his basic insistence on love is admirable, and the very thing that queers him with his stodgily, though by no means virtuously, aristocratic kinfolk. Only Tucker, the old family retainer, sympathizes with him; he has been left a goodly inheritance but, as a thoroughbred servant, cannot leave and, even though he now drinks and sneers openly, knows too much to be fired.

The family conspires to have Jack committed for good, yet can do so without grave financial loss only if he has a male heir, whose guardian Sir Charles can become. Sir Charles, the late earl's half brother, marries off his own mistress, the showgirl Grace Shelley, to Jack, while Charles's wife, Lady Claire, proceeds to seduce his psychiatrist, Dr. Herder, to keep him safely silent. The scheme almost suceeds, but Dr. Herder is piqued when the Gurneys high-handedly proceed to ignore him, and he manages an eleventh-hour cure by confronting Jack with another madman who thinks he is God: McKyle, the Electronic Messiah. Jack is a loving God, all benevolent laissez-faire and let copulation thrive; McKyle is a God of vengeance for a rotten world, who believes he is giving off deadly electricity. He conquers Jack and shocks him into admitting, "I am Jack." He is on the way to being cured.

What does recovery mean? It means that he has adopted another persona, that of a typical reactionary British lord. He wants flogging and capital punishment reinstated, and advocates sexual repression and strong class distinctions. He secretly identifies himself with Jack the Ripper, too, and his mind and verbiage still intermittently wander. All of which, alas, establishes him as a perfect member of the ruling class. When Lady Claire makes advances to him, he stabs her to death and lets Tucker, the old family retainer, take the rap. He delivers a sanguinary, seminonsensical harangue in the House of Lords and receives a thunderous ovation. At last, his wife, the loose chanteuse turned devoted mother and spouse, tries to woo him back; since his return to sanity, he has neglected her sexually. As the camera pulls away, we hear a terrible scream. The fourteenth earl of Gurney has murdered Grace.

What Peter Barnes has done in his screenplay is threefold. *The Ruling Class* is, first, a riproaring attack on the British upper class—more than just satirical: absurdist. In this sense, it offers little that is new and might be accused of flogging a dead horse. But privilege, of one kind or another, persists throughout the world, and Barnes challenges it wittily and fiercely. The ostensibly cured earl tells his doctor, "Behavior which would be considered insanity in a tradesman is looked on as mild eccentricity in a lord," words barely less trenchant than the famous remark of Beaumarchais's Figaro:

"Because you are a great lord, you think you are a genius. What have you done to earn so many advantages? You took the trouble to be born, nothing more." The bold thing about the film is that its earl gets away, literally, with murder, and lets poor Tucker, a secret "bolshie," take the rap. There is no moralizing cop-out here as in, say, *Kind Hearts and Coronets.*

Secondly, though it is cleverly handled, there is that tiresome thesis of the madman as the only sane person in a world gone mad. This derives ultimately from *King Lear* (to which the film contains discreetly scattered allusions), whose hero had to go insane with grief to begin to see the light through his very ravings. Enough instances of this motif can be adduced in contemporary art to elevate the theme to a modern *topos.* (*Topoi*, you may recall, are the recurrent themes in classical and medieval literature.) We have had it, most recently, in the films *King of Hearts* and—in an even more ignoble variant—*Hammersmith Is Out;* in the play *Marat/Sade,* though there it was not the main point; and in a slightly modified version in the opera *The Rake's Progress.* Personally, I am more in sympathy with Pirandello's *Enrico IV,* a thematically related work, where the protagonist's putting on the trappings of insanity is viewed as anything but a blessing in disguise.

The Ruling Class, in fact, seems to owe much to the work of R. D. Laing, the British psychiatrist, who perceives schizoid behavior as respectable: the self-defense of the sensitive in a crass world. The assumption is that in a world growing daily more virulent and dangerous, the comparative peace inside the mental institution looks progressively safer and saner. Granted, the psychiatrists and asylum guards may be less normal than most people, sane or insane—that is a corollary of our *topos,* seen recently in, for example, *Candy* and *End of the Road*—but those harmless little inmates with their amiable delusions insuring contentment are clearly better off than the rest of us, buffeted by the world's evil whims. Thus the film's main ironic intent is summed up in this exchange:

> DR. HERDER: Your nephew suffers from the delusion that the world we live in is based on the fact that God is love.
> CLAIRE: Can't he see what the world's really like?
> DR. HERDER: No. But he will, when he's cured.

Yet on closer scrutiny the film goes beyond this somewhat simplistic position.

For one thing, the author, Barnes, notes with clinical correctness that, shocked out of excessive love, the unbalanced person overshoots the mark in the opposite direction. For another, there are interesting metaphysical implications here: Jack is clearly the New Testament God in travestied form; McKyle, the unhinged Scottish puritan, is as clearly a caricature of the Old Testament God who declares Earth "an early failure o' mine . . . where I dump the excrement o' the Universe." Tucker, representing the rising orders, chimes in: "We don't want love, we want a fat slice o' revenge."

In other words, our age, however agnostic and liberated, is seen as still worshiping a fanatical God of vengeance. Our radicals want retribution rather than justice, let alone mercy, and fall in with the McKylean God, a self-styled "holy terror." It is hard to know just who is not mad here, or, at least, less mad than the others.

When, earlier, Jack playfully denied his divinity during a lie detector test, the machine registered this as a whopping lie. Could the machines be demented, too? The very camera seems so when it sabotages one of Tucker's loveliest lines. Asked what the pandemonium following the McKyle-Jack confrontation is all about, Tucker replies, "Life, Master Dinsdale, sir. The rich moth-eaten tapestry of life." But the camera is not on the speaker, and this pregnant summary of the film's outlook gets lost in a hardly audible voice-over.

Perhaps the most impressive feat of the film is that Barnes and his director, Peter Medak, have tackled quite successfully the well-nigh hopeless task of translating a tricky stage play to the screen. There are lightning transitions here from realistic drama to Victorian melodrama, from musical comedy to absurdist black humor, from genuine feeling to poker-faced farce. Just consider the quick-change dialogue. The tone can be high comedy, as when Jack explains how he knows he is God: "Simple. When I pray to Him I find I'm talking to myself." Or it can be wickedly satirical, as when Dr. Herder expounds on why the eleven-year-old Jack felt rejected by his parents: "They sent him away, alone, into a primitive community of licensed bullies and pederasts." Sir Charles stolidly dots the i's: "You mean he went to public school." Or it can get downright scabrous, as when Jack announces his divine agenda for the day: "First I shall command the pope to consecrate a planeload of lightweight contraceptives for the priest-ridden Irish."

The frankly stylized world of the stage is more hospitable to such prestidigitation than the film world, whose chief legerdemain has always been the illusion of reality: making the wildest dream look absolutely real. On stage, blackouts and intermissions help us catch our breaths; on screen, it all becomes a trifle suffocating, especially since the two Peters, Barnes and Medak, have added a strictly filmic level of dizzying comedy. Thus when the supposedly cured Jack and Dr. Herder, who now suspects the worst, engage in a comic duel with their canes, the film takes this out of the living room and onto the ledges and balconies along the manor's façade, in a parody of the old Errol Flynn–Basil Rathbone swordplay. And when the government's Master in Lunacy, Kelso Truscott, subjects Jack to a sanity test that might prove fatal, Jack recognizes him as a former fellow-Etonian and launches into the old school song about rowing to victory. Truscott joins in, and we cut to the two of them in a rowboat that promptly capsizes. Another scene is transferred to a fox hunt, and we see the fox urinate contemptuously in the direction of hounds and hunters.

Yet Medak has found ways of moving and stationing his camera that make the proceedings both theatrical and filmic. There are numerous medium or long shots in which what happens around the edges is at least as important as what goes on in the middle (theatrical); overhead shots that emphasize the enormousness—and enormity—of Gurney Hall (filmic); low- 101 angle shots that turn us into spectators gazing up at heroically strutting players (theatrical); and, above all, brilliantly filmic montages.

Montage has become suspect in the modern cinema. Ever since André Bazin opted against it and pulled auteurist critics and filmmakers with him, the longer sequence, replete with deep focus and panning, has tended to displace dynamic cutting, where the juxtaposition or alternation of shorter takes elicits a network of implications. Even the fast cutting of some New and Newer Wave directors is not truly montage, only restlessness freely indulged in. But consider the powerful editing of the last part of this film, from Jack's ominous farewell to his wife, Grace, as he goes off to make his wildly cheered maiden speech at the Lords, and all the way to the end. In rapid counterpoint, we see Jack's ascent to the pinnacle of acclaim played off against tiny scenes in which his several victims are glimpsed in death, dementia, or police detention; the montage makes Jack's progress look especially sinister and unstoppable, and the victims' fates even more grotesque or monstrous. The soundtrack, in turn, swells, to "Land of Hope and Glory," sinks to the bathos of doddering, skeletal peers chanting "Onward Christian Soldiers" in a hideous recessional, rises to the pathos of Grace's sadly miscalculated wooing song that dissolves into her agonized shriek, and ends with a small child's voice repeating, "I am Jack!"

This is, presumably, Jack's baby inheriting the Gurney curse. But even as this half-formed voice patters on, the camera, in an ironic helicopter shot, soars above Gurney Manor, massive and resplendent in the moonlight—but this, again, is undercut when the soundtrack breaks into, as Jack did when he was still the God of love, "The Varsity Drag." The ditty now sounds like the ultimate sarcasm.

And there are other fine scenes. Jack believes himself married in the sanatorium to Marguerite Gautier, the Lady of the Camelias. (Another "martyr of love," his doctor explains.) Just after our Christ has failed to perform a miracle meant to prove his godhead, there appears at the top of the stairs . . . Marguerite Gautier, alias Violetta Valéry, singing the drinking song from *La Traviata*. Enthusiastically Jesus Christ, alias Jack Gurney, leaps toward her, and joins her in the aria and dance. A miracle we think, after all! No; only Grace Shelley, instructed by Sir Charles on how to capture the mad earl—and also a stunning theatrical, or cinematic, effect.

Yet all this cleverness would go begging if Medak had not assembled a superb cast and obtained seamless ensemble work from them. There is Peter O'Toole, as mercurial as he is incisive, a Jack who does the most outrageous things with a bemusedly introspective air, who gives absurdity romantic-heroic stature, and makes crude farce so dainty and elegant that the film acquires another dimension by his mere presence. Alastair Sim may slightly overdo Bertie, the blithering bishop among the Gurneys; but William Mervyn as Charles, Coral Browne as Claire, James Villiers as their bumbling son Dinsdale, Harry Andrews as the thirteenth earl, Michael Bryant as Dr. Herder, and Graham Crowden as Truscott are paragons each and all: sharp, funny, and also pitiable. And Arthur Lowe, as Tucker, the "bolshie" butler, proves one of the greatest masters of comic underplaying I have ever encountered: he squeezes infinite variety out of the most rigorous economy of gesture and inflection, and if that isn't art, let me sit through *Last of the Red Hot Lovers* three times in a row. It is too bad that Ken Hodges's color cinematography is only adequate.

In its critique of the upper orders (which, however, does not fail to note the complicity of the exploited), in its mingling of sardonicism and wistfulness, in its sense of the abyss where the skid on the banana peel leads us, *The Ruling Class* bears a modest resemblance to a much finer film, Jean Renoir's *The Rules of the Game*. Even to approximate, in broader brushstrokes, Renoir's masterwork is achievement enough.

And Now for Something Completely Different is based on England's popular TV show "Monty Python's Flying Circus." Five young ex-Oxbridge comics—a somewhat less pungent and purposive version of the inimitable "Beyond the Fringe" quartet—perform a number of their own short, swift skits that range from well-aimed satire to mere outrageous playfulness. An American, Terry Gilliam, has interspersed this with ingenious, often devastating, cartoon sequences.

Even the mere grotesqueries, however, have satirical overtones. When someone publishes an English phrase book for Hungarians where things like "Which way is the railway station?" are rendered as "Please fondle my buttocks," numerous Hungarians in London come to comic grief. But there is a final satirical thrust at the bowler-hatted Englishman who, accosted by a foreigner asking him to fondle his buttocks, calmly and nasally replies, "Ah, yes. Pass the Post Office, then take. . ." Nothing can penetrate a Briton's carapace.

Again, we are introduced to a poetic English landscape, and a complacent TV narrator's voice intones: "In this picture, there are forty-seven people, none of whom can be seen." They are enjoined to reveal themselves. As each of them emerges from hiding, he is shot down. Sweetly the voice pontificates: "This demonstrates the virtue of not being seen." The camera focuses on a row of three bushes. "Mr. E. W. Lambert has presented us with a poser: we do not know which bush he is behind," the voice says with melodious BBC unction. Whereupon all three bushes are blown skyhigh, the central one with the biggest detonation. "Yes," warbles the voice with quietly understated satisfaction, "it *was* the middle one."

The skit drives home the use of anonymity in a hostilely officious society. It also satirizes the blandness with which the media view organized inhumanity—as does another skit, in which a TV show called "Blackmail" plays incriminating films of people's indiscretions. The victim can stop the film by phoning in and agreeing to pay a sum that increases every few seconds as the film unfurls. With typical British sporting spirit, the host of the show is full of admiration for the victim who resists calling in till the last moment.

This English import does not merely lampoon institutions and other near-abstractions; its comic vitriol becomes bitingly specific. It boldly and funnily 103 affirms accountants to be boring, tough lumberjacks or policemen prone to homosexuality, great explorers quite possibly half mad, sweet old ladies a social menace, and so on. It reeks of what may be prejudice, but resounds with what is certainly laughter. It dares to offend in what it considers the pursuit of comic truth. *And Now for Something Completely Different* is indeed different from the usual movie satire, whose eye is bleary, whose teeth are made of rubber, and whose heart has sunk to its heels.

September 10–October 2, 1972

Close to the Soil

IT IS almost impossible for me to write about Jan Troell's beautiful film, *The Emigrants,* choked up as I am with rage at Warner Brothers for cutting one hour from its running time. A curse seems to hound the extraordinarily talented forty-one-year-old Swedish director in America. Originally a school-teacher, then a very fine cinematographer, Troell came to the forefront of younger European directors with his very first feature, *Here Is Your Life,* based on Eyvind Johnson's tetralogy *The Novels About Olof.* Troell's next feature, *Eeny, Meeny, Miny, Moe,* was never shown here.

Now Troell has made the film version of another major Swedish novelistic tetralogy. Vilhelm Moberg's epic about a group of Swedes who emigrate to the United States circa 1850, and again he is being cruelly shortchanged by his American distributors. This time Troell filmed the entire tetralogy in two three-and-a-half-hour installments, *The Emigrants* and *The New Land.* European reviews and reports from friends tell me that they are magnificent and require—indeed, demand—no cutting. The logical thing would have been for Warner Brothers to import both films and show them uncut on alternating days—at least in the bigger cities, whatever else might be done in smaller towns. Instead, though it has prints of both films, the company is showing only the first, with forty minutes worth of cuts, and will decide whether to show the second at all on the basis of the box-office returns.

I realize what the problem is, of course. Exhibitors are loath to get involved with a film so long it can be screened only three or four times a day, rather than a more lucrative five or six. The alternative is turning the film into a "road show," i.e., treating it as a touring stage play: one daily matinee, one evening performance, and jacked-up prices. But whereas this might work handily for the filmization of some long-run Broadway musical the masses are yearning to see, it is risky business with an untouted foreign-language picture starring no sure-fire box-office names and dealing with a serious subject. So we reach for that perennial Hollywood panacea: the scissors.

Is this necessary? *The Sorrow and the Pity* runs four and a half hours, and is nicely recouping its outlay. True, it cost only $135,000 to make, and was

104

probably acquired quite inexpensively by its distributor. Yet Warners could surely afford to pay a little more for *The Emigrants* and could sustain a smaller immediate profit; moreover, aside from prestige, there would be steady long-range returns from reruns, college film societies, all kinds of special showings, and TV sales. (I wonder why the New York Film Festival did not select this film rather than, say, Jacques Rivette's dreary, four-hour *Mad Love;* but knowing who the festival judges are, I do not really wonder.) If a publishing house can bring out numerous works for prestige purposes, so, once in a while, could a film company. But among American film companies, greed and benightedness predominate.

As a result, they end up cutting their own throats. Vincent Canby's all-important *New York Times* review—imperceptive and barely lukewarm—accuses *The Emigrants* of being only "a succession of short, cryptic, high-point scenes . . . which have the effect of tableaus that evoke the look of events instead of the emotion." With the *Times*'s facilities at his disposal, Canby must, or certainly ought to, know how truncated the American version is. How many of the films he admires could survive at all after having almost a third cut out of them? It is a supreme proof of Troell's artistry that *The Emigrants* is still a lovely and remarkable film, even though a certain roughness and depletion can, regrettably, be felt in it.

Under the circumstances, I cannot write my usual critique; I will not do an artist like Troell the injustice of reviewing a film of his that I have not really seen. But there are some things I can affirm nevertheless. I can say that the struggles of a bunch of Swedish peasants to survive—first on their own arid soil, amid a harsh climate and social conditions; then through an inhumanly hard trek across land and sea; and, finally, on foreign ground against linguistic and other handicaps—are compassionately, stirringly, and even humorously evoked. I can say that Troell's direction, and his and Bengt Forslund's script, avoid both sentimentality and gimmickiness, and are patient, sympathetic, and incisive.

Further, the large cast, headed by Max von Sydow and Liv Ullmann, is superb almost without exception. Again acting as his own cinematographer, Troell has, without any recognizable camera trickery, toned down his colors to the point where the Swedish landscapes look like undernourished pastels, beautiful but coldly misted over. The interiors, on the other hand, have a good, country glow to them, as in Dutch genre paintings: an aura of cleanliness and decency rather than warmth, but that too, what with all those comforting russets and trusty browns.

When America, the promised land, is reached, the palette runs well-nigh wild by comparison; the brilliant greens, blues, and oranges are jubilant without being overwhelming. This is accomplished through mastery, not just luck: although some of the American scenes were shot on location in Minnesota and elsewhere, others were filmed back in Sweden. As a fine finishing touch, there is the intelligent, laconic, always musicianly score of Erik Nordgren, best remembered here for his sparing, graceful score for *Smiles of a Summer Night.* The film, like the Parthenon, is still a noble ruin.

More Moral Tales

I REMEMBER seeing one of those inept first movies made by an avant-garde filmmaker—the kind that cinémathèques are quite right to show, for who else would?—and thinking that this one was more than usually contrived, clumsy, old-fashioned, and boring even for its genre. It was the sort of thing where you lay hold of a vacuous story line and a vacant apartment, a few personal friends for actors and the public streets for the outdoors, and go ahead and shoot your first feature. This one was by a noted auteurist critic from the *Cahiers du Cinéma,* and one of his colleagues, Jean-Luc Godard, had a bit part in it. The film was called *The Sign of the Lion,* and I said to myself I would be very surprised if its maker, Eric Rohmer, ever made it as a filmmaker. Well, Rohmer has made it, but I have long since given up being surprised by anything.

The adulation that Rohmer bathes in these days seems to me far from merited, and, like most vogues, largely artificial. His fame rests partly on the propaganda machinery the auteurist critics in France, England, and America set in motion in his behalf, partly on glorification based on the New World's infatuation with the sophistication of the Brave Old World, and partly on the exploitable chic of a filmmaker whose name is not his real name, who rarely gives interviews or allows his picture to be taken, and whose eccentricities of behavior and dress give birth to Garboesque legends.

Rohmer's principal films thus far form a group of "Six Moral Tales," as he calls them, in each of which a man already married or otherwise committed to one woman meets another woman with whom he briefly flirts, but whom he either rejects or is rejected by, and so returns to the original woman. Though I doubt whether this theme is worth six variations, it would appeal to a timid, intensely Catholic, basically puritanical husband and father like Rohmer if he felt strongly drawn to other women during his fifty-odd years of life but clung to unsullied monogamy.

Now there is an obvious value in belaboring such an obsessive theme: it gives you a marked artistic profile that even the blindest bat in the audience can identify, and it enables the auteurist critic to discern structures in your work to his heart's content. It has been the case of some major filmmakers—think of Antonioni's ennui, Bresson's fixation on holiness, Buñuel's love-hatred for the Church, Ozu's familial pieties—and it can prove useful to minor practitioners as well.

But there is something a bit too schematic about Rohmer's schema, not unlike the rigor of those eternal French boulevard farces in which perennial triangles jump in and out of sempiternal beds. In such an earlier "moral tale" as *La Collectionneuse,* the schema is, in fact, imposed with clanking arbitrariness on a protagonist whose ultimate purity is the purest accident. Let us not judge Rohmer, however, on an unfocused, disjointed, and clearly immature work, and turn instead to his next moral tale, *My Night at Maud's,* on which his reputation is chiefly based.

Ma Nuit chez Maud is a film where little or nothing happens, which, by that time, was considered a guarantee of high artistic intentions. It is, furthermore, a film whose hero abstains from intercourse with a highly attractive, intelligent, and extremely willing young woman, and who does so mainly out of religious scruples, for the sake of his moral purity. This must have struck today's moviegoers as something quite remarkable. Abstinence as an ideal? A hero who fails to make it with a woman and emerges the more heroic for it? Suddenly all the puritans, weaklings, sexual failures, self-styled moralists could see themselves vindicated in the movies. If you look more closely at the protagonist, to be sure, he is not meant as such an unqualified moral success, but people in search of vindication don't look all that closely.

The most important innovation of the film, however, was its talkiness. Here was a movie in which people acted minimally and talked maximally. And what highbrow topics; Catholicism, Marxism, Pascal's philosophy, atheism, sexual indulgence versus chastity, and the like. The fact that the talk was on a rather sophomoric plane—Pascal, for example, was discussed on the level of a bull session among French *lycéens*—did not strike many people, so awed were they by the fact that a whole long scene could take place in a room where people sat around and the camera did nothing but wander about among their faces while they debated . . . Pascal. O the wonder of it! The triumph of intellectuality! If you could sit through *Maud* without noticeably falling asleep, you were manifestly one of the elect.

Alas, *Maud* is a rather clumsily made film: a script in which almost everything happens either by caprice or coincidence, people are manipulated like pawns to illustrate the author's preconceptions, the camera technique is static and amateurish, the black-and-white photography mediocre (ah, but doesn't that drive home the mediocrity of French provincial existence?), and the final twist a banality straight out of O. Henry, and one that, moreover, telegraphs itself. But over all this hovered the guardian spirit of Pascal, and, as Maud, Françoise Fabian proved a magnificent actress and most alluring woman, who actually could hold the film together with her almost tangible qualities of intelligence, vitality, and grace.

The next moral tale released here was *Claire's Knee*, a film I found not only feeble but also mildly distasteful. The main action of this equally talky movie concerned the unholy desire of the grown-up protagonist to clasp the right knee of a seventeen-year-old girl. Somehow his whole yearning for not one but two adolescents had transmogrified itself into a craving for that one right knee (the left, apparently, had no appeal). A nasty little subterfuge permits him to fondle that knee; satisfied, the hero can go on and marry his grown-up fiancée.

But this unanalyzed kinkiness is the least of it; the large part of *Claire's Knee* is taken up with endless confabulations among various characters on the nature of love. Rohmer made a dogged effort to write epigrammatic dialogue here, but his epigrams were neither sufficiently witty, nor well-turned and penetrating enough, and suffered, in fact, from a hysterical pregnancy.

But, once again, all this talk on film took the American audience's breath 107 away. For if a tradition has been going in one direction for decades—and in film the tradition was, especially in America, action—then all a fellow has to do is to fly squarely in the face of that tradition and embrace verbose inaction, and he is sure to make a splash. It even worked for the totally zonked films of Andy Warhol and his mindless gang, so why not for the by no means mindless Rohmer?

Yet there was more than the indulgence of all that gratuitous talk in *Claire's Knee;* there was also the glorious setting of Lac d'Annecy and the Savoyard Alps photographed by Nestor Almendros in color this time, with a technique that was getting better, though still rather picture-postcardy. There was something insidiously appealing about watching all these people live not in Hollywooden luxury but in cultured easefulness among sumptuous surroundings and frittering away pearls upon pearls of summer days on graciously carefree chatter. One even saw a mature man and a mature woman actually dallying in a platonic *amour de tête,* the sort of thing the French have learned from a long theatrical tradition of *marivaudage* but that hit middle-class American audiences with the force of revelation: the essence of sexuality without the actual grubby business of sex. And, surely, Rohmer's films are a eunuch's delight.

Which brings us to the current, sixth and last, of the moral tales, *Chloe in the Afternoon.* (Two others were short TV films, and we are, it seems, to be spared them.) This is the least pretentious, least elaborately wordmongering, least metaphysically masquerading of Rohmer's films, and, because of this unassumingness, surely the most likable. Although its protagonist fantasizes and internally monologizes away like other Rohmer heroes, these disquisitions are less fancifully esoteric: they are exclusively the attempts of a happily married man to indulge himself in mental polygamy—transmute the pretty girls on subways, sidewalks, and even among his office staff into extensions of his wife and conduct imaginary love affairs with them.

When Chloe, a promiscuous young drifter who once ruined a friend of his, pops up again in Frédéric's law office, he allows himself to become her friend for the afternoons. For Frédéric is a man afraid of the emptiness of afternoons (this, again, is a bit of grandstand metaphysics), and in the mannish, irresponsible Chloe he is attracted to the exact opposite of his orderly, feminine wife. But when Chloe, finally, throws herself at him in what may be her sincerest feeling for a man ever, he runs back to his wife. Without invoking Rohmer's Catholicism, the film does not make much sense in its resolution: why should a man who has been playing with and helping this girl for months, becoming more and more sexually and spiritually drawn to her, promptly run away when she offers herself?

There is a further failure in the casting of the untalented and unprepossessive Zouzou as Chloe: this French equivalent of Viva is a big void at the center of the film, and testifies, once again, to Rohmer's amateurishness. But the filmmaker has captured something else: the aura and aroma of quasi- and pseudosexuality in our lives. There is an all-pervasive sense of flirtatiousness and covert coquetry, of sexual innuendo and aspiration as they invade most of today's living. Almendros's color cinematography has become assured and distinctive, Rohmer's camera has acquired some fluidity, the verbiage is better than anything previous from Rohmer's pen, the atmosphere of Paris is lovingly caught, and the acting, other than Zouzou's, apt.

But what makes the movie interesting in a minor way is not these things. It is the heightened sense of potential sexuality with which the air is charged, and which lurks behind or beneath the most mundane daily routines. To have caught it on film does not make Eric Rohmer a major filmmaker by a long shot—or even a closeup, which he prefers. But it does make *Chloe in the Afternoon* a film with a strong flavor even if a slight substance.

October 29, 1972

Madness, Public and Private

ALTHOUGH not so great as *The Sorrow and the Pity,* Marcel Ophüls's new documentary about the Ulster troubles, *A Sense of Loss,* is a very considerable achievement. In the earlier film, about World War II, historic perspective had already pretty much sorted things out, and we could make use of Olympian hindsight in distributing merits and demerits to the benighted creatures who thrashed about in horrors and uncertainties. In the new movie, we are plunged right into a bloody chaos, and no one—participants, filmmakers, audience—can be sure of what the solutions are, or how they might be implemented.

The situation in Northern Ireland might seem like mere skirmishing viewed from our transatlantic safety. But it is as sanguinary, desperate, and intransigent as any human violence can be, and can serve as a model for civil warfare or border conflict anywhere: blacks against whites in America, Jews against Arabs, Indians against Pakistanis, plus all the African bloodshed, past, present, and future. The hatred between Irish Protestants and Catholics has many powerful bases: religious, in a country where religion still deeply matters; historical-traditional, where such an issue as union with England versus a free, united Ireland is ancient, ingrained, and hotly contested; economic, given that the Protestants tend to be the haves and the Catholics the have-nots.

Ophüls was faced with problems beyond the fact that the fighting is still in full swing. There is the difficulty of our relative ignorance about Irish politics compared to what we know about the German occupation of France, for example. There is the further difficulty that both among the Catholics and the Protestants there are numerous parties and factions ranging from extremism to liberalism, whose exact platforms (even assuming they exist) are hard to make clear in a 135-minute film—especially when members of the same organization (e.g., the regular IRA—as opposed to the Provisionals, newly formed in Ulster) disagree among themselves. Then, too, people are understandably unwilling to discuss their illegal activities. Finally, despite   109 their proverbial gift of gab, some of these Irish express themselves poorly, to say nothing of accents that are sometimes bad enough to make one yearn for subtitles.

Nevertheless, Ophüls's film takes on a deep significance and fascination once we look beyond the immediate situation, stirring as it may be. At that point, the people involved cease to be Bernadette Devlin or Sir Harry Tuzo, Commander of the British Forces in Northern Ireland; the Reverend Ian Paisley, a rabble-rousing ultraconservative Ulster Protestant leader, or the two Catholic fathers we meet, one fairly chauvinistic, the other reasonable and iconoclastically humane. Suddenly, we are confronted with basic human attitudes in a timeless conflict: the internecine strife that has always divided humanity and set it to murdering itself. *A Sense of Loss* then becomes more like a medieval morality play, only less medieval than eternal, and less a morality than an immorality.

For we can see no moral resolutions to these religious antagonisms, to these acts of violence that, even when the doctrine is half-forgotten, are still doctrinaire and proliferate in all directions. We encounter voices of reason and acts of humanitarianism, but we realize them to be pitifully outnumbered. The four specific deaths Ophüls concentrates on are particularly revealing. One is that of a baby, the archetype of innocence. Another is that of a teen-aged girl returning late from a dance—the most romantic tragedy: Death and the Maiden. Still another is that of an affluent Protestant businessman who, discovering an unexploded bomb in a department store, carried it out in order to save innocent lives and blew himself up in the process; here a member of a presumably reactionary group proved himself most gallantly self-sacrificing.

The fourth death, of a Provisional IRA lieutenant shot by the British troops during an armed engagement, is the only militant one. Ophüls concentrates on the man's funeral and captures some bitter ironies. The family denies his IRA associations, thus, in a sense, posthumously castrating him. Still more terribly ironic are the faces of the mourners: hate-filled rather than grieving. Particularly frightening is a huge, fat termagant—a young woman clearly in the Provisionals—who marches at the head of the cortege. There is enough unthinking hatred in her face and bearing to keep a revolution fueled for decades.

There is also a great deal of talk from people in high and low stations, some of it quite perceptive, but none offering workable solutions. Most of the people ring changes on the refrain: Why did it have to be him, her, us? When a Catholic mother is told that overpopulation among Catholics may have something to do with their problems, her suggestion is that the Protestants should make more babies, too. When a strikingly handsome, seemingly civilized Protestant printer is asked whether the hate-ridden doggerel about Catholics he prints might not stir up deadly conflagrations, he denies this, citing as proof that a (Protestant) court freed him of such charges. And irony of ironies: the militant Catholics and Protestants are equally against abortion and birth control measures that might eventually ease the situation.

110

Perhaps the only thing Ophüls leaves deliberately veiled, though he hints at it sufficiently, is the extent to which religion is at the root of the misery.

A caustic Protestant journalist suggests that all the clergymen and their secular warriors be put on a raft and turned loose at sea. Quixotic as the solution is, it appears only slightly less practical than Bernadette Devlin's barnstorming in behalf of socialism, a movement that seems to leave almost the entire country apathetic, if not downright hostile, toward it.

What Ophüls has accomplished in this invaluable film—possibly more clearly even than in his previous, greater one—is to show how hopeless the human predicament is. And he shows it with excitingly incisive, on-the-spot color cinematography, and with some of the most cogent questions directed at high and low alike. But the answers—however good or bad and, sometimes, even witty—are all short on hope for the human race, even if only implicitly. By way of a final irony, this makes the decent, thoughtful, socially responsible people in the film look all the more touching: saints in the lost cause of sanctifying mankind.

A suitable pendant to *A Sense of Loss* is Ken Loach's *Wednesday's Child,* a title that senselessly deviates from the original British one: *Family Life.* David Mercer's script, based on a TV play of his own, concerns a middle-class London family who manage to drive one of their daughters into schizophrenia. Janice is a confused and not very strong-willed girl, but in no way unusual in either her bad or good traits. She has not broken away from home like her married sister, Barbara, and she is caught among boring jobs, the ossified bourgeois values of her parents, and the radical ones of her painter boy friend, Tim. She is justly dissatisfied with the caricatures of sympathy and understanding she gets from her father, a hard, dull worker, and from her mother, a concerned, not unclever woman, but self-righteous and unimaginative. Yet she does not have the talent of courage—or simply the masculinity—that permits Tim to survive without a family life.

Unfortunately, these basic aspects of the problem are accorded rather sketchy treatment and emerge, if at all, in tiny flashes scattered throughout the film. Handled more convincingly is the attrition between parents and daughter once Janice's behavior begins to take on pronouncedly schizoid characteristics. Best of all is the handling of Janice's clinical history.

She becomes, first, the patient of an R. D. Laing-like radical psychiatrist who treats her sympathetically and conversationally and also has revealing sessions with her repressed parents. Dr. Donaldson finally takes her into his highly unconventional "institution," modeled on Laing's Kingsley Hall. Just as Janice is beginning to make genuine improvements, narrow-minded and, presumably, jealous rivals manage to relieve Dr. Donaldson of his post. Janice then falls into the hands of the behaviorists.

These behavioral psychiatrists subject the girl to old-fashioned, obtuse forms of treatment, which, though restrainedly chronicled by the film, appear horrifying and, alas, believable. The shock-therapy scenes, in their very understatement, are almost unforgettably disturbing; in this artistically un-

111

derstated filmization, they constitute a much more shattering indictment than in previous, more sensational moviemaking. How Janice is ruined for life by official, state-subsidized psychiatry is depicted both faithfully (as a panel of psychiatrists after the picture's screening at the New York Film Festival affirmed) and with a finesse I would not have expected from either David Mercer or Ken Loach.

It is regrettable that, while Janice's worsening encounters with her parents are traced with impressive meticulousness, her relationships with her boy friend and married sister are treated spasmodically and unpersuasively. Why these two benevolent figures fail to help her remains unanalyzed and looks like loading the dice against her.

The film is, nonetheless, aptly photographed and directed. It has a splendid gallery of minor characters, mostly patients and hospital staff, and the major performances ring true. Sandy Ratcliff is a deeply moving Janice, precisely because she remains unsentimentalized. Bill Dean's Father is properly more abjectly helpless than brutish. As the mother, a nonprofessional actress, Grace Cave, gives a performance so detailed, so subtly shaded, so fiendishly and heartbreakingly exact, as to make it—in both senses of the word—stunning.

October 30, 1972

Dizzying Distortions

FRANÇOIS TRUFFAUT's *Two English Girls* is a disappointment, even coming from a filmmaker who has already made ample use of the artist's right to occasional failures. The film is based on the second and last novel of Henri Pierre Roché, whose first was the basis of Truffaut's biggest success, *Jules and Jim*. Roché turned to fiction in his seventies and originally told his life story as the complicated love triangle of one woman and two men. Then, in *Deux Anglaises et le Continent*, he felt emboldened to come nearer to the truth: one man and two women. I have read neither novel, but the two filmizations, speaking approximatively, resemble each other as a glove does its mate turned inside out.

That, in itself, is bad. I get a sense of Truffaut repeating himself here even more than in the weaker segments of his autobiographical films, the Antoine Doinel series. On closer inspection, *Two English Girls* also emerges as a rather unpleasant distortion of its predecessor. For what in *Jules and Jim* had a certain quasi-improvisatory ebullience—the exhilarating unconstraint of a young filmmaker of genius finding himself in full command of his craft—now begins to look like a set of nicely tooled movable parts rearranged into a different contraption. Inventiveness has become slickness; enthusiastic impetus, mere doggedness.

112

In both films, the narrative interest lies in curious permutations curiously arrived at and capriciously resolved. But in the new work there is a sense of calculation—as if Truffaut, taking greater liberties with Roché's text than he did before, were trying to impress us deliberately and weightily with his perceptions of how erratic, irrational, and totally unpredictable the human heart is.

Unfortunately, we know all that already. Such a catalogue of quirks becomes interesting only if the approach is psychologically revelatory, cinematically innovative, or produced with such absolute expertise in all other departments as to make the film overcome its lack of plotting and characterization. What Truffaut (more, I suppose, than Roché) did here is to parade the greatest number of improbable reversals before us; we are supposed to be so overwhelmed by what we did not expect as not to notice the shortcomings in what we have every right to expect.

We are asked to believe, indeed sympathize with, the bizarre involvements of a young turn-of-the-century Frenchman with two English sisters at whose mother's house in Wales he spends a summer vacation. Anne is a lively, outgoing girl, while the younger Muriel is broodingly introverted. For some reason, Claude, who is not exactly the introspective type, picks the less pretty and likable Muriel, whom Anne, herself infatuated with Claude, has destined for him—quirks number one and two. Muriel insists she does not care for the youth, yet presently agrees to marry him—whim number three; a one-year waiting period is imposed by a conclave of parents, during which time the loving and saddened Claude goes back to Paris and promptly starts fornicating around—whim four.

Anne comes to study art in Paris and she and Claude arbitrarily decide to become lovers, then separate for no compelling reason—oddities five and six. Claude, by now in love with Anne, pushes her toward other men whom she, though loving Claude, accepts—caprices seven and eight. Muriel visits her sister in Paris, and startlingly throws herself at Claude, who equally startlingly backs away—shocks number nine and ten. On the eve of her wedding to another, Anne dies of some romantic ailment, whereas Muriel, tortured by guilt about some childish bit of quasi-lesbianism and subsequent indulgences in masturbation, appears in France again and makes passionate love to Claude—surprises eleven, twelve, thirteen, fourteen. The next day, she leaves to marry someone else and will never see Claude again—twist number fifteen. Years later, the aging Claude wanders around the Luxembourg Gardens thinking that an English schoolgirl whom someone calls Muriel might be his lost love's daughter. She isn't—surprise number sixteen, or no surprise number one, depending on your point of view.

Along with these questionable reversals, we get a wealth of quaint details, but details that remain external: unexplored actions, or voice-over narration by Truffaut that records events and data without much speculation, poetry, or incisive formulation. The result is mechanistic and dehumanized. Even if reality can be as odd as this, it is so at a slower pace; in this kind of acceleration, the entire film looks almost like that speeded-up orgy *à trois* in 113

Kubrick's *Clockwork Orange:* a joke. Yet it is clearly intended as an occasionally droll but fundamentally sad morality tale, and it simply fails to convince.

The color cinematography is handsome; place and period are conscientiously re-created. Truffaut constructs his scenes knowingly and endows them with his sense of rhythm. All this is not enough, especially considering another great flaw, the casting of Jean-Pierre Léaud as Claude. The director has written, "In my opinion, Jean-Pierre Léaud is the best actor of his generation"; in my opinion, there never was a more fatal misjudgment.

Léaud's assets consist of a set of stiff, repetitive movements; a breathy, toneless voice; a cocky, proletarian face that can occasionally assume a hangdog expression; greedily beggarly but otherwise inexpressive eyes; the personality of a rather persistent mollusk. As a boy, he was charmingly natural and authentically rebellious in *The 400 Blows;* but he grew up untalented and homely, like so many child actors before him. Nevertheless, Truffaut has identified himself with this bumbling cipher, and there is no greater love than that of a great ego for his alter ego.

Léaud walks through the film, except when he sleepwalks through it; in the final scene, when he is supposed to be a graybeard, he is a high-school student moonlighting as a Macy's Santa Claus. Tracy Tendeter and Kika Markham are fine as Muriel and Anne. There are numerous references to previous Truffaut films to delight auteurist critics. Truffaut has drastically cut the film since its first Paris release, and there are some undeniably nice directorial touches throughout it. But none of this mitigates the essential trashiness of a still seemingly unending chain of tergiversations.

About *The Assassination of Trotsky,* the less said, the better. As directed by Joseph Losey, written by Nicholas Moseley, and enacted by its three stars at hysterical pitch, it seems the collective work of mental patients who, by way of therapy, have misguidedly taken up filmmaking instead of basket weaving. The film has no new theory about the murder, which does not, however, prevent it from fantasizing rather freely. Visually, it goes in for hammily posed tableaus; verbally, for pretentious discontinuities that sound either inscrutable or banal; rhythmically, for periodic forward lurches that soon come to embarrassed halts. One remains pretty much in the dark about events and motivations, but this is not nearly so bad as the fact that one is left not even wishing to understand.

The single unifying element here is that everyone acts weirdly, inconsistently, and as little as possible. Losey has directed with his old heavy hand, this time encased in an iron gauntlet. He allows an image of Stalin to stare at the would-be assassin from the water on which his boat is gliding; ponderously, he intercuts the killing of Trotsky with a matador's expediting a bull in the arena. Romy Schneider looks and carries on worse than ever, but is still far from the unattractive woman she is supposed to be. As the assassin, Alain Delon does nothing but attitudinize sullenly, though given the zonked screenplay, it would be hard to do more. As Trotsky, Richard Burton glowers unfocusedly, and orates away with a kind of absent-minded orotundity. As Mrs. Trotsky, Valentina Cortese, by virtue of sheer personal dignity, contributes the one appealing presence.

November 13, 1972

Why Is the Coeatus Always Interruptus?

Luis Buñuel's *The Discreet Charm of the Bourgeoisie* presents me with a critical poser. Here is a film that has received rave notices from all reviewers, top to bottom, and is doing well with local audiences; yet I consider it absolutely worthless. Why?

The film operates on two levels: as an essentially realistic yet satirical portrait of the French bourgeoisie, and a series of dreams and visions constituting a surreal plane. Not only does the film strike me as a failure on each of these levels, it does not even manage to benefit from contrasting or dovetailing the two. I submit that Buñuel, who has made some splendid and some dismal films, is now an old, exhausted filmmaker.

Since *Belle de Jour,* he has declared every film his last; would that he had retired even earlier, after *Viridiana* and *Simon of the Desert*—he could have exited with a bang. Although the subsequent films have shown unabated technical control, they have not added a jot to their maker's artistic stature. Repetitiousness, self-indulgence, and frequent obfuscation swallow up their occasional wry felicities. With *The Discreet Charm of the Bourgeoisie,* his once considerable but steadily evanescing art has become mere senile doodling, and his besetting sins of lack of discipline and indulgence in private obsessions have gotten quite out of hand.

The present film, totally bereft of true invention, is rich in dredged-up jokes, mutterings into the filmmaker's beard, and desperate pursuits of random senescent fantasies meant to keep an enterprise that has nowhere to go going all the same. The basic notion, as Buñuel declared, is that "some people want to have dinner together; they cannot, and why not?" This may sound like an unfunny joke, but it is, alas, the unfunny truth.

To begin with the satirical-realistic level: satire must, at the very least, be funny. But *Bourgeoisie* is either groaning under old, obvious jokes or coasting along barren stretches of mirthless nastiness. A sextet of rich and decadent bourgeois, including one ambassador from the imaginary Latin American country of Miranda, enjoy eating copiously and well. Yet, for one reason or another, their meals get interrupted. Let's call this the coeatus interruptus theme.

For example, they come to dinner at their friends' house on the wrong day and must leave. They go, instead, to a country inn, but find in an adjoining alcove the dead proprietor's body awaiting the undertaker, and so decide to   115 leave. Or they go, of an afternoon, to a fashionable café-restaurant in Paris, and, successively ordering tea, coffee, and hot chocolate, are told by the returning waiter that the place is out of reach. So they leave.

Where is the joke or satire in that? No decent restaurant is ever out of all beverages, so the scene does not correspond to some ludicrous reality. But what about satiric-comical heightening? Does the scene, by indirection or hyperbole, succeed in ridiculing fancy restaurants? None of the above. Does it, then, make some sardonic point about French society? Not at all. Is it funny? No, only preposterous. In another scene, the group sits down to dinner only to be interrupted by some officers who are to be billeted with them and whose maneuvers have unexpectedly been moved ahead. Dinner is delayed while the hostess improvises additional food and tables, and the meal is about to start again. But now the other mock army attacks prematurely, the officers must leave, and we get an interruptus within an interruptus. And so the provocative sexual fantasies of Buñuel, with sociopolitical and religious implications, have dwindled to mere food phantasmagoria; poetically suggestive prurience has shrunk to digestive esurience, and the entire film is a coeatus interruptus. Absurd, yes; funny, no.

And not meaningful either. What do these and other such scenes tell us? That the French bourgeoisie likes its food and takes it seriously, and hates to be thwarted in its enjoyment of it. So what? The Italian bourgeoisie is just as keen on eating, and so is the German and Austrian, and any other you care to name, with the possible exception of the English and American. But is this telling us anything new or enlightening or needful of iteration? What is so hilarious about people rattling off names of dishes or holding forth on the best way to make dry martinis? Nothing; yet from the way audiences are laughing you'd think the ushers were passing out laughing gas.

With interrupted eating comes also interrupted sex, the archetypal interruptus. A husband discovers his wife on the verge of adultery with his good friend the ambassador; or guests arrive for lunch just as the host and hostess feel so amorous that they must have instant intercourse—so they climb out of the window and have it in the bushes. This is not only juvenile prurience, it does not even make satirical sense: if these solidly married bourgeois can still pant for each other so at high noon, all is not lost. Where the blood stirs, there is hope. But where is the satire, where the joke? Two people greedily pawing each other at an inopportune moment? Compared to that, a man slipping on a banana peel is Wildean wit and Swiftian satire.

On the surreal plane, the equivalent to the interruptus is the shaggy-dog story. In a sense, a dream is always over too soon, before the punchline of fulfillment can set in. But Buñuel shaggy-dogifies his dream or fantasy sequences in every possible way. A young lieutenant pops up from nowhere and relates a childhood vision in which his dead mother and her murdered lover appeared to the boy. They tell him that the dead and bloody man is his real father, and that the evil man he lives with is merely the killer of that true father. At the ghosts' urging, the boy poisons his pseudoprogenitor. He has had an unhappy childhood, says the lieutenant and departs, never to be

seen again.

Another man, a sergeant, is brought on to recount a dream of his. It is full of weird goings-on in a necropolis photographed and edited as in cheap horror movies; the events signify nothing meaningful or related to anything else in the film. The sergeant is asked to tell also his "train dream," but there is no more time for this. He has to leave, and we are left with a shaggy dog within a shaggy dog. Again, a police commissioner we neither know nor care about has a dream about a bloody sergeant, allowing Buñuel to bring on yet another bloody corpse (the film is awash with blood, but you don't hear any of the antiviolence critics denouncing this one!) and to have a sado-comic scene in which the police torture a young rebel by means of an electrically charged piano, which, so to speak, plays him, and from which, suddenly, an army of cockroaches pours out—a shaggy-roach story.

Why should we care about the dreams of supernumeraries? A dream becomes interesting in relation to the waking personality of the dreamer, but if he remains a passing blank, of what concern are his grotesque dreams to us? Yet even the principals' dreams remain in this film unrevealing, unfunny, unconvincing. It would seem (as Buñuel has more or less admitted) that some of those dream episodes were originally intended as strange but real events—as, for example, in *The Milky Way*—but that the filmmaker lost his nerve and explained the thing away as dreams within dreams. Typically, we'll see a character wake up after a grotesque dream, and another, equally grotesque, sequence begins. Then a second character is seen waking up, and he tells us that he dreamed both foregoing sequences, that even the first dream was dreamed by him, the second dreamer. Yet the protagonist of the second dream was really a third character, whose dream that should have been. If this doesn't make sense to you reading it, don't worry—it won't make sense viewing it, either.

The shaggy dogs spill over into the waking sequences. An elderly peasant woman promises to tell a bishop why she hates the gentle Jesus, but is whisked off before she can do so. Again, the police commissioner receives a phone call from the minister of justice to release his prominent prisoners. Why? he asks. The minister explains, but the noise of a low-flying jet obliterates the explanation. Asked for a repeat, the minister wearily obliges, but another jet interferes. The frustrated commissioner passes the order on to his sergeant, who also requests an explanation. As the commissioner answers, the banging of radiator pipes drown out his words—shaggy upon shaggy upon shaggy dog.

All the humor is pathetic. A bishop is summoned to give absolution to a dying old man. He turns out to be the gardener who, years ago, killed the bishop's parents who employed and tormented him. The bishop absolves the old man, then shoots him dead—another blood-spattered corpse. There is an ambassador from Miranda, a fictitious Latin American dictator-ruled country, who imports cocaine into France in the diplomatic pouch, disarms an occasional Mirandan coed who tries to assassinate him, and clumsily dallies with a French friend's wife. There is that friend himself, who, besides being a client for the cocaine, is also a gourmet and bon vivant, and the wife's younger sister who always tags along cannot hold her tongue or liquor, and 117 vomits a lot. And people laugh at this! But they'll laugh at anything. We first glimpse the bishop innocently walking up to a front door to ring the bell; in the audience, hearty laughter. Why? Surely they have seen a soutane before, and the churchman is not walking on his hands or backward or hopping on one foot.

Then there is a visual refrain, a periodically repeated shot of the six main characters walking down a highway. This is no one's dream or vision and may be an auto-*hommage* to Buñuel's own *The Milky Way*, in which a highway was the connecting metaphor. Here, however, the three or four recurrences of the shot with incremental variations tell us no more than that our bourgeois sextet is trudging down the road of life with a different expression on each face. So what else is old? To resort to grandiose symbolism in order to say what plain narrative has already conveyed (and what, anyhow, is self-evident) is arrant pretentiousness.

Coitus or coeatus interruptus and the shaggy-dog story are the two faces of the same debased coin. They are an impotent old man's cacklingly sadistic interference with his own fictional characters, and an exhausted mind's failed search for meaningful conclusions. Buñuel is merely rehashing his earlier and better films (themselves often enough marred by incoherence), without the fascinating love-hate or righteous indignation that informed them. We knew what was assailed in *Los Olvidados* or reduced to absurdity in *Simon of the Desert*. In *The Discreet Charm of the Bourgeoisie* we have not so much a shaggy as an old dog, unable to learn new tricks or even adequately recall old ones. This latest Buñuel film is a haphazard concatenation of waking and dream sequences in which anything goes, and which would make just as much, or just as little, sense if they were put together in any other disorder.

Jean-Claude Carrière once again collaborated on the script, and he may well be Buñuel's evil genius, though perhaps Buñuel himself can now lay claim to that title. Since there is no plot and the characters are just pawns—oily businessman, dissembling diplomat, spaced-out debutante, haughty matron, frivolous wife—able performers are reduced to striking permanent attitudes and hoping they will add up to performances. This makes good actors look poor, and limited ones like Bulle Ogier (who, in her third exposure here, proves a walking tautology) look terrible. The talented Delphine Seyrig opts for one unrelieved smirk from beginning to end. A film that can make her look bad is bad indeed!

November 27, 1972–February 25, 1973.

Gaudy and Gaudier

From aberrant senility in Buñuel's *The Discreet Charm of the Bourgeoisie* we move to middle-aged megalomania in *Fellini's Roma*. In this combination memoir of childhood yearning for Rome; nostalgic reminiscences of Roman boardinghouses, bordellos, and rowdy wartime music halls; quasi-documentary (i.e., mendacious) evocations of Roman ways, byways, and subways; and the usual late Fellinian catalogue of circus freaks and societal grotesques, we find that all roads lead not to Rome but to Fellini.

Egomania has seldom scaled such loathsome heights. In a film where everyone is misshapen, obese or emaciated, gross or desiccated, a dwarf or a giant, we see two absolutely stunning creatures: a beautiful boy and a gorgeous youth—the one portraying Fellini as an adolescent, the other as a young man.

Suppose that an episode in this rambling, amorphous movie deals with traffic entering Rome from the Appian Way on a rainy evening. The film will then trace not so much the bizarre vehicular and pedestrian tumult (itself hardly worth the footage, or mileage, lavished on it) as Fellini directing his cameraman mounted on a boom mounted on a truck, the camera shielded from the rain by a piece of wildly windblown roseate plastic. The boom swings boldly over the stalled and maddened traffic, the pink plastic flaps over it like some giant bird from the Arabian Nights, and Fellini's voice booms, his ego flapping over all.

In the bordellos, young Fellini is the most romantically ardent client; in the music hall, where you do not literally see him, there are plentiful allusions to such earlier films of his as *Variety Lights, I Vitelloni,* and *Nights of Cabiria;* at an absurdly exaggerated, heavy-handedly mirthless parody of a midnight fashion show for the clergy—with everyone from the roller-skating priests and nuns to the fantastically enthroned pope displaying frantically satirized clerical supergarb—we are to recall fondly similar extravaganzas in *8¹/₂* and *Juliet of the Spirits;* at various outdoor feasts, Fellini is the focal character or the graciously self-effacing cicerone (he even allows Anna Magnani to poke playful fun at him); and during excavations for the Rome subway, old Roman frescoes are discovered—looking not like old Roman frescoes but like advertising posters for *Fellini Satyricon.*

Gore Vidal, "the celebrated American writer" and Rome-inhabiting expatriate, fatuously expatiates about Rome being the perfect place from which to observe the decline of the Western world. With observers like Vidal and Fellini, the Western world will need no Vandals and Visigoths to speed it to its fall. *Fellini's Roma* illuminates nothing about the city's life; in fact, it is not unlike its own last episode in which a motorcycle gang endlessly careers and careens through nocturnal Rome, headlights briefly hurling light beams on some historic landmark and, presto, tilting and zooming on. In *Fellini's Roma,* the old master is just another roaring boy.

Equally absurd, if not more so, is Ken Russell's *Savage Messiah,* about the seminal sculptor Henri Gaudier-Brzeska who died in World War I at age twenty-three. This is yet another Russellian artist's biography in which the artist becomes a garish psychopath, and any resemblance to known facts is strictly coincidental. Even more than in his meteoric career, the film revels in the sculptor's relationship with Sophie Brzeska, the tormented, much older Polish woman who became Henri's platonic mistress and would-be in- 119 cestuous mother figure. With what veracity? If, on a joint visit to the Louvre, Henri impressed Sophie by doffing his hat to the Winged Victory, Russell has him shoutingly climb up on the statue to hurl defiance and be chased out of the museum by a passel of unfunny Keystone *flics*.

Russell's notion of being a sculptor is incessant hacking away with mallet and chisel, accompanied by breathlessly iconoclastic discoursing about Art and Life—a view partaking in equal measure of Walt Disney and *Harper's Bazaar*. And, as usual with Russell, the film becomes a torture chamber. He invents a scene where Henri and a nonplatonic mistress grossly copulate before a Sophie forced to watch with horrified fascination. Or Helen Mirren, an actress whose endowments surpass the Hottentot Venus, struts in fulsome nudity along the great staircase of her marbled ancestral mansion. About Vorticism, the movement to which Gaudier and several other important figures belonged, Russell has little or nothing to say; he is content with a passing parade of pseudonymous grotesques, as distasteful as they are unbelievable.

Unfortunately, all this only makes Russell into a public nuisance, exactly as it is meant to, the unhappy director mistaking general obloquy for the hallmark of genius. Regrettably for him, even lack of genius can be reprehended—except, perhaps, in this wretched age whose every vacuous exhibitionist (Russell included) is loudly hailed as an innovator. In Christopher Logue, that overrated, modish poet, Russell has found a scenarist worthy of himself; and Scott Anthony turns Gaudier into the brash scalawag Russell clearly demanded.

A solitary light shines out of this turgid mess: Dorothy Tutin's Sophie. In this homely, prissy, preposterous figure, Miss Tutin finds the urchin under the spinster, the wounded soul within the megalomaniacal eccentric. The performance glows like a jewel inside a pig's bladder.

November 27–December 11, 1972

The Art of Showing Nothing

BOREDOM becomes palpable in Robert Bresson's *Four Nights of a Dreamer,* a free adaptation of Dostoevsky's much-filmed short story *White Nights*. As if the last filming of this tale, by Luchino Visconti, had not been stilted enough, Bresson had to go the Italian one worse by making his short film an interminable parade of pretentious trivia. Pauline Kael once remarked that Bresson's later films have been "dumb," in the sense of stupid; to this I would add that they are dumb in the sense of uncommunicative, inexpressive.

In his earlier films, Bresson tended to convey how, in a troubled world, someone achieves a state of grace; he applied a strictly simple, often static and extremely elliptic technique to complex, involuted, and violent subjects.

The contrast worked compellingly. In his later films, the subject matter has become more mundane and his technique more demonstrative; the effect is no longer that of something transcendent being quietly documented, even if (understandably) not explained, but of something just ordinarily painful, quaint, or neurotic being belabored to the point where it dazzles us through sheer idiosyncrasy and style.

A great deal of what has been called Bresson's Christian mystique or saintliness must, I think, be given a less honorific name: quirkiness. In a highly thought-provoking interview with Charles Thomas Samuels (in *Encountering Directors*) Bresson curiously remarks, "I can't bear to see people kissing on the screen." He also explains that his nonactors often go about with downcast eyes because they are following the chalk marks on the floor. Now it is all very well to choreograph a scene, but this can be done by less enslaving means. What Bresson wants to do, as he has frequently said, is to make his amateurs perform mechanically, without thinking about their parts, without acting. In that way something basic and natural is supposed to emerge quite unconsciously. Bresson has been all too successful in this pursuit of nonhistrionic acting: he has effectively choked the life out of most performances.

Four Nights of a Dreamer concerns Jacques, a young painter, who stops a girl, Marthe, from jumping off the Pont Neufe into the Seine. She tells him she was supposed to rendezvous with the man she loves, a student who had been her mother's lodger and, after getting Marthe to sleep with him, had gone off to Yale on a one-year scholarship. He promised that if he still wanted to and could marry her, he would meet her on the exact anniversary of their parting on the bridge where they had said goodbye. Isabelle Weingarten, who plays Marthe, acts stiff and somewhat dazed, but at least she is not zonked. Guillaume des Forêts (I don't believe that name!), as Jacques, speaks in a stifled monotone, lopes and slouches, is given to vacant stares, and generally suggests a rather timid revenant. Marthe and Jacques spend three more nights on and around the bridge, telling each other their life stories. As Marthe's narrative is acted out, we meet Jean, her seemingly faithless lover. To no surprise of ours, he looks like a ghoul and acts like a zombie.

What a difference real acting could make here! But no, everything must be subdued: speech as if by rote, movements as if produced by strings. Absolute string-pulling is what Bresson the puppeteer is after. God knows, other men have made movies, and good ones, with amateur actors, but they did not compel them to walk, talk, and breathe along chalk lines. Perhaps Jean is such a hirsute, thin-rimmed-spectacled, pinched-looking nonentity to make Marthe belong more truly to the camera and its autocratic wielder, the director.

Thus the big nude scene in the film is not the one in which the unclothed, upright bodies of Marthe and Jean cling together almost motionlessly, but the one where the naked girl preens and cavorts before her pier glass. It reveals, ostensibly, her sudden awareness of her sexuality; but when the camera takes the place of the mirror, it is for the director that the girl seems   121 to put on her sexual dance. On first viewing, the scene appears justified by the heady erotic aroma it exudes; on second viewing, however, I found no special artistry, only the loveliness of the girl's body and the fact that, for once, she is allowed to unfurl her long, dark, sensuous hair.

More than increasingly minimalized acting, the problem may be the progressively more preposterous plots. As in *Une Femme douce,* and, less obviously, *Pickpocket,* the filmmaker goes back to Dostoevsky for his scenario. "Feelings," Bresson told Samuels, "don't change from century to century," thereby ostensibly justifying his modern-dress version of period stories. Although essential feelings remain unchanged, their expression, however, does undergo significant modifications. In the still almost feudal Russia of the nineteenth-century czars and on a bridge across the Neva, things were done and expressed differently from what is enacted and voiced on or under a contemporary Parisian bridge. A girl does not have to sneak out of her house at night for a tryst; a man does not go off—even to the antipodes, even to Yale—for a year to be unheard from until he returns one year to the day of his departure to the same nocturnal meeting place. Marthe would not send the silently loving, masochistically suffering Jacques to deliver a letter to Jean's friends; there are little things like telephones or *pneumatiques* or going there yourself.

If the plot of *Four Nights* seems ridiculous in present-day terms, the time sense—or, if you prefer, the editing—of Bresson has become no less infelicitous. To quote Bresson to Samuels again: "I don't create ellipsis; it is there from the beginning. One day I said, 'Cinema is the art of showing nothing.' I want to express things with a minimum of means, showing nothing that is not absolutely essential."

With all due allowance for hyperbole, there is something absurd about that "art of showing nothing." Bresson is after an ellipsis, a lacuna, something that the viewer's imagination must creatively fill in. The aim may derive in part from Bresson's having been a painter. Where a single image, the painting, is all there is, overtones, implications, suggestiveness will become all-important. But on film, where movement and continuity are of the essence, Bresson's short, rigorously self-contained takes, providing no development, run the risk of becoming self-defeating.

The method works in films like *Diary of a Country Priest* and *A Man Escaped* for a very good reason. In both films, much was going on: in the former, it was emotional and spiritual conflict; in the latter, the intricate, desperate stratagems of a condemned man planning and carrying out a difficult escape. Wherever you apply your sudden, narrow, fleeting focus, you catch a moment of intense psychic or physical struggle. In *Four Nights of a Dreamer,* you keep getting snapshots of lulls, dawdling, gaps between significant activity. Repeatedly, we catch Jacques daubing away at his paltry pop canvases, or confiding his fairy-tale fantasies of a *princesse lointaine* to his tape recorder and then lying on his cot as he listens to them being played back— all of which serves only to make him more wishy-washy, ineffectual, and boring.

122   Another bothersome habit of Bresson's is dragging in private concerns

irrelevant to his plot and, with his seignorial disdain of explanation, turning them into sources of misunderstanding or, at least, confusion. At one point Jacques is visited in his studio-apartment by a fellow painter whom he does not recognize but who proceeds to lecture him about the glories of the minimal art he (the visitor) practices. Since Jacques carries on throughout like a brain-damaged somnambulist, his amazed incomprehension—presumably meant to express Bresson's dismay at such tenets—merges with, and gets lost in, his general vagueness. This inadvertently makes it appear as if Bresson found the friend's opinions acceptable. (On second thought, maybe he does.) Again, a prolonged parody of a cheap, pretentious *policier* in the manner of Jean-Pierre Melville is dragged in out of left field, and may strike some as a tribute rather than the jibe it surely, though distractingly, is.

The one device with which Bresson successfully bridges the gap between Dostoevsky's day and ours is the tape recorder Jacques uses to record his own voice repeating the one word "Marthe." He carries the contraption close to his heart in an inside pocket, and turns it on in unlikely places such as a bus, to the consternation of other passengers. This is an effective transposition of what was once a lover's heartbeat insistently thumping out the beloved's name.

Other equivalents fail. For Jacques and Marthe to watch from the bridge a passing *bateau-mouche*—colorfully illuminated and hauntingly photographed by Pierre Lhomme—is no emotional equal of taking the girl out in a rowboat. And it is quite obvious that the Brazilian *saudades*-singer (or whatever he is) and his bongo band are put on that pleasure ship merely by tricky montage. The whole pretty interlude emerges as an arbitrary decoration, rather like the already mentioned nude scene before the mirror—very different from the nude scene in *Balthazar,* where the ravished heroine cowers against the wall, a shot having both narrative and symbolic significance.

In the end, we could not care less which dreary male the dull heroine goes off with, and feel that our time, like Bresson's talent, has been wasted. The art of showing nothing has become the art of saying nothing.

December 25, 1972

Bergman Off Target

INGMAR BERGMAN's *Whispers and Cries*—or, as the distributor retitled it, *Cries and Whispers*—attempts to do too much. We are given the interacting existences of four very different women to whom extraordinarily painful things happen, and we are to identify ourselves equally with all four of them although the film does not tell us enough to make us feel fully even for one. How does Bergman manage to lose these people as entities despite the fact that the details of their existences are captured with his customary insight and evocative power? By being overconcerned with mood, ambience, visual 123

and histrionic minutiae, and shock effects. These, impressive as they are—
perhaps precisely because they are so impressive—usurp the space in which
people could be people and a life could give the illusion of being lived, not
merely highlighted.

Agnes, a woman in her late thirties, is dying of cancer in her sumptuous
country mansion circa 1900. Her elder sister, Karin, a tough, efficient, withdrawn woman, and her younger sister, Maria, a frivolous but charming
coquette, have come for the deathwatch. The only other person in the house
is Anna, a quiet, almost stolid, earth-motherish servant. Agnes keeps a diary,
permitting Bergman to show us scenes from the past as recorded in its pages.
Thus we are introduced to the sisters' dead mother, a beautiful, distant,
apparently unhappy person, whom Agnes came to understand only by and
by.

The sick woman takes a turn for the worse and David, the doctor, is
summoned; he can offer nothing beyond the compassionate touch of his
hands. Maria, though married and a mother, tries to renew the affair she
had with David. He is momentarily tempted, then leaves with the monosyllable, "No." The word produces whispers of recollection in Maria's ears,
and we return with her to the time when Anna's little daughter came down
with an illness that proved fatal. Joachim, Maria's husband, was away, and
David attended the sick child. He was persuaded to stay overnight, enabling
Maria (who had been his girl once) to share his bed again. But Joachim
found out, and Maria discovered him fumbling with a dagger with which he
had just tried, bloodily and bunglingly, to kill himself. "Help me!" he im-
plored, lurching toward her and collapsing; horrified, she withdrew, uttering
that fateful monosyllable, "No!"

Agnes cries out in pain. The very house seems to echo it with unearthly
murmurs. Maria and Karin cannot help their sick sister, but the mothering
Anna climbs into bed with her and offers her large, bare breasts as soothing
pillows to her surrogate child. Later on in the night, Agnes's horrible wheezing summons all the women to her bedside. Agnes cannot even speak:
ghastly sounds dribble out of her mouth. The ministrations of the others
finally bring her around and she is touchingly thankful; upon being read to
aloud, she dozes off. Still later, the wheezing recommences. To Maria's horror, Agnes echoes Joachim's plea: "Can't someone help me?" Racked with
pain, she piteously beats her breast. Her eyes manage one more quarter-
smile at Anna, then turn toward the window and stop. She is dead. Anna
falls across the body but does not cry; Maria sobs; Karin freezes.

There is a brief bedside prayer for the deceased. The old minister invokes
her as a saint and asks her to intercede for us with God; he permits himself
words of such doubt and despair as no Swedish Lutheran clergyman, especially of that period, could pronounce in public. Now it is Karin's turn to
hear whispers, and she recalls a dinner for two in this very house, when she
and her much older diplomat husband were paying a brief visit. It is a frosty
tête-à-tête, with quiet hatred radiating across the long table. Karin overturns
a glass of red wine; it breaks and stains the tablecloth with a semblance of
blood. The husband goes off to bed expecting her to join him. She remains

seated for a while, playing with a shard. "Nothing but lies. A tissue of lies!" she repeats out loud and, shard in hand, retires.

Anna undresses her in an elaborate, rather servile ritual. Perhaps she permits herself an overbold look. Karin, who cannot now abide such a glance, angrily slaps her, but immediately asks forgiveness. Anna refuses with a vehement shake of the head. A crucial trust seems to be broken here, but the incident is presented too cursorily to bear much emotional weight. Left alone, Karin mutilates her vagina with the shard; her face first registers pain, then something akin to orgasm. She goes in to her husband who gives her a contemptuous look. Smiling, she reclines on the bed and, as he approaches, offers him her bleeding genitals. Appalled, he watches her smear the blood all over her mouth and face—the areas he might kiss—and, once again, her eyes and tongue display sexual ecstasy.

Back in the present, Maria confronts Karin with the fact of their sad estrangement, but Karin rebuffs Maria and maintains her isolation. She reads a passage from Agnes's diary in which the dead sister expresses her thanks for having received the best gifts from life: solidarity, friendship, grace. Karin's tone implies that Agnes, in her saintly naïveté, only imagined such grace to be possible. Maria nevertheless touches her sister's face affectionately, and Karin breaks down: "I don't want you to do that; to be kind to me." She sobs about not being able to breathe any more; in the adjoining room, the dead Agnes lies still and unwheezing.

Later, sitting at the same table where the world once appeared to her a tissue of lies, Karin accuses Maria of smiling callously (is she equating her sister with her husband?) and has a fit. She howls rather like Agnes in her agony. But the two finally fall into each other's arms and exchange caresses, kisses, hugs. We do not hear their words: the soundtrack bursts out with a Bach saraband for unaccompanied cello. This strikes me as a poor shortcut, particularly since the device of bringing in music, often baroque, to avoid dialogue has been used by too many lesser directors.

We hear whispers once more, and something like a child's moan in the night. Anna wakes up—or thinks she does, though she is really dreaming. She looks into the empty crib of her dead child, then walks through the dining room where the studs on the chairs glow eerily in the moonlight (a magnificent shot). In the sitting room next to Agnes's bedroom, Maria and Karin lean against the walls as in a trance. "Don't you hear? There's Agnes weeping," Anna cries out, but the sisters neither hear her nor feel her touch. Anna enters Agnes's room and the camera zooms onto the dead woman's face revealing fresh tear stains. The dead woman speaks (cleverly off-camera): the atmosphere in the house makes her anxious, prevents her from being at peace. She asks Anna to summon her sisters, but both of them repudiate her: Karin angrily, Maria hysterically. It is up to Anna again to put the dead woman to rest, which she does by cradling her against her naked bosom in a tableau, part Pietà, part mother nursing her child.

The whole family returns from the funeral. Karin's husband expresses his unwillingness to give Anna anything: she is young and can easily find other employment. Anna proudly declines even the keepsake of Agnes that was promised her by Karin. They all thank her coldly and leave; only Maria presses some money into her hands and lightly brushes the servant's face in a farewell gesture. Karin asks Maria whether their new-found closeness might not continue, but Maria's thoughts are elsewhere and Karin wheels on her furiously. The two women separate, strangers again, but with coolly dutiful promises of annual get-togethers. Anna is allowed the use of the house a little while longer.

The soundtrack plays the Chopin prelude that was previously associated with Agnes, particularly when she was remembering her mother. Serenely alone now, Anna takes out Agnes's diary and reads the entry for a day when Agnes felt supreme happiness. We see the four women in white, as they were at the beginning of the film, strolling gaily in the park around the house. The sisters settle on the swings, and Anna rocks them gently. "The people I am most fond of were with me," declares Agnes's voice; "I wanted to cling to the moment . . . I feel a great gratitude to life which gives me so much."

The film is first and foremost visual—therein lie its glory and limitation. Bergman says in the screenplay that it all began with a vision of four women in white inside a very red room, and that he had to puzzle out painstakingly the meaning of this image. Actually, the film begins with the camera exploring the park on a misty, chilly autumn morning. It then goes into Agnes's sickroom, where the bed is made of black wood, the bed linen and Agnes's nightgown are dazzlingly white, and the blanket is of a deep red. The color motif of the film is sounded: the black of death and anguish and grief; the white of purity and innocence, of the sacrificial offering; and the red of passion, blood, and the tortured heart.

These uncompromising colors dominate the film, for the walls are mostly scarlet, the furniture and nocturnal shadows supply abundant darkness, and gowns are generally white. Agnes, to be sure, is always white; Maria will switch to red, Karin to black or an ominous, shiny dark gray; and Anna will once wear a pale blue plaid print. Except in the few brief outdoor scenes, a good many colors are barely or never glimpsed in the film; a yellow flower gives us rather a jolt.

This is not to imply that the color symbolism is in any way obtrusive: one's awareness of it remains subliminal. Only the red walls exude a heady fascination that both exhilarates and oppresses; Bergman explains that the inside of the brain always seemed red to him. Surely, the inside of the body, or, indeed, the heart, must seem even redder. And these scarlet and crimson hues suggest the interiors of theaters as well, so that we can perhaps say that the film unfurls in a theatrical inner space—inside the thinking, feeling, suffering organs of humankind. In any case, the three dominant colors, in their various permutations, provide an unusually intense, almost drastic, background against which the pastel colors of flesh take on a more pathetically ephemeral character. The right color always manages to predominate: even the roses in Agnes's sickroom are white, and it is one such white rose that dissolves into the image of the wistfully recollected mother.

With sovereign skill, the three main colors intermingle. For example, when, in Anna's dream, Karin and Maria go in to see Agnes, their darkling figures glide alternatingly past moon-whitened window shades and walls that, even at night, are a solemnly glowing red. Equally marvelous is the framing of the shots. Take the one in the flashback where Maria and David confront each other before making love. They stand, dim red and black figures, slightly out of focus in the background right; to the left, closer to us, an avid fire leaps in the hearth; and closest to us, framing the lower edge of the image, is a huge, soft, white bed with fluffy pillows at one end, and a large, rolled-up, white eiderdown at the other. Bed and fire—sex and passion—are much more real than those fuzzy lovers.

Still more extraordinary is the editing, with image commenting upon successive image. For instance: Agnes has just died, and disembodied hands, in closeup or medium shot, smooth out her matted hair. It is Karin and Anna, but we see them only as hands. They raise the bed covers to reveal Agnes's legs. The nightgown, during the agony, has pulled up, and there is something faintly obscene about these still handsome legs bared in death. One is stretched out desperately straight, the other is bent at a jaunty angle, giving the corpse a torn, struggling look. The hands now join the erring leg to its mate, and pull the nightgown over both.

The camera tilts up to catch, suddenly, Maria, standing at the foot of the bed and sobbing. As the hands lift the pushed-down bed covers to draw them back, Maria is blotted out, as it were, reproachfully. The covers are tucked under Agnes's chin, her hands folded on top; the camera pans upward and there, as before, is Maria, weeping and useless as ever. Now a taper is shown burning in extreme closeup, a hand approaches with another candle to be lighted. The two candles separate and as the camera retreats, we see that holding them are two black-clad women, the layers-out. We see, too, their finished work: Agnes wearing a knitted, babyish bonnet, her hands pressing a fat yellow flower to her breast. By sedulous stages, the ugliness of death has been glossed over.

The film has themes rather than a plot. The nays we utter to those who, in diverse but related desperation, ask for our help; the difficulty of breathing that both the dying and living experience, along with the shared difficulty of speaking. There are the various forms of sexual fulfillment, to which is opposed the simple touch of human hands that we all seek or shun—seek even when we shun it, and cannot keep even when we have it. We lose it in love, in kinship, in death—where, ironically, it is lavished upon us one final time. And this touch (it became eponymous in Bergman's last film) is only one of several recapitulatory motifs.

There is also the hysterical breakdown of Karin with its garbled yet still revealing speech fragments, reminiscent of the nurse's in *Persona*. When David reads the map of aging in the lines of Maria's face in a mirror, he calls her, for some reason, Marie; we are reminded of the ballerina in *Summerplay (Illicit Interlude)*, whose name was Marie, and who sat gazing at her not so young face in her make-up mirror, while the ballet master foretold harsh truths to her. The magic-lantern session goes back to such a lantern in Bergman's own childhood, about which he has written; the embittered minister's reference to this "dirty earth under a cold, empty sky" comes from 127

Bergman's Erasmus Prize speech, subsequently the preface to *Persona*. The image of bright outdoor happiness at the end echoes the last shot of *Wild Strawberries*, where Professor Borg has a radiantly white vision of his parents, still young, in a pastoral setting. There, however, it was a living man embracing his past and becoming reconciled to his life; here, more gloomily, it is the vision of a dead spinster, the posthumous illusion of one to whom life was niggardly and death prodigal in cruelty.

But these and other echoes add little to *Whispers and Cries* (the "whispers" of memory must, surely, precede the "cries" of agony); they trail about the film as forlornly as the white-garbed, wraithlike women. Because Bergman spends so much time on atmospheric details, he is obliged to bring his women to life with a single, striking incident each. Some of these incidents are too strident, some too ordinary, some too vague. Although we perceive distinctions and parallels, we are not given enough material for their comparative evaluation.

The acting of Harriet Andersson, Liv Ullmann, Ingrid Thulin, and Kari Sylwan is superlative both individually and as an ensemble; Sven Nykvist's cinematography may well surpass all color seen so far, and the sets, costumes, and direction are masterly. Only the screenplay is a bit of a miscalculation.

January 22, 1973

In France We Do It Horizontally

I've tried to describe the impact of a film that has made the strongest impression on me in almost twenty years of reviewing. This is a movie people will be arguing about, I think, for as long as there are movies.

—Pauline Kael, *The New Yorker*

When President Doumer (or was it his near-namesake Doumergue?) of the French Republic witnessed an exhibition of a newly imported dance, the tango, his Argentinian hosts inquired what he thought of it. "Very nice," he replied, "but in France we do it horizontally." The tango in Bernardo Bertolucci's *Last Tango in Paris* is clearly not only that sensual dance that gets mocked in the ballroom scene, but also what the two principal characters perform in their hideaway—horizontally, vertically, and sitting down, forward as well as backward. The "last tango in Paris" is the forty-five-year-old Paul's fatal affair with the twenty-year-old Jeanne, and it may even be that last bit of romantic fantasy that the middle-aged are still clinging to but that the under-thirty generation will have no further truck with. A film, then, it would seem (for its meanings, such as they are, are not very clear), about the death of romance, and yet a film strongly championed by women, not to
128 mention critics and the general public.

When *Last Tango in Paris* was first shown on the closing night of the last New York Film Festival, without the customary critics' screening preceding it, all but the most important reviewers were kept in the dark about whether they would get to see that sold-out event at all. They did, finally, sitting on steps and in the aisles. It was further impressed on them by United Artists, the distributor, that Italian censorship would very likely ban or mutilate the film, and that unless New York critical support swayed or shamed the censors, no other audience in America, or possibly anywhere, would ever see it.

Critics went home breathless to write their condign raves. Grandest of these was Pauline Kael's, which proclaimed the date the equivalent in movie history of the first performance of Stravinsky's *Rite of Spring*. "This must be the most powerfully erotic movie ever made," she swooned. In due time, her review, reproduced by United Artists in its entirety in fourteen-point type, became a two-page advertisement in the Sunday *New York Times*. There followed a *Time* cover story on the film and its star, Marlon Brando, and promptly the advance ticket sales zoomed. With its five-dollar tariff, *Tango* took its rightful place alongside *The Godfather* and *Deep Throat*, while more articles on it kept coming out, jointly constituting a universal rave pre-review.

Last Tango in Paris strikes me as yet another pretentious, empty, and dishonest film by that arrogant, attitudinizing, derivative, monstrously slick filmmaker Bernardo Bertolucci. Just before it was released, an earlier Bertolucci item opened in the hope of cashing in on *Tango*. This was *The Spider's Stratagem*, remotely based on a Borges story and praised as the director's best work by numerous reviewers who may have wanted to steal Pauline Kael's thunder. It is poseur's cinema at its worst, all stillborn symbols, pseudoprofound surrealism, and inscrutability, except for an eminently scrutable homosexual sensibility: almost every shot arbitrarily, aestheticizingly posed, and the entire film one long pseudo-intellectual pose. When I asked Borges about it, he said that was the first he had heard of such a movie.

Tango is much less obscure, but just about as posturing a film. Paul, a forty-five-year-old American expatriate, has been kept for the last five years by his French wife, Rosa, who runs a cheap hotel. On the morning after her mysterious suicide, he finds himself inspecting an elegant but dilapidated apartment in Passy simultaneously with another prospective tenant, Jeanne, a frizzy-haired, miniskirted swinger of twenty. Within a few minutes, the two are copulating (she wears no panties), first standing up, then on the floor. Paul rents the apartment, furnishes it with a large mattress and a few incidentals, and the pair propose to meet here for purposes of pure sex, without exchanging names or biographies. "Everything outside this place is bullshit," Paul declares.

We, however, see bits of their outside lives during the three days the film spans. Paul has seedy encounters with Rosa's mother, who has come up for the funeral, and Marcel, Rosa's lover, who also lives in their hotel and wears the identical robe Paul wears—both gifts from Rosa. Paul also keeps vigil by Rosa's corpse laid out in a bed of flowers, and is consumed with recriminations, rage, and, finally, grief. Jeanne meets Tom, her fiancé, a TV filmmaker and movie nut, who is shooting a documentary about a typical Paris girl—Jeanne. Its climax is to be their wedding, but, before that, there are recapitulations of her childhood as a reactionary colonel's daughter. She and Tom have a number of fights, and Jeanne now thinks she is in love with Paul.

In the apartment, the lovers play sexual games, more often than not sadomasochistic. He rapes and sodomizes her, at the same time forcing her to repeat blasphemous and antisocial phrases. Or he neglects her until she is driven to masturbation, or, again, he has her sodomize him with two fingers while he extracts from her declarations of abject enslavement. At other times, he reminisces about his unhappy childhood, or has her relate details of her sexual awakening. He rejects nonsexual feelings, roars when she asks for his name, and preconizes animal noises. Their conversation is mostly taunts and parries.

Tom somehow reclaims Jeanne's affection—we don't know exactly how, but comprehensible acts are few and far between in this long film. Paul vanishes for a while and Jeanne cools toward him; suddenly, he reappears and drags her into a restaurant where a tango competition is in progress. He declares his love and proposes marriage, but now she finds him old, drunk, and emotionally demanding; she gives him one last masturbation under the table, calmly wipes herself off, and prepares to leave forever. Paul pulls her onto the dance floor where they perform an obscene travesty of the tango and are chased away. He pursues her into her apartment where she finally tells him her name even as she shoots him with her father's gun. While he lies crumpled and dead on her balcony, she rehearses her line to the police: self-defense against an unknown rapist.

Almost everything about the film is a lie. Take the locations, to begin with. A fancy apartment like that in Passy would be guarded with machine guns against casual copulators off the street, and the rent would be way beyond a flophouse-owner's means. And Jeanne's apartment, with its lushly leatherbound books, is hardly what this goose would inhabit; when, at one point, she quotes Pirandello ("Tonight we improvise!"), the inconsistency becomes absurd. In her parents' place, things remain preposterously as they were when she was eight: the notebook she secretly kept is still under the table where she hid to write in it.

The characters make even less sense. Paul is a thinly veiled Marlon Brando, who obviously improvised his approximate life story for the auto-biographical speeches. But why a man of such varied talents and accomplishments should end up as his wife's gigolo is made no more clear than why she performed that particularly gory razor-slashing on herself, which turned their entire bathroom into a bloodbath. And why did Paul so love the lewd creature she was, owning diversified orgy equipment ranging from French ticklers to clerical collars? And why should Jeanne have instant intercourse with a shabby, middle-aged stranger with whom she has exchanged only a handful of surly words, then promptly set up bawdy housekeeping with him?

130

Clearly, she falls in love with Paul for mere purposes of dramatic irony, so that when he falls for her, she may fall out of love and reject him. And why should he be proposing love and marriage at a time when bitterness about his wife and matrimony fills him entirely? And what about Tom, the infantile cinéaste who recites litanies of movie stars' names in the pouring rain and is continually framing imaginary shots with his bare knuckles—why should this parody of a Godardian suddenly grow up in the end, turn down the overlush Passy apartment now proposed to him by Jeanne, and come out in defense of maturely facing reality?

There are no real characters here, only movable pegs on which to hang a makeshift plot and shiftless actors' improvisations. The film was first intended for Trintignant and Dominique Sanda, who would have turned it into a very different story, but Bertolucci, evidently willing to drift with his actors, couldn't care less. Brando's ad libs are inartistic and often boring, as actors' improvisations in wholesale quantities always are compared to real writing; Jean-Pierre Léaud's wild, infantile improvisations as Tom are barely warmed-over Godard. Who indeed wrote what script there is? Bertolucci and one Franco Arcalli are listed as coauthors, but Arcalli is the film's editor and cutters have not been known as writers. A young American woman who had a bit part in Bertolucci's *Conformist* claims to have worked on this screenplay; the French dialogue is credited to Agnès Varda.

Whoever wrote what, hatred for women and a pervasive homosexual sensibility characterize the film, which purports to be the last word in heterosexual explicitness and so delights female—even feminist—reviewers! When Paul gratuitously beats up a john brought to his hotel door by a prostitute, he derisively calls him "Faggot!" Is this supposed to be a clue to our protagonist's secret problem? Or is it just an indulgence in some of the filmmakers' not so secret problems? Certainly the kind of sex between strangers hurtled into by Paul and Jeanne is much more frequent among homosexuals, as also would be anal rape. The film altogether wallows in anal references (and if not anal, the next best thing, fecal) dragged in for no reasons germane to the characters as portrayed; and, parallelly, in the insulting and humiliating of women.

For example, while Paul has himself buggered by Jeanne, he rants: "I want to get a pig and have it fuck you. I want the pig to vomit in your face and you to swallow the vomit. Then I want you to go behind and swallow the farts of the dying pig. Will you do that for me?" "Yes, and more!" pants the sodomizing girl in a transport of self-abasement. Earlier, Jeanne explored Paul's body: "What strong arms you have!" "The better to squeeze a fart out of you." "What long nails!" "The better to scratch your arse with." "What thick hair!" "The better to let your crabs hide in." "What a big tongue!" "The better to stick it in your rear." (At a later screening, so help me, I heard this line as "The better to tickle your lid, my dear." Despite statements to the contrary, the film has been tampered with—cut in several places, and the big anti-God scene, in which Brando, impersonating a mad dog, growlingly attacks a Bible salesman, was eliminated entirely.) 131

Gratuitous arse shots proliferate. A bunch of kids are shown defecating; Jeanne crouches during a longish scene with her half-pulled-down pants emphasizing rear cleavage; Paul defies a woman tango contest judge by baring his bottom at her and shouting, "Kiss me, sweetheart!" And so with the dialogue. When Paul frightens Jeanne by making as if to devour a dead rat, he assures her, "I'll save the arsehole for you." Another time he tells her that slaves are branded on the arse, in allusion, perhaps, to *Story of O*. A couple of times he dwells incongruously on his hemorrhoids. Most idiosyncratically, he informs Jeanne that you don't find the ideal man "until you go right up in the arse of death, right into the womb of fear," a remark redolent equally with pederasty, pretentiousness, and meaninglessness.

The film can thus be seen as a product of the closet-queen mentality. Jeanne is, by the well-known Albertine strategy, really Jean, a boy in disguise, and the filmmakers are playing with secret fears, guilt feelings, and obsessions that they want to get off their chests but dare not quite reveal. This theory gets some support from the fact that the scenes of anal sex are accompanied by a hysteria that established homosexuals at ease with such penetration—and even swinging chicks like Jeanne, who presumably would be quite used to it—would not be likely to display.

In this case, the tango-palace sequence takes on a new meaning. The competition in which the contestants perform spectacular but bloodless, robotlike gyrations, becomes the hell in which the repressed homosexual finds himself imprisoned. He is enacting affectless, simulated copulations (in a 1914 circular, the Futurists denounced the tango as "a pantomime coitus for the camera," little knowing how prophetic they were being); Paul's defiant gesture to the tango-contest judge, the representative of repressive authority, is to bare his arse. This becomes the latent homosexual's symbolic assertion of his rights; even the marriage proposal to Jeanne-Jean may be an encoded plea to be allowed out of the closet and proclaim and legitimize a homosexual union. But the less honest partner refuses, and goes to the ultimate length to hide the truth.

Women appear consistently as cold, mean, dishonest, mad creatures. The dead wife was a superbitch, her mother is a pious fool, the Passy concierge a cackling madwoman. Jeanne's mother is a hypocrite, her favorite schoolteacher was a lesbian, her trusty maid is an arrant racist. A handsome young Negress at Paul's hotel is glimpsed being rejected by her saxophone-playing lover as she greedily tries to go down on him; later, Paul insults her as "Miss Blowjob of 1933—she still makes a few scores when she takes her teeth out." And, significantly, Paul's dying gesture is sticking his wad of chewing gum on the underside of Jeanne's balcony railing—an "Up yours!" to her and the world. Already behind the film's opening titles we have seen paintings by Francis Bacon, a painter with a markedly homosexual orientation.

But most homosexual, perhaps, is the scene in which Paul and Marcel, the men who shared Rosa, sit on the lover's bed and exchange beauty secrets about how to keep their hairlines and waistlines looking young—just the sort of thing aging inverts would prattle about. All this, of course, is detrimental only in a film posturing as the revelation of ultimate heterosexual truths, and made by two such supermasculine men: Brando, the heartthrob of even the most ardent feminists, and Bertolucci, about whose alleged female conquests *Time* magazine is still deliciously hinting away.

The worst degradation in the film is Jeanne's. Our heroine first betrays her fiancé, then becomes a masochistic sex object, and, finally, murders her lover. Bertolucci has unfortunately cut out of the released version of the film the scene in which Paul makes as if to strangle Jeanne. She taunts him to go ahead: no one will know who did it because her trysts with him are unknown to the world. (Unconvincing, but no more so than everything else in this preposterous film in which everything must be accepted on faith—bad faith.) But Paul cannot do it and so, or so it would seem, proves the weaker of the two. The tables are turned: Jeanne begins to evade Paul and, after killing him in the last scene, proceeds to rehearse the speech to the police that will establish her motive as self-defense against an unknown would-be rapist. What Paul could not do to her, she has successfully done to him.

This, surely, is the ultimate possession. Subjugating someone sexually may be reifying her, but what is that compared to murdering someone? Reification is only temporary and can be enjoyed masochistically; annihilation is permanent, unenjoyable for the victim and a great sadistic triumph for the executioner. Jeanne has pleasurably sucked Paul dry, then destroyed him and made herself free to marry Tom, the adoring immature lover whom, with her newly gained sexual expertise, she will be able to dominate totally. This can be seen as the filmmakers' attempt, conscious or otherwise, to make Jeanne into a black widow spider figure who destroys her mate. Tom, though he occasionally fights back, she can bully into docility; Paul she simply murders.

Jeanne, like Rosa, is called by Paul every vile name in the book ("pigfucker" and "fucking pig" are special favorites—any connection with *Pigpen*, a similarly oriented film by Pasolini, whose assistant Bertolucci once was?); charmingly, he informs her that "in ten years [she] will be playing soccer with [her] teats." Nevertheless, female critics gush that the film is "the most liberating ever" (Pauline Kael); or that it "does as much—perhaps more—for the woman as for the man" (Molly Haskell). Of course, such enthusiasm may have simple reasons. Brando is still the supreme heartthrob of many professional and lay female filmgoers, and this movie, into which he has admittedly poured autobiographical utterances and in which he lays his body and sexuality two-thirds bare, makes him more present, available, vulnerable than ever before. In fact, almost half of Pauline Kael's rave is a glowing, white-hot tribute to Brando. And Judith Crist, whose review is the acme of undigested ambivalence and self-contradiction ("pop . . . slick . . . self-indulgent, marred by contrivances," she berates *Tango*, while granting it "excellence of . . . achievement . . . bold approach to an intimate experience in terms that cause us to explore ourselves"), nonetheless gushes on about Brando as the one who "brings an aura of greatness to the entire film . . . gives the film its raison d'être and proves his greatness."

But the most revealing delusion takes place in Molly Haskell's mind. She writes: "It is only when [Paul] has her pinned to the wall, screaming that she will do anything, anything he asks her, that [Jeanne] realizes—perhaps—that he is the one man who hasn't used her." The glaring error here is that in this scene it is Jeanne who has Paul pinned to the wall with her two inserted fingers, but so clearly does this film inspire free-floating sexual fantasies in women viewers that they are quite capable of seeing the reverse of what is happening. It then becomes easy to assert that Paul is the one man who hasn't used Jeanne: to the yearning Brando worshiper, rape by Marlon would not be the least imposition, never mind exploitation. And when Miss Kael writes that "if the actor were anyone but Brando many of us would lower our eyes in confusion," she too, I think, is being confessional rather than critical. A performance that would be an affront from anyone else is considered "princely" coming from Brando.

Bertolucci's camera skitters about with considerable chic and relentless ostentation. The colors provided by Vittorio Storaro's cinematography are nice when they are evoking rainy or cloudy cityscapes in grays, browns, and violets; indoors, however, especially in the sex scenes, there is a riot of yellows, golds, and oranges worthy only of a fashion magazine editor's idea of heaven. The music by Gato Barbieri, a saxophonist, is soupy ersatz Nino Rota, and the production design is on the schmaltzy side. Maria Schneider's Jeanne is a buxom guttersnipe, with the face of a perverted cow and the acting ability of a petulant ox; Jean-Pierre Léaud's Tom is his usual home-movies notion of camping it up. That fine actor Massimo Girotti is a bit overrefined as Marcel, and neither he nor Maria Michi, as Rosa's mother, is helped by being dubbed into French by an ultrasmooth voice. Lesser parts offer their interpreters nothing. Then there is Brando. He gives us a star turn in French and English, an anthology of all his best parts or, rather, highlights from them. This has two unfortunate results: we have seen it all before and it does not hang together. The brutish Kowalski, the fallen British gentleman from *Burn!,* the victimized rebel from *The Wild One,* the dogged Chicano of *One-Eyed Jacks* turn up at random and get into one another's hair. The actor goes from exaggerated toughness to undue whininess without ever defining Paul's psychic or cultural identity.

It is not so much that the film is vulgar, though it certainly is, as that it is mindless and pointless. It seems to be muttering something about the need to grow up and abandon childish notions of sexual paradises, yet those are the only things it droolingly revels in. It purports to mock Tom with his fantasies of nonstop tracking shots, yet is itself full of the likes of them. It appears to make fun of Tom's inferior loving through his camera as against Paul's superior lovemaking with his masterful penis, yet ends by vindicating Tom above the broken, sodden, aging suitor of our overgrown teeny-bopper.

There is a line in *The Spider's Stratagem:* "Tripe is a dish that, well done, is very good; badly done, should be thrown in the face of the cook." If you ask me, everyone involved in this *Tango* deserves the tripe in his face.

February 19, 1973

Verse and Worse

FILM HAS its own poetry, which does not accommodate itself to any other kind of poetry, except perhaps Shakespeare's, with any alacrity. That is why to make a movie out of *Under Milk Wood*, a radio play by Dylan Thomas, the most lyrical and bardic of bards, was to court failure. True, *Under Milk Wood* is written mostly in prose, but a prose that eschews the strictures of meter and rhyme only to be more gorgeously, frenziedly poetic, in both the good and bad senses of the word. Thomas exuded poetry; even in a bread-and-butter note he could write of being "miraculously home again now in this tumbling house whose every broken pane and wind-whipped-off slate, child-scrawled wall, rain-stain, mouse-hole, knobble and ricket, man, man-booby-and-rat-trap, I know in my sleep."

As you can see—or, rather, hear—from that typical shred of mere epistolary prose, Thomas was a poet always, and always the poet of onomatopoeia. However brilliant his other gifts may have been, supreme among them was onomatopoeia. For him this was not only what the device usually means—painting with sound, something like "the murmur of innumerable bees," where you are meant to hear the buzz of the insects. Rather it was a magisterial orchestration of vowels, consonants, and syllables into rapturous bundles of words that tripped or thundered off the tongue, frolicked or fulminated across the palate, to issue as something both waterfall and symphonic orchestra.

Of course, there was meaning wrapped inside this sound; but the sound itself was an image, not so much of the rattling of rain or nibbling of mice or whatever, as of the glory of and exultation in language—language as it gathers up the delirium of feeling, thinking, being, and converts it into fountains and fireworks of sonority. But just try to put this on film!

There are, essentially, three approaches. In the case of the first two, you take a line like "And you alone can hear the invisible starfall, the darkest-before-dawn minutely dewgrazed stir of the black, dab-filled sea . . ." addressed to blind Captain Cat, and you either match it with cinematic images that illustrate the words, or you contrast it with more or less discrepant images. You create verbal-visual unison, or you create counterpoint. The obvious difficulty with the former procedure is that you get duplication, as in those hideous TV commercials where the words on screen are also boomed out at you with hectoring redundancy. The latter has the disadvantage of dumping the audience in a two-ring circus where, trying to catch both the verbal and visual acts, it ends up missing both.

Something analogous happens even with the third and best method, where word and image function in close harmony, similar yet dissimilar and, ostensibly, reinforcing each other. Here one becomes so fascinated by the cunning interaction of sight and sound that the virtuoso interplay largely overshadows both the poetry and the spectacle. Suppose someone were to 135 recite a poem about the heart as a tightrope walker while performing complicated stunts on the high wire. Both the poetics and the acrobatics would lose out to the overall wonderment, though the greater loser, surely, would be the poetry. And so it is in the movie *Under Milk Wood,* an honorable failure, a truly beautiful loser.

Dylan Thomas initially entitled his play *Llareggub, A Piece for Radio Perhaps.* It evokes a typical day in the life of a tiny Welsh coastal town, Llareggub (really Thomas's own Laugharne), but the quintessentially Welsh-sounding name is actually "bugger all" spelled backward. The word is supposed to have come to Thomas when an importunate host, Professor William York Tindall, asked the departing poet to write something Welsh in his guest book. In a similar put-on, the life of the Welsh town hides ribald jokes inside its rapt, onomatopoeic lyricism. It is to the credit of Andrew Sinclair, who adapted the work for the screen and directed it, that he meticulously preserved both aspects, the Rabelaisian and the neo-Swinburnian.

There are a few avoidable lapses in Sinclair's film. The biggest flaw is the handling of the two narrators Thomas wrote into his radio play—two because the BBC, to avoid monotony, tended to provide a pair of alternating voices for its political and cultural broadcasts. Sinclair correctly perceived that, on film, these narrators had to become physical presences, and so made them into two wanderers, former Llareggubians, who return to the town in the morning, rove, booze, mingle, wench, and comment about everyone and everything until, at nightfall, they depart again. But he has not succeeded in integrating them perfectly, and, worse yet, he gets them involved with a young woman who looks like a higher type of London secretary, complete with pants suit. The two narrators proceed to penetrate this pants suit in the course of a mini-orgy that clashes stylistically with the general tone.

The other avoidable major error, but this one only seemingly avoidable, was the deadly casting of Elizabeth Taylor as Rosie Probert, old blind Captain Cat's dead sweetheart, a girl of easy virtue yet difficult to forget. Miss Taylor wears enough eye shadow on each lid to shame the dome of Sultan Ahmet's renowned Blue Mosque, and is altogether gotten up to look like Zinka Milanov trying to play Tinker Bell. She lounges about amorphously and drips some eminently un-Welsh-sounding verbiage in her customary margarine-*cum*-molasses delivery. This blot on Sinclair's scutcheon was, in fact, unavoidable, because Richard Burton could be gotten for the first narrator only at the cost of this cameo role for Liz—and Burton, besides looking good on a marquee, is considered the mandatory Thomas interpreter.

I have never admired Burton's readings of Thomas all that much: compared to Dylan's own, they are an overinflated second best—though, to be sure, nothing comparable in overinflation to Liz Taylor. Burton, moreover, gives us his by now standard performance: an expression of vaguely suffering, congealed remoteness, and a voice that resonates like a moody, muffled trumpet played by an absent-minded musician. Peter O'Toole, however, is charming as the memory-haunted old seadog, and a large cast of famous English and not so famous Welsh actors is uniformly delightful. It is wrong to single out anyone in such a tactfully directed, tightly knit ensemble, but I cannot resist calling your attention to Meg-Wynn Owen as Lily Smalls.

The cinematography of Bob Huke (who shot *The Virgin and the Gypsy*) is full of colors that seem to ripen before your eyes without ever growing over-ripe; the musical score performs efficaciously; and Sinclair's direction is, for the most part, quietly assured. There are also many felicitous inventions, such as the license plate on the English tourist bus that invades Llareggub: ACH 1066.

Still, for all the pleasures the film provides, not the least being the un-spoiled coastal village of Fishguard, lovingly explored and caressed by the camera, the basic problem remains. As Thomas described the play to Princess Caetani, it is "an impression for voices, an entertainment out of the darkness." It is meant to recreate a day in the life of this village, a day in the life of this world, by means of voices emerging from a dark silence, then returning into the silent darkness. The movie is too much with us, too swaggeringly, brawlingly specific; it does not convey, as the more evanescent radio play does, our little life as shrouded with a sleep.

César and Rosalie is highfalutin trash, admirably summed up by the German term *Edelkitsch*. Claude Sautet's new film, like his *The Things of Life,* purports to deal with relationships among men and women that cannot be readily resolved no matter how civilized and mature—or, conversely, primitive and intemperate—those embroiled in them may be. Romy Schneider, a more or less idly rich divorcée and mother, is torn between a jolly but somewhat coarse-grained tycoon, Yves Montand, and a younger, more artistic but also less rich, cartoonist, Sami Frey. She cares for both of them in different ways, and so shuttles helplessly between them.

Montand becomes violent and destructive, Frey melancholy and self-effacing, Romy more and more withdrawn and unhappy. Finally, Montand sets up a *ménage à trois* that Romy rejects. It looks as if she is going to settle down to a job in another town, while the two men, now warm friends, begin to keep house together, united by their lost love. But Romy is drawn back to them, and *ménage à trois* it is.

All this is shown superficially and repetitiously, with the emphasis on the chic aspects of life—fast cars and attractive dwellings—not on probing the characters. The woman in particular is a blank, either fixing drinks for the card-playing tycoon and his business friends or making coffee for the cartoonist and his late-working fellow "artists." The film does not hark back to the incomparably more accomplished *Jules and Jim,* as has been suggested, but to those cliché-ridden French boulevard farces, as well as to the muddy boulevard love dramas that men like Henri Bataille and Henry Bernstein used to churn out with depressing regularity during the early decades of this century.

There is splendid color cinematography by the dependable Jean Boffety once we get beyond the monochromatic blue of the title sequence, and Sautet keeps the film hopping. But there is no more reason for us to care about   137 how these three ciphers will rearrange themselves than about watching someone work out anagrams for a three-letter word.

March 5, 1973

A Flat Trio

LET ME ADDRESS myself to some minor cinematic disappointments I had to bypass for the sake of some major ones. Biggest among these smaller letdowns is Jacques Tati's *Traffic.* After *Jour de fête* (1948), *Mr. Hulot's Holiday* (1953), and *My Uncle* (1958), the French comedian and filmmaker seemed to run out of steam until 1967, when he made *Playtime* (not yet shown here), and now *Traffic.* The film again features Tati's comic persona, the officious but bumbling Hulot, who, this time round, must get a newly designed French vehicle to a motor show in Holland.

Naturally, everything goes wrong with the trip, particularly because Hulot is being preceded or trailed by a sexy and dizzy press agent in her little sports car—a young woman with a genius for creating, no matter what the snarl-up, additional trouble. Sadly, however, the film strikes me as almost totally unfunny. Tati tries to evoke the absurdities of the highway life for the most part, but the subject has been rather exhaustively covered from, say, Dino Risi's *The Easy Life* to Godard's *Weekend.* The film, quite poorly photographed, gets so desperate in the search for humor that it devotes a goodly sequence to showing how various drivers, while waiting for the traffic light to change, pick their noses: furtively, maniacally, absent-mindedly, etc. In its quiet way, the scene is about as repulsive as can be.

Twice *Traffic* rouses itself from its feebleness. In a truly epic bottleneck, whose dimensions, intricacy, choreography, and only slight exaggeration lift it into the realm of the surreal, a Volkswagen with its hood snapping open and shut like some monstrous shark or crocodile pursues one of its wheels that has come off and seems to be escaping for dear life. The other funny scene concerns the PR girl's pet dog, hidden by some hoodlums who leave in its place a cleverly improvised mock-up of the dog's cadaver. It is somewhat cruel fun, but it does bring into amusing focus the girl's superficiality even in grief. For the rest, *Traffic* is stalled all the way.

I haven't read Graham Greene's *Travels With My Aunt,* which sounded as bad as other recent Greeniana, but I doubt if it could have been as poor as the film George Cukor made from it. The screenplay by Jay Presson Allen out of Hugh Wheeler is unmitigated claptrap, and the *mise en scène* has that horrid look of cut-rate lavish: glossy, gaudy, cluttered, but not elegant, opulent, sumptuous. The all-corners-cut appearance extends to the very casting and acting; such highly capable actors as Robert Stephens and Lou Gossett perform here as if they were criticizing the material rather than embodying it.

Still, I cannot really blame them, though I must admire Alec McCowen for transcending his surroundings and turning into a credible and lovable figure the prissy, avuncular nephew whose life is glamorized by becoming attached to an eternally youthful, reckless, and totally extravagant aunt. These spectacular aunts à la Mame have a way of ringing as theatrically rigged as fairy godmothers (pun, alas, intended), and Maggie Smith gives an absolutely shocking performance as the current one. Perhaps it is because Miss Smith is too young and cannot play this older woman without patronizing and caricaturing her—or for whatever other reason—almost every one of the actress's gestures, intonations, tricks is hollow or pasted on, artificial without the conviction that would make it artistic. It is play-acting that hurts one in every part, especially the teeth—even if they were as false as the performance itself.

About *Lady Caroline Lamb* it takes a supreme effort of the will not to remain speechless. The life story of this nineteenth-century lady who managed to be both a scandalous eccentric and a dullish bluestocking is not without interest. Her marriage to the thoroughly decent William Lamb, who was to become Lord Melbourne, and her brief, sterile (and, as has recently been suggested, possibly unconsummated) affair with Lord Byron, could have made a nice, sardonic film. For the story is a wry, essentially ludicrous, antiromance, even unto her death in early middle age after an attack of madness triggered by encountering the funeral cortege of the poet with whom she had had a liaison that was more publicity than passion, and most of all mutual recrimination.

But Robert Bolt has turned this into a soggy romance, a super-*Ryan's Daughter,* and since he has now taken over as director as well as scenarist, there are no dime-fiction holds barred. The author of that very respectable play, *A Man for All Seasons,* and of the dishonest but impressive script for *Lawrence of Arabia,* has become a sentimental hack; while he can still turn out an occasional neat epigram, it won't sustain us through layers and layers of platitudinousness and posturing. In fact, the last scene, in which a still young Lady Caroline is eulogized for having died of a (hold on to your hats) broken heart, is a sequence to be enshrined in the Museum of Cinematic Absurdities, along with such duck's-egg-sized zircons as the ending of *The Red Shoes* and the Sarah Bernhardt sequences from *The Barkleys of Broadway.*

I have the uneasy feeling that Bolt, the long-suffering husband and purveyor of scripts to the capricious Sarah Miles, is giving us a piece of encoded and perhaps therapeutical autobiography here, but that does not make it better for the rest of us. As the tempestuous Caroline, Miss Miles tosses off the most pasteboard performance of her upsy-downsy career, and is outfitted with the most condignly pasty make-up ever—as if the whole woman were made of stale marzipan.

Nevertheless, she comes out ahead of Richard Chamberlain, whose Byron is simultaneously so rotten and so ludicrous as to make one wonder about the more recent peregrinations of the casting couch, which used to be shoved under bosomy and willing starlets, but seems now to have wandered off in other directions. Jon Finch is improving with each performance, and his William Lamb, albeit not outstanding, is dignified and persuasive. A number of England's finest actors and actresses are drowning in this film; only Laurence Olivier and Margaret Leighton manage to keep their heads above all that watering down.

March 19, 1973

Junk Epic

POOR LUDWIG II of Bavaria! However mad, he was the sponsor of Richard Wagner and made the *Ring* and Bayreuth possible; this is to have done handsomely by the arts. To be turned into *Ludwig,* a three-hour film by Luchino Visconti, is to be repaid in niggardly, indeed scurvy, fashion. Even a mad king deserves sane examination.

Because Visconti is known also as an opera director, one would have expected at least Ludwig's nexus with Wagner to be portrayed with precision and solicitude. But although there is a fair amount of footage on Wagner and Hans and Cosima von Bülow, Visconti puts his foot in it and stresses only the scandalous aspects of the affair or the irrelevantly grandiose ones, such as the famous musical birthday offering to Cosima that has nothing to do with the story of Ludwig. Wagner's music rattles around the soundtrack, but the implications of a sovereign's emptying the state treasury not for public welfare, not for warding off Prussian impérialism, but for lavish patronage of the arts, are never really gone into.

Even those extravagant castles in the air that Ludwig managed to build on solid ground—castles combining every conceivable style into pure Disneyland—are not properly scrutinized: Why and how were they built, and what did they mean to Ludwig and the people of Bavaria? In fact, you do not even obtain as good an idea of what Neuschwanstein looks like from the film as you can from a German travel poster. Nor does the film afford more than a glimpse of the fantastic Lindehof grotto with its underground boating lake and Wagnerian tableaus for decoration—Madame Tussaud's, the Tunnel of Love, and Capri rolled into one. And this despite location shooting and no expenses spared.

Surely, you might think, there is some consideration of how and whence that notorious madness came, and a cataloguing of the stages by which it grew. But all we get is something about its running in the family: a scene or two showing Prince Otto, a younger brother, going off his rocker. How, if at all, was this derangement related to the king's homosexuality? To be sure, this aspect of the monarch's life concerns Visconti more, but even here there is no serious effort to see deeply into the problem. Instead, an unhappy, frustrated romance is dreamed up by the scenarists, Visconti, Enrico Medioli, and the ubiquitous Suso Cecchi d'Amico. They would seem to imply

140

that the nineteen-year-old, just-crowned Ludwig's rebuff by his cousin Elizabeth, who represses her feeling for him so as to remain faithful to her husband, Emperor Franz Josef, starts the teen-aged king on the road to homosexuality. Granted that Romy Schneider plays the young empress rather more boyishly than necessary, this explanation is as factitious as the romance itself is fictitious.

The king's subsequent homosexual affairs with various youths in his service are treated with similar superficiality, without exploration of how they affected Ludwig's psychic and political status, or what it must have meant for these youths to shed the royal uniform for the royal pleasure, and all this in an illiberal Catholic country. There is room here for a tragicomedy of psychological tremors and social repercussions; instead, we get Ludwig gazing yearningly at some bathing groom or sleeping adjutant and occasionally conducting a dialogue fraught with ambiguities. Just as in *The Damned,* Visconti climaxes with melancholy shots of the aftermath of an all-male orgy, but his customary tightrope act between nausea and nostalgia lacks the honesty and incisiveness of art.

This long, creeping film is such an overdressed vacuum that it affords the bored viewer a perfect opportunity for assessing how plodding a director Visconti is. Although Armando Nannuzzi's color cinematography is at best competent, the rest of the technical staff is first-rate, and Ruggero Mastroianni is a master editor. So if the movie lacks a good sense of rhythm either in individual scenes or in their concatenation, if the camera angles and movements are as predictable as the performances are conventional, the fault is clearly the director's.

Typical of this kind of filmmaking is the handling of the king's infatuation with Josef Kainz, who was a nobly cerebral actor—*ein niebezauberter Bezauberer,* an unenchantable enchanter, Hugo von Hofmannsthal was to call him—nothing like the insignificant stripling reciting himself hoarse for an imperious, insatiable sovereign as the movie would have it. And Folker Bohnet is hardly the actor to impersonate Kainz, especially not when obliged to recite in awkwardly German-accented English.

But the script itself is never far from ludicrous. Elizabeth will pontificate prophetically: "Rulers like us have nothing to do with history. We are only for display, unless someone makes us seem important by assassinating us"—which is immediately followed by a flash-forward of her laid out, assassinated and mourned over. The fact that this is the film's only obvious flash-forward makes the scene even more incongruous and clumsy. And what are we to make of this advice to Ludwig when his homosexual inclinations begin to surface: "It happens to most young men—to all when they are so sensitive—but usually they get over it with help"?

Even more problematic is the counsel of Ludwig's chaplain and confessor upon hearing that the king would break off his engagement to a princess he does not love: "In the darkness of your room you will realize that the warmth of one body is the same as any other's." Are we to be wowed by the profundity of this or roar at its absurdity? Whatever its intentions may be, this epic leaves us with only a few mouthfuls of snickers.

Helmut Berger plays Ludwig earnestly and haughtily, except when overcome with reverence for Elizabeth or Wagner, or with tantrums that never grow up into rages. Instead of aging as the film progresses, he merely becomes more slovenly, and though, from overindulgence in candy, his teeth become more rotten, his performance remains pretty much the same. He does, however, look as pretty as anyone in the film, which is not hard, considering that his most serious competitor, the usually lovely Silvana Mangano, gives a disfiguringly hammy portrayal of Cosima von Bülow. Adriana Asti, still listed in the credits, was cut out of the film altogether, unless perchance I slept through her appearance. Trevor Howard, thoroughly British as he is, does make Wagner into a believable, complex figure, and that, in this context, is quite an achievement.

April 2, 1973

Art vs. Propaganda

THE BIG brouhaha of the month was George Stevens Jr.'s dropping of *State of Siege* from the gala opening roster at the American Film Institute's new theater in the John F. Kennedy Center for the Performing Arts. The film, the AFI's director explained, "rationalizes political assassination." This was vehemently denied by the filmmaker, Costa-Gavras, his associates, and Don Rugoff, the American distributor. Both sides rate demerits: Stevens for scheduling a film with whose contents he was evidently unfamiliar; the filmmakers and distributor for disingenuousness. The film is patently anti-American and does, up to a point, sanction political assassination.

State of Siege is taut, effective, easefully assured filmmaking. Costa-Gavras, the young Greco-French director, has learned quickly and well. *The Sleeping-Car Murders* was mere clever folderol; *Z* was a good piece of charismatic special pleading, with nice human touches, but a bit too pat and cute. *The Confession* went too far in the opposite direction; it was too arid, monotonous, predictable. The new film strikes a good balance: it moves swiftly in time and space, but avoids nervous jumpiness and does not refrain from lingering over some tragic or wryly comic incidents. There may be a few too many shots of the routine ugly aspects of a state of siege, yet even these retards have their atmospheric value.

The director handles his camera with a nice sweep, achieving psychologically satisfying patterns that are not too geometrical or repetitious and manage to pick out significant details without unseemly overemphasis: during an action shot, we casually notice the children of the poor playing on a dumping ground full of rusty junk with ominously sharp edges. Costa-Gavras is ably assisted by Pierre William Glenn's color cinematography showing a Latin American winter with a slightly misty and grainy look, just inconsistent enough with the lushness of vegetation and general pigmentation.

Everything appears a bit frazzled, shopworn, overcast—subtly, ineffably un-pleasant. The cast, headed by Yves Montand, is right in aspect and perform-ance; only Jean-Luc Bideau looks more like a Parisian lout than a Latin American revolutionary. The adroit script is by Costa-Gavras and Franco Solinas, and if the dialogue by Solinas (of *Battle of Algiers* fame) sounds epigrammatic, it still rings sufficiently true.

The film deals loosely with the Mitrione case, though Mitrione becomes Santore, and Uruguay an unspecified Latin American country. Santore, an ostensible AID man, is kidnapped by an underground organization consist-ing mostly of young leftists. His captors demand amnesty for all political prisoners in exchange for his freedom. When it becomes evident that he is actually a police expert teaching the local police counterrevolutionary tac-tics; when many of the underground's leadership are captured; when the government, despite a crisis, does not fall and refuses any deals, the revolu-tionaries must reluctantly execute Santore. Little is accomplished by this; a new American policeman in AID clothing arrives. But underground eyes are alert and watchful.

This broad outline is filled in with lively, pungent, and reasonably con-vincing details. Yet what does the film achieve? It is, to begin with, so unremittingly political that people in it exist only as political antagonists, with just a suggestion of a private life glimpsed, here and there, in passing. For all the toughness, leanness, and bitter wit of the dialogue, it is all about political concepts and activities, revolutionary and counterrevolutionary measures, unjustified governmental violence and allegedly justified insur-gent, popular violence in behalf of the exploited people against capitalists, fascists, torturers, abrogators of human rights. And unless politics means more to you than people—which, even to the dedicated young revolution-aries of this film, it is not supposed to—the movie will leave you emotionally unfulfilled.

The problem, though, is more than the politics: it is the propaganda. God knows, I deplore U.S. interference in the political, social, and economic structures of foreign countries—in short, U.S. imperialism—and applaud the film's intention of showing how, under the cloak of economic aid, we support repressive local governments and poach on all kinds of natural resources. Nevertheless, it will not do to show all the figures in the country's govern-ment and almost all Americans as villains. Montand does portray Santore most skillfully as a not unintelligent and not really evil man, so eager to uphold conservative middle-class values that he becomes a tool of evil. And there is a well-meaning American agronomist who is shown as a befuddled, innocent supernumerary. The rest, however, range from smugly exploitative to dangerously vicious.

Conversely, the members of the underground are exemplary in their disci-pline, scrupulousness, courtesy to prisoners, and absolute fair play. They make occasional mistakes, but are much smarter than their oppressors; their documentation of such elusive data as the training in violence administered to their policemen in U.S. police academies is nothing short of prodigious. Their self-control is admirable, and they conduct Santore's questioning and 143 condemnation in the most humane and parliamentary manner; idealistically, they release two other, less guilty prisoners. They form one big family and their own elderly parents support them to the death. After a film like *The Sorrow and the Pity,* the unambiguousness of *State of Siege* simply will not wash.

Thus the underground executes Santore only as a last resort, when their government and the United States leave them no alternative; to spare him would make the revolutionaries look ridiculous and impotent. Characteristically, while we see the Brazilian and Uruguayan governments torturing the freedom fighters as well as murdering a few, we do not see the execution of Santore. This has been called tastefulness but is, I am afraid, tendentiousness. And it won't do to say that in *The Confession* Costa-Gavras showed us the evils of Communism exactly as he now shows us the evils of American imperialism and its puppets. In the earlier film, the Communists were not presented as monolithically bad; there were nasty *Stalinist* torturers and killers, but if only the *anti-Stalinist* victims were to come into power someday, as they might, the Iron Curtain would rise on a rosy spectacle. In the U.S.-dominated Latin America of *State of Siege,* the underground is not part of the system, and *all* parts of the system are bad: the few liberal deputies in Parliament are outshouted and overruled.

The film has every right to be anti-American, only let no one pretend that it isn't. My own question concerns the efficacy of such filmmaking. As entertainment, it is too meager. As art, it is much too impersonal. And as propaganda, it preaches to the converted, but can it sway the unbelievers? "A bunch of Greeks, Italians, and Frenchmen," I hear Middle America sneering, "probably all Commies, make a film in Chile (where else?) about what is supposed to have happened in Uruguay. What do they know? And how fair do you think they are to us?" Even as propaganda, art is more effective.

And art is what *Love* is. This Hungarian film, directed gracefully by Károly Makk, conveys much more vividly the agonies of life under a totalitarian regime. There is less political terror than petty meanness that, on no specified charges, indefinitely imprisons a loving husband and affectionate son, inflicting the horrors of separation and loneliness. The man's widowed old mother is sickly and may die any day; his wife, to keep the old lady going, tells her her son is in America directing a movie, and actually fakes letters and costly gifts from him to his proud, happy mother. Theirs is a bristling, precarious relationship of shared love for an absent man, each woman jealous of the other yet also admiring and, ultimately, loving of the other.

How condescending the old lady is, how grandly she takes her daughter-in-law's sacrifices for granted! And while the latter must humor her, she loses, as an undesirable's wife, her job, her friends, and the best part of her apartment, requisitioned and assigned to others. But she keeps her dignity, and out of despair and anger fashions more love for the old lady, who, in turn, teaches her how to cling to life and endure. The two women share memories of a copious past, imagine a beautifully fictitious present, and hope for something of a future. As gratuitously as they jailed him, the authorities release the husband. His return as a broken starveling, his hardly daring to aspire to his wife's renewed love, are almost unbearably moving because they are stripped to a minimum of words and to awkward, tentative gestures completely bereft of histrionics.

The film is buoyantly witty in the midst of its earnestness; its remarkable screenplay is, even after heavy losses in the subtitles, recognizably the work of a major novelist, Tibor Déry. (It is actually based on two short stories by Déry, cleverly combined.) The acting is superlative. Lili Darvas, drolly stiff and stubborn as the mother, Austrian by birth and speaking flawed Hungarian, constructs from petty tyrannies, barely smiling satisfactions, and crumbs of grudging praise a great inner luminosity. Iván Darvas (no relation) fills the screen with the fearful emptiness of his eyes that gradually fill up with humble happiness. Best of all is Mari Törőcsik as the wife. There is such vitality in her despair, humor in her rages, adorable pigheadedness in her generosities, and indomitableness in the fidelity she comically threatens to discard, that she embodies the epitome of vulnerable, buffeted, inextirpable love. Love, manifold yet one, is a felt presence in this film that quietly but devastatingly condemns political injustice.

April 30, 1973

Offbeat or Deadbeat?

ONE OF my favorite schoolboy boners runs: "Q.: Who said 'Kiss me Hardy!'? A.: Laurel." "Kiss me, Hardy!" were, of course, Lord Nelson's dying words to his trusty second-in-command; but *The Nelson Affair,* the movie version of Terence Rattigan's play, *A Bequest to the Nation,* sorely lacks the presence of Stan and Oliver. With them, it could have been deliberately parodic instead of unintentionally ludicrous. Directed by the British television director, James Cellan Jones, from Rattigan's own screenplay, the movie is so bad as to be occasionally funny, but not nearly often enough.

Hal Wallis, the American producer of pseudoprestigious trash, ravages British history: *Becket, Anne of the Thousand Days,* and *Mary, Queen of Scots* were progressively worse travesties, but *The Nelson Affair* is downright repugnant. In bygone days, cinematic pseudohistory was always, in the most vulgar sense of the word, a romanticization: in Sir Alexander Korda's *That Hamilton Woman* (1941), for instance, Laurence Olivier and Vivien Leigh turned Nelson and Lady Hamilton into wonderfully storm-tossed and star-crossed lovers, the glamour of whose relationship more than compensated for the sadness and sordidness of their respective ends. The new trend is to make everything seedier and nastier than even history could make it, and earn high marks for realism.

Rattigan's Emma Hamilton, however—a boozing, brawling, slatternly, foulmouthed fishwife—is not much more believable than the radiant crea- 145 ture of high romance. Nor is this Horatio Nelson—decent, pompous, conventional—more convincing than the matchless hero of quasi-legendary history. In both cases a formula, a fabrication to suit the presumed temper of the times, takes over, and no effort is made to let the imagination reinvent the truth. Even after her fabled beauty had faded and the woman had become coarse, there must have been some remnant of femininity in Lady Hamilton; but this Emma, as played by Glenda Jackson, is a termagant and guttersnipe whom the most sex-starved old seadog would think twice before accosting. On a wall, we perceive Romney's breathtaking portrait with the actress's idealized face painted in. That idealized Jackson face is a sacrilege; the real one is a scandal.

Peter Finch's Nelson is straight man to Miss Jackson's farcical spitfire—a pretty dull performance. Yet what finally does in Finch, as well as everyone else, is the dialogue: congealed *sauce piquante* over a basic witlessness, as if a little rancid seasoning could turn stale mutton into venison. And Jones's direction is amateurish, especially in the Trafalgar battle scenes, which were not even shot in a studio tank but, manifestly, on dry land. Margaret Leighton does a professional job with the thankless role of Lady Nelson, and Gerry Fisher's color cinematography is competent.

After that, the merest trifle, like Truffaut's *Such a Gorgeous Kid Like Me,* is a welcome diversion. It is sad that Truffaut should be so enamored of rubbishy novels (showing that, for all his intelligence, he rather lacks taste) as to base film after film upon them. It worked twice, in *Shoot the Piano Player* and *Jules and Jim;* it also yielded such clinkers as *The Bride Wore Black, Mississippi Mermaid,* and *Two English Girls.* The present film is made from an American novel of the same title by one Henry Farrell, and although Truffaut and his coscenarist, Jean-Loup Dabadie, have wrought numerous changes, the triviality remains.

The basic idea is not without merit: a sexy, irresistible, amoral girl's progress from conquest to conquest; her rise, despite minor setbacks, from obscurity to the heights of success over the dead or incarcerated bodies of various fall guys and patsies. It is an old story, but can always be made new. Here it does acquire a slangy flavor and some fresh twists: because Camille Bliss, the Machiavellian heroine, is only moderately clever and wears her untrustworthiness practically on her sleeve, her victims have to blind themselves and do most of her dirty work for her. When one among them finally sees the light—an absurd little romantic ratcatcher played amusingly and touchingly by Charles Denner—he falls, as if by divine providence, off a church tower. It is almost as if we were living in a Sadian universe, where virtuous Justines are abhorrent to the Creator himself and struck down by lightning bolts, while the evil Juliettes triumph.

There are two main problems with the film. Although it is funny, it is not all that funny, or that original in its gags; and though we are meant to sympathize with the young sociologist who falls haplessly in love with Camille, he is too much of a moral and intellectual booby to elicit real sympathy. Yet the film does move along at a splendidly breakneck pace;

even when we do not particularly admire what is included, we marvel at the judiciousness of what is omitted. As Camille, Bernadette Lafont is no longer the juicy young strumpet of *Le Beau Serge,* but she retains a toothsome body and a humorous energy, both of which she brandishes with true flair. André Dussollier, still a drama student, is perhaps even paler than his part, but color is supplied by Pierre William Glenn's cinematography and Georges Delerue's first satisfying score in years.

May 14, 1973

The Dignity of Ordinary Life

YASUJIRO OZU, best known for *Tokyo Story,* is the most haunting filmmaker I know. With almost unnoticeable pinpricks, he insinuates himself ever deeper into our consciousness, touching us a little here, amusing us a little there, making us face up to ourselves everywhere. Gradually, we fall under his beneficent spell, understanding life as seldom before, realizing the smallness of our achievements, but also the greatnesses in that smallness, which is all we have. Very often in Ozu's films people wear an expression that is inscrutable—not because it is Oriental, but because it is rock-bottom human. It might be the outline of a wry and weary smile or the prelude to tears, or just bemused abandonment to the buffetings of life. It is the Ozu expression, and occurs not only in his characters' faces—his very films are impregnated with it. As we watch them, it imprints itself also on us.

Although we may not remember his individual films clearly—they are so very much part of his recurring concerns as to merge into a shimmering continuum—we do recall scenes, moments, and the bittersweet awareness that informs them. What makes these self-effacingly titled films so universal and basic, so totally what soap opera would be if only it knew how: art in its primary colors, embracing every human situation, fitted to everyone? Ozu's films keep us continually cognizant of our life span as a whole; they show how people change yet remain themselves: grow up, grow aware, grow old, grow resigned—not necessarily in that order, and not always all the way.

These films are in touch with childhood and old age no less than with what lies between. If not in a single person, then in a family circle or group of friends, we see all the ages of man connecting and interacting. And even as all the stages are juggled as neatly as a prestidigitator's balls, we realize there are not, after all, so many of them—that life is shorter, plainer, sillier, and sadder than we would think; yet also sweeter, even in its sadness. For it is the fathoming of this sadness that enables us to make that Ozu face with which we accomplish, as best and most gracefully we can, the transition to the inevitable next stage. Put most simply, Ozu paints with primary colors, but applies them with utmost subtlety. Everything in his films is profoundly telling, yet remains only a detail. Even death, when it is recorded, comes   147 imperceptibly: less as an event than as a transition. Ozu seems to deal in wavelets; what he captures is a flow.

As people change, so does the Japan of the forties, fifties, and early sixties that he records with such affectionate melancholy. The traditional values are slowly disappearing as Japan becomes Westernized; the process is, as in a film (though not one by Ozu—he uses no such devices), a kind of slow crossfade from one image to another. Or, perhaps, a superimposure, where old manners and trappings mingle with new ones. But the new is gaining on all fronts. Ozu has often been identified with the principal patriarch in his movies—usually played by Chishu Ryu, a lean, delicate-featured man, diffident, affable, and philosophical—surrendering graciously, yet not without regret for the old modes, to the unavoidable. Ozu, however, was quite Westernized, as Masahiro Shinoda, who used to be his assistant before becoming a prominent director himself, has told me; so much so that, instead of soy sauce, he put butter on his rice.

An Autumn Afternoon was Ozu's fifty-third and last film, made in 1962, shortly before the director's death from cancer at the age of sixty. It concerns Hirayama (Chishu Ryu), a widowed business executive; his daughter Michiko, who keeps house for him; and Kazuo, his student son. There is also Koichi, the elder son, married to the spirited Akiko and plagued by money problems that keep them sparring, though in the end Akiko always gets her way. Hirayama eats and drinks at a restaurant with his two best friends: Kawai, another businessman, who urges him to agree to a good match that he could arrange for the twenty-four-year-old Michiko; and Professor Horei, who has just married a girl only a couple of years older than his own married daughter.

The main locations are Hirayama's office, his home, Kawai's house, Koichi and Akiko's apartment, the abovementioned restaurant, and Torys Bar. After he and his friends arrange a dinner for an old schoolteacher of theirs nicknamed The Gourd, Hirayama has to take the drunken old man home to his noodle shop, run by his joyless spinster daughter, who has grown old and sour caring for him. There Hirayama meets a man who served on the destroyer he commanded during the war; the delighted fellow invites him for a drink at Torys Bar, where the barmaid reminds Hirayama of his dead wife—"if you don't look very closely." The former chief petty officer plays the old navy march on the jukebox, and they reminisce and muse about what would have happened had Japan won the war. "We'd be in New York now, the real thing, not an imitation," the younger man speculates, "and the blue-eyed ones would be wearing wigs and chewing gum while plucking their samisens." "It's lucky we lost," Hirayama remarks.

Actually, the film begins at the office, where a secretary is about to get married and leave. She is twenty-four—Michiko's age. Yet Hirayama insists on thinking of his daughter as a baby, so he can hold on to her. Through a number of vaguely, sometimes imperceptibly related episodes, we follow Hirayama's awakening to the fact that Michiko must go off and marry if she is not to become a cold, unhappy creature like The Gourd's old-maid daughter. Not that married life is all that smooth and easy, as we see by Koichi and Akiko's example, and the sheepish way the elderly Horie defers to his young wife. But it is right for Michiko to leave.

Not much of a plot, yet it all hangs together, even such apparently random incidents as Akiko and Koichi's spats over some secondhand golf clubs that Koichi wants to buy but cannot really afford. For it turns out that Miura, the intermediary in the golf-club deal, is the man Michiko has secretly loved. So Koichi takes him to lunch and sounds him out; it emerges that he is already engaged. He had been interested in Michiko, until Koichi had implied that she was still too young. "It is my fault!" Koichi exclaims ruefully, but soon amends this to "It's the hand of fate," as they settle down to serious eating and drinking. "It is *my* fault," old Hirayama later declares, but is promptly relieved when his daughter receives the news with composure. Upstairs in her room, Michiko cries, and keeps heartbreakingly twisting a tape measure around one hand, then around the other. She will accept a prearranged marriage.

Always life goes on. Ozu photographs it mostly from that famous low angle of his, as if the camera were squatting on the tatami, watching everyone and everything go by. This static use of the camera is riveting: the viewer must remain more passively observant, a bit detached, as meanings rather than happenings register on him. Locales are established by long shots, showing first the surrounding outdoors, then the indoors where the real business of living takes place. Finally the characters appear, usually in medium shots, and frequently looking straight into the camera. There are no dissolves and no tracking shots, minimal pans and only the necessary crosscutting. We seldom go outdoors. The camera just squats in those half dozen or so locations successively, observing and listening. Life meets it more than halfway, though withholding most of its climaxes. We never even glimpse the man Michiko marries.

But we do get revealing surprises. After having seen Michiko mostly in Western garb, we go up with Hirayama and Koichi to her room on her wedding day; in a corner, we barely note part of a mannequin clothed in the elaborate traditional wedding attire. There is a reverse-angle shot, and the mannequin turns out to be Michiko, immobile and more exquisite and pathetic than ever, yet also resolute. "Be a good wife and be happy," her father lamely instructs her, exactly what he said to the secretary who was getting married. How poor our best wisdom is; but at least the wedding costume links Michiko to the tradition, to all those women married off and told to make the most of it.

There are about as many lighthearted sequences in *An Autumn Afternoon* as grave ones. Yet a tearful scene will contain something droll, and in the middle of a gay one something claws at our hearts. Often the moment is both funny and sad, as when the barmaid, seeing the formally dressed Hirayama arrive from his daughter's wedding, asks whether he's been to a funeral. The humor can be tough, as when, at the end, young Kazuo, from his bed, warns his father, still drinking away in his formal attire, to go easy on the sake—"Can't have you dying yet!" Though Kazuo promises to fix breakfast in the morning, we know that, for all her domineering, Michiko   149 took better care of the old man. Hirayama drinks, sings the naval march, and almost dozes off at the table. "Yes, all alone in the end," he murmurs sadly.

The camera cuts to several quick shots of Michiko's vacated room, where her abandoned pier glass remains—as if to reflect the emptiness into infinity. Hirayama goes into the kitchen and pours himself some cold, weak tea out of the kettle. Then he sits down at the kitchen table with his back to us: he and the film have nothing further to say. We have had intimations of his life back to his school days and forward to his lonely death. The color photography is beautifully unassertive; the music honky-tonk but suggestive of life's ultimate indifference. The acting is superlative. Ozu could not have asked for a finer epitaph.

May 28, 1973

Caveat to the General

The Day of the Jackal, Fred Zinnemann's thriller, based on Frederick Forsyth's bestseller about an attempted assassination of Charles de Gaulle, is much better than I expected. The film concerns the efforts in 1963 of an English hired killer paid half a million dollars by the OAS to gun down the general. He is an elegant, cold, unshowily efficient professional, with a multitude of skills but no supernatural powers, who goes about his work in the most businesslike manner. Kenneth Ross's script is spare and intelligent; it details the successive stages of plotting and detection meticulously, shifting ingeniously from strand to strand of the various actions that make up the web of events, and so creating a feeling of breathless simultaneity.

There is no suspense of the ordinary kind, for we know that De Gaulle was not killed. But we are kept involved in the techniques and stratagems that the several parties use: the OAS, led by some not unclever fanatics; the French governmental, military, and police forces, which finally come to depend on Inspector Lebel, the sort of undashing French policeman (a figure that goes back to Louis Jouvet in Clouzot's *Quai des Orfevres*); the assisting Britishers across the Channel; the sundry accomplices, such as gunsmiths, forgers, even ordinary citizens inveigled by the assassin; and, finally, the killer himself, operating under the code name Jackal. The complaint that this film lacks Hitchcockian wit seems to me irrelevant, for it capitalizes on something else.

That something is the fascinating interaction of skill and luck, of know-how and pure chance. We are allowed to witness and speculate upon the way the greatest cleverness is often less important than sheer good or bad luck; on what little incidents and coincidences life and death—the very fate of nations—may depend. It is the ironies of fate, the happy guesses or miscalculations, the sudden windfalls or stumbling blocks, the labyrinthine ways by which plans and people reach their unforeseeable ends, that *The Day of the Jackal* traces with exemplary nonpartisanship. The Jackal is not made particularly likable (but, then, neither was De Gaulle), yet he earns our grudging admiration for his cold-blooded temerity, his great versatility and inventiveness, his professional dedication to his monstrous task, his controlled viciousness that kills only when necessary.

Zinnemann sagely keeps the human element at a minimum, concentrating instead on a process and counterprocess, on the minuteness and unpredictability of the events that tip the scale now in favor of the Jackal, now in favor of Inspector Lebel. The film is, in other words, as nearly like a documentary as a story film can be. Its only flaws are the improbabilities, impossibilities, and occasional unexplained bits that always dog this genre; they are relatively infrequent here, but they are troublesome. The final irony, in particular, proves a manifest phony on closer inspection. Still, much of the film is persuasive and all of the 142 minutes hold one's interest; there is, moreover, a prevailing restraint and finesse that suggest the requisite violence and sexuality quite sufficiently without unduly dwelling on them. I for one would have liked to know how the Jackal seduced the chilly baroness, but I can sacrifice such points to matters of graver import.

The acting is impressively smooth throughout from a Franco-British cast whose accents do not always make sense, but whose acting always makes up for this. Edward Fox is a fitting Jackal: not too charming, sinister, brutish, or urbane, but enough of all of these, and consistently cool and lucid. He looks like a cross between Burt Lancaster and Jean-Pierre Aumont, so that his very face is a neat synthesis of tough guy and subtle technician. Lebel is played by Michel Lonsdale, the Englishman who became an archetypal French actor in the films of Truffaut, Malle, and others; heard for the first time in English, he makes one wonder whether that slight French accent is put on or, by now, inescapable. Lonsdale's is the only less than perfect performance, a trifle too studiedly teddy-bearish and rumpled.

I especially enjoyed Alan Badel, Tony Britton, Michel Auclair, Olga Georges-Picot, Cyril Cusack, and Delphine Seyrig. The entire cast of histrionic celebrities and near-celebrities, however, achieves not only fluid ensemble work but also that anonymity required for such quasi-documentary filmmaking.

Still, there is no getting away from the fact that when the outcome is foreknown (as also in *State of Siege*), this kind of movie incurs a loss. For the only thing that could absolve the film entirely from the need for conventional suspense would be art—something the movie neither has nor, fortunately, pretends to. Yet it need only be compared to a similar film about hired assassins and international intrigue, Michael Winner's *Scorpio*, to reveal unmistakably how chaste, sensible, and suggestive it is. Photographed in no-nonsense colors by Jean Tournier, and edited at a lively but unrushed pace by Ralph Kemplen, it is a civilized and thought-provoking treatment of a highly uncivilized activity.

A Woman Who Left, a Man Who Stayed

IT IS NOT surprising that Ibsen's *A Doll's House* should enjoy such renewed popularity all of a sudden—with a current film version based on a successful off-Broadway and London revival of the play, and another movie treatment due here shortly. The work's supposed message fits the women's liberation movement's aims, and its heroine, Nora, has been the symbol of the new, emancipated woman ever since her first appearance in 1879. From then on, women leaving their husbands, and perhaps also their children, had Nora's name on their lips for their battle cry, and Ibsen's rebel doll-woman became the patron saint of reformers fighting for feminine rights.

Yet, when you come right down to it, Nora is a curious women's libber. She leaves because her husband, Torvald Helmer, refuses to assume chivalrously the guilt she incurred on his behalf, and rants and roars instead about the scandal and setbacks he must endure. It is Torvald's selfishness and lack of gallantry, rather than his narrow patriarchalism, that drive Nora away. But Nora, too, is a fine little egoist. When her friend and admirer, Dr. Rank, reveals that he is dying of syphilis inherited from his father, she proves quite callous, being interested only in whether he might not first bequeath to her enough money to pay off her debt. When he ever so faintly hints at some erotic compensation, she is shocked. Rank, of course, is not very generous, either. But that is Ibsen's point. Most people are not brave or strong or nice; their unselfishness, if any, lasts only until it is put to a real test.

Beyond that, to be sure, is the theme of the doll house (which is what the play's title should be in America, but the Britishism "doll's house" has stuck). Ibsen did not believe in a marriage based on lies: on role-playing, make-believe, and childish games, such as Nora's pretending to be Torvald's little squirrel. This is why Nora replies to Torvald's "Nobody sacrifices his honor, not even for the person he loves" with "Millions of women *have.*" The point is that in a world of dishonesty, women have been forced into still greater dishonesty by being rushed into marriage without first acquiring experience, self-knowledge, and concomitant pride; rectify this, and some, though not all, hypocrisy will be eliminated. As Michael Meyer has correctly noted, *"A Doll's House* is no more about women's rights than . . . *An Enemy of the People* [is] about public hygiene. Its theme is the need for every individual to find out what kind of person he or she really is and to become that person." It is, therefore, to the credit of Patrick Garland's direction and Christopher Hampton's adaptation that the women's lib angle is not played up in this movie version, as it is in the one by Joseph Losey.

Still, the basic problem remains: that you virtually cannot transpose a great play successfully to the screen. In the play, for example, you never see Nora's children—wisely, because it makes their mother's abandoning them more acceptable. In setting all of the action in the Helmer living room, the playwright conveys the notion that he is not telling you the whole story, only such significant parts of it as take place in this strategic spot. Once, however, the camera starts moving around the house, including the nursery (which, in a film, seems inevitable), and even steps outside (which, though avoidable, happens here), we begin to wonder why so little is shown us—why, for instance, there is no more than an occasional glimpse of the children, and why nothing is made of their mother's farewell to them. The conventions of the stage work toward making the story more credible; the conventions of film work against it, at least in its present form.

The problem is compounded by the director and the cast. Garland has no cinematic experience and does a great many things schematically, as a neophyte would. Thus in the great final confrontation scene there is steady cutting from closeup to closeup of whoever is speaking, until we get, predictably, a capping two-shot in the end. Then, to preserve the famous final stage direction, we hear the front door closing behind Nora from Torvald's point of view—or, rather, nonview—as the camera peers into the empty hallway and comes to rest on Torvald. A bolder director would have ended with Nora, and disturbed us more by suggesting the ostracism, hardships, and life in a *déclassé* demimonde that await her.

As for the cast, Edith Evans may well be too old to be the children's nanny, and Ralph Richardson, with what seems to be Parkinson's disease (does he have it, or is this his way of suggesting terminal syphilis?), is certainly too old for Dr. Rank. Anthony Hopkins would be a very good Torvald if he did not try too hard to make him jolly and likable and downright cute. When he is serious, though, he is fine: conventional and stuffy but not insufferably smug; self-centered but not, like so many other Torvalds, to the point of repugnance. Although Anna Massey is a decent Mrs. Linde, Denholm Elliott makes Krogstad unduly slimy rather than just ordinary and desperate.

Claire Bloom was an enchanting Nora on stage; she just about carried off the near-impossible task of growing up in the play's short time span and changing from self-avowed squirrel and secret macaroon-eater into a sad yet determined woman willing to pay the high price of freedom. Her performance on screen is just as good, but the camera records her age with merciless candor, and Miss Bloom is simply too old for the part, so that some of her youthful mannerisms affect us unpleasantly. Arthur Ibbetson, a usually competent cinematographer, has apparently been instructed to keep his colors cool to convey the chill of Scandinavia; his palette of almost unrelieved blues and greens makes the Helmer home not so much a doll house as a sparsely lit aquarium.

Following a troubled history with our Treasury Department, the Cuban film, *Memories of Underdevelopment,* has finally reached us five years after it was made. It is an ingeniously constructed, quietly eloquent film, whose only and very minor fault it is to leave us excessively hungry for more. Sergio, a wealthy, upper-middle-class Cuban, refuses to join his wife, parents, and friends in emigrating to the U.S. when Castro takes over. He is no Marxist and even less a revolutionary, merely someone fed up with the banality of bourgeois existence. Once long ago he let the right girl slip by while he 153 concentrated on acquisitiveness; now he is bored with the material goods he will soon be stripped of anyway.

He has turned into an interested but skeptical bystander, vaguely deluding himself about becoming a writer, but really kept alive in his idleness by curiosity concerning the new regime's ability to remedy Cuba's underdevelopment, and by some real or imaginary sexual escapades. He remembers the past with amusement, observes the present with irony, and reflects about the future with the detachment of someone who no longer belongs anywhere.

The script, from the novel by Eduardo Desnoes, was written by him and the able director Tomás Gutierrez Alea. A great deal of teeming, multifarious material has been packed into some 90 minutes of running time, giving the film an extremely rich, as it were novelistic, texture. Documentary footage of the Bay of Pigs invasion and the subsequent trials, bits of staged but very realistic cinéma-vérité, voice-over interior monologues, flashbacks, clandestinely recorded tapes of marital fracases, brief scenes from the protagonist's fantasy world, overlappings of past and present, television screens showing Castro hurling defiance and U.S. race riots, titles introducing the names of certain characters as chapter headings, short takes nevertheless containing key incidents—these and other devices are intermingled smoothly and often amusingly to give the film the shape of a neatly rolled-up ball made of variously colored pieces of string: the disparate incidents become unified because they are the constituents of a human life.

The film is daringly free of party-line cant, though its cinematic freedom is more impressive even than its political one. Gutierrez Alea's camera can glide broodingly over the past-ridden accumulation of objects in Sergio's apartment, or dart about the streets to the accompaniment of tart observations by the hero. Its sense of rhythm is matched by its sense of humor, sometimes irreverently reiterating an awkward image on a screen grown obsessive or redundant, sometimes saucily foreshortening an episode that might have used some lingering over. Little discrepancies creep in between images and words; political or social paradoxes are fixed in a verbal or visual epigram.

The characters are sharply but not unsympathetically observed, including those who are morally unprepossessing; situations and dialogue are seldom lacking in wit or speculative penetrancy. The acting is always spontaneous yet proficient, whether it is Sergio Corrieri's protagonist quietly and sardonically going to seed, or Daisy Granados's superficial, silly, ultimately touching little schemer who almost traps him into marriage. There is a sparingly used but remarkably evocative score by Leo Brower, and the black-and-white photography by Ramón Suarez captures equally well the exhausting white heat of the exteriors and the enervating shadowiness of the interiors. If *Memories of Underdevelopment* lacks a clear resolution, the density of its texture and the very palpability of its aliveness are nonetheless immensely satisfying.

Working-Class Woes

COWINNER with *Scarecrow* at the Cannes Festival, *The Hireling* is certainly the better film of the two, faint as that praise may be. Like Joseph Losey's unfortunate *The Go-Between*, it is based on a novel by L. P. Hartley, and likewise exudes a subdued but rancorous class hatred that, in one way or another, infests every scene. The plot is simplicity itself. A neurotic young widow, Lady Franklin, hires a struggling chauffeur to drive her about in his gorgeous but as yet unpaid-for Rolls-Royce. She is at odds with her world, especially with her egotistical widowed mother, and takes some comfort in the sturdy simplicity of the hired driver.

Leadbetter, as the fellow is called, thinks that Helen Franklin is falling for him because she rides up front and indulges in candid talks with him. This misunderstanding grows until Leadbetter is rejected in an acutely painful scene. Lady Franklin is going to marry Captain Cantrip, an unscrupulous but socially acceptable opportunist. In a frenzy, Leadbetter beats up his successful rival, then proceeds to wreck the Rolls in a symbolic massacre. He drunkenly drives it into a wall again and again while singing the army songs of World War I, in which he distinguished himself, and which marks the beginning of the end for the old, aristocratic England.

The screenplay by Wolf Mankowitz probably oversimplifies and exacerbates Hartley's tortured indirections: though I do not know this particular novel, I know Mankowitz all too well. The young director, Alan Bridges, a newcomer from television, has captured the atmosphere and look of England in the twenties most conscientiously; but he wears his social purpose, if not on his sleeve, on almost every frame of his film. During the early scenes, when the lady is being driven about suburban and rural sections of England, no opportunity is missed to surround the Rolls—that stately English home on wheels—with images of abject poverty: peasants and workers moiling slavishly, or milling about in front of dilapidated hovels, or gazing at the lady's progress with hollow stares. The color cinematography by Michael Reed is moody and evocative, yet the effect is that of a dyspeptic British Bruegel training a lowering camera on a Dance of Death-in-Life.

Most effective is the film's very beginning, with the recently widowed, guilt-ridden Helen Franklin being released from a genteel sanatorium after a nervous collapse. The awkwardness of the staff's attempts to reconcile professional firmness with social deference toward their near-somnambulistic patient is fraught with eerie humor. Sarah Miles—known hitherto for her excellence in relatively simple, bitchy parts, and for her routine competence in all others—achieves genuine histrionic stature through a splendid fusion of dazed abulia and lurking vulnerability in her portrayal of Lady Franklin. Beginning with a cow-eyed, quasi-inert anxiety prone to instant relapse, she reactivates Helen by fine, tremulous degrees, first into humanity, then into womanliness, thence into giddy flirtatiousness and, finally, into upper-class, 155 commanding toughness. But Miss Miles never obscures the basic decency that the character maintains even in her misguidedness.

Almost equally good is Robert Shaw's Leadbetter: slightly ambitious, ever so faintly calculating, and a bit of a bully, but with a cockiness that does not exclude human warmth and a rather touching frangibility. Shaw, an old Pinterian hand, knows how to make inscrutability perform for him, how to let a single seed of irony sprout from a fallow field of noncommittal imperturbability, and how to be threateningly sexual even while executing some menial or humdrum task. His final intoxication with liquor, love turned to hatred, and a sense of social outrage is brilliantly managed. The ludicrous, piecemeal demolition of that noble Rolls contains in equal measure comic absurdity and an awesome lust for destruction that may, soon, cease to be inward-directed.

Fine cameo performances are delivered also by Elizabeth Sellars, as Helen's mother, whose chill envy of her daughter's youth masquerades as carping maternal concern, and Peter Egan, who makes the feckless Cantrip indomitable by that spineless, impudently graceful insinuation that somehow infiltrates stones. Yet the reason that *The Hireling* isn't better than it is, or even as good as the foregoing paragraphs imply, is that the nature of class hatred is only hinted at and not profoundly explored.

It would have been possible perhaps simply to establish this class hatred and allow things to work themselves out. But once you start scrutinizing it, you must analyze its workings more incisively, deeply, and, yes, poetically than this film—whose makers may not even be aware of how corroded by class hatred they themselves are—begins to do. *The Hireling* steers an uneasy and unsatisfying middle course, and is particularly remiss about developing its potentially revealing minor characters. It latches on to footling irritations instead, and feverishly attempts to inflate and aggrandize them. The mere interruption of an upper-class conversation by workers banging away outside the windows is stretched and underlined to a degree of portentousness the incident cannot be expected to bear. Marc Wilkinson's score itself, good as it initially is, succumbs to this inflationary mania.

The big spring disappointment is Lindsay Anderson's new film, *O Lucky Man!*, which has already had more phases than the waning moon. It started out at Cannes with a running time of 192 minutes, decreased during New York previews to 178 minutes, and wound up being released at 166. Though I saw the middle version, longer or shorter are meangingless terms where at best only 30 minutes are salvageable. The idea for the film comes from its star, Malcolm McDowell, on whose early misadventures several episodes are based. Like Anderson's last film, *If . . .* (it also has the same scenarist and cinematographer), *O Lucky Man!* moves from heightened realism to disheveled surrealism and back again, until it ends—this time not with a bloodbath, but with one of those Felliniesque cop-outs.

Mick Travis, the youthful hero, is a sort of working-class British cross between Candide and Sammy Glick, albeit neither quite benighted enough for the former nor cunning enough for the latter. The film is a kind of "How to Fail in Business Without Really Trying," with Mick enjoying numerous tiny successes that quickly turn into whopping fiascoes. He goes from coffee salesman to spy suspect; from near-victim of a mad scientist to lover of the feckless daughter of an unscrupulous multimillionaire; from being that mogul's secretary to becoming his fall guy; from prison to the movie studios. The film concludes with an open call for actors in an audition hall, presided over by Lindsay Anderson himself. He tells Mick, who catches his eye, to smile; when Mick asks what there is to smile about, he is gruffly coerced into smiling. The audition turns into a ball—laughter, shouting, dancing, and balloons (getting to be the dreariest of film platitudes) going off merrily, while the entire cast of *O Lucky Man!*, the picture that is about to be made, gleefully rampages away.

There are several directorial tricks involved. A pop composer and singer, Alan Price, backed up by his group, is often heard, and fairly often seen, performing the film's score. Sometimes the scene is a recording studio, sometimes the rock group's digs, sometimes the van in which the musicians travel; occasionally this is worked into the plot, frequently it is just there. The device proves wearying, particularly since only a couple of the songs have satirical and musical bite.

Again, the leading actors keep popping up throughout the movie in different parts. Some reviewers found this doubling fascinating; it strikes me only as arbitrary. By way of variation on the device, Helen Mirren, who plays Patricia, the spoiled heiress, always appears in the *same* part—which doesn't please me much either, since I find her singularly ungifted and unappetizing. But at least in this film, unlike in her two previous ones, she unveils only four fifths of her remarkably gross body.

O Lucky Man! is pretentious and excruciatingly monotonous. Its class warfare is couched in inadequate satire, and its absurdism is never exhilarating. David Sherwin's script offers no new insights into corruption, social strife, venality, obtuseness, mutual mistrust, the triumph of carnality over feeling, and other ill-assorted targets—far too many for anything more than random potshots. The desperate rushing from episode to disparate episode without developing anything would be justified only if the vignettes built up to some spectacular climax or punchline; but they don't. Some of them do not even register clearly, like the *caritas Romana* sequence, where I find it hard to determine what the vicar's wife feeding the hungry hero by suckling him is supposed to signify.

Good actors get little opportunity to act here. Ralph Richardson is not allowed to make more than a stereotype out of the rapacious nabob, and his other role amounts to nothing. Rachel Roberts has had the third and best of her bits cut, and Arthur Lowe can do little with three meager roles, one of them (by today's standards, rather objectionably) in black-face. Malcolm McDowell is adroit and winning as usual, but Mick is a dimensionless and predictable booby with whom our patience wears out quickly. Some quite notable character actors do their level best with even sparser and more thankless parts.

Anderson must have been improvising the film as he went along, incorporating driblets of his composer's life as well as his star's, and goodness knows what else. As the movie fluctuates between class hatred and all-around misanthropy, naturalism and wild hyperbole, bitter earnestness and jaded nonchalance, the sense of pointless accretion becomes oppressive and finally smothering. Only Miroslav Ondriček's color photography works to perfection; the cinematographer is surely the Czech freeze's greatest gift to Western filmmaking.

July 9–23, 1973

Tatty Tati and Beri Berri

WITH *Playtime,* Jacques Tati finally becomes what he has long threatened to be: a crashing bore. *Playtime,* released abroad in 1968, is considered by many his masterpiece. It certainly is a major effort. For this wan satire on contemporary living, Tati had to build a section of a modern city of glass and steel, including high-rise apartment buildings, office towers, a replica of Orly airport, a luxury restaurant, and streets that include a traffic circle around which traffic (rather unfunnily) keeps biting its own tail. Much had to be fully, functionally constructed, and the film took three years to make. It takes about equally long to sit through.

In a preface added to the English-language version, Tati explains his intentions, always an evil omen—remember Vadim's preface to *Les Liaisons Dangereuses* and Clouzot's to *La Vérité?* We are informed that the comic hero can no longer be one individual, Chaplin and Keaton having done that sufficiently; it is now humankind in general, little people resisting, or becoming prey to, universal mechanization. But all this, regrettably, is only an excuse for not having a comic plot, a humorous narrative (always Tati's chief problem), and scattering one's shots all over the place in the hope of hitting something funny somewhere. And for all this, Tati, in his Hulot persona, is still a sad throwback to Keaton and other silent comedians. What soundtrack *Playtime* has is a sorry hodgepodge—snatches of poorly synced polyglot babble indistinctly blown about on the winds of despair.

Playtime takes place in and among five main locations: the airport, where absurd foreigners arrive as arrogant VIPs or pitifully herded-about tourist groups; an office building, where Hulot wanders about forever missing the functionary he is looking for; a trade fair, where Hulot and others are buttonholed and browbeaten by various hectoring exhibitors; opening night at a fancy, newfangled restaurant, where everything—service, cuisine, the building itself—goes to pieces, but the guests live it up undeterred; and a drugstore, where one rallies for a wee-hour snack before the tourist buses move on.

158 A few bits of slapstick are genuinely hilarious, but they are so very rare

that one experiences Tati's company not as that of a truly witty person, but as that of a bore who has memorized several good jokes. Routines are stretched out and repeated endlessly, gags fatally resemble other gags of just a few minutes before, what is ridiculed is often a cliché (bossy Germans, sheeplike American tourists, a drunken Texas millionaire brashly treating everybody), much of the humor is not firmly based in reality, and absolutely everything outstays its welcome. Tati himself ambles about as Hulot, not only acting but even looking like a man who has used up his last comic resources. Several other figures crisscrossing the film are equally lackluster, and Barbara Dennek (a bovine German au pair girl whom Tati picked up to play the heroine) looks scarcely good enough for the casting couch, let alone the screen.

There are two bigger problems yet. First, a twice-repeated gag has someone open a soulless glass door to reveal in it a reflection of the Eiffel Tower or Sacré Coeur, which the person blithely ignores. This makes me wonder: In the name of what does Tati lampoon modern architecture and society? Are quixotic eccentricities like the Eiffel Tower and Sacré Coeur that much better than regimented efficiency? Is the bumbling Hulot really superior to the despotic headwaiter or pedantic bureaucrat? And, further, can one still make films that are copies of silent comedies? Can one still compose even good imitation Beethoven symphonies, paint even impeccable Rubens nudes?

You will not want to buy anything at Claude Berri's *Le Sex Shop*, a supposedly delightful little comedy that purports to celebrate the rewards of innocence and marital fidelity in a world of nasty sophisticates, sexual swingers, and perverts. Berri's own screenplay tells the story of Claude (played by Berri), a little Parisian bookstore-owner who is losing money on his business and cannot keep his cute wife Isabelle (Juliet Berto) and cute children in the cute style they are accustomed to. Our *chenouque* (which might be French for schnook) is told by a successful friend to convert his operation into the eponymous *le sex shop* (which is Franglais for a place that sells pornography, erotica, and kinky sex gadgets) because "Proust or positions, a book's a book." He agrees, and is soon adrift on a sea of erotic temptations provided by his sexiest clients, a swinging dentist (Jean-Pierre Marielle) and his sexually multivalent wife (Nathalie Delon), not to mention an adorable lesbian salesgirl (Béatrice Romand) he has hired.

Claude and Isabelle remain pure through temptations that might have fazed a Saint Anthony or a Britomart; but, in order to have it both ways, we are treated to fantasy sequences in the best Woody Allen style, where sex is consummated titillatingly just off-camera, while in reality—Berri's reality, that is—nothing untoward happens. Few jokes come to the rescue of this candied Candide and grisly Griselda, and even Berri's acting and personality are far from prepossessing. The others, however, are deft, notably Berto, Marielle, and Romand, and there is one winsome scene when that fine old character actor Jean Tissier, in charming words and gentlest tones, extols the 159 beauties of violent perversion. We are, at some remove, reminded of Charlus, and fleetingly wonder whether the distance beween Proust and positions might not, after all, be shorter than the film believes. If, indeed, it believes anything.

August 6–September 3, 1973

True and False: Troell and Truffaut

I HOPE that you have seen Jan Troell's magnificent film *The Emigrants*, which is almost a prerequisite for its still more magnificent sequel, *The New Land*. I hope, further, that you saw *The Emigrants* before it was dubbed into English, and that you will rush to *The New Land* before it, too, falls prey to the dubber's dismal trade. But, first, about Jan Troell. At forty-two, he has clearly established himself as second only to Ingmar Bergman among Swedish filmmakers, and so one of the world's finest. He comes from a humble background and was for years a grade-school teacher in his native Malmö, the town in which Bergman first proved himself as director of the City Theatre. By symbolic coincidence, Troell came to live in the very house Bergman had once inhabited.

The most remarkable quality of Troell's films—shared only with those of the great, underestimated Italian master, Ermanno Olmi—is that they make you love not only them but also the man who made them. For they make you deeply conscious of human goodness in a way that is neither saccharine nor dull, neither holier-than-thou nor too-good-to-be-true. Throughout these films, you feel you are in the hands of a human being who cares about other human beings, who renders the truths of their lives without rending the veils of their privacy, who has sympathy even for what he deplores, and the great tact not to skip over the foibles of his favorites, lest they become big, boring saints. Troell's films have such feeling for life and understanding for humankind as to envelop the viewer in a warm friendship with the filmmaker (which he—a shy, retiring man—nowise solicits) and a gentle pride in belonging to that race up there on the screen.

Troell, who coscripts, photographs, edits, and directs all his films, has not fared well in America. His first important short, *Stopover in the Marshlands* (1965), was shown here only at special screenings, even though this superbly accomplished and quietly moving short film may be the best I have ever seen. It is adapted from a story by the great Swedish novelist Eyvind Johnson, whose autobiographical tetralogy, *The Novels About Olof,* became the basis for what is still Troell's favorite film, *Here Is Your Life* (1966). Its 167 minutes were cut to 110 by the American distributor to make it more commercial; it merely made the latter part of the film a truncated mess. Even so, the earlier sections remain among the most beautiful examples of poetic realism I have ever seen on film. The development of a young writer from poor backwoods orphan through a variety of odd, arduous, underpaid jobs—which, however, lead him to sexual, social, and existential self-realization—is followed with the most exquisite blend of toughness and sensitivity, lyricism and wry humor, as a series of tragic and droll episodes point his way toward maturity.

Troell's next film, *Ole dole doff (Eeeny, Meeny, Miny, Moe,* 1968), won the grand prize in Berlin and displayed the great Per Oscarsson in top form, yet it was never bought for this country. It deals with the attrition between a schoolmaster and his pupils who finally drive him to his death. Into it Troell poured his own experiences, even using his old Malmö schoolhouse for the schoolroom scenes. One tetralogy leads to another, and Troell next turned to the masterwork of the other giant of modern Swedish fiction, the recently deceased Vilhelm Moberg, whose four-novel sequence about Swedish immigrants in mid-nineteenth-century America is to the Swedes what *Moby Dick* and *Huckleberry Finn* are to us. Actually, Troell tells me that he feels closer to Johnson's lyricism than to Moberg's epic—which did not, however, prevent him from creating another masterpiece.

The four novels became two long films, *The Emigrants* and *The New Land,* from each of which Warner Brothers made Troell cut some forty-odd minutes for American release. Troell is characteristically modest and generous about this, and says *some* of the cuts may actually constitute improvements, but he does resent those made exclusively to obtain a PG rating. Personally, I resent all the cuts, having never felt more at home with film characters than with the Nilsson family whom Troell follows from being starving peasants in the barren Swedish backwoods to becoming settlers, first struggling then prosperous, in the woodlands of Minnesota.

Sitting alone through *The New Land* in a screening room on the Warner lot at Burbank, I never once looked at my watch or wished the film would end. One is much less easily affected when viewing a film alone, but in that empty little room I repeatedly wept and rejoiced; only upon finishing two of my favorite long novels, *The Magic Mountain* and *Remembrance of Things Past,* did I feel such a sense of loss as at my final leave-taking from Moberg and Troell's Nilssons.

The New Land begins with Karl Oskar, Kristina, and their two surviving children arriving at the miserable hovel on that glorious midwestern land he has acquired for cultivation. There is a harmless quarrel between the devoted couple, as there are going to be other, fiercer ones, often involving Karl Oskar's restless younger brother, Robert, who will leave them to seek gold in the West and come back only to die. But always there will be loving reconciliations. We see the growth of this family through almost insurmountable poverty, their relations with other neighboring settlers and the Indians that come usually peacefully but once in terrible wrath, their involvement with the soil and the harshness or munificence of the seasons, the births and deaths that lead to the final merging with America: shocked, we realize that the language on screen has become English, that the original settlers having died, the Nilssons have imperceptibly turned into non-Swedish-speaking Nelsons.

It is a movemented story, full of incidents that encompass the gamut of our emotional repertoire. Faithfully, though obliquely, it records several important but painful chapters of our history. Yet the greatness of the film lies not chiefly in the excellence of its plot or characterizations, in the majestic sweep of human destinies across a near-empty land to give birth to a society and new civilization; it lies rather in the breathtaking sensitivity to detail in every single scene of this still long film, and in the extraordinary sense of rhythm with which they are joined together. Happy scenes follow sad ones, luminous sequences tread upon tenebrose ones, lively action yields to brooding stasis, words dispel ingrained silence or, conversely, long stillness settles upon speech. But none of this is schematic, deliberate juxtaposition of opposites; everything flows into everything else with appropriate alacrity or reluctance. Consider, for example, a montage of autumn, where the flight formations of wild geese are contrasted with the patterns of falling leaves, one such leaf seen falling in superimposition both in slow motion and at natural speed, so as to evoke that strange compound of durability and transience that is the leaf's life and our own.

Or observe how Troell ends the scene in which Kristina sobs because she must not have any more children, and her husband comforts her. From a two-shot of the sobbing woman bent over her bed and the husband leaning toward her from behind, we pick up their hands, reddened by toil, in extreme closeup. Kristina reaches back over her shoulder toward Karl Oskar's hand that has climbed up her back. We focus on the hands awkwardly united and, as Kristina is shaken by a final sob, a sudden tremor in those tightly fused hands. Then cut. That single, brief, shared paroxysm of two hands that clumsily sought each other out is infinitely moving. So, again, is the episode with the desperately needed ox, a patient, serviceable brute whom Karl Oskar must kill in a heart-rending scene to save his son's life. But Troell can pack poetry into the briefest shot: a nocturnal landscape where everything is inchoate and obscure, only in the foreground a single branch looms refulgent with its hoard of moonlight.

The sparing but evocative music, the minutely exact costuming, the tenderly incisive make-up, the precise yet lyrical color, and the simple, humane performances of Max von Sydow, Liv Ullmann, and the rest go to the heart of artistry and truth. No wonder Miss Ullmann told a colleague that her favorite role was not in one of several great Bergman films, but in Troell's two-part masterpiece.

It is interesting to note how much has been written about Jean-Luc Godard, the sick mother of the New Wave, and how very much less about François Truffaut, who has a good claim to being its putative but healthy father. The image is faulty, however, because the New Wave stemmed not so much from a marriage as from a *ménage à trois,* with Alain Resnais as third partner. The vastly influential films with which it all began were Truffaut's *The 400*

Blows, Resnais's *Hiroshima, Mon Amour* (both 1959) and Godard's *Breathless* (1960). In many ways, all three showed their makers at the top of their form, and were scarcely, if at all, surpassed by later films from the same hands. All three contributed greatly to today's revolutionary, or at least revitalized, approaches to filmmaking.

But Truffaut, from the very beginning, had something the other two lacked: sweetness. As we look back over his twelve feature films and two important shorts, we notice a basic quality of Truffaut's films that has remained inimitable: the mixture of emotional tenderness stretched sometimes to the point of sentimentality with a witty toughness in matters of technique that undercuts the emotionalism. In Truffaut's best films—and even in the good parts of the others, e.g., *Mississippi Mermaid*—we are often conscious of a double rhythm produced inside us: the mental speed with which certain ideas, visual effects, or bits of verbal cleverness have to be absorbed, and the measured, deliberate pace with which we attach ourselves to the characters and linger over the joys and heartaches. The counterpoint achieved by these disparate tempos is the savor and hallmark of Truffaut—a bittersweet quality that can as readily sink into dumb suffering as rise into delirious delight.

It is this duple rhythm that we remember about Truffaut rather than the technical astutenesses with which he studs his films; just as from Godard we carry away the technical tricks and the atmosphere of nihilism that gradually yielded to anticinematic Maoist agitprop foolishness, whereas Resnais's chief contribution remains the almost voluptuous scrambling of time and place.

After the solid achievement of his first three films, Truffaut became uneven: sometimes lost in the pointlessness of *The Soft Skin,* the aridity of *Fahrenheit 451,* the vulgarity and preposterousness of *The Bride Wore Black;* at other times infusing the slight *Stolen Kisses* with considerable charm, and the constricted, somewhat thin *The Wild Child* with moments of ringing integrity and insight. Lately, Truffaut has truly floundered, with *Two English Girls,* a forced, arch, oversentimental attempt at a repeat of *Jules and Jim,* and *Such a Gorgeous Kid Like Me,* a well-paced but crass and rather obvious piece of slickness. Now, with *Day for Night,* his thirteenth feature, Truffaut is on to an important, if somewhat trendy, subject; but this rather better film makes us regret the excellence that it could have attained. If what Truffaut said in a 1962 interview is true, that a director, having made his biggest hits before then, becomes, at forty, more detached, more abstract, lost to the industry but most fascinating to film students, *Day for Night,* made in Truffaut's fortieth year, should mark an important turning point. I doubt if it does.

The English title corresponds exactly to the French one, *La Nuit américaine,* the technical term for the method whereby special filters make a scene shot in daylight look like night. Thus the title cleverly suggests the resourceful artificiality of filmmaking, and the film is, on one level, a record of a film being shot at La Victorine studios in Nice. This film-within-the-film, *Meet Pamela,* concerns a young Frenchman, Alphonse, who brings a new English bride, Pamela, to introduce to his parents on the Riviera. The girl and her   163 father-in-law, Alexandre, fall in love and run off to Paris, where the youth follows them and kills his father. In showing the shooting of the key scenes of *Meet Pamela, Day for Night* concentrates on both the ingenious inventions and random infelicities that accelerate or bog down the work, make for creative exhilaration on the set or threaten to shut down production altogether. In this sense, the film is a combination guided tour and gossip column, documentary and exposé, guaranteed to please both young people interested in making movies and older folks curious about the mysteries of the film studio.

Interwoven with this are the life stories of the people making *Meet Pamela:* the producer, director, actors, technicians, as well as sundry spouses, reporters, and hangers-on. Actually, though the film is fairly reticent about some lives and not all that explicit about others, it does convey the impression that the secrets of those fascinating, temperamental, violently neurotic but lovable film people are laid bare for us. We are introduced to the troubled relationship of the juvenile, Alphonse, with his mistress, the assistant script girl; to the double life of the leading man, Alexandre, an on-and-off-screen Don Juan of long standing now revealed as the anxious lover of a young man he wishes to adopt; to the drinking problem of Séverine, the aging Italian actress who plays the mother, and who, unhappy mother and unfulfilled woman in real life, gets drunk on the job and bungles scenes; and to Julie, the Hollywood-based British star who comes to play Pamela, and brings along her brand-new doctor husband who pulled her through a recent nervous collapse.

These people get involved with one another, or other cast and crew members, and some end happily, some not. In this respect, the film becomes the equivalent of a dime novel for vicarious thrill-seekers in the roller-coaster lives of movie stars. But *Day for Night* also means to capture the fancy of fancier filmgoers—sophisticates who enjoy fiction about the writing of fiction, plays about the nature of playwriting, films about the making of films. It is in the self-referential mode that culminated in Fellini's overblown *8½*, but Truffaut, lacking Fellini's megalomania, contents himself with playing the director, Ferrand, and does not choose to make him the central and most fascinating character. Yet since art whose subject is its own making tends to be sterile stuff (think of the horrors of action painting!), Truffaut and his fellow scenarists, Jean-Louis Richard and Suzanne Schiffman, try to wriggle toward a higher, truly speculative segment of the audience.

So the movie accosts that old but ever-absorbing subject with which serious art has often concerned itself: the relationship of art and life. What self-denial and sacrifices must the artist bring to his art? What toll does life exact from his work? Where does spontaneous living become grubby research? To what extent must the artist turn his loved ones into guinea pigs? To what degree must he himself become the victim of a materialistic society? Henry de Montherlant was that rare artist who claimed—through his fictional alter ego, the novelist and womanizer Pierre Costals—to be able to turn on at will the faucets Work or Life, though one might wonder if his recent suicide does not, after all, indicate that the Hot of life and the Cold of art emerge from, or dry up in, the same spout. Certainly Truffaut has felt the compulsion to mix a great deal of autobiography into his films—not only into the fairly obviously autobiographical Antoine Doinel series, but even into such adaptations of novels as *Shoot the Piano Player*.

The question here, however, is to what extent do the vicissitudes of personal life help or impede one's efficacy as a film actor or technician, and this somewhat shallow concept of the relation in terms of mere output, rather than in more searchingly psychological and existential terms, proves a limitation. Even such a climactic scene as the one wherein the director lectures his self-indulgent juvenile who has gone to pieces over being jilted lacks both the wit and poignancy of a similar scene in Christian-Jaque's *Un Revenant* (*A Lover's Return*, 1946), where, to be sure, the actors were the incomparable Louis Jouvet and the gifted François Périer, rather than the always slightly stiff François Truffaut and the profoundly untalented Jean-Pierre Léaud. In fact, the trouble with this aspect of *Day for Night* is that, just as the film-within-the film is unqualified trash, so the film proper is trivial and hackneyed. What gets represented is not so much the relationship of life to art as of pseudo-art to hackwork. Or, if you prefer, of trash to trash-within-trash.

Nevertheless, the film is far from a total waste. When it comes to conveying how movies are made, no one could seize the very aroma of filmmaking, its changing moods and rhythms, more magisterially than Truffaut, whose specialties are sensitivity to human moods and captivating use of changing rhythms. There is, for instance, the episode in which Ferrand-Truffaut is trying to shoot the big scene of the aging actress Séverine (splendidly portrayed by the excellent Valentina Cortese) who has secreted a bottle on the set—and for whom pages of dialogue have to be pinned up in secret places—and who, out of drunkenness or nervousness, repeatedly flubs either her lines or her business. Three things make this scene particularly gripping. First, we see the touching patience that director, fellow actors, and some crew members have with Séverine—notably the gentleness toward actors for which Truffaut is known; second, the ingeniousness with which Truffaut manages to balance this scene between comedy and pathos; and third, the imaginative camera movements and editing through which even the tedium of re-iterated takes is kept seemingly various and suspenseful.

Jean-Pierre Léaud, whom Truffaut considers the most interesting actor of his generation, and whom I perceive as an eternally callow, crashing bore, luckily has no big part here; Jean-Pierre Aumont is graceful and moving as Alexandre, and several others do nicely. I regret the merely fleeting presence of the delectable Alexandra Stewart, and am rather disappointed in Jacqueline Bisset as the Hollywood star: she proves neither so pretty nor so talented as I remembered her. The film is, finally, no more, no less than a charming trifle. What happened to the credo Truffaut expressed in a 1970 interview with Charles Thomas Samuels: "I have become more interested in my characters, in their situations, and in what they say"? The characters here are stereotypes, the situations scantily explored, the words less than pregnant or penetrating.

Polishing It Off

ROMAN POLANSKI's *What?* confirms me in the belief that this gifted film-maker is the sad victim of his supreme lack of discipline. In Poland, under restrictions that proved salutary to him, Polanski made the powerful *Knife in the Water* and several impressive shorts; in the West, he succumbed to the corruption absolute freedom wreaks on frenetic characters and erratic minds. Usually in collaboration with the scenarist Gerard Brach, Polanski proceeded to make films that were progressively more muddled, pretentious, gratuitously nasty, and pointless. Obsessed with sex and violence, Polanski, who often acts in his movies, looks like a diabolic sophomore, and makes films the way other sophomores scribble graffiti. *What?*, coscripted with Brach, pretends to make some sort of statement in absurdist terms about bourgeois decadence and human stupidity and meanness. Actually, the plot is a meaningless agglomeration of ills visited on an innocent heroine who, in escaping from a bunch of rapists, lands naked in a mysterious seaside villa full of idly rich eccentrics and maniacs.

The trouble with this heroine, pretentiously called The Girl, is that she is not so much innocent as imbecile—just as the creeps to whom she is exposed are not so much representative types of bourgeois materialist vices as of the irrelevant lucubrations of Polanski's unhinged fantasy. The film is rather like Sade's *Justine* rewritten by William Burroughs and filmed by a slightly cleverer Andy Warhol. Invoking absurdism is no excuse. Serious absurdists have a view of the world; Polanski's horizon is bounded to the north by his unsavory psyche, to the south by his overactive crotch. The fatuities and nastiness perpetrated by the film's characters have little or no resonance beyond the wasteland of Polanski's id. Marcello Mastroianni and Hugh Griffith are gifted but erratic actors, yet even as dependably skilled a per-former as Romolo Valli is made ludicrous by this movie. The presence of Sydne Rome, the heroine, can be justified only in terms of Polanski's taste in women, not in terms of anybody's taste in acting. The carelessness and self-indulgence of *What?* are epitomized in the scenes where The Girl plays the piano: the fingernails of the hands that play in closeup are an inch shorter than those of Miss Rome in the longer shots. A filmmaker so flagrantly sloppy about matching his shots testifies *in parvo* to his matchless irrespon-sibility.

But all this is as nothing to Marco Ferreri's *The Grande Bouffe* (very unfreely translated from *La grande Bouffe*, meaning "The Big Feed"), winner of this year's Critics' Prize at Cannes and already the hit of Paris and some other Western capitals. Ferreri is the director of several distasteful films, among which *The Conjugal Bed (L'ape regina)* is perhaps the least loathsome; here he has surpassed himself. Four men, a jaded commercial pilot (Mastroianni), Marcello; a vaguely effeminate TV producer (Piccoli), Michel; a sexually infantile judge (Noiret), Philippe; and a restaurateur whose marriage seems unhappy (Tognazzi), Ugo, resolve to commit suicide by overeating. They repair to the abandoned villa of one of them, which they furnish with comestibles worthy of a feast given by Harun al-Rashid. For a while they also move in a trio of whores, but these get disgusted and leave. Only a fat, seemingly naïve schoolmistress (Ferreol), Andrea, comes to visit and stays triumphantly on.

The film now chronicles the eating prowess of this quintet of superpigs, gormandizing that is occasionally interrupted by Michel's working out at the barre, Marcello's tinkering with a Bugatti in the garage, Philippe's griping, and Ugo's cooking up storms of ever more Rabelaisian dishes. Eating and fornicating are the main actions, though there is also a lively subplot of vomiting, breaking wind, and pelting one another with food. (The film should be a smash in Bangla Desh!) The whores switch to lesbian activities and finally leave; but the meaty Andrea gets Philippe into bed and, during a bout of fellatio, receives his solemn marriage proposal. This does not prevent her from carrying on with the others, usually under her intended's nose, in one large, communal bed.

The humor consists of automobile parts being rammed up a girl's crotch, of Michel playing the piano to the accompaniment of his own shattering anal detonations, of Marcello and Andrea kicking a plethora of plates off the bed in which they copulate, of the three whores voluptuously spoon-feeding one another, of various foods being made up in the shape of giant breasts or the Baptistery in Florence, of having a tart molded by Andrea's naked behind. One capital jest has the toilets backfiring and covering the floors with a lava of excrement. Finally the four begin to drop off. Marcello freezes to death on a snowy night at the wheel of the Bugatti, Michel flops over a balustrade like a beanbag toy and expires in a pool of feces. These two corpses are propped up inside the kitchen freezer through whose glass doors they continue to watch over Ugo, Philippe, and Andrea as the feast goes on.

Philippe has become feeble-minded and cannot tell people apart any more; Ugo eats one of his most monumental creations single-mouthed, and dies in a simultaneous orgasm of food and sex: the one provided by Philippe's feeding spoon, the other by Andrea's masturbating hand. Philippe sits in the garden talking to a stray dog as if it were Ugo; Andrea feeds him a huge pink gelatin in the likeness of her bosom (it is hard to say whether it is an enlargement or a reduction) and he promptly yields up the ghost on the warmly proffered original. More prime meat is delivered in a truck and Andrea has the butcher boys scatter it across the garden for the stray dogs to eat. She herself withdraws into the house, and the film ends as meaninglessly as it began.

Like Polanski's junk, this, too, is being peddled as a satire on capitalism, the bourgeoisie, mankind itself; on the materialism, vulgarity, and suicidal madness of our society. I am not quite convinced that our society is all that sick as this film's exegetes would have it, but assuming that it is, cures like this "satire" are considerably worse than the disease. The four gluttons are crude caricatures and not even representatives of prime bourgeois meatheads: the homosexual TV producer who spouts tags from Ecclesiastes, the lecher who prefers old cars to women, the middle-aged but virginal judge are not really prototypical specimens of middle-class malaise. And here, if anything, they are presented as amiable zanies, whose pranks Ferreri and his two coscenarists seem to enjoy or even envy.

There is, of course, a way of castigating grossness or of observing it dispassionately without becoming gross oneself. There is also a way of being unpretentiously funny without trying to make profound statements. And there is a way of jettisoning psychological realism for the sake of significant metaphors and symbolism. This movie, however, misses all those boats. It doesn't even adhere to a logic of its own: after the house has been covered with detritus and inundated with offal, we suddenly see the kitchen spotless and in immaculate order. But the basic problem is that the film's image does not work on either level: neither on the literal, because the four men have no cogent reason for wanting to die; nor on the figurative, because bourgeois society's death wish (if it has one) is expressed not in overindulgence but in strife and resultant starvation, in mutual exploitation and concomitant moral despair. Ferreri, with his birdbrain, has bitten off more than his pig snout can chew.

December 1973

England Made Me, France Unmade Me

THE ONLY current film of any significance is Yves Boisset's *L'Attentat* (The Assassination), foolishly retitled *The French Conspiracy*, presumably on the dumb notion that people will mistake it for a sequel to, or even revival of, *The French Connection.*

Boisset's film, made several years ago, aroused various threats from the French government; at the very least, it was to be denied an export permit. Yet if it arrives here late, this has more to do with lack of interest on the part of American distributors: Boisset, a serious young filmmaker whose one previous work you may have seen was the gravely underrated *The Cop*, has none of the glamour and flashiness that a Costa-Gavras pumps into *Z*, and sprinkles over *State of Siege*. *L'Attentat* (I cannot bring myself to write *The French Conspiracy*) is based on the true story—as far as it is known—of the 1965 abduction and murder of the Moroccan left-wing political leader Ben Barka, who was lured to Paris, to be killed there, it would seem, by a cabal of high-echelon Moroccan and French officials, abetted by the CIA and the Parisian underworld.

The screenplay, based on a story by Ben Barzman and Basilio Franchina, is by Jorge Semprun, who wrote all of Costa-Gavras's political scripts, as well as Resnais's *La Guerre Est Finie*. It is not a brilliant script, and is not superlatively directed; but it is an honorably imaginative re-creation of a major political and human scandal, and it has throughout the aroma of

168

verisimilitude. Its heroes and villains are not supermen, not even great conversationalists; they both make glaring mistakes as well as adroit moves, and the awkward, amateurish means by which someone escapes from his enemies, and the relatively naïve ways in which clever men walk into traps, have the believability that grander heroics and diabolical cunning no longer hold for us.

There is, in fact, an artlessness about the film that we can accept as the untidiness of fate in a world where life imitates more and more the art of the absurdists. The hero, Darien, a seedy journalist turned police informer to evade political imprisonment, is bamboozled by his lawyer and a French television bigwig into going to Geneva to convince Sadiel, an important exiled North African leader, to come to Paris for a set of significant telecasts about the Third World's problems. Boisset uses a deliberately slow pace in these early scenes, in which American, French, and the unnamed North African country's officials plot genteelly, while the gray figure of Darien, who thinks he is at least in part serving the cause of his old friend Sadiel, becomes the spider's surrogate. Though he is suspicious, he does not realize what he has been doing until the truth dawns on him, hideous and humiliating, in a look of utmost contempt from Sadiel, whom his torturers are marching off to his death.

Jean-Louis Trintignant, as this once capable, now grubby character shocked back into decency, gives one of his better performances: the less romantic his role, the better Trintignant is, and here his heroism is mostly an angry despair, the indignation of a muck-swallower handed one mouthful too many. Sadiel is played by Gian Maria Volontè, by far the most absorbing Italian actor today, because he is at least as much character actor as leading man, with a touch of very contemporary maniacalness that spans and combines the two. (His voice, by the way, is dubbed into French by another fascinating actor, Charles Denner.)

Almost everyone else is equally good. Michel Piccoli, as Sadiel's rightist nemesis; Philippe Noiret and Michel Bouquet, as the chief French intriguers; François Périer, as an honest policeman hamstrung by corrupt superiors; and several others. As a supposedly left-wing American newscaster, Roy Scheider is perhaps a mite obvious (but, then, the dubbing doesn't help him); as Darien's noble mistress, Jean Seberg, for all her ripe years, still acts like a starlet (but, then, her own voice doesn't help her: a Marshalltown accent does even less for French than for English). Ennio Morricone, whose scores range from horrid to superb—the avant-garde usually sounding much worse than the traditional ones—here, unfortunately, contributes one of the former. But Ricardo Aronovich, whose camera work we remember affectionately from *Murmur of the Heart*, provides unassuming color photography.

The CIA, one of the villains in *L'Attentat* (*The French Conspiracy*), becomes in *The Serpent* something rather more curious: simultaneously brilliant and imbecile. Henri Verneuil's film, based on Pierre Nord's novel *The Thirteenth Suicide* (and, since the film contains nothing approaching thirteen suicides, 169 presumably very loosely based), is utter hokum, in which this old-hat director, most recently representd by *The Sicilian Clan,* specializes. But *The Serpent* is extravagant even for Verneuil. We are asked to believe that one of the high officials of the Russian secret service—and seeing that he is played by Yul Brynner, asked twice as much—would more or less fool the CIA into believing that he seeks political asylum, and then feed them enough false information about supposed double agents among the Western nations to cause these agents' prompt demises, even though they later turn out to have been loyal to the West. His chief collaborator, more improbably yet, is a high-ranking British secret service chap who, in due time, defects to Russia. Most improbably, the CIA all along has enough lie-detector and other evidence to make the ingenious Russian's fingering of supposedly unfaithful agents appear, at the very least, questionable.

This is altogether one of those lamentable films in which false clues are constantly tossed at the viewer—events that could not have happened in this particular way in the light of the explanations given later. But the script, by Verneuil and Gilles Perrault (another fairy-tale writer?) is uninteresting even more than unbelievable, and cannot even refrain from playing silly jokes on its supposedly serious self: a married playgirl is called Annabel Lee; a German secret service chief, Lepke, after an American gangster; a French intelligence officer, Tavel, after a *vin rosé.* The one arresting thing about the film is that it takes us inside the CIA's headquarters outside Washington; whether it is anything like the real thing, or merely dreamed up by one of France's most illustrious production designers, Jacques Saulnier, hardly matters.

What we see is a glorious amalgam of super-penny arcade, a technological exhibition with automated displays to be puttered about with, and an Orwellian dystopia working away full blast. It is presided over by Henry Fonda, under the semifictionalized name of Allan Davies, and a dull Davies it is who, in one scene, does not know the difference between a Turk and an Armenian. Because he allowed so many good agents to infiltrate Heaven prematurely, this Davies ends up resigning from his job and going off to California. That, the film implies, is the American equivalent of being sent to Siberia, and, for once, it may have a point.

The cast boasts some expert actors, including our old friends Bouquet and Noiret from *L'Attentat,* without whom, it seems, international intrigue is inconceivable. It is nice to see again, even if in small parts, that fine German stage and screen actor, Martin Held; the pungent Italian actress, Paola Pitagora, remembered from the gifted Marco Bellocchio's *Fists in the Pocket;* and the lovely Elga Andersen, who, however, because of bad make-up or inconsiderate camera work, looks less than her best here. Not so welcome is the reappearance of the untalented Farley Granger, who, in an official CIA briefing session, mispronounces the common Russian Christian name Semyon as "semen"—but this may be the kind of seminal error the CIA is prone to. The film also features Claude Renoir's most lyrical landscape photography, and three nasty surprises: a score by the apparently overworked Ennio Morricone that is bad even when it turns melodious; a title sequence utilizing solarization, one of the most unappealing current cinematic clichés; and an egregiously effete performance by the once-admirable Dirk Bogarde.

A slightly better but still quite unsatisfactory film is *England Made Me*, an adaptation of the 1935 Graham Greene novel by Peter Duffell and the pseudonymous Desmond Cory, and directed by Mr. Duffell, who is definitely not my bag. The novel takes place in Sweden; the film, in Germany, during the rise of the Nazis. Duffell, who shot it over two years ago, insists that he was not trying to cash in on the success of *Cabaret,* but merely shifting the locale to make use of a time and place full of "tensions and pressures . . . which provide a *mise en scène* that marvelously evokes the special atmosphere of 'Graham Greeneland.' " And off they went to get this marvelous German atmosphere in Yugoslavia.

I must guiltily confess to not having read the novel (correction: not guiltily—there is nothing all that necessary about Graham Greene), but it is obvious from what is left of the plot that Sweden was required for the film, too. Not only is Erik Krogh, the millionaire financial manipulator, modeled on Ivar Kreuger, the Match King, but also prosperous Sweden, culpably clinging to its lucrative neutrality, is a far better example of the moth-eaten moral fabric—the trimming, temporizing bad faith—that is much more Graham Greeneland than is Nazi Germany, with its grandiose satanism. By mixing up the story of a former English public-school boy, who dishonestly pretends to be an old Etonian but honestly boggles at the peculations he finds his sister involved in, with the horrors of nascent Nazism on the rampage, the shabby little personal dilemmas (How many flyspecks are reconcilable with an unblotted scutcheon? At what point must even a rumpled conscience start to protest?) become unduly, and undramatically, trivialized. In a letter to the critics, Mr. Duffell, an English TV director whose one previous film was *The House That Dripped Blood,* writes that in 1971 there was only Visconti's *The Damned* with "a similar background" but "quite different concerns."

To be sure, *England Made Me* is not concerned with pederasty, but, otherwise, it shares some of the sensationalistic aspects of Visconti's vulgar and stupid film—only, of course, on a more modestly immodest scale, given the difference in budgets. Here, too, we have a climax consisting of a Nazi orgy, and one that is staged, photographed, and edited just as crassly. But, for the most part, this movie suffers from undernourishment: not enough plot, characterization, notable dialogue, visual interest—not even enough costume extras—to keep the mind and eye properly occupied. Better than die of malnutrition before our eyes, it should have, like Chaplin in *The Gold Rush,* eaten the shoestring on which it was made.

Peter Finch, who plays the dapperly turbulent financier, is given so little to work with that, for all his intelligence, sensitivity, and good looks, he cannot make the part interesting, let alone moving—for, surely, Greene intended us to see the pathos as well as the squalor of corruption. As his English assistant and mistress, a girl with inchoately incestuous feelings for her brother who must die to save her, Hildegard Neil is not up to either the seductiveness of the woman or the complexities of the part. And as the scapegrace, scapegoat brother, the personification of the charming, feckless, unemployable English gentleman—whose one redeeming feature, a sense of fair play, is precisely what undoes him—Michael York is deplorable. Looking more than ever like a blond rat, and overdoing both the vacuous jollity and the nonplussed petulance, he does not so much convey arrested development as exhibit it. There are, however, two supporting performances worth any price of admission: Michael Hordern's as Minty, a seedy, cadging, slatternly journalist—a Greenelander down to the permanent shiftiness of the gaze and the edgy tone of wounded self-esteem; and Joss Ackland's as Krogh's strong-arm man, a faithful brute dispensing uncouth services to his employer with the no-nonsense solicitude of a British nanny.

About the only person I can recommend this film to is myself. For Berlin, it uses Belgrade, where I grew up; for the Riviera, Opatija, where I was taken for my Easter holidays; for Krogh's summer residence, Lake Bled, where we, too, had our summer house. But one man's sentimental screen journey can easily be everyone else's bum trip.

February 1974

Malice Toward All

SOME FILMS are merely bad, others actually loathsome, still others loathsome without being literally bad. In this last category belongs *Going Places,* the second feature film of Bertrand Blier, son of the noted character actor Bernard Blier. Based on Blier's own bestselling novel, *Les Valseuses* (slang for testicles), the film is already a big hit in France.

Two petty hooligans in their twenties—Jean-Claude, the leader, and Pierrot, the follower—pass the time molesting women, snatching pocketbooks, appropriating cars for joyrides. A beauty-parlor owner, less than grateful when the punks return his Citroën DS at a pleasure trip's end, shoots Pierrot in the groin. The boys escape with Marie-Ange, a pretty beautician who is the boss's apathetic mistress, and whom, in exchange for a car, they hand over to a spectacularly unsavory character. Jean-Claude forces a doctor to patch up Pierrot's bullet-grazed scrotum, then robs him of his money; next, the boys embark on a cross-country flight, stealing vehicles, obliging a nursing mother encountered on a train to suckle them as well, taking turns belaboring Marie-Ange sexually and verbally (she is incapable of orgasm), and breaking into an empty beach house where they sniff a young girl's abandoned panties, and Jean-Claude, *faute de mieux,* sodomizes the loudly protesting Pierrot.

When they're not using Marie-Ange or cursing her for not coming, they torture her to find out whether her boss has recovered the Citroën, one of whose axles they have sawed almost through so he'll end up killing himself; they rob and wreck the beauty salon, where they shoot Marie-Ange in the leg, tie her up, and abandon her. Two girls in a bowling alley refuse to go to bed with them, so they lie in wait outside a women's jail for a released prisoner: she, poor sex-starved thing, will gratefully give them everything. Out comes Jeanne Piroles (Jeanne Moreau), whom they pick up, spend a lavish day with, and take to a hotel; after a grand *folie à trois,* she kills herself with a bullet up the vagina. They fetch her son, presently released from another prison, and take him to the rural hideaway they share with Marie-Ange; amazingly, he brings the frigid girl to a shrieking climax. But he, too, has gone stir crazy, and implicates them in the revenge murder of his humane prison guard. Again the boys and Marie-Ange are on the run across the country in stolen cars, but now with the added viaticum of noisily happy consummations on the back seat for whoever isn't driving.

The trio relieves a vacationing family of their car and of their more than willing teen-aged daughter, Jacqueline, who might be the owner of the panties that once afforded the boys olfactory delights. Now they not only sniff and taste the thankful girl's pubes, but also deflower her while Marie-Ange cradles her head; then they send her off, reluctant but fulfilled. Once again the threesome is ensconced in a nice Citroën DS, and we bid them goodbye as they drive not into the sunset, but into a tunnel toward what new adventures? In the novel, the car was the very one they had "fixed"; not so in the movie, where picaresque bliss must prevail.

I give you all this not as a plot summary, in which I do not believe, but as a moral indictment, in which I do. My objection is not so much to the film's amorality as to its untruthfulness and dishonesty. Almost every woman in it relishes the vile treatment she receives. Marie-Ange, when they're not pinching her nipples to make her talk, is glad to take good wifely-motherly care of the youths. Jeanne Piroles is so sad at being too old and, presumably, unable to hold on to them that she dispatches herself after one perfect night together. The young nursing mother, on the way to share a furlough with her soldier husband, becomes enraptured as she's worked over. The train, totally empty, must be the Flying Dutchman; the soldier husband turns out to be a mangy specimen, more in line for a medical discharge than for a furlough. Little Jacqueline loves every moment of her brutalization. A crazy guy fresh from prison, with no previous sexual experience, brings chronically frigid Marie-Ange to instant thawing out.

Along this happy journey, veracity and feeling for anyone but the two hoods fall by the wayside. When the beauty-parlor owner has them covered with his gun, "cowardly" neighbors, who make nasty comments on the boys' long hair, come to *his* assistance. "You better believe that this is France!" exclaims Jean-Claude, casting an outraged glance heavenward. To show clearly that he is on their side, the filmmaker forthwith allows the boys to escape against overwhelming odds. When Marie-Ange, for once, protests, Pierrot explains that they are ordinary guys, not very *fleur bleue,* which is not a Guerlain fragrance, but the symbol of Romantic purity for Novalis and his spiritual heirs. The cute wording is supposed to make the ruffians lovable,   173 and chivalry ridiculous. When our heroes promenade their ennui through a vacant resort town in the *morte saison* (a scene perhaps derived from Patroni Griffi's wretched *Il Mare*), their frustrations are blamed on France itself. Next, they disport themselves in front of disused German bunkers—are we to stretch chronology, and view the poor boys as war babies, as guiltless victims?

The filmmakers have assured me that the kids are really ludicrous, lost mother's boys, so risible that enlightened French bourgeois audiences merely laugh at them. I am not surprised at French audiences any more than at ours (have they not loved such clinkers as *Benjamin, Le Bonheur, The Umbrellas of Cherbourg, The Things of Life, Claire's Knee, The Discreet Charm of the Bourgeoisie,* to cite but a few). Yet I am amazed by some ardent feminists who, I hear, endorse this movie. Blinkered by fanaticism, they seem to ignore its ongoing reification of women, merely because in the end Marie-Ange appears to have her lovers well in hand.

I am not asking, of course, that *Going Places* be banned or censored, but I do believe that the other side should be given equal hearing, if not in the film, then at least after it. The only woman who is not shown enjoying molestation is fat and middle-aged, and presumably knows she cannot expect the bliss of ravishment. (In broad daylight, by the way, the housing development where she is tormented is completely deserted; Blier is cheating again.) The beauty-parlor owner is detestable; Jacqueline's parents are spineless, dreary bourgeois, whose savage indictment by their multiple-dropout daughter is presented as entirely just. When our heroes, in turn, drop her, we wonder what fate awaits her. But the filmmaker doesn't bother his witty head over such trivia.

The escapades are shot in seductive color by Bruno Nuytten; particularly effective are a sandy beach through whose pallor black-clad figures cut a starkly imposing swath, and a willow-lined canal that evokes thrillingly both Corot and the Impressionists. The violin score, composed and played by Stéphane Grappelli, once in the band of that legendary gypsy musician Django Reinhardt, is bewitchingly insinuating. Blier and his editor have paced the movie soundly, and there is good acting, especially from Jeanne Moreau, who can make both saturnine world-weariness and offensive word leakage (as when she horrifies a restaurant proprietress with a paean to menstruation and an elegy for her loss of it during incarceration) seem winning. No less right is Miou-Miou as Marie-Ange, whose part consists mostly of pouting, stripping, and fornicating, and who yet manages to invest it with variety and an inchoate dignity. There is a quiet intense bit from Brigitte Fossey (the unforgettable little girl of *Forbidden Games*) as the nursing mother, and Gérard Depardieu and Patrick Dewaere are convincing wise guys and louts.

Yet the film is quite undone by its fundamental dishonesty. If the boys are the petty criminals—cute, if you like—they seem to be, they do not deserve the two hours of sympathy lavished on them; if they are the pathetic little jesters Blier claims they are, where is the single feature to endear them to us—other than clever impudence, which hardly qualifies? If, at least, these characters were taken from life instead of coming out of a Godard movie, say, *Breathless* or *Pierrot le Fou*. And it is not even as if such films depended for their success on the criminal classes, which would make some sense; worse, they live off the bad faith of a bourgeoisie panting to display its swinging savvy by embracing trendy trash.

No less repugnant, and not even well made, is *Malizia* (Malice), the sixth film of Salvatore Samperi, for my money one of the world's most unappetizing directors. Now twenty-nine, he made his debut several years ago with *Grazie, Zia*, an inept, vaguely demented little film, which tried to treat incest both as a sick joke and as no laughing matter, and merely debased the lovely Lisa Gastoni as a beautiful aunt manipulated by a very young, psychopathic nephew. In *Malizia*, Samperi deals with a gorgeous young housemaid who comes to work for a fresh widower with three very fresh sons. The middle son, of high-school age, enters into a voyeuristic, faintly sadomasochist relationship with the maid, finally resolved in intercourse just as she is marrying dad. We need not dwell on the seamy details of the plot characterized by (a) vulgarity of the most prurient sort, which has the gall of posturing as artistic restraint; (b) absolute blindness and deafness to how human beings feel, think, speak, and act anywhere in the world, including even Italy; and (c) photographic crudities and excesses typical of Vittorio Storaro, Bertolucci's pretentious cameraman.

Point (b) is most conspicuous because it is a lack exhibited in its total, congenital state—like color blindness and tone deafness. Samperi and his coscenarists unfailingly make a character do or say the opposite of what any normal person, and most abnormal ones, would say or do in a given situation. Even visually they are utter fakers, making the boy and the maid so stunning as to exclude the possibility of any locale other than a film studio. (Laura Antonelli certainly, and Alessandro Momo probably, deserve better vehicles.) As for point (a), the opening scene will serve as a handy example. Mamma's funeral is to show that the deceased was less than lovable, and that the mourners, indeed folk in general, are a scruffy lot. So Samperi gives you the youngest son playing ball all over the house, a disgusting fly buzzing from one face to another, various people furtively smoking or picking their noses, eye shadow grotesquely running down cheeks, a callipygous neighbor being lewdly ogled, the bereaved husband displaying instant hypocrisy, and, to top it all, a candle setting fire to the coffin. It is as loaded a concentration of facile condescension in a short preamble as a director of merely average vulgarity could make do with for an entire film.

And there is also point (d). Samperi's movie derives almost slavishly from the work of Pietro Germi, who for decades now has been giving us Bruegelesque canvases of Italian carryings-on. But except in his worst films, like *The Birds, the Bees and the Italians* and *Alfredo, Alfredo*, Germi does not permit himself anywhere near such wholesale crassness. And even at his lowest, Germi differentiates between sickness and health; in his best films, inhuman behavior is induced by inhuman circumstances, e.g., the (nonexistent) Italian divorce law of *Divorce Italian Style*, or the Sicilian social inequities of *In the*   175

Name of the Law. Samperi, on the other hand, saddles the human animal with meannesses that are, at best, improbable (as opposed to others that are, alas, quite common), then revels in them to his heartlessness' content, and to the delectation of countless Italians—and now perhaps others as well—pouring in to see *Malizia.*

The Apprenticeship of Duddy Kravitz is Mordecai Richler's adaptation of his own novel, about which I heard good things. These are only partly—very partly—borne out by the movie, directed by Richler's fellow Canadian and friend, Ted Kotcheff. The film is a combination *Room at the Top* and *What Makes Sammy Run?,* Canadian style, chronicling the fortunes and setbacks of David (Duddy) Kravitz, an overenterprising youth from the Montreal ghetto. The schema is by now fairly rigid: the hero of such films will sacrifice everything—friends, family, the Good Woman—to scaling the socioeconomic ladder, until he finds himself on top, or well on his way toward it. The only optional elements are the proportions in which the author mixes grimness and humor, squalor and farce; and whether he will end with a hero oppressed by his aloneness (which this genre takes for granted) or smirking at it defiantly. *Duddy Kravitz* opts for the smirk.

The film has going for it a well-observed mileu, a rich gallery of colorful locals (English-, French-, and Jewish-Canadian, plus a sprinkling from Old and New England), and a wealth of incident that sometimes gets out of hand. Kotcheff, who made at least one film deserving more attention than it got (*Outback*), does not have a sure directorial hand, and lets some scenes go on too long, others not long enough. At other times he exhibits tidiness and economy in making a point—though not, as they say in Washington, a point in time: the chronology, indeed the very seasons, remain disquietingly vague for such a naturalistic film. Brian West's camera work often lapses into picture-postcard lushness, but the acting, except for Richard Dreyfuss's Duddy, is, if anything, understated. It is also generally compelling, though the once remarkable Jack Warden comes across here as a lesser Keenan Wynn. A young French-Canadian, however, named Micheline Lanctôt, gives a performance of exemplary humanity and restraint.

September 1974

Passion and Skullduggery

SOME DIRECTORS spring full-fledged from Jupiter's brow—indeed film, for such a complicated art, is remarkably rich in practitioners whose first works were technically and artistically commanding. That is not the case, however, with Maximilian Schell, the accomplished screen and stage actor who has been gradually evolving into a filmmaker. His first movie, an adaptation of Kafka's *The Castle,* he merely produced; the next, *First Love,* derived from

176

Turgenev's novel, he coscripted and directed. Apparent in this film were culture and literacy, but also overeagerness, overambitiousness, the need to cram the film full of "Art."

Wisely, Schell had engaged Sven Nykvist, Bergman's superb cinematographer, and together they set about making a movie as rich in colors as the story is in the hopes and pangs of first love. They succeeded too well, producing a surfeit of gorgeousness beyond the digestive power of two fragile human eyes. Other things went wrong, too, not least a corollary crowding in of incident, some of it too obliquely and allusively presented, and the faulty or altogether lacking rhythm in the film's unfurling. Some of these difficulties persist in Schell's new picture, *The Pedestrian;* some of them have been overcome, but often at the cost of new ones. Still, the film is markedly superior to its predecessor: a worthy failure. But failure all the same, as proved to me by the fact that it gets worse on second seeing. A good film holds its own on renewed exposure, and a great one gets better with each return visit.

Schell is not fond of linear narrative and, accordingly, the film is loosely strung together, full of flashbacks to the same scene but with a difference, flash-asides to what might be happening but isn't, extreme closeups in soft focus for visual *dépaysement*, omission of establishing shots so that we must unscramble both time and place. Such stratagems are in themselves neither good nor bad (although much contemporary film criticism esteems them for their mere existence), but rather like parentheses, ellipses, and aposiopeses in writing—good if put to good use, bad if misused. In *The Pedestrian* there are examples of both.

What plot there is concerns a German industrialist, Giese, who was present as a German officer at a massacre of Greek women and children during World War II. His exact role in this inhuman reprisal is unclear. An unscrupulous newspaper editor, Hartmann, digs up some facts, among them the existence of a female survivor of the holocaust, the identity of another now solid burgher involved in the mass shooting, and the possible connection between this and the recent death of Giese's elder son and heir, Andreas, during a shadowy auto accident while Giese was driving. The film follows the final stages of the paper's investigative operations, and the movements of Giese himself, spied on by reporters. The tycoon's day proceeds from a visit of the old man and his grandson to a science museum, then to Giese's unexpected dropping in on his young mistress whom he catches or almost catches *in flagrante delicto* with a young man, then on to a compulsory illustrated lecture for automotive delinquents, then to a trolley ride during which the old Greek woman observes Giese but cannot positively identify him, and, further, to a return home and his unsympathetic dropout of a younger son, his patiently forbearing wife, and some confrontations with the prying reporters.

There are numerous other scenes, including such curious set pieces as a dream of Andreas's about death, which provides a kind of leitmotiv—far from fully integrated into the film, however; a dialogue with the grandson about the meaning of history, which never makes the pregnant pronouncement on whose verge it hovers; a scene in which seven old women, including 177

Giese's mother and other relatives and friends, discuss the nature and morality of war; a flashback in which Giese, vacationing in Greece with his mistress, is reluctantly persuaded by her to join in a folk dance under the suspicious eyes of the natives; and another, matching scene, narrated but not shown, in which a similar event took place in a Spanish flamenco joint, but this time on a trip Giese took with his wife.

One problem with all this is the overabundance of literary and cinematic influences. The way in which the opening dream is photographed derives too obviously from the beginning of *Hiroshima, Mon Amour,* with the camera hugging an unidentifiable object so tightly and blurringly that it looks mysterious, otherworldly, downright metaphysical. Meanwhile the voice-over narration of the dream's content sounds like a cross between a Kafka parable and an early Rilke story. Even when we figure out what is going on, we cannot relate it to the rest of the film. Again, a bedtime story Giese tells his grandson seems too heavily indebted to the old woman's tragic fairy tale in Büchner's *Woyzeck,* and strikes a tone inconsistent with Giese's other talks with his grandchild. The scene in which an aged actor and actress recite the balcony scene from *Romeo and Juliet,* as they once long ago acted it on the stage, fills me with an uncomfortable sense of déjà vu, although I cannot actually trace its derivation.

Other scenes suffer from excessive staginess. There is something de trop about dredging up a handful of famous old actresses from all over—including Germany's Lil Dagover, Austria's Elisabeth Bergner, England's Peggy Ashcroft, France's Françoise Rosay, and several others scarcely less celebrated—and seating them at a round table to discuss war. It is hard to make them appear to belong there, and the grand manner in which they act betrays them as prima donnas preserved in their pride. It is all too good to be true. Still other scenes belabor an obvious irony, as when a little girl runs from one side of a street to the other to push a pedestrian's button, and at the mischievous brat's interminable red light the whole law-abiding German economic miracle seems to come to an obedient standstill.

The little girl is a pedestrian, and pedestrians in this film are privileged beings. Giese, because his driver's license has been temporarily revoked, has become a pedestrian, too, and makes discoveries that as a driver he would have zoomed past unseeing. There is the realization that his mistress cheats on him, and that there is a whole world of trolley riders, initiates in a mystery of the impecunious about which he knows nothing. As a pedestrian, too, he is confronted with the horrible images of vehicular homicide, which put him in touch with the truth of Andreas's death: his son was trying to kill both of them in a crash after learning about Giese's war guilt. The truth, then—but does it bring happiness, or even peace?

This might well have been the theme of the film; instead, it keeps getting sidetracked and hopping all over the place. The device of incremental repetition—flashbacks telling a little more each time—is indulged in both in the car-crash episodes and in the scene of the massacre, and begins to look gimmicky. The metaphysical issue—What is death?—keeps popping up in various guises, yet remains as unintegrated as it is unresolved. The grandson's questions—"What is history?" "Where is Daddy now?" "Is Daddy's death part of history?"—are not made germane to the master themes of truth and guilt. There are beautiful moments, like a tracking shot of Giese walking past the Krupp Works that finally makes no point; Godard notwithstanding, a tracking shot is not ipso facto a moral choice. Other shots are held too long, like the darkening image at the end of the Greek-dancing sequence, or the film's closing shot with the camera pulling back to reveal a heated debate as having been no more than a TV panel show. A Viennese waltz inundates us, the formerly furibund panelists shake hands, and the camera loses itself in surveying the television equipment.

There are even graver lapses, like a sentimental flashback to Andreas, his wife, and their child playing in a blissful landscape while the death of Greek children is discussed on the soundtrack in facile irony. But the film has its virtues, too, in Schell's skillful writing and directing of certain vignettes. Thus the relationship of Giese and his mistress tells itself by nice indirections; his relation with his wife is sympathetically developed in a few swift scenes; the television debate, largely improvised, achieves considerable power through eloquent spokesmen on both sides. The cinematography by Wolfgang Treu and Klaus Koenig is effective throughout, but downright breathtaking in certain snowscapes—how photogenic the color white is when shot with color film! Dagmar Hirtz, who charmingly plays the small part of Andreas's wife, has edited the film sensitively, and the excessively slow fades doubtless represent the director's wishes.

Much of the acting is excellent, owing in part to Schell's clever intermingling of amateurs, professionals, and displaced professionals; thus the unsavory Hartmann is played by the English stage and screen director Peter Hall, and Giese himself by Gustav Rudolf Sellner, a stage and opera director. The results are interesting: from the directors one gets a more cerebral kind of acting than from the actors, from the amateurs something more spontaneous, and so a whole spectrum is established. Still, *The Pedestrian* remains a disjointed movie, with moments of pretentiousness, exaggerated improbabilities, and too many questions raised. Granted, an artist is not obliged to answer questions, but he must shed light by asking them more clearly.

Yet Schell, at least, is not afraid of engaging serious subjects, and does not become so absorbed in their seriousness as to forget the free play of the style-giving imagination. He does not, generally, allow importance to evaporate into slickness or ossify into ponderousness. The German film entered the postwar years with a distinct promise in the works of Helmut Käutner, Wolfgang Staudte, Bernhard Wicki, and a few others, a promise that was completely derailed in the hands of such overcerebral or simply unhinged experimentalists as Alexander Kluge, Rainer Werner Fassbinder, Werner Herzog, and Jean-Marie Straub. It would be nice to hope that Maximilian Schell might contribute to recouping its flagging fortunes.

To the French, the drama of adultery is what the western is to Americans. And no Frenchman in recent times has churned out more of these dramas 179 than Claude Chabrol, whose specialty is adultery seasoned with murder. Chabrol is an interesting case: a charter member of the New Wave, he is, in terms of camera movement, framing of shots, and subtle sense of how to play on the viewer's sensibility, very nearly the equal of his idol, Hitchcock. He falls decidedly short only of the true artists: the Welles of *Citizen Kane* and the great European and Japanese masters. In his finest film, *La Femme infidèle,* Chabrol may have achieved that intensity of perception, sympathy for human joy and suffering, and economy of expression without histrionics that are three of the hallmarks of art. But for all his basic elegance, Chabrol has made some remarkably trashy films.

His characters often behave with an absurdity or perversity that is artistically unacceptable and even clinically inconceivable. It surpasses mere stupidity but falls short of genuine pathology, coming off instead as deliberate, meaningless auctorial manipulation, producing on the audience numbness rather than shock. Along with this dehumanization of his characters, Chabrol goes in for plot developments and endings that are worse than simple-minded—almost imbecile. People who have managed to function with appreciable ingenuity suddenly commit inordinate errors or become profoundly untidy; are unmasked by their most primitive opponents, or voluntarily turn themselves in for no good reason.

Chabrol's exegetes have interpreted this as Christian, mystical, miraculous—justice and morality asserting themselves by supernatural means, simple yet inscrutable. To me, it always looks more like laziness and failure of the imagination: Chabrol's unwillingness or inability to work out the details of a plot, and concern only with grand final effects. It is as if an automobile inventor were interested merely in his car's getting somewhere, and did not mind if it had to be drawn there by a team of oxen. To be sure, the plot of many a thriller suffers from overingeniousness. If things were really as they are shown in such movies, either the supercops would have made crime obsolete, or the supercriminals would have completely done away with law enforcement.

But one extreme is never the corrective for the other. If criminals collapsed as easily as they do in Chabrol's new *Wedding in Blood,* very few would have the nerve to commit a crime in the first place. The adulterous killers of this film are caught out so easily that one cannot avoid the impression that Chabrol's real concern was only with the ironic concluding closeup of their hands fatally united by manacles, and that it hardly mattered to him how to bring this about. His *deus ex machina* is the woman's pretty, staring-eyed daughter, whose behavior is generally puzzling, but whose final maneuver is not so much beyond as beneath credibility.

Yet *Wedding in Blood* is still among Chabrol's better films, despite, or because of, its simple-mindedness: at least it avoids the elaborately excogitated absurdities of some of the others. Actually, what makes the film interesting, over and above the sheer technical expertise, is its evocation of physical passion. Its hero and heroine, played with suasion by Michel Piccoli and Stéphane Audran, are sometimes grotesquely, sometimes shatteringly in the
grips of a fleshly craving for each other such as has seldom if ever been

conveyed on screen—least of all in pornographic movies. *Last Tango in Paris,* poor as it was, had something of this lust in its first mating sequence; but that was rather an impersonal compulsion, sex for its own sake. Here it is a fierce and unique attraction that two particular people have exclusively for each other: its very grotesqueries—bellowings, grunts, moans, nuzzlings, nibblings, clawings, and bites—achieve a crazy, pitiful, magnanimous dignity: the sense of a physical love for which all must be sacrificed, so absolute that it makes considerations of morality, safety, self-respect irrelevant.

What renders these lovers especially winning is their great, centripetal sensuality. Down to the remotest rattle in their throats, to the farthest tremor of their anatomies, they have become eroticized, so that Audran's right foot makes love to Piccoli's back as Piccoli's mouth and hands pay affectionate tribute to Audran's left foot and toes—in a cheerfully natural manner, without any hint of fetishism—while the owners of these extremities converse with loving casualness. It is a splendid lesson for puritanical or amatorily retarded Americans (whose numbers must still be legion, else why the phenomenal sales of sexual self-help books?) in what I can only call total, energizing, revitalizing sexuality.

Too bad, however, that all this is not at the service of a more imaginative plot or more fully developed characters. Outside their exemplary passion for each other, these two beings are not accorded much personality, and the fact that their respective spouses are so gross or so dreary makes for a sadly unequal contest. Jean Rabier's cinematography has been steadily improving, but it's still too unrelievedly pastel for my taste; as for the able Pierre Jansen's score, it is haunting but sometimes overloud and portentous. The supporting cast is adequate and the fluidity of the camera truly impressive, except in one of those overfanciful circular pans that have become Chabrol's personal signature, like Hitchcock's walk-ons. A beautiful film, then, with no baroque effects, but, ultimately, empty.

Lina Wertmüller, the Italian film director, has been represented here in rapid succession by *Love and Anarchy* and *The Seduction of Mimi,* in reverse order to the one in which they were made. Both films have the same strengths and weaknesses. Miss Wertmüller is perhaps the first totally unfeminine female director: no one would guess these films to be the works of a woman. That is a mixed blessing, for what they gain in masculine toughness, they lose in feminine sensitivity. At this stage of her development, the director is good at unsentimental tragedy and uncomplaisant comedy, and has an admirable visual sense. This last is exemplified by the scene from *Mimi* in which the rejected would-be lover woos his implacable Dulcinea while she is selling handmade sweaters and machine-made Communist propaganda on one side of the street, and he gazes at her with eloquent yearning from the other.

It is a finely rhythmic pantomime: on one side the man's slow, crawling gaze; on the other, the woman's fast, grotesque gestures of deprecation; and, in between, the cars zooming past almost subliminally. Call it a game of comic-romantic tennis, glances and gestures slapped back and forth across a net of blurry traffic at spectacularly unequal speeds. The scene is remarkable for its compression of the large part of a courtship into one wordless sequence. But Miss Wertmüller hardly ever relaxes; most of her scenes try to say or do equally much, and have rather more individual vitality than ability to flow into one another. They are like magnificently athletic runners in a relay race who somehow neglect to make contact with the next teammate. Yet she handles her camera, dialogue, and actors with such sturdy control and incisive intelligence that one must hope she will eventually relax into a more easeful fullness.

July–October 1974

The Tragic Deterioration of Fellini's Genius

THOSE whom the Catholic Church did not prevent from seeing Rossellini's *The Miracle* (the ban on it was reversed by the Supreme Court, but the film has been shown very little, all the same) will remember the mute figure of the Stranger, a handsome, delicate-faced, sensitive-looking man whom the heroine, a simple peasant woman guarding the villagers' sheep, could understandably mistake for Saint Joseph. His visage had rare dignity and subtlety, and the mysteriously ironic expression with which he responded to the adoration of the shepherdess was worthy of the Mona Lisa's countenance. That tall, slender man, who was none other than the not-yet-director Federico Fellini, was in every way the antithesis of the gross sensualist—double-chinned and bulging-bellied, though still in his early fifties—Fellini of today, the has-been director. It is not so much that he was younger and had dyed his hair blond for the film; it is rather that there was no vulgarity in his appearance or demeanor.

But if the physical change was great, how much greater yet is that between the earlier Fellini films, starting with *Variety Lights* (1950), and the later Fellini films, culminating in the current, critically overpraised *Amarcord*, made by that grotesque yet idolized figure wearing vaguely "artistic" apparel, and seen lording it all over Rome followed by a sizable sycophantic entourage. "I want to surround myself with acrobats, storytellers, and jesters, as in a medieval court, but there will be no despotism," Fellini declared thirteen years ago in an interview in *Films and Filming* magazine. A retinue of servile clowns may not be the creation of a despot—it may even be that the despot is the creation of his toadying followers—but Fellini "the King of Rome," as the late, highly respected critic Charles Thomas Samuels described him, is too crudely despotic a creature to have much of the artist left about him.

Looking back over Fellini's career, one can see that in a sense he has always made the same film, because, as he has often remarked, all his films are autobiographical in spirit, sometimes indeed in their letter. This need not be a drawback if only the basic themes undergo sufficient variations, and if they are not so self-centered as to exclude awareness of other people. If, in short, the films are concerned with transmuting felt life into art. This was the case, to a greater or lesser extent, with all of Fellini's films through *Nights of Cabiria* (1956), and including even a number of scenes in *La Dolce Vita* (1959), where some episodes were already tainted with dishonest sleight-of-hand, bathetic pretentiousness, pseudo-intellectual attitudinizing, and a kind of bloated self-imitation. Thus the latter's phony miracle episode was only a more melodramatic reworking of the pilgrimage sequence from *Cabiria;* the various orgies were more diffuse revampings of the New Year's Eve party in *Il Bidone* (1955); and *La Dolce Vita*'s structure was so overextended and rambling as to be rather more than the largely passive central figure, the quasi-autobiographical Marcello, could hold together.

Fellini was already cheating. True, there may have been something contrived even in *Cabiria,* what with the one seemingly devoted man in the prostitute-heroine's life turning out to be the biggest crook of all, and her unduly speedy arousal from blackest despair to dancing jocundity by the rather too fortuitous appearance of a band of merry revelers. But at least the transformations occurred on camera, and were there for us to believe or disbelieve on ocular evidence. In *La Dolce Vita,* Marcello's deterioration takes place between the film's episodes, and must be taken entirely on faith—the filmmaker's tendentious bad faith.

There followed a series of ever more frantic, garish, and unsatisfying films, with the partial exception of *8½* (1962), which, though also overloaded, posturing, and intellectually confused, had at least the virtue of admitting, in scarcely disguised autobiographical outspokenness, that Fellini had nothing more to say, no more films to make. (This very virtue, however, has had a vast and nefarious influence, encouraging all sorts of cinematic no-talents who have nothing to say to make grandiosely self-serving films about that uninteresting fact.) For *8½* was a film about a great director's spiritual and physical paralysis, about his inability to make the film he is supposed to be making, and his incapacity to make decisions or choices in art and life. In every possible way the protagonist, Guido Anselmi, was equated with Fellini, and the film would have been a perfect confession of present, and presage of future, impotence, had it not been enshrouded in an opaque, hocus-pocusy *mise en scène* and furbished with one of the most dishonest endings in the history of cinema: a circular procession of all the characters—creatures from the hero's past and present, and anonymous additional figures—all led by a band of clown-musicians in a capering parade of bustle for its own sake, of what the Canadian critic Peter Harcourt has called "the impulse toward life without demanding why."

But aside from the glaring schematism with which this was staged, there was its total incredibility. Although partly yet another fantasy of Anselmi's, it was, like other fantasy scenes in the film, meant to function also on the level of truth; but it was a truth unearned by anything that preceded it. Why the demanding mistress and the dissatisfied wife, the dead parents and   183 the morally rigid, exacting, and possibly fraudulent churchmen, and all the other ghosts and bugbears, victims and tormentors in the protagonist's life, should suddenly turn into a tractable, docilely cavorting roundelay could be explained only as the meretricious concoction of an arbitrary happy ending.

When a potentially major filmmaker, such as Jean Vigo or Andrzej Munk, dies young, is the loss as great as when a former giant of the cinema lives on to make some of the world's worst films? More than any art form, film has had its masters who deteriorated pitifully—Welles, Renoir, Bresson, Rossellini, De Sica—but no one who made the likes of *The White Sheik, I Vitelloni,* and *Nights of Cabiria* was ever reduced to turning out the pompous and arrogant trash that Fellini has shoveled at us, with one partial exception, since *La Dolce Vita.*

The tragic deterioration of Fellini's talent—indeed, genius—can be traced in his handling of any one of the recurrent motifs on which his films are based. In several of Fellini's works, for example, we encounter the town simpleton, Giudizio, who first appears in Fellini's masterpiece, *I Vitelloni* (1953), as a harmless halfwit, a fisherman whom the young provincial idlers sometimes watch at his work. When the leader of the gang of *vitelloni* (fatted calves, i.e., drifters) steals and tries unsuccessfully to sell the statue of an angel—a piece of cheap, mass-produced religious art—he ends up leaving the angel with the ecstatically worshipful Giudizio. We now get a lovely shot of Giudizio carrying this vapid-looking angel out to the beach, squatting down beside him, fondling him with his hands and eyes, and raptly murmuring the one word, "Angel." In a world of turmoil and frustration, Giudizio is an image of simple-hearted contentment.

But look at this same Giudizio in *The Clowns* (1970). He has become a mere grotesque, the typical village idiot, whom Fellini's camera examines with cold curiosity as one of those malformations by means of which everyday life impinges on the circus. Finally, in the current *Amarcord,* Giudizio has become a laughingstock, a poor harebrain whom the crowd at a spring festival entrap on top of the pyre on which the effigy of winter is about to be burned. They scare Giudizio out of his remaining wits by pretending they'll immolate him too, and his fear only heightens their hilarity. Notice how Fellini's heart has hardened—not only toward Giudizio but also, and more disturbingly, toward his and Fellini's own fellow human beings.

Take another festivity: the outdoor wedding feast, a meal consumed somewhere in the open countryside under an awning, or in front of a farmhouse, where a long table is set up, and food and drink are liberally ingested in honor of the newlyweds. *Amarcord* concludes with such a scene, but all it tells us is that the town belle, getting long in the tooth (or, because we are in Italy, broad in the beam), finally marries the likeliest available man: a plain and dull *carabiniere* who at least sports a fine uniform. Nothing happens during this entire scene except chitchat, teasing, and a little horseplay; finally the married couple and most of the guests take off, leaving behind a few stragglers, and allowing Fellini to end with a facilely bittersweet dying fall. In *La Strada* (1954), there was a similar al fresco wedding feast, but it served as backdrop to the activities of the main characters, to reveal their

184

troubled, nomadic lives in counterpoint and contrast to the texture of busy yet normal stationary existence.

In *Amarcord*, Fellini draws more and more on ill-digested surrealism or expressionism. The townsfolk go out in boats to watch some grand maritime event, nobody quite knows what. It gets to be night, and most of them are dozing when, suddenly, the new superliner *Rex* sails by, tier upon tier of dizzying lights looming skyward from sea level, as if the Milky Way were reascending after a whimsical midnight dip. The image has crude visual power—the figures of the pigmy fleet frantically cheering and waving to the colossus sweeping by unconcerned—but it is nowise integrated into the rest of the film and does not justify the minutes of screen time it consumes. The movie clutches avidly at any gratuitous effect—surrealism, expressionism, caricature, nostalgia, whatnot—in feverish succession, anything at all to keep its chin above the watered-down platitudes. Indeed, it tries to compress several of them in a sort of last grasp, so that both the indolent young men of *I Vitelloni* and the mischievous schoolboys of *8 1/2* are squeezed into the same classroom scenes in which subteens are made to rub posteriors with strange benchfellows in their thirties.

If some feeble, or feeble-minded, jokes are reluctantly dragged out, others are tossed in with bewildering haste. Thus, a wealthy upper-crust family of three, in advanced discord and disrepair, are introduced from time to time just sitting or skulking around, as if their mere grotesque presence made some exquisitely satirical point. Worse yet are scenes in which schoolboys gape at ample female behinds riding about on bicycles, or masturbate in close harmony in a parked car as they call out the names of movie stars or local charmers, and the abused vehicle rocks as in a palsy, while its headlights blink suggestively. Here, connoisseurs of the abyss will agree, Fellini sinks to the level of Mel Brooks.

Granted, Fellini was always drawn to the excessive, the baroque and bizarre, he nevertheless handled it with taste and control. Take the figure of the fat woman that seems to have haunted his childhood and, apparently, affects him still. I am not thinking of such comic fat women in that early masterpiece, *The White Sheik* (1952), but of La Saraghina, the woman-mountain, seated before whose rhumba-dancing form the schoolboys of *8 1/2* get their first significant as well as funny intimations of female flesh in action. But in *8 1/2* the heaving of that ultra-Rubenesque flesh is not dwelt on in extreme closeup, and our noses are not figuratively rubbed in it as the nose of the autobiographical boy-hero of *Amarcord* literally is. In the latter, the fat woman inundates the wide screen with her bared mammoth mammae, between which she imprisons the boy's head, nearly suffocating him as well as nauseating the civilized filmgoer, while around him *hoi polloi* laugh their heads off.

The difference is obvious: La Saraghina was, as Fellini told Charles Thomas Samuels, "sex [as] seen by a child ... grotesque, but also seductive"; in *Amarcord* her counterpart is merely good for a few belly laughs from those whose stomachs remain unturned. And, furthermore, she becomes an object for kids to masturbate over, in a scene that is particularly tasteless and, in   185 more than one way, heavy-handed. But one can go to any of Fellini's later films for unending parades of ghastly grotesques, which preponderate especially in *Juliet of the Spirits, Satyricon,* and *Toby Dammit,* though such a sequence as the outdoor diners wolfing down their food in *Roma* should not be overlooked either. And this living wax museum of horrors does not even serve a symbolic purpose.

There is in *I Vitelloni* a marvelously funny and humane carnival sequence in which the most clownish of the five drifters, superbly played by Alberto Sordi, gotten up in drag, drunkenly drags after him a huge papier-mâché clown's head. "Come, my beloved *testone,*" he apostrophizes it, and the audiovisual pun is perfect. *Testone* means large head, blockhead, and obstinate fellow, all of which Alberto is without facing up to it, and the image of him dragging the symbol of his own folly through the dust behind him is funny and moving without being patronizing or vulgar.

But by 1969, in *Satyricon,* Fellini allows us to glimpse several times an enormous marble head that has no other meaning than its own oddity; in *Amarcord,* we get an immense head of Mussolini, a kind of float made of flowers, which, in the fantasy of a porcine boy, opens its flowery mouth to promise him a glorious future. A motif that had a sound psychological, dramatic, and even symbolic raison d'être in an early film is dragged in, later, merely for show, for visual grandiloquence, and, still later, just for a corny gag. If these three heads symbolize anything to me, it is the pitiful decline of Fellini's mind and sensibility.

Quite rightly Peter Harcourt speaks about the "imaginative emptiness of Fellini's later films," of which *Amarcord* is the perfect example. Rather than stopping at "I Remember," Fellini's title should have gone on: "I Remember, I Reuse, I Rereuse, Until I Don't Even Remember What It Is I Am Rerereusing." *Amarcord* is as episodic and disjointed as all of Fellini's more recent films, but without even the saving grace of admitting it.

Everything in the film has either been done before by Fellini, in many cases more than once, or else it wasn't worth doing in the first place. Consider, for instance, the much-lauded scene in which the family takes an insane uncle out of the asylum for an afternoon in the country. The scene has possibilities, but Fellini makes nothing of them. The humor is either, as in much of the rest of the film, puerilely scatological-obscene, or virtually nonexistent. Thus the carriage in which they are riding must stop for the uncle to urinate in a field. The comic grandfather (he has earned his comedic stripes earlier by breaking wind and illustrating his sexual prowess with suggestive gestures) joins him in the act, but notices that his son, having failed to unbutton his fly, has befouled himself. There is much pseudocomic to-do about this, and when the coach finally moves on, we are shown that the horse, too, has left behind a large memento. Now, though the audience laps it all up, does it deserve being called by some reviewers equal or superior to scenes from Fellini's early masterworks?

Is any part of the film worthy of such kudos? When the mad uncle climbs up a tree, keeps shouting he wants a woman, and pelts those who would remove him with pebbles, I begin to wonder by what ingenious and humanly significant device the fellow will be brought down to earth. But the best Fellini can come up with is a midget nun who climbs up into the tree, utters a banality, and, pronto, down comes uncle like a lamb. True, the midget nun is played by a man, as certain normal-size nuns in early Fellini films were played, but does this, even so, make any kind of usable comment? At most, it makes nuns look ridiculous, which is neither germane nor humane.

And so it goes throughout this crude, unfunny film, in which the father, in moments of frenzy, beats his head or tramples his hat, something I thought went out with Chester Conklin or, at the latest, Leon Errol. *Amarcord* is even considered by some misguided souls to make a deep comment on Fascists, by showing them as nothing more than petty, spiteful, and ludicrous; but since just about everyone else in the film is mean and risible, the Fascists end up no different from the good guys. Because both *I Vitelloni* and *Amarcord* deal with the provincial life of Rimini, where Fellini grew up, some reviewers have sacrilegiously bracketed the two films. Yet they are as different as bread and mudpies, the early film dealing sympathetically with human beings, however fallible, and allowing the funny-sad life of the town to emerge through their tales, whereas the recent movie starts with some abstract notion of The Town, and, as in *Roma* (1972), slaps together some warmed-over autobiography and a few burlesque set pieces into a stillborn self-parody.

Yet the worst thing about *Amarcord* and its immediate predecessors is that the chief joke is human ugliness. Whether it is the aforementioned obese women displaying their behinds on bicycles; a ridiculous-looking uncle (another one) making himself more obviously repugnant by sporting a hairnet; a female Goliath using her naked bosom as a weapon; a family dinner scene in which almost all the faces, even those of the youngsters, are profoundly unprepossessing; a school in which every teacher is some kind of puppet or gargoyle; a town populated mostly with freaks; or, saddest of all, a little schoolgirl whose homeliness is paraded about as a source of delicious mirth—the joke is always on humanity, and almost always on the easiest, cheapest, and, finally, most witless level.

There is no denying that witty satire thrives on savaging mankind, but where in *Amarcord* is there witty satire? Alternatively, where is compassion? Even the figure of the whore, whom Fellini used to depict with almost excessive, often sentimental, sympathy, has become a ghoulish, nymphomaniacal madwoman, wallowing in a crude parody of auto-eroticism. Time was when Fellini could tell the journalist Anita Pensotti that he had to make movies in an atmosphere of fun, confidence, and enthusiasm. More recently, he told Charles Thomas Samuels that his films were tormenting imps to be got rid of, that "the sign I have to make a film is given by my hatred of it." The hatred, alas, extends to all humankind, and, lacking the wit of a Swift or a Voltaire, the best Fellini can look forward to is equaling the dismal record of a Ken Russell.

In the early Fellini films, mankind, all of it, was encompassed by the filmmaker's love: no one was too stupid or frail, too guileful or beastly, to forfeit Fellini's comprehending care. Not a sappy, slavering love, still less a patronizing pat on the head, it was a sadly, tenderly all-pervasive compassion. Of course, one can make as good films out of fury, despair, indignation, passionate mockery, or any other strong feeling; what one cannot do is make a good film out of self-serving smugness and general indifference.

And to think that this once great artist is still only fifty-four, an age at which one hasn't even earned the right to the excuse of senility.

November 24–December 1974

Growing Up Absurd

ANOTHER NOTED DIRECTOR, Louis Malle, a slightly lesser member of the original New Wave, continues his steady advance. Though he made his name with the undistinguished but sexy *The Lovers,* it is with *The Fire Within, Murmur of the Heart,* and the Indian documentaries that Malle earned his true credentials; now *Lacombe, Lucien,* although hardly a flawless work of art, marks another step in the right direction. It is a kind of fictional companion piece to Marcel Ophüls's powerful documentary *The Sorrow and the Pity—* more appendix than pendant, perhaps, but important, all the same. It concerns the last six months of a seventeen-year-old boy, Lucien Lacombe, or, in the peasant way of giving your name, as well as in the officialese of the Nazi occupation, Lacombe, Lucien.

A callow and untutored village youth in southwestern France, Lucien excels at shooting hares and, in April 1944, as the Allies begin to overrun France, conceives of joining the *maquis.* But the underground, represented by the teacher from whom Lucien mostly played hooky, doesn't want kids ("War isn't like poaching," as the teacher says and the subtitles do not translate), so he drifts into the camp of the Vichy police, disaffected or fanatical French servants of the Gestapo. Gotten drunk by the policemen, impressed to find among them an idolized former cycling champion, and warmed by the seeming respect he is shown for the first time in his life, Lucien betrays his teacher and joins the police. So begins an unthinking but gratifying life of raids, torturings, confiscated wealth, and status.

When a spineless young aristocrat and fellow policeman, Jean Bernard, takes the boy to have his first real suit made by a former leading Paris tailor, a Jew now hiding in this provincial town with his surly mother and pianist daughter, Lucien's manhood begins. Albert Horn's child, France, is twenty, pretty, and spoiled. Lucien woos her childishly and crudely, while her sophisticated father, who has given up almost all hope, looks on with disgusted fascination. When Lucien commandeers the girl for a farewell party at headquarters for Jean Bernard and his ex-movie-actress girl friend (the two are escaping to Spain with money extorted chiefly from Horn), France is manhandled and cruelly humiliated for being a Jewess. Out of her ensuing despair, and the realization that Lucien is, after all, the best of the lot as well as enamored of her, but also because her flesh has needs of its own, France becomes Lucien's mistress, and the boy moves in with the Horns. Albert treats him mostly with a horrified irony, but there is also a latent affection between the cocky, uncouth little peasant and the refined, morally and physically attenuated master tailor. During a last, reckless attempt to get Lucien to help with an escape to Spain, Albert is apprehended by Faure, the beastliest of the French policemen, and handed over to the Germans.

Meanwhile, Lucien ignores all warnings about his own impending execution once France is liberated. Part enjoyment of his ghastly work, part sense of fatality, something draws him on, let the heads fall where they may. In reprisal for a successful underground raid, the Germans, in the person of a Wehrmacht soldier and Lucien, round up France and her granny, who are allowed to take along only some essentials. From out of these Lucien scoops up a looted watch he once gave Albert, but the German insultingly takes it from him. Lucien kills the soldier—it is hard to say whether to recover the watch and his honor, or to save his girl—and escapes with France and the grumpy grandmother. Somewhere in the country their car breaks down, and the trio settles into an abandoned farmhouse to live off Lucien's poaching skills. Now a family provider, Lucien enjoys a summer idyll in the teeth of approaching catastrophe. By fall, an inscription tells us, he will be captured and shot; we are not told what becomes of the Horns.

Lacombe, Lucien is remarkable, first, because it brings to a fiction film perhaps better than ever before (including even Bergman's powerful *Shame*) the sense of the banality of evil. Art did not need Hannah Arendt to alert it to an insight the great visual and plastic artists always possessed. In one of his finest poems, W. H. Auden evoked this awesome, almost callous, serenity of the Old Masters in whose paintings "everything turns away/Quite leisurely from the disaster"; so Malle's film will have a montage of the torturers at work in the police headquarters' bathroom, dunking a manacled man's head in the full tub, then a big, lazy dog sprawling contentedly on the staircase while we hear the victim's screams, then a couple of giggling brats scampering down the stairs while below, at the bar, black marketeers negotiate and, in the next room, Jean Bernard and his dumb Betty play a sloppy game of table tennis. And with the exception of the loathsome fanatic Faure, the collaborators are crass and selfish rather than deeply vicious. Villagers and townsfolk lead harassed but stupidly normal lives: while her husband is a prisoner of war, Lucien's mother lives with one of the village bigwigs; a town landlord is stolidly pleased to keep raising the rent of the Jews he is harboring. Somewhere there are *maquisards* fighting and dying, but they are the exception; the norm is adaptability, mean-spiritedness, and survival.

Furthermore, the film is daring enough to show the victims, too, as less than perfect lambs or brave martyrs. Horn is suffocating in apathy: his efforts at escape have slackened, he has relaxed his control over his daughter, his acceptance of exploitation by Jean Bernard is almost too willing. He cannot work up righteous indignation even at the snotty Lucien, whose tepid   189 champagne he guzzles, and his only weapon is a maudlin irony. France has had some previous unsavory love affair, and now this with Lucien; for all her finer stirrings, she is overindulged and willful. And not noble: when a servant lass whom Lucien jilted for her publicly berates her as a dirty Jew, France simply goes to pieces and sobs out her loathing for her Jewishness. She runs up to hide and weep in the bathroom where prisoners are tortured; she is doubled up in pain like them over the same bathtub; and in this bathroom she becomes Lucien's concubine. As for the grandmother, she has become a perfect grouch, refuses to talk French (the Horns are German Jews), and sulkily withdraws into the solipsistic game of solitaire. The tragedy of war is not so much that it makes some into heroic victims; it is rather that it makes most end up soiled and ugly.

Malle is, I think, saying that good doesn't have to be all that good, or bad all that bad, yet there is a right distinguishable from wrong. Only it's so very hard sometimes to make the distinction. How admiringly one of Lucien's chums, the village priest's acolyte, gazes at our hero after he has wrought bloody carnage among the rabbit population. How aroused France is by an animal trap Lucien is resetting even as she caresses a wood dove that was caught in it; as she sweetly fondles tonight's dinner, she has a look of positively sexual excitation while contemplating the next entrapment. And once, when Lucien is asleep, she picks up a rock and thinks of bashing in his head; but his eyes open to gaze at her, and she becomes powerless.

Ambiguous gazes, ambivalent attitudes prevail. Lucien's mother, who comes to warn her bad boy that death awaits him unless he runs, is nevertheless glad to accept ill-gotten moneys from him. Although Lucien likes Albert, he is not above threatening him in nasty playfulness with his submachine gun. Though Albert feels that he ought to, he cannot manage to hate Lucien. People are more benighted than wicked, like the womenfolk of that upper-class partisan about to be led off and shot, who cannot understand why their man doesn't call up the police prefect to complain about mistreatment. Queerest and creepiest are the letters of denunciation Frenchmen send in about fellow Frenchmen, some of which we hear. In one of them, a chap writes that as a good Catholic and Frenchman he cannot tolerate black-marketeering and must report so-and-so. "Someone," says a dried-up policewoman, "even denounced himself. It's a sickness."

But art does not oversimplify; rather, it faces up to complexity and duality. The sordid little affair between Lucien and France has its poetic side, nevertheless; on some levels, they are still young, still innocent. Lucien, who thinks nothing of killing a songbird with his slingshot, pityingly caresses the hideous carcass of a dead horse. Some of those scurvy Frenchmen working for the Germans still have their moments of grace. The only certain evils are stupidity and ignorance, and Lucien is saddled with both; but how guilty is a person of innate cloddishness or environmentally absorbed backwardness? We do not rejoice when an intertitle superimposed on the final shot of Lucien lying in a meadow and watching the naked France announces his execution on October 12, 1944. If anything, we look at him as France does in the penultimate frames, both chilled and concerned, seeing past and future, cause and effect, in unsettling palimpsest.

There is a fine sense of detail here, yet Malle will go wrong through repetition and overexplicitness. Twice, when Lucien is at his most ominous, he sits down on the piano keys France has just been playing and produces a brutal sound; it would have been very effective—once. Twice during crucial scenes a couple of kids come chasing by. Twice a symbolic pun on France the girl and France the country is rubbed into us. Two or three times, Lucien, trying on his first custom-made suit, transfers his handgun from one inside pocket to the other, twice missing a pocket.

There is one occasion when repetition *is* significant—though it may be lost on American audiences thanks to poor subtitling. When Albert Horn is delivered to the Gestapo by Faure, the latter first humiliates him with viciously anti-Semitic remarks softened (perhaps deliberately) by the subtitles. Horn fights back with dignified irony; what breaks him, however, is that the rotten fellow keeps addressing him with the familiar *tu*, horribly condescending from a stranger. His last, shocked words—to the man who is sending him to his death—are, "But why do you keep calling me 'thou?'" which the subtitles skip altogether.

Later, when Lucien gets his last chance from a captured officer of the underground, who, in return for being freed, might save him from the firing squad, the officer makes the mistake of addressing him as *tu*. "I don't like being addressed as 'thou!'" Lucien roughly replies—twice. We need this emphasis to realize that he is throwing away his life to maintain his mistaken sense of dignity, and that he may have gotten the importance of the *vous*, at least in part, from the example of Albert. The subtitles render this with "I don't like strangers talking to me," which loses all the implications.

The film has brilliant moments—like his mother's visit to Lucien at the Horns'—and rather less brilliant ones like, say, the bitchy carryings-on of Betty, the stupid and bored movie actress. Yet its main weakness is its hero: Lucien is a bit too crass for us to care about him deeply. The problem is almost insuperable; make him more sensitive and you lose your point: the exploitation of dumb kids by power politics. Were Lucien more perceptive, his tragedy might never have occurred, or it would have taken a very different form. Here the idea was to show that even such humdrum creatures carry with them a modicum of pathos, a touch of tragedy, all the sadder perhaps for being so commonplace and frequent. Thus Lucien must be as he is—except that a great artist, which Malle isn't, or isn't yet, would have made him more moving even in his brutishness.

Among the many things in the movie's favor, let me mention only the outstanding acting of almost everybody down to the smallest parts, even if I single out here merely the grandmother of Therese Giehse, one of the stars of Brecht's Berliner Ensemble. With very few lines (and those in German), she manages to make her near-silent part convey a whole quirky, selfish, petulant yet extraordinary, undauntable old woman. And now a few words for the masterly cinematography of Tonino Delli Colli, who has worked for various directors and always for Pasolini, whose unpalatable films he imbued with great visual beauty. Here he makes the countryside look vital and attractive but not lushly romantic. A sunset, for example, that elicits a response even from Lucien's inchoate soul is not all that resplendent: more burnt orange than glorious reds and pinks, but by this very burnished quality earthier and more likely to appeal to Lucien, with his pawky eyes seldom opened beyond a slit. Or consider the Horns' interior: how exactly poised it is between gloom and a certain cozy nonchalance. You are never aware of gimmickry; when the young lovers are naked on their first morning after, bathed in an ever-so-slightly chilling blue light, this derives from the blue bathroom tiles. If Aristotle was for Dante *maestro di color che sanno*, Delli Colli is for me *maestro dei colori che sono*.

Malle's film, to its final credit, raises a question even more troubling than the political ones: whether this rough boy, in a full life span in his rude village, could have lived as intensely and excitingly as he did by selling himself to Evil for one violent, miraculous spring and summer.

December 1974

Made in Heaven?

INGMAR BERGMAN'S *Scenes From a Marriage* is not as released the great filmmaker's best film, and may not even be the best film of the year. But it is almost certainly one of the most important films ever made, if by importance we understand the possibility of art's influencing people in a positive way—a slight, elusive possibility, perhaps even an impossible one. But one that we must believe in if we are not to give up on art or humanity, either of which strikes me as giving up on life.

Originally, *Scenes From a Marriage* was six fifty-minute television episodes, which, broadcast once weekly in Sweden, virtually stopped all other activities. The series had to be rerun a couple of times, and everyone watched, brooded on, debated the programs. The marriage of Johan and Marianne became an exemplar, like a great chess game, a political crisis, or the struggle for survival of men trapped in a mine shaft. People who previously were scarcely aware of Bergman's existence now buttonholed him on the street to discuss his new work. Under its influence, some marriages broke up, while others were re-examined and mended. Bergman had always wanted his films to be a craftsman's artifacts for people's use, like tables or chairs. With *Scenes From a Marriage* he succeeded beyond all expectations.

The television installments were trimmed down slightly and fused into a four-hour film. This was initially meant to be shown in theaters, either in one or in two parts. Eventually, though, Bergman cut the film to two hours and forty-eight minutes (the hardest thing he ever had to do, he says), and, blown up from 16 mm to 35 mm, it was commercially released. I shall refer to the original version as O, to the middle version as M, and to the final one as F; having read O in the published screenplay and seen both M and F, I confess that they have merged in my mind, and that I can no longer speak about anything but a fused version with the fullness of O, the encompassability of M, and the wide-screen spaciousness of F. I advise moviegoers to buy O (Pantheon Books) and read it; then see F and enjoy it more than they could otherwise; then start a write-in campaign to Cinema V for the theatrical release of M or the televising of O, or better yet, both.*

Only in such an exceptional case do I recommend reading the script first. Even though *Scenes* was shot as a movie (this is an important distinction), it was intended for television, which means that it consists mostly of closeups and two-shots, and a great deal of dialogue. What was Bergman to do when this went abroad? A full complement of subtitles would detract much needed attention from the faces, if not actually obliterate them. Dubbing in such steady closeups would be distractingly recognizable, and, besides, what voice-dubbers could match the vocal perfection of Liv Ullmann and Erland Josephson? He settled for sparse, selective subtitles as the least of evils, allegedly designating exactly which lines were to be translated. I think he underestimated our capacity: we are able to see all we need to and still read much more than is given us, some of the omissions being crucial (I shall cite two of these later). So, please, read the book first.

Scenes From a Marriage is for our time what *Everyman* was for the Middle Ages. In its simple way, that medieval morality play embodied all the eschatological knowledge the average person needed to live and die by; in a quite similar, though less simple, way, Bergman's film sums up for us all there is to know about love, sex, marriage, divorce—the life of a man and woman together and apart. In that sense, it is perhaps closer in its capaciousness to the great medieval synthesizer, Thomas Aquinas, and can be viewed as a *summa psychologica* and *summa erotica* and, most of all, a *summa matrimonii*. Alongside the major literary tracts on love by such writers as Stendhal, Kierkegaard, and Ortega y Gasset, we must now place this cinematic treatise on married love—indeed, on basic man-woman relations—by the giant of Swedish and world filmmaking.

The six "scenes" of the film chronicle ten years in the life of Marianne and Johan, a middle-class Swedish couple; he is an associate professor at the Psychotechnical Institute (whatever that may be) and she a lawyer specializing in family law. In the first section, "Innocence and Panic," the two are firmly married to each other, with the husband dominant but neither spouse particularly aware of it, and with an undercurrent of frustration under the sweepingly normal flow of marital life. In one sequence, the couple, parents of two daughters, are being interviewed for a women's magazine as an ideally married pair; later we see them as dinner hosts to another couple, much unhappier than they are yet desperately needing each other even as they prepare for divorce; finally, we see Johan and Marianne getting ready

---

*M was, alas, never released theatrically. But O was televised by PBS, both in a subtitled and in a dubbed version, which sounded dreadful, as such things always do.   193

for bed, with all their psychological uncertainties, but also with the comfortably formfitting delusions that enable them to continue together. (O contained an abortion sequence, but it seems to me less than essential.)

In the second section, "The Art of Sweeping Under the Rug," we get a sense of how tiresome social and family obligations impinge on marital plenitude, and a hint that Johan may be having a clandestine affair. We see the couple at work: Marianne counsels, and is disturbed by, an older woman who, after a long and unfulfilling marriage, seeks a divorce, even though loneliness is all she can look forward to; Johan uses a young woman professor—a colleague who is also his lover—as guinea pig in a psychological experiment. She tells him that his poetry, for which he harbors secret hopes, is mediocre, which enrages him. In the concluding sequence, we see Johan and Marianne at sexual odds with each other, but carrying on as best they can without probing into their difficulties.

"Paula," the third section, takes place at the couple's country house, where Johan informs his now more than usually ardent wife that he is leaving her tomorrow for Paula, a young language student with whom he is off for a year in Paris. Johan disgorges his hostilities; Marianne brings out all her devotion, jealousy, pathos, and almost morbid curiosity about Paula. They spend an odd night together and have an even stranger breakfast; then he goes, inexorable though rather shaken. On the phone Marianne finds out that her friends knew about the whole thing for some time, and rage is added to her grief.

In the fourth section, "The Vale of Tears," Johan, now living with Paula, comes to his old home for dinner with Marianne, now the mistress of David. It is an exotically titillating tête-à-tête: though still married, they are also strangers; though discussing the prospect of his probable three-year guest stint at an American university and the concomitant advisability of a divorce, they end up inordinately loving with each other. They try lovemaking, but she backs out. She reads him her memoirs of childhood and youth (set down at her analyst's instigation, and brilliantly illustrated by Bergman with snapshots of Liv Ullmann at various ages), but he falls asleep in the middle of it. Still, they end up in bed together, but, as they both sense, only transiently, inconclusively.

In the fifth and most shattering section, "The Illiterates," they meet in Johan's austere office to go over and sign the divorce papers. Johan's American job has fallen through, the Paula business is a failure, and the man's self-esteem is at its nadir; Marianne has lovers, successes, imminent independence, and is riding high. One last time, she seduces Johan on his office floor to prove to herself that she no longer needs him; when he catches on, he beats her savagely, and there is a hideous physical and verbal fight. Instead of reconquering her, he signs the papers icily; she leaves with the observation: "We should have started fighting long ago. It would have been much better."

The sixth and concluding section, "In the Middle of the Night in a Dark House Somewhere in the World," takes place ten years after the first. Both
Marianne and Johan have remarried quite other people than their earlier

lovers, and are, on the whole, satisfied with them. But a year ago they met at the theater and precipitately became lovers again. Now, with their spouses away on trips, they will have a weekend together in their old summer house. The memories are too painful, and they switch to a friend's cottage, which, however, is a mess. Still, they bed down quite pleasantly, exchanging sexual and other confidences. She tells about her marriage to a go-getter and sexual athlete (which makes Johan uncomfortable), and confesses also to some early infidelities in her first marriage. He admits to his repressed desire to be a small-town bookshop owner and live in uncomplicated calm. They have found an amazing new gentleness with each other, and wonder whether this is love, happiness, the best one can hope for. They say cozily wise things, but fall asleep intertwined, with the great questions barely, if at all, answered. The last few minutes of the film (identical in O, M, and F) are among the most profound and moving moments I have ever experienced anywhere, but *must* also be read in the screenplay, where they constitute three or four pages of writing that is richly mellow, incantatory, and sublime.

Let me deal first with an objection to the film one hears occasionally: that it is too commonplace; that these people are so Everyman and Everywoman that they cease to be specific individuals; that the whole thing is too much of a faceless generalization. I disagree emphatically—especially after reading O and seeing M, both of which, alas, are superior to F. But do not let this serve as an excuse for skipping the released version. No, Johan and Marianne are not platitudes; they are encyclopedias. Let us face it, great art, as Cocteau was first to point out, is made up of commonplaces. What is new is their form and style, the changes in sensibility and in expressions of feelings. But the bringing into focus of human needs, inchoate awarenesses, twilight long-ings—their being made manifest for today's understanding—is always only great art's playing variations on what great art has said before. Man changes in some ways, but where the subjects are love and transience, the two funda-mental themes, originality will always be only a commonplace given time-lier, more elegant, more piercingly poetic expression.

The fact that we have all known Johans and Mariannes—the fact that we ourselves are, to a greater or lesser extent, Johan and Marianne—only in-creases their value for us. This would not be so if mere recognition were everything, but something significant has been added: Johan and Marianne are more vividly, juicily, exemplarily what we ourselves are. They represent our flaws and quirks, weaknesses and virtues, more brilliantly and per-spicuously than we can. Early on Marianne remarks: "Sometimes it's as if husband and wife were making a long-distance call to each other on faulty telephones. Sometimes it's like hearing two tape recorders with preset pro-grams. And sometimes it's the great silence of outer space. I don't know which is more horrible." Very perceptive, we say, but not yet brilliant. The brilliance is in the sentence that precedes it: "I'm always coming across it in my work." In other words, Marianne, who shrewdly identifies the three horrors of marriage, can do so only in that of someone else, not in her own.

Later, when Johan announces he is leaving, Marianne blames herself. "Stop that," he says. "It's an easy way out always to take the blame. It   195

makes you feel strong and noble and generous and humble." This is penetrating, but then the man is a psychologist and clearly understands. Yet
only a moment earlier this canny man said: "I know that we've had a good
life. And actually I think I still love you. In fact in one way I love you *more*
now since I met Paula. But can you understand this bitterness? I don't know
what to call it. This bitterness, I can't hit on any better word." This man
who knows so much actually knows nothing.

What Bergman perceives devastatingly clearly is the continual jockeying
for power in the most intimate of relationships. But he knows also how
unconsciously it all happens, how unaware these characters are of what they
are doing. And so he makes them utter truths that are truer than they
realize. When Marianne shows Johan a letter she got from Paula in which
the mistress describes compassionately Johan's bravado underneath which
he is so unsure, Johan mutters, "I've noticed that actually you can say
anything you like about anyone at all. Somehow it always fits." Though on
the simplest level this is merely a way of sloughing off Paula's insight, there
is a greater verity here; we are all of us so alike and yet so idiosyncratic that
it is perfectly true: some conventional or contrary feature in us will make
every aphorism at least partly hit the mark. But in another way, Johan's
clever epigram merely proves Paula's point: it is an intimation of its truth
that makes him want to ridicule it—precisely the reaction of a man with a
fine façade covering a basic softness.

The marvelous thing about *Scenes* is that while showing only two characters in great detail, and a few others only peripherally, it manages to convey
a whole bourgeois consumer society—its economics, politics, social structure,
feeble idealisms, and thriving insecurities—through casual remarks, offhand
allusions, the feel of a room, the look of a piece of furniture. Particularly
telling is the yearning of these highly urbanized, intellectual, sophisticated
personages to achieve a pastoral naïveté, which they suppose to be hopelessly
beyond them. "Why can't we be big and fat and good-tempered? Just think
how nice it would make us," Marianne lets slip, when things seem still quite
all right. A year later, close to divorce, she wishes: "If only we could meet as
the people we were meant to be. And not as the people who play the parts
all sorts of powers have assigned us." Several years and two new marriages
later, they spell it out more clearly. Johan talks about the small provincial
bookshop he would have been happiest running, and Marianne agrees:
"How content we'd have been. We'd have grown fat and comfortable and
had a lot of children . . . and never quarreled." But Johan hates even the two
children they do have and, oh, how they quarrel!

Yet Utopia of a sort sneaks up on them. With their respective spouses
abroad, they are in a country hideaway, serene lovers again. They tell each
other truths that had to be suppressed before or else hurled out as lethal
projectiles; now even the most painful ones among them emit a penumbral
satisfaction, a soothing phosphorescence of decay. "Everything's fine. . . . It's
just that I can't stand it," Johan complains; but in the new-found intimacy
with Marianne, the lament becomes a respite. "Just think if everything

really is too late," Marianne moans as they lie in bed together. Johan replies: "We mustn't say things like that. Only think them." (The subtitles, damnably, don't translate the second statement.) This is maturity: knowing which truths to tell the other person, and which ones to tell only oneself. "I feel a great tenderness for you and forget about myself," says Marianne, "even though I don't efface myself." And Johan: "I think that you and I love each other, in an earthly and imperfect way." Without knowing it, and though they can only do it furtively and intermittently, these two have become, in spirit, the fat, comfortable little people of their longings. As they go to sleep, they murmur sensible, sustaining things to each other, such as: "If we harp on it too much, love will give out." They have become loving friends.

Scenes From a Marriage is a journey into friendship: a sexual, adulterous, untidy friendship, if you will, but a genuine one. "Perhaps one day we'll be very good friends," the divorcing Marianne has exclaimed. And it has come to pass. Several years ago, while lunching with Bergman, I told him of the sadness of staying in the same Stockholm hotel room without the woman who had shared it with me before, and who was now marrying another man; surely Bergman, the great mystagogue of the human heart, would come up with the profound, specific solace. "That's all right," he said, "you'll remain friends." I was disconcerted: Is that the best he could do? It may indeed be the best; at least, as Johan and Marianne prove, it is good enough.

The film is superlatively directed. Bergman, who has always proclaimed his love for the human face on screen, has never had this love more lovingly reciprocated than here by the faces of Liv Ullmann and Erland Josephson. Bergman's *The Magician* is called *The Face* in Sweden, and in the present film, truly, the face meets its magician. Yes, Miss Ullmann is a great actress, as we know from her majestic work for Bergman and Jan Troell, and creditable performances even in such Anglo-American atrocities as *The Abdication;* but never before has such variety been elicited from her.

She is fragile and tough not only by quick turns but also, if needed, both at once, as in a magisterial scene in M (unfortunately cut from F) where her husband tells her about how their faithful cleaning woman found him in bed with Paula and was first shocked, then madly solicitous. Miss Ullmann must register not merely a kind of abashed, involuntary amusement and a sophisticated cheerfulness to maintain her pride, but also a lacerating pain underneath; she brings off all three by turning her face into a living palimpsest, one of the most stunning pieces of acting I have ever encountered on stage, screen, or in life. But never mind, there are scenes galore left in F where she can display—though never ostentatiously—her endless range and infinite subtlety.

Erland Josephson is a more cerebral actor, with something more deliberate, *voulu,* about his performance, but this is both appropriate here and done with great command. He is not an unduly handsome man (as Miss Ullmann is meltingly lovely), and so must work harder on winning us over, but he does—by a reticence fraught with implications, expressions that seem to sink into his face rather than sally forth. It is great ensemble acting by a quicksilver pair, through which one always feels Bergman's presence, as one *hears* the conductor in great orchestral playing. The framing of shots, the alternation of closeups and two-shots, cool and warm colors, light and dark, the changing camera angles—above all, the ravaging effect when at a crucial point the camera pulls back to reveal, for instance, the disarray of an office floor that served successively as lovers' bed and haters' battlefield—these are the most easily overlooked yet least deniable hallmarks of a master self-effacingly at work.

There are also beautiful supporting performances and, as always, the unsurpassable cinematography of Sven Nykvist, who tames colors as a lion tamer does his royal beasts: now keeping them harmless pussycats, now urging them to display regal powers. And it is photography so sharp as to survive unimpaired in translation from 16 mm to 35 mm. But, then, the film oozes one or another beauty through every pore. Take the terrible moment when Marianne is about to halt the divorce, but Johan, with an irony more sneakily cutting than a knife—say, a piece of paper's edge—sneers, "God, what a sermon!" (untranslated by the subtitles) and starts her hatred rolling again. Or the scene when Johan, about to go off with Paula, learns that his gray suit is at the cleaner's, and Marianne asks touchingly, "Can't you travel in your jacket and flannel pants? They give you a nice youthful air." It is a moment when you can almost hear a pizzicato on the audience's heartstrings.

With sovereign wisdom, Bergman limits himself to the drama of the two beings that really matter. The other lovers and mates are merely spoken of, only once glimpsed. Even the children and in-laws are felt rather than seen. For as Rilke recognized, the Third "who goes through all lives and literatures . . . has no significance. . . . Living among people . . . are the Two, of whom there would be so unbelievably much to say, of whom as yet nothing has ever been said, although they suffer and act and do not know how to help themselves." It is this Twosome that Bergman has captured in *Scenes From a Marriage,* a superspectacular like *War and Peace,* complete with Battle of Borodino and all the rest, for a cast of millions played by two players. And, for the most part, only by their faces, voices, words—and their great creator, Ingmar Bergman.

January 1975

Nothing Fails Like Excess

Luis Buñuel is a difficult director to evaluate. At seventy-five, his oeuvre might well be completed, yet new films, each heralded as his last, keep pouring from him. Although these late films strike me as vacuous and unnecessary contraptions, each is hailed as a masterpiece, often even by critics I respect. What film in recent memory garnered such unanimous raves as *The*

Discreet Charm of the Bourgeoisie? Yet I found it a pretentious, often pointless, mostly crude and witless rehash of everything Buñuel had done better before. It was filled with the cackle of an old man laughing at his own feeble, oft-repeated joke, and with a palsied indignation, lacking focus and potency.

Now along comes *The Phantom of Liberté* (the most absurdly macaronic American title since *The Grande Bouffe*), and though not making its predecessor's claims to definitive statements about the bourgeoisie, and possessed of a few amusing moments in its early sequences, it is, ultimately, just as exhausted, disconnected, repetitious, and ineffectual a film as *Bourgeoisie*.

Two forces have always been operative in Buñuel: his adherence to surrealism with its celebration of the irrational in dreams and fantasies, and his war on oppression and repression, social, political, or sexual. What complicates this schema, however, is that Buñuel has variously cast in the chief oppressor's role the Catholic Church, Franco's Fascism, the upper classes, the middle class, and human nature itself, perceived as predominantly evil— ruthlessness being the very condition of survival. All of these hostile forces may appear in one and the same Buñuel film, confused and even contradictory, and the director scatters his shots at so many-headed, chimeric, and shifting an adversary.

What complicates matters further is Buñuel's assumption that surrealism is the real weapon for his particular warfare, which, more often than not, it isn't. He is confusing two kinds of liberation: liberation from conventions, taboos, and crippling psychic fears, for which hauling out the secret, repressed images of the unconscious may indeed be the proper strategy; and liberation from political or religious oppression of a specific sort, which, if it yields to anything (doubtful as that is), yields to a clear and reasoned attack, either serious or satirical. This presumed all-purpose surrealism works best in the framework of mischievous banter (*The Age of Gold, Simon of the Desert*), or when a sense of the tragic keeps it at a minimum (*Los Olvidados, Viridiana,* and perhaps *Land Without Bread*). It works least when Buñuel's always uncertain tone shifts most (*Diary of a Chambermaid, The Exterminating Angel, Belle de Jour*). In such recent films as *The Milky Way, Tristana,* and *Bourgeoisie,* the tone is painfully vacillating, the surrealism has a senescent, worn-out look, and there is much deliberate obfuscation.

So, too, in *Le Fantôme de la liberté* (to give the new film at least the dignity of its original title) things get thoroughly out of hand. Continuity of any sort is achieved only by the most desperate stratagems, and the attempt to give shape or savor to individual episodes or to the whole film results in the dragging in of shabby jokes, the milking of dried-up devices, and a dismally schematic repetitiousness. The film's first episode is based on a vignette by G. A. Bécquer, Spain's foremost Romantic poet. In it, a Napoleonic officer feeling up the statue of a Spanish noblewoman is clouted on the head by the marble arm of the adjoining statue of her husband. This is filmed against a background that re-creates Goya's famous painting: Spanish patriots shouting, "Down with liberty!" at a French firing squad, as they choose death rather than Napoleon's kind of liberation.

So far, so good. But the avenging statue reminds Buñuel of Don Juan's

Stone Guest, and off he goes into an episode about the French officer violating Doña Elvire's coffin, where the corpse is revealed in miraculous preservation. This has nothing to do with Bécquer's story, and merely indulges Buñuel in one of his favorite motifs, necrophilia (as in *Belle de Jour* and elsewhere). A private fantasy obtrudes on what began as a veiled allusion to Spain's present political predicament. An off-screen female voice tells us that Elvire had been buried with all her paraphernalia, and another woman's voice asks for the meaning of that word. We now see two present-day Parisian nannies reading this old romance, while a suspicious character accosts the two little girls they should be watching. He gives the girls postcards whose apparent filthiness makes one child let out a knowing exclamation as the other stares spellbound. Herewith another Buñuelian *topos*, child molestation (as, for instance, in *Chambermaid*); but what has this to do with the much more genteel and grown-up upper-class decadence the rest of the film lampoons?

Next we meet the children's rich, sophisticated parents. Daddy is a passionate arachnologist, has a huge spider framed on the mantelpiece, and catechizes his daughters in spider lore. The call of the dark, sinister instincts, we assume, and recall the fighting scorpions with which *The Age of Gold* begins. But the tone changes as the parents stare in horror at the confiscated postcards, and a reverse shot reveals the cards as depicting well-known landmarks like the Eiffel Tower and Sacré Coeur. Mildly funny, these bourgeois viewing the monuments of their own class and society as scabrous monstrosities. But, then, why the leering character who distributed them, and the girls' clearly sexual response? Surrealist game-playing? But how does this jibe with the immediate firing of the governess, an instant switch of tone to one of nasty social satire?

One mode continually undercuts the other, and repetitiveness undoes them both. There is, to be sure, another moderately amusing scene in which some monks in a hotel, having gambled with rosaries and sacred medallions for chips, are forthwith shocked to their hypocritical marrows by the kinky sexual practices of their neighbors. Thereafter the film goes irremediably wrong. The reversal ploy, as with the postcards, keeps returning ever more jarringly and meaninglessly. Thus a polite company sits around the dinner table discussing ecology, and as one of them raises the threat of accumulations of human excrement, all of them are revealed to be seated on toilet bowls, presumably excreting in unison. Presently, they start excusing themselves, as one or another locks him- or herself into a bathroomlike cabinet, where, however, a dumbwaiter provides an avidly consumed meal.

Note that this doesn't work on any level. A portrayal of social irresponsibility: people who worry about the threat of excreta blithely increasing that threat? Nonsense. Feces, on the contrary, provide useful fertilizer. A depiction of human hypocrisy and foolish arbitrariness: pretending to philosophize while actually excreting; doing one private thing (defecation) in company, the other (eating) in concealment, though the reverse would make just as much, or just as little, sense? But hypocrisy and arbitrariness are very different faults, and to attack them thus bracketed is, to say the least, arbitrary. Mere dreamlike, surreal illogic? Then it is all much too neatly anti-thetical, much too pat to resemble the spontaneous, heterodox modes of surrealism and dreams.

In further episodes of *Fantôme,* we encounter, for example, another set of parents who claim their daughter did not return from school, ignore her protesting presence right beside them, and go, *with her,* to the police to report her as missing, and so on. This means, if it does anything, that we ignore our young, the truth that comes from the mouths of babes. But what a clumsy way to make a dubious point: the paradox is so witlessly gross, is belabored with such ponderous persistence, that the discriminating viewer must consider the procedure as untrustworthy—philosophically as well as artistically—as a pair of loaded dice.

Another sequence has a boy seducing his elderly but well-preserved aunt to no visible point, except perhaps to scoff at the incest taboo; still another, with the reversal technique, has a mass-murdering sniper exonerated in court and courted by an adoring public. If the sniper were shown as some sort of Mansonish cult figure, a point could perhaps be made; but Buñuel rushes through the sequence with mechanistic uninvolvement. Yet another episode offers us a police commissioner in duplicate, played simultaneously by two different actors. One seems very proper, the other not—yet just what kind of impropriety is aimed at by his receiving a phone call from his dead sister who used to play the piano for him in the nude? More necrophilia and incest; but do these recurrent motifs tell us something about police commissioners or about Buñuel? The commissioners go off to quell a political upris-ing at the zoo—not by the animals, but by some invisible revolutionaries heard shouting, "Down with liberty!"

So the film ends, having come full circle—or has it? Something is supposed to have been brought home to us—perhaps that, now as then, though a few will die for liberty, the majority will repress or persecute freedom. But what is freedom to Buñuel, anyway? To be able to bed one's aunt, or practice sadomasochism as a parlor game with the active or passive participation of the clergy? All this, like so much of Buñuel, is not really surrealism but Dadaism, which, though not inferior, was something different. Its purpose was not to explore and liberate the unconscious, but to jolt the middle class out of its smugness by mocking all its values, and especially its notion of art. But today's bourgeoisie has given up most of its notions of respectability, and tolerates—when it doesn't downright revere—the most preposterous forms of "art." So who is there left to be shocked by these late Buñuel films? It is 1975, but you cannot teach old Andalusian dogs new tricks. Perhaps this dated daring succeeds through its quaintness: doing what the porno films do, but with a little mystery added; perhaps even through its conserva-tism: displaying statelier, more respectable production values, and greater restraint.

What can we say about a dream sequence that merely introduces an emu (or is it a cassowary?) into the dreamer's bedroom, followed by a mailman with a letter that is there even after the sleeper awakes? What feeble, etio-lated bits of surrealism or Dada from a filmmaker who once gave us *Viri-*

diana! Can any of this be blamed, perhaps, on Jean-Claude Carrière, Buñuel's coscenarist on all his worst films, beginning with *Chambermaid?* Or is it that, besides what I have said above, Buñuel has grown old and soft—though not quite so obviously senile as the Renoir of such late films as *Le Petit Théâtre de Jean Renoir.*

I think also that much that has been hailed as Buñuel's profundity is merely self-purgation: catharsis for himself rather than for his audience. Though this may be the commonest motive for artistic creation, it is, by itself, insufficient. Too often Buñuel seems merely compelled to let his sadism or foot fetishism or love-hate for the Church out of the bag, and it is only the combined stupidity of critics and audiences that reverently endows this with supposed universal significance. Yet some of Buñuel's most effective (though not most profound) sequences were derived directly from the Marquis de Sade—thus the thread-and-needle incident in *El* from *La Philosophie dans le boudoir,* and the conclusion of *The Age of Gold* (with a little extra sacrilege, to be sure) from *Les 120 Journées de Sodome.* Perhaps someone should commission from Buñuel the filmization of one of Sade's works. It might bring out the worst in him, which is easily his second best.

Collectors of supreme cinematic monstrosities had better keep a sharp lookout for Ken Russell's latest, *Mahler,* which may yet set a quick-disappearance record even for a Russell film. This one surpasses in absurdity and hollowness even *The Music Lovers* and *The Devils,* though in sheer loathsomeness it may fall just a bit short of that emetic duo. Once again Russell gives us the alleged biography of a composer—his favorite subject both on film and on television—a special Russellian brand of biography that adds a mere truffle's worth of fact to a huge pâté of invented inanity. In the case of Gustav Mahler, Russell becomes his own scenarist, which may be mandatory for a film artist, but spells disaster for a mere clever phony. (If Russell were to resent that appellation, I would be willing to compromise on "nut," but further than that I couldn't go.)

The film is in such demented and rotten taste that I do not wish to waste much space on it; but I must point out that the entire dinner-table scene culminating in the boy Gustav's locking himself into the toilet, along with much of the kids' outdoor swimming scene, repeats almost word for word dialogue and incidents from Isaac Babel's short story "Awakening," and this, shockingly, without any acknowledgment in the credits. Similarly, the nightmare funeral sequence is derived partly from Dreyer's *Vampyr,* and partly from Truffaut's *Jules and Jim,* though, to be sure, with a good deal of Russell's own pornographic vision superimposed on it. As for the Mahler–Cosima Wagner sequence, it ranks for sheer rankness with Russell's lowest, and does not even contain a grain of truth.

Mahler's very music is heard here in disconnected fragments, which is permissible, I suppose, but what excuse is there for singing the lovely *Kindertotenlieder* poorly in a jarring English translation, while the screen offers crudely literal shots of parents and children running around buffeted by a storm? Bernard Haitink conducts the score, and proves once again that the illustrious Concertgebouw Orchestra is under an unsteadier baton than in times past.

February–April 1975

Enforced Journeys

VITTORIO DE SICA, who died last November, is represented posthumously by his penultimate film, *A Brief Vacation*. It would be nice to be able to report that this charming man, gifted actor, and once outstanding filmmaker (*Shoeshine, The Bicycle Thief,* and, especially, *Umberto D.*) regained at the end that cinematic power that had been steadily seeping away from him. Not so, alas. *Two Women* (1961) remains his last distinguished film, though I also liked, in its simple-minded way, *Marriage Italian Style* (1964). After that, it was the deluge of mediocrity and worse; still, that inept film, *The Garden of the Finzi-Continis,* managed to please a lot of people, though it considerably worsened the feeble, overrated novel it was based on. The present film has a screenplay by Cesare Zavattini, one of the biggest names associated with Italian neo-realism and De Sica's collaborator on his best films, but, like the director, a man whose originality and vitality have been severely sapped.

A Brief Vacation, based on a story by Rodolfo Sonego, concerns Clara, a poor young working mother from Milan, who out of her measly factory wages must support her children, her invalided husband, his loafing ex-jailbird of a brother, and an obtuse, grasping mother-in-law. When her lungs become afflicted, a government physician sends Clara over the protestations of her wickedly selfish family, to Sandalo, an Alpine resort, for however many months it will take her lungs to clear up. At a well-appointed sanatorium, where rich paying guests and a variety of sick workers, including some committed Marxists, mingle among idyllic surroundings and all the creature comforts, Clara perks up—not only pulmonarily, but also psychologically, humanly. She even has a fleeting love affair with a poetic young worker, but after two months is found healthy again and sent back to— what? The same old penury and drudgery, or something better? The film ends with her looking from the window of her Milan-bound train at huge red graffiti racing by; they are Maoist slogans, and her expression is mysteriously ambiguous.

De Sica and Zavattini were both men of the Left, and their profound sympathies for the common people, free from ideological straitjacketing, filled their best work with a gallant, passionate populism that could move even the most inveterate elitist. But what has happened to these men over the years, besides aging? In an autobiographical essay of 1963, Zavattini wrote: "Signor Rossi said my finding everything beautiful prevented me 203 from drawing useful considerations from reality." This is relevant here; although Clara's family are a nasty lot, the implication is that toil and deprivation are to blame. Clara, on the other hand, and her gentle lover, Luigi, as well as all other abused workers promoted by sickness into the leisure class, are shown as thriving, learning, progressing from cheerful vacationers into dedicated self-improvers. Clara reads Manzoni and Tolstoy, inherits some fine clothes from a fashion model who befriended her, and is on her way to becoming a signora. It is all a bit too easy and too beautiful, and in their younger, tougher days, Zavattini and De Sica would have done it differently—would not have settled for an ambiguously bittersweet ending.

But never mind the ending: everything would have been harsher, sadder, more sardonically, mirthlessly funny, and more truthful. Compare the sharply etched characters in *Umberto D.* with the clichés and caricatures that drift through this film: the quasi-emancipated model who sinks to her knees before her greasy millionaire the moment he comes to fetch her; the flighty little debutante who falls madly in love with every young doctor, causing the immediate transfer of the unfortunate fellows; the rich, recklessly merry, shockingly outspoken chanteuse who is trying to conceal her fast-approaching end (rather overplayed by Adriana Asti); and all the rest. What are they but figures from a comic-strip version of *The Magic Mountain?* And what of the fact that evil coincidence dogs Clara throughout the film? And how about the casting of the too beautiful, too aristocratic Florinda Bolkan as Clara? And of the sickeningly sweet Daniel Quenaud as Luigi?

The late Charles Thomas Samuels's 1971 interview with De Sica ended on a shattering note. Said the then sixty-nine-year-old director: "All my good films, which I financed by myself, made nothing. Only my bad films made money. Money has been my ruin." The factory scenes in *A Brief Vacation* have an authentic, abrasive asperity; later on, in Ennio Guarnieri's deliquescent cinematography, the snow-clad Alps look virginally seductive. But those are slim pickings compared to what De Sica and Zavattini could have given us if they had come up with a fictionalized but honest retrospect at De Sica's career: the story of a superior filmmaker who can sell only his trash. It could have been a far better film than *8¹/₂* (to say nothing of *A Brief Vacation)*—truer and much more important.

Two French films about the plight of the Jews in occupied France have reached us simultaneously. They both differ from *Lacombe, Lucien* in that the focus is on the victims rather than on the persecutors; they further resemble each other in having been made by Jews and having a strong biographical or autobiographical flavor. They are *Les Violons du Bal,* by Michel Drach, and *Black Thursday* (*Les Guichets du Louvre*), by Michel Mitrani. Yet, ultimately, the two Michels and their films could not be less alike. Seen together, they provide an excellent object lesson in how such—or, perhaps, any—films should or should not be made.

Drach's film is sentimental, mendacious, self-serving, pretentious, and arty, the very things to make a film look like art to reviewers and other people who don't know what art is. It is very much what a clever—but not so very clever—kid fresh out of film school and stuffed to the gills with Godard, Resnais, Robbe-Grillet, etc., might make to prove his cleverness and originality. So, for starters, we get a frame story in which Drach, playing himself, tries to persuade first a swinish French producer to finance a film about the Drach family under the Occupation, then takes the idea to a scarcely less odious, but more enterprising, Italian producer. It is to concern his, his mother's, and his grandmother's escape to Switzerland; Drach wants to play himself directing the film; his real-life wife, Marie-José Nat, is to play both his wife and his mother; and David, their small son, is to play Michel when young. The producers raise various scurvy objections (some of them actually quite sensible), and insist that a star must play the director. Promptly, Drach turns into Jean-Louis Trintignant.

The film proceeds to oscillate between the present, in which we see it being made, shot in black and white; and the past, the story itself, shot in color. Sometimes the jumps from present to past, from monochrome to color, come so thick and fast, back and forth, that you literally get seasick from watching. There are also all kinds of zoom-ins and zoom-outs, shots of figures gradually coming into focus, tricky camera angles. Even David's screen test becomes part of the film, and smart-aleck philosophizing runs through both the main and the frame story. Whenever a scene can be shot through frosted glass, smoke, steam, fog, whatever, that's how it is shot; if an arriving train produces the merest wisp of steam, you may be sure that the camera will be plunked in the middle of that wisp. Typical is a sequence in which two characters converse on parallel running bands headed in opposite directions, requiring that one man run backward on a forward band; mirrors to either side proffer an image of two figures converging in some demented perspective.

And what self-glorification! As a child, Michel spouts profound cutenesses (or cute profundities) galore, e.g., "But I can't be like the other little boys, I have too many things in my head," and often acts more maturely than his mother. As an adult, Drach is shown risking his neck for a Communist student demonstrator, even though the youth keeps sneering at him for being a bourgeois liberal. As for lovely Mother, she walks through the horrors of war, frequent near-capture, arduous escape in exquisite haute-couture creations, her hair and make-up immaculate—though it must be admitted that another refugee woman, in the direst extremes, is also bountifully rouged and mascaraed. The hat and clothes Mother wears for the great escape might be rather too dressy and cumbersome for a picnic with the president. Unpleasant things are glossed over: Elder Sister's becoming a fashion model and fraternizing with Nazi officers is made to look quite platonic and harmless. Heavy symbolism and irony are rampant: when her beau's aristocratic mother tells pregnant Elder Sister that the boy cannot marry a Jewess, we see in back of her a freshly killed and trussed deer hanging from the wall; when we first see unhappy Sister as a mannequin, she is modeling a bridal gown!

It is worth stressing that when the film finally shakes off its nauseating artinesses, it hurtles straight into a routine, derivative tale of border escape, 205 lacking even clarity. The peasants who help with the escape are presented as greedy pigs who rob Mother blind, and either deliberately or accidentally (it is unclear which) almost let their clients be caught by the Germans. Yet these same peasants convey Granny very smoothly to safety.

Black Thursday, on the contrary, is, except for an occasional lapse into self-conscious poeticism, an honest and harrowing film. It makes horror not a glamorous adventure, merely horrible and, worse yet, banal. The Jews in it are not attractive: they have strange, Semitic faces, wear outlandish clothes, gibber in harsh Yiddish. Though not exactly cowardly, they have no sense of self-preservation. They have little understanding of what awaits them, walk into traps or obey deadly orders like sheep, and suspiciously reject lifesaving help from non-Jews. This is precisely what makes them moving, and the crime of the largely, though not wholly, collaborating French truly monstrous. For lethal anti-Semitism toward gorgeous mammas and adorable kiddies looks like fairy-tale fantastications, the acts of wicked witches and sorcerers. But this bundling off to death of less than prepossessing people by xenophobic Frenchmen and Frenchwomen (or by you and me) is dreadfully human, dreadfully believable, and unutterably sad.

The very heroine of *Black Thursday* is a plain, stubbornly unheroic Jewish girl; that her final self-sacrifice is due in part to absurd clannishness makes it all the more credible and heartbreaking. Mitrani has directed with restraint and strong suspensefulness, and re-creates historic events with a panoramic eye, without, however, losing sight of individuals. If only he had rejected the derivative, obstreperous, attitudinizing, and ugly score by that American no-talent, Mort Shuman! It is published, a screen title tells us, by Industrial Music. Worse than industrial—computerized.

April–May 1975

Was This Trip Necessary?

IF VACUITY had any weight, you could kill an ox by dropping on it Michelangelo Antonioni's latest film, *The Passenger.* Emptiness is everywhere: in landscapes and townscapes, churches and hotel rooms, and most of all in the script. Never was dialogue more portentously vacuous, plot more rudimentary yet preposterous, action more haphazard and spasmodic, characterization more tenuous and uninvolving, filmmaking more devoid of all but postures and pretensions. In his great films (*L'Avventura, The Eclipse*), Antonioni managed to show real people gnawed on by aimlessness, boredom, self-hate, against backgrounds of gorgeous isolation or bustling indifference. They were people whose words and gestures we recognized, whose obsessions or despair we could understand, especially as they were surrounded by vistas or artifacts that objectified their malaise.

In *The Passenger,* however, everything must be taken on the say-so of the filmmakers, on the slender evidence of a pained expression or a painfully written line or two. David Locke is both a big-time BBC documentary filmmaker *cum* journalist and a hollow existential failure, but these two givens either remain unsubstantiated by the few attitudinizing words or images, or actually manage to contradict each other. We meet him first somewhere in North Africa, bogged down in his vain search for a guerrilla stronghold, and disgustedly changing identities with a hotelmate dead of a heart attack. This only briefly encountered stranger, Robertson, resembles him, and so it is, apparently, child's play to change places: you just drag the corpse into your own bed, switch rooms, possessions, and passport photos, and assure the lethargic hotel clerk and manager that you are Robertson and the dead man Locke. The fact that Locke is a famous BBC reporter certainly known to the authorities of this unnamed state investigating the death does not seem to matter in the least.

So Locke-Robertson returns to England where he does not look up his wife, Rachel, or producer, but does catch a glimpse of The Girl (as she is known—or unknown—in the film), and proceeds to follow the indications of the dead man's engagement book, which take him, first, to the Munich airport and a specified locker, where he finds an illustrated invoice (!) for sundry armament for the aforesaid guerrillas; Robertson, it appears, was a gunrunner. In an empty Bavarian church, our hero is accosted by a German and a black, the latter none other than Achebe, the leader of the insurgents. In exchange for the pictures and itemizations of armament, Achebe gives David a lot of real money.

Here let me interrupt to identify the scriptwriters. The chief one was Mark Peploe, younger brother of Antonioni's former girl friend, Clare, who had contributed to the wretched script of *Zabriskie Point.* He was assisted by Peter Wollen, a British film buff and author of one of the worst film books ever written, *Signs and Meaning in the Cinema.* No ordinary worthless film book, it is one crazed with semiology, the science of signs, and extols the trashiest films of Howard Hawks in terms of stylemes, semantemes, plerematic stratums, and other such semiological tidbits. I suppose that if an African insurgent leader pays good money for diagrams of weapons, that is his tribute to semiology.

To continue. David, ostensibly trying to run away from his real self, nevertheless leaves a trail behind him as plain as footprints in the snow. His old life, apparently, was that of a compromised observer; now he has opted for active commitment by trying to keep the many (and improbable) appointments in Robertson's pocket diary; but no Daisy shows up in the designated place in Barcelona. Instead, David's producer is at the same hotel as the supposed Robertson, trying to find out more about Locke's death. David evades him with the help of The Girl, whom he picks up at the Palacio Güell, now a theater museum, into which he has ducked to escape the producer. She is a swinging architecture student traveling all over Europe with one smallish handbag, nevertheless containing a goodly number of different   207 albeit flimsy outfits. Soon she and David are lovers, now evading Rachel, who has come to Spain and enlisted the police to help her track down Robertson, whom she has figured out to be her husband.

There are all kinds of near-meetings, chases, narrow escapes. David and The Girl keep further appointments with the names in Robertson's diary who all fail to materialize. They separate, but meet up again in a sleazy hotel in Osuna, called with symbolic irony Hotel de la Gloria, where David tells her a symbolic but unironic parable about a blind man whom regained sight drove to suicide. He sends The Girl away, and while she lingers about in the courtyard there is a famous scene (about which more anon) during which David is murdered off-camera by agents of the African state Achebe's insurgents are fighting (the same agents, in an earlier scene, abducted and tortured Achebe). When Rachel and the police arrive, the latter ask both women whether they know the dead man. "I never knew him," answers Rachel with ironic symbolism. "Yes," says The Girl, shattered and loving to the last, by way of a final, tragic irony.

When Antonioni made *Zabriskie Point,* pitiful as it was, I was willing to make excuses. *The Passenger* is even more pitiful, and I am no longer willing or able to find excuses. Only a very foolish, humorless, and self-serving man could have made this abomination. The screenplay has two layers, both bad, and each, as it were, polluted by the other's company. There is, first, the Peploe-Wollen layer, the kind of script any mindless film buff (if that isn't a pleonasm) might write—made up of recollections of other screenplays, without visible writing talent or feeling for lived life. Take the opening sequences. Locke is searching for the guerrilla camp and is directed from one nest of mysterious Arabs to another in exchange for cigarettes, and eventually finds in his Land Rover a boy who doesn't speak to him but makes him drive to and stop in the middle of the desert and there disappears, we don't know how. Another native guide pops up and starts leading Locke up into the hills toward the camp, but when seven Bedouinish-looking camel riders go by at a distance, the guide inexplicably bolts. If he is willing to take Locke to an entire campful of them, why run at the sight of these far-off, unheeding seven? As he starts the trek back through the desert, Locke gets his vehicle stuck in the sand. Stranded in the middle of nowhere, he, too, breaks down, but is, in the next shot, back at his hotel. How?

I suppose we are not meant to ask such mundane questions of a profoundly existential, arcanely symbolic film. But when the whole thing smells, not so much of the midnight oil as of the midnight celluloid devoured by bleary addicts, I do ask questions. The symbolic superstructure had better rest on a little basic believability before reaching for the higher metaphysics; but *The Passenger* is using its pseudo-Hitchcockian framework without any of Hitchcock's ability to couch machinations in ostensible reality. At every turn of the plot, Peploe and Wollen rely on coincidence, a crude device crudely justified by having Locke remark to The Girl: "I never used to notice [coincidence]. Now I see it all around." But if you make chance your protagonist, you forfeit sympathy for the characters, reduced to insignificant particles buffeted about by happenstance. It is, moreover, quite improbable that, for example, David can just run into some Gaudí building and again find The Girl there, and more preposterous yet that she can check into a hotel by herself as Mrs. Robertson—her passport could as soon identify her as The Girl.

Motivation is as scant as probability. One quasi-stenographic scene is supposed to convey what went wrong between David and Rachel; we are to believe in the basic dishonesty of David's work because he does not ask hard-nosed enough questions of an African dictator (yet he gets some pretty electrifying footage of an execution); we hear—just once—about his troubles with an adopted son whom we never even see; we witness Rachel's involvement with a particularly repellent lover, and wonder why; we wonder even more at David's fake identity fooling Achebe so easily. And so on: human behavior is reduced to mere uncompelling idiograms, which may be more of Wollen's semiology.

But there is another layer here, the Antonioni-autobiography layer, where the director unconvincingly superimposes his own problems on those of his characters. Thus the Rachel of Jenny Runacre is made to look as much as possible like Monica Vitti, which may explain why, by way of *revanchisme,* her current lover is turned into such a beast; the Africans whom David interviews are made out to be particularly devious—presumably Antonioni's evening the score with the commissars who made trouble with his documentary, *China;* everything seems so dreary and frustrating to David, yet except for his failure to reach the rebel camp, he really is doing well enough. This, then, is Antonioni's own ennui being grafted onto the protagonist, who, as Jack Nicholson plays him, seems to be smoldering with energy and enterprise to burn. Thus Antonioni's self-pity preempts the chance of genuine pity evolving for the characters. Even The Girl may have become such a fantasy figure—unfettered, available, assenting, and loyal, idealized out of any kind of reality—only to make Rachel-Monica look worse.

Peploe and Wollen cannot begin to tell a coherent story, and Antonioni does not care to. But what about dialogue? When David first accosts The Girl at the Palacio Güell, here is their initial exchange: "I was trying to remember something." "Is it important?" "No." "What is it, do you know? I came in by accident." "The man who built it was hit by a bus." "Who was he?" "Gaudí." "Was he crazy?" I cannot say whether the scenarist who has two people meet like this is crazy, but he might easily have suffered a concussion when hit by a bus. When the dialogue isn't being coyly lunatic, it is dismally platitudinous, as in this bit between Rachel and David's producer: "We hadn't been very close the last couple of years." "Did he love you?" "Yes. It's just that we didn't make each other very happy." And a little later: "It's stupid. I didn't care at all before. Now that he is dead, I do."

And then there is the pretentiousness, as when The Girl walks up to the window of the ultimate hotel room. "What do you see?" David asks from the bed on which he sprawls. "A little boy and an old woman. They are having an argument about which way to go." A bit later he asks again: "What can you see now?" "A man scratching his shoulder. A kid throwing stones. And dust." Compare this with John Peale Bishop's poem, "Perspectives Are Precipices," from which it might almost derive, and you'll see the difference between genuine symbolism and mere attitudinizing. There follows that dreadful parable about the blind man who regains his sight, in which Locke, quite out of character, waxes garrulous and grandiloquent, and which runs in part: "First he was really elated, really high. But then things began to change. No one had really told him how much dirt there was—how much ugliness. . . ."

What, then, are the film's contributions? It plays around fairly effectively with video tape and the tape recorder, but this sort of thing was handled better in *Blow-Up* with still photography. The film's vistas are beautiful enough, as always in Antonioni, and are well chosen to evoke moods. But without any human beings we can feel for, these sights, including some interesting interiors, remain no more than the interior and exterior decorator's art. There are some bravura shots: David in a cable car over Barcelona harbor, shot from above as he spreads his arms like wings against the blue waters; The Girl's face and bust in a speeding, open-top car, seeming to float into the row of trees bordering the road—though this is somewhat damaged by sudden massed violin music, when elsewhere we hear only this or that single instrument. And then, at the end, the seven-minute take in which the camera first looks out through the barred windows, as if it were from the vantage point of David's shoes, and then gradually approaches and passes through the bars, circles around the yard and, eventually, returns into the hotel room. It catches the paltry goings-on in the yard as well as the coming and going of several cars: one with an advertising billboard, then one with the killers, finally those of the police. Then the camera comes back in to confront David's dead body.

Now, this is all very ingenious, involving a crane and a special camera that can dangle perfectly horizontally, and some fancy choreography. But what does it mean? That time passes and brings with it equally trivia and tragedy? That life tramples indiscriminately big and small events? But this could be done much better (as it was at the end of *The Eclipse*) if we were not obliged to wonder, "How in hell did he get that shot?" or to exclaim, "My, isn't that clever!" It is directing that calls attention to itself for its own sake, and, among other things, serves to obscure from us the killing and wrap it in adventitious mystery. The sequence, with all its cleverness, is ostentatious and obfuscatory. Technique is to be admired only when it submerges itself in dramatic necessity.

Maria Schneider, The Girl, looks simian and unwashed, and speaks her English lines with almost total incomprehension and incomprehensibility. Jenny Runacre's Rachel comes across merely drab, Ian Hendry is wasted on the colorless part of the producer, and Jack Nicholson is intense or ironical or exasperated, but cannot mold a character out of nothing. He is, moreover, a highly unlikely Englishman, even for one who has been living in America but working for the BBC. Luciano Tovoli's camera work is very fine, such as the exacting Antonioni has been getting from all his diverse cinematographers. But nothing can save *The Passenger* from stewing in its own juicelessness.

July 1975

Sucker for Punishment

Two MEN have been lost inside Claude Chabrol. One was a devout Catholic, obsessed with sin and righteousness, guilt and expiation; the other was a clever but perhaps too flashy interior decorator. I would not have missed either of them very much had they not been somehow embalmed, and did their remains not show through Chabrol's glossy but transparent filmmaking. As things stand, I rather abhor them. In *Just Before Nightfall* (*Juste avant la Nuit*), a film that reaches us four years late, where never might have been better, both the spoiled Catholic and the modish decorator have a field day. For the Catholic, there is Charles, a middle-aged advertising executive, who strangles Laura, his best friend's wife, with whom he was having a sadomasochist affair. Though he is racked with guilt and confesses first to his wife, the devoted and understanding Hélène, then to François, the friend, they both insist on forgiving him. Nobody will denounce him to the befuddled police; everyone offers discretion and help. He dies, as it were, of aborted expiation. For the interior decorator, there are the houses François has designed: his own, where he says at one point Laura's funeral will take place, and which looks indeed like a swinging mortuary; and Charles's, in which he was pushed to surpass himself, because Charles egged him on with the idea that a bit of avant garde around oneself keeps arteriosclerosis away.

The interiors of these houses, as well as (less appropriately) some of the other interiors, are particularly rich and fruity, with lush brown and purple predominating, the latter color negotiating a happy marriage between Catholic ritual and far-out decoration, thus satisfying both of Chabrol's buried personas. Particularly grating on my eye is Charles and Hélène's bedroom: against a patterned brown wallpaper, invariably brown silk bedsheets. It all looks rather like a literal interpretation of the words of Yeats's Crazy Jane to the Bishop: ". . . Love has pitched his mansion in/ The place of excrement." And when Charles broods on these brown sheets in his perennial purple silk pajamas, we seem to get the Bishop, too.

Chabrol himself is less than fond of the two mummies whose walking sarcophagus he is. He gives it to the failed Catholic by means of the horrible torture of Charles, who wants justice and punishment and keeps getting absolution instead; he lets the interior decorator have it by means of the cruel mockery he splatters across the *haute bourgeoisie,* whose lives are shown as all dissembling, hypocrisy, and cold comfort behind gorgeous but superfi-   211 cial façades and décor. So the efficient marriage of Charles and Hélène seems hollowly ritualistic in some ways (like failed faith?), so François and Laura's marriage was just a civilized cover for their divergent sexual activities, so Charles and Laura's affair was only a game of reciprocal torture of the sort into which the jaded bourgeoisie might easily fall. But the trouble is that Chabrol himself is much too deeply fascinated, indeed possessed, by the things he would satirize and excoriate to get beyond playing with superficially scintillating sin and sinfully beautiful surfaces.

There is room here for an absorbing movie, but Chabrol's too externalized screenplay, based on an obscure novel, barely begins to touch it. The novel's title, *The Thin Line,* provides the clue. It is the thin line between morality and perversity, repentance and masochism, playfulness and wanting to kill or be killed, justice and self-torture, love and hate. But instead of pursuing one or two of these ominously intertwined opposites in analytical detail, Chabrol spreads across the screen ironies within ironies, ambiguities upon ambiguities, paradoxes inside paradoxes, and the heaviest set of symbols you have ever seen, from rat traps to handcuffs. The actions of all the main characters (including some minor ones, like the embezzling employee Bardin) are submerged in a lavish bubble bath of ironic ambiguities instead of being accorded the hard soap of analytic insight. We seek illumination and get more easy symbolism and ironies: a commercial made by Charles's firm is for Culpa (as in *mea*) soap, and features Satan.

"I desire to judge no one," says Charles early on; later he exclaims, "I can't bear not being judged!" Did he kill Laura because of the ghastly exhilaration of the lethal game into which she drew him, or simply because he came to hate her? Does François forgive him out of deep friendship or a deep-seated loathing for his faithless wife? Is Charles's need to be judged an admirable bow to justice, or only a perverse piece of self-torture? Does Hélène forgive him because she loves him, or merely to maintain the hideous bourgeois proprieties? Does she finally kill him out of love or, again, for the sake of appearances, to avoid scandal? Does the closing shot of her and her dreary mother-in-law swathed in identical plaids mean that Hélène's nobly sacrificial deed was her first step toward becoming the same kind of snobbish hypocrite as the older woman?

A few such thin lines of demarcation closely examined might make for artistic depth; the substitution of quantity for quality merely cheapens everything. Chabrol moves his camera about brilliantly—sometimes overstepping the thin line into mere cleverness—and he has some splendid actors; if Stéphane Audran (Mme Chabrol) falls a bit short as Hélène, the others, led by the magnificently suggestive Michel Bouquet as Charles, more than make up for it. But the film, with erratic cinematography by the sometimes saccharine Jean Rabier, and erratic music by the often superb but sometimes bathetic Pierre Jansen (an aptly named collaborator for a Jansenist moviemaker), dwindles into irritating triviality. Out of that many thin lines you make crosshatching, not movies.

There is, on the one hand, something obsessive, perverse, fascinated by evil for its own sake, in Chabrol; on the other, something slick, superficial, childishly fond of odd juxtapositions and quaint non sequiturs. In between, there is his curious cult of stupidity: dumb people doing dumb things for dumb reasons and suddenly trapped and helpless. Hence the perverse admiration for killers in, say, *Les Bonnes Femmes, Le Boucher, The Beast Must Die,* but also for petty creeps usually embodied by such untalented Chabrol regulars as Henri Attal and Dominique Zardi, who appear here as a stolid detective and a nasty, outlandish advertising man. The result is a mixture of the nastily, flashily melodramatic, the jarringly banal, and the commercially slippery. In his new book, *Directors and Directions,* John Russell Taylor sees *Just Before Nightfall* as "in many respects a very funny film . . . because Chabrol obviously regards Charles's plight as absurd." I disagree: I think Chabrol regards *everything* in life as stupid and amoral, or, at best, grotesque. Lacking seriousness, he gives us not the Beckettian Absurd, but Chabrolian kinks.

August 4, 1975

Lear Without Lyricism

GREAT PLAYS lose even more on screen than great novels. Though the rhythm of the film is different from both the novel's and the play's, at least the verbalized space of the novel is comparable to the photographed space of the film. But box in the movie to simulate the stage, and you create claustrophobia; open up the filmed play for the sake of cinematic values, and you dilute the action and defuse the words. For these among other reasons, the late Grigori Kozintsev's *King Lear,* a nice try in some ways, ultimately fails.

Shakespeare was served best on screen when the adapted play was a relatively minor one—so lesser novels thrive on film, while major ones come to grief. Olivier's *Henry V* and *Richard III* strike me as the best filmed Shakespeare, far superior to the same Olivier's *Hamlet* and *Othello.* But Shakespeare is at least as much of a temptation to filmmakers as a sheer cliff wall is to mountaineers, and takes a greater toll.

Kozintsev was an intelligent, civilized, cosmopolitan stage director who founded, when not yet seventeen, with Leonid Trauberg and the painter Sergei Yutkevich, the experimental theater workshop FEKS (Factory of the Eccentric Actor), whose purpose it was to combat the academic influence of the Moscow Art Theater by introducing elements of surrealism, vaudeville, and the circus into the drama. In a few years, FEKS turned out some interesting movies along with provocative stage productions. By the late twenties, FEKS was dead, but Kozintsev and Trauberg went on to make the three noteworthy *Maxim* films in the thirties. When Stalin banned one of their pictures in the forties, they split up, and, on his own, Kozintsev continued to work in the theater, and to direct the internationally acclaimed film versions of *Don Quixote* (1957) and *Hamlet* (1964). In both, mood predominated at the

213

expense of other elements, and though allowances were made for the medium of cinema, Dwight Macdonald could still rightly criticize the "academic style" of the *Hamlet,* a "conventional work" with only a couple of "flashes of the old FEKSian fire."

King Lear, finished in 1970 and only now shown here, burns with an equally pale fire. Its felicities are modest, sporadic, and often tangential, its deficiencies fundamental and almost omnipresent. It cuts the play quite heavily, and, of course, it is the long poetic speeches that get it in the neck. Thus, though it is nice to see the storm scene introduced by restlessly careering wolves, bears, and mustangs, I don't want this at the cost of decimating Lear's lyrical-tragic outbursts in Act III, Scene II. A *Lear* without lyricism, as we saw in Peter Brook's stubbornly wrong-headed stage and screen versions, is no *Lear* at all.

Kozintsev has written a less than earth-shaking but more than sensible book, *Shakespeare: Time and Conscience,* in which the basic idea of his *Lear* film is adumbrated: "Hordes of vagabonds, terrible caravans of human grief, roamed the country. They were ragged, exhausted from hunger, and vainly sought work. They dragged themselves along the road, leaving by its edge the corpses of those who did not have the strength to go farther. So went the future army of hired labor." This is one compromise Kozintsev may have been obliged to make with socialist realism: throughout the film, we see this army of the poor marching, dragging, or being pushed around. In the hovel in the storm, there is not just one Poor Tom—scores of such unaccommodated men lie about. When mad Lear and blind Gloucester wander forlornly, there are battalions of bare, forked animals following them. It seriously undermines Shakespeare's vision of man cut off from his fellow men except for some equally isolated companion in misery, who cannot, for all his devotion, restore a lost sense of community.

But Kozintsev is no party-line hack, and he tries for something greater: the flimsiness of human grandeur he has written about in his essay on *Lear.* And so we get skies that are almost always ominous, parched ground crisscrossed by fissures, views of an agitated sea, and bonfires cropping up in the unlikeliest places. The bleakness is extended to the various castles, although there seems to be only one, made to stand in, confusingly, for three. But then Kozintsev goes too far: there is no initial pomp and splendor against which Lear's later downfall can be measured. And Yuri Jarvet, the Lear, not only looks eighty (which Shakespeare, exaggerating, asks for) but also the frailest eighty ever to face the epic endurance test of the action. Jarvet, moreover, looks a bit like a court jester himself, while the Fool resembles an actress in drag—to be exact, Falconetti as Dreyer's Saint Joan. He behaves like a bona fide madman, rather than the cynically merry fellow, progressively sadder and more bitter, we find in Shakespeare. To make matters grimmer yet, the actresses playing Goneril and Regan look old enough to be mothers rather than mistresses to Edmund (the Goneril, Elsa Radzin, was in fact Gertrude in Kozintsev's *Hamlet,* six years earlier), and characters like Cornwall, Burgundy, and Oswald have sinisterness emblazoned on their evil mugs.

214   Kozintsev's direction is curiously uneven. Lear's angry departure from

Goneril's castle is shot with a fine sense of movement for both actors and camera, and our first sight of Lear in the storm, with the camera tracking rapidly backward as he comes suddenly into view forging ahead at a forty-five-degree angle to the camera's path, is a brilliant effect. But at other times things seem much too random for comfort, and the big action sequences— the blinding of Gloucester, the battles scenes, the Edmund-Edgar duel—are muddled, uncompelling, and poorly edited. Strange continuity: the reunited Lear and Cordelia are seen in their modest finery; next thing, they are escaping amid a throng of refugees; another shot, and they are ragged, bare-foot prisoners. Is the English army so desperate that they would strip the very shoes off their royal captives?

Dmitri Shostakovich's score, though used in moderation, detracts when-ever it is heard. It is thoroughly undistinguished music, except for the Fool's flute solo, which, however, is too loud. Particularly infelicitous are the word-less choral writing for the battle scenes, and the sudden, ostentatious cre-scendo for Edmund's death. A wildly unroyal wedding for Cordelia on a desolate heath, complete with officiating monk, and Edgar's primitive burial of his father, complete with makeshift cross, are references to Christianity of the kind the play hasn't got. The love triangle Goneril-Edmund-Regan is perfunctorily and clumsily handled; Gloucester's attempted suicide is cut altogether; and though the deaths of Cordelia and Lear are well enough managed (even if I don't relish the echo's adding several further *nevers* to Lear's quite sufficient five), the ending is tendentious and wrong: instead of Edgar's gloomy last speech, we get an upbeat shot of the poor dousing the last flames of warfare and beginning to rebuild. That is not what tragedy is about.

The humdrum cast, in which only Kent, Cordelia, and Edmund can pass muster, allows many of the great poetic lines that aren't cut to be thrown away. That is not what dramatic poetry is about. Finally, and most distur-bingly, Jonas Gricius's black-and-white photography is merely gray and grayish (it was much better in *Hamlet*), and along with lack of tone contrast, there is no depth of field. That is not what cinematography is about.

September 1, 1975

Caste Away

SEVENTY-THREE YEARS have elapsed since Barrie's *The Admirable Crichton,* years fraught with Freud, Marx, Mao—even *No Orchids for Miss Blandish* and *Story of O.* So when, in 1975, Lina Wertmüller makes *Swept Away by an Un-usual Destiny in the Blue Sea of August* (her titles tend to be long, at least in the Italian original), her version of *The Admirable Crichton,* things become, politi-cally and sexually, more complex, daring, and, at any rate by implication, subversive—but also less admirable. In repressive turn-of-the-century Britain, 215 when an able and impeccable manservant and a haughty, impractical young lady of the aristocracy were shipwrecked on an exotic island, there may have been some "sentimentalising" going on, as one of Barrie's characters puts it; but when the hierarchic order reasserted itself, one did not curse England, and one never, never lost one's courage. Now, when a capitalistic prima donna of a Roman wife and a Neapolitan Communist of an assistant yacht steward get similarly shipwrecked, the goings-on are much more naked and brutal, both physically and ideologically, and both parties end up defeated and discouraged. And the air is thick with curses. Have things become better or worse?

To begin at the beginning, we have in the forty-three-year-old Miss Wertmüller a valuable addition to that small band of filmmakers who never run out of surprises. There is in her work such intelligence, intensity, and basic sense of cinema as to make it look better than merely good: wholly original. She makes films that do not look like anybody else's—not even, as one might have assumed, those of Federico Fellini, who launched her on her filmmaking career by appointing her assistant director on his *8 1/2* in 1963. Though she still reveres her master, even if, to my mind, he has long since grown useless, she manages not to resemble him, except perhaps in that quality of hectic humor that distinguished such an early masterpiece of his as *The White Sheik.*

In no way, however, does she resemble the other prominent Italian woman director, the profoundly untalented and coarse Liliana Cavani, best known for the abysmal *The Night Porter.* (And since the New York Film Festival is once more upon us, permit me a slight digression: whereas Cavani's work and she herself have been very much in evidence at the festival, the judges have blithely and consistently ignored Miss Wertmüller.) Of Wertmüller's eleven films, only the two preceding ones have had commercial distribution here: *Love and Anarchy,* and the crassly retitled *The Seduction of Mimi.* Not content with crudely chopping down the title, the distributor of *Mimi,* New Line Cinema, greedily and irresponsibly cut twenty-odd minutes from the film itself, thus severely damaging that fine picture's continuity.

Swept Away has certain things in common with these last two Wertmüller films: it is a tragicomedy about love and sex and politics, and their significant interaction; it is an attempt to see through to the saddening core of the subject while remaining cheerfully alive to its comic ramifications; it has impressive control over both vocabularies, the visual and the verbal (Miss W. both writes and directs her movies); it allows a minimum of characters to conjure up an entire society; and the leading players are, once again, Mariangela Melato and Giancarlo Giannini. But here, with its shipwreck-begotten *folie à deux,* the film is more than ever centered, for a nearly two-hour duration, on just two principals. Miss Wertmüller's ability to make us believe in her somewhat farfetched plot device and stay involved with the permutations of Donna Raffaella and Gennarino's relationship is all the more striking when we consider that there are really no surprises in this plot—indeed, that both the filmmaker's ideology and our own experience tell us that there cannot be surprises: the rich wife must return to her luxurious ambience, the poor fellow must be reabsorbed by his constricting circumstances. Yet, like other Wertmüller films, *Swept Away* is not depressing in the last analysis; there can be no happy ending, but the struggle for betterment is both heartbreaking and exhilarating, and, who knows: someday perhaps society will make it, even if this particular hero and heroine didn't.

There are a few weaknesses in Miss Wertmüller's work so far, the prime one being, paradoxically, her strength. There is such an overabundance of energy here, such unquenchable enthusiasm for the matter at hand, such facility with camera and words, that the filmmaker herself gets swept away, does not know where to stop. In the early parts of the film, the Signora's arrogance and exploitativeness know no bounds. Though almost equally hard on her own class, Raffaella indulges in nonstop sneers at the Left, which, with her demands for ever more slavish service, make her behavior a kind of inexhaustible but exhausting cabaret turn, consisting of garrulous mockery, cruelty, and narcissism. She is also quite funny most of the time, but one comes to long for a little economy and finesse of means—in fact, for a little more plausibility. On the other hand, Gennarino, the maltreated factotum, is delightfully conceived and executed, with his slow burns, sudden impotent rages, and mixture of shrewdness and innocence.

After a very droll, but even more exaggerated, set of mishaps while drifting on the Mediterranean, the two land on a deserted island; the bitchiness of the Signora is overcome by the superior adaptability and strength of the underdog, who proceeds to pay her back in full. As Gennarino becomes master—politically, sexually, even verbally—it is the conception of *his* part that becomes overobstreperous with directorial emphases that tend toward schematism, predictability, monotony. But Wertmüller's wit and imagination never abandon her for long, and some fine new maneuver soon reengages our interest. It is to the director's very considerable credit that she can even make use of a sequence about sodomy in a tasteful, funny, and humanly revealing way.

But there are other problems. Miss Wertmüller falls into the unfortunate trap of letting explicit and otherwise well-staged scenes of intercourse be played with unlikely integuments covering the players' loins. This looks quite distressingly unreal in such naturalistic filmmaking, where, I think, one must either take on the censors and rating boards with, so to speak, a frontal attack, or else show less and suggest more (which may, however, be less funny). A bigger lapse yet is the background score. Though never quite at the summit of Italian film music, with Nino Rota and Ennio Morricone, Piero Piccioni belongs (with men like Aldo Cicognini and Carlo Rustichelli) on a decently high plateau, and has some enjoyable scores to his credit, particularly where his slightly street-organish, improvisatory-sounding compositions fit into the character of the action. Here, on a desert island, the music obtrudes too loudly, too sweetly, and too often—sometimes even with those soupy vocalises—constituting a surprising piece of banality, despite the grace of the melodies derived in part from Purcell.

Surely the way to handle the island sequences would have been either with Antonioni's method in *L'Avventura,* where Giovanni Fusco's wry score was used almost subliminally, two or three bars at a time; or in Bergman's later manner, omitting music altogether and relying on exquisite orchestrations of natural sound. After all, "the isle is full of noises, sounds and sweet airs" played by wind and sea; no need to bring in Piccioni's twanging mandolins—to say nothing of those disembodied voices.

On the positive side, though, is Wertmüller's excellent dialogue, with which, alas, the subtitles have difficulty keeping up even when they are not being sluggish and treacherous in their own right. To Donald Rugoff's credit be it said that the film is to be released with new subtitles that will, I hope, dispense with some of the gratuitously added obscenities. Even so, they will have a hard time coping with the wonderful contrasts Miss Wertmüller gets between the blasé, upper-class northern Italian of the Signora—who, on top of everything, has the speech defect of the aristocracy, *r*'s turned into *w*'s— and the southern, déclassé but zestful lingo of her servant-turned-lord-and-master. I doubt whether it is possible to capture in English such things as the full social and sexual implications of Gennarino's triumphal cry during intercourse: *"Signora, io te futto!"* But other things should work just as well in translation—whether it is the litany of major social injustices inflicted by the upper on the lower orders that Gennarino recites while raining blows on Raffaella, among which he includes "all those TV programs!"; or whether it is the flights of true demotic lyricism he bestows on her during lovemaking, such as "my sweet and tender eel" and "milk-fed piglet."

The film reaches its psychological and dramatic heights during the lovers' quandary about whether to signal a passing yacht or let this natural (or is it unnatural?) paradise endure. Here the writing, directing, and acting are beyond possible improvement. The penultimate sequences are somewhat untidy and confusing, but the final ones (including Gennarino's perfectly cast wife) reattain full mastery. The very last shot in particular is laden with suggestivity. Indeed, it is the strength of the film that, even on the occasions when it gets vexingly obvious, it can still intromit a troubling whisper beneath or beyond all the shouting. It is as if the gayest moments were edged with a barely visible black border, even as the saddest ones are still bathed in the reflection of a far-off smile.

Ennio Guarnieri's cinematography is up to his best efforts: not great, but good enough. Miss Wertmüller uses with amazing effectiveness the old device of shots of the sky for purposes of time lapse or mood setting, and here Guarnieri's tendency to prettify comes in handy, undercut as it is by the director's irony. For a moment, we are coaxed back to memories of *The Blue Lagoon* and similar romanticizing trash, only to be jolted forward into Wertmüller's whimsical or sardonic realities.

Fond as I am of both Mariangela Melato (nasty rodent's face and all) and Giancarlo Giannini (with his trick of distending his eyes more and more— now they are saucers, now saucepans), I wonder whether seeing them three times in a row, playing leads under not dissimilar Wertmüllerian circumstances, does not put too great a burden on their genuine talents. How riveting it might have been to watch the more understated approach to these roles of, say, a Bibi Andersson and a Jacques Perrin—to pull out of the hat two slightly improbable and all the more tempting names. Still, Melato and Giannini are never unworthy, and, in the farcical moments, quite inspired.

Whether one chooses to be more severe or more indulgent with Lina Wertmüller, one cannot ignore the happy combination of a filmmaker who knows both how to make films, which isn't all that rare, and how to think, which is. Moreover, how many filmmakers who can do both can still do it after several good movies? Consider the more recent work of directors like Bresson and Antonioni, whose cerebration has turned into obsession and whose obsessions have proved crippling.

Miss Wertmüller runs the risks of being faulted by both the political and the apolitical crowd, the Left and the Right. She will be reviled as a feminist, antifeminist, anticapitalist, and anti-Communist. In truth, she is concerned mostly with the politics, the injustice, of power. The capitalist paradise on the yacht is as unstable as the populist utopia on the island; neither the tyranny of the rich wife nor the supremacy of the proletarian caveman can last forever. As it is, both parties are losers in the end—and will be, the film implies, until some kind of social justice based on neither privilege from above nor force from below prevails. *Swept Away* does not advocate any panaceas; it merely unmasks with insight and laughter the limited efficacy of all our solutions. Even the seemingly beneficent patriarchal despotism of Gennarino proves precarious, and practicable only on desert islands. Yet the film is not cynically despairing but a witty and earnest call to further exploration and discovery.

September 22, 1975

Red Coats in the Sunset

Conduct Unbecoming, the play by Barry England, made it in London's West End mostly because it offered a few kicks in the rear of the departing British Empire, and the last thing lost power is always good for is a few parting kicks to show that one didn't want it in the first place. The play did less well on Broadway, but still benefited from its British prestige (in America, even a lost empire is something to contemplate with romantic envy), and there was some commendable craftsmanship mixed in with the factitiousness and fadedness of the enterprise. That Barry England is not a writer of stature, though, is demonstrated by his insensitivity to language: "I fancy I can survive without sympathy," a character says to another, "yours least of all!"—where what is meant is, of course, "yours most of all."

But what could this play offer to the screen? It deals with a kangaroo court-martial in the British Indian Army of a century ago trying an aristocratic young officer for allegedly molesting the charming but frivolous widow of a fellow officer. Lieutenant Millington, the accused, wants to get out of the army and picks for his defense counsel the very "bourgeois" Lieutenant Drake, who worships the regiment while despising Millington and is sure not to defend him very hard. Captain Harper, the regimental adjutant and president of this infralegal but recognized "subalterns' court," is a martinet who detests Millington's flippancy, and all would go smoothly if (a) it did not emerge that Millington, if found guilty, will have something much worse than dismissal in store; and (b) Drake did not have a good "bourgeois" conscience telling him that an innocent man's honor is about to be besmirched to save that of the regiment.

Not a bad thing, this: a movie that concerns itself with questions of honor—of individual versus institutional honor, of comradeship and esprit de corps combining into an instrument of injustice. It is a worthy and (alas) always timely topic, and one that (double alas) is particularly relevant to American society today. But, even on stage, there was too much spurious gimmickry surrounding the central issue; in the movie, directed by Michael Anderson from a script by Robert Enders, the often pungent dialogue is cut and weakened, whereas the gimmickry is ponderously enhanced. Partly, of course, it is the old insoluble problem of how and how much to "open up" a one-set courtroom play—and with India in the background, the temptation was great. That the opening-up here was undertaken in minimal doses was wise; that it was undertaken at all dissipates the essential tension.

Moreover, Enders and Anderson have put in a great deal of labored suspense about who the actual culprit is and what he did and why, which is all of minor importance, and means deflecting attention from the more interesting moral and political issues of *Conduct Unbecoming* toward shopworn devices and a basically contrived plot. A brilliant director and scenarist would have made the film more constricted, more claustrophobia-inducing, to convey more powerfully the constrictions of militarism, the unhappy side effects it heaps on dubious primary ones. That would have required, above all, more sophisticated directorial skills than evidenced in the simplistic reaction shots, for example, with which the film is liberally and unappetizingly peppered.

Yet *Conduct Unbecoming* can be viewed with modest pleasure, if only for its performances and for the cinematography of Bob Huke. The sole disappointment in the cast is Stacy Keach as Captain Harper. That he manages to sound completely American despite awkward attempts at Britishness is the least of it. What matters is how outclassed he is, not only by tried and tested English veterans, but also by such a nowhere-near-veteran as James Faulkner, who endows Millington with a justly measured cockiness beneath which the right amount of susceptibility and vulnerability remains discernible. Keach, however, goes for the obvious choices and fails to communicate the terrible conflict by which this monolithic career soldier is eventually riven.

The others fall into two groups: those, like Trevor Howard and Christopher Plummer, who go through their undemanding paces with a fine display of accumulated trickery—the cardsharp's rather than the actor's art, but sufficient for the purpose and great fun to watch; and those like Michael and Susannah York (relations in name only), who come up with genuinely rounded performances. S. York has nothing very profound to do, but she does it with grace and insight and something I can describe only as spiritedness, a lovely quality either on or off the screen. M. York, whom I have often found wanting, brings to the role of Drake a shyness that may be a mite exaggerated, but his inner and outer struggles are recorded with a meticulousness and finesse I was most pleasantly surprised by. Altogether, a great day for the White Rose of York.

Bob Huke, who did beautifully with much more photogenic material in *The Virgin and the Gypsy* and *Under Milk Wood,* was here confronted with the ungrateful task of having to shoot mostly in an officer's common room at night, sparsely illuminated for the sublegal activities conducted in it. That he managed to make all those red tunics in chiaroscuro look so very much better than, say, a bellhops' convention during a power blackout is a testimonial to what conscientiousness and imagination can do even with a severely limited palette; in a film about honor, Huke's cinematography is by no means the least honorable feature.

About *Royal Flash,* the less said the better. It marks yet another step in the steady decline of Richard Lester, whose rise consisted mainly of one movie, *A Hard Day's Night,* and whose downfall was just about his entire subsequent oeuvre. Neither his attempt at repeating his initial, Beatle-studded success (*Help!*), nor his forays into quasi-serious drama (*Petulia*) or quasi-philosophical black comedy (*How I Won the War*) panned out, leaving him only period slapstick to sink into ever deeper: *A Funny Thing Happened on the Way to the Forum, The Three* (or *Four*) *Musketeers,* and now this desperately chugging, puny Ruritanian farce, *Royal Flash.*

With the help of his *Musketeers* scenarist, George MacDonald Fraser, and based on one of Fraser's own "Flashman" novels, Lester has fashioned yet another of those farcical derring-do movies, where the idea is, so to speak, to smelt *The Prisoner of Zenda* and the Three Stooges. I doubt whether anyone could have gotten a funny full-length feature out of this, though it might have made an amusing silent two-reeler once long, long ago. Even then it would have needed a funnier protagonist than Malcolm McDowell, who can be very effective in lower- or middle-class comedy-drama, but who seems to lack all period sense or ability to project himself into the upper orders. Here he is Captain Flashman, a mid-nineteenth-century rake and opportunist mistaken for a hero in London, then abducted and forced to impersonate a duke he resembles in the imaginary principality of Strakenz, and so facilitate Bismarck's metapolitical designs. He is constantly beset by a barrage of villains, all of whom—and especially Alan Bates—prove much more pleasing than McDowell.

Some able British actors are given inadequate direction and nothing much to do, while such egregious nonperformers as Britt Ekland continue to nonperform. Even the always arresting Florinda Bolkan's steady fascination is arrested by Lester's mismanagement of her; indeed he makes her look positively undesirable. So, too, the always dependable and sometimes brilliant cinematographer Geoffrey Unsworth provides merely routine camera work, not helped by the exaggerated yet unwitty production design of Terry

Marsh. But the ultimate fault is Fraser and Lester's. The director's success was based largely on applying the techniques of the TV commercial to feature films—a dazzling one-shot gimmick that could not be elevated into a style and swiftly outstayed its welcome. In *Royal Flash,* Lester's very opening shot is copied from the opening of *Patton,* and anyone who would steal from Franklin Schaffner would probably not hesitate to rob a blind newspaper vendor blind. About Fraser, the production notes tell us: "Challenge his knowledge of cinetrivia and you lose. Who else can remember Chester Clute, Charles Lane, and Chris Pin Martin? Or what Claude Rains threw in the wastebasket in *Casablanca?*" Not content with memorizing cinetrivia, Fraser seems hell-bent on adding to it; what Claude Rains *should* have thrown into that wastebasket is the script of *Royal Flash.*

October 6–13, 1975

Cinematic Illiterates

ONE OF THE New York Film Festival's favorite directors is Werner Herzog (Herzog, incidentally, is not even his real name), several of whose movies have, in the course of the years, alternately bored and incensed festival audiences. I myself have, by turns, fought to stay awake or struggled to control my bile through such items as *Even Dwarfs Started Small, Fata Morgana,* and *Land of Silence and Darkness,* in which a combined effort to shock, mystify, and hypnotize neutralized itself eventually into numbing dullness out of which only an intermittent spurt of pretentiousness or bloody-mindedness would rouse the stomach or the soul to renewed retching. True, Herzog is personally very charming, and true, I have not seen *Aguirre, the Wrath of God,* which some consider his best work; but I have now seen *Every Man for Himself and God Against All* at the festival, which, retitled *The Mystery of Kaspar Hauser,* is about to be launched on the general public, and I can report that, under either title, it is an offense against God and man.

The first thing to be noted about this choppy, capricious, ponderous, and attitudinizing film is that it is an utter betrayal of its magnificent historical subject. Kaspar Hauser was a boy of fifteen or so who showed up out of nowhere in the main square of Nuremberg in 1828. Inarticulate and clutching a letter that obscured rather than clarified his provenance, he was taken in by members of the intelligentsia and aristocracy after having revealed exceptional intellectual powers. It appeared that he had been kept in a dark hole and in a state of ignorance; now, under the patronage of Lord Stanhope and the supervision of the jurist Anselm von Feuerbach, he became an internationally famous prodigy. There were attempts on his life, and in 1833 he was murdered under circumstances as mysterious as those of his birth and childhood. He may have been the heir to the Principality of Baden, relegated to a living death for the sake of another claimant, but the facts are hard to ascertain under the incrustation of legend.

Numerous scientific and literary works, in various languages, were inspired by this meteoric trajectory. They began with Feuerbach's memoir, *Caspar Hauser, Example of an Outrage Against Intellectual Being*, and culminated in the celebrated novel by Jakob Wasserman, *Caspar Hauser, or The Sluggishness of the Heart* (1909). Kaspar—the *K* is not the Kafkaesque, only the modernized spelling—became the prototype of the gifted outsider (intellectual, artist, man of feeling) whom society persecutes and kills: a bright, romantic candle snuffed out by the dark mass its individuality defied. One of Verlaine's loveliest lyrics celebrates him as Gaspard Hauser, the archetypal Romantic, born too soon or too late.

What has Herzog wrought from this rich ore? He found a halfwit he identifies as Bruno S.—well into his forties, physically gross, with impaired speech that sounds like that of a crudely constructed automaton—and has tried to palm off this intellectually, aesthetically, and histrionically unappetizing specimen as Kaspar Hauser. Bruno S. may be a sad or instructive case in his own right, but he has nothing to do with the historically fascinating and mythically absorbing Kaspar, who represents the tragedy, the doom, of brilliance, not the drama of the sincere but clumsy misfit, the honest brute in a hypocritical ambience—not that Herzog can handle *this* subject any better. Though his Kaspar is at times allowed to deviate into sense, Bruno S. makes it all sound mildly cretinous and so blend in with the posturing, ponderous shallowness of the film as a whole.

Granted, something about a generally insensitive society remains. But it now looks as if the peasant who kept Kaspar imprisoned was also his subsequent murderer for no good reason; Kaspar now seems to be the victim of a few specific, particularly odious, low charlatans or high-society hypocrites, rather than the tragic butt of some ecumenical, basic incomprehension and envy; his treatment by real or fake benefactors is shown without any sense of the subtlety and complexity of human motivation; and the coarseness and insufficiency with which his learning process and growing insight—and the eventual clash between natural man and codified citizen—are represented become even more glaring when contrasted with *The Wild Child*, where Truffaut handled a similar case with much greater humanity and artistry. Here it all resolves itself into a few caricatures of churchmen, some facile swipes at nineteenth-century medical practitioners, a few potshots at oafish villagers and callous members of the upper classes, and an unspeakably dreary running (or limping) gag lampooning the bureaucracy in the figure of a ridiculous scrivener.

Incident upon incident is written, directed, and acted with overwhelming banality or, worse yet, heavy-handed irony, and Herzog has no sense of texture, of the fabric of life, only a feeling for the weird. At best, he can show you a near-catatonic Kaspar leaning against a door with his head, or a supposedly cured and educated Kaspar playing the piano with the same kinetic and expressive aberrations he exhibits in his speech. Worst of all, 223

Herzog, like other young German filmmakers, seems to be influenced by the American cinematic underground and its tendencies toward self-indulgence, irrelevance, and meaninglessness posturing as symbolic profundity. So, in the guise of Kaspar's fantasies and dreams, we get some wholly unimaginative visual and verbal non sequiturs, scenes shot (Herzog says) by the director's brother on a trip to the East, and enlarged from Super-8 film with the customary graininess. These sequences, and the pretentiously hollow verbiage that accompanies them, manage to be even more boring than the rest of the film.

Although postwar Germany has produced an appreciable number of fine writers, she has not been blessed with any resident filmmakers of merit (although Wim Wenders shows promise), and there has yet to come a story film out of postwar Germany for which one can have genuine enthusiasm. But the dullest filmmaker not only in Germany but also in the whole world (if we discount such a universal no-talent as Warhol, and Marguerite Duras, the second-rate novelist turned arrogantly tenth-rate filmmaker) may very well be Jean-Marie Straub, the Alsatian cinéaste whom Richard Roud, the New York Film Festival's director and dictator, has promoted year after year, and even written a book about. It is hard to say whether Straub is more German than French (he speaks both languages with the same uncouth Alsatian accent), but more of his films are made in German, and the excruciating, gut-parching uncinematicness and dryness of all of them seem Teutonic rather than Gallic. The current festival showed his *Moses and Aaron*, an attempt at making a film out of Schönberg's opera, just as Straub had previously put Corneille's *Othon* on screen with equal damage to dramatic and cinematic art.

As with certain abstract painters, of whom one knows that they could not draw if their lives depended on it, one can readily deduce that Straub cannot begin to tell anything resembling a story. He tried it once with *Not Reconciled*, based on a perfectly workmanlike fiction by Heinrich Böll, which Straub reduced to mincemeat—and indigestible mincemeat at that. After various other ways of evading narrative, Straub has hit upon the flat-footed transposition of dramas and operas onto the screen as his latest desperate remedy. Yet even before we get to Straub's film, which he codirected with his equally immodestly untalented French wife, Danièle Huillet, we must briefly consider the opera *Moses und Aron* itself.

Schönberg's libretto is wordy and undramatic; the relatively lengthy score seems to me to deserve a phrase of Ned Rorem's about the works of George Crumb: "sonorous canvases—skillfully stretched sheets of sound effects offered as ends in themselves." It has a few moving choral or exciting orchestral moments; otherwise, it is either *sprechstimme*, a kind of ululating *recitativo estrasecco*, or lively but distracting background music for a movie—a movie that Straub failed to make. He did not even avail himself of the opera's one indubitable blessing: that Schönberg never got around to composing the last act. Straub proceeds with Schönberg's musicless libretto for

Act 3—more lifeless, biblico-metaphysical maundering—and succeeds in making the last part of the film drearier yet.

In effect, Straub has put the performers of the recent Michael Gielen recording of the opera into an empty, semiruined amphitheater and shot a pseudoperformance of the work with costumes, props, and minimal movements, which, nevertheless, occasionally become naturalistic. But whether the style is kept rigorously, hieratically static, or whether things open up a bit and even go beyond the arena, the camera work is mostly closeups from often unlikely angles or, contrariwise, very ordinary long shots and excessive circular pans. It would have been a wonderful change to let the Golden Calf scene become a real orgy, or even just to show us at times the able Gielen conducting the fine Orchestra of the Austrian Radio—watching musicians at work would have been a hell of a lot more dramatic than staring at deadly shots of soloists and choristers opening and closing their mouths. Let me say simply that opera on film is a pretty impossible affair, that *this* opera on film is more impossible yet, and that this opera on film as directed by Mr. and Mrs. Straub is the ultimate impossibility.

Straub, whom I imagine to be devoid of all humor, begins with an extreme closeup of a Bible in Gothic type, or, to be exact, of the passage with which the opera deals. Simultaneously, Luther's stern German is read on the soundtrack by Mme Huillet-Straub's voice in a fruitily inapposite French accent—but where is such comic relief during the subsequent 104 minutes, when we could really use it?

October 20, 1975

Unwatchable and Watchable Madness

WHAT CAN I SAY about Ken Russell's latest, *Lisztomania*, that I haven't said about his previous outrages? Russell is like a plague of locusts: whether it settles on fiction (*Women in Love*), drama (*The Devils*), poetry and painting (*Dante's Inferno*, a TV film about Rossetti), sculpture (*Savage Messiah*), or, as most often, music (for film or television, Russell has by now done, or done in, ten or eleven composers), this winged pestilence makes its subjects ridiculous and then devours them. That he may be the single internationally known British director today only goes to show that in a topsy-turvy world, nothing succeeds like excess.

But excess of what? Mostly of vulgarity, I fear. And what kind of vulgarity? Well, there is the whoring after success—the realization that with even relatively sober-minded pseudobiographies, like the ones of Frederick Delius and Henri Gaudier-Brzeska, one does not make it big with the unenlightened multitude; there is the terrible straining for Art (with a supercolossal, not just capital, *A*), without really understanding that some form of   225 restraint must be imposed; and there is the unhinged craving for gaudiness, opulence, superfluity of a boy on whom the puritanical controls and genteel pieties of a British lower-middle-class upbringing were thoroughly inflicted.

Still, to overreact to this extent presupposes something more: an excess of universal contempt without the leavening of love, and envy of one's artistic superiors with the consequent need to cut them down to one's own size. One element of the typical Russell cinebiography is the reduction of ordinary people to unappetizing caricatures, and of some genius or near-genius to a mere eccentric, as if artistic greatness were simply a psychic deformity expressing itself in violently unconventional behavior and creations molded from rage. There have, to be sure, been artists to whom this applies, though even then not quite so crudely; and they were not necessarily the artists Russell pounced on—not Gustav Mahler, for instance, and still less Franz Liszt. The (for lack of a worse word) style that Russell foists on his subjects, the quasi-plots he spins around them, the brazenly infantile lies, can perhaps best be described as comic-strip baroque, or the dungeons of Piranesi as animated by a Disney gone bananas.

Liszt, in this dreadful *Lisztomania,* is a nonstop fornicator and glitter rock star (appropriately played by Roger Daltrey, with a face as long as a mule's, and a talent considerably shorter) who spends his life shuttling between boudoirs and Mick Jagger–style concerts for tiny-brained teeny-boppers to go wild at. He meets a sailor-composer, Richard Wagner (why sailor? The Flying Dutchman?), whose cap, in Gothic letters, misspells Nietzsche as "Nietszche," and who becomes his protégé, son-in-law, and, eventually, mortal antagonist. Foiled in love, Liszt turns abbé, while Wagner turns into Dracula, complete with castle and fangs, and creates a combination Frankenstein-*Heldentenor*-Hitler monster that lays waste the world until it is destroyed at last by Liszt (now an angel) and his main mistresses (ditto) by means of a contraption half space ship, half organ.

The symbols of music, sex, and religion are everywhere, in such grossly travestied forms as to make all three ridiculous and repellent. Thus much of the clothing on, and furniture around, Liszt displays or apes musical instruments or notations, if not, indeed, distorted phalluses or vaginas. Columns are almost invariably giant penises, their pediments testicles; Liszt may be swallowed up by a gargantuan vagina or sprout a monster penis that several of his mistresses ride toward a guillotine. The guillotine is briefly superimposed on, and identified with, the vagina of Franz's current mistress, who, dressed in a see-through bat costume, proceeds calmly to decapitate the unhappy member. (Russell's hatred of women deserves a lengthy study unto itself.) The pope, played by a deranged-looking Ringo Starr, who doesn't even try to act (or perhaps he does—on Starr, the difference doesn't show), appears in vestments decorated with film clips and a large portrait of Judy Garland.

When Russell runs out of even such ideas, he resorts to still more irrelevant lampooning: a flashback to Liszt and Marie d'Agoult's happy days becomes an inept takeoff on Chaplin and *The Gold Rush.* That anachronism is all-engulfing, that history is just so many toy building blocks for rotten

226

little Ken to kick about or smash, that we have to look at Daltrey and Starr and their likes and listen to their Cockneyfying of words well beyond their ken (though just within that of their Ken) is less important, however, than the fact that basic human truths are made into a mockery that is neither genuinely funny nor at the service of an even remotely tolerable cause.

For Liszt was, above all, a decent fellow, always helpful to other musicians, especially struggling young talents, and his relationship to Wagner was by no means war unto the death. Yet the film makes him grotesque, Wagner evil, and Cosima (who, from Russell's point of view, has the further misfortune of being a woman) worst of all: already in *Mahler* she was a Nazi beast; here she is also a mass murderer and patricide. Nor is Russell trying to make any significant comment about Liszt's music—in fact, almost all of it here is Liszt's worst—*Liebestraum*, the rhapsodies—and even that mostly transmogrified into garish rock by Rick Wakeman, and croaked out by Daltrey. For possibly the first and last time in my life I wished I could have heard some real Liszt.

Russell is impartially unfair to whatever he touches, so Wagner's music gets it as much as Liszt's. He seems, on the evidence of *Mahler* and now *Lisztomania*, much exercised by the Nazis, yet he must clearly relish them under the pretense of censure, otherwise why drag them in irresponsibly twice, and why linger with such evident delight on their every carefully itemized atrocity? His treatment of the Jews is, in any case, no better; all of them are pawnbrokers who, smoked out by Wagner-Hitler-Karloff, try to escape, not with their wives and children, but with their gold clutched to their breasts.

Huw Wheldon, who gave Russell his start at the BBC, has remarked that "the capacity to analyse and rationalise Ken doesn't begin to have" (quoted by John Baxter in *An Appalling Talent: Ken Russell*), and the deficiency seems to get exacerbated with every passing year. In *Lisztomania*, for example, Berlioz says little and Chopin nothing, but the former is absurdly represented as an outrageous swish, the latter, equally absurdly, as a rabid algolagnist. It is all vastly more sickening than *Tommy*, because it is perpetrated on serious music and musicians. But do not get the idea that the conspicuous vulgarity and waste in this movie are somehow fun to look at: "Madness in great ones must not unwatched go," says Claudius of Hamlet; but the madness of an arrogant pipsqueak hardly bears watching. The one fascinating thing in the film is the mouth of Fiona Lewis, who plays Marie; exquisite as it is, it does not justify the rest of this noisy, noisome movie.

In the domains of silliness and posturing, though well below Ken Russell, *Down the Ancient Stairs* earns a foothold. Mauro Bolognini has made some notable films; of those shown here, the gripping *La viaccia* (cut though it was) and, especially, the wonderful *Il bell' Antonio* were superior achievements. But, then, the former was based on a novel by Pratesi; the latter, on a novel by the still undervalued satiric genius Vitaliano Brancati. (I wish we could see the film Bolognini made from Svevo's *Senilità!*). In *Stairs,* Bolognini is working from a novel by Mario Tobino, obviously vastly inferior even to those novels of Pasolini from which he made two of his best known, but not best, pictures: *La notte brava* and *La giornata balorda* (*From a Roman Balcony*). Of such films, *Cahiers du Cinéma* could justly complain that they displayed a "morbid world . . . of misogyny and homosexuality," to which *Down the Ancient Stairs,* at least in its morbidity, is a throwback. The script is by a quartet of scenarists, including two of Fellini's: Pinelli and Zapponi. The locale is a rather sumptuous provincial mental hospital during the early Fascist era, circa 1930. This elegant institution houses some of the most harrowing cases of madness along with a couple of gorgeous doctors' wives and one stunning head nurse, all three of them carrying on with Doctor Bonaccorsi, the star psychiatrist of the hospital. Bonaccorsi, poor thing, is scared of going bananas himself, and trying hard to discover the schizophrenia virus between bouts with his toothsome paramours.

To these a potential fourth is added in the person of a young woman psychiatrist, Dr. Bersani, who has come to study under Bonaccorsi. (I am speaking figuratively.) She is a Freudian, Bonaccorsi is not, and one hopes that the film will turn into a good contest, dramatic and verbal, between a Freudian and an anti-Freudian. But no; except for a few ludicrously simplistic thrusts and counterthrusts, we get the standard Snake Pit movie (picturesquely spine-tingling scenes of life in a madhouse), the standard romantic-melodramatic claptrap gotten up in the kind of fancy dress supplied by the House of Visconti & Bertolucci, and the customary allegorical overtones for the sake of artistic and intellectual cachet, in the style of the same furnishers. *Stairs,* then, is exactly as hollow, as ultimately banal, as any film by them, or by Pasolini and Zeffirelli, and does not even know which genre it falls into; whether the cutely mendacious, madness-is-saner-than-sanity one of, say, *King of Hearts;* or the pretentious allegory-of-Fascism one of, say, *The Conformist.*

Either way, the movie is preposterous, but with some compensations. There are four extraordinarily lovely women in it: Lucia Bosè—as bad an actress as ever, and showing her age, but still a noble presence; Françoise Fabian, a bit too mature for the part of Dr. Bersani, and not allowed to deploy her magnificent hair, but what a joy to watch, anyhow; and Marthe Keller and Barbara Bouchet, as sacred and profane lovers of Bonaccorsi, equally though differently beautiful. The last three are dubbed into Italian, so it is hard to judge their acting; the same goes for the late Pierre Blaise. As for Adriana Asti, one could tell she is overacting even if she were dubbed into Maori. And then, as Bonaccorsi, there is the one and only Marcello Mastroianni. Even in this basically laughable part, he commands respect and belief. The doctor may be an ass, but the actor makes us understand what those women see in him. Bonaccorsi may be craven and hypocritical as well, but how human and forgivable Mastroianni can make those vices seem! What he cannot do is convince us of his intellect and scholarship, but for this the script may be more to blame.

Bolognini's direction is, on the whole, assured, except in the scenes of passion and perversion, which even Visconti could not have made more ridiculously unconvincing. But the mental patients are handled effectively, and, as always, Bolognini is expert at getting the period look and flavor, here with the help of décor and costumes by Piero Tosi, one of Visconti's stalwarts, who gives the film an uncannily Visconti look. Ennio Morricone's score daringly juggles three different styles for three different aspects of the story, but is less affecting than some other Morricone scores. Ennio Guarnieri's cinematography is up to its old tricks, favoring pastel effects of a dubious sweetness. The dialogue is primitive when not downright foolish, and when things start bogging down seriously, nudity is hauled in to the rescue. So, with things to giggle and gawk at, one cannot be exactly bored by *Down the Ancient Stairs;* neither, however, can one honestly like it.

In *Sweet Movie,* Dušan Makavejev tells parallel parables of capitalist exploitation and Communist brutalization; being of a Rabelaisian temper, he also includes a good deal of scatology and obscenity. For Eastern audiences, the film would be a revelation, but they'll never see it; for Western ones, after some pruning by the director, it is mildly distasteful and not a little dull, so that not many will *want* to see it. For Makavejev, I hope, it is just right, so that having gotten it out of his system, he can go on to the better things of which he is capable.

October 27, 1975

Dispensable Deviltries

The Devil Is a Woman (and the English title-giver is a plagiarist from Sternberg) is a film so appalling as to be profoundly unworthy even of such a journeyman director as Damiano Damiani. Having missed *Confessions of a Police Captain,* and discounting a negligible short, I know Damiani's work from his two other features shown here: *Arturo's Island,* which was untidy but not uninteresting; and *The Empty Canvas* (*La noia*), which was slickly competent and utterly vacuous. But the latter was based on one of Moravia's typically empty novels, whereas the former was derived from a novel by Moravia's rather more talented ex-wife, Elsa Morante. The natural assumption was that Damiani was improving in technique, but worsening in choice of material. Unfortunately, his well-received adaptation of a novel about the Mafia, *The Day of the Owl,* was never distributed here, though it marked a return to adapting the work of a good novelist, in this case Leonardo Sciascia. If jackals, dolphins, and condors could all have their days among us, I can't see why owls should have been discriminated against.

In the case of *The Devil Is a Woman,* though, there is no novelistic source; the script, from a story by Damiani, was written by himself in collaboration with Fabrizio Onofri and Audrey Nohra, whom I suppose to be the wife of the producer, Anis Nohra. Idea and treatment, characterization and dialogue are of staggering banality, schematism, and preposterousness. We are 229 asked to believe that a writer (nationality mysterious: actor Italian, name of character Spanish, dubbing British but with attempts at a Latin accent) has been invited to stay in a Roman convent to help an inmate, a Polish Monsignor, write his memoirs, meant to clear him of charges of voluntary collaboration with the Nazis. This convent is also a kind of sanatorium for prominent but disturbed Catholics from both the clergy and the laity. It is ruled with merciless discipline by icy Sister Geraldine (nationality unspecified but played very Glenda Jackson by Glenda Jackson), whose secular arm is the austere but toothsome Signora Contreras (Bolivian, with a British mother—played very English by Lisa Harrow). The regimen at this institution is that of a rather more than usually rigorous medieval monastery, ranging from Sister Geraldine's hair shirts (actually, hair belts) to denial of dessert to the mildly gormandizing Polish Monsignor, from holding a princely patient incommunicado to driving him, through an obnoxious kind of ecclesiastic group therapy, to suicide.

It is, of course, Sister Geraldine who is the post-sex-change Devil of the title, and Glenda Jackson need only trot out her icicle-hung "serious" performance (as opposed to her better "comic" one—she has only one of each) to make me cry uncle. If she continues like this, she will surely become the sub-zero-temperature Gale Sondergaard *de nos jours*. But to go on with the story (which is all there is): Sister Geraldine manages to ruin the lives of all she touches—even of those who temporarily elude her grasp; yet the film makes equally explicit that her seemingly more enlightened ecclesiastic superiors pay for their loss of fanaticism by becoming cynical careerists.

What is most clear is that this film is motivated by cheap anti-Catholicism. Now, anti-Catholicism is practically the hallmark of the Italian filmmakers; the sole notable exception is Ermanno Olmi. (Zeffirelli, another exception, is not notable; Pasolini, though occasionally somewhat notable, is too slippery for his ideology to become assessable.) Yet controlled, intelligent church-baiting—usually humorous—has never done harm to a film; this sort of crass anti-Catholicism, however, is humanly stultifying and artistically stunting.

Anyhow, Signora Contreras, who is expiating the shooting of her Fascist husband to save her rebel lover, and whose symptoms are general coldness and excessive masturbation, falls madly and defiantly in love with Rodolfo, the ghost writer. The young prince, incestuously in love with his sister, is driven to a particularly unappetizing form of suicide by Sister Geraldine; the incestuous sister, at the viewing of the corpse, kisses it passionately on the mouth, which, in due time, lands *her* in Sister Geraldine's care. The Polish Monsignor rebels, escapes, stuffs himself on assorted foods, repents, returns to the convent. The contrary Signora Contreras flees with Rodolfo, promptly turns atheist and nymphomaniac, then likewise crawls back to Sister Geraldine, who, despite the injunction of her superiors, resumes her medieval methodology. Only Rodolfo is able to make the *gran rifiuto* and evade Sister G.'s chilling blandishments to find apparent peace (the editing is elliptical) with a blonde who scoffs at rosaries.

230   The acting, further marred by dubbing, is without distinction, and Da-

miani's direction ranges from the pedestrian to the platitudinous. Sad to say, even the worthy Ennio Morricone misses with his score; he pitches it somewhere between Palestrina and Carl Orff, where it plops between two styles as badly as if they were stools.

In *Black Moon*, the talented and adventuresome filmmaker Louis Malle has been seduced into making a surrealist film, based largely on some of his dreams, on some bad advice by the late Therese Giehse (to make a movie without dialogue), and on the desire to shoot on his own farm. There is a war going on between men and women, and Lily, the teen-aged heroine, seeks refuge at a farm run by a seemingly incestuous (again!) brother and sister, who do not speak, though he sometimes sings Wagnerian arias. In an upstairs bedroom, a sick old woman listens on a two-way radio to reports about the Trojan War, or argues with a giant rat in an unknown language. Odd animals and brattish children do strange things, together or separately; an obese and mangy unicorn keeps dropping in and making Pythian pronouncements; the old woman is breast-fed by the silent sister. Children in Wagnerian costume are singing *Tristan;* the brother slashes to death an eagle with his saber, repeating the theme of a Persian painting on one of the walls; Lily ends up by suckling the unicorn.

This and more is superbly photographed by Sven Nykvist, and Malle knows how to compose a scene. But it is finally all pointless and uncompelling: surrealism seems to have exhausted its cinematic potential, and whoever resorts to it nowadays—Buñuel, Malle, or some young filmmaker—emerges as an instant epigone.

Exhibition purports to be a cinéma-vérité examination of the life, work, and private world of France's leading porn-film actress, Claudine Beccarie. The director, Jean-François Davy, who is also the interviewer, does not probe deeply enough, but does unearth a few curious details, such as the all-baring Mlle Beccarie's fierce refusal to reveal anything about her politics. Does that make politics the ultimate obscenity? The scenes from a hard-core film in the making, with their ritual groupings and gropings in closeup, have become as defused as the icons of surrealism.

Although Mlle Beccarie masturbates with a stylish rubato, my mind wandered idly from Beccarie to "peccary"; *that* might still hold interest: the intimate biography of a peccant wild pig, to be entitled *The Day of the Peccary.*

November 10, 1975

Strictly From Hunger

THE CASE OF THE Bengali filmmaker Satyajit Ray is rather more interesting than his 1973 film, *Distant Thunder,* currently on exhibit; more thought-   231 provoking, in fact, than any or all of his films. It is a case as notable as that of India itself, a prime example of a contemporary barrenness trying to cash in on a culture it once had. The India of the past sheds as little luster on Indira Gandhi's India as the Hellas of Aeschylus, Pericles, and Plato does on the Greece of more recent years. In a cultural desert, and in one more heavily censored than if Victoria sat on Indira's throne (in India, films are not allowed to show a kiss), it was indeed a miracle for even so modest a talent as Satyajit Ray's to emerge with *Pather Panchali* two decades ago. It is not so much that Ray's films are slow, or pallid, or derivative, or choppy, or technically rudimentary—though they are all of these things, too—as that they are, for the most part, dull. *Pather* and the other two films of the so-called Apu Trilogy seemed better than what followed, perhaps because of the novelty of seeing films from India. What impressed me in Ray's later films was the infallible gift for making things come out less varied, dimensional, moving (in both senses) than life.

Some of this is not the fault of Ray, but of the political mess and cultural wasteland, the underfinancing and overcensoring he must contend with. But all this oppressiveness works, in some ways, to his advantage: it precludes a lot of competition, excuses many crudities. And, true, there are cultural differences that may make it harder for us to apprehend Ray's meanings, yet given the bending over backward with which every supine bit of Indian mysticism is hailed by our budding Buddhists, yearning yogis, and transcendental meditators, Ray, for all his secularism and even socialism, cannot help benefiting indirectly from his Indianness. I have no room here for a detailed consideration of his work, but let me mention merely that such recent films of his as *Days and Nights in the Forest* and *The Adversary* have demonstrated to me with how primitive, indeed nonexistent, a sense of humor he turns to comedy, with how insuperable an inability to get inside his characters he adverts to drama.

In *Distant Thunder,* Ray proposes to tell the story of some villagers during the 1943 famine, while World War II was rampaging across the border from India. The last image of the film is, in fact, a silhouette shot of dark figures advancing across a convex nocturnal horizon, while a title tells us that five million died during what some called "the man-made famine of 1943." That final image sums up Ray's inadequacies: it is, first, meretricious poster art, just as that title is sheer didacticism; second, it reminds us that the film did not show how this famine was any more man-made than any other in India's hunger-ridden history. Yes, we learn that the villagers are dimly aware of a war beyond the frontier, but we do not begin to see how that war affects shortages within the noncombatant country. There is, to be sure, a rich merchant who hoards rice and causes an ineffectual riot, but, surely, there are such hoarders in all famines.

Ray's lack of acuity is everywhere apparent. The obvious thing to attack in India is inadequate birth control, but this Ray flagrantly fails to do—indeed, he ends with a paean to philoprogenitiveness. The film's hero and heroine are a young Brahmin and his wife; as the only Brahmin around, he is teacher, physician, priest, and village elder, and rather smug about it. His wife, the prettiest woman in the area, is likewise somewhat complacent. Hunger, near-rape, having to take on menial work, increased suffering all about them teach them a lesson or two. Still, when a mooching old beggar descends on this well-nigh starving couple with nine of his relatives, what does the husband say? That having managed to survive as a couple, they'll also manage as a dozen. Sweetly smiling in the direction of her belly, his wife corrects him: "Thirteen!" So the implication is that even when millions are starving, it is still wonderful to bring further potential starvelings into the world. Nor does it seem to occur to Ray that India, even with a famine, might have been better off than those neighbors who were being bombed by the very planes his villagers gaze at with childish delight. In fact, it is not wars beyond or within the borders that cause famines; rather, it is universal stupidity that causes war, famine, and films like *Distant Thunder*.

By Western standards, none of the actors gives anything like a rounded performance, not even Soumitra Chatterji, who played the grown-up Apu, and who does a routine job here as the Brahmin. But, in all fairness, the script and direction by Ray are no help. How pathetic is the attempt to whip up excitement by crosscutting between what happens to the husband and what goes on with the wife on a given day, as if two sets of events pedestrianly told could become more interesting by intercutting. Note also how stiltedly and listlessly the riot scene is executed, how melodramatically the lurking would-be rapist is introduced, yet how simplistically he is then disposed of. A hideously burned face is disfigured only on one side, leaving the other improbably handsome (shades of Preminger's *Junie Moon*); and though it is always hard to get actors to appear starved, here the women look downright roly-poly.

What Ray lacks most is the ability to build, to shape the film toward a climax by proper dovetailing, rhythmic patterns, and a sense of purposive urgency. Instead, at any moment he will drag in, say, a recurrent shot of two gamboling butterflies, about as poetic as the works of Laurence Hope. And his cinematographer, Soumendu Roy, reinforces this uncertainty of touch: within one shot, the color values will suddenly bleach out, so that we seem to shuttle between the palettes of Maurice Vlaminck and Marie Laurencin—to pick artists sufficiently second-rate to bear comparison with Roy and Ray.

There must have been a contest on between the producers, Reader's Digest Films, and the composer-lyricist-star, Anthony Newley, as to which of them could ruin *The Old Curiosity Shop* more thoroughly. Not that the novel is one of Dickens's best (although when it gets away from its two central characters, it is good enough), but it deserves better than it gets in this movie-musical disincarnation. *Reader's Digest* spreads enough cheer across the story to make Disney look like John Calvin by comparison, and Newley smears himself so distastefully from end to end as to make all the sugar-coating turn to wormwood in your mouth.

With remarkable modesty, this musical *Old Curiosity Shop* was retitled *Mr. Quilp*, the part Newley happens to be playing—which is rather like turning *Hamlet* into *Mr. Polonius*. After all, they could have renamed the film *Mr.*

Newley. Of course, to justify the title change, the part of Daniel Quilp had to be blown up until it balloons out of and over the rest of the movie, which, what with cutting other roles partly or entirely and letting Newley write most of the songs for Quilp, was easier done than said. True enough, Dickens's Quilp was a dwarf, but no matter: what Newley adds to the character in size, he subtracts in talent.

Oscar Wilde once observed, "One must have a heart of stone to read the death of Little Nell without laughing." The filmmakers, to prove that they have soft hearts—to say nothing of their heads—have remolded the whole thing into one big, happy comedy. You might assume that the death of Nell, which, as George Sampson put it, caused "a tidal wave of tears that washed across these [British] islands and across the Atlantic," resisted glossing over. Not a bit of it: Nell sickens suddenly, worsens almost instantly, and dies blissfully under the loving gaze of Kit Nubbs, who, after he comes to own the curiosity shop, sings a final, faithful tribute to her memory, and is certainly not shown married to Barbara. Nevertheless, there is a wedding here: Newley's songwriting manages to marry off bits of "On the Street Where You Live" to bits of "I've Grown Accustomed to Her Face," and so it all works up to a happy blending after all.

The prevailing mood is serene and cheerful. Quilp robs and brutalizes serenely and cheerfully; Grandfather Trent and Nell go begging as if on a month of Sunday picnics through an England that might as well be Oz; a perky Sally Brass wears lipstick, and an overstuffed Dick Swiveller, exquisite clothes; the Marchioness—but, hold on! The Marchioness is no longer that because too many American parents might have difficulty explaining to their children what a marchioness is, so she has become "the Duchess." Elliot Scott's décor is authentically conceived, but executed and lighted so lavishly, made to look so brightly unlived-in, as if it were pure marzipan and, any moment, the actors might start eating it—except that, down to the last beggar, they look far too well fed. Anthony Mendleson's costumes, if you disregard the upgrading, are pleasingly designed, but Christopher Challis's cinematography is only conventionally competent, and Gillian Lynne's dances, if anything, out-White Onna White. The screenplay, by Louis and Irene Kamp, is a family affair, and is distinguished only by its blurring of topography and chronology.

In Michael Tuchner's direction, blandness and banality go sweetly hand in hand, and the one attempt at originality (belated, at that) is the jump-cutting of some of Quilp's song numbers, so that a verse during which he swings from the rafters is followed by one during which he is voluptuously lolling in an armchair. The songs themselves surpass the ones Newley used to write with Leslie Bricusse. Your Bricusse-Newley score would have at least one song that, however unoriginal, was at any rate ingratiating and clung to the memory, if only like a burr. This Newley-Newley score is not only oldly, oldly conceived, it also persists in being tuneless and unmemorable even where it is lifted from the most respectable sources. The lyrics are on the order of: "My Somewhere is/Anywhere with you" and "I've forgotten how she looked/Except she reminded me of spring."

234

The "she" is, of course, Little Nell; as played by Sarah Jane Varley, she is a strapping girl, mature of mien, and so lacking in expression as to seem truly aged in the wood. Sarah Webb, as the newly promoted Duchess, is better, but it is hard to see this urchin as the vis-à-vis of a Dick Swiveller played by David Hemmings grown peculiarly portly and prematurely *embourgeoisé* in appearance; at least it is lucky that we do not see the two getting married, lest we should think ourselves transported into a *Reader's Digest* version of *Lolita*. To be sure, in no British-made film are the character parts played wholly without interest, and so Yvonne Antrobus, Mona Washbourne, and a few others do very nicely, but further stalwarts such as Michael Hordern, Jill Bennett, Paul Rogers, and David Warner perform at the minimum of their potential. Perhaps they do it by way of tacit protest against Newley's maximum pitch from start to finish: a Quilp meant to be the most delectable, scrumptious, *gemütlich* villain who ever didn't live. Watching Newley leer, growl, cavort, and jack-in-the-box his way through *Mr. Quilp* (complete with visual and verbal allusions to Nixon and Watergate), you'd have to have a heart of stone not to want to hurl one at him.

March 17, 1975

Facing the Music

RECENTLY I wrote that opera on film is an impossibility; now that even Ingmar Bergman comes to relative grief with *The Magic Flute,* my case seems very nearly proved. Let me hasten to add that this may well be the best filmed opera ever, though that, unfortunately, does not mean very much. The trouble with putting opera on film is that even when you do it right, you are wrong to do it at all: you are only reminding us how much better the thing is in the opera house, where it belongs.

Bergman has loved *The Magic Flute* ever since childhood, and he introduced a bit of it in puppet-theater form into *Hour of the Wolf.* Altogether music has been important to him (as painting and poetry have not), and marriage to the pianist Käbi Laretei taught him still more about music. He has staged operas here and there, and his *Rake's Progress* for the Stockholm Opera was—by all accounts, including Stravinsky's—one of the great operatic productions of all time. In his films, he has used music wisely and ever more sparingly; in his latter ones, he has usually limited it to preexisting music played by someone on an instrument, the radio, a phonograph, as the plot requires it. (In *Cries and Whispers,* he departed from this practice, and though the Chopin played on the soundtrack by Käbi Laretei worked very well—being presumably a memory of the women's mother playing her piano—the Bach cello music did not fit in believably and felicitously.) In his earlier films, Bergman commissioned music from some able Swedish composers, the most distinguished of them Karl-Birger Blomdahl, who supplied   235

The Naked Night with an exemplary score—and to think that his fascinating opera, *Aniara,* from a poem by the Nobel laureate Harry Martinson, has never been performed in New York!

But back to *The Magic Flute.* Bergman's first decision was clearly to cast attractive singers in all the roles. Since the film was made for television, where the closeup is king, good faces were all-important. But that is right up Bergman's alley, the face being the prime ingredient of his mature filmmaking. "I am always interested in faces," Bergman explained to me. "I just want you to sit down and look at the human face." Assuredly, these faces are quite good even for movie actors; for opera singers, they are nothing short of remarkable. Josef Kostlinger is a handsome, manly Tamino, and Håkan Hagegård's Papageno is just this side of adorable. Irma Urrila, as Pamina, is a composite of Liv Ullmann, Bibi Andersson, and Ingrid Thulin, though without the fascination of any of them. Elisabeth Eriksson is so charming a Papagena that Bergman, apparently, didn't have the heart to turn her into the required crone in her first meeting with Papageno, and let her get away with only partial downgrading into a homely country wench. The Sarastro of Ulrik Cold is positively young and much too sensual for a priest of Isis and Osiris (who, like other things Egyptian, are pretty much left out of Bergman's version of the text); only the Queen of the Night, Birgit Nordin, is allowed to look run-of-the-mill Queen-of-the-Nightish, and is sometimes photographed with exaggerated cruelty.

Two problems immediately arise. Nice as these faces look, they are not quite animated and versatile enough to hold our attention through so many tight shots. And even though they open their mouths relatively discreetly for opera singers, we are soon peering into them—discovering that Papageno is a bit snaggle-toothed; that the Queen has quite a few crowns on her teeth but none of them gold, which confirms us in our notion that these are not expensive singers. And that is the second, and bigger problem: for more alluring faces, we are paying with inferior voices. There is only one major voice in the lot of them, Ragnar Ulfung, and he is squandered on the small part of Monostatos; he is alone, too, in having the full polish and discipline of a trained Mozart singer. Hagegard sometimes approaches this, and Kostlinger and Eriksson have agreeable vocal moments. Urrila remains pallid-sounding throughout, and Nordin simply cannot cope with the high tessitura of the Queen, and often sounds strained and harsh. As for Cold, he actually croaks through *"In diesen heil'gen Hallen,"* and is not much better later on, even though he can look as soulful as the young Edmund O'Brien, whom he rather resembles.

What the presence of a Gundula Janowicz, a Sena Jurinac, and a few such others, could have done to heighten the level of vocal musicianship! But there is something even more basic involved here: you just know that the singing has been postsynced and electronically amplified, and that takes the joy out of the affair. It is almost as bad as dubbing foreign-language acting into English: what you hear is not the natural voice of the singer spontaneously and continuously deployed. You cannot trust what you hear. And the sound in a movie theater (at the Coronet, by the way, there is worse: even the tops of the heads often get chopped off) does not have the fidelity of the best hi-fi equipment. So you end up feeling variously cheated.

The opera is sung in Swedish, which is fine, since the German libretto by Schikaneder and Giesecke is about as beautiful as those worthies' monickers. The English subtitles, though they take considerable liberties, are in quite suitable doggerel. Bergman often introduces, in sundry ingenious ways, cards with the verses printed on them, and these overtones of the community sing are dopily endearing. But, oh, that hopeless libretto, which, as the movie brings us closer to it, becomes more ridiculous yet. Bergman has tried to improve it in various ways, first of all by cutting: one duet and a great deal of dialogue (in which the Masonic stuff is put on with a trowel) have bit the dust.

While this is all to the good, I doubt the wisdom of attempts at greater psychological relevance. Sarastro is turned into the father of Pamina, who becomes the pawn in some kind of internecine parental power play between him and her mother the Queen. The eponymous flute becomes more phallic even than magic, and also something like Prospero's staff in *The Tempest,* which this Sarastro-Prospero sadly relinquishes in the end, even as he bequeaths his worldly goods to Tamino-Ferdinand and Pamina-Miranda. There are overtones even of the Fredrik-Anne-Henrik triangle from *Smiles of a Summer Night.* Papageno and Papagena are no longer semi-avian, to make things a little more realistic, I suppose (but why precisely here?); whereas the ordeal by fire and water, where more realistic liberties might well have been taken, is routine stuff except for some nudity in the corps de ballet.

Bergman is at his best with the overture. It is evening in one of those opulent Swedish parks surrounding a magnificent building, the opera house, and there is a fine statue silhouetted against extraordinary reddish orange light—only the first of the restrained miracles the magic camera of Sven Nykvist performs throughout. Then we go inside the building, a kind of reproduction of that jewel box of a Drottningholm Theater, built in 1766, and indeed not much bigger than a jewel box. Inside this compact theater, Bergman's adroit cutting from face to face in the audience suggests that the whole world is united in Mozart. The anchor face is that of a thrilled little girl (Bergman's daughter), whence we proceed to any number of other faces, young and old, beautiful and plain, white and yellow and black. Then there is another key face: that of Mozart surveying his constituency from a portrait. The rhythm of the editing matches that of the music, the faces assume or reflect the mood and coloring of the melodies, and for final punctuation there is always the little girl or Mozart, though other faces also recur. Sometimes there is even a panoramic shot of the theater from without, or a shot of the proscenium, reminding us of the date of the opera, 1791. This is brilliant filmmaking, conveying the ecumenical spirit of the music, and its transcendence of time, both historic and human. These faces have tasted eternity.

Alas, once the libretto is upon him, Bergman has a tougher time of it. Still, he makes marvelous choices, hits on splendid *trouvailles.* Keeping most of the action on a smallish eighteenth-century stage, with mostly contemporary sets and props, and only at times, almost imperceptibly, broadening the scope to studio dimensions (with one glimpse of genuine outdoor snow) is a judicious wedding of the needs of opera with those of film. Delicious, too, are the occasional sidelong glances into the wings and beyond, into the dressing rooms; a montage of how the various performers while away the entr'acte is particularly amusing and ingenious. Throughout, Bergman the distinguished stage director comes to the aid of Bergman the master filmmaker. Consider, for instance, that delightful Sesame Street dragon; or how well the Three Ladies are moved about the stage, and the Three Genii above it. How delectable are the animals (with children inside them), including those three up-side-down Chiroptera that I felt quite batty about. And what of the enchanting stage transformation from the winter of Papageno's discontent into sudden springtime with the arrival of Papagena, and the reciprocal striptease as the comic pair remove each other's hiemal integuments for a vernal embrace.

Yet a good many other things do not work; in fact, none of the serious parts of the plot. These, of course, would be incredible enough from the farthest seat in a large opera house, but there the camera wouldn't rub our noses in them; nor would we be reminded of the kind of drama most of these singers aren't actors enough to provide. There are other errors of judgment. I don't think Papageno's glockenspiel should be housed in a box with a flagrantly erotic painting on it; nor do we want Bergman's daughter cropping up again and again in closeup after the overture.

Finally, though, both good and less good points pale beside the fact that *musically* this remains an undistinguished event, especially under Eric Ericson's unmagic baton. "Mozart helps me enormously," Bergman has said; I doubt whether, for all his good intentions and considerable cinematic achievement, Bergman has been much help to Mozart.

From even farther north, the lower reaches of Finnish Lapland, comes a most curious film, *The Earth Is a Sinful Song*. Based on a novel by the late Timo Mukka, who came from those Hyperborean parts, it relates the crude, violent, puzzling ways of poor peasants and Lappish reindeer herdsmen, whose lives are pared down to rough essentials: hard work, hard sex, hard death; primitive talk, humor, and religion; strange indulgences and inhibitions. Motivation is at its most inscrutable this side of Nō drama. The actors, if that is what they are, are as unprepossessing as they come, yet slowly they claim, and then clamp down on, our attention.

A remote landscape and remoter ethos come disturbingly alive. We are reminded of what human nature is, reduced to it lowest animal denominator. Yet these people are never condescended to, never made cute or picturesque. The cinematography uncannily gets across the feel of Nordic light and Northern murk; some of the outdoor scenes seem not photographed but painted on translucent glass. The continuity lurches about and skips over needed details, though some of this the director, Rauni Mollberg, may have justifiably wanted. Certain things are plainly unbelievable: Why can't a Laplander swim, or at least outrun a much older Finn? Two scenes involving the killing of animals are very hard to take, but not gratuitous. Lopsided and lumbering, the film nevertheless raises questions about ourselves beneath our civilized veneer—questions we had better confront.

November 24, 1975

Unholy Writ

CALLING the pseudonymous Pauline Réage's sadomasochist "classic," *Story of O (Histoire d'O),* incorrectly *The Story of O* in the movie version is the first mistake. The absence of the article is deliberately depreciatory: in French, "histoire de———," means "just a——— story" or "one of those——— stories." In this case, it is a *mere* story about a woman who rates no more identification than an initial, and that initial, O, an ideogram for the aperture—any aperture—through which a woman can be possessed. (Before NOW, or some other group, starts protesting, let me explain that I am only summarizing "Pauline Réage," who *appears* to be Dominique Aury, and *must* be a woman, for no man could so project himself into the microcosm of feminine minutiae of make-up, clothes, etc.) In any case, the book may not succeed as a novel, and may indeed contain passages calculated to arouse; yet it also has literary merit, and is certainly an attempt to understand the meaning of masochism and, to a somewhat lesser extent, its complement, sadism. The movie, just as trashy as Just Jaeckin's previous *Emmanuelle,* is none of that.

Jaeckin, a once and always fashion photographer (it would appear that fashion photography has a permanently debilitating effect on the eye or mind), has made this film into something like *The Story of Vogue,* resembling the original less than Bowdler's *Family Shakespeare* resembles Shakespeare. Whereas the novel examines in painstaking and painful physical and psychological detail the partly voluntary, partly compulsive feelings and acts through which a woman becomes a total masochist and ends up either as an object or as a suicide (one of the few "literary" tricks of the book is to have alternative beginnings and endings), the movie, with a script by the well-known hack Sébastien Japrisot, is something entirely different. It is a fairytale depiction of the beauties of sadomasochism, presented as a cross between a sexual finishing school for adventuresome young ladies and a non-stop vacation at some more sumptuous version of Club Med. When its heroine is asked why she behaves as she does, she quotes *Alice in Wonderland* with a knowing smirk.

The Story of O was made as soft-core pornography for the sake of hard cash, at a time when censorship in France was already permitting things like *Exhibition.* But Jaeckin preferred to avail himself of the celebrity of the novel for the sake of his kind of film, shot through a whole drugstore's worth of   239 gauze and Vaseline, with everything bathed in a warm amber glow, dressed, decorated, and furnished according to the latest slick-magazine styles, and with the plot, dialogue, and outcome all on the sentimental love-story level. There is a wondrously happy ending for the infantile heroine: by a few perfunctory ordeals she rises to the top, and becomes the smiling master and manipulator of both her male and female lovers, a kind of Cleopatra of Sunnybrook Farm.

On the physical side, the book records assiduous whippings, oral and anal ravishments, and various ever more elaborate techniques for making the heroine's apertures ever more permanently, distendedly open, more continually offered up to her master and the men he bestows her on. But there is also a strong lesbian coloration, especially in the episode at Samois, where a strict sado-sapphic discipline is imposed, and which, in the movie, becomes a kind of Barbizon Hotel for women. It is now run by a Gallic Spring Byington rather than by a tough butch lesbian who has devised a way of so tying up a woman that only her vagina and anus are exposed for slow, refined flogging of which men, impetuous brutes that (according to the author) they are, would not be capable.

In the movie, none of this. No oral or explicitly anal sex, and even the whippings are of the most artistic and decorous sort, leaving only a few, highly ornamental, marks, and taking place in opulently overdecorated surroundings. There is gourmet cooking, and the kind of service well beyond the means of a four-star hotel; the most expensively tasteless clothes and jewelry are provided free of charge, and a kind of Muzak that ranges from imitation baroque through semiclassical to genuine pop. In the book, every nexus, hetero- or homosexual, is and remains a love-hate relationship: the victim feels a combination of fear and love and, sometimes, hate; the tormentor experiences sexual gratification, malign triumph, and, sometimes, a fleeting tenderness. But by eroticizing pain and sinking ever deeper into all-accepting slavery, by basking in the abandonment of will and reification to the extent that the least crumb from the master's table becomes an emotional feast, Réage's O achieves a paradoxical victory in abject defeat.

Not so Jaeckin and Japrisot's heroine, who remains a cutely shallow young thing from beginning to end, revels in having all kinds of men and women, dominant or slavish, falling Hollywoodishly in love with her, becomes more manipulator than manipulated, and ends up the laughing *domina* of her self-deposed master, Sir Stephen. Even her chains are usually made of delicate-linked, glittering chrome, suitable for necklaces; the posts to which she is tied are apt to be arty statues of adorable blackamoors; the whips have handles in the shape of elegantly carved dogs' heads, which are much more in evidence than their lashes; intercourse of any kind is photographed in the most incorporeal style; the heavy irons and austere ring with which O's labia and finger are subjugated become diminutive vaginal ornaments and digital jewelry soon to be sold at better department stores everywhere; and the large, deep initials with which both of O's posterior cheeks are branded become a single discreet monogram on the small of O's back, in a handsome but unaggressive display type, probably Gravure Open (Typefoundry Amsterdam). Most important, however, the book's philosophical, theological, psychoanalytical, and existential speculations are reduced to snippets of voice-over narration in a tone befitting a documentary about deep-sea fishing.

One of the things that distinguish pornographic films from the rest is that one does not get acting from them, only faces, bodies, and the ability to simulate pleasure and, in this case, pain. Corinne Clery, as O, is quite the prettiest young woman I have seen in such a film, even if she is rather swaybacked and has breasts lacking in absolute firmness—but though they might just pass the pencil test, her acting flunks both the agony and the ecstasy tests. As her first lover, René, Udo Kier seems uncomfortable even in a moderately macho role; as Sir Stephen, Anthony Steel looks suitably civilized and sinister—British-brutish—but is obliged to play a lamb in wolf's clothing. Truly, here is a film that deserves to have unleashed on it both Susan Brownmiller and her followers and the Eulenspiegel Society, so that between them they may tear it frame from frame.

December 1, 1975

Overblown, Underdone

IF COSTA-GAVRAS'S and Joseph Losey's reputations were balloons, they could hardly last another minute, so overblown are they. But since they are filmmakers' reputations, they can probably go on forever without being exploded—which is what is, or ought to be, known as the Preminger Syndrome. Have one big hit under your belt, like Costa-Gavras, or a couple of seemingly solid minor ones, like Losey, and you can coast along on that ad infinitum. Now, I have nothing against a person's achieving only one impressive work (or, in Losey's case, one half); that is always better than nothing. But nothing is worse than having a film director's every subsequent work touted as a major accomplishment, even if it is as paltry and dreary as—to pick random samples from an all too crowded hat—late Tati, Bresson, and Welles.

The Franco-Greek director Costa-Gavras is a man full of worthy intentions. His first film, *The Sleeping-Car Murders,* was trivial hokum, but even into this gimmicky and attitudinizing murder story Costa-Gavras was able to sneak some politically gilt-edged stances, and introduce marvelous performances from actors sometimes cast against type, sometimes more famous than their parts would warrant, and yielding stunning results. The next C-G film, *One Man Too Many,* was virtually uncatchable over here; it certainly slipped by me. Then came the big one, *Z.* True, it was slick and, again, fairly gimmicky, but it worked and was something new: a political film with a serious subject and aims handled partly as a thriller, partly as an outrageous farce. The novelty was arresting and, on top of that, the film fitted neatly   241 into the political temper of the times: no one was more hated than the military rulers of Greece who had come into power through the misdeeds *Z* recorded, and the relatively discreet leftism that pervaded the film was in line with the American liberalism that ran high in the late Vietnam years.

Another aspect of *Z* made film history: its ending. Not since Truffaut concluded *The 400 Blows* with that celebrated freeze frame did an ending enter cinematic vocabulary as did *Z*'s: a bluntly matter-of-fact summary of what happened to the film's principals afterward, both printed and uninflectedly narrated, while from beside the titles the face of the mentioned character peers out at you immobile, as in an illustrated TV newscast. It is an effective device for driving home a bitter historical irony, as in *Z*, though questionable in more fictional films such as *American Graffiti.*

Neither of the next two C-G movies came off, althouth they employed the services of the same writer, the anti-Franco Franco-Spanish novelist Jorge Semprun. In both *The Confession* and *State of Siege,* the director tried to make more soberly straightforward, quasi-documentary films, with humor almost totally absent. There was an effort toward impartiality in making the Stalinists in the former film uncommonly rotten even for Stalinists in a leftist film, and by giving, in the latter, the part of the "ugly American" to that most charming of Frenchmen, Yves Montand. Still, there was a great deal of dubious political hanky-panky in both films, along with some rousing verities; what was more damaging, though, was that neither film could shed new light on well-known historical incidents, or make its characters as real humanly as politically. In *The Confession,* the chief device for gaining audience sympathy (or was it comic relief?) was having the pants of a little man on trial for his life drop periodically in court.

With *Special Section,* Costa-Gavras and Semprun return to their *Z* mode, trying to graft suspense and black humor onto a record of true and appalling political machinations. This is the tale of that monstrous law engineered shortly after the German Occupation by a collaborationist French minister, making minor or imaginary offenses punishable by death, with immediate execution without chance of appeal, and without adequate legal representation. Even more unconscionably, the law was made retroactive, so that some prisoners already tried and doing jail stretches could be retried and sent to the guillotine for crimes they obviously could not have committed, in retaliation for a political murder by unapprehended Communist students. This law, passed without any real pressure from the Nazis, ostensibly to avoid never-mentioned executions of "respectable" upper-class hostages, was to be the ignominious Special Section of the French judiciary that executed countless innocents merely for being leftists, Jews, or members of the lower class. It was administered, with few abstainers, by respectable French jurists, who were never under a special threat, and were not punished after the Liberation.

For bringing this to public attention, hats off to the filmmakers; but neither the attempt at suspense nor the black humor can be praised. For we know from the start that no one can prevail against Pétain and his entire government; and whereas the gags in *Z* worked because they were confined to the later, nontragic part of the movie, here a runaway chicken is distastefully chased past politicians plotting the death of innocents, and big laughs are to be derived from the discomfiture of executioners soon to be chopping off guiltless heads. Slickly and scurrilously, the movie holds our interest; yet in the end we wonder whom to resent more: the filmmakers, for turning tragedy into a *divertissement,* or ourselves, for falling for it.

As usual in a C-G film, some things work. There is, once again, splendid cinematography, this time from Andreas Winding, who knows how to make a brutal scene look spookily beautiful. And Semprun's dialogue is clever—too clever—as when a defense lawyer accuses a corrupt presiding judge of *"quelques détails rocambolesques, même Courteliniens,"* where the first epithet has lost its literary overtones, but the second is a bit too literarily fanciful (not to mention injudicious) even for such Gallic circumstances.

Costa-Gavras is a skillful director. He knows, for example, when using a long shot is more dramatically chilling than coming in tight, as a cruder director would; but he has no taste, as when he shows a political assassination in slow motion, complete with pounding heartbeats on the soundtrack, the worst sort of cliché. He has a good, although somewhat excessive, sense of pacing, and a tidily selective eye, though some fine details get unfinely milked. And he has again obtained a prodigious cast, in which even such very known actors as Louis Seigner and Michel Lonsdale manage to surprise you as if they were uncannily apt unknowns, indeed nonprofessionals. And actors of different styles are made to fit together into an ensemble that works with a precision that nowadays even machines are beginning to lose. Here it would truly be ungracious to single out anyone.

Credit for this must go to the director, too; but the basic idea remains sick. You cannot tell a story that concerns a few individuals with such fatal intimacy in terms of so large a canvas, and keep picking up and dropping people with alienating nonchalance. To treat human lives with such narrative casualness is to make the film partake, on however much smaller a scale, of the same depersonalizing evil its main thrust commendably attacks.

Joseph Losey is an interesting case: had he not been a victim of McCarthyism, forced to leave Hollywood and the B-pictures he turned out there, he would have most likely remained a minor coterie director, rising at best to the modest heights of films like *The Prowler.* McCarthy propelled him into becoming a *major* coterie director, for in British exile Losey teamed up with that prince of phonies, Harold Pinter, with whom he contrived his two *succès d'estime, The Servant* and *Accident* (I buy roughly one half of the first), and his principal failure *d'estime, The Go-Between.* How wretched a Pinterless Losey can be is best seen in such recent efforts as *The Assassination of Trotsky,* despite a most interesting subject; and in *A Doll's House* and *Galileo,* despite such distinguished collaborators as Ibsen and Brecht, though a less pretentious hack than Losey would probably leave theatrical masterpieces to the stage.

In his current film, *The Romantic Englishwoman,* Losey has again latched on to a prestigious playwright as collaborator: Tom Stoppard, who coscripted the film with the author of the underlying novel, Thomas Wiseman. It is 243 very hard to determine, without having read the book, where Thomas ends and Tom begins. But since Stoppard's stock-in-trade is infernal cleverness with words (which allows so trivial and misshapen a play as *Travesties* to be hailed as a masterpiece), one hopes that Stoppard's contribution was no more than an occasional highlight on the otherwise glossless dialogue, e.g., "The bourgeois life has its compensations."—"What would it be without them?" In any case, the dialogue aims mostly for the Pinteresque pause-ridden innuendo rather than the Stoppardian shower of verbal shooting stars. And Stoppard could nowise be so effective on screen as on stage: although words are much more important to film than our younger (and frequently illiterate) cinéastes would have it, the words have to be fewer than on stage, to allow attention to the increased number of visual elements. Moreover, *The Romantic Englishwoman* is too commercially slanted a vehicle to allow for Stoppard's characteristically abstruse interests.

So I hope that such gems of wit as Glenda Jackson's appraisal of how she loves her supposed-poet-and-actual-gigolo lover, "Let me count the ways: you're a fucking poet, you're a poetical fuck," is non-Stoppard stuff. Assuredly what the film has most of is the old Loseyan paraphernalia: the distorting convex mirror from *The Servant,* the blatantly nudging zoom shots (particularly zoom-outs) from *Accident,* and a hyperextension of the device Losey has sometimes used effectively: positioning actors at greater than customary distances from one another so as to logically justify fewer closeups, and creating a greater sense of isolation, or reciprocal alienation. But here the device gets to be ludicrous, as when one partner in a dialogue is merely a distant head jutting above a stairwell in the lower left corner of the frame. No less felicitous is making Miss Jackson play the concluding reconciliation scene with her husband with her head almost sticking out of the lower left corner of the frame, the angle creating further disharmony in an already jarring face.

Nor does Losey get performances, either from the principals or from most of the supporting players. The casting itself is senseless: Glenda Jackson as a romantic Englishwoman? She who generally looks and sounds like a washerwoman taking inordinate pride in a laundry strike she has just organized, has nothing romantic about her inner or outer persona—unless a moon-surface complexion, bricklayer's hands, and the walk of a hoplite can be construed as romantic, to say nothing of a near-perpetual sneer. And just when we had every right to hope that the infelicitous body, which used to be exhibited nude in her earlier films with the regularity of a cuckoo emerging from a Swiss clock, would be spared us (Miss Jackson having attained the kind of star status above the call of gratuitous nudity), we are plunged again into the old unsightliness. Helmut Berger looks customarily gorgeous in his usual Saint Laurent wardrobe, and is getting to be quite proficient at portraying everything about the uppity gigolos he is always playing, except perhaps their presumed heterosexuality. Michael Caine's once genuinely cocky Cockney charm has worn precariously thin, even as his face and frame have become thick with flab. Béatrice Romand is wasted on a small, rather gratuitous role, and out of Nathalie Delon not even a better director could get that bedeviling sexual ambivalence that Jeanne Moreau and Delphine Seyrig so abundantly dispensed in earlier Losey films.

Perhaps the chief distinction of the picture is the number of things getting defenestrated in it: an overnight bag, a book, some manuscript pages, an attaché case; a bagful of dope, moreover, gets not only stuck through a window but also, like the rest of the movie, washed down the drain.

December 8, 1975

All's Unfair in Love and Politics

WITH *The Story of Adèle H.,* Truffaut has again undertaken an intimate film like *The Wild Child,* but pared down his principals even further—to one. The attempt is calmly grandiose: to film a love story for one player, Adèle, the younger daughter of Victor Hugo. The girl grew up in a double shadow: that of her father, a great literary and political figure, and also great lecher, who could get girls of Adèle's age even in his advanced years; and that of Léopoldine, her beautiful older sister, drowned at nineteen along with her young husband, who, unable to save her when their boat capsized, deliberately died with her. Growing up in the godforsaken Channel Island of Guernsey, whither her father was banished, this Miranda had the misfortune of encountering the British lieutenant Pinson; a little more than Caliban and a lot less than Ferdinand, he dallied with her both on Guernsey and in London, where she followed him. Tiring of her, he was glad to be transferred with his regiment to Halifax, Nova Scotia. Adèle then did something wildly daring for a young woman of her day: without telling her parents, who disapproved of Pinson, she sailed across the ocean to try to reclaim him.

Living in a modest boardinghouse (Truffaut's screenplay, with the collaboration of Jean Gruault and Suzanne Schiffman, follows Adèle's diary rather closely), Adèle set out on the task of reconquest with a mixture of methodicity and fanaticism. When she finally cornered Pinson into admitting bitterly that the Great Man, her father, would never give his consent, she managed to wrest it from Hugo by mail. She paid Pinson's gambling debts, sent love messages to him in bizarre forms, including a paid prostitute to spend the night with him as a gift from her, watched through the window as he made love to other women, built a cande-lit shrine to him in which she worshiped his photograph, and defied his and her father's pleas that she go back home. Soon she who had been offering a unilateral open marriage if only he would have her was resorting to monstrous stratagems: trying to humiliate him before his soldiers, attempting to get a hypnotist to mesmerize him into marrying her, breaking up his engagement to a wealthy young woman. All this time, too, she was writing mendaciously optimistic letters   245 home and horribly truthful entries into her diary, as well as having night-mares in which she was the drowning Léopoldine. Though receiving regular money orders from home, she kept getting slovenlier and shabbier.

Truffaut, too, is negligent. By concentrating on Adèle, he fails to show how her family background induced her imbalance. Moreover, she was thirty-three and plain when she came to Halifax—by contemporary stan-dards a spinster left hanging on the vine. Instead, Truffaut casts the gifted, adorable, rising young star Isabelle Adjani, under twenty when she made the film. This makes Adèle's monomania less believable, more capricious and unhinged. There are no excuses for it; no claustrophobic life on Guernsey, no Electra complex, no love-hate for her sister, no fear of growing old un-wanted. Further, Truffaut makes Pinson (Bruce Robinson) into an ephebic pretty boy, devoid of sympathy for Adèle or anyone else, rather than into an ordinary, shallow man, somewhat pitiable himself for all this unwanted ado-ration and persecution. The story becomes less complex, then, less worthy of our compassion.

I think Truffaut errs, too, by not conveying that Adèle's pursuit lasted seven years, before ending (in scenes that he does show) with her as a ragged, demented figure who has followed the now married Captain Pinson to Bar-bados. Here, a derelict who calls herself Mrs. Pinson, she no longer even recognizes the man over whom she went mad. In a series of rather ineffectual stills and with voice-over narration, we learn that she was brought back to France, placed by her father in a genteel institution, where she puttered away a long life until 1915.

Unfortunately, Truffaut has opted for swift, short episodes, trying to make out of lean, restless vignettes a sweeping canvas of love, madness, personal tragedy. Within every short scene the tempo is hectic: even if Adèle is merely writing or pacing in her room while expressing her thoughts, the scene zeros in on its purpose like a cropped photograph. It is all *in medias res,* nervous camera movements, and punch lines. There is no sense of dementia as a slowly ripening bitter fruit inside one, something eating away from within rather than goading the victim into constant gadding about. A more brood-ing approach—staying with a scene, mood, condition longer—might have conveyed the pathos, horror, and ultimate humanity of the situation more shatteringly.

But something even bigger is missing from the movie: the sense of what Rilke called the shooting up of the beloved beyond the paltry object of her love. As he once put it (in *The Notebooks of Malte Laurids Brigge*): "Always the beloved transcends the lover, for life is greater than destiny. Her giving herself will be immeasurable: this is her happiness. The ineffable suffering of her love, though, has always been this: that what is demanded of her is to limit this giving of herself." What Adèle feels and deploys is both greatness and insanity: a love too great for its object. For the clinician, this is aberra-tion; for the poet, greatness. Sadly, dreadfully, both are right.

Truffaut sides with the poet—out of love for Adèle, or Isabelle Adjani, or love itself. But his art is not up to the nobility of his intentions; we do get

Adèle's craziness and poignancy, sometimes also her repulsiveness; we do not get her greatness. Mind you, much is done very well. There is no excessive use of closeup, and the reliance on medium shots creates an illusion of Adèle and the world being equally important, battling to a draw. With the help of his skilled cinematographer, Nestor Almendros, Truffaut has kept both the outdoor and indoor color schemes predominantly nocturnal, mauve, brown, dark. In the brilliantly lit Barbados scenes, conversely, only the mad Adèle is a black scarecrow. And Truffaut has latched on to an unused score by one of the great film composers, Maurice Jaubert, who died prematurely in World War II, and whose music here, even when it doesn't quite fit, is gripping. If only what radiated from the lovely and talented but too young Isabelle Adjani's face were tragedy, not merely exquisite pouts.

André Cayatte has made three or four effective films: *Justice Is Done*, *We Are All Murderers*, *Tomorrow Is My Turn* (*Le Passage du Rhin*), and possibly *Avant le Déluge*, which I have not seen. He is a former lawyer and journalist, and his pictures tend to be works of enlightened propaganda: pleas against the fallibility of the jury system, for the abolishment of capital punishment, against war or political hysteria. These movies were well constructed, often superbly acted, and directed competently even if without great artistry. They were easily the equivalent of boulevard drama, and if auteur criticism (starting, in effect, with André Bazin) had not turned against Cayatte, his reputation would not have suffered so badly. But it is true that Cayatte has always tended toward gimmickiness, as in an updated version of the Romeo and Juliet story, *The Lovers of Verona* (in which, however, the sixteen-year-old Anouk Aimée proved unforgettable), or *La Vie conjugale*, in which the failure of a marriage was examined in two separate films, one from the husband's, the other from the wife's, point of view, and both equally humdrum. But as Cayatte went on, he got worse, developing a tract-writer's shrillness that left little room for quieter tones. The air in his films was thick with polemic, which only pawns, not people, could breathe.

This made Cayatte's penultimate film, *To Die of Love*, self-defeating: the characters were drawn in simplistic black or white. Gabrielle Roussier, the complex and contradictory real-life woman whose story this was meant to be, emerged as a martyred saint—a plaster one, in fact, but for the humanizing authenticity of Annie Girardot's trenchant performance. But even that fine, humanly ornery artist could not desanctify the odor of the film. In Cayatte's latest, *Where There's Smoke*, we are up against similar problems. This is the tale of an intrepid and able reform candidate's enforced withdrawal from a mayoral campaign against a thoroughly corrupt incumbent and his murderous political machine. The challenger's innocent wife is smeared with a tricked photograph making her out to be an orgiast; later, the physician-hero himself is tricked into taking a murder rap. There are only the most perfunctory attempts by Cayatte to endow his all-black or all-white characters with a touch of human gray, and there is virtually nothing in the film that isn't purely plot (i.e., thesis) oriented. One recalls wistfully 247 the flesh-and-blood reality of the aging woman with a lapdog—especially as incarnated by the great Valentine Tessier—Cayatte could create in *Justice Is Done;* all this has gone up in *Where There's Smoke.*

As the spotless wife, here, once again, is Annie Girardot; as her doctor-husband, the likable Bernard Fresson. And here, too, is a distressing double standard: whereas the husband is allowed some past extramarital activity, the wife must be shown as simon pure, lest someone lose sympathy for her. Who? Cayatte is indulging either a male chauvinist audience or himself; either way, things are being rigged for primitive reasons in a film that, by its very theme, demands the aura of truth. Such primitivism embroils Cayatte in all kinds of difficulty. The heroine must be a saleswoman in a fashion boutique, already a mite improbable for a French doctor's wife; she must also be friends with her fellow saleswoman, the decadent designer-owner's wife, who throws the wildest parties and seems to have nothing in common with our chaste heroine—a friendship that is more than a mite unlikely. In order to get his series of black-and-white illustrations, Cayatte must drag his plot from one improbability to the next, the thesis to be illustrated being, first, that an honest man hasn't got a chance against the machine; second, that even the irreproachable person cannot remain unscathed by ingeniously trumped-up calumny: the loving, trusting husband can't entirely disbelieve photographic fakery so clever that no detection device can penetrate it.

Even as a *pièce à thèse,* this thesis goes to pieces—partly because of the excess of contrivances, and partly because the human problem is so much more absorbing than the political one, but gets fanatically swept under the ideological carpet. The direction is uninspired but adequate; Annie Girardot is getting a bit too old for this kind of role, and an unflattering hairdo does not help. Still, she is as genuine and unactressy as ever. André Falcon and Michel Bouquet are wonderfully triple-dyed heavies, and there are more picturesquely rat-faced policemen and judges than you have seen in a rat's, if not a coon's, age. But it is all too much of a muchness; for a mere suburban mayoral race, Cayatte gives us enough villainy to outfit an international scandal.

December 22, 1975–January 12, 1976

Is the New Wave Washed Up?

WHAT HAS HAPPENED to the French film? That was the question that haunted me after leaving Claude Pinoteau's *The Slap,* though it has also worried me fairly persistently over the last ten years. The French film had achieved a greatness during the thirties that not even the catastrophe of war, not even the tyranny of the German Occupation, could quell. Right under the noses of the conquerors, Marcel Carné, with the help of a magnificent script by Jacques Prévert and with the support of a brilliant cast, was able to create one of the great films of all time, *The Children of Paradise.*

It can be argued with some cogency that adversity breeds ingenuity, that oppression elicits the passion for freedom, which, in turn, inspires artistic creation as an act of at least covert political value. Still, after the Liberation came a yet more fertile period of filmmaking, which led to one of the major contributions to French cinema, the New Wave, though certain old-wave directors proved themselves no slouches either. I think of films like René Clément's *Forbidden Games,* another masterpiece untarnished even by Clément's subsequent lapse into insignificance. Here, the joy of liberation, the postwar ferment, had a great deal to do with cinematic invention.

Indeed, the *Nouvelle Vague,* intoxicated by the old films (many of them American) to be seen at the exemplary French Cinémathèque run by Henri Langlois, and by the often absurd but generally provocative articles in *Cahiers du Cinéma* (some of them written by the very same young men who were soon to become leading filmmakers), was about to turn into the most exciting component of Western cinema in the fifties. There were then a host of young cinéastes full of hope and hopefully embraced by the media and enthusiasts alike, although only a handful of them were to continue making successful or, at any rate, noticeable films after the first flush of enthusiasm turned pale. These men are François Truffaut, Louis Malle, Alain Resnais, Eric Rohmer, Claude Chabrol, Jacques Rivette (whom I consider, finally, unimportant), and most curious and controversial of all, Jean-Luc Godard. Though by far the most influential, Godard, I think, was also in many ways the most poseurish of these filmmakers, as well as the least disciplined. Becoming more and more of a Maoist, champion of the Palestinian terrorists and everything else that indulged his fanatical hatred of the bourgeoisie, Godard managed to phase—or craze—himself out of cinema altogether. In the end, with a revolutionary filmmaking collective of the most *outré* sort, he was making only agit-prop movies that seemed to have as little bearing on cinema as on mental balance. Now even that has stopped. Nevertheless, Godard has made at least two films that transcend mere historical interest— *Breathless* and *A Married Woman*—and as a theoretician of film he has likewise made a challenging contribution, even if his influence will be found partly liberating and partly misleading.

What has happened since then? I can think of only seven memorable films made by post–New Wave French directors, excluding such things as the new type of documentary, the cinéma-vérité film, which, though important, does not quite belong in this discussion of the mainstream film. These seven are Serge Bourgignon's *Sundays and Cybèle,* Alain Jessua's *Life Upside Down,* Jean Eustâche's *The Mother and the Whore,* and two each by Robert Enrico (*At the Heart of Life* and *Zita*) and Jacques Tati (*Jour de Fête* and *Monsieur Hulot's Holiday*)—although there may be some that I am forgetting. The New Wave masters, as well as some of the older directors, went on making some good films, too, but as I look back over the past decade of French filmmaking, I am far from overwhelmed.

Economics has something to do with it, of course. Much of French film-making depends on foreign capital and various coproductions, so that non-French elements are imposed on the local industry. I am not, of course, arguing for some kind of nationalist purity as a virtue, nor am I in the least against every kind of salutary crossbreeding. I am merely saying that if Buñuel, for instance, makes a film in France, it takes rather a herculean stretch of the imagination to call the result a French film. And (perhaps wrongly) I am not including on my list such a very beautiful and moving film as Raoul Coutard's *Hoa Binh,* because it was made in war-torn Vietnam, and depends too much on the expressiveness and nobility of the Vietnamese amateur actors—indeed, of the entire population—to be considered, strictly speaking, a French movie. On the other hand, I am less than happy about some forms of cross-pollination, as when large bundles of (usually American) money encourage prototypically commercial French filmmakers like Claude Lelouch and Jacques Demy, or assimilated foreigners like Costa-Gavras, to make relatively expensive, sometimes quite decent, but always sub-artistic movies, chiefly for export purposes.

Yet the reason for the paucity of excellence in current French filmmaking must go even deeper than that, and is probably not unrelated in the end to a universal backsliding that, with rare exceptions, engulfs the entire world, even such recently superbly productive countries as Japan. Even so, the French economy is not that bad, and although Gaullist France was dealt a considerable cultural blow by the puritanism of the late general and his good wife, the political circumstances were never so oppressive (except in the sexual area) as to preclude serious filmmaking. The real cause of tiredness of the French film, then, may have to be sought in a certain cultural exhaustion, in an explosion of materialism, and even, as far as moviemaking is concerned, in an inferiority complex vis-à-vis foreign outputs, especially American. Most, if not all, of the New Wave directors modeled themselves so insistently on American filmmaking—whether big studio, independent, or underground—that the juice went out of their work. A great many of the major French successes of the sixties and seventies (whether deserved or undeserved) could be classified as imitation American, like, say, *Day for Night* and *The Umbrellas of Cherbourg,* or else as slightly updated versions (usually quite disastrous, e.g., *Le Bonheur* and *Benjamin*) of the great domestic films of yesteryear.

All the same, some aspects of cinema continue untarnished in France, notably acting and cinematography. I could list here a long row of very fine performers and cameramen who have come to the fore in quite recent times, and, though they are less easy to spot and recall, some extremely able set and costume designers. In one other field in which the French film used to shine, however, there has been a notable decline; I am referring to background music. This has been provided lately either by such established vulgarians as Michel Legrand, or by such sadly fading former talents as Georges Delerue, or by such promising one-shots as Philippe Sarde and Michel Magne, who then peter out. Maurice Jarre, whose work in France augured so well, has gone both literally and figuratively Hollywood, with lamentable results. In fact, the only score by a Frenchman in a movie of recent years that really stays with me is that of *Going Places,* by Stéphane Grappelli, a seventy-year-old former member of the Hot Club de France. That *was* a score.

These reflections, I repeat, are occasioned by Claude Pinoteau's *The Slap,* which is not a particularly good or bad movie, and is rather typical of the technical proficiency the better French directors maintain along with sprightly dialogue, but without the saving gift of imagination that alone can give a film a quality of true aliveness and individuality, and thus of art. It is not such an obvious genre film as, say, *Borsalino* (or even Pinoteau's previous, undistinguished *Escape to Nowhere*); neither, however, is it such a pretentious piece of goods as, say, *The Things of Life.* There is, in fact, a certain liveliness in its tempo that is quite attractive though it does rather wear you out. In 98 minutes you are whisked through so many comic and dramatic climaxes, reversals, and anticlimaxes that you feel like one of those bicycles racers who, unlike God, do not even have the privilege of resting on the seventh day.

All this would be justified if only the film had much of anything to show. We are given here eighteen-year-old Isabelle, in the process of flubbing her premedical-school requirements, while she also makes a mess of trying to move in with a boy friend, and of her relations with her father and mother, who have separated. The other principal character is her father, Jean, a secondary-school geography teacher with book-writing ambitions, who is torn between memories of his wife who left him and the nice woman he lives with, who gets into trouble with the school authorities for helping out a student in a fight with detectives, and who loves his daughter deeply, but is as unable to express that love as any other he has ever felt. There is more than enough material here for a decent film, if only Pinoteau and his co-scenarist, Jean-Loup Dabadie, did not feel obliged to go into too many lesser characterizations, rather too many unimportant incidents, a quick look at various aspects of the French school system, and even into an attractive but excessive travelogue.

Both Isabelle and Jean are superlatively incarnated. No one could do the charming, flighty, not very intellectual but bright girl—drifting among parents, boy friends, and vocations—better than Isabelle Adjani. That she is of the same age, roughly, as the heroine has only very little to do with it. Clearly she is a thoroughly accomplished actress who knows what can be done with the eyes, with evocative body movements, and with a great range of vocal inflection. She also has superbly healthy good looks, and that rare and scarcely definable ability of great actresses (and women) to be at their most irresistible when they are most exasperating. This is a skill you cannot learn—it is something you are born with, and it is part of Mlle Adjani's extraordinary equipment.

As Jean, Lino Ventura proves yet again that he is the true successor of Jean Gabin, one of the supreme unwobbling pivots of French movies. He is a tough guy—*un dur,* as the French put it—but he can always suggest a softness within, and a wonderfully strangulated tenderness seeping through. He can do comedy up to a point, and all sorts of drama suggestively, in a way that gets under your skin. He is of that splendidly indeterminate age at which a   251 man supposedly appeals to women of all ages, and he has been the same age ever since I can remember, and won't relinquish it very soon. He can make a gesture count: note how he lowers his head in embarrassment when he bids his mistress adieu, and again as he waits, at the end, for his wife to make a call to her Australian lover, a call that may signify a partial or total reprieve for Jean.

But that brings me to the queasy aspect of the film. It carefully eschews obvious happy endings: Isabelle may have found the right man to go off with permanently, though another friend's remark that she'll come running home in a fortnight may also be true. Jean's wife may come back to her marriage, although she may be saying (we don't hear her words) only that she'll rejoin her Australian a day or two later. This is not a bitter, not a sweet, not even a bittersweet ending for either Jean or Isabelle, but a whatever-you-want-to-make-of-it ending: fairly tough for the "modern" viewer, quite hopeful for the "old-fashioned" moviegoer. And this having it both ways runs, I am afraid, through much of the film, leaving it less gripping and even less touching than it might have been. And certainly less conclusive.

Still, there is lovely supporting work from Annie Girardot, Nicole Courcel, and Georges Wilson, and a film in which a principal encourages his disenchanted geography teacher by evoking to him the satisfaction of seeing a student state that " 'Burma produces tungsten,' where the day before he did not know a thing," is not without its wry, ironic charm. And wry, ironic charm is so much of what we have always gone to the French cinema for.

January 26, 1976

Wertmüller's *Seven Beauties*—Call It a Masterpiece

THERE ARE, broadly speaking, two kinds of greatness in art: that of transcending previously known boundaries, of defying all norms; and that of perfect taste, of working with exquisite tact within one's limitations. In music for example, this would be the difference between a Wagner or Mahler on the one hand and a Fauré or Ravel on the other; in painting, between a Michelangelo or Picasso and a Botticelli or Degas. The artists of pure taste seem, rightly or wrongly, to possess a smaller greatness, though I often prefer them to the other sort. But there exists, fascinatingly, even a rare third kind that combines aspects of the two divergent greatnesses—artists who are, somehow, both big and small, fierce and civilized, beyond taste and yet also, miraculously, tasteful. I think of Goya, Delacroix, and Debussy in this way, of Stendhal and Proust and Rodin.

Without wishing to make odious and extravagant—or, at any rate, premature—comparisons, I must still declare that *Seven Beauties* (*Pasqualino Settebellezze*), the new film by Lina Wertmüller, strikes me as the work of this third kind of artist: one who amazingly blends great force with something that, even if it is not exactly delicacy and finesse, is still a mischievous piquancy, a penetrating slyness that borders on a kind of refinement. If *Swept Away* marks a considerable step beyond Wertmüller's earlier, very fine films, *Seven Beauties* is an upward leap in seven-league boots that propels her into the highest regions of cinematic art, into the company of the major directors. Not since I saw Ozu's *Tokyo Story* was I so overwhelmed by a film, but in Wertmüller's case we have yet to wait and see whether she can go on to other comparable achievements, and I think she can. Yet whatever happens hereafter, this is a milestone that future filmmakers will have to keep an eye on, that future filmgoers will have to—will *want* to—keep in mind. With this film, Wertmüller has succeeded where Brecht has failed, in creating a work that can be called *The Adventures of the Good Soldier Švejk in the Second World War*.

At this point, people who have not yet seen the film may want to stop reading, or let what goes in one eye go out the other. Suit yourself. In any case, the story concerns Pasqualino Frafuso, a very minor Neapolitan mini-*mafioso*. We meet him first escaping from a troop-train wreck in World War II somewhere in a dark, rainy Teutonic forest, where he bumps into a fellow escapee, Francesco. As they wander across inhospitable terrain, seeing Jews being shot in mass graves, Pasqualino explains that he is here because he, too, killed—for a woman. We expect something romantic, but nothing like that applies to our man. A wonderful matching shot cuts away from the looming German treetops back to Naples, a bulbous red-white-and-green paper corsage on the thigh of a chanteuse in a low-down vaudeville house. The thigh and the woman are more bulbous yet: his sister Concettina is quite a beast.

The Neapolitan half of the film deals with how Pasqualino, "Seven Beauties," as he is called, must, out of a sense of "honor" and "dignity"—two of his favorite words—kill "Eighteen Karats" Totonno, the brothel owner who, supposedly, promised marriage to Concettina and started her off on the primrose path. But here, immediately, a shower of ironies drenches us. Concettina, poor thing, is a horror, and only too happy in her decline—the alternative being a sweatshop where, along with her mother and six sisters, she has to work hard, hot and cramped, sewing and stuffing mattresses, while Pasqualino primps before a mirror, delivers moral sermons, pats arses, puts a gun grandiosely in his belt without really thinking of using it, and walks about Naples under the adoring and ironic gaze of women, women, women, and even a very young innocent girl, whom he earmarks for his future fiancée.

This Pasqualino in Naples is a curious character, with his dapper mustache, slicked-down hair, and a swagger that stretches from eyes to toes. His whole personality seems to have fallen between Adolf Hitler and Rudolph Valentino, as between two stools. When he challenges Totonno, in a brilliantly filmed scene, he is knocked out cold; it is almost only by accident that 253 he later manages to kill him. When the Mafia boss urges him to use some imagination in disposing of the corpse, he bungles everything. But fleeing across Germany, a cowardly, scampering little animal, he exhibits the lowly, somewhat repellent, talent of the inveterate survivor. The film continually crosscuts between Germany and Italy, the past and the present, but not merely for purposes of suspense—not even just to explain how Pasqualino got to be this way. Rather it is to show that the life of the preening little *mafioso* was just as preposterous, in its own way, as that of the escaping survival artist, except that the weird things are now being done in the name of staying alive and not in that of *onore* and *dignità*—and survival is probably a worthier cause.

In Germany, after a curious adventure in a hunting lodge where a half-naked woman sings Wagner's "*Träume*" to her own piano accompaniment, and Pasqualino chooses food over sex—our hero and Francesco are caught and thrown into a concentration camp run by an enormous and ruthless female commandant, a golem turned Ilse Koch. The camp is evoked with horrifying accuracy by bleak set design and color (or lack of it), the clatter of hectoring German voices, and editing—the horror of hanged men made greater by their being perceived only for a second or two, and looking grotesque rather than tragic—but what makes it all the more appalling is the crosscutting to Italy when it does occur: yellows and pinks making the grays and blacks retroactively grimmer. And then comes Pasqualino's insane (and yet saving) idea: to seduce the horrendous commandant, because even at the heart of that elephant made of ice there must be a woman wanting to be loved. The idea—worthy of both Swift and Tod Browning—is also typically Italian, and there lies its appropriateness to Wertmüller, who is, like all great directors, her own writer.

Cutting away from the camp, we get further installments of Pasqualino's story—the steps by which he arrived at his present state. The trial, where a clever shyster gets him off with a twelve-year sentence on a plea of insanity; the feigned madness that takes the form, among others, of impersonating Il Duce (irony within irony: feigning being "the Savior of Italy" is to be truly mad, but Pasqualino actually approves of the man he is crazily imitating!), and leads to a madhouse full of tragicomic adventures, from which one can be rescued only by transfer into a worse madhouse: the army. The seduction of the commandant, a story of sadomasochist, comic-horrific grotesquerie, is counterpointed by the humorous-serious philosophizings of Pedro, a Spanish anarchist who is a fellow inmate at the camp. Pedro preaches a cogent sermon in praise of the New Man who must be born soon in order to put an end to overpopulating the world, which will shortly result in people killing one another over an apple. Is it order that the world needs, then? asks Pasqualino. "No, no, no, no," says Pedro (Fernando Rey), "that's what the Germans have." And he delivers a paean to *l'uomo in disordine,* man in disorder, the creative disorder of absolute individuality. "It's a pity about man," says Pedro, who has been tortured and castrated by his fellow men; "I did like him so much."

254   Pasqualino is all ironic contradictions. He explains that he is ugly, but

that he was still irresistible to women in Naples, and so was nicknamed *Settebellezze* (Seven Beauties). But that nickname is just a typical hood's monicker and has nothing to do with true sexiness. Yet he *does* have seven sisters, who, however, are seven frumpy uglinesses. His "dignity" is what gets him into murder, and his imagination (*fantasia*) is what lands him in jail. He is really a worm, as the commandant tells him; but in a short, incisive speech of hers, which is a counterpart to Pedro's, she decries the fact that this little worm (which is what Totonno the pimp had also called him), this "subhuman Mediterranean larva," will survive because it can, half dead, still produce an erection vis-à-vis a bestial giantess; whereas the master race, with its dreams of a world-encompassing order, will collapse and perish.

Here I must speak of the technical expertise. Wertmüller is a master of both camera placement and movement, and of editing or montage. She would have delighted Bazin as much as Eisenstein. Consider, for instance, Pasqualino's cocky descent down the steep streets and stairs of Naples under the doting gaze of women, to the marvelous musical underpinning by Enzo Iannacci's score; the tracking and panning, interlarded with female closeups, is a psychological as well as cinematic triumph. But soon our man has to ascend some stairs to the great hall where Don Raffaele, the Mafia boss, holds forth, and the upward movement is more precarious, the colors become darker. The boss is perceived against enormous antique sculptures—a superhuman Heracles embattled with centaurs—even though he himself is a puny figure. Always the camera catches significant, ironically commenting details in an art work, an inscription, a photograph. When the commandant (Shirley Stoler) is sexually using Pasqualino, who thinks he is seducing her, there stands at one end of the room a looted masterpiece redolent of supreme Mannerist sophistication: Bronzino's Cupid and Venus in a frigidly incestuous, icily obscene sexual act; on the opposite wall hangs the sternly disapproving photograph of Hitler. And on the Victrola, Zarah Leander, the Führer's favorite chanteuse, is singing *"Nur nicht aus Liebe weinen"*—only do not weep for love. And Tonino Delli Colli's brilliant cinematography, in the curtained lighting for this unholy sex act, turns faces part green, part purple, as in some "decadent" Expressionist painting by Kirchner. Meanwhile, the commandant's whip becomes as much, or more, of a sexual organ as Pasqualino's starved, pitiful, but indomitable penis. It is a room in which ironies buzz about, contradictions attain vertiginous heights of the grotesque.

Faultless, too, is the rhythm with which the film shuttles between Germany and Italy. This always occurs when one story has become unendurable or stalemated, and any change is welcome. Even within individual episodes, though, the sense of contrast is marvelous: after the claustrophobic chopping up of the dead Totonno in his den, we move out into a gorgeous dawn panorama, as if the old adage were sardonically reversed: Die and see Naples. There are splendid matching shots: from the "love-crazed" prisoner, made to stand in the empty assembly area of the *Lager*, his hands, by way of punishment, at the back of his neck, we cut to Pasqualino acting "crazy" in the Naples prisoner's dock, and hitting on the identical gesture. And what of the glory of having the entire trial scene done in pantomime? In a baroque 255 palace of justice, covered with grandiose frescoes, a puny mockery of justice takes place—and trust Wertmüller's camera to discover among the painted figures a bemused ostrich, the symbol of evasion of reality and truth. And what comic puppet's gestures everyone is making (Wertmüller started as a puppeteer), and how they're all gotten up! The ugly sisters have all dyed their hair blond, to convey the golden radiance of angelic purity; only it makes them look even more sluttish. And since people, separated by space, cannot talk to one another, what a veritable ballet of eyes! Glances from client to lawyer, from lawyer to Mafia boss, from tearfully happy mother to son; glances, above all, between the adoring Girl, promising to wait, and Pasqualino, being hustled away, promising to return and claim her. *Oeillades* leap toward one another; gazes of longing, smugness, hypocritical piety intertwine in a wordless dance. How comic it all is. And how pathetic.

Even the music backs up these points. *"Träume"* (Dreams), which the half-naked woman at the hunting lodge played in isolated yearning, is taken up again by the commandant as she is serviced by Pasqualino. In between, however, when the prisoners are being brutalized in the death camp, we get "The Ride of the Valkyries." Well, those are the two extremes of Wagner's music, or of the Germanic soul: its most voluptuous sentimentality, and its most shrilling violence. To be caught between these antipodes is analogous to being hemmed in by Bronzino and Hitler, by bestial sex acts if one wants to survive, and by being gunned down in a trough of liquid excrement if, like Pedro, one chooses anarchy and humanistic defiance. Even the slogans on the wall join in the cruel mockery: in a preposterous Italian prison, we read: NOT JUST TO PUNISH, BUT ALSO TO IMPROVE; in the monstrous German *Lager,* we are apprised that WORK MAKES FREE.

There is more going on in a minute of this film than in an hour of *Hustle* or *Hester Street* or *Barry Lyndon.* By "more" I do not mean plot, of course. I mean things like symbolic geometry, the way the movements of the escaping Italians are opposed in direction and speed across the film frame to those of the Jews being herded to slaughter. Or things like color: the way Delli Colli's camera can make you forget that color is color and believe that it is black and white; or experience a forest in the cold rain as more gray than green, and Naples after the Liberation as all red and gold. Here again the inestimable contribution of Enrico Job, Miss Wertmüller's artist and set-and-costume-designer husband, asserts itself. Or consider the way the camera, watching the suitcases containing the hacked-up Totonno being lowered jerkily, clumsily, from a window, jerks nervously downward along with the valises. Or how the escaping Pasqualino is framed in long shot by an open door and a corridor: his irresolute scamper this way and that comments ironically on the frightened gaze of the crone from whose point of view the single take is shot.

Throughout the film, Miss Wertmüller's view moves in and out of her characters, creating a magnificent contrast between one shot in which things are seen subjectively, grandiosely, by a character, and the next, where they are perceived punily, objectively, by the eye of history. Thus in the brothel confrontation scene between Pasqualino and Totonno, which at one point is like the shootout in some John Ford western, and at the next like some pratfall in a Germi comedy. And what sense of detail: the shriveled old woman doctor at the madhouse still vainly wearing a hairnet; the German soldier finishing his cigarette before machine-gunning the Jews; the croaking, strangulated hum with which the enfeebled Pasqualino (superbly played by Giancarlo Giannini) serenades the commandant; and so many more.

The final sequences are the most moving. The Yankee liberators have made whores of everyone, from Pasqualino's mother down to the pure young girl; the prevailing jollity is as disturbing as it is gaudy. And when the Girl appears in the doorway—bedizened, soiled, ashamed—and still stares with unblemishable love at Pasqualino; and he, remembering uncomprehendingly Pedro's lesson, declares they must get married at once and have thirty children, so that when overpopulation and hunger set in, their family will be able to hang on to those apples, you are left in tears at what, after all, is a kind of happy ending. But oh, the sadness of it: these two who have come through so much, who have been changed so utterly, and who still haven't learned anything. She is still the submissive, worshiping, sentimental Italian girl; he is still the macho, huge-litter-begetting Italian male, even though she has been had by everyone, and he has been alerted to the dangers of overpopulation.

Just as at the start of the film historic stock footage imperceptibly changed into a personal story to the accompaniment of a satirical Wertmüller lyric worthy of Jacques Prévert, so the freeze frame at the end, showing Pasqualino's face as a compound of anguish and incomprehension, returns us to history, to mankind's danger of being frozen into misconceptions and headed for extinction, for all the shrewdness of dumb survival artists. How many comedies have ever made you cry?

That is the ultimate greatness of Wertmüller and her film—that it transcends all conventional categories. It is neither comedy nor tragedy (its saddest parts are funny; its funniest, heartbreaking), and it makes nonsense of the very need for classification. Above all, perhaps, it is grotesque—like a gargoyle that is ugly, beautiful, frightening, and ludicrous. It is even two entirely different kinds of filmmaking: the Italian scenes are early, prime Fellini; the German sequences are out of those somberly, tearingly sardonic Polish masters, Wajda and Munk. Yet the astonishing thing is that such divergent modes could be made to complement and nourish each other, bodying forth a most ancient wisdom about the ambiguity and self-contradictoriness of things. For in this film there is no absolute right, except for the need for creative disorder and the New Man; otherwise, both the commandant and Pasqualino, both the Mafia boss and an obscure socialist intellectual condemned to half a lifetime in prison, both the simply decent Francesco and the complexly perceptive Pedro, are right, or partly right. It is right to die defiantly in a vat of excrement; it is also right to survive by swallowing excrement. The solution, if it exists, will have to go beyond these half-truths.

Seven Beauties is also a film about the power and duality of love—love of   257 sex, of passion, of survival—that is both angelic and bestial, both giving and selfish, gentle and terrible. It is a theme that runs through all Italian art— say, from that song to Love that Machiavelli lovingly inserted into both his *Mandragola* and his *Clizia,* and that ends with "... How equally men and gods/Fear the weapons with which you are armed," all the way to the remark of the centaur Chiron in Pavese's *Dialogues With Leucò:* "What was bestial then, if the beast was in us like the god?"

February 2, 1976

Scentimentality Italian Style

IN ITALY now you find an astonishing number of directors who qualify for the term *homo unius libri,* a man who has produced only one memorable piece of work. Thus there are quite a few filmmakers who have made one outstanding film, then little or nothing; and even more of those depressing cases who, after one or two remarkable achievements, barrage us with trivia or trash. A good example of the former type is Vittorio De Seta, whose *Bandits of Orgosolo* is a small masterpiece, but who in the fifteen years since then has made only two less distinguished films, and was, I imagine, swallowed up by Italian television. Of the latter type, there are too many examples to list; let me offer as specimens only Luciano Salce, who made the magnificent *Il federale,* and then nothing but rubbish, and the rather more serious Valerio Zurlini, who never remotely approached his superb *Family Diary (Cronaca familiare).* Of course, I am not talking here of such brilliant filmmakers whose only problem is not being able to get financing because their work, however good, does not sell—men like Ermanno Olmi somehow managed to make three great films and one or two very good ones.

Dino Risi, too, is a prime example of the second type of director: although prolific, he hasn't generally risen above the proficient comedy level of *Love and Larceny (Il mattatore),* though *Una vita difficile,* not shown hereabouts, may have been something better. But once, in 1962, with *The Easy Life (Il sorpasso),* Risi surpassed himself. This was one of those rare cases when a film functions beautifully on two levels: as a perfect commercial entertainment and as a work of art. Since then, however, Risi has done nothing of note, and his new film to reach us, *Scent of a Woman (Profumo di donna),* is no exception, despite a certain liveliness, even wit, in the early parts. Based on a novel by the respectable but less than major writer Giovanni Arpino, this is the story of a handsome, well-to-do ex-army captain who, in a freak accident, lost one hand and his eyesight. He now lives sequestered with an aunt in Turin, whence he ventures forth on occasional trips. On such occasions he gets hold of soldiers on leave who are willing, for due compensation, to act as his orderlies, or seeing-eye boys. He always calls these boys Ciccio, and the current Ciccio, a nice young fellow properly awed by the aristocratic and vehement Captain, is to accompany him on a trip to Genoa, Rome, and Naples.

The Captain is a man turned bitter and domineering, but with a good deal of humor and generosity still left in him. Above all, he is proud, and will do anything to keep people unaware of his blindness, even if it means buying newspapers he pretends to read, and dispensing misinformation to people who ask him for directions in the street. His greatest horror is of someone pitying him; otherwise, he is almost a normal Italian male, obsessed by women, all the more so since he has learned, literally, to smell them out. But he will get involved only with whores; he is morbidly afraid of inflicting his infirmity on a decent woman. He terrorizes Ciccio, but also educates him, somewhat cynically, in the ways of the world. The early stages of their journey are rambunctiously amusing as the Captain curses or assaults most of the world around him, or tracks down a suitable prostitute with Ciccio's befuddled help. There are nice touches here, as when the Captain steps in front of a zooming car in Genoa, assuring Ciccio that "This is a civilized city—he'll stop"; or when the train halts at Pisa, the station is loudly announced, and Ciccio tells his boss they're in Pisa, to which the Captain responds with "I know. I'm not *deaf*." Most of the humor, though, stems from the Captain's pursuit of not so much the *profumo di donna* (scent of women) as of the more basic *odor di femmina* (exhalations of female flesh).

There are curious parallels here to *The Easy Life*, where the same star, Vittorio Gassman, likewise played a more experienced, cynical sensualist who undertakes the antisentimental education of a young and naïve admirer, played by Jean-Louis Trintignant. But the earlier film was incomparably richer in wit, social implications, psychological complexity, and, finally, honesty. Its crazy, catastrophic ending was far more believable than the drawn-out, mawkish, improbably sentimental concluding passages of *Scent of a Woman*, which even the fine acting of the principals cannot make palatable. I don't know whether Arpino's novel ends as stickily (though its title, *The Darkness and the Honey*, rather suggests it: the honey of love coming to sweeten the lonely dark of the blind), but if ever a film cheated with its happy ending, this is it. Gassman is extremely winning as the Captain, making his asperities not just tough but also vulnerable, allowing a wild despair to show through his jocularity. The way he tries to make the pupils of his eyes converge, as if two blind eyes could fuse into one seeing eye, is particularly moving, as is the fragile balance he strikes between being frightening to and frightened by the young girl who adores him. That girl is played most appealingly by the lovely Agostina Belli; Alessandro Momo, who was so good in the ghastly *Malizia*, is perfect at rendering Ciccio's contradictory feelings and unsentimental innocence. But life is much harsher than this film written by Risi and Ruggero Maccari, with a stilted score by Armando Trovaioli, and doggedly pastel cinematography by Claudio Cirillo. For, in reality, this highly promising young actor was killed in a motorcycle accident at the age of eighteen—almost as if life were giving the lie to Risi by imitating the ending of *Il sorpasso,* which was art, and rejecting *Profumo di donna,* which is a mere confection.

February 9, 1976

No Miracle in Milan

To TELL THE TRUTH, I would almost prefer not having to write about Lina Wertmüller's *Tutto a posto, niente in ordine* (1973) after having written about her new masterpiece, *Seven Beauties.* The earlier film, whose title means "Everything in Its Place, Nothing in Order," has been retitled *All Screwed Up* by its American distributor, New Line Cinema. Neither the retitling nor its nature is anything new for New Line Cinema, a firm that distributes a good many sex films as well as a few prestige items. So when an earlier film of Wertmüller's, *Mimi the Metal Worker, His Honor Betrayed,* was turned down by several other American distributors, they bought it for a song from Euro Film, the Italian producers. They did not proceed to distribute it, however, and Miss Wertmüller believes they intended it as a tax loss. Meanwhile the next Wertmüller film, *Love and Anarchy,* was acquired by Peppercorn-Wormser, trimmed by seven or eight minutes with Miss Wertmüller's approval, and shown in New York to great critical acclaim, even if the audience response was, at best, tepid. At this point, Robert Kenneth Shaye, the president of New Line Cinema, quickly brought out the film, with cuts amounting to, according to Miss Wertmüller, somewhere between twenty and forty minutes (closer to forty, she thinks), and retitled salaciously *The Seduction of Mimi.* As an experienced distributor of erotica (which *Mimi* is not), Mr. Shaye knew what he was doing: American audiences would naturally assume that Mimi was a girl rather than a male metal worker, and that "her" seduction constituted a pornographic movie.

When in my review of *Swept Away,* which included some retrospective observations, I accused Mr. Shaye of being exploitative, he wrote me a vaguely threatening letter in which he described the title change as a "legitimately provocative double entendre" I had apparently missed, and both implicitly denied making any significant cuts and explicitly admitted his thorough recutting of the film with his editor, so as "to make it playable for American audiences." Well, *Mimi* is so good a film that even crippling cuts that damage the continuity could not make it fail.

So when another Wertmüller film, *Tutto a posto,* did not do very well in Italy, Mr. Shaye and his company rushed in and bought it for a pittance, and held on to it again, only to release it suddenly and with no advance publicity as *All Screwed Up.* Clearly Shaye had got wind that what Cinema 5 was about to unveil a week later, *Seven Beauties,* was a major achievement, so he was going to scoop them with this incomparably lesser work, again provided with a "legitimately provocative double entendre" for a title. But, as I wrote to Mr. Shaye in reply to his letter, one man's "legitimately provocative" is another's "crassly exploitative."

Tutto a posto, which I cannot bring myself to refer to as *All Screwed Up,* has apparently not been cut by New Line Cinema, though it must be understood that a European film director, unless he enjoys the status of a Fellini— or, better yet, has his own production company—has no real control over what deals his European producers negotiate with American distributors, and when Mr. Shaye writes me that his cuts in *Mimi* were made with Miss Wertmüller's "full understanding and consent," he either doesn't know, or doesn't want to know, what he is talking about. But back to *Tutto a posto.*

This is a film about impoverished southern Italians coming up north to make good, a standard theme in Italian cinema as in Italian life. The migration usually leads to the heavily industrialized city of Milan, the locale of Visconti's *Rocco and His Brothers* and of Wertmüller's film, which could be described as a comic *Rocco* with serious overtones. In *Tutto a posto,* a bunch of young workers, male and female, form a commune, and the film examines their adventures both inside and outside the apartment they have taken over and refurbished. This includes, besides tricky parietal regulations, marriage, love affairs, and hostilities within the commune, and all kinds of jobs outside it, legitimate and highly illegitimate.

The film does not truly come off for a number of reasons. The writer-director has, first of all, bitten off more than she can chew: there are too many main characters, stories, big and small problems crowded into a relatively narrow compass; moreover, there are times when the invention simply flags. There is, furthermore, a certain inconsistency of aim and style. Thus we get some De Sica-ish neorealist dwelling on human misery along with Felliniesque comic-poetic episodes topped with a quasi-documentary evocation of various types of work (mostly unpleasant) in the manner of Ermanno Olmi. And there is even a scene at a modern, expensive housing development where the outdoor shots have a curiously Antonioniesque look. Lastly, there is a lot of straight farce, very much in the manner of lesser Germi or Monicelli. In her other films, Miss Wertmüller can reconcile such stylistic vagaries—in fact, create her own style out of inspired eclecticism, out of such fused contradictions—but this material does not blend smoothly. Even her usually uncanny sense of casting forsakes her here, and though most of these professionals or amateur actors look right, there are no memorable performances such as we usually get even from her mere supporting players.

Yet this is not to say that the film is without merit. There is an overpowering sense of what drudgery feels like in some scenes, notably those that take place in the kitchen of a large, busy restaurant. I asked the director whether she was influenced by Arnold Wesker's *The Kitchen,* and, sure enough, she directed an Italian production of Wesker's lively play. But, like a true artist, Miss Wertmüller transforms her borrowing into something very much her own, and life in this Wertmüller kitchen is just as idiomatic, idiosyncratic—indeed, aromatic—as in the Wesker one. And the kitchen shot with which the film ends, a circular pan that accelerates until it becomes a blur, is a positive 261 masterstroke summarizing this mini-world as well as the larger world it symbolizes: the increasing frenzy, the blotting out of individuals, and the maddening circularity.

We really share in various kinds of work: in the spookiness of the abattoir where production-line killing of animals is casually taken in one's stride; in the oppressive heat at some jobs, and the lacerating cold at others. And there are the ironies of labor, as when a chambermaid keeps dusting the *objets d'art* of a luxurious apartment while explaining to her lover over the telephone why even their combined salaries are not enough to get married on. There is also a very funny and brilliantly photographed scene in which the desperate father of a too numerous brood goes out to be a male whore for an evening, and another scene, somewhat less funny (because less original), about a ludicrous robbery. I also liked a scatological vengeance scene and a lyrical-elegiac leitmotiv, whereby one of our needy heroes keeps encountering, at greater or lesser distance, improbably beautiful and impossibly rich young girls. Sometimes he catches their eye; always they make him, painfully, catch his breath. Sometimes they merely flit by in expensive cars; at others, as students, they join in the poor folk's protest activities, and still remain inaccessible. Ingeniously, they are played by the same very young girl, but made up so differently as to be almost unidentifiable as the same person. This is that one Beauty that has many faces and disguises, that can temporarily lure a working-class lover from his beloved, but that can never, never be attained by the underprivileged. A powerfully symbolic visual refrain, this.

But there is much that is less good. A comic seduction scene that, for all its ironic commentary on consumerism, is both trite and gimmicky; and scenes involving an overproductive couple, including a near-abortion, that are neither original nor trenchant enough. And, as already noted, there are barren stretches that even the frenetic pace and the eye-catching cinematography of Giuseppe Rotunno cannot quite make up for. Yet, admirably, Miss Wertmüller neither patronizes nor idealizes her working-class characters—she does not even feel *for* them, only *with* them. But dearer to me than much of *All Screwed Up* is this incident that occurred while we were lunching in a New York restaurant. "Why aren't you proud of your Italian origin?" she asked a headwaiter, who answered in good Italian that it was because, like so many of his fellow émigrés, he ended up not as some kind of cultural ambassador but as a servant. "We are all of us both servants and ambassadors," Miss Wertmüller retorted, "and, frankly, I have met more idiots among ambassadors than among waiters."

It is a wicked shame to cut the work of so genuine, so humane an artist, and I shall never forgive New Line Cinema's Robert Shaye for the twenty to forty minutes he cut from *Mimi,* a far superior film. And I repeat, for the benefit of other distributors who might emulate him, what I wrote to Shaye in response to his statement that he was making the film "playable for American audiences." "Who are you," I wrote in part, "to determine what American audiences may see and what they may not? Don't misunderstand: although I consider film scholars and critics better equipped than businessmen to make such decisions, I do not wish them to have such power either. The decision should be up to the filmmaker, who clearly made the best movie she was capable of, and aimed it at people; not Italians, Americans, or Eskimos, but people, who everywhere are divisible into sensitive and insensitive, perspicacious and obtuse. Now, if the film was aimed at clods, why import it in the first place? If it was aimed at discriminating viewers, who are you to interfere with full communication? Do you assume that even intelligent Americans are dumber than Italians? Do you think that your money gives you moral and aesthetic rights over the film?"

A practice almost as abominable as cutting fine foreign films is adapting great plays for the screen, even if, as in the present case, we deal with the lesser evil of mere transfer, not adaptation. I refer to Trevor Nunn's stage production of *Hedda Gabler,* now transposed to the screen as *Hedda.* Peter Eyre's excessively absurd and sniveling Tesman and Patrick Stewart's brash and boring Lövborg are exceptionally wrong-headed, Timothy West is a persuasive Judge Brack, and the other supporting players are adequate. But even though she is better on film than in the stage performance I caught, Glenda Jackson continues to strike me as a vastly infelicitous Hedda. She has none of the true aristocratic *hauteur* of General Gabler's daughter, and exudes instead a kind of amusing bitchiness, which has nothing to do with what Ibsen wrote. And though she does not commit the typical stage performer's error of acting "too big" for the camera, she utterly lacks that comeliness and allure that make men die for Hedda and women fawn or cringe.

Nunn's direction is neither embarrassingly stagy nor particularly cinematic; Douglas Slocombe's cinematography is, as always, undistinguished; and there is an inept score. But the basic problem is that a great stage work belongs to the stage alone. Its space, time, and dialogue are inextricably wedded to the dimensions and expectations of the playhouse, and any kind of tampering can only upset the delicate balances involved. Even a mere transposition to the screen that in no way "opens up" and pads or dissipates the work is bound to be disastrous. At the very least, it is like having to drink one's wine not from a glass but a soup plate.

February 16, 1976

From Appealing to Appalling

MANY YEARS AGO in Paris, at the Rose Rouge, I caught Yves Robert performing his own riotous take-off on westerns. I knew then that the young actor's talent was for skits, an estimable genre, much harder to pull off than many a longer form. Robert has since done some fine acting and directed a number of movies, of which we saw only *The War of the Buttons* (a charming film, undeservedly ignored here), *Very Happy Alexander* (a rather too consciously charming film, beautifully acted, and quite successful here), and *The Tall Blond Man With One Black Shoe* (a contrived, mostly unfunny picture with the insufferable Pierre Richard, but rather successful). Now we get his 1973 film, *Salut, l'Artiste!,* small but delicate, with some lovely insights as well as an occasional bit of heavy-handedness. It is what Robert is best at: a collection of loosely related sketches, some quietly moving, some sharply funny, some both. It is a film that has pertinent comments on actors, which is what all of us are, whether by profession or not.

Nicolas Montei is a middle-aged Italian actor whose triumph came in a Chekhovian role on tour in Strasbourg, where, however, it failed to register amid all that goose-liver pâté. He has settled in Paris to the unsettling life of a minor actor doing everything from nightclub acts to entertaining at banquets, from TV commercials to bit parts on stage and screen. He has left his *couturière*-wife, Elisabeth, and their two sons, and now lives with Peggy, his sound-recorder-mistress, who has left her husband. His best friend is Clément, a struggling forty-three-year-old fellow actor who never even made it in Strasbourg. The film is about the often comic but nonetheless desperate fight to survive on the fringes of show business, and the curious way in which life and art get tangled up, so that no one—least of all a struggling artist—can tell them apart. But it is also about something deeper and more moving: about the fact that even those who fail at both art and life, who play badly in both domains, believe in, suffer for, and truly live only in their restless playacting.

The film begins with a wonderful dolly shot across the outdoor and indoor splendors of Versailles, to arrive at, in one of the great halls, a man in Sun King apparel with his back to us, talking—but to whom? His first words are, "They said what, the cops?" After a while he turns around and we see that he is an actor talking on the phone; soon we learn, through a mildly amusing episode, that he is a bit player in a dumb movie. Clearly, this Nicolas Montei lives in different worlds simultaneously; is it any wonder if his private life unfurls in blurry superimpositions?

But the pangs of the artist are lacerating even couched in minutiae. Concerning a cigarette commercial, Clément worries intensely whether it was artistically right to have done it with his gloves on. During the dubbing of an animal cartoon, Montei, who does one of the silly animal voices, complains that the line "idiot turtle" does not feel right in his mouth. About bigger problems, one kids oneself; so Montei blames his lack of success on his Italian-accented French, is blissfully unaware of what it means that at grave, emotionally charged moments he can get sidetracked by a pair of random breasts or legs. The chase after women is not that different from the pursuit of jobs; when you live on quicksand, permanence is good for paying lip service to, dull when you get it. So when Clément lands a steady job doing on-the-spot publicity for a department store, he gets out of it as soon as he can; when Nicolas enjoys the love of a woman one could love for a lifetime, he stops having the time of his life.

The problem, a profoundly human one, is *volupté,* for which there is, alas, no proper English equivalent. When Clément explains to Nicolas and Peggy why he is leaving show business, he concludes, *"Je n'éprouve plus aucune volupté"* "I no longer experience any———." The French word means bliss, ecstasy, sexual fulfillment; it suggests a protracted, intense, and sensual delight, for which "pleasure," the customary translation, is much too weak. What Nicolas and Clément get, or want to get, from their work is this voluptuous pleasure, both physical and spiritual, which is hard to attain and almost impossible to sustain. Nicolas has a chance at it with either of his two worthy and beautiful women.

This, however, is where the film misses out importantly. Elisabeth, the wife, is conceived as an infinitely gentle and sympathetic woman, a devoted mother and good worker, and very attractive, too; we would like to know why the marriage broke up. We can guess, of course; but guesswork is not what is wanted here. The mistress, Peggy, is another serious, understanding, devoted woman, even more beautiful, though perhaps not quite so patient and tolerant. Again we are shown less than we would like to know about how this relationship breaks up. The main problem is that the two women emerge a trifle undifferentiated, and also a bit too good to be true; as a result, Montei's psychic maneuverings do not come quite clear. We can tell that he is infantile, fickle, emotionally greedy, but the dynamic details that would lend full definition and dignity to his failures are not forthcoming.

Yet what marvelous acting! Carla Gravina, unfortunately dubbed into French, is impeccable at conveying a "good woman" without making her in the least sappy or spineless. There is just a touch of amused irony in her regard; she is still very fond of Nicolas (though the script by Yves Robert and Jean-Loup Dabadie errs in not clarifying exactly to what extent), but she is not taken in by him, and Miss Gravina has a smile that is enchanting in its unaggressive worldly wisdom. Marcello Mastroianni, who does his own French speaking, gives a very satisfactory performance as Nicolas, although he relies rather too heavily on that befuddled hangdog expression that was always one of his specialties, but now threatens to become his stock-in-trade. Still, his work here is very apposite, even if a shade unsubtle. Jean Rochefort, on the other hand, is perfect as Clément, with the precise blend of cockiness and ruefulness, self-assurance and hurt. I am filled with admiration for this actor's range, for his histrionic and human maturity. Yet the miracle of this film—as of any she is in—is Françoise Fabian as Peggy.

If I had to choose the most irresistible actress in cinema today, I would pick Françoise Fabian after only slight hesitation. Her intoxicating, black-haired and blue-eyed beauty would have something to do with my choice, but other factors would be of far greater importance. She has a quality I can describe only as superabundance of soul, an outpouring of inner riches with every look from those eyes, every tremor of that face and body. But never mind the eyes—with her mere eyelids, Mlle Fabian does more acting than many other performers with their entire equipment. There is an almost terrifying rightness about when these eyes gaze steadily ahead, and when the lids are lowered like a canny dramatist's curtain at exactly the proper moment. These large, hugely aware eyes look at you searchingly, sadly or hopefully, demanding that you be yourself, your sheerest self; when they look down or away, it can both make you weep and feel infinite relief at being granted a moment's guilty respite from so much beauty, so much truth.

This may explain why Montei is afraid of Peggy, though it does not begin to explain why an actress whose presence spreads across a film like a benediction should have been in so few and such inadequate vehicles. It is not Eric Rohmer but she who made *My Night at Maud's* a night to remember; it is she (along with Lino Ventura) who made *Happy New Year* worth seeing despite Claude Lelouch's soulless slickness. Sometimes we see her in films as awful as *Down the Ancient Stairs,* where, dubbed and miscast, even she cannot fully register; at other times, though the film is a worthy one, like Yves Boisset's *The Cop,* it unjustly fails and vanishes before we get a chance to go back for another look at the actress's fine work in a small part. And in *Belle de Jour,* though she steals the show from Catherine Deneuve, her part is infinitesimal. She must have been in quite a few movies that never made it to the U.S., but I am sure that she has not been seen enough even in France, and certainly not in films up to her gifts. Since I consider her one of France's major artistic assets, her underexposure is one of the great losses of French, indeed world, cinema.

There is a scene in which Miss Fabian stands under a large poster of Nicolas Montei and, distracted by the way their relationship is malfunctioning, absent-mindedly answers the phone. "I don't know. No, I don't know," is all she says, and *we* don't know to whom and about what. But the look on her face and the tone of her voice, combining with the off-center framing of the shot, and the huge poster face of Nicolas looking indifferently away, makes this one of the saddest and most beautiful moments I have ever seen caught on film. There are also longer sequences that work remarkably in *Salut, l'Artiste!* There is a melancholy walk on a gray day along the beach at Cabourg, where every line of dialogue (by Dabadie), every camera angle (by Robert), every detail of Fabian's and Mastroianni's movements and expressions (especially the way Fabian half leans toward yet half backs away from the man), and every cheerless tone of the photography (by Jean Penzer) pierces one's heart.

And there is another scene, also melancholy but very funny, too, in a recording studio where an animal cartoon is being dubbed, and where the silly cartoon images fall across the human actors' faces, painting—or branding—them with the colors of clowns. Still other scenes range from excellent to strained, the last one, meant to summarize the overlapping of life and art, being downright facile and pretentious. What the picture, without being anything like a masterpiece, shares with the very best films is a fine sense of rhythm, and that, more than anything else perhaps, is what makes a film a film.

Salut, l'Artiste! has a haunting score by Vladimir Cosma, the only thing it has in common with *Catherine & Co.*, which also has a—rather less good—Cosma score. Even so, it is the best thing about a film that is surely the most loathsome, the most offensive dung heap masquerading as a movie I have

seen in years, perhaps ever. It presents sexuality as smirking, sweaty, mercenary, bestial, exhibitionistic, completely selfish—a way of either humiliating
your partner or tormenting the aroused onlookers in the public places where
this sex is often performed. The heroine, played by a nasty baggage called
Jane Birkin, goes from being a vicious little tease to becoming a corporation
for the corporeal pleasures of her stockholders and her personal enrichment.
Her men range from crude businessmen to kinky aging aristocrats, from a
callous young playboy she adores to a supposed adolescent who appears to
be really a misshappen gnome. This kid suffers from premature ejaculation
(good for lots of laughs) promptly cured by sex with Jane. Through clever
investments, she ends up a millionaire, still plying her trade with her contented customers.

The movie is mostly about Miss Birkin's behind, which is worked into
every shot in ever more gross ways. The anal emphasis is necessary because
Miss Birkin has minimal mammaries and a second-rate face (upper half
sightly, lower half un-). Sex is made into something hideous in this movie,
much less elegant and sexy than amassing money, which is the body's
primary function. And Jean-Pierre Aumont gives Jane lessons in anti-
intellectual snobbery almost as repellent as the film's sexuality. This horror,
which gets an R rating (so much for ratings!), was directed by Michael
Boisrond, and coauthored and produced by Leo L. Fuchs, which is a funny
way of spelling it. The other scenarist was Catherine Breillat, a woman who,
I think, needs her consciousness raised.

March 8, 1976

Stags at Bay

Vincent, François, Paul and the Others is an undistinguished film that is nevertheless worth seeing for its performances. It concerns a group of three older
men (the ones named in the title) and Jean, the son of a dead fourth, and
their friendship that endures through the difficult period of coming-of-
middle-age, despite various letdowns and minor mutual betrayals. It is a
hymn to the persistence of masculine loyalty while wives and mistresses
become adulterous, defect altogether, or remain devoted yet somehow outside the magic circle of camaraderie. It is not a theme I find particularly
appealing, but my real objection is to the basic quality of the screenplay by
Jean-Loup Dabadie, who now seems to write every other French script,
Claude Néron, who also wrote the underlying novel, and Claude Sautet,
who also directed.

The quality of that screenplay can best be described as upper-middlebrow
soap opera, or, if you prefer, commercialism with a touch of class. It is not,
needless to say, that friendship isn't worth such close scrutiny. Anything that   267

stumped Socrates, who had to conclude the *Lysis* with that exemplary aporia, "We have not as yet been able to discover what we mean by a friend,"
is surely worthy of speculative investigation. What I do not like about the
movie, though, is that the level of writing is fundamentally trivial; that even
though women are treated with respect, they are excluded from the inner
sanctum of male bonding; and that the filmmakers never take a stand on
what seems to be the central issue: is the infantilism that so strongly colors
Vincent's personality a worthy manifestation of that "child in man" preconized by Nietzsche, or is it a tragic or, rather, tragicomic flaw? Yet if we
allow Socrates to end on a note of dubiety, why castigate Sautet for something similar? Only because, as I see it, he does not think the problem
through with the rigor demanded by scrupulous comedy.

For comedy is what the film essentially is. The friend who won't help you
financially today, will offer to do so tomorrow; the wife who leaves you now
may come back one of these days; when you end up bankrupt, you can
always sell out to a nice guy rather than to a greedy swine, and an old pal
will come through with a job scarcely less desirable than the business you
have lost. The beautiful mistress, less than half your age, who walked out on
you, comes back in the end; the boxing career, for which you are not cut out,
nevertheless allows you to retire ahead of the game, after a spectacular
though only half-deserved technical knockout; the girl you have knocked up
stays around faithfully while you decide whether you'll marry her; the heart
attack that knocks you over does not prove fatal. Even the wife who whored
around to punish you (it seems) for the abandonment of your youthful
ideals, ends up happily with one of your dedicated friends; sobered by this,
you still have a good chance to start anew, supported by your loving friends.
And if you do not manage to finish the great World War II novel you have
been fitfully working on for thirty years, at least you thrive as a nonfiction
writer and the husband of a model wife.

What I have encapsulated above does not, of course, happen to one man,
but is distributed among the four principal characters; still, since the hero of
the film is really that male quartet, one is entitled to see these fates as
befalling "Man" with a capital *M,* whom you may or may not judge a
capital fool. No doubt the characters of comedy have a charmed life, as do
the figures in this *comédie larmoyante;* but they are also to be perceived as
at least as laughable as lovable, and not, as here, sentimentalized into endearing big children, sometimes even pathetic sufferers. Certain devices,
moreover, are used a trifle too mechanistically for comfort. So, for example,
the contrapuntal structure, predictably alternating between cheerful and
worrisome episodes; or, again, the incomplete sentences in which Vincent is
always speaking, with the three dots of the ellipses palpably hectoring you
into filling in the unspoken pregnancies.

Still, there are compensations. There is the cinematography by the admirable Jean Boffety, often taking discreet but not inconsiderable risks in the
direction of imaginative stylization—as in the monochromes behind the titles
and during a reverie based on black-and-white photographs, or during a

particularly painful flashback wherein Vincent recalls his wife, Catherine, packing up to leave him even as seductively pretty pastel colors deliberately mock the somber gravity of the incident. There is also the at least intermittently effective direction by Claude Sautet, an action director with misplaced ambitions. The scenes in which there is no pronounced physical activity are managed rather routinely; but let there be even the most mundane intensification in the goings-on, and Sautet's *mise en scène* leaps to life. By far the most noteworthy sequence in the film is the boxing match, which, along with similar sequences in Huston's otherwise unmemorable *Fat City*, constitutes the most honestly, unexaggeratedly gripping representation of prizefights in recent filmmaking.

And, to repeat, there is the acting. Yves Montand is in peak form, allowing rasping uncertainty to break through the suave façade, finding always different and attractive ways of suggesting something more individual than the filmmakers have provided him with, and able to grow strikingly older or younger on camera as the particular scene demands. Michel Piccoli keeps his characteristic edge of sinisterness well in hand, and plays his two major outbursts with flawless finesse. Serge Reggiani, whose batrachian visage always grates on me, is nonetheless on target in the most difficult, because most passive, of the principal roles, and effectively resists the pull of his few big moments toward overplaying. It is interesting to note that all three of these inexhaustibly popular French leading men are Italian by birth or descent, though I am not quite sure what to make of this. Young Gérard Depardieu, in any case, is French through and through, and here continues to demonstrate his easygoing versatility.

Most winning among the women are Stéphane Audran, who has perfected that heavy-lidded, sensual-lipped, all-forgiving look of hers that implies both limitless compassion and heroic refusal to give in to the *lacrimae rerum;* and Marie Dubois, who has a marvelous way of suggesting the lower-class intensities that lurk beneath an upward-mobile complacency. I am less taken with Ludmilla Mikaël, who remains a bit schematic, and Catherine Allégret, who exudes an uncalled-for sluttishness; but it may be that the script is short-changing them. And I am saddened by Antonella Lualdi, who, unlike other youthful stunners, is middle-aging into bovineness.

Here and there I get a surprising impression of downright carelessness from Sautet. For a man who knows a good deal about music, he allows his composer, Philippe Sarde, to get away with yet another of his pea-soupy piano concertos (what became of the Sarde who once managed the buoyant score for *La Chamade?*); and he permits the costume designer to make every man at Clovis's restaurant-reopening party wear identically blue shirts. (Later on there are scenes with nothing but white shirts.) Yet for all its mediocrity, the film is not boring, and certainly better than Sautet's trashy *The Things of Life* and *César and Rosalie*, though I cannot comment on his early *Classe tous risques* (1960), often considered his finest contribution, but never seen by me.

Revisionist Tales

WHO WOULD have believed that the time would come when we would long for the good old days of Cecil B. De Mille and Charlton Heston? Well, it has come to pass. Sir Lew Grade has produced for television a *Moses,* directed by Gianfranco De Bosio and starring Burt Lancaster; they make De Mille and Heston look like mighty men towering over this puny latter-day breed. Somewhat refurbished, this television *Moses* has been allowed to enter the promised land of cinema, there to disport itself as a great religious epic.

To give you some idea of the magnitude of the project, let me proclaim unto you that the splendor of imperial Egypt seems to consist of two sets: set A is made of imitation stone blocks; set B is constructed of genuine plywood. For the more martial aspects of pharaonic grandeur, extending from a throne room to a riding academy, the false granite of A is pressed into service. For the more intimate scenes, involving worship of the gods or mourning for a dead firstborn, the plywood of B is dutifully hauled out. The mighty armies of Egypt feature no fewer than two chariots, and half the Egyptians are incorrectly pigmented. The dubbing was done in England, and when a black messenger talks with an accent befitting the Master of Baliol, or when the members of Moses' family speak with American, British, Swedish, Italian, Greek, and Israeli accents, the sense of *dépaysement* becomes overpowering.

And what the characters say is every bit as remarkable as their surroundings. For example: "This punctilious observance, as you so grandiloquently term it, is of the very essence." Or: "The world took six days to make; to make laws for the Israelites may take longer." Or this, from Moses overruling Aaron's misgivings about becoming high priest: "Take this not in the manner of a punishment, but in the manner of a promotion." Parenthetic phrases proliferate: "I have, may the gods forgive me, spoken," says the pharaoh; finespun metaphor is prevalent, as when Moses notes that he is "clothed in the garment of liberty of choice." (Actually, I prefer Liberty of London.) There is also a good deal of secularist demythifying: "A miracle, I suppose, is something you need happening that happens," Moses supposes. This dialogue is made truly astonishing, however, by the fact that the first screenwriting credit goes to Anthony Burgess, a writer of genuine distinction. Whatever his exact contribution may have been, his willingness to lend his name to this junk confirms me in my long-held belief that his love of money is as transcendent as his love of art.

While we are on the subject of writing, I should mention that along with this King Features version of the Bible story, we also get one major theological revelation: "The tablets of the law," says Moses, "so slowly, so painfully inscribed . . . ," suggesting that the Supreme Being, on top of his well-known stylistic problems (e.g., redundancy—"I am that I am"), suffered also from writer's block. Yet, deficient as the movie is in illumination, it has even less to offer by way of those dependable biblical spices—the salt and pepper of religious cinema—sex and violence. There is a fairly good stoning-to-death sequence, and even Moses gets one whopper smack between the eyes, but all this is kid stuff by currently accepted G or PG standards; as for the fully clothed revels around the Golden Calf, they might have been choreographed by Cotton Mather.

What, then, is left? A superb demonstration that in a rotten movie even actors as substantial as Ingrid Thulin, Mariangela Melato, Irene Papas, Anthony Quayle, and Laurent Terzieff are rendered worthless; if the dialogue or dubbing doesn't get them, the direction surely will—no one escapes this 3-D menace. But poor Burt Lancaster achieves dismalness over and above the line of inevitability. While the others look mostly like actors trying to do their best with unspeakable rubbish, he always manages to look and sound like someone actually—slowly and painfully—thinking up the tripe he is uttering. Even *his* dreadfulness is surpassed, however, by that of his son, William, who plays the young Moses as someone rather more frightened by the camera than the toiling Jewish slaves by the bullwhips of the overseers.

The film has uninspired cinematography by Marcello Gatti and inept special effects by Mario Bava. Both the music by Ennio Morricone and the "additional music" by Dov Seltzer are trashy, though I loved the lyrics of a marching song that run, in their entirety, "Ee, ee, Eesrael!" repeated as many times as there are grains of sand in the desert. Richard Johnson narrates the film with apposite perfunctoriness, but the voice of God (uncredited in the program, perhaps to suggest a cameo performance by the Prime Mover himself) is that of a typical American radio announcer; portentously pear-shaped tones emotionlessly delivered, but with a whiff of the echo chamber to give them that empyrean quality.

If you care to know what happened to the descendants of the gallant settlers of Canaan some few millennia later, there is a new Israeli film, *My Michael,* by Dan Wollman, to provide you with a few sketchy, less than satisfactory, answers. Based on a novel by Amos Oz (allegedly more cogent than the film), it tries to depict the frustrations of middle-class intellectuals in today's Israel as reflected in the marriage of Michael and Hanna. To be conveyed in particular are the difficulties of being a sensitive, imaginative young woman in a patriarchal, unliberated society. Michael is a decent enough young man impecuniously plodding his way toward a doctorate in geology while neglecting the needs of the wife he is passionately fond of; Hanna must give up her study of Hebrew literature in order to be a housewife, mother, and victim of unfulfillment and corroding boredom.

The situation is both specific and universal, the problem genuine and potentially moving. That it all remains unrealized must be blamed equally on the direction by Wollman, and on his and Ester Mor's script. The attempt to focus on small incidents, unnerving details, and compose them into a mosaic of despair is sound; the execution, however, is faulty. No rhythmic flow unites the discrete episodes; the observation of detail lacks freshness and acuity; Wollman does not find the proper objective correlatives for spiritual attrition. The overexplicit sexual fantasies of Hanna, Michael's timidity

271

about his research, their young son's inability to stroke a kitten properly are other poorly chosen or insufficiently concrete vehicles for the psychic content.

In Wollman's favor, though, be it said that this is a more serious try at social comment than usual in Israeli filmmaking, that some small dents in Israel's terrible puritanism are made here, and that *My Michael* is something more adult than the usual combination of kibbutz conviviality, young love in bloom, and endless rows of unforgettably sly characters and picturesque vistas of old and new Israel. Alex Cagan's score is engaging despite its derivativeness, Adam Greenberg's cinematography is respectable, and there is one outstanding performance by Efrat Lavie as Hanna. Cinematic acting is largely the ability to convey through certain unfussy expressions the illusion of inner riches; in Miss Lavie's case one feels that the rich inner landscape actually exists.

Degrading is the word for *Man Friday,* a movie presented by Sir Lew Grade, responsible for quite a number of lew-grade entertainments. The idea of retelling Defoe's classic tale from the point of view of Friday could just barely have made sense if some historic perspective had been retained. But the idea of the not so much noble as swinging savage trying to civilize the prosaic and uptight Englishman could only appear viable in these revisionist days, hot for reinterpreting some well-known work from a new and freakish vantage point. This kind of meddling is generally the work of hacks eager to cash in on trendy shortcuts that obviate the need to think up something original while allowing you to batten on the prestige of the underlying classic. It usually leads to reductionism, not only because lesser men are retelling the works of greater ones, but also because the new angle depends for its stability on being tricky, cute, or shocking. So we are likely to get "The Story of Dick Whittington as Told by His Cat" and, ultimately, "The Tale of Puss as Told by One of His Boots."

In the case of *Man Friday,* the scenarist is Adrian Mitchell, a minor British poet more noted for his politics, which is to the left, than his poetics, which is all too often left behind. Friday and his tribe are a fun-loving, pantheistic, socialist, polymorphously sexual hippie commune, while the whites are, at worst, fiendish slave traders and, at best, like Crusoe, well-meaning but smug, prejudiced, God-ridden killjoys with ridiculous public-school notions of fair play that nowise interfere with their condescending colonialism. The ending manages to fudge over things quite considerably, but this much at least is clear: Crusoe, even when penitently recognizing the superiority of the blacks, is too infected by his white "sickness" to qualify for admission into the tribe. Cheerless separatism is the best he can look forward to.

The plot is a string of Crusoe's moral defeats in spite of material victories over Friday, until, in the end, the defeats become material as well. Friday may be guilty of cannibalism, but he eats only accidentally deceased comrades—what he does with his enemies is passed over in silence. In all other ways he is markedly superior to Crusoe, not least in offering him his own friendly body to assuage his sexual frustration—a kindly offer met with an indignant rebuff. When Robinson has finally been outperformed, out-smarted, and, as it were, outhumaned by Friday, the audience is meant to be in total sympathy with the black when he tries to kill the white and, at least, prevents the tribe from accepting the humbly suing postulant.

A film in which the best white is still absurd, whereas blacks are wise and generous and can learn fluent English overnight would have been a huge success some years ago, when black militancy was surpassed only by white liberal self-hate. In a period of interracial collaboration, however, I hope that this film can look forward to the failure it so richly deserves for artistic as well as ideological reasons. The satire and humor, for example, are both sophomoric and leaden, and the simplest points are made in the slowest and heaviest ways. I have seen one other film directed by Jack Gold, *The Reckoning,* and I am again unimpressed by Alex Phillips's camera work. Peter O'Toole gives yet another one of his tormented performances, while Richard Roundtree remains much too flip and urban. The score by Carl Davis, however, is refreshingly different.

No need to belabor the already departing *French Provincial* with too many kicks in its vanishing rear. It is a product that smells of the film school, with the tricks and techniques of famous directors copied, exaggerated, and displayed with the kind of complacency that few genuine creators would indulge in. Written by its young director, André Téchiné, in collaboration with Marilyn Goldin—an American film enthusiast and occasional writer about film who had a walk-on part in *Last Tango in Paris*—it is aggressively antirealistic in every aspect, from its gracelessly contrived studio sets, through its totally nonensemble acting, to its (putting it kindly) incompetent direction. Worst of all, though, is the script, which tries to relate the last forty years of French political and social history in terms of the fortunes of one family, while it experiments with all kinds of techniques, orientations, and juvenile persiflage of past cinematic styles. But the writers are sorely lacking in wit, wisdom, and discipline—to say nothing of lucidity, which they spurn utterly—and the result is an unsightly and irritating farrago. Jeanne Moreau's fleshly genuineness juts out of the film as ostentatiously as Marie-France Pisier's stilted posturings are accommodated by it.

March 22–April 5, 1976

Private Problems

INGMAR BERGMAN's new film, *Face to Face,* is doubly disturbing. First, because it may be the most harrowing portrayal ever of a nervous breakdown, and, second, because it shows a supreme filmmaker in total control of his medium merely marking time. To begin with my second point: Bergman's technique, which is now capable of rendering the most painfully intimate agonies, the 273 most elusive glimmers of unease, the slightest changes in the outer or inner atmosphere, can, one feels, convey even the sound of grass growing. But Bergman seems to have reached a plateau of self-copying after the summit achievements of *Persona, Shame,* and *The Passion of Anna,* beyond which he has not progressed. God knows, it is a plateau higher than most people's peaks, and *Scenes From a Marriage* represents even a bit of extra elevation. But in *Face to Face* there is precious little that Bergman has not done before, as well or better.

Indeed, like the somewhat inferior *Cries and Whispers,* and probably more so, the new film is a compendium of Bergmanian themes and motifs, going back at least as far as *Thirst (Three Forbidden Stories),* whose theme, "Hell together is better than hell alone," is resumed by *Face to Face's* "We're thankful for the horrors we are used to. The unknown ones are worse." Detailed comparisons to numerous Bergman films—especially *Wild Strawberries, Persona,* and *Hour of the Wolf*—can and will be made, but not often, I think, to the present film's advantage. It does, however, continue the experimentation with color symbolism that reached previous heights with *The Passion of Anna* and *Cries and Whispers.* In this area, Bergman and his master cinematographer, Sven Nykvist, have forged well ahead of Antonioni's *Red Desert* and *Blow-Up,* to say nothing of the naïve experiments of Jacques Demy.

"Color symbolism," to be sure, is not quite the right term. Take the scene where the nervous breakdown of Dr. Jenny Isaksson, the young psychiatrist, begins: it is nighttime in the bedroom of her more than friend and less than lover, Dr. Tomas Jacobi. Everything in the room is either brown or green, the basic earth colors. But the variations of shade and texture, especially as dramatized by the single source of light, Tomas's bedside lamp, make these colors assume an austere harmony, an appropriateness (the two colors have been traditionally and effectively combined) that is made a mite unearthly by the colors' being a trifle out of place here; dark browns, for instance, are not usually associated with pajamas and bedding. Against the formal severity of this color scheme, Jenny's terrifying fit, made up of something that is both sobs and guffaws—something blended into a sound and look that are frighteningly inhuman in their otherness, and yet, I am convinced, the very essence of psychic collapse—seems even more uncontrolled, chaotic, and devastating. But alas, the most magisterial efficacy in one province of filmmaking is no substitute for total expressiveness in all departments.

Although Bergman gives free vent to his most personal obsessions—notably the supreme traumatic experience of his childhood, being locked into a closet by way of punishment—the idiosyncratic vision of the film is insufficiently supported by an armature of plot, character, and dialogue. The story of a poised professional woman's going to pieces, attempted suicide, comatose nightmares, and precarious recovery is valid enough, but deliberately leaves out too many key incidents; instead, it gives us either intensely private images of anxiety, such as the many, rather uncommunicative dreams; or vaguely suggestive but overgeneralized commonplaces about the tragic human condition, such as lack of communication between generations and spouses, confusions of liberated sexuality, inchoate fear of dying. There is, in

274

fact, a capricious arbitrariness in the storytelling. When, for instance, Jenny asks Tomas, "Tell me about yourself," his response is an anecdote about how he learned to belch at the age of nine, an incident that ended badly; beyond that, nothing: "My life has been pretty uneventful." Now, that strikes me as *recherché*, the author's willful intervention to make the characters odd and mysterious—leaning on eccentric details at the expense of human wholeness.

The problem makes itself felt even more in the treatment of character. For example, when Tomas has saved Jenny's life and helped nurse her back to health with exemplary devotion for so recent a friend, and when she finally evinces stronger feelings for him, he announces, as a bolt from the blue, that he is off to Jamaica to pursue unleashed, presumably bisexual, indulgences. More amazing yet, he may not come back at all. I find this manipulative: not a piece of organic character development, but a trumped-up device to force Jenny into a corner.

Lastly, the dialogue. Swedish literary friends have often astounded me by declaring Bergman's language old-fashioned and second-rate. Though dependent mostly on translations, I could not hitherto accept this contention. Yet, by some strange prolepsis, it does apply to the published screenplay of the new film, vastly more prolix and attitudinizing than what is in the movie. Bergman has a genius for paring down his scenarios and immensely improving them by the time they reach the soundtrack; even so, in *Face to Face*, the few pregnant or poignant utterances are surrounded by much barren verbiage.

A few valuable technical achievements are indisputable—thus a brilliantly understated near-rape scene in which a pair of adjacent open doors reveal simultaneously two rooms, each with its complementary image of quiet horror (all that is visible of the assaulted woman is an anguished right foot)—in other words, the multiple screen naturally arrived at. There is also a new kind of fadeout, faster than usual, and conveying the ease of falling from one type of consciousness into another.

Yet the one incontrovertible splendor of the film is Liv Ullmann's performance. Great art, we know, destroys its scaffolding, hides its artifice; but seldom has an actor been called upon to perform so awesome a set of self-revelations, to cut through to that inner nakedness that is no longer beautiful—mere animality at bay—and executed it so simply, so utterly without self-indulgence or pleas for audience sympathy, with such harsh truthfulness. It is not just sublime acting; it is a piece of great, invaluable daring.

April 12, 1976

Bitchcraft

Jean Renoir's earliest sound film, *La Chienne* (1931), now in its first American public release, is quite a technical achievement. At a time when sound was in its puling infancy, there are atmospheric existential noises; when lenses were primitive, there is considerable deep focus; when equipment was heavy, there is much effective camera movement. And there is more: a story in which conventional concepts of good and evil are treated with a flexibility bordering on iconoclasm—which was most innovative of all.

Renoir says in his autobiography:

> The story [concerns] the downward drift of a clerk who robs his employer to satisfy the demands of a little tart. The clerk is an amateur painter whom the art dealers find to have a certain amount of talent. He gives all the money to the girl, whose pimp is insatiable in his requirements. When he finds out about the pimp, the clerk stabs the girl with a paper-knife. The pimp is arrested, convicted of the murder, and guillotined. The real murderer becomes a beggar.

La Chienne is far from a great film. Based on an insignificant novel, it has a rather preposterous plot; its characters are, for the most part, either too stupid to follow up on options that any fool would grab at, or, like the hero's wife, so simplistically exaggerated as to lose all humanity. Even key details are unconvincing: the totally illiterate heroine will be reading a great big book, just so that the paper knife needed to cut its pages can provide Legrand, the protagonist, with an innocent's murder weapon. Poor Lulu! What a price to pay for having once in her life read a book!

Not even the acting, which in later Renoir films became superb, is particularly noteworthy. Michel Simon is a good befuddled Legrand, but was to do much more subtly detailed work later on. As the pimp, Georges Flamant gives a fussy performance, with some juicy mannerisms that are milked too hard. As the eponymous bitch, Janie Marèse is as uninteresting histrionically as visually. Yet by 1931 standards she was an intoxicating *femme fatale*.

La Chienne is fascinating, though, for a variety of nonartistic reasons. First, as a lesson in how unseriously cinema was taken not so long ago. The name of the actor playing the pimp is given by reputable authorities variously as Flamant, Flament, and Flammand; the leading lady's is reported by half the experts as Marèse, by the other half as Marèze. Some sources say that one reel of the soundtrack was lost during infighting with the producers, others dispute this. Even who the main technicians were remains unclear. The mist that shrouds ancient literature still envelops the films of the thirties.

Then there are the curious anecdotes and legends that surround this movie. We have it on Renoir's word that Simon, Marèse, and Flamant lived in real life a tragic triangle not unlike the one they enacted on screen. Yet another example, you might say, of life imitating art—or, in this case, pseudo-art. As Flamant told Renoir,

> He kept his hold on Janie by the use of methods that were in the best romantic tradition of the [underworld] milieu. He would make her undress and lie naked on a couch while he crouched at her feet. He would stay like that for hours, "without touching her" . . . "You see, mate, all I do is look at her . . . with devotion, but I don't touch her. After an hour I can do anything I like with her. Without touching her—that's what's important.

A couple of weeks later he took her out driving in a large new American car he couldn't handle by not touching it. There was a crash, and Marèse died. Here is Renoir again: "Michel Simon was so heartbroken that he fainted during the funeral and had to be supported. . . ."

The great character actor was suspected of unorthodox sexual practices. He would say, according to Renoir, that "there's only one thing on earth that has a little life in it . . . a woman's clitoris." Nevertheless, he was rumored to be carrying on with his she-monkey. Renoir doubts this: "I can bear witness to the purity of their relationship. That charming animal had a real affection for him, a need for love that was touching and utterly chaste."

All this would have provided a much better basis for a film than that potboiler by Georges de la Fouchardière. But, irony of ironies, *La Chienne* gathers pretentious critical exegeses as an old hull does barnacles. That the slain woman's mother remains silent under questioning inspired from André Bazin one of his most opaque lucubrations: "This is realism of manners, not of psychology. Psychological realism works in relation to the freedom of the *mise en scène.*" Renoir loved the puppet theater, and, perceiving the absurd aspects of our life, gave this and others of his films a puppet-theater frame, which elicits the following farfetched pontification from Leo Braudy in his Renoir book: "By this reassertion of the puppet-show frame Renoir wryly mocks the order of art that is so totally separate from human anguish, while at the same time enhances the striving for art that constitutes a kind of salvation by its perspective."

To show the crampedness of Legrand's lodging, a little girl is revealed playing nursery songs on the piano in a room across the airshaft. From that master obfuscator, Raymond Durgnat, this prompts the following: "Thus [Legrand's] confined space opens. His 'corruption' is an integrity like her innocence. They are two artists together (yet unknowing). This doubleness, not to say duplicity, of composition might tempt one to comparisons with . . . Masaccio," a temptation, along with many others, that Durgnat blissfully yields to. If you can, however, go to the movie without the expectations aroused by such exegetes, do.

Clotilde, the heroine of Alberto Lattuada's *Bambina*, learns to make love, but does not come of age. Clotilde is a wealthy sixteen-year-old retardate, who urinates equally in her bed, in her panties under the gaze of her mother's guests at an elegant soirée, and on her lover's best suit when she rides him as they play horsy. *Bambina* is a semipornographic *Lolita*, with lots of southern Italian gusto and a curious happy ending: Saverio, the mature, materialistic land developer, has given up everything for his sexy kewpie doll with the underdeveloped brain; Clotilde has learned to say "I love you" as she heads for wedded bliss consisting entirely of nursery games and serious copulation. For such love, apparently, it is worth losing the world.

This is, you may have gathered, a fairly demented little film. But it believes in itself with remarkable singlemindedness. The world around Saverio is all scheming, greed, loveless sex, voyeurism, big business on the rampage. And not only around, but inside him, too. Until, that is, he goes ape over

Clotilde, the luscious little monkey who can't talk, and cannot even go beddy-bye unless her nanny masturbates her to sleep. Even if the particular exemplar is unconvincing—what will happen to Clotilde and Saverio's marriage after six months?—there is something to be said for the notion that a shared private obsession is preferable to endless public exploitation. Unlike, say, *Malizia, Bambina* is not evil.

It is not, however, a good film, and deserves only the kind of sympathy we grant madmen from whose mouths drop flashes of insight. There are some good performances. Luigi Proietti is an amusing Saverio, who gets both comedy and pathos out of his conversion from acquisitiveness to Humbert Humbertism; Irene Papas is a compelling presence as Clotilde's rich, mercilessly mercenary yet not unmotherly mother. As Clotilde, Teresa Ann Savoy is amazing: the face more wholesome than comely, the much-bared body unbearably perfect, the unslim ankles and irregular teeth flaws that, in context, are humanizing. More important is Miss Savoy's ability to convey maximal hedonism and minimal thought with a naturalness that places everything beyond moral judgment: childishness with a child's amorality, animality with an animal's innocence, mindlessness permitting the body a pristine candor and eloquence.

Lattuada is a director who, besides having made some respectable movies on his own, gave Fellini his start by collaborating with him on *Variety Lights.* There are some genuinely Felliniesque moments in *Bambina,* which also has competent cinematography by Lamberto Caïmi, who used to be camera operator (though not, as credited, cinematographer) to the great Ermanno Olmi. The screenplay, by Ottavio Jemma, Bruno De Geronimo, and Lattuada could use more wit and invention, and Fred Bongusto's music is only serviceable. Still, there are moments of life-enhancing eroticism here, and I disagree with the *Times* review that would have them aimed at people with a fetish for imbeciles. Not having a fetish for Miss Savoy would seem to come nearer the mark of imbecility.

May 10–May 17, 1976

Skier Enskied

THERE IS A POEM by the contemporary Japanese poet Saijō Yaso in which the "hills . . . blaze/Savage and red" with "a single red leaf." So, too, Mount Everest blazes with the solitary red patch of Yuichiro Miura, the Japanese skier in his crimson windbreaker, schussing down the highest, most dangerous, most inaccessible slope of all. It is the last of the many wonders of *The Man Who Skied Down Everest,* but not necessarily the greatest, for this delicate, awesome, and humane film is brimful of miracles.

Only the Japanese could have realized this project. Miura, in conceiving and executing it, proves himself a combination kamikaze in the service of peace, athlete of the sort Pindar celebrated, Oriental philosopher, and Japanese poet fusing epic and filigree. The narration of the film is ably extracted from Miura's diary by Judith Crawley. It takes a little getting used to, for a characteristic Miura thought sounds like a cross between a Zen kōan and a haiku or tanka; gradually, though, we are completely won over. When Miura plans to attach a parachute to himself to convert certain suicide into mere mortal danger, and muses, "I would like to use a parachute: it would add grace and beauty to the adventure, like an airy lotus blossom on the sacred mountain," we already know the man; we know that this is neither phrasemaking nor exhibitionism, but his way of thinking and being.

Yet the feat is not only Miura's; it is also that of the gallant band of Japanese cameramen and skiers, of the eight hundred barefoot Nepalese carriers who lugged their ponderous loads across difficult terrain to the base camp, and of the Sherpas who then took over. It is, in a special way, the glory of the six Sherpas who were swept to their deaths in a crevasse by an expectably unexpected cave-in while reconnoitering a route across the treacherous icefall; and also the magnanimity of the brother of one of the dead Sherpas declaring, "A Sherpa is not a Sherpa if he's afraid of the mountains; so I will continue to climb so long as my Japanese brothers need me." There is a luminous double entendre in that word "brother": for a lost brother, new brothers are born of the common enterprise.

Why would one undertake to ski down Everest? And why make a film of it? To answer the second question first: arduous as it is to get heavy Cinema-Scope equipment to those almost unattainable, hard-to-breathe-in heights, to have a record of this achievement, to make all mankind partake of this victory, is the final, ecumenical goal; what would otherwise have remained a personal, unsharable achievement becomes a world-uniting event. Yes, but the basic idea that came out of a bantering conversation with Sir Edmund Hillary a few years earlier—skiing down the twenty-nine-thousand-foot mountain—how is one to explain it? The famous words of the tragic George Leigh Mallory, "Because it is there," remain as good as any explanation; not even the moving play that Auden and Isherwood wrote about Mallory, *The Ascent of F6*, has a better one to offer. Miura will occasionally wax particularly poetic: "I dreamed of skiing down the virgin snows of the Himalayas. It's almost like the beginning of love: you can do anything." Well, anything you can do racing down a sheet of ice at a forty- to forty-five-degree angle through which protrude jagged rocks, and at whose end is the fearful abyss called Bergschlund (the German for "mountain maw"); unless you can stop before it, it swallows you forever.

Miura was the right man: a Hokkaido University phys-ed graduate, world ski record-holder, conqueror of mountains from Alaska to Chile, first skier down the sacred Mount Fuji, he was, at thirty-seven, tired of merely working for the Ministry of Physical Fitness, hosting his TV show about skiing, and being a celebrity. "I fear for the human spirit if man surrenders his indomitable drive to conquer the unknown," Hillary had said. And much was still unknown—even how a parachute functions, if at all, at such thin-aired, previously unparachuted altitudes. And what of the wind up there, and of having to ski in an oxygen mask? But the same force that drew Childe   279

Roland to the Dark Tower inexorably summoned Miura to that towering peak, called Chomolungma by the Tibetans, i.e., Mother Goddess of Earth—perhaps *das Ewig-Weibliche* itself? For as he nears the summit, he feels oddly closer to his wife and daughter back home.

Consider the difficulties: the three-million-dollar cost, the twenty-seven tons of equipment, the needed eight film technicians, of whom only three had climbing experience, the task of getting three mighty CinemaScope cameras (two of which were to become inoperative at the crucial moment) to the sixth and topmost camp on the South Col of Everest, those rocks the size of four-story buildings along the downhill course, and the Bergschlund. And all this had to be filmed and edited down to tractable length. That the movie lasts only 87 minutes and yet manages to catch the various aspects of the trip—from the flowers underfoot to the birds of prey overhead, from scientific experiments to minutiae of daily living, from intense physical and technical preparations to sundry forms of recreation—this is in itself a miracle of tact, and typically, superbly Japanese.

The Japanese influence must have spread also to the Canadian and American technicians who worked along with the Japanese on assembling and editing the film (earlier achievements of Miura's are also touched upon); but special respect is due Mitsuji Kanau, the chief cameraman, whose Arriflex faithfully dogged Miura's lightning descent. All the cinematography is beautiful, however, both in what it shoots and in how it shoots it, from the expedition's arrival in Katmandu on February 25, 1970, to those ultimate moments when Miura, now sliding on his back—one ski, off his foot, is schussing down on its own—somehow manages to come to stop 250 feet from the Bergschlund.

There are views of trekking across high foothills, of fighting one's way up ice walls with ropes and crampons; there are crossings, with heavy packs, of slender bridges slung across nightmarish chasms, scenes among huge ice blocks that might be a Cubist vision of hell. And there are scenes of tranquillity by day or night: without wind, when you are adrift in absolute stillness; and with wind, which recalls you to the task at hand. There are inner experiences made visible: the well-being that comes of shared danger overcome; the fellowship that arises from watching *The Seven Samurai* on cassette television together with Sherpas who have never seen it; the consanguinity that stems from burying and mourning six dead men. There are dreamy rituals of communal dance, of dentistry and haircuts in a high chair jutting more than twenty thousand feet into the sky, of erecting cairns to the precious dead with mirrors placed in them to represent the soul of man in which the great mountains can view themselves. For here a strange union takes place and is captured on film; as Miura says, "I cannot tell where the mountains end and I begin."

Splendor of the seen, and also of the heard. Of the many remarkable sound effects, the finest are the narration and the music. The former is spoken by that marvelous Canadian actor Douglas Rain; if there were a prize for the difficult art of narration (as there ought to be), the first one should go to him. Never does he sound orotund and portentous, never is he an announcer or a pontificator. He simply becomes Miura: experiencing, cogitating, living. He is exhilarated or apprehensive, contemplative or aroused, but never, never actorish. How touching he is when he says, with understated solicitude, "I worry about failing more than about dying," or when, after some spectacular skiing and a descent finished on his backside, he wonders, gravely yet unassumingly, whether he has succeeded or failed. Rain, like Miura, must know that this is one of those rare exploits that transcends such considerations.

And then the music by Larry Crosley; a group called Nexus, using Eastern, Western, and strange, newly invented instruments; and the flutist Robert Aitken. This could have been sticky: pompous, patronizingly ethnic, trendy, or just excessive. Instead, like the expedition, it avoids pitfalls, and sounds mysterious and lovely, Oriental and Occidental, companionable yet otherworldly. As friend and comforter, it interprets unfamiliar landscapes and customs; it authenticates moods and feelings discovered in unknown, skyey regions; and it knows when to fall discreetly silent.

I could go on, but even if my words could convey what the film lets you feel, I would be advised to leave you to your own discoveries. As well as any film ever, *The Man Who Skied Down Everest* conveys how the heroic deeds of individual explorers—skiers, mountaineers, filmmakers—unite the lot of us by converting the dangerous curiosity, restlessness, and violence within us to peaceful uses. To the most peaceful and wonderful use of all: the conquest of the impossible. It is what Pindar heralded in his Third Nemean Ode: "The end shines through/ in the testing of actions where excellence is shown. . . ."

From the sublime to the ridiculous. First, Claude Chabrol's *Une Partie de plaisir* (*A Pleasure Party* or, as mistranslated by the distributor, *A Piece of Pleasure*), with a script by Chabrol's frequent collaborator Paul Gégauff, who, along with his wife, Danielle, also stars in it. The story of what happens to the quasi-marriage of a male chauvinist when, at the gander's prompting, the goose helps herself to some sauciness, is partly trivial, partly unbelievable. The people are too bad, too good, or too stupid to be true, and neither plot nor dialogue comes to the rescue. Granted, there are good-looking faces, elegant clothes and furniture, and catchy land- and townscapes, photographed by Jean Rabier with his usual imitation–Marie Laurencin palette, but none of that is enough, not even a very winning performance by Mme Gégauff.

What this contrived and banal film elicits, though, is a sense of regret. Chabrol is truly a master of technique: watch closely how he moves his camera about, how he intercuts an extreme closeup of a detail with a sequence in medium long shot, or how he dazzlingly switches camera angles in midstream. This man can do everything with his camera, but where in heaven's name is his sense, his taste? What know-how lavished on utter claptrap!

In Fernando Arrabal's *Guernica*, conversely, there is something like anti-know-how. This unspeakable phony, whose plays and movies are equal 281 garbage, thinks that his anti-Franco politics is enough to excuse sordid perversions masquerading as poetic metaphors, inane dialogue posturing as eccentric profundity, and the most inept filmmaking carrying on like avant-garde originality. Actually, that must be what his defenders think; Arrabal manifestly fancies himself an unqualified genius. He does manage, however, to make the noble cause of antifascism look like some ghastly disease. Mariangela Melato should know better than to appear in such trash, but actors and actresses, I guess, seldom do.

June 7, 1976

The Unkindliest Cut

ONCE, as a youngster, I came across an illustration in one of Magnus Hirschfeld's sexological tomes; it was captioned "St. Origen castrates himself for the sake of the Heavenly Kingdom." Insufficient grounds as that seemed to me then as now, it made vastly more sense than doing it for the sake of an idiotic script, which, as far as I can tell, is the only reason for it in *The Last Woman,* Marco Ferreri's abominable new film. Gérard, the hero, having practiced up with his electric meat carver on many a hunk of roast beef, expertly applies the tool to his tool. The trick photography is excellent: it really looks as if he held aloft his bleeding, severed penis by way of a senseless but sensational climax to an otherwise dull and pointless movie.

Ferreri has a certain ferocity that, in his earlier pictures, endeavored to be satirical. I have not seen his two first features made in Spain, but did view two of his early Italian efforts, *The Conjugal Bed* and *The Ape Woman,* which, however witlessly, still tried for satire. Their only effect on me was to make me feel sorry for the two gracious actresses, Marina Vlady and Annie Girardot, entrapped in them. The one middle-period Ferreri I experienced was *Dillinger Is Dead;* here he had begun to move in the pretentious direction of Bertolucci and Pasolini (in whose *Pigsty* he played a vulgarian without apparent need for make-up). What distinguishes *Dillinger* and other Ferreri films of the period (I gather) is lack of clarity.

I caught up with Ferreri's latest phase when I saw *The Grande Bouffe,* which remains in my memory as one of the two or three most unappetizing films I have ever sat through. In it, four men commit suicide by gorging themselves to death, with forays into a few other forms of bestiality along the way. The film did not succeed in making even an iota of social comment, and, as for satire, it reached its high point with Michel Piccoli's repeated breaking of wind. What in Rabelais and Lina Wertmüller manages to be outrageously funny—because it becomes part of plot and characterization—is in Ferreri adventitious and gross.

The Last Woman has a script by Ferreri and his frequent collaborator, the Spaniard Rafael Azcona, and you can tell right away that something deep is afoot when the engineer hero, played by Gérard Depardieu, having defied the bosses of his factory whose workers are on strike, proceeds to defy also a horde of police dogs, and then bursts in, most defiantly, on the factory nursery school, where the pretty teacher Valérie is just giving her breast to his little son, Pierrot. Now, why should a boy who is almost old enough to walk still need suckling; and why must one, just because one is a nursery-school teacher, do the nursing? These, however, are only the first of many impenetrable mysteries.

Gérard's feminist wife having walked out on her husband, Valérie moves in, for no apparent reason. And why did the wife run out, leaving the small son mostly in his father's care? And what is her relation with a girl friend, from whom she seems to be inseparable? Why, if Valérie appears to be so fond of the worthy Michel, does she so lightly throw him over for Gérard? And why does she so quickly run back to Michel? And so very quickly back to Gérard? And why does Gérard, who seems to thrive on his promiscuous independence, suddenly need Valérie around all the time? Is Gérard impotent? Is Valérie frigid? Or is that the effect they have on each other? Sometimes there seem to be great and happy orgasms; sometimes, ignominious fiascoes.

Why is the wife's feminism, as it influences Valérie, made to look like the cause of trouble, when trouble was manifest all along? Why does Michel show up with a new girl friend who is supposed to be English and not speak a word of French, yet utters her few English words in a thick French accent dubbed into the mouth of an Italian actress? Why must Gérard and Valérie, when they are not having mostly faulty sex, conduct mostly defective conversations? Why doesn't anything in this damned movie have a damned bit of apperceptible motivation?

But whenever characters in a film have the same names as their portrayers (Gérard—Gérard Depardieu; Michel—Michel Piccoli; Nathalie—Nathalie Baye; René—Renato Salvatori), we should know that we are in for misery. For it means that the filmmakers could not even be bothered to imagine original names for their creatures, so little interested were they in conceiving genuine people. What they were after was merely a new, modish thrill and, of the few modish thrills still left over, they happened to seize on castration. It need not be in the least clear whether Gérard performs it to spite himself, Valérie, or women in general; or whether the act is to be viewed as a triumph or a defeat. Real people and convincing actions have long since become expendable; what is needed is a suggestive background of evil capitalism, idling factories, soulless high-rises, men and women simultaneously at one another's genitals and throats, and oodles of suburban despair.

Your film must have that anguished sense of frustrated consumerism; that neurotic *Red Desert-cum-Two or Three Things I Know About Her* look; that surfeit of boredom begotten by Moravia upon Antonioni, and, if possible, a bit of Sartre Resartus thrown in. To this end, it is advisable to find for your locale a brand-new, preferably unfinished-looking, suburb; and for your cinematographer, someone who has worked with Antonioni—in this case, Luciano Tovoli, who shot that supreme amalgam of angst and ennui, *The* 283

Passenger. You also commission a modernistic score—though here, for some reason, from Philippe Sarde, the master of the neo-Rachmaninovian mode. Sarde, no slouch, goes ahead and concocts something modernistic—and so godawful that you wish he had stuck with his umpteenth reworking of the Second Piano Concerto.

Gérard Depardieu, who was delightful when I last saw him in Claude Goretta's *Pas si méchant que ça*—a charming film that, typically, has not yet been released hereabouts—is a revolting slob in this one. If the script calls for a revolting slob, the performance is impeccable. Ornella Muti, as Valérie, is a beautiful young woman with, however, the thick lips of a heathen idol, the heavy legs and ankles of a Maillol nude, and breasts like large but not quite solid gourds. She is dubbed into French by a voice much too sophisticated for the part she is playing, or, rather, the body she is baring, which is what she mostly has to do. At that, she bares it less than Depardieu does his—a twofold pity.

The infant Pierrot is enacted or entoddled by David Biffani. His part consists of being buffeted hither and yon, or watching Depardieu and Muti roll over each other. If this kid can grow up unstunted by the experience, it will have to be considered a major miracle. For having farmed out their offspring to Ferreri and his unsavory enterprise, Mr. and Mrs. Biffani deserve the sternest chastisement—say, a month in the current equivalent of Devil's Island, or three or four sittings through *The Last Woman.*

If Marco Ferreri is the most dependably vulgar filmmaker I can think of, Claude Berri is the most consistently lowbrow and unimaginative. Ever since he made that crude short, *The Chicken,* which gave goose pimples of delight to Bosley Crowther, he has regaled us with movies that were either crass bits of fictionalized autobiography or lame attempts at titillation through clean dirty jokes. Examples of the former are *The Two of Us* and *Marry Me! Marry Me!;* of the latter, *Le Sex Shop* and now *Male of the Century,* which may represent both dreary autobiography and clean dirty jokes—the fusion of two lamentable genres.

The film is "based on an idea by Miloš Forman," which isn't an idea at all, only an old Jewish joke that has been kicking around eastern Europe for ages. It's no wonder Forman gave it away; the question is merely why anyone—even Berri—would want it. As Berri has developed it, with the help of Jean-Louis Richard, it concerns a pants merchant in Lyons whose faithful, long-suffering wife, on whom he freely cheats, finally has a fling of her own. He cannot forgive this, and, on top of it, she is now held hostage by a couple of bank robbers. What if she had sex with one of them? Our hero fantasizes about this, agonizes a little, and tries some hanky-panky with a willing nurse.

If you think there is little promise in the foregoing, how about jokes involving mothers-in-law, panties, and birth-control pills? And what jokes! Wifey's mother tells a reporter that if her daughter is in danger of being raped, she would gladly take her place. When hubby suffers from insomnia, his mother, by mistake, gives him one of wifey's birth-control pills. Hubby ikewise imagines himself taking his wife's place, and we presently see him aking off his drawers to sit in the chief robber's lap. If this hasn't yet turned our stomach, consider that hubby is played by Claude Berri himself, with a ace, physique, and personality that could deter a nymphomaniacal she-nonkey. For me, to watch him in the dual capacity of director and star (his name in the film, by the way, is Claude!) is the equivalent of a severe case of beri-beri.

Our director is as fond as John Cassavetes of casting himself and members of his family in his movies, and so here we are exposed also to his own progeny playing his progeny, and his own mother, Mme Langmann (Berri's real name), playing his mother. Their services could, no doubt, be had for free; but, considering their performances, that may not have been cheap enough. There is also mediocre photography and worse music; however, Juliet Berto plays the wife. Mlle Berto is well on her way to becoming a very considerable actress; she performs with an intelligence and economy—a certain melancholy incisiveness—more eloquent in one shot than Berri in his entire output.

June 21, 1976

Untenable Tenant

THERE IS SCARCELY a more depressing case in movies than that of Roman Polanski. A filmmaker of considerable talent and not just bad but downright repellent taste, he could well have become a major artist had he remained in his native Poland. Polanski, a naughty little fellow with bizarre preoccupations, desperately needs Big Brother to watch over him. Polish censorship provided him with just such a restraining superego, and never did curtailing of an artist's freedom yield more salutary resuts. His single Polish feature, *Knife in the Water* (1962), and the best of his Polish shorts, *Two Men and a Wardrobe* (1958), are original and pungent achievements, quite possibly major works. In these films, his taste for the perverse in life and (as he sees it) nature is confined within the boundaries of suggestion, saving him from his bent for grossness.

These early films contained also a certain amount of social criticism— Polanski's resentment of Communist restrictions on human and artistic self-expression—and this, too, happily deflected some of his attention from his favorite topic: sexual kinkiness, sometimes laced with supernatural overtones, though only as pretexts for greater sexual outrageousness. Yet even into these early Polish works Polanski could sneak references to his scabrous or obscene predilections; thus *When Angels Fall* (1959) takes place in a public latrine. His first Western work, a short called *The Fat and the Skinny*, was already an outright piece of sadomasochism under its Beckettian veneer.

It is useful to recall how Polanski's faults were often transmuted by overin- 285 dulgent fans and deluded reviewers into shining virtues. When his first Western feature, *Repulsion* (1965), came out, many serious critics were impressed by the fact that this study of a murderous female psychopath devoted little or no attention to why the girl got that way. I remember arguing this point with Robert Brustein, who declared himself fed up with the Freudian explanations of madness that, he claimed, had been done to death, or at least to deadly boredom, and welcomed the emphasis on the systematic working out of the morbid symptoms. To me, the film was just one sensational effect after another, however brilliant on occasion. Without psychoanalytical or some other form of humanistic insight, there was no human interest; without prime concern for human motivation, the violence of the film was as senseless as a mass murder, and just as inartistic.

I missed Polanski's first Hollywood-sponsored film, *The Fearless Vampire Killers* (1967); recut as the release print was by the studio, Polanski himself disowned it. His previous British-made feature, *Cul-de-Sac* (1966), struck me as odious, as did his first big Hollywood hit, *Rosemary's Baby,* despite scattered touches of dazzling dexterity. Quite aside from all other considerations, these films were so sensationalistic and exploitative that there was very little room for art in them. With *Repulsion,* by the way, Polanski had begun collaborating with his regular scriptwriter, Gérard Brach, who has been, as far as I can see, at best a trivial, at worst a nefarious, influence on his work.

Meanwhile, Polanski married the lovely actress Sharon Tate, and lost her in the way everyone knows: the Manson murders, which, along with Vietnam and Watergate, though on a smaller scale, alerted America to its bad conscience. At the time of the Manson murders, Hollywood was rife with rumors to the effect that Polanski's life-style was responsible for what happened, that the Manson gang's choice of victims was no mere accident. When Polanski next made, with Kenneth Tynan, his quirky and overbrutal version of *Macbeth,* it was interesting to find Pauline Kael speculating on that excess of lovingly dwelt-on ferocity as an attempt to exorcise the memory of personal tragedy. It seemed to me that Miss Kael was putting the cart before the horse; Polanski's by then legendary "unconventionality," rather than some almost fortuitous consequence, seemed to be at the root of things, a theory that appeared to gain confirmation by Polanski's electing to play the sadistic little punk in *Chinatown.* Yet with that film Polanski redeemed himself in part even for the deeply rotten *What?* that had preceded it, in which his appetite for kinky filmmaking, unmitigated by any artistry, reached its apogee.

Chinatown, however, was different: of all Polanski's later films it most closely resembled *Knife in the Water.* There was much criminal evil suffused through the movie, along with quite a lot of psychic cruelty; but it was all kept in check by wit and understatement, even by a certain kind of gutter romanticism, all of which may have been contributed by the screenplay of Robert Towne, who also was responsible for the welcome social implications. Doubtless, too, the then Paramount bigwigs breathed heavily down Polanski's neck, reincarnating the Polish state as a felicitous controlling factor. (Lest anyone misunderstand me, let me make clear that I am not for controlling the artist; I am only saying that in Polanski's atypical case such controls have proved inadvertently beneficial.) Though not quite a work of art, *Chinatown* comes close to being one in its best moments: it is, in any case, a well-made film, which is nothing to sneeze at, and shows no signs of sloppiness except for a few final improbabilities conveniently glossed over by good acting.

It is thus all the more surprising how thoroughly sloppy *The Tenant*, Polanski's latest venture, has turned out to be, even granted that he is reunited with his scenaristic nemesis, Gérard Brach. As always in Polanski's worst pictures, something that looks very much like stupidity takes over, though it may be nothing more than near-total lack of interest in whatever merely leads up to the kinky and maniacal sequences, the film's true raison d'être. We are given here the utterly improbable story of Trelkovsky, a little Parisian office worker of Polish origin, who, for no convincing reason, rents expensively a small, dismal apartment without so much as a toilet to it on the top floor of a respectable-looking house, whose owner, concierge, and tenants, however, seem to be, at the very least, unappetizing, if not downright monstrous. They make the kinds of demands that no halfway normal tenant nowadays would begin to accept. To be sure, the film is based on a novel by Roland Topor, a distinctly unwholesome illustrator and writer, but even that cannot explain and excuse everything.

Nothing makes sense, in fact: the suicide of the apartment's previous tenant, Trelkovsky's urge to move (his earlier lodging is never even mentioned), the protagonist's lopsided relationship with Stella, the suicide's best friend. Why can Trelkovsky take off from work whenever he wants to? Why do his pals suddenly fade from the scene? Why can everybody intimidate him much of the time, even though at other times he can be quite spirited? These absurdities and others are not even presented consistently: that Trelkovsky, whose windows give on the communal toilet, sees various tenants just standing there and seemingly staring at him could mean that he was demented from the outset—but, then, why do his office mates treat him as perfectly normal? Why does the striking Stella promptly fall in love with him? Of course, the entire film could be perceived as Trelkovsky's hallucinations, but what concern can we deploy if everything is the ravings of a madman, if we are not even accorded a normative view of reality, and if that mad protagonist is far from being a sympathetic, or merely believable, madman?

Yet even technically the film is not well made. Thus Trelkovsky's fantasies are shot so explicitly and naïvely as to lose their chance for scariness. Some of them are holdovers from *Repulsion*, like that arm and hand coming out of nowhere; others are just too funny to be frightening, like Jo Van Fleet's ineptly camped-up performance as a supposedly sinister neighbor. Particularly clumsy, too, is the English dubbing. There is something abysmal, however, about *all* dubbing, and the speech from the film in which the hero speculates about how many of his parts need to be lopped off for him to cease being himself can be answered categorically for actors: without your voice, you are no longer yourself. Moreover, the American voices that were engaged here lack all finesse.

Script, direction, and dubbing join in making all performances insignificant, if not indeed ludicrous. As for Polanski himself, who started out as an actor, he can be good in small, usually unsympathetic, roles. But he does not have the stuff of a leading man, even for such an oddball lead as Trelkovsky—though it would certainly tax the ingenuity of our most accomplished actors to make the farfetched changes in Trelkovsky appear even momentarily credible. Yet the saddest thing about *The Tenant* is that it employed the services of Bergman's great cinematographer Sven Nykvist, and managed to make even his inspired work look stilted or irrelevant in this context. One final note: the head nurse is played by Helena Manson. Coincidence or . . . ?

June 28, 1976

Extra- and Intramural Warfare

A MAJOR DISAPPOINTMENT is *The Old Gun,* by Robert Enrico, a director of genuine, but rather intermittently deployed, talent. At his best, he has made such films as *In the Midst of Life* (three Civil War stories by Ambrose Bierce, of which only one, *An Occurrence at Owl Creek Bridge,* has been given appreciable exposure here, even though this tripartite work is remarkable as a totality) and *Zita,* as well as some absorbing, mostly scientific, shorts. At his less distinguished, he has still managed to turn out some better than fair adventure thrillers (of which the most recently seen here, *Le Secret,* uneven as it was, received unduly short shrift). But *The Old Gun* is in every way a most unfortunate film, and its huge success in France, with both critics and the public, is even more shameful than the mere audience success of *Midway* in America.

The Old Gun is a film of blind hatred for the Germans, telling of the atrocities a bunch of them commit in and around a ramshackle castle in the South of France. Evacuation before the advancing Allies is imminent, making the wanton and extremely brutal murder of (among others) the protagonist's wife and daughter even more ruthless and gratuitous than other wartime horrors. This protagonist, a surgeon previously possessed of only middling commitment to the French cause, now becomes a human murder weapon of utmost—and not a little incredible—efficiency, exterminating a good dozen Germans singlehandedly. These killings, mostly with an unlikely old hunting gun of his father's, are intercut with reminiscences of his wooing of his second wife, and of family joys and contretemps with her and a small daughter from his previous marriage.

These memory flashbacks are extraordinarily flat and uninventive both in content and in the way they are fitted into the present action, and for this, the script, chiefly by Pascal Jardin, must take its share of the blame. As for the manner in which the Germans are eliminated, even granted a certain diversity along with the preposterousness, there is, needless to say, nothing

288

life-enhancing about it. Its appeal is not only to brutality, but also to chauvinism—one justly aroused Frenchman being the equal of any number of superiorly armed krauts—and its obviousness remains virtually unalleviated.

There is one, only one, interesting moment in all this. The French underground appears on the scene, preliminary to attacking the castle, and temporarily withdraws. The *maquisards* come across our hero, who has already done in a few Germans and is about to tackle the rest. These Frenchmen recognize him as their absentee *châtelain,* and treat him with a puzzled, somewhat patronizing, deference. He, in turn, wanders about among them, abstracted and barely aware of them, wishing only to be rid of them so as to go on wreaking his personal vendetta. There is a strangely illogical, nightmarish quality about these potential allies not getting together that briefly captures the senseless sterility of war.

I am not saying, of course, that the German atrocities depicted here are in the least inconceivable, even though the film goes a long way toward making them seem unconvincing; what I am saying is that *The Old Gun* re-evokes them without sufficient cause. A film like *Lacombe, Lucien,* or the even more imperfect *Special Section,* recalls Nazi cruelties in order to make some new points about the war, to explore hitherto overlooked areas of swinishness or nobility, to elucidate aspects of human nature for which the war serves only as a particularly apt background. This movie, however, merely reawakens the old patriotic lies, stirs up again the ancient, bloody bitterness leading to no understanding, no peace.

The film won the César, the French equivalent of the Oscar, which only shows that, in any language, Oscar means nonsense. Similar awards went to Philippe Noiret, for his portrayal of the hero, and François de Roubaix, for his score. Noiret is one of the finest comic and character actors in movies today; he does everything possible to infuse a dram of humanity into the proceedings, but all to little avail. To his credit be it mentioned that, in Rome last winter, he told me that he had avoided seeing the finished film. As for Roubaix, whose mostly solo guitar score for *Zita* was lovely indeed, his music here is just serviceable. Like the Oscar, again, the César rewards, even in the occasional right person, the wrong achievement. Romy Schneider behaves appealingly as the wife; in the brief part of the mother, Madeleine Ozeray, once Louis Jouvet's leading lady and mistress, looks almost as pretty as ever.

Alpha Beta is an English play by E. A. Whitehead, transposed onto the screen pretty much unchanged from the way it was performed at the Royal Court, and again directed by Anthony Page. It zeros in on an unhappy Liverpudlian lower-middle-class marriage at three dates: in the early sixties, late sixties, and early seventies. It is a Catholic marriage, full of guilt feelings, a sense of entrapment, and the need and inability to let go. There is infidelity on the husband's part, jealousy on the wife's, and bitter recrimination from both sides. The situation is not so much sad or funny as it is absurd, and not so much absurd as hair-raising when you consider how many marriages and other relationships nowadays are as lamentable, ludicrous, and locked-in as this. Whitehead's writing is not quite one-of-a-kind, but it has both the feel of reality and a sense of form, which, together, are not to be dismissed lightly.

The direction is incisive, but there remains the incontrovertible fact that this is a filmed play that one should have seen on the stage. Failing that, however, it is still a magnificent experience to watch Rachel Roberts and Albert Finney reenact on film the union, in George Meredith's words, of this ever-diverse pair. It is acting at its very highest: anyone who cares a rap about performance penetrating to the essence of humanity owes himself this experience. Watch Finney change from act to act (the movie preserves the act division): he goes from a baffled but still belligerent young husband to a cocky, irresponsible lecher, and thence to a man prematurely old and exhausted but clinging to some illusion of independence. It is not one but three glorious performances rolled into one; I promise you that you have never seen an actor change more drastically without benefit of make-up—bulge out so in one scene, and cave in on himself so utterly in the next. Notice how the eyes go dead, the voice gets blunted, the very outline of the body blurs with defeat. Rachel Roberts is no less superb, but her part has fewer dimensions. Yet how piteously she ages, becomes more thrall to despair, and still preserves a spark of pugnacity, however dulled and enfeebled.

The film simply reeks humanity from every frame or pore: battered, smelly, hopelessly soiled humanity, yet somehow luminescent in its very putrescence.

For rock bottom, we have Philippe de Broca's *Le Magnifique*. I have never shared the admiration of Stanley Kauffmann and Pauline Kael even for early De Broca, though I could see a slender talent in *The Love Game* and *The Five-Day Lover*. Subsequent items either left me cold, like *The Man From Rio,* or, like *King of Hearts,* repelled me. This current take-off on James Bond movies, however, is bestially stupid, most humorless when brutishly reaching out after cheap laughs, as obvious as anything devised by a five-year-old lover of the worst kinds of movies. And though its gore is meant to be farcical, it is explicitly and viciously gory enough to make the movie unsuitable even for the small, unbright children it seems intended for.

Jean-Paul Belmondo, the hitherto always at least desirable Jacqueline Bisset, and the previously no less oafish Vittorio Caprioli play the leading parts as badly as they deserve to be played. If your choice is, say, between *Le Magnifique* and bubonic plague, you might pick the movie.

July 19–26, 1976

Kissing Kin

CINEMA is not yet dead in France, after all. Suddenly there are two French films of real worth: one, *Cousin, Cousine,* a comedy that nevertheless doesn't lose sight of the drama of living; the other, *The Clockmaker* (see next article), a drama that, however serious, manages to hold on to its sense of humor. I admire both these films and am amazed that both won the Louis Delluc Prize: Could it be that there is hope for French film criticism as well?

Since there are direct or indirect references in both films to the great French turn-of-the-century humorist Alphonse Allais (whose unavailability in English is a great and inexplicable loss), let me start my discussion of *Cousin, Cousine,* Jean-Charles Tacchella's second film, with a quotation from Allais:

> There are, in this world, complicated people and simple folk.
> Complicated people are those who couldn't move their pinkies without assuming the air of someone setting in motion the most mysterious mechanism. The existences of certain complicated people appear to be extended networks of coils and counterweights.
> That's what complicated people are all about.
> Simple folk, on the contrary, are people who say yes when you should say yes, no when you should say no; who open their umbrellas when it's raining (and they've got their umbrellas), and who close them as soon as the rain stops. Simple folk proceed straight ahead as the path leads, unless there is a barricade forcing them to make a detour.
> That's what simple folk are all about.

Complicated people have since become even more self-embroiled, while the few simple ones are now just as likely to climb over the barricade. Such simple ones, in *Cousin, Cousine,* are Marthe and Ludovic, married to other people who are complicated, and each with a child. They are distantly related by marriage and meet at a family wedding; they fall, not exactly in love, but in sympathy with each other. Or, perhaps, in tune. Ludovic, who is married to Karine, a sexually unfastidious hysteric happiest when taking sleep cures, is a teacher of social dancing—temporarily. He periodically changes jobs the way others change sexual partners and so keeps spiritually fresh: from mycological research, say, to playing in a jazz band. Marthe is a solid working wife and mother who has had only one brief affair with an office mate who "amused" her, although Pascal, her husband, is a fancy salesman and an even fancier confirmed philanderer.

Whereas Pascal and Karine have a vehement, quickie affair, Marthe and Ludovic embark on a long-range platonic friendship. Both families are large and given to little bourgeois celebrations, besides marriages and funerals, where Marthe and Ludovic meet. Soon they start seeing each other for the sheer enjoyment of being together, and the only reason they don't go to bed is the apprehension that this might shorten the relationship. Not only do they do things that please them, they also indulge—modestly—in things that displease their spouses. She buys him a loud tie of the sort Karine loathes; he buys her a picture hat of the kind Pascal detests. So subtle are Tacchella's writing and direction that the preoccupied Pascal doesn't even notice the hat whereas the neurotic Karine, by now eager to hold on to Ludovic, salutes the blatant necktie.

The friendship becomes an affair, inevitably. But, far less inevitably, it keeps providing felicity. It even drives the errant Pascal and Karine to reform, as nearly as such creatures can, by turning absurd in the opposite direction. I must not tell you how it comes out, but remember that what appears to be a fairy-tale ending is not, if you look closely, all that fairy-tale-ish. Perhaps not even all that happy. And certainly not an ending.

If this were all there is to *Cousin, Cousine,* it would still not be inconsiderable; but there is much, much more. There is, first off, a large gallery of supporting characters of widely divergent ages and importance, yet all are observed with the same light, but not casual, good-natured lucidity that cuts to the bone. Only "cuts" is too harsh; could we say *caresses* to the bone? For these·people—good, bad, silly, sensible—are treated with an insight finely balanced between mockery and compassion; but the mockery is never cruel, the compassion never weepy.

More remarkable yet is the sense of French bourgeois family existence that is evoked in all its ramifications and permutations without the slightest self-importance and with a fluid rapidity that obliges you to keep your eyes and ears wide open. For existential truths reveal themselves untheatrically, with a minimum of to-do, to those who can read the fine print and hear the confidential whisper on the wing. Beyond that, the film is full of the funny little roughnesses and smoothnesses that make up quotidian, universal living. Call it the aroma of happenstance, the feel of being alive, or just plain miracles—oh, very humble, unradical miracles—along the path from morning to night to morning, from light to dark and back again. Tacchella records them astutely and sympathetically, a few times with a little exaggeration, just enough to make us realize they are miracles as well as daily occurrences.

There may be something in the basic mismatedness of the two main couples that is a trifle schematic and improbable; there may also be something oversimplified about the ending, though it is wisely enveloped in ambiguity. But everything in between is both totally believable and freshly observed, down to the very looks of the actors that are as unactorish as they are palpably right. The possible exception is the Pascal of Guy Marchand, who, even for his second-rate conquests, could be an iota more attractive.

Do not conclude from this that the virtues of the film are somehow literary. Nothing could be more filmic than Tacchella's extraordinary pacing made up of those discreet rubatos and accelerandos that help convey the exquisite little eccentricities of *Cousin, Cousine,* and here the expert editing of Agnès Guillemot was of paramount help. Even the interiors and landscapes seem free of premeditation, and Georges Lendi, the cinematographer, uses his often unconventional-seeming subdued or back lighting not because it is unusual, but because that is the way things often are lit, if only we stopped to consider. Gérard Anfosso's music is prankish without being coy, and generally uninsistent. In its least utterances, gestures, or silences, the film is saying something; nothing goes to waste.

There are large observations: the first weekend in bed of Marthe and
292 Ludovic (played with bursting authenticity by Marie-Christine Barrault and

Victor Lanoux) is quite possibly the most accurate representation of happy, healthy sensuality I have seen on film—because it is only partly about actual sex, and much more about the exhilarating sexualization of words and actions that surround the act, cradle and cushion it. There are filigree observations: Marthe coming to the Christmas party with a prim brassiere under her see-through blouse, and leaving, after happiness has struck, without that confining garment. This liberation is in no way underlined; you catch it, if you do, to your own conspiratorial delight.

How does Alphonse Allais figure in this? Ludovic's smiling account of why, in his bachelor days, he never locked his door at night comes from one of Allais's humorous sketches. And why the title, *Cousin, Cousine*, male and female cousin? Because in large, tight European families the first chance of an adolescent to fall in love is with a cousin of the opposite sex. Some of this is actually glimpsed in the film, but the very love of Marthe and Ludovic, who are distantly related, is as unworldly, undiluted, and surprising despite its expectability, as that of cousins.

My Friends was carefully planned by Pietro Germi, who died before he could shoot it; Mario Monicelli directed it very much to Germi's specifications. Germi was a fine but less than great director whose best films, such as *In the Name of the Law* and *The Road to Hope*, are not so well known as his merely good ones, e.g., *Divorce Italian Style*. Monicelli is the same sort of director, whose *Big Deal on Madonna Street* is justly remembered as an uproarious comedy, but whose best film, *The Organizer*, is hardly ever revived (how sad that young people are growing up knowing by heart every film of Hawks and Ford, but ignorant of *The Organizer!*), and whose second-best, *The Great War*, was shown here only briefly, and then in a badly cut version.

Well, *My Friends* is hardly up to either director's best, even though it has outgrossed *Jaws* in Italy—in fact, become the Italian *Jaws*. The subject is, you might say, *I Vitelloni* a quarter century older (though without any of the genius of Fellini's masterpiece): five amply middle-aged men who refuse to settle into predictability and prefer to go off periodically "gypsying" together on shorter or longer pilgrimages to their not quite irretrievable youth. These journeys backward, but also forward into the unknown, tend to end up as oversized schoolboy pranks: some screamingly funny, some tasteless, and some dragged out beyond comic justification. Since Germi's Florence is larger than Fellini's Rimini, and these men older and (with one exception) more affluent than the *vitelloni*, the escapades are on a grander scale, though no less ludicrous.

The problem, aside from the tendency of the humor to flag, is a certain lack of rhythm and form. Though the death of one of the practical jokers provides a kind of ending—albeit an open one—there is no beginning or middle, what with flashbacks within flashbacks and a time sequence not artfully enough scrambled, so that instead of a wonderful, crazy continuum, we actually get confusion and anticlimax. Moreover, the minor characters do not come sufficiently alive; not only are they merely pawns, but they also fail to add up (as they so richly do in *I Vitelloni*) to a panorama of the society   293 against which our anarchic "gypsies" play out their madcap games, rebelling not so much against conformity as against the process of aging.

Furthermore, the film is deficient in emotional shading. A neglected wife and children, a schoolgirl with sexually ambidextrous tastes, a mean little man whose greed turns him into a most malleable dupe, a humorlessly academic son—these figures deserve a little melancholy commiseration, a touch of that pathos that would make *My Friends* ultimately not less, but more of a comedy than it is.

Even so, I was astounded by the hate-filled obtuseness with which the film was received by the majority of a sneak-preview audience. American movie-goers, I suspect, don't mind outrageous escapism, but are disturbed by real-looking social irresponsibility. For *My Friends,* however mildly, glorifies antisocial behavior. But there are unquestionably fine performances from Gastone Moschin as an amorous architect, Philippe Noiret (badly dubbed into Italian) as a devil-may-care crime reporter, Adolfo Celi as a cynical surgeon, Bernard Blier as a querulous patsy, and several others. Only the gifted Ugo Tognazzi is not quite right for the part of a down-at-heel aristocrat that would have suited Vittorio De Sica to perfection. Luigi Kuveiller has photographed with decent restraint, Carlo Rustichelli's score is palatable soda pop, and Ruggero Mastroianni proves again that he is one of Italy's most dazzling editors.

August 2, 1976

Time Measured in Heartbeats

I CANNOT RECALL offhand another first film quite like Bertrand Tavernier's astonishing *The Clockmaker.* Based on a Simenon novel, it might have been no more than a suspense melodrama—which it still is, only turned inside out, to become a conspectus of the social and psychic problems underlying so-called senseless violence. The *scènes à faire* are deliberately omitted: the murder is not shown at all, the trial scene reduced to a few seconds. What the film does show is how Michel Descombes, watch dealer and repairer and solid citizen of Lyons, comes to understand what made his son kill an industrial policeman, what bourgeois capitalism really means, and what love between a boy and a girl, or a son and a father, is all about. A crime novel is converted into a film about understanding.

The Clockmaker cannot be consumed as a popcorn-drenched, Saturday-night movie—though even that way it cannot fail to register. Tavernier's film is more like a poem taking place in a world of details: visual and verbal details, and, above all, envenomed pinpricks of irony. There is nothing "big" about the film: physical violence never exceeds inexpert punches among middle-aged men; voices are raised only once or twice, and then quickly slink away; though sadness comes to displace oxygen in the air, no one ever cries. Yet the film is bursting with barely contained moral, social, and political indignation, love that cannot quite find the right words, pain too proud to strip in public.

The pretitle sequence magisterially sets the tone. A little girl is looking out of a speeding night train when not wandering forlornly through its corridors. Nothing much catches her eye until, quite casually, an automobile is burning in the night. As if aware that a world order has gone awry, the camera leaps off the train to concentrate on that disturbing bonfire. Two master images have been introduced: a small child alone in the disorienting night; a formerly healthy car, not overturned, the victim of vandalism.

With measured, dignified tempo, but through scenes bustling with life and insight, the film proceeds to catch up with this brace of symbolic images. Michel Descombes, first seen enjoying some hearty food and pungent but mostly uncommitted political talk with friends in a bistro, is presently drawn into a police case. His son has made off with the pickup truck and abandoned it after a flat tire. Commissioner Guiboud gradually reveals the known facts: young Bernard Descombes and his girl friend Liliane, of whose very existence the father was unaware, killed a man named Razon, set a torch to his car, and escaped.

Here the film, as it were, trifurcates. What it emphatically is not is a tale of pursuit of the missing pair. What it depicts is, first, Michel's painstaking development of awareness that his son's estrangement from him (after the boy's mother left and, subsequently, died) is not an incomprehensible and unbridgeable gap; second, a process of sociopolitical discovery, whereby Michel learns what bourgeois society does *for* its fat-cat beneficiaries and *against* those who are at their mercy; and, third, a burgeoning relationship between Commissioner Guiboud and Descombes that, finally and sadly, comes to nothing—even an honest cop, it would seem, is no fit company for a man of goodwill in today's society.

The three themes are cunningly imbricated and implicated with one another, and wrapped in a visual refrain of urban affluence. At irregular but strategic intervals, the city of Lyons, famous for its southern comfortableness, stodgy prosperity, and Rabelaisian eating, makes its appearance through opulently sunny townscapes, massive monuments, or the omnipresence of comestibles: outdoor or indoor markets, ubiquitous food shops and restaurants, people eating in all kinds of surroundings while, in newscasts or conversations, the essential events of life whiz by them. The food image becomes more and more obsessive and—in a film in which even small incidents, overheard snippets of talk, trivial utterances of radio announcers echo one another with seemingly fortuitous but incisive irony—eventually dominates the action.

We first meet Descombes at a bistro where, in the company of his cronies, he particularly revels in the onions, so prevalent in meridional cookery. As a bachelor, he boasts, he can consume them more unrestrainedly than his married friends can. With extreme gustatory relish, he pronounces the first syllable of *oignons* as a diphthong, contrary to modern French usage. By drawlingly diphthongizing it, he not only indulges in escalation of esurience   295 but also forces us to attend to and recall the (unstated) locution, *c'est mes oignons*—it's my business: eating well, solipsistically enjoying myself, is my affair.

But life, as Michel Descombes is soon to learn, is not just his affair. A decent man, a good and tolerant father, a citizen of liberal though inactive persuasions, he finds that the world is a more constricting, restrictive, brutally unjust place than he ever realized. "The big clocks are always the most off," he says at one point, without yet fathoming that the world is the biggest clock of all. And Tavernier proceeds to unfurl in manifold but subtle ways the insidious modes of social oppression that frustrate the human soul. In what is—incredibly—his first film, he deploys uncanny tact and resourcefulness with camera, dialogue, and cast.

Take the camera first. When Guiboud is about to tell Descombes that his son is wanted for murder, he considerately makes him sit in his, the commissioner's, car, with its door left open. The standing Guiboud now tells the seated Descombes the shattering news, then closes the car door on him. From a two-shot, the director cuts to a long shot of the car in the rural setting, positioned at a diagonal in the frame. In the next shot, Guiboud is sitting beside the dazed father. The long shot, accompanied by the slamming of the door, suggests the sudden isolation of the previously easeful burgher in an alien countryside (where the truck was abandoned), the diagonal creating further asymmetry and distanciation. It also tactfully averts the eye from the first and most dehumanizing shock and grief. Finally, by hiding Michel inside a car and letting the slammed door speak out, it conveys enclosure and entrapment.

Or consider the visual refrain of Razon's car, first sighted as a burning, inexplicable, almost surreal mystery. Soon it is viewed objectively as a charred symbol of snuffed-out privilege, having belonged to a murdered management spy among factory workers who was also a Fascist, rapist, and swine. But already a grinning yellow journalist is urging his photographer to take tendentious pictures of the burnt upholstery, the incinerated "corpse" of a car, as he calls it with fulsome gusto, adding that there is nothing like a car carcass, glimpsed in news photos or on television, to make housewives cry. The killing of a car proves much more heinous—as we get to see from televised reactions—than that of a man. But this image of a helpless victim of "leftist" assassins is not the dead vehicle's last avatar. Soon it becomes a tourist attraction where mindless couples pose for snapshots.

Tavernier's visual sense is acute in camera movements and placements alike. There is, for instance, the slight titubation of the camera when Michel comes home after a night of carousing, or the way the camera catches its last sight of Guiboud from an unexpected vantage point, as if over the shoulder of the departing Michel, who has broken with the commissioner forever. And notice how the camera observes Michel in self-effacing, peripheral profile in the little police waiting room at St.-Brieuc, while a secretary officiously banging away on her typewriter is in the center of the image, dominating the frame. Again, how fleetingly the camera takes in Liliane, as she and Bernard are being flown back to Lyons, fastening her seat belt—we only just notice the handcuffs. What could be more grim than a chained girl supererogatorily strapping herself to her seat? And it is caught with an off-handedness that makes it all the sadder.

The script is brilliant. Note, for example, how Descombes eats less and less as the movie progresses, even as Guiboud keeps eating, sometimes from Descombes's very plate. Or think how much is told about Guiboud's relationship with his unseen daughter by her spoiled Afghan he takes for a grumbling walk, and by the quiet defiance with which he, who rebuked a subaltern for littering, litters the daughter's palatial doorstep. Consider, too, the scene where Descombes and Guiboud exchange confidences about experiences they have had in public with small children: how revealingly each interprets such an incident his own way, and how, digressive as the scene seems, it tells us all about why the abyss between these two worthy and considerate men will have to widen irreparably.

The dialogue shines throughout, is full of unexpectednesses that nevertheless ring true—whether Guiboud reads a jingoistic poem found on the murdered man and exclaims, "I knew it was Claudel *before* I saw the signature," or whether a disenchanted Descombes says to the fancy, hypocritical lawyer defending his son, in a tone quiet with disgust, "And I don't like your pink shirt." Every minor character has his own language or tonality, which the competent but curt subtitles cannot quite render. Dry wit is always there: "France has fifty million inhabitants and twenty million informers"; poetry is never far away, as when, in the noisy prison visiting room, Bernard calmly tells his father, "Don't shout, articulate!" At the end of their all too brief exchange, the son cuts through the din with: "Finally you hear what interests you." Such plain-sounding dialogue is poetically charged with double entendres; at the very least, it echoes some previous statement with a significant, ironic difference.

Tavernier had the intelligence and courage to seek out for his coscenarists Jean Aurenche and Pierre Bost, who, before the New Wave swept them out of office, had worked with many major directors, often on literate scripts adapted from famous novels. The old boys emerge from retirement reinvigorated: merely in what they have put on the walls of Bernard's room they display as much ingenuity as other scenarists in pages of dialogue. There, writ large, are quotations from Céline and Alphonse Allais; by encompassing the antithetical bitterness and joviality of these writers, Bernard's personality stands out clearly even in his physical absence.

From the overworked, and lately underinspired, Philippe Sarde, Tavernier has elicited a splendid score: fitful and sparing, changing idioms from jazz to baroque, but always remarkably apposite. Pierre William Glenn's fine cinematography could have profited perhaps from a more decadent lushness; the performances, however, could not be bettered—alas, space confines me to nods to the two principals. Jean Rochefort is stunningly able to make a civilized and sympathetic cop still exude an aroma of oppression and malaise; Philippe Noiret is dazzling as the protagonist who goes from stolid decency to contained heroism through intense anger and suffering, never once overacting in the slightest, yet packing worlds of meaning into a tiny   297 change of expression, a minimal hesitancy of tongue, an almost microscopic gesture.

I hear that Tavernier's third film, *The Judge and the Murderer,* is even better; if so, it must be a masterpiece. Meanwhile, we have *The Clockmaker* to give thanks for. "I love madness and anger," Tavernier has said, and even if we don't quite accept his radical (but not party-bound) views, we respond to his love of stifled souls driven to homicide because "if you can't breathe, you must break the windows." Tavernier nearly convinces us that the plate-glass windows of our society can't be opened, only broken.

August 9, 1976

Suffering Artist, Smiling Dictator, and Smaller Fry

IF ANY FILMMAKER could do justice to the tormented genius of the great Norwegian painter Edvard Munch (1863–1944), it is Peter Watkins, who, leaving aside the question of genius, could match Munch obsession for obsession. In films (the first two for television) such as *Culloden, The War Game, Privilege, The Gladiators,* and *Punishment Park,* Watkins has explored political and social injustices past, present, and future, always with laudable intentions but often with a political paranoia that managed to undermine all of his films except *The War Game,* a harrowing quasi-documentary about what atomic bombs could do to England and, by extension, the world.

Edvard Munch is a half-documentary, half-fiction film about the earlier part of the painter's life. Its excesses are not of the Ken Russell variety: Watkins does not use an artist and his life for irresponsible, indeed masturbatory, fabrications having little or no bearing on fact. If anything, Watkins's problem is the opposite: he tries to crowd in too many facts of every sort—relevant, barely relevant, irrelevant—in a compulsive need to give his subject the vastest possible ramifications. If Watkins were making a film about a pebble dropped into a pond, he would not only show every last circular wave stirred up, he would also give you all other waves on that pond, all similar waves on neighboring ponds, copious reference to past waves, and perhaps a brief course in oceanography.

The present film is 2 hours and 47 minutes long, which is a lot, but not enough for all the things Watkins sets out to encompass. They include: social conditions in Christiania, the capital of Norway, in 1884; a medical dissertation on tuberculosis, of which the painter's mother and sister died; the ideas of Hans Jaeger, poet and reformer, who influenced Munch; a brief survey of the major artists during Munch's formative years; techniques of drawing, painting, etching, and woodcutting utilized by Munch; shots of many of Munch's works, often dwelling on details; Munch's childhood, youth, and

298

early middle years as retold from his diaries or dramatized by Watkins and his Norwegian cast, often in improvisations; summaries of the lives of Munch's family, famous and obscure friends and acquaintances, love affairs and would-be love affairs; numerous accounts of, and opinions on, Munch's works in the press and in books, or from known and unknown observers of his art; references in the voice-over narration to historic dates concurrent with the stages of Munch's life—dates culled from art, science, politics, etc. Thus if the year Munch went to Paris was, say, the year Hitler, Göring, D. H. Lawrence, or someone else famous was born, this is duly noted, as is the invention of a new weapon, a war in the Orient, or labor unrest in southern Italy.

On top of this, of course, there are the events of Munch's life, his views and feelings and, above all, reminiscences: blood-spitting tubercular attacks of his mother's, sister's, and his own; an early love affair with a pseudonymously labeled "Mrs. Heiberg" (which Watkins considers crucial for Munch's spiritual and artistic development); and experiences in the circle of young social and sexual rebels known as the Bohemians of Christiania. These three sets of themes are shown as haunting Munch's youthful and psyche, and are either repeated (with or without variations) over and over again throughout the film, or sneaked, often as mere flash frames, into almost every major episode of the movie. Thus *Edvard Munch* becomes simultaneously a biography, psychography, and iconography of Munch, as well as a kind of *monologue intérieur,* verbal and pictorial, of what went on inside the painter's mind.

An undertaking of such boundless, such manic magnitude is clearly doomed to failure, even if spread across the considerable canvas of a 167-minute film. But even if the work is ultimately a failure, it is the most magnificent failure I have seen in years, and one that nobody interested in any aspect of artistic creation can afford to miss.

For this failure comes nearer than any film I have seen to the impossible task of conveying what it means to be a painter, an artist; what creating feels like, and how it is done. To be sure, Watkins commits factual errors—from small ones, like turning Félix Vallotton into Paul Vallotton, to bigger ones, like making Munch into the only begetter of Expressionism. True, he was the most important precursor, but Gauguin, Van Gogh, and Toulouse-Lautrec also made their contributions. But this is unimportant compared to what Watkins does convey by interlocking means.

First, he shows some of Munch's masterworks actually being made—ingenious re-creations of the artist's hand drawing, brushing, jabbing—and accompanies this by voice-over explanations of the strategies involved. The explanations, though somewhat oversimplified, are still miles ahead of what we get in the standard film biographies of artists. Next, Watkins uses a great deal of extreme closeup, showing the brush, pencil, or gouge doing its work in such magnified fury or intense intimacy as other filmmakers deploy to get at some natural cataclysm or wild beasts in their lairs. Here the use of sound is particularly inventive, indeed expressionistic. Sound gets amplified, too, in aural closeup, so that a brush or pencil rages across the canvas, a knife 299 explodes inside a block of wood. At the same time, images from Munch's mind, in a stream of consciousness, are interwoven with the making of the artwork, and connections—disputable but highly suggestive—are established.

Most important, there is the cinematography of Odd Geir Saether, assisted by no fewer than three lighting experts. What these men and Watkins have achieved, with the inspired aid of various designers, is the closest possible filmic re-creation of the world of Munch's paintings and engravings. The shapes and colors are there and, better yet, the hazinesses and deliquescences, the near-abstractions and emotional charges. The film—the world—actually becomes Munch's oeuvre: every frame is perceived through Munch's eye, Munch's brush, Munch's state of soul. This is an overwhelming accomplishment that easily overcomes the awkwardnesses in the storytelling and the not infrequent clichés and banalities of the voice-over commentary.

There are other virtues. For instance, the achronological, seemingly disjointed back-and-forth movement of the film, the deliberate discrepancy between the visual and aural elements, the frequent use of music as contrasting commentary rather than mere emotional underlining, the way some memory scenes gradually build to fuller significance and understanding—all highly evocative devices, even if they do sometimes fall flat here. There is also the excellent likeness of the actors to their historical prototypes; thus August Strindberg is effectively embodied by an actual Strindberg descendant. Yet there are miscalculations: some reiteration becomes tediously repetitive; some incidents are too remotely related and fragmentary to be enriching, and rattle around distractingly if not, indeed, ludicrously.

Moreover, Watkins's hysteria—different in kind but not in degree from his protagonist's—does distort things somewhat. For example, Watkins the radical wants to show how the inhuman working conditions of the time and the resultant proliferation of TB influenced Munch's gloomy world view, further exacerbated by a stern, reactionary father. Yet much of Edvard's early exposure to TB stemmed precisely from his physician father's charitable treatment of many impecunious patients, visits on which he took the boy along, however misguidedly, to foster his Christian charity. Then, again, though Watkins does not face squarely the fact of Munch's intense misogyny, he does try to make connections between prostitution and the painter's malaise, thereby minimizing the unsettling importance of the frenzied "free love" cult—though, to be fair, this, too, is in the film.

There are only two real acting parts: Munch and Mrs. Heiberg, as the painter called his first love and mistress, a married woman. Gro Fraas is wonderful in this role: not beautiful, but intensely real, sexual, disturbed and disturbing in her ambivalence about Edvard. As Munch, Geir Westby is a good likeness even if less handsome than his prototype; his performance is conscientious but a little too subdued and inexpressive at times—which is still preferable to the customary overacting in the portrayal of neurotic artists. Watkins himself delivers the extensive narration with nice understatement and vocal suavity, though he does mispronounce foreign names and words fearsomely, and even manages to utter the last name of the poet Sigbjørn Obstfelder in two different ways.

I must repeat, however, that the very cinematography in *Edvard Munch* is a joy and an education in itself, not to mention all the other rewards of the film. Only those who insist on tidy, perspicuous 90-minute packages had better stay away. You don't get that from Watkins—or from Munch, either.

No less wholeheartedly recommended is *General Idi Amin Dada*, Barbet Schroeder's 1974 documentary about the Ugandan dictator. That statement raises two questions: Is the film really Schroeder's, and is it a documentary? It had to be made with the collaboration and complete approval of General Amin, very much to his own specifications. Certain scenes were staged especially for the film, and several cuts were coerced. Amin wasn't kidding: he held a hundred Frenchmen as hostages in Kampala, and an uncut film might have resulted in a hundred cut throats.

It's no use trying to describe this film; it has to be seen and heard as it is proffered by Amin to the eyes and ears of the camera, with his intonations and facial expressions. The general is an odd mixture of monstrousness and charm, shrewdness and stupidity, arrogance and eagerness to captivate. He is both a liar and a visionary, sordid and grandiosely unhinged, a man of many talents: murderous, hilarious, some even likable. That the Israelis scored so brilliantly off him at Entebbe should not blind us to his continuing menace; that his risibility is a fairly close real-life equivalent to the uproarious fiction of Evelyn Waugh's *Black Mischief* should not make us forget the thousands of lives the man has taken and will, no doubt, go on taking.

There are scenes in the film as funny as you have ever witnessed, but, in retrospect, you will laugh out of the other side of your mouth. This man is a scary, horrible illustration of what happens when a primitive mentality acquires absolute power—which may not be all that different from what happens when a sophisticated mind gains similar supremacy. What is eminently clear is that the very real obtuseness and the no less real acuity, which coexist in Amin, are equally dangerous. And as you watch him—governing, threatening, laughing, playing Napoleon, winning a bogus swimming event, talking to elephants—something terrible happens: some part of you ends up liking this megalomaniacal tyrant, this bloody fantast. His ugly face veers into charm, his faulty English clambers into dignity.

Is it his difference from us or his resemblance that makes Amin so fascinating? I don't know, but I'll have to think about it. And so will you, for a long time. If a film's value is measurable by its ability to linger in the memory—not the worst yardstick—*Idi Amin Dada* is decidedly something of value.

Lovers and Other Relatives is another piddling film by the distasteful Salvatore Samperi, whose obsession with incest or near-incest and leering approach to his lurid material are not quite sufficient to disguise his basic incompetence. Still, Laura Antonelli and the late Alessandro Momo are enormously charming in the leads, and one or two others also please. Remarkable, though, is the ineptitude of the distributor, who allows the name of the famous cinematographer Tonino Delli Colli to become apocopated in the American-made credits into Tonino Delli!

There is not much to be said for Lina Wertmüller's decade-old *Let's Talk About Men* beyond that it shows a playwright and stage director making her uneasy transition to film (when have four unrelated episodes, perfectly acceptable as one-act plays, ever come together into a good movie?), and that it contains some of the themes and devices that Wertmüller was to elaborate into such efficacious cinema later on. There is racy acting from Nino Manfredi, occasionally verging on excess; and there are pleasant flashes of wit, as when a bankrupt husband tells his spoiled wife who bravely announces that they can be happy in a garret, "All you know about garrets is what you saw in a production of *La Bohème* by Zeffirelli."

It is curious, though, what misunderstandings Wertmüller's work elicits. I have already heard feminists say that this is the filmmaker's only truly feminist film. Rubbish. On closer inspection, the women here are just as guilty of botched marriages and lives—through indolence, passivity, refusal to use their brains—as the men are through their "masculine" vices. The director is nothing so limited as a feminist or antifeminist; she is a wary, skeptical, ironic humanist.

But the most grandiose recent misreading of a Wertmüller film came from Dr. Bruno Bettelheim, who covered pages and pages of *The New Yorker* to tell us that *Seven Beauties* is all wrong because (a) concentration camps were not really like that, and (b) Pasqualino is approved of for having the right attitude because, at no matter what cost to his humanity, he survives. But nothing in the film indicates that Wertmüller sides with her antihero; indeed, that pitiful, forlorn expression of his on which the last frame freezes should make clear to all what a lost soul he has become. As for the view of the camps being *literally* wrong, maybe so. But so, for instance, was Shakespeare's history; yet who—except perhaps a distinguished psychiatrist—would argue that *Richard II* and *Antony and Cleopatra* are sinister misrepresentations of fact?

August 23–September 13, 1976

A Very Living Fossil

MASAKI KOBAYASHI has made at least two films of great artistic merit: *Harakiri* and the exceptionally moving trilogy, *The Human Condition*. True, his currently showing 1974 movie, *Kaseki* (Fossil), is not quite so successful, but it is still an engrossing and perhaps even ennobling piece of work whose three and a half hours go by almost too quickly. We come to know the protagonist, the rich and self-made businessman Itsuki, so well as not to want to relinquish him; since the film's end is a kind of beginning, we would gladly stay on and find out what happened. It is the feeling we have at the close of very long, gripping novels—that a world we wanted never to end has uprootingly run out on us. This is rare in the cinema; more power to Kobayashi and his scenarist Shun Inagaki for bringing Yasushi Inoue's novel to such quietly persuasive screen life.

Itsuki, the construction-business bigwig, flies to Europe with his secretary Funazu on business and pleasure. Aside from a brief trip to Spain, they stay mostly in Paris, putting up at the beautiful old St. James and Albany Hotel, and taking in everything from the Rodin Museum to the Crazy Horse Saloon. Itsuki, a widower, is a martinet, bossing around his secretary as he does his married daughters back home, yet he also has a sense of beauty and a yearning for rest. He is captivated by the quietude of Córdoba and the loftiness of Chartres, but he may be most impressed by an unknown young Japanese woman whose path in Paris occasionally crosses his. In the Ritz bar, he gets an excruciating pain that, when he is almost dragged to a physical checkup by Funazu, proves to be an inoperable duodenal cancer. He locks himself into his room, contemplates suicide, drinks, and conducts long, desperate conversations with the image of the Japanese woman (whom he has since discovered to be a Mme Marcelin, wife of an immensely wealthy, older Frenchman): she has become for him the angel of death.

Gradually, he recovers his serenity on a car trip through Burgundy, on which one of his accidental companions turns out to be Mme Marcelin. They go visiting the famous Romanesque churches; in one of them, Itsuki has a sudden sense of calmly blending into the stonework, into eternity. Returning to Japan, he does not reveal his condition, not even when his business turns out to be on the verge of bankruptcy. He works harder than ever, watches an older associate die of cancer and exchanges ideas about life with him, travels to his hometown to make up with his stepmother because of whom he ran away from home, and hopes to live long enough to go see the cherry blossoms with Mme Marcelin, who will be coming to Japan with her husband. Her image has never forsaken him; they still conduct searching imaginary dialogues.

An old army buddy shows Itsuki a piece of marble made of many-million-year-old fossils, and reminds him how, after the two of them had survived the war, they concluded they were living on borrowed time. Itsuki now sees himself doubly humbled: as a fossil whose life was but a moment to a fossilized eternity, and as a true cadaver living on scrounged time. Then the miracle occurs: the cancer proves operable after all, and he will live. The vision of Mme Marcelin no longer materializes for him, and he, in turn, begs off the trip to the cherry blossoms. He must start afresh. But how?

I have summarized the plot because it is probably the weakest element of the film, and knowing it in advance will make you concentrate on what really matters: the loving attention to character, the intense communication through concise images, the sense of the underlying sadness of existence recorded with eloquent understatement, and the earnest struggle to comprehend the meaning of life and death. In this last respect, the film is not so

303

much in the tradition of movies about people who foresee their imminent deaths, like *Dark Victory* or *Ikiru*, as in that of *The Seventh Seal*, with its pressing existential and eschatological concerns. Like Bergman's film, *Kaseki* is unable to provide final answers (as what honest work of art can?), but, unlike it, it commendably refrains from a last-minute epiphany. On the other hand, the fossil analogy does not quite work; the Japanese scenes tend to lack the richness of the European ones; and the ending is a bit arbitrary, rushed, and perhaps too inconclusive.

But how brilliantly the perceptive outsider, whether he is the protagonist Itsuki, or the director Masaki Kobayashi, perceives the essences of France and Spain; and how imaginatively we are shown the approach of death sensitizing a dying industrialist from a moderately observant tourist into a poet-philosopher. There is a Japanese finesse that, applied to the landscapes and culture of Europe, brings out certain details with an almost unprecedented sharpness. Kobayashi, moreover, is a master of mood; thus the people glimpsed in the Tuileries Gardens before Itsuki's negative prognosis exude something very different from the aura of a lonely old man awkwardly eating on a bench, seen after that death warrant. The peace of Córdoba is much more mundane than that of the cathedrals of Vézelay and Tournus; the similarities and differences between the imaginary Mme Marcelin and the real woman, who sometimes appear to Itsuki simultaneously, are strikingly and touchingly observed.

This is a film made mostly of suggestive minutiae: two hands colliding accidentally for a second on a rough-hewn stone column; a beefsteak seen alternatingly as invigorating or obscene, according to whether it appears to thwart or abet the progress of the cancer; a Burgundian landscape (explicably or inexplicably?) turning from snowy to verdant; the grim view of a room from the floor when a man has sunk to it in shock or pain; the brusque finality of a handshake between people who will never see each other again. Rarely has a man's growing understanding of what he did or failed to do been conveyed so incisively and movingly; seldom have the stages of inner development been externalized so wholly without a slip into sentimentality. And the words are worthy of the images, whether in the voice-over narration or dialogue. Take: "I used to think all women in mourning are beautiful, but women knitting are nice too"—one fewer dram of poetry, and the statement is prose; one more, and it is too fancy for a tycoon. Or: "If it was profitable, I did it. If not, I didn't. I'm not sure that that was work."

It is hard to evoke the loveliness of a film where still lifes of the most mundane objects are composed with the delicacy of Japanese flower arrangement. The texture of things is embraced by the camera until those things yield up their essences to it. And the acting is no less purposive than the camera: no intonation or expression is extended by a single unnecessary second. Shin Saburi is most affecting as he makes Itsuki deepen from toughness into fineness, always avoiding easy sympathy; Keiko Kishi is equally appealing as vision and woman, in gentle wisdom or buoyant vivacity. The supporting cast is equally fine. And always there is that marvelous rhythm of
the film: slow and stately in its general progression but often quite nervously

agitated in the individual sequences. The score, by the distinguished modernist Toru Takemitsu, aptly harks back to the chamber music of Fauré and Debussy, and is used sparingly for emotional heightening. Even if it falls short of absolute greatness, as compared to *The Human Condition,* Kobayashi's own overwhelming masterpiece, the film fails us neither artistically nor humanly.

September 27, 1976

Stereotypes, or Nearly

AN INEPTITUDE of an exotic sort is the Dutch film *Keetje Tippel,* directed by Paul Verhoeven, whose previous hit, *Turkish Delight,* I managed (luckily, it would seem) to miss. This one is based on the autobiographical writings of Neel Doff (1858–1942), a woman who rose from penury, pulmonary illness, and prostitution in Holland to wealth, respectability, and a certain literary reputation in Belgium and France. The film follows her story from the arrival of her Frisian parents and their numerous brood in Amsterdam for a life of squalor, venomous bickering, and sordid occupations—from menial jobs through whoring to posing for artists, thence to being a kept woman polished by her lover until he drops her, thence to Socialist demonstrations and marriage to a fine and very rich young man who had his eye on her all along.

What Doff (conceivably), the scenarist Gerard Soeteman (certainly), and Verhoeven (if possible, even more certainly) have wrought is a series of clichés from the lives of the poor and oppressed, and particularly the upward-mobile poor, female division. These lives are sad and touching, but, alas, not impervious to platitudinous treatment. What may have worked as a three-volume novel full of detailed and fresh observation, compressed into 104 minutes of a passing parade of novelistic and cinematic commonplaces—predictable disasters and no less predictable moments of respite—emerges amateurish and ludicrous on screen.

No one here has found a way to shake the stereotypes off the wooden shoes with which he or she plunged into the enterprise; even the score by Rogier van Otterloo (son of the famous conductor?) is, though catchy, warmed-over Georges Delerue. If there is anything original about the film—to our eyes—it is the rather crass way of treating sex and the bodily functions: a foursquare approach that may well be typically Dutch and manages to make sex almost indistinguishable from defecation. The way Verhoeven dwells on the anus and pudenda gives a whole new meaning to the word "Netherlands."

Keetje-Neel is played by Monique van de Ven with a saucy charm and the face of an indomitable urchin, but without histrionic depth. The other parts are inconsequential; only the role of the mother escapes total superficiality in one or two scenes. The virtues of the film, such as they are, are the 305 cinematography of Jan de Bont, somewhat arty but still impressive; and the many views of Amsterdam, one of the world's most watchable cities.

For total incompetence, however, there is nothing like *The Spirit of the Beehive,* by the Spaniard Victor Erice. If you have admired such fine Spanish films as Bardem's *The Death of a Cyclist* or Saura's *The Hunt* and *The Garden of Delights,* don't go to see this one, which is so bad that I only wish I could blame it all on the repressiveness of the Franco regime (the movie was made in 1973) rather than on the filmmakers. But, let's face it, a picture whose four principal characters all bear the Christian names of the performers who enact them immediately proclaims its lack of even the lowest kind of inventiveness.

This is the story of two little sisters, one good (Ana), one bad (Isabel), who see the movie *Frankenstein* in their small Castilian village circa 1940. It incites them to speculate about spirits while their father tends his bees and may work at some unspecified job somewhere in the city, and their mother does nothing visible except write letters to a French Red Cross worker who once, presumably, was her lover. There is a maid who is not afforded any personality, an anatomy lesson in the classroom that does not connect with anything, a mushrooming expedition by the father and two daughters where we are accorded a mycology lesson that does not connect with anything either.

Then Ana discovers and shelters an escaped prisoner in an abandoned barn (one of the older clichés of "serious" children's films) who gets shot by the police, and about whom we learn nothing. Thereupon Ana runs away from home and has a vision of Frankenstein's monster accosting her. She is found next morning in a coma, but is saved. The mother burns a letter destined for her ex-lover and shows a little more interest in her husband who continues to brood about his bees. The wise local doctor pontificates about the values of survival, but even the pontifications in this film are meager, almost monosyllabic. Ana goes out onto the balcony and calls for the spirit (the slain prisoner?) to come to her. End of film.

Ana is played by a pretty, haunted-looking kid, and we do find out how dark it always is inside Spanish country houses, so dark that even we take a siesta during most of the film. Erice's camera seems to suffer from arthritis, and almost never dislodges itself. Neither, for this film, should you.

Italy is represented by a pair of current offerings of no more than passing interest. The more ambitious of the two is *The Sunday Woman,* directed by that reliable but uninspired craftsman Luigi Comencini, from a script by those amiable polygraphers Age and Scarpelli. This is supposed to be a quaint murder mystery with social-critical overtones, where the milieu is meant to matter more than the mystery. Unfortunately, neither is developed with much incisiveness or believability, though there are isolated flashes of wit (sometimes ponderous) and a few pointed observations.

The basic given is the involvement of the decent, middle-class police inspector Santamaria, in the process of solving a murder, with the upper classes of Turin: industrialists and their idle wives, wealthy scions and their dubious protégés, fancy art dealers and pompous academics. Santamaria, who tries to be civilized and tolerant, is nevertheless slowed down more by the quick than by the dead, ending up as a nettled sociologist as much as a lucky criminologist. The murders are duly solved, though the plot is riddled with holes and sins against most of the canons of mystery writing; we are supposed to regale ourselves primarily on adultery, homosexuality, eccentricity, and chicanery among the upper crust, and more of the same at the bottom.

Alas, the film is more interested in surfaces than in cores, in effects than in causes, in cleverness than in clear-sightedness. Homosexuality in particular is treated in a way that is both unconvincing and patronizing, but heterosexual relationships emerge schematic and trivial too, without much laughter as the reward of this reductionism. We do get to see quite a lot of Turin, which is good news insofar as we don't usually get to see Turin in the movies, but bad news inasmuch as Turin is not that fascinating. The cinematography by Luciano Tovoli, who was launched by Antonioni's *The Passenger*, is competent but nothing more, and, in one lush garden scene, so violently green as to pass for a Saint Patrick's Day parade.

The acting is lively but not necessarily distinguished. Marcello Mastroianni plays Santamaria with his habitual mixture of suavity and diffidence, which decades of practice have refined into a choice blend, but the role offers him no chance to extend his repertoire. As a bisexual playboy, Jean-Louis Trintignant is not quite sure about when to be edgy, when jaded, but at least he resists any temptation to flashy excess. Jacqueline Bisset, with an uncharacteristic upswept hairdo, manages to look wonderfully Italian and patrician, but keeps her acting to a minimum. Whereas Trintignant loses by being dubbed, Miss Bisset seems to profit from it. Lesser roles are played either blatantly or perfunctorily, though Aldo Reggiani makes a commendable effort at infusing depth into the role of Trintignant's young lover, albeit not without occasional overacting.

The film is haunted by ghosts of similar but better films; it does, however, shine in one department. Ennio Morricone's score is possibly his best since that for *Investigation of a Citizen Above Suspicion*, which was a minor miracle. Morricone can fall flat when he tries to be symphonic, and be dull when he strives to be "modern"; but when he sticks to his graceful yet insidious (yes, insidious) little melodies, usually scored for a percussive piano cavorting against a background of sparse but mellifluous strings, he creates wonders worthy of Nino Rota and Kurt Weill. Here, again, the melody consists of a mere handful of recurring bars, but with enough subtle variations in tempo and texture to make each reiteration sweetly old and spanking new. One could do worse than go to this movie mainly as to a concert.

How Funny Can Sex Be? marks yet another step down in the always uneven but formerly sometimes dazzling oeuvre of Dino Risi. In his best films, Risi could attain a modest profundity; here, in a script he concocted with Ruggero Maccari, he is profoundly tasteless, yet not entirely unfunny. We are given eight sexual vignettes ranging from healthy vulgarity to perfect swinishness that should delight the pig in everyone in direct proportion to 307 the development of his pig-factor. Rarely, very rarely, there is even some less crude humor, and there are two irresistible performers. Giancarlo Giannini proves yet again what a varied and delicious comedian he is, switching faces, voices, and accents as you or I might change underwear (I could have said shirts, but that would be less swinish); he has, besides, more charm than a barrelful of kittens. As for his equally role-changing leading lady, Laura Antonelli, she is a more than competent actress with an incomparable loveliness that is both ribald and innocent enough to turn saints into fiends and vice versa. Armando Trovaioli's music is his usual claptrap, and the cinematography by Alfio Contini, another Antonioni discovery, is workmanlike. There is, moreover, a tremendous performance by Alberto Lionello as a transvestite, and Enrico Job's (Lina Wertmüller's husband's) make-up and costumes are joyously outrageous.

François Truffaut's fifteenth feature, *Small Change (L'Argent de poche)* is small potatoes, and this not because most of the performers are small fry—kids from two to fourteen, disporting themselves in the small town of Thiers in central France. Rather, it is a matter of nothing happening in the movie despite its continuous busyness. Some dozen principal child performers and countless ancillary ones engage in escapades ranging from falling in love with one another's mothers to falling out of windows, from administering disastrous haircuts to schoolmates to stealing the other kids' possessions, from tangling with teachers to getting their parents all tangled up. We see kids being cute, rowdy, smart, raunchy, funny, prematurely cynical, hiding deep-seated wounds—in short, running through the whole repertory of childhood as Truffaut has rehearsed it so often since his early short *Les Mistons*. Next to romantic love, in fact, the beleaguered dignity of childhood is Truffaut's principal theme; but childhood is a subject far from inexhaustible, and Truffaut's belaboring of it begins to smack less of deep understanding than of a failure to understand the meaning of growing up.

Small Change is a totally unstructured agglomeration of episodes, some charming, some ordinary, some tired and rather tiresome. It all leads up to nothing more than a lengthy tirade or homily by a sympathetic teacher who lectures his pupils about the need for parental comprehension and love. The lecture is as unimpeachable as it is platitudinous; it should be delivered, if at all, to parents rather than children, and preferably not in the presence of a paying audience whom it will bore to distraction. The film ends on a high-angle shot of a smiling throng of children, a visual commonplace to cap a verbal one. True, the film does have its brighter moments, and the kids are so well-directed as to seem entirely undirected, but that is still small change from a director who has given us the estimable *Wild Child* and the magnificent *The 400 Blows*. In the history of French cinema, which has so often brilliantly addressed itself to the problems of children—notably in *La Maternelle, Poil de Carotte, Forbidden Games,* and the seminal *Zéro de Conduite—Small Change* is rather less than a ripple.

Which is not to say that there is no audience for this movie: fanatical
Truffaldians, people nostalgic for their childhood, folks who at the mere

sight of a wide-eyed youngster outburble any infant, and miscellaneous sentimentalists. Sure, there are some gifted kids on the screen, as well as winning adults; what is lacking is a film. *Small Change* could be longer or shorter, its episodes could be totally rearranged, without making an appreciable difference. And a final word of execration must go to Helen Scott's subtitles for introducing into the already extensive repertoire of subtitular failings a new and particularly odious one—that of "free" translations. When a great writer or translator renders another writer freely, i.e., more idiosyncratically and idiomatically than the best strict translation could do, well and good. But when a hack arrogantly departs from the text in order to be "creative" as she benightedly perceives it, woe betide.

October 4–18, 1976

Of Men and Justice: A Platonic Relationship

MARCEL OPHÜLS is a sort of genius in spite of himself. Left to his own devices, he would turn out movie musicals and screwball comedies. His all-time favorite movie is *Top Hat*, and his own best-known fiction film is *Banana Peel*, on which, I'm afraid, he rather slipped up. But when he could not raise the money for more of that sort of thing, he was forced into TV documentaries to make a living. The result was *The Sorrow and the Pity*, the most important historical documentary to date, and a work of art that revolutionized the concept of nonfiction filmmaking.

The Memory of Justice is an even more ambitious undertaking than *The Sorrow and the Pity*, and the immensity of its aim is virtually the only reason for its not quite coming off. But the film is no more a failure than Pheidippides, the runner who happened to die as he delivered to Athens the stirring news of the battle of Marathon. It is a film that makes me shudder that but for a little money Ophüls might be turning out *Top Hats* and *Band Wagons* (good or bad) instead of being the magnificently mad hatter of nonfiction filmmaking who refused to get on the bandwagon of TV-style documentaries.

The new film, which appropriately takes its title from Plato, is a quest for the Platonic idea of justice. Devoting the major part of its attention to a reconstruction and reconsideration of the Nuremberg trials, it attempts to assess who was guilty there: what collective and individual guilt was in Nazi Germany, whether the prosecutors themselves were blameless (at Hiroshima, say, or Dresden, or Katyn), and what the lessons of Nuremberg were—if any. How, if at all, have they been applied to Vietnam, Algeria, Chile, and wherever else crimes are being excused in the name of war?

The two main characteristics of Ophüls's documentary work are, first, not   309 setting out with all the answers in your pocket, and, second, restlessly searching on in ever widening circles of investigation. These would seem to be standard parts of a documentarist's equipment, but are, in fact, rare as can be. Few documentarists are willing to end on a Socratic aporia, an ironic uncertainty leaving the question at least seemingly open; still fewer dare make a 287-minute movie, letting the chips fall where they hurt.

In *The Memory of Justice* there are five principal ingredients: (1) the old piece of documentary film, used as it was shot, but changed by a new commentary or a new context; (2) the old filmed material crosscut with new footage, usually of the same person or place as he, she, or it is now; (3) film clips from the past, but not directly related to the matter at hand, yet shedding a fascinating oblique light on it; (4) interviews with prominent or obscure people now, who were somehow involved with the events of the past; (5) talks with quite ordinary people uninvolved with the historic events, except by sometimes being in the places where those events occurred.

The results are prodigious. The fact that a crucifix is discernible on Admiral Dönitz's wall as he tries to justify now his former un-Christian deeds strikes a strong discordant note; that Karl Brandt, the officer in charge of Auschwitz, removing his earphones after hearing his death sentence, should carefully smooth his thus ruffled hair back into place—a small, precise military gesture—sends chills down the spine. These are *objets trouvés,* certainly, but they become, in the new context, overpowering presences, pieces imperiously demanding to be fitted into the puzzle.

Other things stem from judicious interventions of the filmmaker. Dr. Gerhard Rose, a high medical officer implicated in the inhuman experiments performed on camp inmates, relates that he was condemned to a life term in "prisons or appropriate places of confinement," and Ophüls cuts away from Rose's attractive living room to an outside view of his exquisite house and garden. The irony is quiet but devastating, and entirely the product of the filmmaker's intelligence. The aging but still beautiful Marie-Claude Vaillant-Couturier talks about that moment when, after testifying at Nuremberg about monstrous crimes she miraculously survived, she walked past the prisoners' dock with the top Nazi brass in it, and suddenly stopped in amazement: these murderers seemed to be—were—ordinary human beings. We watch the young, striking-looking woman in a sequence from a period newsreel walk past the dock, and Ophüls freezes the frame. It seems like a very tiny bit of ingenuity, but it is a stroke of genius. In that freeze, a tremendous historic and philosophical insight solidifies for us forever. And since the way a movement resumes after a freeze frame has something slightly unearthly about it, a mechanically exaggerated "life goes on" quality, the effect is even more penetrating and indelible.

I could go on enumerating high spots for pages, but better let everyone be his own Theseus in this maze. What exploring this film will also uncover is the happy sense in which Ophüls's idiosyncrasies work in his favor. Being the son of the famous movie director Max Ophüls, Marcel is very concerned with artists and show-business people, and so extends his inquiry to the absorbing related field of what the artist's role was or should be in a totalitarian society. Marcel's eagerness to direct movie musicals makes him smuggle all sorts of musical passages into his soundtrack, all kinds of show sequences into his film. This may seem frivolous at first, but soon reveals a twofold purpose—to introduce much-needed relief among demanding or harrowing stretches, and to remind us of our great gifts for escapism.

At the very least, the film is a spectacular gallery of characters, and the ideologies, insights, and delusions whose carriers they are. Abstract or seemingly abstract questions—for who can fully comprehend the idea of genocide even if it is documented by tragically eloquent film clips—become perspicuously embodied in the cogently chosen people of the film. All of them are something more than merely good or bad, right or wrong: surprising. For hardly anyone whom Ophüls examines, however briefly, fails to disclose some element of the unexpected, some extra dimension, lovable or hateful, but always the opposite of what the rest of him made us expect. Whether we agree or disagree with them, these supposed personifications of human virtues or vices are all more complex than we would have thought. Thus we become aware of what may be Ophüls's greatest insight: not so much the tragedy or comedy as the irony of the human condition.

There are some minor flaws. Ophüls brings in his family and himself in a way that crosses the line of usefulness into mild awkwardness. Certain shots are, I think, held too long, and the insouciant background life that sometimes surrounds the talking heads may get leaned on too heavily, as fine irony becomes smug sarcasm. The students in Ophüls's Princeton film seminar are too dense to deserve that much time, whether or not their denseness is the point of those scenes. Sometimes an ambience around a speaker seems too tendentiously composed; at other times, as around the wonderful Noël Favrelière, it remains too puzzling.

But these are venial errors in a film that leads up, much faster than its hours would make you think, to a sublime conclusion, Yehudi Menuhin's profound remark that "judgment should really come from within the person who has committed the crime." Most people are not up to that task, not even if a work of art like this one points the way for them. But some characters in the film are big enough for it, and even the average viewer of *The Memory of Justice* should leave the theater a little richer than he entered. That is the achievement not only of the facts so skillfully tracked down here, but also of the subtle rhythm, the dialectical progression, the all-encompassing sweep with which they have been endowed. The conclusion is something every spectator must write for himself; I hope the public will be wiser than those critics who have expressed facile contempt for this or that one among the dramatis personae. Surely the lesson of the film is that the true enemy is, with rare exceptions, within us ourselves. The rare exceptions are saints, and *they* are not likely to cast stones.

Kings of the Road is a three-hour film by Wim Wenders who, with Hans Jürgen Syberberg, is one of the two interesting German filmmakers. This movie, however, is an aimless and self-indulgent account of two supremely inarticulate youths riding through Germany in a moving van, the only moving thing about the picture. Once in a while Wenders does capture the stirring of an emotion, an incipient dilemma, some vestige of humor or pathos, but nothing is allowed to come of it. The most memorable scene is that of a man defecating in a quartz mine, with the dark feces dropping dramatically onto the white quartz. Chalk up another first for German filmmaking.

Solaris, a Russian sci-fi film by Andrei Tarkovski, is another Russian movie cut for export to about half its original length. Based on a novel by the modish Pole Stanislaw Lem, the film is inscrutable, preposterous, and rather dull. Sci-fi needs, as a bare minimum, good special effects and a big budget, neither of them forthcoming here. The film abounds in existential and metaphysical anguish and esoteric pseudoscience, both of them impenetrable and uncompelling. Eduard Artemyev's score is the usual Russian movie-music bluster, Vadim Yusov's highly-touted cinematography is routine stuff, Tarkovski's direction is plodding, and the subtitles are practically nonexistent. The acting is generally unimpressive, though Natalya Bondarchuk is nice-looking, and in one scene you can almost see her breasts through a diaphanous fabric. Chalk up another first for the Soviet cinema. The film has met with considerable displeasure in official Russian circles, which is not quite sufficient reason, I'm afraid, for our liking it.

About *Mad Dog*, an Australian western in which Dennis Hopper brings Method acting to the outback, only this: Philippe Mora, its director, is surely unsurpassed in his inability to tell a story. Whoever can find me a film more arhythmic and incoherent—indeed inept—gets a reward in the shape of the ears of a wombat. Other films by Mora are, of course, *hors de* wombat.

October 25, 1976

Coming Close to Kleist

GREAT WORKS OF ART should not be tampered with. To adapt a supreme fiction to the screen is an act of *lèse majesté*, serving the purposes of unscrupulous filmmakers eager to cash in on prefabricated glory, and audiences either too lazy to read or too impoverished in imagination to visualize what has been written. Even less than great lyric poetry can withstand translation into another language can the verbal artwork survive transposition into another, alien form. Still, if such recasting into new molds there must be, Eric Rohmer's film version of Heinrich von Kleist's 1808 novella, *The Marquise of O . . .* , is as intelligent, honest, and successful as such an undertaking can be.

Kleist's style is one of the most idiosyncratic and remarkable in German literature. In his stories, Kleist was giving vent to his romantically over-heated temperament while imposing on it strict stylistic constraints. His aim was to relate extraordinary tales in the swiftest, baldest, most factual manner; there was to be no psychologizing or editorializing, only essential narrative data, a few needed descriptive details, and a bare minimum of dialogue. But the sentences, straining hypotaxis nearly to its breaking point (in *The Marquise of O . . .* one of them is twenty-seven lines long), carry along their heavy burden of information propelled by a dire emotional urgency. True, the unusual prevalence of indirect discourse with the syntactical subordination it requires, and the extremely formal, almost forensic or hieratic, tone in which narrator and characters express themselves, suggest painstaking circumspection, if not indeed tranquillity. But the frenzy and agony of the reported actions and reactions, combined with intermittent lapses into near-monosyllabic ejaculation or nervous stichomythia, convey a quite antithetical passion and violence. In a typical Kleistian sentence one can literally feel the convulsive struggle between a vision of total disorder and a desperate rage for self-control. Kleist's very syntax moves one profoundly, and when one further recalls his short, tragic life, the pathos of even so ultimately happy a tale as that of the Marquise of O . . . becomes unbearably sad.

There is no way for a filmmaker to convey the Pyrrhic victory over chaos of Kleist's utterance on screen, even if, like Rohmer, he wisely makes the film in German and follows the text with almost fanatical fidelity. The very fact of Kleist's obsessively indirect discourse, with the wonderfully alienating device of those conditionals and subjunctives its use in German requires, cannot be rendered on film; it has to be put into direct discourse and into the characters' mouths, thus conventionalizing, de-electrifying, and slowing down the speed of thought to that of action. Rohmer's insistence on dissolves—which may be necessary to convey the passage of time—further delays what in the text hurtles ahead. Resolutions and attitudes, which Kleist can describe with tight-lipped brevity, demand on film some sort of dramatic demonstration—at the very least a tracking shot or a sudden cut to a closeup—and forthwith the well-nigh impersonal rush of the prose becomes dissipated.

Yet even the quasi-Chinese formalism of the spoken words is jettisoned by the subtitles, which modernize, abridge, and, above all, break up the hypotactic flow into parataxis. This is, for the most part, inevitable in English and in subtitles, but there is also excessive flattening as when (to give only two elementary examples) *"so wird sich das übrige finden"* shrinks to "then we'll see," and highly ceremonial *"gesegnete Leibesumstände"* shrivels into "pregnancy." Rohmer's own liberties taken with the text are minimal, and generally inventive as well as dramatically justifiable. So he changes the condition of the Marquise when impregnated from a faint to a drugged sleep that is more credible, adds a little comic relief by spelling out the jokes in which a reconciled mother and daughter indulge themselves behind the back of their unsuspecting coachman, and saves most of the story of Thinka the swan for the end, where it serves as a fitting denouement. I am rather more dubious 313 about Rohmer's rejection of suspense by making clear from the outset who the father of the unborn child is, but even this may be relatively unimportant.

What does distract and detract is the comic tone Rohmer gives to a good many scenes that are absolutely earnest in the text. This may have been all but unavoidable: a mass audience cannot help being amused by the moral scruples, the fineness of compunction, the exaltation of etiquette evinced by a bygone age. Too bad, then, for the mass audience—if not, indeed, for our overpermissive society—but in turning, however unavoidably, *The Marquise of O . . .* from a rigorous study of individual moral growth to heroic dimensions into a protocomedy, Rohmer has, charmingly and cleverly, cheapened Kleist's work. The mindless guffaws of the theater audience with which I saw the film turned my stomach just as they no doubt caused Kleist to turn in his grave.

Rohmer's direction is, as always, theatrical, but that fits in with the major part of this material. The frequent use of diagonal composition within a frame is a nice compromise between the lateralness of the stage and the depth of the camera's field, if not, indeed, the randomness of life. Note, for example, the effective shot in which the Marquise's family, diagonally lined up before her bed, are pleading with her, while her face remains hidden by the canopy, giving her noncompliance a greater inexorability. Or take the lovely recurrent long shot of a corridor in the paternal house, at the far end of which, usually in the shape of the arriving hero, drama irrupts. The effect suggests—and is worthy of—Ozu.

The casting is partly inspired—Edda Seippel as the mother, several minor parts, and especially Edith Clever, as the heroine; partly poor—Peter Lühr as the father, Otto Sander as an inappropriately yokelish brother, and, worst of all, Bruno Ganz as the Count. Ganz's popularity on the German stage and screen, which lately extends all the way to frequent appearances in French movies, seems to me inexplicable. An unprepossessing young man, the flatness of whose achingly asymmetrical face is worsened by a preternaturally cleft upper lip, he is given either to staring blankly or to whirling his eyes about patronizingly. It may be that his raffish homeliness and faintly regional accent reflect a current trend away from the typical matinee idol; even so, this poor, blunt instrument is a far cry from Kleist's aristocratic hero, described once as looking like a young god.

Edith Clever, however, besides looking delightfully like a young woman out of an Ingres or David painting, and thus fitting neatly into the tastefully devised period sets and costumes, is also a consummate actress who here conveys the needed amalgam of delicacy and strength, fusing supposedly feminine and allegedly masculine qualities (with both of which Kleist has endowed her role) into the seamless whole of a model human being.

The much-lauded "internationality" of the film proves a liability: Rohmer's Italy looks like Bavaria (where the film was shot) in its buildings and church interiors; the furniture, though delightful, is French, not Italian; the faces are strictly Teutonic. Even the priest's Latin has a German intonation.

314 The cinematography by Nestor Almendros is a bit too prettily deliquescent,

but the absence of a musical score adds sobriety to the proceedings. Rohmer's transposition of Kleist, then, is not without fault but generally impressive; it would have been even better, however, to have desisted.

November 8, 1976

A Kiss for Cinderella

Fairy tales tend to make flimsy or flabby cinematic fare. Recall only the disastrous film versions, to cite recent grievances, of *The Little Prince* and *The Blue Bird*. Amiable fantasy is harder to create on film than either the starkest realism or the most sophisticated stylization. For fantasy has to be superreal enough to make us catch our breath, yet also real enough not to make us mutter snide comments under it. And fantasy must get to both adults and children, which requires a long reach. Further, it must not remind us of fantasies gone before, because, with the possible exception of romance, nothing is more endangered by familiarity.

Bryan Forbes's *The Slipper and the Rose: The Story of Cinderella* very nearly succeeds on all counts despite a title that sounds more like a doctoral dissertation than gossamer and stardust. Forbes is a director whose achievement tends to depend directly on the quality of his scripts; he is not the kind of brilliant megalomaniac who can transform trash into a cockeyed wonder, but he is cleanly workmanlike and faithful to what is decent in a scenario, whether it is by his own hand or handed down to him. He has made some good and some undistinguished films, but almost all contain fine passages, and at least one, *The Raging Moon* (ineptly renamed *Long Ago, Tomorrow* in the United States) is a minor gem.

Forbes's last movie, *The Stepford Wives,* was calamitous, but not much more so, if at all, than the Ira Levin novel and William Goldman screenplay it was based on. That, too, was a sort of fantasy, but of a singularly mean-spirited type, with a cold kind of nastiness that eluded the director. Yet the leadenness of that film is seldom if ever present in *The Slipper and the Rose,* even if the new work does at times put its foot in it, and is not quite devoid of thorns.

The script Forbes devised with some help from his composers—for this is a musical—is both a reasonably faithful retelling of the story and a mild elaboration and modernization of it. The fabulous and the quasi-realistic or slightly deflationary elements do not quite fuse, but there is something here both for the kids around and the kid inside us, whether it is fanciful and lush or gently satirical. The film is good enough to make the brightest child laugh heartily, but even a cagey adult will find himself smiling out loud. If the disparate components fail to coalesce, they can be savored bit by bit.

There is, first of all, a feast of performances. Forbes, himself a former actor, chooses often unexpected but always apt interpreters, and gets them 315 to believe in the material and flesh out whatever may be thin and precarious. As the King, Michael Hordern, surely the cinema's most scrumptious fussbudget, grouses, blusters, and dithers away to frantic perfection, regardless of whether he has funny, unfunny, or no lines at all. Scarcely less enjoyable is Kenneth More as the Lord Chamberlain, comic yet also wistful. More, a delightful quondam comic leading man, has lately been condemned to few and feeble pictures, from which, thanks to Forbes and himself, he is herewith resoundingly rescued. And Forbes has literally coaxed out of two decades of cinematic abstention Margaret Lockwood, who had finally petered out as a sexy menace in the mid-fifties. Now, with a touch of comedy to spice up the wickedness, she plays the evil Stepmother both stylishly and with fetching restraint.

Then there is Annette Crosbie as an exquisitely harried Fairy Godmother, muddled but always muddling through. Part addled, part wryly efficient, Miss Crosbie is entirely irresistible. As the Prince's staunchest friend, Christopher Gable is youthful and winning as ever, and puts his balletic expertise to shining use. Lally Bowers makes a gracious yet unsticky Queen; as an *outré* cousin to the Prince, Julian Orchard turns snobbish oafishness into a jet of comic effervescence. And in what must be her last film role, as the Dowager Queen—so old and fragile as to make even her crotchetiness ethereal, and her celebrated querulous tones downright translucent—there is Dame Edith Evans, whom Forbes used to such good effect in *The Whisperers,* and to whom he seems here to be bidding an affectionate and affecting farewell.

But what of Cinderella and the Prince, you ask impatiently, are *they* bearable? Yes, surprisingly, despite the fact that Gemma Craven might at times be Shirley Temple (as Shirley was then), and that Richard Chamberlain actually is Richard Chamberlain. He looks good, wears his elegant costumes fastidiously, dances (and seems even to sing) creditably, and appears altogether more at home in a fairy tale than anywhere else. As for Miss Craven, she is sweet without being cloying, and—I don't know whether she is acting innocence or innocent of acting—works out handily in her prettily undemanding role. In tiny parts, such established actors as André Morell, Valentine Dyall, and not a few others, quietly heighten the general tone.

Robert and Richard Sherman's songs are less than memorable, and much less than original, but at least they are not by Leslie Bricusse (i.e., embarrassing), and one highly derivative waltz as well as two even more eclectic comedy songs do worm themselves into one's acceptance. Lyrics that rhyme "castles" and "vassals" have at least an impertinent charm, though I wish they would refrain from the bad grammar of a refrain that runs: "The rules and regulations we respect/Must be treated circumspect." Angela Morley's orchestrations lack finesse; Marc Breaux's choreography has an equal number of high and low spots, and is occasionally entrusted to such capable hands and feet as Wayne Sleep's. Julie Harris's costumes are good for the women and better yet for the men, though the glass slippers (did she design them?) are decidedly gimcrack.

We are never let down, however, by Raymond Simms's production design, helped by two mightily photogenic Austrian castles that belong in movies every bit as much as Monument Valley or the Golden Gate Bridge. And we are steadily sustained, too, by Tony Imi's marvelous cinematography, which goes from somnolent soft focus to sharply limned opulence at the drop of a slipper, and for all its flights of fancy never transgresses against good taste. There are indoor scenes that look as burnished and homey as an old pipe, followed by outdoor sequences in which nature runs riot without the colors ever becoming oppressive. Forbes moves his camera along with relaxed assurance, and errs only now and then by overextension and dawdling. Nothing great here, but generally satisfying work all around, not least from a personable cairn terrier named Fred.

Alain Tanner has always struck me as a filmmaker who conveys the dullness of Swiss life so seemingly well only because his films are so genuinely dull. This is no small achievement in its unappetizing way: it takes something to make the picturesqueness of Geneva and the eloquence of Renato Berta's cinematography add up to a little heap of misery. Tanner's scripts (which he coauthors with John Berger, the British Marxist art critic and novelist) have a way of piling up mildly absurd, faintly paradoxical incident on incident without any compelling structure or dynamic development until the mediocre or defeated people they tend to deal with end up as uncomfortable to watch as a straight-backed wooden chair is to sit in. What we experience is not so much pity for wasted human potential as tedium and the waste of our time. We end up cursing the creatures with whom we were meant to commiserate.

Jonah Who Will Be 25 in the Year 2000 is, as customary with Tanner and Berger, composed of rambling episodes from the lives of eight good people, more or less Left-oriented Genevans or French from across the border, all of whom will act as mentors to Jonah, who is about to be born to two of them. It is a vaguely revolutionary octet, whether its members work in classrooms or offices, workshops or supermarkets, or out on the land. Because all eight, as well as an older ninth, are meant to be of equal importance, they end up equally underdeveloped and unimportant. They act and fornicate in moderation, and talk incessantly and rather less compellingly than their creators seem to imagine. For all their idiosyncratic ways of teaching, interacting, and copulating, the better socialist world whose harbingers and engineers they are supposed to represent appears to be one doomed to quixotic sporadity and pretentious wordmongering. I doubt whether it can even be constructed, let alone made to work.

Typical of the invention of the film is that each character's name begins in *Ma* (e.g., Max, Mathilde, Marco, etc.), which may be a tribute to Marx and Mao or to mania and mannerism. The film is riddled with quotations from and references to everyone from Diderot to Piaget, from Rousseau to Neruda, without, however, appreciably enlivening the routinely capricious proceedings. There are a few pleasing performances, notably from Jacques Denis, Raymond Bussières, and the incomparable Miou-Miou. This bizarrely named actress, first seen to good advantage in the otherwise distasteful *Going Places*, is here nothing short of quintessentially feminine. Not all

317

that attractive or histrionically remarkable, she simply exudes the sort of naturalness, warmth, and easefulness that one has seldom encountered on film or in life. Playing a cashier who gives away supermarket goods to needy customers, she is such a perfect blend of confidence and vulnerability that we experience her legitimate prison sentence as an affront to our very well-being.

Barbet Schroeder, whose *General Idi Amin Dada* was a gruesomely fascinating documentary, now gives us *Maîtresse,* a grisly and unabsorbing tale about a professional dominatrix and her well-to-do clients who come to her to be subjected to bondage and torture, and with whom she lives in a peculiar symbiosis, though her own love affair with a young thief is relatively straight. She also has a marriage with an older man who, from afar, is both her protector and exploiter, but the details of this remain hazy.

Now, the intention seems to be to show some sort of parallel between so-called normal and so-called abnormal relationships, but this does not come off for two sovereign reasons. The "story" part of the film is superficially conceived and jerkily executed, and we never find out much more about the lovers (mechanically played by the able Bulle Ogier and Gérard Depardieu) than that they favor more or less kinky forms of lovemaking. But the "sadomasochist documentary" part of the film is told in copious detail yet without any sort of directorial inventiveness or moral or intellectual passion. Here too there is a signal lack of curiosity about getting beyond the sensational surfaces, so that the accumulation of scabrous details emerges, whether intentionally or not, as a piece of wan sensationalism. And because sensationalism cannot afford to be lackluster, *Maîtresse* fails both as serious filmmaking and as pornography.

November 15, 1976

More Than They Can Chew

Is IT POSSIBLE to have watched Jeanne Moreau's development from a band singer, through a light comedienne often playing the part of the other woman, into a leading dramatic actress of stage and screen without having fallen in love with her? The qualities she exhibited were intelligence, independence of spirit, sexual availability, and an intensity of feeling that could make her a great lover or a great whore, depending on the part. Of course, those were the roles she played, but something about her sultry, almost sulking sexiness, the dots of mockery and dashes of languor supplying her eyes with their own Morse code, the low-pitched and slightly raucous voice that could as easily taunt as promise torrid and utterly disreputable forms of bliss, suggested that, for once, the real woman could not be far behind what the actress was playing. Or that, at any rate, is what we told ourselves.

It is, therefore, sad to see this angel of eroticism grow middle-aged before our eyes. And the aging of screen idols is particularly cruel because it proceeds, as it were, by jump cuts. A woman we live with grows older almost imperceptibly, through gentle daily transitions smoothed over by love that do not catch us unaware—if we notice them at all. But to see a Moreau deeply lined, tautness grown saggy, all shapes uncertain . . . *that* hurts; no use pretending otherwise. Perhaps if she acted her age a little more, it would not bother us so much; if she did not carry on as if she were still irresistible to all men, young and old.

These melancholy reflections are prompted by *Lumière,* a film that offers us Miss Moreau as scenarist, director, and star, and disappoints us to a greater or lesser degree on all counts. The film concerns four women friends, all actresses, though one, Laura (Lucia Bosé), is married to a big-business man and semiretired. The other three are active; Sarah Dedieu (Moreau) is the most prominent of them. Already the arrogance of that name is somewhat alienating: Sarah, as in the Divine Sarah, and Dedieu yet—of God—lest we miss the point. This fiftyish Sarah is passionately loved by at least two young men: Thomas, who seems to be a set designer or assistant scriptwriter, and Heinrich Grun (which should be Grün), a brilliant young German *littérateur.* She is loved no less, though tacitly and platonically, by an older man, Grégoire, a physican.

Women adore this God-given Sarah as much as men do: they seek her advice, keep snuggling up to her, buy her presents, and part with their favorite possessions if she so much as looks at them. And Sarah is dazzling. She entertains her friends exquisitely at her gorgeous country house; reads Heinrich Grun in the original German (which Miss Moreau mispronounces heartily); puts nasturtiums in her salads and a collection of exotic cutlasses on the walls of her sumptuous Paris flat; is awarded the Diamond Prize at a grand party at the Plaza-Athénée (which the film's closing credits manage to misspell, as they also misspell the name of the composer); and when an elderly admirer, incurably ill, kills himself, his farewell letter is addressed, naturally, to her. In fact, as she says, she has everything but a child. Considering the age and mentality of some of her lovers, she may have that too.

The elder of the two other actresses is Julienne (Francine Racette), a divorced mother and quite successful performer, about to make a film with the prestigious young director Saint-Loup (note the Proustian allusion), who also courts her. Saint-Loup, needless to say, was Sarah's lover while making an earlier film with her; at the end of the shooting she, presumably, dropped him, though she says she found him good as a lover. Julienne is seduced in the crudest and most obvious way (meant to be funny) by a crude and obvious American movie star, played by Keith Carradine crudely and obviously.

The youngest woman of the group is Caroline (Caroline Cartier). She lives with Nano, a struggling scenarist, who jealously torments her when she is 319 considering a small movie role involving total nudity, or behaving flirtatiously with an American director who might cast her, or just minding her own business. Eventually she asserts herself by paying the rent for the apartment she shares with Nano and kicking him out.

It all begins at Sarah's country house as the camera circles around the outer walls of the building in a Marguerite Durasish shot, catching the women intermittently through consecutive windows, and losing them when a bit of wall obtrudes. Things soon get even more portentous, with Moreau and Bose sitting back to back in chiaroscuro, and Moreau intoning: "There are always partings. . . . There is death." The next scene has the women lunching together in the sunny garden, and the camera pans and tracks like crazy—as if standing still for a moment would relegate the shot to the nearest mausoleum. The talk is about sex. Next we have two women in artfully adjoining hammocks; the talk is again about men. Then a kite flies skyward to the accompaniment of Astor Piazzola's moody accordion score. Well, that is the kind of movie it is.

There are many learned allusions and erudite artinesses. When Sarah and Heinrich kiss in a park, the camera does a semicircular track à la *Vertigo,* to which God knows how many movies have already paid homage. Heinrich Grun gets his name from Gottfried Keller's novel *Der grüne Heinrich,* and a hefty volume of Keller's works appears mysteriously on a bedside table in the room at the Plaza-Athénée where Sarah is awaited by Heinrich for their first night of love—a room into which he checked with only a toiletry case barely large enough to hold his shaving equipment. Saint-Loup lectures Julienne: "Have you read Conrad? You must read Conrad. Not right away; maybe later on." The American movie for which Sarah does preliminary tests is entitled grandiosely *Misconnection,* though that may just be a French misconnection with the English language.

The cause of feminism receives a few perfunctory obeisances such as Laura's *cri de coeur,* "I'm sick of being my father's daughter, my husband's wife, my children's mother. I am Laura!" But the old order also gets its due when Sarah glues her ear to Laura's pregnant belly and asks, "And the baby, how is it?" "It's fine." "That's the main thing." The height of the ludicrous is reached, however, when Sarah and Heinrich interrupt their first love night to walk out onto a bridge across the Seine, where Sarah recites verbatim Bergman's rather pretentious epigraph to *The Hour of the Wolf,* and the German exclaims ecstatically, "You are the woman made for me! I am the man made for you! We must go to sleep now." If only Bergman had rhymed, we could say things go from bad to worse and from verse to bed.

No point in adducing further absurdities and pretensions. There are three authentic scenes: the one where a laconic Grégoire learns that he is doomed by leukemia, the one where a demure Julienne goes to see her ex-husband, and the one where a rejected lover clumsily proposes to Sarah. Otherwise, despite some good performances, especially from Francine Racette, there is not much to recommend this film, unless one takes the position that any film made from the feminine point of view is something to cheer about. And so it might be if it were made better, as was, for instance, Antonioni's *Le amiche*.

Dream City by Johannes Schaaf is a misadaptation of the only novel by the great Expressionist graphic artist Alfred Kubin, *The Other Side*. The novel is conceived along philosophical lines and beautifully written; the film is scarcely more than a bizarre visual fruit salad. Blessed are those who can say, "I haven't seen the movie, but I have read the book."

Sérail is picture-making of the most deplorable sort about a haunted house that consumes its tenants with the help of some mysterious women. It was written and directed by Eduardo de Gregorio, the scenarist for the atrocities of Jacques Rivette and the highfalutin obscurantism of Bertolucci's *The Spider's Stratagem*. Besides being a modish ghost story, it is also part paean to oral sexuality (perfectly all right in its place, but why here?), part feeble in-jokes, such as calling the hero, an English novelist, by the unlikely name of Eric Sange. Why? Because of the well-known producing company, Films du Losange, owned by Barbet Schroeder, the boy friend of Bulle Ogier, one of the actresses in *Sérail*. Nothing here makes much sense, nor does the film play fair with us, freely trampling across the thin line separating legitimate ambiguity from willful obfuscation. *Sérail*, moreover, is a good deal less virile in approach than its title might suggest and plays havoc with Bulle Ogier's and Marie-France Pisier's sexuality. Leslie Caron tries to act mysterious instead of trying to act; Corin Redgrave strikes poses. The picture comes to us via the New York Film Festival, where it should have stayed, along with other epicene favorites by Rivette, Fassbinder, *et al.*

December 6, 1976–January 17, 1977

Improvident, Imprudent, Impossible

ALAIN RESNAIS is a filmmaker I have always wanted to like; he has, after all, made the documentary *Nuit et brouillard (Night and Fog)*, which, along with Paul Celan's poem "Todesfuge," is one of the two best artistic treatments of the death camps I know: elegiac yet restrained, understated yet terrible. But apart from this powerful short film, how many sometimes interesting but ultimately irritating full-length failures Resnais has given us.

There was *Hiroshima, Mon Amour*, which started so well, and treated time and space in such truly innovative fashion, only to turn into simplistic propaganda and end in dragged-out dreariness. There was *Last Year in Marienbad*, where style was everywhere, but no amount of it could cover up the pretentious banality of Alain Robbe-Grillet's script and the fatuous mystification it exuded. There was *Muriel*, a sincere attempt at coming to grips with 321 the tragedy of Algeria in oblique and personal terms, but Jean Cayrol's script was not up to the task it set for itself, and Resnais's mania for fragmentation and time-scrambling was too much for the slender narrative.

Then came *La Guerre Est Finie,* a try at a more commercial film with a more commercial scenarist, Jorge Semprun; despite good performances, it was never far removed from middlebrow banality. *Je t'aime, je t'aime* represented Resnais's obverse, anti-intellectual side—his obsession with comic strips and dime novels—and was basically a piece of trivial science fiction gussied up with feeble metaphysical cant. Most disappointing of all was *Stavisky,* where an absorbing real-life story was turned into an interior decorator's fantasy, with some irrelevant Trotskyana added to give the film pseudosignificance. The script, again, was by Jorge Semprun (who has contributed his highfalutin obviousness also to the films of Costa-Gavras, in whom, however, he has found a perfect match), and seldom has fiction so trivialized fact.

Still, there remained the Resnais of *Nuit et brouillard* and some other nicely turned short films; meanwhile I had also met the man and found him quietly appealing. So when a new film of his comes along—*Providence,* in this case—I cannot encounter it without expectations engendered by his manifest directorial contributions and a certain intelligent seriousness, barring that fascination of his with Dick Tracy, Harry Dickson, and the like. Alas, *Providence,* Resnais's first English-language film, with a script by the playwright-scenarist David Mercer (best known here for *Morgan!*), strikes me as his first unmitigated disaster. There is not even the cinematography of Jean Boffety or the beauty of Olga Georges-Picot that palliated the absurdities of *Je t'aime, je t'aime.*

It is always a dangerous thing for two obsessive types to join hands. Resnais has an absolute horror of linear narration, which obliges him to graft stylistically jarring flash-forwards onto such a simple tale as *La Guerre Est Finie,* or compels him to insert gratuitous bits of Trotsky into *Stavisky,* making that film into a kind of Stoppardian *Travesties* without the humor. Mercer, on the other hand, seems wedded to the tiresome notion that this society drives decent chaps crazy, but that their craziness is better than other people's sanity—an oversimplification and distortion of complex truths with lasting appeal for simple-minded audiences, as witness the tenacious popularity of *King of Hearts* and much similar claptrap. Of this ilk were *Morgan!,* how forgotten now for all its quondam success, and several other Mercer works, notably *The Governor's Lady,* where the governor turns into a gorilla, just as the eponymous Morgan had donned a monkey suit and proceeded to behave in ever more antisocial ways.

In *Providence* no one turns into an ape, but some people turn into hairy creatures, possibly werewolves, even if it subsequently emerges that this happens only in the imagination of the dying old novelist Clive Langham (John Gielgud), who is the partially hidden narrator of the first four fifths of the film. But if these were only the boozy fantasies of a moribund ex–*bon vivant* and sophisticated author, the result might be quite amusing. Unfortunately, social and even religious allegory pullulates throughout. The novelist who pulls the strings of this imaginary plot is not only a father; he is also, in certain senses, *the* Father, an always seemingly dying but never dead God, with two more or less prodigal sons, a dead wife named Molly (for Mary?), and a mansion called Providence.

The old man imagines a convoluted scenario involving a love triangle made up of Claud (Dirk Bogarde), his legitimate son, who is or appears to be a ruthless district attorney; Kevin, his illegitimate son (David Warner), who is or appears to be a soldier-turned-revolutionary; and Claud's wife, who is or appears to be Ellen Burstyn, a fish out of water in these highly stylized Anglo-French surroundings, and giving her one thoroughly bad performance in a distinguished career. This is the sort of part that Delphine Seyrig could play in her sleep—and usually did—but which (I am guessing) does not jibe with Miss Seyrig's new-found feminist militancy. Claud has an affair with an older woman (Elaine Stritch), who may be entirely a figment of Clive's imagination and is an alter ego of Molly, even though she resembles Clive in that she, too, is dying of an incurable disease.

These fantasies, which form the insubstantial substance of the film, are sometimes interrupted by concentration-camp or police-state nightmares of the bibulous oldster, intended, I suppose, as the apocalyptic side of this film about the decline of the bourgeoisie, heightened even beyond the expressionist texture of the rest. To all of this, the concluding sequences add a kind of bittersweet, realistic descant. Matters are not helped, however, by the first four fifths of *Providence* being something like Noël Coward rewritten by Harold Pinter, and the last fifth like David Storey rewritten by Arnold Wesker.

You may have gathered that the worst thing about the script is its tone, situated at the intersection of drawing-room comedy with existential undertones, social satire with ominously metaphysical overtones, and high camp. I submit the following examples for your consideration without comment, for none is needed. "Kevin, I'm not overawed by the universe." "Going to meet an old flame, carrying a thundering prick." "You look well."—"I'm dying." "We [spouses] live in a state of unacknowledged mutual exhaustion behind which we scream . . . silently."—"Sounds binding." "Do you approve of violence, Miss Boon?"—"Certainly not!"—"Neither do I. (Pause) It reeks of spontaneity." "Do you like the way he masticates?"—"I am more interested in the way he fornicates." "What, then, is this huge, huge sense of spiritual emptiness?"—"Triviality." "I once knew a woman with tits like a spiral nebula." "The point about being conventionally unconventional is that it provides a mask behind which one can live in peace—relative peace." And so it goes, reams and reels of it.

To this, Resnais adds his own trickery, such as a camera endlessly prying into treetops and shrubbery, cityscapes carefully depersonalized so as to become a mythic Anywhere, bits of brutalist architecture, elaborate and overpowering interior decoration (Claud Langham's home is made to combine the less endearing features of a mausoleum and a set of catacombs), a terrace in front of changing painted backdrops that disorient us, an irrelevant character popping up in inappropriate locations, identical speeches repeated in different settings, and so on. There is some cleverness in the way the shots are 323 assembled, and Jacques Saulnier's décor as photographed by Ricardo Aronovich is impressively oppressive, but it all comes to very little. "How do you regard suicide?" somebody asks. "Terminal," is the supposedly witty answer, and this kind of filmmaking is, I am afraid, pretty terminal too, especially as embalmed by Miklos Rozsa's bombastically old-fashioned score.

There is also a certain insistence on unnecessarily unpleasant details, such as an extremely realistic post mortem performed on one of the actors, with whose inner organs there seems little reason to acquaint us in such loving detail. Nor is there a pressing need to show us Gielgud on the toilet, stuffing suppositories into himself, and belching—although this last may be David Mercer's *hommage* to one of his stage works, *Belcher's Luck*.

Dirk Bogarde is not particularly good at sophisticated comedy, something resembling which he is mostly called on to do here; David Warner is a little too pat in his rendering of the Mercerian crazed rebel, whose archetype he created in *Morgan!* Kathryn Leigh-Scott is pretty, but present only briefly and with nothing to do; there are also cameo appearances by two very fine dogs I take to be Belgian tervurens and an enchanting hedgehog, but the only sizable contribution is made by John Gielgud. He alone wins out over the material, and makes old Langham funny, touching, and even, for the most part, believable.

Veljko Bulajić is Marshal Tito's favorite director, and he goes in for large historic canvases of an epic character and with, whenever possible, international casts. His *Battle on the Neretva* was a gigantic tribute to a partisan victory in World War II—a film in whose enormous magnitude there rattled around a pea-sized brain. Though it seemed to have scant historic value, it had some paleontological applicability, demonstrating why the dinosaurs died out. Now Bulajić is back with *The Day That Shook the World*, based on a script he cowrote with another Yugoslav, and which was then Anglicized by Paul Jarrico's adaptation and questionable British dubbing. This time the subject is the assassination of Archduke Ferdinand at Sarajevo, which precipitated World War I.

The movie, produced by the hapless Oliver A. Unger (strictly from Unger), is a model of everything an historical film should not be. It does not make historical and political data sufficiently clear, it does not involve us in the lives of the participants, it invents some cliché figures (like the Bosnian patriot Šarac, named after a legendary horse and showing rather less intelligence) and stereotypical incidents, and it is shot with a dogged literalness and ponderosity that, though the subject is nominally libertarian, should endear it to all authoritarian heads of state. If you want a more informative and believable account of these events (even though it, too, is fictionalized), I can recommend Hans Koning's novel *Death of a Schoolboy*.

Archduke Ferdinand is played very decently under the circumstances by Christopher Plummer; Florinda Bolkan is regal as always as Duchess Sophie; and Maximilian Schell gives one of his more routine performances as the noble Šarac who does not break under the cruelest tortures. The various Yugoslav actors appear to be able enough except that Gavrilo Princip and his chums look a bit too mature for high school kids, and their having been dubbed by perfect British public-school voices is, to say the least, undermining. The cinematography by the Czech cameraman Jan Čuřík is undistinguished but competent; the music by Juan Carlos Calderón and Libuš Fišer is beastly. But the Bosnian land and townscapes—all too sparing as they are—are quite wonderful.

January 31, 1977

No Holes in the Swiss

It is sad but unsurprising that the mediocre and pretentious Alain Tanner should be considered Switzerland's premier filmmaker when that title clearly belongs to Claude Goretta. Goretta's second feature film, *The Invitation,* had that eccentric, slightly incongruous quality that characterizes human behavior when it is latched on to by an eye that is both penetrating and poetic and recognizes the quirk-atoms of which matter-of-fact reality is composed. This dazzling but still slightly unsteady work is now surpassed by Goretta's third feature, *Pas si méchant que ça,* for which the banal English title, *The Wonderful Crook,* is totally unacceptable. A true, even if seemingly farfetched, tale is told here with unaffected brilliance, with stunning control of both the cinematic medium and a *vérité* far beyond mere *cinéma.*

Not So Bad As All That, as the film should be called, is the story of a small manufacturer of wooden furniture who can no longer meet his payroll owing to competition from plastics. He resorts to a double life—a cloak of outwardly respectable Swiss-bourgeois family living lined with secret Robin Hoodish crime. With his official life come a sweet wife and child and responsibilities to a difficult father; with his clandestine one, breakneck adventure and a funny-romantic love affair that ultimately turns heartbreaking. *The Wonderful Crook* (ugh!) is a film to which laughter and tears come in the most natural way: unpredictably, pell-mell, and irresistibly.

What makes this picture so extraordinary is the amount of truth and poetry it carries with such unostentatious ease that casual moviegoers will miss a great deal of it, though even for them there is enough inventive clowning to make the experience worthwhile. For underneath the clever yet apparently simple plot lies the most acute analysis of human differences and similarities within differences, of the clash between legality and morality, of the contradictions in various lovers' attitudes toward one another and toward love itself—the very thing that gives love its bittersweet, tragicomic, and wholly irreplaceable savor.

The Wonderful Crook is a film about some of our most vital problems, stated so quietly, subtly, and originally that the worst mistake would be to see in it only its wistfully delicious story. It is, first of all, about the impossibility of   325 doing good—all the good that is within oneself—without falling afoul of someone or something. Pierre, the hero, loves both his wife and mistress, and manages, miraculously, to satisfy both these women who believe in the indivisibility of love. Nevertheless, with the best of wills, he is almost intangibly depriving them both. For his true love is for wood: living, breathing wood, which, when converted into furniture, continues to make little sighing, wheezing sounds at night; wood with grain running through it like veins that Pierre can trace with his eyes and fingers as lovingly as he ever scrutinized the skin of a beloved woman.

But there are many themes here, harmoniously interwoven. Take the relationship of Pierre and his father, a dour, taciturn man who cannot verbalize his feelings. While Pierre merely toils in the paternal furniture workshop, he has no true understanding of the work of his father. Then, when the old man has a stroke, loses his speech, and becomes partially paralyzed, Pierre has to take over the business and begins to understand what it is to care and be unable to share one's worries with even those nearest to one. But the father dies and there can be no communication. And this entire father-son nexus is given an ironic, comic-strip commentary in the playlet about William Tell that Pierre and his cronies put on at a children's benefit (note the irony in that, too!)—a skit about Switzerland's legendary hero whom paternal love leads to the liberation of his country from the Austrian yoke. Yet that country is apprehending and punishing Pierre for fulfilling both his filial obligations to his father's business, and his "paternal" duties to his employees. All this, however, would be of little avail without the director's technical mastery.

The chief components of Goretta's style are foreshortening and pregnancy. Scene after scene is pared down to its essentials, forgoing establishing shots and incidentals for the sake of suggestive reverberations from the preceding scene; even as we are working out the full meaning of what we see, it becomes enriched by what went before. An entire bank robbery may be captured in a single concentrated image, with sound effects and visual elements aptly complementing each other. Some new furniture in Nelly's, the postmistress's apartment, tells us about the developing relationship between her and Pierre; scenes of domesticity with Marthe, the wife, are cut from to similar scenes that, we discover suddenly, take place in Nelly's apartment. A fire at a happy picnicking ground evokes fires at a garbage dump where Pierre had to burn brand-new, unsold furniture. A funny light beam dances on the window of a bank; only by degrees do we realize that Pierre is in mid-robbery, receiving a signal from his new accomplice, Nelly.

Such sudden insights or gradual revelations need to be backed up by intensity of images and evocative juxtaposition. Consider the following bit of montage. We watch Pierre holding Marthe as she practices cycling around in small circles, a mysterious activity whose meaning will become clear only later, though it already conveys a playful complicity between the spouses. Cut to Pierre's father, mute in his wheelchair, being read to by a servant; she is reading from a trashy erotic novel, for which the father's reprehending eyes, unobserved by the excited reader, express utter contempt. Ironically, the passage concerns lovers who communicate wordlessly with their eyes. In the next shot, the father seems to be better; he has recovered enough to be planning a piece of furniture. Cut to Marthe as she falls off her bike. An omen? In the next shot, the father is motionless beside his work. Cut to a factory boy with a funeral wreath merrily cycling toward the boss's residence—a bike again, but how differently used.

The next shot is even more highly fraught with meaning. We see Marthe in the darkened bedroom where, we assume, she has withdrawn in grief. And she is indeed visibly mourning. But Pierre's head comes into view from below the frame, and the bereaved son pulls his wife down with him toward lovemaking. Is this disrespect for the dead? Not so, we gather; a grief, rather, to be assuaged only with something equally intense and life-affirming.

And what a remarkable sense of rhythms Goretta has! I say "rhythms" because I perceive two main kinds of rhythms in a film: one alternating between fast and slow movements, and one fluctuating between brightly lit and darker sequences. This crucial matter of rhythm in film requires more investigation than it has received so far, but I have no doubt that film needs a variety of tempos as does a piece of music, as well as the interplay of light and dark exhibited by great paintings.

Thus Goretta will slow down the frantic movement of the film to allow Pierre to brood over a foaming glass of something like Alka-Seltzer; as against that sparkling brew, his expression is doubly weary and inert. Or consider a series of shots where Pierre and Marthe are interrupted in their nocturnal lovemaking by a noise from their little son's room, and we move among the child's dark room, the brilliant whiteness of the bathroom where Pierre fetches some water for the child, and the partly illuminated bedroom where a small lamp is just enough to make Marthe's naked body incandescent against the surrounding shadows. Then, in a bit of sex play, a pillow knocks over the lamp, and all is dark again. This sequence is the equivalent of chiaroscuro in painting, cinematically spread out over several shots rather than being confined to a single image. It also corresponds, I believe, to our profound need for variety, but with a rhythmic progression giving it order.

The film is full of tiny triumphs, such as the funny little animal noise Nelly makes when Pierre asks her whether she is frightened, or that piercing image when Pierre is being hustled off by the police while in a neighboring garden someone is indifferently watering his lawn with a jet that describes niggling curlicues. There is more lightly worn penetrancy, casually tossed-off beauty, in this film than in anything since *The Clockmaker*. And the performances, exquisitely photographed by Renato Berta, could not be better. Gérard Depardieu, fresh from playing callous louts, is superbly moving as a befuddled, decent man straying ever so sweetly, but with no artificial sweetening added; note, for instance, with what minimal inflections and ever so slight hesitancies he delivers the paean to doomed wood about to be replaced by plastics.

No less fine are Marlène Jobert as Nelly, whose gradual change as she falls ever deeper in love with Pierre is delineated by almost imperceptible degrees, all the more compelling for sneaking up on us, and Dominique Labourier as Marthe, the wife who can be both generously loving and—such are life's paradoxes—blind to what is going on. The supporting players are equally impeccable, especially Michel Robin, who was so good as the hero of *The Invitation.*

Alas, the subtitles are horrible. It should have been obvious right away that someone who repeatedly uses "lay" for "lie," "alright," and "the day rises" is not the person for the subtleties of Goretta's script. This hack knows neither French nor English: *se passer* does not mean "to pass" but "to happen," *filer* is not "to go" but "to scram." You cannot render the slightly amused *"C'est plutôt rare, une demoiselle de votre genre"*—something like "It's not every day you meet a young lady of your kind"—as "I never met anyone like you"; still less does the allusion to Christ's last words by a man whose wife has left him, *"Tout est consommé"* ("It is finished"), bear translating as "Everything is burning." An important shade of meaning is lost when Nelly's *"Etre libre, ce n'est pas forcément coucher avec tout le monde"* ("To be free doesn't necessarily mean sleeping with everybody") is Englished as "I'm free. I don't sleep around." To reduce *"Je te trouve drôle quand tu te mouches"* ("I find you funny when you blow your nose"), spoken under intimate circumstances by a loving woman, to a charmless "You're strange," is not economy but sabotage. And so on, pitifully. But a director who, among other things, can come up with that superb, uninsistently symbolic final freeze frame, whose iconography I leave to you to analyze, can survive even this malpractice.

The Cookies (Les Galettes de Pont-Aven), written and directed by Joël Séria, makes every effort to be whimsical, touching, and outrageous by turns, but ends up showing mostly lots of effort. Here and there, though, a bright moment peeps through. The plot is a kind of comic version of *The Moon and Sixpence,* even if its umbrella-salesman-turned-painter does not get any closer to Tahiti than Pont-Aven, and does not even begin to approach Gauguin in talent. Still, the whimsy, on the whole, is more convincing than the pathos, and even the pathos is more so than the basic hold on reality. But Jean-Pierre Marielle has a graceful comic gift, even if he is less good at moving us, and there are juicy supporting bits from several players. Still, *galette,* besides meaning cookie, can also mean nonentity. Consider yourself warned.

But, then, *cookie,* in English, has a second meaning, too, and Dolores Mac-Donough and Jeanne Goupil are certainly sweet on the tooth.

February 7–14, 1977

Dead Film in a Dead Language

TIME AND AGAIN I have written that since *8½,* a deeply flawed but suggestive and, in a scene or two, even affecting film, Federico Fellini has become a burnt-out case. There were signs of decline even before that, but few major filmmakers have, after two or three great films and as many estimable ones, gone on to a series of abominations comparable to what Fellini has spewed out since *8½*. This, for me, includes even his one subsequent success, *Amarcord*, which I found a gross, witless, ham-fisted rehash of earlier Fellini movies, especially the incomparable *I Vitelloni*. Whoever puts these two films side by side without perceiving the later work as a lumpish travesty of the earlier one is, in my view, tasteless, mindless, or blind.

Now Fellini has become almost too obliging: as if to prove me right so palpably that even the tasteless, mindless, and blind can get it, he has dropped *Casanova* like a ten-pound weight on our toes. This film, lasting over two and a half hours, may well be the most ponderous specimen of imaginative miscarriage from a major filmmaker in cinematic history. Particularly offensive and depressing is that Fellini has taken a fascinating protagonist and very rich story only to make them as hollow and aimless as he himself must have become. If this artistic fiasco were not accompanied by boundless arrogance in Fellini's behavior and recorded utterances, one could feel profoundly sorry for the man; as it is, one can only feel revulsion.

Consider, first, Fellini's remarks about his hero, as reported by (among others) Paul Schwartzman in the *New York Times Magazine:* "There is nothing in [Casanova's] *Memoirs* . . . nothing. . . . There is no ideology, no feeling, no sentiment of even an aesthetic character; there is nothing of the eighteenth century, hence no historical or sociological critique." For Fellini, Casanova "is a stereotype . . . a meaningless universality." Well, consult any handbook on literature and learn otherwise. Thus, in *The Reader's Encyclopedia* you find that the *"Mémoires* . . . are of great interest historically"; in *The Oxford Companion to French Literature* (Casanova wrote in French) the work is called "a highly entertaining account of eighteenth-century European society." And so wherever you look.

But why not go back to the text itself, whose mere "Preface," by way of giving Fellini the lie, contains more genuine artistic expression, canny insight, and authentic human flavor than the entire movie. The seventy-two-year-old Casanova is justifying his youthful conmanship: "We avenge intelligence when we deceive a fool, and the victory is worth the effort, for a fool is encased in armor, and we do not know where to attack him." Where amorous escapades are concerned, it becomes "reciprocal deceit [that] cancels itself out, for when love enters in, both parties are usually dupes." Sophistry, to be sure, but with more than a grain of truth. And it is no man without spirit and wit who wrote: "I should consider myself guilty if I were a rich man today. I have nothing; whatever I had, I have squandered; and this consoles and justifies me." And again: "The cruelty of boredom! It can only be because they had forgotten it that the inventors of the pains of hell did not include it among them." Almost no part of this twelve-tome work is boring, whereas virtually every minute of Fellini's long film is hellishly dull.

And now read these words, so touching, poetic, elegant, and wise:

> Worthy or unworthy, my life is my subject, my subject is my life. Having lived it without ever thinking that I should take a fancy to write it, it may have an

interest which it might not have if I had lived it intending to write it in my old age. . . . Remembering the pleasures I enjoyed, I renew them, and I laugh at the pains which I have endured and which I no longer feel. A member of the universe, I speak to the air and imagine I am rendering an account of my stewardship as the majordomo does to the master, before vanishing.

If Casanova prevaricates and embellishes a little, why, so do the majordomo and the poet. But what does Fellini offer us as equivalent for such beautiful sentences? Casanova in prison, recalling an erotic adventure—retold in the movie as an abjectly animalistic parody—and wildly masturbating away.

Take only the three opening episodes of the film. First, the carnival in Venice, re-created how? Mostly as a crowd, including the doge, watching a huge sculptured female head being hoisted from the waters of the lagoon. What does this tell us? Something about a dream Fellini once had of such a head—it appeared, equally disconnectedly and gratuitously, in *Satyricon*—but nothing whatsoever about Casanova, or even about what that dream might have meant to Fellini. It is merely that he dreamed it, and, having happened to him, unexamined and uncomprehended as it remains, into the movie it goes.

Next comes the episode of the fake nun, M.M., which takes up more than half of Volume IV of the *Memoirs* but is reduced in the movie to one extended session of fornication, exhibitionism, and voyeurism. In the book, this is often touching, psychologically subtle, sociologically and historically revealing stuff that could stand by itself as a consummate short novel or piquant comedy of manners. If Fellini's version has a point, it is that Casanova and his bed partner could carry on like perverse bunny rabbits and still remain isolated from each other, each in his own game, fantasy, self-love. That is a very small point to make, particularly when you consider that most of the film—at least insofar as it is intelligible and does not strike one as mere egomaniacal improvisation—keeps making it, over and over again.

Next comes the famous incarceration in the Piombi, the notorious dungeons of Venice, and the spectacular escape. This constitutes most of the remainder of Volume IV and must be considered a true and brilliantly told adventure story. Fellini, partly because he begrudges his protagonist genuine ingenuity, determination, and fortitude, and partly because he seems no longer capable of telling a consecutive tale full of narrative incidents and human particulars, reduces the whole thing to a few picturesque shots, thus turning a rare and valiant achievement into something barren and pointless.

Surely it is time to ask ourselves where the stereotypes are here, the "meaningless universality" and, above all, the nothingness Fellini complains of. In the protagonist? In the material? Or in Fellini himself, who, having admitted to creative bankruptcy in *8½*, insists on dedicating the rest of his career to ever more crashing demonstrations of it? As the film continues, it has progressively less to do with the *Memoirs* and indulges more and more in fantasies that manage to be meaningless without even the benefit of universality.

330   Take one example out of many. There is an episode with a giantess who

puts on a circus show with a couple of dwarfs. At first she seems to be ferocious, as she Indian-wrestles with Casanova and other men, or takes on eight sturdy fellows simultaneously in an exhibition of catch-as-catch-can. Later, Casanova spies on her as she and the dwarfs take their evening bath together, and she seems to be not a bad sort at all. Our hero falls asleep outside the tent; next morning the trio has vanished, to his dismay.

What in God's name does this tell us about Casanova? Or even about Fellini, except what we already know: that he is obsessed with dwarfs and giantesses, who appear, singly or together, in almost every one of his later films. And then what? The episode doesn't even add anything to the ostensible theme of the film—a kind of antisex or antipromiscuity sermon, as Schwartzman tells us in the above-mentioned article on the basis of conversations with the director. It does not even suggest the horror of sex (if anything, the giantess, the mother figure, seems attractive but taboo—which may be Fellini's real but unanalyzed problem); it just sits there, dreary and self-indulgent.

Well, what about this antisex business? Yes, the couples are always shown copulating with most of their clothes on; they are shot as if they were in separate rooms while making love to each other; and some or all of them seem to be on a kind of trampoline during the act. This makes for the sort of bouncing that, along with bestial panting, grotesquely distended and rolling eyes, and hideously contorted mouths, might well put an impressionable soul watching it off sex altogether. But why? Is Fellini in the pay of some ultra-puritanical hellfire sect? Has he gone mad with repressed sexuality or overindulged lust? Or has he become impotent and determined to spoil what he can no longer enjoy for everyone else as well? Whatever the purpose—assuming there is one—the result is more unstructured, repetitious, witless, and ugly than most moviegoers can endure, except perhaps as some extreme form of penance. You do not go to *Casanova* when you see this film; you go to Canossa.

There are still intermittent displays of technical mastery, but much of the direction, too, smacks of reckless improvisation with no certain goal in mind; and, as usual, only possibly even more so, Fellini has not worked from a script but drifted with his moods during shooting, and urged his actors not to speak lines but mouth anything at all—numbers, names—with the real dialogue to be postsynced. Actually, the actors' own gibberish might have been more interesting.

What a mess the soundtrack is—at any rate, in this English version by Christopher Cruise, supervised by Anthony Burgess—with every kind of British, American, and foreign accent, not to mention a number of fragments of other languages, alive or dead, and often mispronounced. But every word that is supposed to come out of an on-screen mouth manages to sound like voice-over narration—quite, quite dead. Even the words are inept: "I find your improprieties facetious and totally devoid of humor." How can something facetious be totally devoid of humor?

Giuseppe Rotunno, a distinguished cinematographer, has become progressively coarsened by his services to Fellini; the vulgar effects demanded of   331 him he supplies all too dependably. Nino Rota, the once dazzling composer of Fellini's (and others') scores, seems to have become exhausted also; moreover, the attempt to blend period and present-day styles makes the music come out tentative and constricted. Danilo Donati, another old Fellini faithful, comes off best with the sets and, especially, the costumes. But outward opulence merely emphasizes the inner impoverishment.

There is very little acting from the cast here: from some because they are amateurs or because their parts are poor; from Casanova because he is Donald Sutherland. The Canadian actor is not helped, of course, by Fellini's having succeeded in making him look even less prepossessing than usual. Wooden he always was, but in the final sequence, Fellini transforms him into a kind of automaton, as he imagines himself dancing once more with a life-size doll he once made love to. But when it comes to being an automaton, Sutherland is ahead of Fellini by a good many years.

For the rest of the cast, Fellini continues, with a few exceptions, to seek out some of the most freakish and nauseating actors and amateurs and to stuff his films with them. For this sort of thing, his genius remains unabated, which may come in handy when he flunks out of movies: it should get him a job running a circus or a freak show. At least he will then be rid of Bernardino Zapponi, the Latin teacher who became his usual coscenarist starting with *Satyricon,* and whose ideas are as dead as his language, though not half so beautiful.

February 21, 1977

German and Gimcrack

A FESTIVAL of a dozen films by Rainer Werner Fassbinder at the New Yorker Theater has been launched with the American premiere of *Mother Küsters Goes to Heaven.* Fassbinder, who started in the avant-garde theater, is a thirty-one-year-old German filmmaker who turns out movies the way other people shed dandruff, and is generally considered the new Godard or, at the very least, the *Wunderkind* of the German cinema. The main influences on him would seem to be Brecht and Warhol, the unendurably static Jean-Marie Straub and the souped-up second-rate American action directors, which shows that, if nothing else, he is catholic to the point of self-contradiction. He works with a repertory company of nonactors who speak with minimal inflection and move with a certain excess of jerkiness or lethargy, whether deliberately or because they can't do any better would be hard to say. He adapts, writes, or coauthors his screenplays, which are usually fairly static, and tend to take place within extremely narrow confines. This cuts production costs, but also makes for feelings of claustrophobia in the viewers.

The plots are usually simplistic tales of the decline or, more rarely, salvation of marginal figures from the petit bourgeoisie or proletariat. These characters are often quite appreciably stupid, and almost always embroiled in sordid family squabbles or squalid lovers' quarrels. Though only one film deals overtly with homosexuals, what strikes me as a militantly homosexual atmosphere hovers over the others: a detached, almost deadpan, rendering of outrageous goings-on among people in whom a single characteristic is often exaggerated to the point of camp. Obligatory scenes of campy grotesquerie take place in seedy bars or kitchens, Fassbinder's favorite locales, and *Mother Küsters* has its share of these.

The movies are made on extremely low budgets and show it. The Fassbinder acting company, which sometimes includes the director himself, is made up mostly of rather unappetizing specimens of both sexes; one of the few exceptions is Karlheinz Böhm, the son of the noted conductor, who has both looks and talent. An aura of arrogance is everywhere, as if Fassbinder were saying, "I can slap movies together as fast and loose as I wish because I am a *Wunderkind.*" The procedure, I am afraid, makes him into a bit of *Blunderkind.* He turns out, as I see it, two kinds of movies: bad ones and not-so-bad ones. *Mother Küsters* is one of the latter.

This is the story of elderly, working-class Mrs. Küsters, whose husband suddenly goes berserk and kills one of his factory bosses and himself. While the press exploits the good woman in various ways, her children more or less abandon her. She seeks help wherever people will talk to her and aid her in restoring her husband's good name. This is offered her first by the Communist party, then by the anarchists, but both finally leave her high and dry. At last, she goes home with the janitor at the magazine building where she has gone to stage a sit-in; the chap is a widower and has a good dinner waiting at home.

It is a perfectly serviceable story, but Fassbinder develops it with his customary mixture of heavy underscoring and cavalier offhandedness. Occasionally there is some satiric bite, but more often the film contents itself with facile and predictable observations, which the director now shoots with greater assurance than before, but still without particular distinction. Here the ending happens to be happy; it could just as easily have been otherwise. The acting is generally rudimentary or, in the case of the repellent Irm Hermann and Gottfried John, downright poor; only the aforementioned Böhm and, at times, Ingrid Caven seem to know what they are doing and how to do it. Michael Ballhaus's cinematography is just adequate, and does nothing to counteract the general air of stasis and insignificance. Still, the film is not offensive, which, for Fassbinder, is pretty good.

Aguirre, the Wrath of God, is a 1972 film by the German director Werner Herzog about a 1560 expedition by Spanish conquistadors in search of El Dorado. Based on some available historical data (I gather), the film recreates what might have happened when, the jungle having proved impenetrable, Don Pedro de Ursua was appointed to lead a scouting party of forty Spaniards and Inca slaves to explore the Amazon on rafts. Ursua took along his wife, the brave and beautiful Iñez, while Don Lope de Aguirre, the second-in-command, took his adored fifteen-year-old daughter, Flores. 333

Among the forty men were also a priest and the nobleman Don Fernando de Guzman. Ursua was apparently overthrown by the crazed Aguirre, who, with the connivance of the priest, appointed Guzman emperor of the new realm of El Dorado.

Eventually, Ursua was hanged and Guzman assassinated, and the fair Iñez walked off into the jungle to certain death; Indians, disease, hunger, and other calamities slowly decimated the little troop. At last, the by now totally insane Aguirre, one of the last dying survivors, declared himself the scourge of God and proposed to found a dynasty with his dead daughter as the last remaining raft drifted toward doom.

Even some of these basic facts may be products of Herzog's imagination, though the trouble with the film is not the excesses but the insufficiencies of that imagination. We never get inside anyone's mind, and come to understand neither Aguirre and his madness nor why the others trusted him so long. Equally incomprehensible is why Ursua and his supporters put up so feeble a defense, or why the rest of the men are so sheeplike. The two female characters remain especially nebulous, and Flores, if memory serves, doesn't even speak. Aguirre is creepy from the very beginning and surely no one Ursua would agree to as a traveling companion, let alone a second-in-command. As for the priest, he is only an easy excuse for Herzog's simplistic anticlericalism, just as the stupid, self-indulgent Guzman is an easy mark for the director-scenarist's anti-upper-class (for which read antibourgeois) sentiments. The soldiers are all lumped together as pathetic pawns of their exploiters along with the enslaved Indians and the one black slave brought along to frighten the natives.

The dialogue is rudimentary, but even the action is inchoate, draggy, almost as if shot in slow motion. There are long periods of dawdling, after which the film has a brief, spastic forward lurch, only to sink back again into lethargy. No doubt Herzog thinks this is Art, and perhaps it is even meant to convey heat, uncertainty, helplessness. But what it really does is to make it all look not like a river expedition but like underwater exploration, with the helmets and bits of armor more like divers' suits, and the movements peculiarly suitable to a deep ocean bottom. These men seem to be following not so much Ursua or Aguirre as Jacques-Yves Cousteau. And there is no finer insight into individual motivation than the simplistic assumption that greed for power and gold explains everyone and everything. So the film becomes just the slow picking off of the explorers by here an arrow, there a poison dart, yonder a spear—call it "Ten Little Non-Indians."

Now and again Herzog hits on a powerful image, as when a special trap hoists a man in the jungle to death in the treetops, or when a swarm of squealing, scrabbling marmosets invades a raft of dead or dying men. But, by and large, there is not even much visual imagination here, and the very location photography by Thomas Mauch conjures up little that could not just as well have been faked by studio technicians. Moreover, the quality of the color never transcends mere adequacy. If this was a matter of insufficient funding, my condolences to Herzog; if a deliberate notion of minimal art, the back of my hand to him.

There are no performances to speak of. There is mostly glowering and ponderous posturing, some speechifying and virtually no conversation. As Aguirre, Klaus Kinski scowls, slouches, or rants, and generally comports himself in the manner of silent-movie villains. Among the others, Ruy Guerra (Ursua) and Helena Rojo (Iñez) at least get a chance to suffer with aristocratic hauteur. About the most interesting thing in the movie is the Indian folk-style music, played on a quaint instrument that looks like a cross between an ocarina and a sea urchin.

March 14 and April 18, 1977

Northern Light

Man on the Roof is a civilized, understated thriller, of a kind that is all too rare these days. Bo Widerberg's film, based on a novel by the well-known Swedish husband-and-wife mystery-writing team of Sjöwall and Wahlöö, is made with a wary intelligence all the way. It is fully aware that however perilous and even spectacular police work can get, it is seldom if ever romantic, either in the glamorous or even in the darkly sinister sense. This is no bogus epic in which Charles Bronson or Clint Eastwood as Superstick performs wooden wonders; nor is it a lurid, picturesquely ominous *film noir*. If anything, it is a *film gris*.

Not that the weather in Stockholm, where the scene is set, is particularly gray. The light is rather of that northern, oyster-colored sort—off-white; it is the moral climate that is pure *grisaille*. The bad men are not unilaterally, unequivocally bad; at the very least they are staunch upholders of law and order whom their kinfolk and admirers consider model beings. Or they may have been driven off their rocker by injustices so great as to be clarion calls to madness. As for the good people—who, for the most part, wear the same uniform as the others, namely that of the police—they are all somewhat irritable, tired out by long work hours, and often getting so little sleep that they function in a state bordering on somnambulism. They have their internecine antipathies and, unlike in dumb Hollywood police movies, do not particularly relish their unsavory jobs.

The atmosphere, then, is not dissimilar to that in certain French movies based on Simenon novels, or indeed in that remarkable Kurosawa thriller, *High and Low*. For what is even more important than the film of fatigue that coats this film is the sense of human detail: that crime and its detection go on in an everyday world full of ordinary human frailties and decencies, ordinary shrewdnesses and stupidities, even ordinary idiosyncrasies and oddities. So we get the savor of existence surrounding and seeping into the plot and the horror of violence and bloodshed becomes both more real and more mysterious when encased in quotidian happenstance.

There are wonderful scenes here—for example, a detective waking up and finding his baby's bottom in need of wiping. Half naked, he gets out of bed and performs the rotten task; still half naked, with his genitals jiggling foolishly under his T-shirt, he tumbles back into bed with his equally half-naked and only half-awake wife for some quickie matutinal sex. Seldom have I seen sexuality so demystified on screen, but not for that reason made cheap. And the film does the same with other things. Thus when the killer of a police inspector turns by crazy yet inexorable logic into a rooftop sniper decimating the police force, the boys from homicide, though capable and hardworking, are just a little too slow to prevent major mayhem. I particularly love a scene in which a typical TV-watcher following the pursuit of the sniper on his set suddenly looks up to see the murderer look down at him through a chink in the roof. Now, there is a parable for our time!

Bright deductions are made almost as often as costly mistakes. There are no masterminds on either side of the fence, and though there are sudden, astounding twists, there are decidedly no miracles. Widerberg, who wrote as well as directed, is a man of exemplary economy: panic is conveyed by a solitary eye peering from between nocturnal curtains; an actual murder scene is extremely brief, but all the more scary for it, with the real terror lingering on—in the victim's blood that keeps reappearing like a refrain in several subsequent scenes, quite logically and presented in the most matter-of-fact way, as when fingerprints are being taken or floors washed. Departing dread drags its feet.

Particularly enlightening are the various loyalties, animosities, feuds, or just states of indifference among collaborating policemen, which turn the police world into an emblematic microcosm with its own personal and political frictions and amenities. This is superlatively conveyed by actors who are all unknown to me, but who, I am sure, would exude, even if I knew them, a marvelous sense of anonymity—of being *what* they are rather than *who* they are. Not one of these faces or voices is too good to be true, or too stereotyped to be worth attending to. Yet these people say witty or wise or searing things, but always imbued with so much spontaneous humanity as to make none of what is said feel written down or acted out.

The resolution may be somewhat obvious and anticlimactic, and the ending uncomfortably abrupt, but even this may have its justification in lifelikeness. If one or two things at the very end seem to remain unexplained, this may be a matter of missing subtitles, or of a momentary lapse in the editing (by Widerberg himself, and very canny most of the time), or of something that would be manifest to Swedes and puzzling only to us. But these are trivia in a film that is perhaps most distinguished by its lucidity, by its determination not to leave anything to chance, sleight of hand, or plain sloppiness. Robert Benton, for instance, who made *The Late Show*, might profitably have his nose rubbed in *Man on the Roof.*

This is good, solid, heartening work from Bo Widerberg, whose previous films I have found always interesting, though even the best of them—*Raven's End* and *Ådalen 31*—were slightly marred by showiness or sentimentality. None of that here. And the cinematography by Odd Geir Saether, the wizard behind *Edvard Munch*, is just right, too: none of the splendors of *Munch,* only workaday realities with an occasional marvel randomly impinging on them—exactly as in life. A special commendation must go to the score by Björn Jason Lindh, so subtle and sparing as barely to sound like music— more like the sound of Scandinavian efficiency humming through lovely but cool Stockholm.

Jabberwocky, a movie by and with some of the Monty Python crew (mostly Terry Gilliam, who directed, and Michael Palin, who stars), plummets to new depths. What wretched jokes it contains revolve almost exclusively around blood, slops, and obesity. Gore, garbage, and fat spread across this medieval pastiche as substitutes for wit, humor, and invention. If you can laugh at this, you can laugh at anything and might as well stay home working up great guffaws over the spots in your kitchen sink.

The problem with Monty Python is that their scattershot, scatterbrained approach works best—or only—with random skits going off on all sorts of tangents. They lack the breadth and persistence of vision required for a tale of some length and consistency.

April 11–May 2, 1977

Well Intentioned, Ill Conceived

JACOB THE LIAR is such a well-intentioned film that one heartily wishes it were also well done. Alas, it is plodding from beginning to end, except for one fantasy sequence that is worse—almost totally lacking in imagination. Imagination is the key: even in strictly realistic movies some kind of inventiveness is needed, some kind of delicacy, poetry, vision. Or language—in this case, a cinematic language better than humdrum, slow-moving literalness.

This East German film by Frank Beyer, from Jurek Becker's screen adaptation of his own novel, strives to remain understated in every way. Though it concerns dreadful events in a Polish ghetto in World War II just before the coming of the Russians, it scrupulously avoids any kind of sensationalism or tearjerking. When a Jewish worker is shot by a Nazi guard, we do not even see the moment of death. When another Jew hangs himself, we see his corpse only after it has been decorously laid out, the neck covered with a muffler. When a girl's parents are deported and a lover prevents the dutiful daughter from joining them, or even seeing them being marched off, it is all directed and played with the minimum of emotional self-indulgence.

These are virtues, no doubt, but they are negative virtues, perhaps even crippling ones, when there is no artistic heightening to take the place of the missing melodrama. In Greek tragedy, it was the poetry that did the trick; in Renaissance paintings of martyrs, it was the symbols of their martyrdom; in the films of Carl Dreyer and Ingmar Bergman, it is the suffering human face 337 in agonizing closeup. But *Jacob the Liar* just plods along from the grimly comic to the wryly wistful, never hitting an absolute low point and never attaining a major high one.

Jacob Heym, a former café owner and chef, is now a slave laborer like all other remotely able-bodied men of the ghetto. By a fluke, he overhears a German broadcast announcing Russian attacks on a not so very distant Polish city. He leaks the news out to the ghetto, which gives him the idea of pretending to own a strictly forbidden contraband radio and fabricating ever more encouraging accounts of alleged Russian advances. He becomes a bit of a hero and savior: the formerly mounting Jewish suicide rate drops to zero.

There are several subplots: the impeded love affair between a couple of young Jewish lovers; the little sickly neighbor girl whose parents have vanished and for whom Jacob cares; the nexus between Jacob and his best friend, Kowalski, a former barbershop owner; flashbacks to Jacob's prewar affair with a mistress he loved but wouldn't marry, so that she ended up emigrating to America with another man. All of these relationships are presented soberly and decently enough, but without true inspiration—without the telling detail, the striking image, the powerful words that would lift them out of mediocrity. There is no strong sense of either narrative progression or visual rhythm; incident follows incident unsmoothly and without cumulative force, with flashbacks turning up erratically at less than compelling moments.

The story is not especially original; it is only on a smaller scale than most such tales. It is rather impoverished in terms of incident, and what happenings it does possess are generally known to us from other movies, plays, or books on similar subjects. There is even an unwelcome similarity to *Lies My Father Told Me*, and the film may well capture the same audience. Yet *Lies*, though much more sentimental, at least did not invoke the Holocaust for added prestige and impact.

It is depressing to find people admiring a movie or other work because of the magnitude of its theme, regardless of the level on which that theme is engaged. *Jacob the Liar* has none of the slickness and crassness of *Voyage of the Damned*, for example, but it is likely to benefit from the same stock response audiences bring to "big" themes: the atom bomb, the six million Jews, black slavery and roots, a hospital for the terminally ill, and so on. Such subjects mean to elicit our automatic awe, clamor to be viewed ipso facto as lofty achievements, even if they are such poor fare as the play that just won the Pulitzer Prize and the book that garnered both a Pulitzer and a National Book Award.

Jacob is better than either *The Shadow Box* or *Roots*, but it is still pedestrian stuff: a tragic subject accosted without the requisite greatness. It is not unlike the recent movie, *Brothers*, a fictionalized version of the story of the Soledad brothers, which at least had a remarkable performance from Bernie Casey. Here, Jacob is played by the Czech Vlastimil Brodsky, best remembered for his Councilor Zedníček, the collaborationist functionary in *Closely Watched Trains*. Brodsky is a competent actor whom I have enjoyed in character parts n various Czech films. But he is not great enough to fill in what *Jacob* is lacking; his protagonist is grimy, gruff, amusing in his vaguely petulant melancholy, and sometimes even a bit touching. He does not, however, truly move us—we do not get a sense of feelings more profound and complex than the surface view communicates. On top of that, Brodsky is dubbed into German.

There is rather better work from Erwin Geschonneck, a Brechtian actor, as Kowalski. Unlike Brodsky, Geschonneck has a face and voice that impart more than the prescribed expression and the specific words. This "more" is conveyed by less—by withholding certain conventional strategies, by simplifying and muting effects, by giving us the bovinely inarticulate quality of dumb animals in pain that is singularly affecting. There is quite good work in some supporting roles, too, although the child Lena is played with a slight excess of cuteness by Manuela Simon. The cinematography is no better than the writing or direction, and the subtitles by Melvin Kornfeld are grossly inadequate. The film is recommended to people who mistake intention for achievement.

Something similar can be said about the West German movie version of Ibsen's *The Wild Duck,* adapted and directed by Hans W. Geissendorfer. It is just about impossible to transfer a great stage work to the screen for reasons I have expressed so often that my readers must be as tired of reading them as I am of writing them. But Geissendorfer has committed errors well beyond the call of the inevitable.

First, he has cast two important roles disastrously. Hjalmar Ekdal, a charming, ineffectual dreamer, must be played by a winning actor who can convey why this failure of a human being nevertheless commands so much affection and loyalty. To cast in this part Peter Kern, an obese, tallowy, devious creature with little rat's eyes is to undermine Ibsen's intention completely. For it is not the creepiness of a creep that Ibsen took pains to write about here, but the terrible inadequacy of a typical respectable citizen—just like you or me. Equally wrong is Anne Bennent as Hedwig. The girl is supposed to be fourteen (Juliet's age)—a sensitive, impressionable, romantic soul in the throes of puberty and with a strong father fixation. The part is usually played by somewhat older actresses, and, considering its demands, for good reason. To turn it into a twelve-year-old who looks in some ways very, very old and, in others, still totally childlike is to miss the point. It is to make the suicide into a freak occurrence or into a piece of heavy metaphysical symbolism in the manner of Little Father Time in *Jude the Obscure.* The effect becomes shocking rather than moving.

An even graver error is one of which Geissendorfer, as he said in an interview, is particularly proud: the slight opening up of the play to include scenes in the attic where the wild duck and other animals live. This is meant by Ibsen to be a symbolic realm, the unnatural domicile of natural forces man cannot fully harness; to show it on film does not open up a new dimension, as Geissendorfer claims, but deprives us of a greater and more important dimension—one of which he evidently knows very little—namely, the 339 imagination. With the theatrical means at his disposal, Ibsen could have easily put the attic on the stage, had he not known better than to do so.

The third inexcusable error is the omission of the last few lines of the play's dialogue with their important summation of the main theme. A less grave error is the not exactly ideal casting of some lesser parts. Jean Seberg, dubbed into German, at least looks and sounds right as Gina; but Heinz Bennent (Anne Bennent's, the Hedwig's, father) is a poor Relling, making that sensible doctor into almost as much of a fanatic as Gregers, played barely passably by Bruno Ganz. The best performance comes from Heinz Moog as Werle Senior, but I doubt that the play was intended as old Werle's tragedy. A useful contribution is made by Harry Nap's moody cinematography, which captures some of the author's implications missed by the director-adapter.

Infinitely worse yet is Walerian Borowczyk's *The Beast*, which falls at least as far below as it purports to ascend higher than pornography. The Paris-based Polish filmmaker has all the prurient vulgarity of his fellow émigré Roman Polanski, without any of the latter's talent. *The Beast*, which Borowczyk also wrote, is an awkward, stupid, schoolboyishly salacious, and, above all, pretentious and ludicrous tale about copulation between woman and beast, dwelt on lovingly, lubriciously, and, most of all, ineptly. The use of the camera, the handling of actors, and the quality of the dialogue do not exceed the abilities of a slightly backward erotomaniacal choirboy who has never before seen a movie.

The only possible reason for Borowczyk's being taken seriously by a few critics is that the poor fellows cannot believe that anyone could make such bad movies other than deliberately—scenes of supposed high tragedy emerging as outrageous farce, moments of intense eroticism making you laugh to split your sides—and thus assume that there are hidden intentions here that they must not appear to have missed. As for Borowczyk's frequent showings at certain film festivals, I can explain it only in terms of his fanatical misogyny (though, apparently, heterosexual) striking responsive chords in some homosexual festival directors. In one of the highlights of *The Beast* a woman tries to masturbate with a rose—unsuccessfully; so, as long as we have Borowczyk, at least we won't have to go around making up Polish jokes.

May 9, 1977

Only Man Is Vile

CAN A FILM—or any work of art—affect our manner of thinking and acting? More specifically, can a film about war change in any way our attitudes toward war, and thus the course of history? Probably not. The greatest works seldom even try. If I name a few truly magnificent films off the top of my head—*The Rules of the Game, Persona, I Vitelloni, L'Avventura,* Jan Troell's *Here Is Your Life,* Ermanno Olmi's *One Fine Day*—none of them tells you what to do, what the solution of your existential problems is (although Olmi's film comes close to making a statement of the sort). But these works perceive the problems of living with such minuteness and grandeur, such a sense of detail and overarching vision, that no one with an iota of sensitivity can walk away from them without his pockets crammed full of insights. How insight is put to use—if at all—remains, of course, up to the person in question. Some pockets have holes in them.

To get back to war, however, we have this week Jean-Jacques Annaud's *Black and White in Color,* a film subtle and rich in implications and creatively disturbing. It is deeply and uncompromisingly disgusted with war.

Black and White in Color is an absurd English nonequivalent for *La Victoire en chantant.* The French title comes from Marie-Joseph Chénier's *Chant du départ,* a patriotic song of the revolution sometimes called "the second 'Marseillaise,'" which begins, "Victory, singing, lifts the barrier for us." Even if this French equivalent to "America the Beautiful" does not mean much hereabouts, a title like "Victory With a Song" might still convey some ironic impact stupidly lacking in a title that merely announces a color film about blacks and whites.

Annaud's movie—his first, and all the more remarkable for it—takes place in French west central Africa at a trading post near the border of the German-held territories. World War I has already broken out, quite unbeknown to these somnolent colonies. While the Germans are training their blacks to be good little Prussian soldiers, the French allow everything except business to deteriorate: at the general store and elsewhere, mulcting the natives is the order of the day, and that is just about the only order there is. Though some blacks grumble, most of them proudly perceive themselves as true Germans or Frenchmen. In an early scene, a German officer arrives with some thoroughly drilled black porters to pick up supplies from the French, and the concision, wit, and forcefulness with which the differences between mentalities are conveyed are exemplary indeed.

The one person who is seemingly unique is Hubert Fresnoy, a young Frenchman assigned to this outpost to conduct geographical research. He is a bit of a failed *normalien,* and it must be made clear to Americans that the Ecole normale supérieure is not only the breeding ground of teachers and professors, but also the launching pad of many a French genius in the arts and sciences. As such, it has it own special slant on things, its own jargon, even its own brand of cynical humor. We encounter Fresnoy writing a letter to some distinguished master of his back at the renowned school, and sardonically informing him that Africa is not so very different from Europe, and that the geographical research to which poor results at the Ecole normale condemn one may not be so vastly inferior to the lot of a provincial schoolmaster back in France. Fresnoy also asks for the cultural news: What is our beloved Debussy up to, and what's with our dear Charles Péguy?

There is irony here, for as Fresnoy doesn't yet know, the great socialist-pacifist-Catholic poet has already fallen, gallantly leading his men to attack   341 at the Battle of the Marne. At the outpost, however, life is "normal": Rechampot, the store owner, conducts his tidy business with his near-idiot brother; Mme Rechampot, blowsy and bathycolpic, is the local slut; Caprice, another merchant, finds his marriage to the local belle going stale; the military commander, Sergeant Bosselet, drinks steadily and allows Fidèle, his native orderly, to supply him with girls, Fidèle's sister not excluded. Two missionaries, Father John of the Cross, a German-hating Alsatian, and Father Simon, an archetypal Frenchman under his cassock, haughtily trade worthless religious images for invaluable native art, in scenes worthy of Evelyn Waugh's *Black Mischief.* Yet these colonials, morally bankrupt as they are, are not the ludicrous abstractions we have met elsewhere; they are flesh-and-mud humanity, like it or not.

Six months after the outbreak of the war, the news, by accident, reaches the outpost. With immaculate idiocy, a sneak attack on the Germans, presumed to be still in the dark, is planned under the guise of patriotic fervor, though actually as the culmination of simple everyday greed. The only one to warn against this, sensibly and courageously, is Fresnoy; he is dismissed as an irrelevant and ineffectual "brain." The rest of the movie chronicles the abject failure of the coalition of soldiers, churchmen, and solid citizens putting their best black cannon fodder forward, and the emergence of Fresnoy as the one competent leader.

Too competent—for intelligence and organizational skills lead to power, which neatly corrupts our man who was so profoundly affected by news of the assassination of Jaurès, that sublime Socialist leader, himself a *normalien.* Of course, there were ominous signs: Fresnoy had written that these blacks were *almost* human, and would carefully wipe a glass handed him by a black. Fresnoy develops into a perfect military martinet, but, such is the film's artistry, we never lose sympathy for him, even as we begin to feel sorry for his worthless compatriots, whom, along with the blacks, he ruthlessly dominates. The French have become quite brave now: "Certainly we won't surrender—unless there is no alternative." The film moves forward to an ironic ending that I would rather not reveal.

Wherein lies the mastery of this matter-of-fact satire? First, in that it is unceasingly, impudently witty. Second, in that its sharpness does not exclude accurate representations of emotionally charged happenings. Above all, there is, third, the fairness: Germans and French are equally culpable and corruptible, equal exploiters of the Africans. As for the blacks, they are simpler and less spoiled but, in their way, just as absurd: they allow themselves to be led by the nose by the whites and to have yokes put around their necks by their own black brothers, who sell them into slavery. There is a total absence of knee-jerk liberalism and problack sentimentality in this film, which ought to infuriate equally all unthinking people, regardless of race, religion, or nationality. What is under attack is human nature: the root, not the branches, of our condition.

This would still not be so remarkable, were it not executed with great
artistic know-how. The script by Annaud and the novelist Georges Conchon

is admirable: full of sophisticated, literate facetiousness, yet accessible enough to any viewer possessed of an open mind. It is almost all vignettes: brief scenes that make their strong points unobtrusively, fleetly moving on without dawdling over their devastation. A litter-borne priest has, under his big, dangling crucifix, a gun resting in his lap; as the black carriers improvise a song about his stinking feet, he, uncomprehending, extols the sweetness of their singing. When the colonial war is already quite ugly enough, our Frenchmen see newspaper pictures of the horrors of European trench warfare; wistfully they observe that they have nothing so glorious to show for their effort. In the next scene, they have their own terror in the trenches.

Annaud's direction is astounding: in its general swiftness that yet knows when to linger awhile; in its attention to detail without rubbing our noses in it; in its cunning use of ambiguity and even confusion; in its absolute control of moral indignation, whose strength is in remaining unstated. The cinematography by Claude Agostini (I wouldn't be surprised if he were Tony Agostini's, that fine painter's, son) splendidly emphasizes mellowness: the great gift of the land that remains unreciprocated by its inhabitants. Pierre Bachelet's music is just right: amusing, original, and unpretentious.

Except for a somewhat monochromatic performance from Jacques Dufilho as the archcapitalist merchant, all the acting is wonderfully shaded. Most marvelous is the evolution of Jacques Spiesser's Fresnoy into a dictator. Even though he genuinely hates war, he clearly enjoys the transformation of himself. Like any good—or even bad—*normalien,* he approaches the task scientifically, determined to excel. The much more primitive Bosselet, who underneath it all is not such a bad fellow, nevertheless falls completely under Fresnoy's frigid spell, as do also the other French people, especially the wives. But Spiesser's characterization is not simplistic: Fresnoy continues to be almost chivalrously polite to these wives, even while allowing his black mistress to lord (or lady) it over them. His tidily slicked-down hair and open-faced youthfulness gradually assume an air of trig bully-boyishness and smart insolence: we can watch the change as we might the growth of a tumor under a microscope.

Equally good is Jean Carmet as the boozy Bosselet, whose first defeat, it turns out, was also his first engagement. Carmet punctuates his disreputableness with vestiges of gallantry, his disintegration still allowing for spurts of decency or even energy; he is very much a Gallic Graham Greene character on the way to absinthe-soaked dry rot, redeemed not by Catholicism but by despotism. The smaller roles are all ably filled, and, for once, even the English subtitles are adequate except when the jingoistic, warmongering lyrics of the "Marseillaise" are bowdlerized into nobly correct sentiments. It is instructive to compare Annaud's use of the anthem, by the way, with its exact opposite in such movies as *Casablanca* or Renoir's *La Marseillaise.*

Black and White in Color might conceivably be faulted for treating death and other horrors of war as casually as everything else. But this is right; the greater horror is reserved for survival. The way one survives here may be a worse kind of dying. But can we believe that such films will avert even a 343 single blow from falling anywhere in this world? I doubt it. Still, we must keep trying, just as we keep pressing our trousers, even if all we do in them afterward is sit and accumulate wrinkles.

May 16, 1977

Failed Loves

CARLOS SAURA is the most interesting director working in Spain today; his *The Garden of Delights* (1970) was a near masterpiece. I have since seen three of his more recent works: *Elisa, My Love,* at Cannes and the following two released in America. I must confess I am not happy about the way Saura has developed, or failed to develop, since *The Hunt* and *The Garden of Delights.*

Cousin Angelica, his eleventh film, is the story of a family that was split by the civil war. As a boy, Luis, a man from the republican branch of that family, loved his cousin Angelica, but was sundered from her by the war. The narrative is somewhat confused and a little too superficial.

Luis, grown up, returns to find Angelica unhappily married, and the film shuttles between nostalgic recollections and uneasy confrontations. Franco and the Catholic church cast their shadows on both past and present, and lost happiness proves irretrievable. There is a fine performance from José Luis López Vazquez, who was so good in *The Garden of Delights,* but neither the grown nor the child Angelica is sufficiently developed or compellingly enough enacted. The cinematography, worthy of the palettes of Ribera and Zurbarán, is remarkable.

Cría, which is the awkwardly abridged form of *Cría cuervos (Brood of Crows),* is a 1975 film and the best of the three. In all of them Saura is concerned with apprehending the continuity between the past and the present, and, if possible, finding a resolution for Spain's political tragedy, the civil war that must have been terrible even for a five-year-old, and whose consequences manifestly haunt him still.

One of those consequences, alas, is Spanish censorship, which, during the Franco years, was just about insuperable, and has not become all that superable yet. As a result, one must read a Saura film to some extent as a coded document; the hateful father figure, for example, that figures in several of these movies is, surely, a symbol also of the Generalissimo and the conditions he imposed; the sundered and emotionally riven families must also be viewed as symbolizing a country rent apart. *Cría,* like other Saura films, has too much mood in it and too little event, but it is hard to tell whether the cause is a lack of things to say or a lack of freedom in which to say them.

The film shuttles between Ana the child and Ana grown up, but is complicated by the fact that the same actress, Geraldine Chaplin, plays both little Ana's mother and Ana herself grown adult, while the child actress Ana

Torrent plays little Ana. Saura leaps freely back and forth between periods and places—or, more precisely, Anas—and the dreamlikeness is intensified by the fact that real events and others merely remembered or imagined are shot in the same way and intertwined. It may all be less of an artistic gain than an aestheticizing game.

Saura does not distinguish clearly between a nicely observed atmosphere with fine textural details and all-important plot elements, of which, in any case, there are too few. Thus three little sisters dancing to a pop record are lingered over just as extendedly and lovingly as little Ana's traumatic discovery of her father dead between the sheets from which the half-dressed wife of his best friend has just run screaming. So cavalier is the author-director about plot that a whole conversation between the child and the maid Rosa, a fat earth mother, is based on Ana's having been the third girl child born to her disgusted father—when all along it is quite obvious that Ana is in fact the second of three daughters. And though the film tries, with commendable restraint and control, to tell the entire story from the child's point of view, Ana simply does not see enough, and the verbal and visual languages of the film remain undernourished.

Teodoro Escamilla's photography is lyrical and brooding as always, but the Misses Chaplin and Torrent both have, along with sensitive faces and suggestions of ample inwardness, a limited acting style that borders on monotony. Once again, Saura puts some good music on his soundtrack; in this case, a piano work by the all too little known Catalan composer of distinction, Federico Mompou.

Hitherto titling mistakes in foreign films were usually limited to the subtitles; now they are beginning to infect the very titles. *We All Loved Each Other So Much* would have been more grammatical and faithful as *We Loved One Another So*—shorter, too. Its director, Ettore Scola, was represented this year at Cannes by *A Special Day,* a much more interesting film, as was his last year's contribution to Cannes, *Brutti, sporchi e cattivi,* I gather, though I did not see it. This one, which played in Cannes two years ago, is a fuzzy, untidy affair, with a script by Age and Scarpelli, who seem to be responsible for (or should I say guilty of) half of Italy's screenplays. Even they, however, have been known to do better than this story of three World War II buddies who all loved the same girl at various times, and sometimes simultaneously.

The movie is founded on a major lie: the assumption that three close friends, one of whom marries a millionairess, can lose track of one another for years in Rome, which, as everyone knows, is a village—the world's most magnificent village, but a village all the same. Subsidiary lies abound as well, such as the right answer on Italy's version of "The $64,000 Question" being overruled by both quizmaster and judge panels. The injured party sues the network five times and keeps losing in court, too. Since the question pertains to *The Bicycle Thief,* since everybody in the movie world knows the answer, since De Sica himself would have promptly called the network and confirmed it, since later in the movie De Sica publicly tells the story and the 345 former loser still doesn't collect, you can gather how loaded the film's comic dice are.

There is psychological inauthenticity to boot. We are meant to believe in the solid friendship that binds these three men and one woman together, yet we never see them happy with one another for more than a minute or two before the shouting, punching, and kicking begins; unlike in, say, Monicelli's *My Friends,* we do not get a sense of true affection, of what it is that makes people care—only of what makes them fight.

Furthermore, Scola, who collaborated on the screenplay, frantically gimmicks up things: there is fiddling around with the time sequence, repeating of the same scene, changing from monochrome to color and back, trying to suggest primitive-period cinematography, cutting off scenes at midpoint, and so forth, all of which, unfortunately, cannot disguise the basic hollowness of the film—quite the contrary, in fact. Unfortunate, too, is the camera work of Claudio Cirillo, my least liked Italian cinematographer, which manages to look faded even when it tries, eventually, to rouse itself into fullfledged modernity. And the music by Armando Trovaioli is typical of this composer's work, a kind of sonorous dandruff.

Stefania Sandrelli is not at her best here, though she has some good moments; as the high school teacher turned film scholar, Stefano Satta Flores is irritatingly obvious. But Nino Manfredi as a perpetual hospital orderly and Vittorio Gassman as a careerist lawyer are marvelous, conveying equally well what changes in people with time and what remains obdurately unalterable. They are splendidly supported by Aldo Fabrizi, as a porcine millionaire, who wears his very grossness with a charming flourish and by Giovanna Ralli, who can invest a silly and useless woman with touching humanity. If, as I hope, there are still people left who enjoy good acting for its own far from inconsiderable sake, they can spend a couple of rewarding hours with this film. My sincerest compliments also to the make-up department, which seems almost godlike in its ability to make people grow older, younger, prettier—if it could only have had a similarly rejuvenating effect on the dulled wits of the screenwriters!

May 23 and June 20, 1977

Berlin Stories

BACK IN 1936, Bertolt Brecht jotted down the following sentence: "I thought I could study screenwriting, but realize that it will take me one morning—the technique is on that primitive a level." At the conclusion of the Twenty-seventh Berlin Film Festival, forty-one years later, one was still inclined to agree; the general level of films suggested that their makers had learned their craft in one morning or, in cases of extreme sedulousness, a morning and an afternoon. No doubt these directors had also put in years of moviegoing and worshiping at such diverse shrines as the old Hollywood, Godard, and Andy Warhol; but from this sort of thing one usually learns imitation rather than creation, which is not the same thing.

The festival itself was decently organized, having in its favor vis-à-vis Cannes, say, that there were fewer films to see: thirty-two in the official part, thirty-eight in the International Forum of the Young Film, twenty-five in the retrospective dedicated to Marlene Dietrich and the Fantastic Cinema, and over a hundred in other sections. Still much more than a single person could encompass, but at least one did not feel, as at Cannes, in the middle of an avalanche—only in a downpour. The films were of all sorts and from all over. Professional visitors were far less numerous than at Cannes, tended to know one another, and exchanged hot tips over cool drinks along the Kurfürstendamm.

Two years hence the festival will have sumptuous new lodgings, but even now the premises were tolerable, except for there being no suitable room for press conferences. At Truffaut's press conference, for example, I found that beyond the first few rows of the narrow, packed little room you could see nothing, and, what with a defective sound system, hear only pretty much the same as at other such events the world over, having to do mostly with women's lib, production costs, and the meaning of the color blue in a certain shot; or else they were not questions at all, but self-serving little orations.

The audiences, again as elsewhere, consisted of professionals, buffs, and just plain folks, and responded in the customary manner with overzealous applause interspersed with a varying quantity of boos. The German taste in movies, among both initiates and outsiders, struck me as a little worse than ours, though this is the roughest of estimates; yet even if it were a bit superior to ours, it would still be quite bad enough. The bad taste did not, however, overestimate the domestic product, as it tends to in the United States; instead, it groveled mostly before the French and, especially, American output. There was lavish enthusiasm for films as trivial as Truffaut's *The Man Who Loved Women*, and as colossally pretentious and supercolossally vacuous as Bresson's *The Devil, Probably*, to say nothing of gobbets of praise for *Nickelodeon* and *Between the Lines*.

Indeed, a festival that opened with Peter Bogdanovich's appalling *Nickelodeon* presented severe doubts about what might follow. What followed immediately, however, was a giant party at the Berlin Hilton—indoors and in the garden—with excellent food, reasonably interesting-looking guests, and a dreadful band. It was so vast and crowded that I actually managed to miss Senta Berger, one of the members of the jury, who, I am told, looked ravishing. Among the many notables and near-notables there were relatively few Americans, always a refreshing phenomenon for someone in search of new faces.

Of the films shown during the festival's twelve days, I saw all but three in the competition, and caught a handful in other sections. Nothing impressed me quite so much as two films screened unofficially and representing the recent work of the noted Hungarian director Zoltán Fábri, who, now sixty, has acquired a technique that, though perhaps not entirely original, is han- 347 dled by him so magisterially as to become quintessentially individualized. He determinedly chooses for filmization brilliant novels that are not particularly cinematic, but so well written as to be a magnificent challenge to the filmmaker. Fábri meets it honestly and imaginatively, and gets riveting results even though by all rights such transfers should fail.

There was Fábri's 1976 film, *The Fifth Seal,* based on a novel by the outstanding fictionist Ferenc Sánta; and also Fábri's 1975 film, *The Unfinished Sentence,* based on the masterpiece of Hungary's most internationally recognized modern novelist, Tibor Déry. The former deals with a very few people in the narrowest scope—a period of two days and only two main locations. In it, four average citizens of Budapest do a lot of theorizing and temporizing, only to be suddenly confronted by the Fascist government of 1944 with a brutal and terrifying test. The latter concerns an entire society, covers considerable space and time, and focuses on the progressive disillusionment of a rich and prominent young man with the right-wing capitalism of pre–World War II Hungary. In both novels, the dialogue is copius, highly elaborate, and of paramount importance; it is to Fábri's great credit that he found visual effects that bolster or summarize the dialogue, much of which he also, respectfully and wisely, retained. Never, however, is there mere visual duplication of the spoken word; rather, there is ever more developed counterpointing. The director was able to infuse movement into the surface stasis of *The Fifth Seal,* and find a shorthand of images for much of the necessarily omitted action in *The Unfinished Sentence,* whose modest Hungarian title, taking account of the omissions, is *141 Minutes From the Unfinished Sentence.*

Even if neither film could, axiomatically, be a total success, both films are powerful and provocative; thus I was stupefied to hear a bright young Hungarian critic declare them both uninteresting failures. If there is anything truly useful to be learned from international festival-going, it is how tastes function nationally. By and large, clever people tend to get tired of what their national cinema purveys wholesale. (Americans may be an exception, there being no end to their craving for westerns, thrillers, and other familiar Hollywood genres.) In Hungary, Fascist brutality, Communist dedication, and the ultimate decency of little people are probably stock stuff; even so, an astute observer ought to recognize the ability of some films to use them only so as to transcend them.

Such use was made by one of the two Russian films in competition, *The Ascent* (or *Ascension*) by Larissa Shepitko.* The thirty-nine-year-old Ukrainian director and occasional actress (married to the important Soviet director Elem Klimov) was a student of Dovzhenko, and it may be that it is from him or from their common Ukrainian heritage that she derives her profound sense of man's oneness with nature. To most Anglo-Saxons and avant-gardists in the audience, *The Ascent* looked like an old-fashioned story about Russian partisans in World War II, decked out with even more antiquated Christian symbolism, the heroic partisan becoming a Christ figure, while his

---

* 1982: Shortly afterward, Miss Shepitko was killed in an automobile accident in Bulgaria—a great loss to the world of cinema.

riend who would save his own skin at any cost becomes identified with Judas.

But what these hostile viewers overlooked is that Shepitko was not allowed to make films for six years (a common enough occurrence in the U.S.S.R., alas) and had to pick a subject that seemed safe to the comrades. What she did with it, though, was to turn it upside down, not only into a Dostoevskian allegory, but also into a tale where, of the six main Russian characters, four are wholly or partly traitorous—something unheard of in past Soviet war films. It takes more than that, of course, to make a work of art, but this, too, Shepitko achieved (with some flaws) in her movingly human document shot in black and white, in which snowy landscapes set off equally dazzlingly dark human figures and black, leafless trees. The ability to reduce a story to absolute essentials and still elicit suspense and compassion is no mean accomplishment, and the three principal roles were superlatively acted by Boris Plotnikov, Vladimir Gostyuzhin, and Anatoly Solonizin, who also played the protagonist in Tarkovsky's famous *Andrey Rublyov,* and here did as stunningly by an icily inhuman collaborationist investigating judge, a sort of unjesting Pilate.

It is not worth dwelling in detail on the other films; far more interesting was the announcement of prizes at the Zoo Palast, the large and efficient theater where the last film in competition had just been shown (a Moroccan version of Lorca's *Blood Wedding* transposed into the Sahara, with the bridegroom's mother played by today's international tragic sufferer extraordinary, Irene Papas; and the hero, by that unlikely blue-eyed Bedouin, Laurent Tertzieff). The nine-person jury came on stage eight persons strong, the Spanish filmmaker Basilio Martín Patino failing to show, and sat stage right; stage left were the recipients of prizes. In the middle were the jury's two (count 'em: two) presidents, the Senegalese filmmaker Ousmane Sembene and our own Ellen Burstyn, handing out Silver and Golden Bears, while Senta Berger acted as M.C. The short-subject awards went off eventlessly enough, the Golden Bear (first prize) going to a well-meaning West German effort about a senile crone's vain search for her long-gone domicile among unsympathetic city-dwellers.

But the feature awards, which Miss Berger, temporarily thinking in French, referred to as "long films," thus causing an outburst of merriment she quickly stopped by emending her Gallicism, were more eventful. Silver Bears went to a Mexican film about masons I had missed (I was told reliably that it held no interest except as a populist document, but populism is big in Berlin these days), whose director bestrode the stage in a pronouncedly unpopulist Pierre Cardinish outfit; to Pál Sándor's Hungarian film, *A Strange Role* (with a brilliant idea insufficiently exploited by the director, and still less by the scenarist); to Fernando Fernán Gómez, for the best male performance, in an intelligently entertaining Spanish film, *The Anchorite,* marred only only by an awkward ending; to Lily Tomlin, in *The Late Show,* for the best female performance; and, for best direction, to the Spaniard Manuel Gutiérrez Aragón, whose film about the making of a young Fascist in today's Spain, *Black Brood,* is still banned in his country—it is extremely courageous and somewhat inept, and the enthusiasm it elicited has probably little to do with artistic reasons.

When Miss Berger announced the special prize of the jury to Robert Bresson for *The Devil, Probably,* both applause and booing became stentorian. Hushing the audience, the actress and jury member stated that the jurors R. W. Fassbinder, wearing his notorious leather-boy outfit, Derek Malcolm, *The Guardian*'s flowing-locked critic, and Madame Vager, the French producer, wanted it known that they had voted for giving Bresson the Golden Bear; however, the jurors Ousmane Sembene and Humberto Solas, the Cuban filmmaker, wanted it on record that they had voted against any prize whatever to Bresson. Again pandemonium. With the announcement of the Golden Bear to Larissa Shepitko's *The Ascent* (which also won the International Film Critics' and Catholic Film Jury's awards, the Protestants, true to their name, crowning Mrs. Silver's *Between the Lines* instead), Miss Shepitko, a striking and statuesque woman, her comeliness only slightly lessened by an excess of red hair dye (for political reasons, one hopes, rather than aesthetic ones), stood calmly smiling, even though it was further announced that four jurors—the absent Patino, and by now familiar Fassbinder-Vager-Malcolm trio—had voted against the Golden Bear for Shepitko. Perhaps they felt that bears to Russia were like coals to Newcastle.

More clapping and catcalls. Someone called Wolf Donner, the festival director, a dumb dog. Donner responded to the hubbub by sourly announcing he hadn't realized award presentations could be so merry. Actually, the film scene was considerably livelier in Munich, where Fassbinder had just been fined for assault with a broken bottle in a gay bar, and his colleague Werner Herzog was about to stand trial for taking potshots at his wife. He missed her, proving that he's equally inept at shooting spouses and film.

August 1, 1977

Sexcess

TOO MUCH of a muchness is only one of the problems with *In the Realm of the Senses,* although that is only one trouble with Nagisa Oshima's dreadful new movie. It is a fictionalization by Oshima of a case that supposedly rocked Japan in 1935: a prostitute cut off her lover's genitalia and ran about the streets of Tokyo with them for three days. Acquitted in a sensational trial she became a national heroine.

That, and that the man was married, is as much as the press releases will tell us. I imagine that he promised the girl marriage, abused her variously, and then set about leaving her; in any case, he must have done her a lot of dirt for the Japanese judiciary of the time to have freed her. Oshima, instead, has tried to tell a story about a man and a woman who love each other with such an insane passion that, as it becomes ever more fanatical and all-consuming, nothing will satisfy it except death. Well, why not? Such tales have been a staple of literature since narration began, and have made it even onto the screen, from *Duel in the Sun* to Cocteau's *The Eternal Return*. But Oshima set out to do something more difficult: to concentrate almost entirely on the two lovers, show their passion in constant closeup, as it were, and deal with the matter realistically, head on. A gallant conception, but one for which he is quite the wrong man, having neither the artistry nor the psychological insight.

Relentlessly throughout the film, Sada and Kichizo, the husband of the owner of the brothel in which Sada is one of the girls, fornicate, talk about fornication, or indulge in kinky sexual games. On the rare occasions they don't, she is in bed with a rich, elderly client (the lovers need money), or he is copulating with an old woman in the presence of Sada, who has commanded it ("I had the feeling I was holding my mother's corpse!"), or with a fat, unsightly whore, because the whore, when Sada was briefly away, mentioned her name to Kichizo, by way of an aphrodisiac. Sada, in turn, will make love to Kichizo's kimono on a trip away from him; at other times, she makes him swallow her menses or eat food that she first introduced into her vagina. ("If you really love someone, you must eat like this.") And already she threatens him with the knife with which she shaves him. They have met cute: Sada watched Kichizo have sex with his wife. It is for not giving up this moonlighting that Sada seems to kill him in the end, though, of course, the deed is supposed to be fraught with metaphysical significance.

To make this monomaniacal passion credible and interesting, you need, first of all, two persuasive interpreters. Eiko Matsuda, as Sada, has a fine body but an insignificant face with uneventful expressions, and she does not suggest depth of feeling or even a neurotically gnawing passion. In a typically awkward bit of dialogue, she says: "I was only hypersensitive"; her lover, equally inspiredly, comments: "I love your hypersensitivity." It may be that hypersensitivity is meant merely as a euphemism for nymphomania, but even average sensitivity is beyond Miss Matsuda's ability to convey—though, to be sure, Oshima in no way assists her.

As for Tatsuya Fuji, as Kichizo, he is even less interesting. A slick-looking man, he does show a certain adroitness in smoking a cigarette while making love, but that is pretty much the limit of his acting ability. At times, he sings gutturally, or smiles and smiles with a certain insipidity that goes well with his dialogue. As Sada is first going down on him, he remarks reflectively, "You're a strange girl." Later, when she is beginning her experiments in strangling him with a sash and complains, "I'm frightened; say something," his reply is redolent of Zen wisdom: "Stupid, I'm being strangled, and you expect me to talk!" Characteristically, after extensive choking, his neck shows not a mark. Much the same goes for his face; Fuji's namesake, the mountain, would have been equally animated.

It will not do, I think, to talk of cultural differences and the inscrutable East. My devotion to the Japanese cinema is enormous, and I have seen countless films in which intense feelings came through the looks and sounds of Japanese actors in ways that were familiar to my Western sensibility. Nor

351

will I be swayed by the contention that Oshima looks at passion dispassionately, and so deliberately keeps the temperature level down. In the first place, any number of needlessly graphic details leave little doubt about Oshima's pornographic intentions; in the second, what would be the point of making a film about passion in which one set out *not* to convey what passion is like? As soon make a film about beauty in which all the sights are ugly.

Rather, judging also by several other films of his, Oshima strikes me as a profoundly untalented director who can even take such fascinating material as that which went into his movie *Boy* and come up with only one or two scenes that have any life in them. Conversely, Oshima talks insufferably pretentiously about his artistic intentions and the philosophical content of his films, e.g., describing himself as "a mixture between a form of asceticism and an ineffably epicurean feeling."

Next, an able director would have understood that the film, for aesthetic no less than psychological reasons, cannot be all sex scenes, many of them involving group sex or exhibitionistic copulations before various observers, unless other things were also revealed to us about the principals. But no such information is forthcoming, and we might as well be expected to care about the obsessions of cockroaches. For if we can neither find the lovers magnetic enough in their presences, nor learn about what it is that propels them, what they are sacrificing, what else they might have done with themselves, we must simply feel for their fanatical drive because it is there, or because we ourselves have such pathological obsessions—in which case we are poor judges of the film's artistic or humane values.

Above all, the writer-director should know better than to plunge us into ludicrousness. If Sada cannot walk with Kichizo without holding on to his penis, all right; if the conjoined couple cannot separate even for their meals and don't want their room cleaned ("But that's what we like, this smell!"), okay, I'll bend over backward to go along. But I have to double up forward in laughter when Sada won't let Kichizo go to the toilet to pee because she can't stand being parted from him that long: "Do it here." "Where?" "In me." "Both at once [i.e., making love and water]? But it's impossible!" "Try it, anyway." And they try. One cannot help wondering what happens when it is time for number two.

You might hope for some humor to relieve the aridity, or even to provide some ironic commentary. Well, the most Oshima can muster is Kichizo's comment after Sada eats some of his pubic hair, "Careful, you'll grow a beard." Nor is there relief or commentary from the few peripheral characters and incidents. With his wife, Kichizo does more of the same sort of copulating; a filthy old man who comes to the brothel for Sada is obsessed in the self-same way as Kichizo. Always, moreover, a deadly symmetry: if Kichizo smokes while coupling, Sada plays the samisen with like ambidexterity.

If indeed this were a story about passion that could find its fullest expression only in death—as it is being touted—then, surely, some kind of joint *Liebestod* would be in order at the end. Instead, we get, in hideous detail, Sada's strangling of her lover, cutting off all his genitals (even Marco Ferreri, in *The Last Woman,* was willing to settle for the penis), and writing on the body in his blood: "Sada and Kichi, the two of us forever." A lopsided *Liebestod* if you ask me: How in tarnation will they be together if she survives? Clearly there is vindictiveness and perversion at work here rather than romantic heightening.

It is typical of Oshima's feeble imagination that he ends his film here, where he ought to have started it. For if anything could have been interesting, it would have been the trial: what the woman said, why they acquitted her, how she became a national heroine, and how, if at all, she made good on "the two of us forever." Instead, we get this inept attempt at pornography that would justify its failure at eroticism by calling itself art. Even the production design and photography are considerably below Japanese standards. As for the critics who perceive in this obtuse film the supreme expression of sex, passion, love, eroticism, or what have you, they deserve not so much our contempt as our commiseration.

August 8, 1977

Bolognini, or Is It Baloney?

La Grande Bourgeoise is, like most of the films of Mauro Bolognini, failed art, the sort of thing that leaves a bad taste in the soul. It is not quite so ridiculous as Bolognini's last movie shown here, *Down the Ancient Stairs;* but it is a far cry from the one truly fine Bolognini film, *Il bell' Antonio,* and the lesser, but still not inconsiderable, *La viaccia.* Many of his films did not reach America: I am sorry that we were deprived of his famous *Senilità* (based on Svevo's great novel, which, I gather, it manages to betray almost as much as serve), and that we were not spared his worst pictures, based on *La notte brava* and *From a Roman Balcony,* by Pasolini and Moravia, respectively.

Three things seem obvious about Bolognini's films: (1) They are mostly based on novels and short stories, often celebrated ones, and depend on the quality of the fiction and, even more, on its adaptability to the screen. (2) As an article in *Cahiers du Cinéma* noted way back in 1962, "[Bolognini's] morbid world . . . is a world of misogyny and homosexuality." (3) Bolognini's forte is historical recreation, especially a fine sense of décor and costumes, which he shares with other directors of like sensibility, e.g., Visconti and Zeffirelli. But be it said for him that his taste is less erratic than Zeffirelli's and more subdued than Visconti's.

In *La Grande Bourgeoise,* the director, alas, has no novel to adapt. Instead, he works from a poor script by Sergio Bazzini, based on a scandal that hit Bologna at the turn of the century. Professor Murri (Fernando Rey), a distinguished teacher of medicine at that illustrious university, and a Socialist and atheist, was the father of Linda (Catherine Deneuve), a brilliant young woman unhappily married to a beastly physician, Catholic and reactionary, to whom she had borne two children. For their sake she stayed with him, 353 although keeping separate quarters, and while actually the mistress of another, older doctor, a friend of her father's. Her brother Tullio (Giancarlo Giannini), a bright young lawyer (though the script makes him rather doltish) and Socialist political candidate, adored her as much as he hated his brother-in-law.

When Dr. Bonmartini made Linda's life insupportable, her doting brother, with the help of yet another doctor friend, a weak and profligate failure of a man (most convincingly portrayed by Corrado Pani), killed Dr. Bonmartini. Through the almost maniacal efforts of an investigating magistrate (played by Marcel Bozzuffi with wonderfully subdued, icy class and religious hatred), brother and sister and various associates were finally caught—the honesty and mutual love of the Murris proving the ultimate tools of their self-destruction—and given heavy jail sentences. The political circumstances—it was election year, and the Christian conservatives used the case, spiced by calumnies in their journals, to destroy the Socialists—further aided the Murris' downfall; guilty and innocent were alike condemned, and only Linda got off because her father's medical skill saved the king's stricken daughter.

It may be that the facts of the case have never fully come to light, or that for legal, political, or personal reasons, the filmmakers cannot tell the whole truth, or even what they take it to be. So the crucial incidents remain veiled in deliberate obscurity, and the killing itself is shot and edited in a completely inscrutable way, with a subsequent divergent flashback compounding the confusion. I am nevertheless convinced that much of the shapelessness and fuzziness of the narrative is due to a wishy-washiness in Bolognini's approach—his primary concern with making the Bologna of 1902 look both opulent and right, and relative indifference to the rest.

Not quite all the rest, though. The director, characteristically, toys with incest, homosexuality, and a general atmosphere of decadence; he also brings in, rather more perfunctorily, conventionally liberal, anticlerical sentiments. In the opening sequence, Tullio and his mistress (Tina Aumont, better than usual), who is Linda's personal maid, are in a state of postcoital languor when an agitated Linda enters their room. Across the half-naked body of the young woman, brother and sister exchange intimate confidences and finally clasp hands in a way fraught with unstated eroticism. Had the film continued on this note, it might at least have had an evil fascination; instead, it soon gets lost in vapid ostentatiousness.

Some of the acting is up to the sets and costumes. Deneuve, although (or perhaps because) dubbed into Italian, displays, along with a new hair color, a new, late-blooming aptitude for acting. Giannini performs with his customary careful intensity, somewhat top-heavy for this flimsy context. Fernando Rey is suavely contemptuous and nobly paternal by turns, and the supporting cast is studded with famous Italian actors insufficiently known here. Among these, only Laura Betti overacts her scenes of vengeful jealousy.

The film might have had a modest appeal despite everything, were it not for the horrendous cinematography of Ennio Guarnieri. Always leaning toward delinquently deliquescent effects, Guarnieri here shoots almost the entire film through a luminous haze that resembles nothing so much as incorrect exposure and lack of focus. While making too few demands on the mind, the movie strains our eyes beyond endurance.

August 15, 1977

Don't Shoot the Actor, He's Doing the Best He Can

WHAT DOES a good actor do in a stupid film? Take the case of Giancarlo Giannini in *The Sensual Man*. This atrocious movie, whose English credits are extremely chary of divulging information, is actually based on *Paolo il caldo*, the last, unfinished novel by one of the most remarkable writers of the first half of our century, Vitaliano Brancati (1907–1954), possibly underrated even in Italy, and virtually unknown in this country because his books are either untranslated or out of print. He did make it twice to American screens: with *Il bell'Antonio* (1960), based on his novel, which is Mauro Bolognini's finest film; and with his screenplay for *Difficult Years* (*Anni difficili*, 1948), a flop here, though it was considerably superior to Luigi Zampa's other major film, *To Live in Peace* (1946), an enormous hit. But the latter was upbeat rather than satirical and scorching; it also had a lovable black ex-G.I. tootling his horn, and was not burdened with an English narration by Arthur Miller.

Paolo il caldo, rechristened *The Sensual Man*, to make it sound like a Lyle Stuart handbook of sexual self-help, is about as removed from the spirit and subtlety of Brancati as a lumpish director-screenwriter like Marco Vicario could make it. It is the tale of Paolo, a wealthy Sicilian who ends up a Roman Casanova. We begin with his amatory initiation in boyhood by a vital young chambermaid who prefers the tenderfoot's tender ardors to his powerful grandfather's senescent lechery. The maid is played by the (in this context) improbably beautiful and genteel Ornella Muti, setting the tone of incredibility that prevails throughout.

But incredibility is only one problem; corniness, epitomized by young Paolo and the maid's ecstatic roll in the corn, is another; a third is vulgarity. Episode after episode is pounded home with a heavy obviousness that turns the camera into a blunt instrument; no point is allowed more than a second or two to be made, or more than two or three further seconds to be remade. What may have been retained of Brancati's language is coarsened by the visual ambience, and further cheapened by Armando Trovaioli's score, banal and insistent to the point of insolence.

Consider the night scene in which Paolo's mother, just widowed and desperately missing her husband's lovemaking—even though the film barely got through telling us that sex between the spouses had ceased long since—masturbates wildly and noisily with her pillow. This is staged and shot with a heavy-handedness no self-respecting porn film would stoop to. Paolo, sleepless, listens apprehensively through the wall of his adjoining room; presently, he hears his raffish uncle enter the bereaved and deprived woman's bedroom, and with most wicked speed mother and uncle are at it, panting and grunting, while Paolo, though already a young man, suffers with infantile intensity. Brancati could bring off something like this thanks to his expert blending of satire and gracefulness, and because prose, a nonvisual medium, operates differently from film; in Vicario, the grotesque promptly becomes gross.

Perhaps the most obvious example of the director's blatancy is the father's deathbed scene dragged out unconscionably, peppered with predictable shots, and rendered more ineffectual yet by Riccardo Cucciola, an actor whose every scene is a deathbed scene. Scarcely less flat-footed is the affair between Paolo and a rich, young parlor Communist, filmed in clumsily staged staccato sequences. (Communist headquarters, for instance, are bedizened like a Komsomol Stalin's Birthday pageant) whose literal-mindedness chokes out every shred of satirical wit. Vicario leaves us with only the vicarious, vestigial pleasure of watching women in various stages of undress. The most enchanting of these—in the role of the apothecary's niece whose daughter Paolo later marries—is unbilled in the skimpy English credits, but is none other than Barbara Bach of *The Spy Who Loved Me*.

It is nice to welcome back Rossana Podestà after an overlong absence, and discover, furthermore, that she has a genuine comedic gift besides her still undimmed good looks; but Vicario elicits the worst from such unsubtle performers as Vittorio Caprioli, Lionel Stander, and, above all, Adriana Asti, as a society matron combining nymphomania with exhibitionism. Always an overwrought and underimaginative actress, Asti here lets loose a *spumante* excessive enough to be nauseating.

Yet it is Giannini, as the protagonist, who ultimately comes off worst. In the already described eavesdropping scene, or in a sequence near the end where panic grips him at the wheel of his car, he enacts with his characteristic concentration a carefully gradated and ever more painfully contained agony that results in a terrific implosion—something simply too much for this flimsy picture. Other performers, admittedly in easier parts, manage to keep us outside their emoting—thus Gastone Moschin as the uncle, and the charming Yugoslav actress Neda Arnerić as the girl Paolo marries and gets his sexual comeuppance with. Giannini's performance is too genuine, too aching, and becomes in this shabby context an embarrassment to watch.

August 29, 1977

German Measliness

Pity the national cinema whose summit achievements are the films of R. W. Fassbinder and Werner Herzog (to say nothing of a Straub and Schlöndorf)!

True, Germany also has the extremely promising Wim Wenders, who has still to make a memorable film (his *The American Friend* is not it), and Hans Jürgen Syberberg, a man of idiosyncratic, ornery talent who has made, among other things, one remarkable feature (*Karl May*) and one probably overlong but in many ways extraordinary documentary, *Winifred,* and whose forthcoming *Hitler* (a feature film not to be confused with the already finished documentary by Joachim Fest) may turn out to be his "breakthrough" film. Notable, too, is the intermittently interesting Alexander Kluge, more important as a writer.

Recently, at the Berlin festival, I did get to see several German films by such established directors as Bernhard Wicki and the East German Konrad Wolff, and by newer names such as Niklaus Schilling and Helma Sanders. Wolff's film, *Mom, I'm Alive!,* despite obvious tendentiousness, was not shameful; the other three were. Miss Sanders's *Heinrich* won West Germany's top cinematic award, the Golden Bowl—I would barely have awarded it a used toilet bowl. This film, about the last days in the life of one of the world's most unfortunate and magnificent geniuses, Heinrich von Kleist, had a surefire story: all you had to do was to follow the facts and available documents that would practically write your dialogue for you, get the right actors, and know something about directing.

All this by way of introduction to the latest Herzog and Fassbinder offerings, diverse but characteristic fiascoes. To start with the lesser evil: *Stroszek,* starring once again Bruno S. (S., presumably, for Stroszek), the middle-aged *lumpenprole* who has spent considerable time in both correctional and mental institutions, and whom Herzog first cast, with sublime inappropriateness, as the lead in his Kaspar Hauser film. In *Stroszek,* Bruno, a habitual minor offender who more or less plays himself, gets out of jail once again, returns to playing and singing (actually, croaking) in courtyards for coins tossed out of windows, teams up with a prostitute (Eva Mattes) seeking refuge with him from her two bestial pimps who keep beating the daylights out of her, and continues his friendship with the frail and senile Scheitz, who looked after Bruno's place and his talking myna, Beo, while Bruno was in jail.

The pimps continue to harass and brutalize Eva and, for good measure, Bruno as well. Since old Scheitz has an invitation and ticket to America from his nephew, who runs a garage somewhere in Wisconsin, and since Eva sells herself profitably to lowly Turkish workers in Berlin, the trio can sail to America together. How those Turkish laborers could in a very short time subsidize two tickets to America, and why even they would want the most unprepossessing Eva Mattes (the star also of Fassbinder's appalling *Jail Bait*) are only two of the film's many insoluble mysteries. Why, for example, does one not denounce the pimps to the police, there being enough evidence to put them away for a while? And why is America the only alternative to Berlin?

The U.S. Customs start the dirty work by quarantining Beo—a talented bird, which, if its utterances are not dubbed, speaks rather better than the mentally beclouded Bruno. The threesome has money enough to buy a car, and makes it to the Wisconsin backwoods, where the nephew proves to be a 357 mighty dimwit too, whose garage and body shop is hardly thriving, and whose Indian assistant may be the one person around even more feeble-minded than his boss. Bruno putters about a bit at the shop, Scheitz goes about with a voltameter measuring animal magnetism in fence posts and dead deer, and Eva works as a counter girl in a hash house.

Once again there is money enough, miraculously, to make a down payment on a mobile home as long as a comet's tail and a TV set to match, but Eva is soon back plying her old trade among the truck drivers, with two of whom she leaves for Vancouver. Next, the bank, in the person of a farcical employee who would look unconvincing in a Woody Allen movie, repossesses the home and telly, whereupon Bruno and Scheitz make a feeble attempt at a holdup to get even with "them." Scheitz is apprehended, but Bruno, implausibly, is not. He steals the garage's tow truck and sets off on a blind journey with some stolen cash and a frozen turkey lifted from a supermarket, which is either symbolic compensation for the impounded myna or sheer madness.

Bruno ends up on an Indian reservation in North Dakota, where an amusement park features, among other things, domestic animals in slot machines performing dances or playing instruments. While activating a deserted chair lift for a ride, he shorts out the machines with the animals. As he drifts up and down on the chair lift, the hapless animals must perform without respite—the police are unable to stop the mechanisms. Bruno has a gun with him and may shoot himself or do someone else harm; the unhappy chicken in a machine just keeps dancing.

I had to go into the plot in some detail to convey the ineptitude and dishonesty, and, above all, fake humanity of *Stroszek*. Much has been made of the unsentimentality of Herzog's approach to his characters, a supposed proof of his sense of human dignity. But the unsentimentality is really an inability to deal with sentiment at all: we are never shown what Bruno and Eva's relationship is like beyond the cliché of two abused outcasts banding together. These people, however, cohabit; yet we are never afforded the least glimpse of any real intimacy, of what and how it is when they are alone together. Of course, Bruno the "actor" may be too unbalanced for such scenes—indeed, he speaks even some of his ordinary lines as if the words were pumped into him by ventriloquism or hypnotism—but, if so, why use this pathetic creature at all?

Eva, too, is a crude and underdeveloped character. We see her expending more emotion on the pimps who abuse her monstrously, or on the truck drivers who want her only for sex, than on Bruno, with whom she is supposed to have her one genuinely human relationship. The nearest she gets to visible closeness with Bruno is that she polishes his beat-up old piano in Berlin. Later, in Wisconsin, she tells him that she would sometimes like to sleep alone; otherwise, we might not even have known that she and Bruno were lovers. Moreover, Eva Mattes, the actress, is not only supremely unappetizing physically, she also lacks any sort of emotional depth or technical subtlety. She can look sulky; she can look pleading; she can smile broadly; and that is about it. That she should have won all manner of top German acting awards is perhaps the most eloquent indictment of the state of film and theater culture in the Federal Republic.

And what about the alleged "deep" theme of the film—that in Germany "they" brutalize your body, whereas in the United States, where things are superficially better, "they" brutalize your spirit. If this is so, the movie certainly does not demonstrate it. The prison authorities are indulgent enough with Bruno and his eccentricities; yes, they may be a bit self-righteous and paternalistic, but that is an understandable occupational disease, and a relatively mild one. The pimps, on the other hand, are barely believable in their calculated yet unreasoned brutality; in any case, they are not representative of Germany, and there are various ways of dealing with them that Bruno and Eva seem merely too stupid to come up with. In America, it is their fault that they overextend themselves financially; that Scheitz and Bruno don't manage to learn English; that Scheitz is senile to the point of dementia, Bruno more than a little unhinged, and Eva addicted to sluttishness. Why doesn't Bruno make music in America, where his rather spastic playing would win him fame and riches? Why must the nephew be close to cretinous? Why does America owe this undynamic trio a living?

The answer is that Herzog loads his dice. He peddles discontent with Germany to Germany's disoriented youth, as well as facile anti-Americanism that always strikes a responsive chord in European envy, in European love-hate for America, and doesn't do so badly either with our own counterculture and would-be swinging bourgeoisie. Neither by dialogue nor by imagery, nor by any other means, does Herzog make his characters anything more than slightly pathetic, rather ludicrous, and heartily repellent. Thomas Mauch's cinematography is routine, and there is, except in certain effects involving the mobile home, no compelling use of the camera.

That Herzog does not generate sympathy for the characters becomes painfully evident in the end, when the dancing chicken, the fire-fighting rabbit, and the drumming duck, each turned into a *perpetuum mobile,* move us much more than the human characters. In fact, the plight of that dancing chicken, in a shot held for an offensively long time, is heart-rending; but this is no symbolic comment on America, or Bruno, or the human condition, as Herzog's crass overemphasis would have us believe. It is much the same kind of torture of animals that was lovingly cataloged near the end of *Even Dwarfs Started Small,* and again in the treatment of the horse in *Aguirre.* But, then, human beings are not treated much better in Herzog's movies, and whatever sympathy there is, is always for those who merit it least.

The same sort of profound amorality informs the films of Rainer Werner Fassbinder. In *Satan's Brew,* moreover, Fassbinder tries his hand at farce, for which he evidently has even less talent than for anything else. Here there is not one joke, I submit, at which someone even remotely connected with normality can laugh, and few at which he wouldn't take offense. Subjects for jokes: an idiot who kills flies and offers them as love gifts; a woman who revels in being insulted, injured, almost killed; another woman who pays handsomely for mock rape and assassination; a married couple in which the 359 husband keeps offering his wife to the creepy hero who claims to be a poet but who is a total no-talent and charlatan, and whom most of the world admires and subsidizes nevertheless. This hero's relationship with his equally repulsive wife consists mostly of their shouting nonsense words at each other (hilarious, that!). There is also an epicene police inspector who makes Clouseau look like Sherlock Holmes, and a pervasive aura of pederasty, which is also treated as a subject for crude farce. The hero fancies himself a reincarnation of Stefan George, and there are numerous tasteless jokes about that great but admittedly eccentric man (thus some of his best poems are recited as if they were doggerel), and one of the female characters is an obvious travesty of Andrée Hacquebaut in Montherlant's *The Girls*—an impudent, witless parody of what in the novel is already ruthless, but shrewd, dissection.

Most of the acting is appalling, the direction stodgy, and the basic mode a reveling in physical and spiritual ugliness. Misanthropy of this kind has to be earned by genuine suffering turned into salient wit—as in the case of Swift. Coming from Fassbinder, who, for all his facile quotations from Artaud plastered across the screen, is supremely callous, it is a nonpareil of moral bankruptcy.

September 5, 1977

The Rain and the Grass

Sandakan 8 is a small, scruffy Japanese film, poorly written, directed, and photographed on the whole, but redeemed by a number of by no means negligible virtues. It is the story of a *karayuki-san*, as girls until not so long ago sold into prostitution and shipped across the seas—in this particular case, to Borneo—were called. After being abused in sordid colonial brothels, those who came back were shunned by their fellow citizens, not least by their very families to whose upkeep they painfully contributed. There is something so shattering about this subject that even a picture worse than *Sandakan 8* could not fail to be somehow dignified by it.

Kei Kumai's film deals with a woman graduate student in history or sociology who, for the sake of a thesis, coaxes out an old *karayuki-san*'s life story, while first hypocritically, then sincerely, befriending her. The script, by Kumai and Sakae Hirozawa, shifts among the largely melodramatic past of Osaki, the now seventyish heroine; the recent past in which Osaki and the student shared the former's fearfully dilapidated and vermin-infested domicile, while the crone's tale is told over a number of days; and the present, when the student is exploring Borneo for the remaining traces of Osaki and other women like her. These very shifts in time are awkwardly enough managed to leave us often confused; but worse than Kumai's opacities are his excessive obviousnesses, as, for instance, the scene in which Osaki is deflowered by a rude and fiercely tattooed fisherman, who has hung the key with which he has locked the girl in around his neck, so that during her physical ravaging the heavy iron key keeps, as it were, raping her thrown-back face—which we see in a low-angle shot, upside down and tear-stained, as it hangs off the bed, always with that key cruelly jiggling against it. If this key were introduced briefly as a final outrage, it could be heart-rending; insisted on far too long, it becomes a ponderous gimmick.

Many a scene is marred by such obvious effects, or by being heavily staged and mangled by some of the minor characters (only a few of whom can act); but there are also moments of bare, essential, incandescent humanity where details are acutely observed, and occasional images—such as her one true lover coming upon Osaki just after the crew of a battleship has, as it were, steamed across her—that have a lacerating beauty about them. Some land-scapes, too, of Kyushu are seductive, and the developing relationship between the former prostitute and the young scholar who comes to respect and care for her is far from unaffecting.

Although the student is indifferently played, both Kinuyo Tanaka, as the old Osaki, and Yoho Tahashi, as the young one, perform with enchanting genuineness, in a style that seems almost too forthright to be anything but lived life itself. Beyond the numerous rough edges, and the fairly numerous rough innards of *Sandakan 8,* there are nevertheless moments of disarming directness, of stumbling but penetrant honesty.

Suspiria is one of that alarmingly increasing legion of movies distinguished above all by stupidity. Dario Argento, who wrote and directed it, may think that it is marvelously campy, and, certainly, it is unmarvelously campy, too. But, above all, it is imbecile. It is a horror movie that is really a horror of a movie, where no one or nothing makes sense: not one plot element, psychological reaction, minor character, piece of dialogue, or ambience. Yet it is precisely in horror movies, where we are asked to believe in something basically incredible, that whatever surrounds this nucleus of absurdity must be made rigorously, palpably recognizable.

Argento—and his whole family, who seem to produce and collaborate on his movies—must also take the blame for three previous horrors shown here, culminating in *Deep Red,* which they did not even dare show to the critics. Here he has imagined a ballet academy in Freiburg, Germany (a likely place!), where terrible things happen to an innocent American student, played with ill-disguised disbelief by the appealing Jessica Harper. Argento's mental grasp—in which I believe as much as in witches—cannot even make the topography of this place believable, to say nothing of the town that sometimes surrounds it, and sometimes not. The director is mostly concerned with creating grisly demises, creepy effects with bats in women's hair, de-composing bodies, a shower of worms raining on people, and dreadful-looking personages hanging around. In short, he much prefers the disgusting to the frightening.

Worst of all, he makes performers whom one has enjoyed in the past appear thoroughly distasteful. I have always liked Joan Bennett and loved

361

Alida Valli: the former here reveals a totally synthetic personality and zero acting ability, which she and her directors have previously managed very tactfully to conceal; the latter is turned into a kind of lesbian golem that might have scared the daylights out of Gertrude Stein. The ballet scenes, executed by people who have only the most rudimentary acquaintance with dance and who seem to be performing something we might call "The Dying Goose," are good for some barbaric belly laughs—as are other things in the movie—but such laughter is hardly wholesome enough to be encouraged. Argento, moreover, has collaborated with a group named the Goblins on "music" that seems to be scored for electronically amplified kitchen utensils, loud enough to qualify as a foreground score.

Although Luciano Tovoli is a competent cinematographer, the garish, fake art nouveau sets he is most of the time compelled to shoot here debase the cinematographic skill he possesses. Besides, Argento hasn't the faintest idea of how to use a camera or cameraman: he will, for instance, shoot a perfectly ordinary conversation in alternating low-angle closeups against a minatory sky with people's hair ominously wind-blown, as if something awesome were about to happen. But there is only awfulness, for one of the conversationalists is Udo Kier, whom I don't take to be an actor at all, but a female impersonator's impression of Alain Delon.

September 12, 1977

Turn of the Century, Turn of the Stomach

WHEN BERNARDO BERTOLUCCI's *1900* was pared down for release from 5½ to just over 4 hours it was an act not of commercial vandalism but of simple human mercy. Even at 245 minutes this sprawling chronicle of two families is close to unbearable. Not because it is overlong, but because it is too short on truth and art. And because it overflows with the kind of naïve Communist propaganda that one would expect only from a Chinese opera about the life of Mao, but which, evidently, is not beneath such parlor leftists as Bertolucci, his brother, Giuseppe, and his film editor, Franco Arcalli, the coauthors of the script.

This is a sort of "Parallel Lives": the decline of the rich Berlinghieri family over the first half of our century, even as their tenant farmers, the Dalcos, rise to the top—thanks to their faith in Marx, the manifold gifts of young Olmo Dalco, and the ineluctable march of history. The two particularly parallel lives—albeit in opposite directions—are those of Olmo Dalco and Alfredo Berlinghieri.

The Berlinghieris are pigheaded autocrats, greedy weaklings, or artistic homosexual drug addicts, until we reach the grandson Alfredo (Robert De Niro). He is well-intentioned but irresolute, undermined by idleness and, after marrying the beautiful but unstable Ada (Dominique Sanda), by jealousy and frustration at not being able to dominate his wife. Olmo Dalco (Gérard Depardieu), by contrast, is strong, brave, generous, impassioned, and, of course, a Communist. Ada, dissatisfied by Alfredo's feeble, capitalist way of loving and living, naturally seeks solace in getting drunk on cheap but good Communist wine (red, of course) in the company of workers, and longs for Olmo's manly embraces. But though Olmo is clearly attracted, his Communist sense of honor precludes adultery.

Don't get the idea, however, that any relations between men and women are of major importance to Bertolucci. Although he purports to make fun of Uncle Ottavio's overt homosexuality, the writer-director's strongest feelings are reserved for the passionate, just barely platonic love-hate between Olmo and Alfredo. For a film that all but equates Fascism with pederasty and sadism, *1900* dawdles curiously over male nudity and waxes peculiarly sentimental over the quasi-sexual closeness of its two central figures. The boys play, fight, kiss each other, and masturbate together; later they possess an epileptic whore simultaneously. When this whore runs into Alfredo and Ada years afterward, Alfredo remembers her name—after all, he shared her with Olmo! He and Ada, who have been drifting apart and quarreling savagely, are immediately lovingly reconciled, and Ada expresses a fervent desire for children by Alfredo—let's not forget, the whore is Plain Folks, and there is nothing like Plain Folks as an instant remedy for all ills—social, sexual, and spiritual.

The lengthy last part of *1900* is an apotheosis of the Communist partisans (who apparently won the war single-handed) and partisan justice. Alfredo is tried by a people's kangaroo court, presided over by Olmo, and found guilty but is allowed to live stripped of his possessions. The film ends with an absurd montage of Olmo and Alfredo simultaneously children, mature adults, and oldsters, continuing to fight their childish battles in surreal fashion. De Niro and Depardieu, good actors both, have never been worse.

But no less important to Bertolucci than leftist propaganda is wallowing in sexual perversion and quite literal excrement. In the guise of censuring rich, Fascist decadence Bertolucci revels in sadomasochistic and drug-inspired orgies, often ending in brutal murder; in the guise of extolling the homely but honest life of the people, he gives us detailed scenes of animal slaughter and animal excrement, including shots of how to elicit fresh offal to throw at a Fascist by manually stimulating a horse's anus. For all its cloyingly beautiful cinematography, *1900* is one of the more stomach-turning films around.

Particularly odious is Bertolucci's concept of a typical Fascist couple, played more repulsively than would seem humanly possible by Laura Betti and, especially, Donald Sutherland. Their homicidal and otherwise perverted acts are dawdled over with a relish well beyond mere propagandizing zeal. Altogether, the film suffers from a moral blur: it is hard to tell whether Bertolucci is praising or reprehending something.

A frame-by-frame analysis of *1900* would reveal Bertolucci's tiresome adherence to derivative and often platitudinous devices—for example, the trick of denoting the passage of time by panning up to the sky, then back down to another landscape some years later. Extreme long shots and boom shots are used with particular ostentation; in fact, the handling of the camera reminds me of the arrogant massiveness of Mussolinian architecture, so ponderously satirized by Bertolucci in *The Conformist.* His customary cinematographer, Vittorio Storaro, provides his usual studied effects that have a way of choking out what little humanity Bertolucci might inadvertently have let squeak through.

And what dismal performances the director gets from talented performers! Specialists in stolidity like Burt Lancaster and Sterling Hayden do not suffer greatly; Robert De Niro and Gérard Depardieu, as mentioned before, fall very much short of their high standards; and lesser lights, such as Dominique Sanda and Stefania Sandrelli, disappear under Bertolucci's bushel. From a brazen ham like Donald Sutherland, we get a performance so appalling that we wonder whether he was directed with a cattle prod.

To give only one sample of how in this supposedly historically accurate film about the passing of the padrones and coming of the comrades Bertolucci falsifies facts, consider that all his Fascists are wealthy middle- and upper-class types, whereas all his Communists are poor peasants or workers. Which is about as far from truth as this clumsy director, who cannot even get good performances from those natural actors that children are, is from art. Moreover, the film (even in its uncut version) has more loose ends than a cashmere jacket used as a scratching post by a litter of kittens. Burt Lancaster, the old Berlinghieri patriarch, says, while hanging himself in a barn full of mud and cow dung, "Everything is milk and shit." Not quite everything: there is very little milk in *1900.*

If it is depressing to see how respectfully even reviewers who disliked *1900* treat young Bertolucci, it is downright ludicrous to note the critics and audiences groveling before every new piece of gratuitous tomfoolery that comes from the aged Luis Buñuel. His films have become progressively more guilty of what the late Charles Thomas Samuels (in a fine essay reprinted in his *Mastering the Film*) defined as "narrative opportunism," as a "commitment to incongruity" often consisting of nothing more than "a succession of switcheroos," titillating but self-contradictory. Yet most critics and many moviegoers accept the label "Buñuel" as a guarantee of quality, proving the charming indiscrimination of the bourgeoisie.

Buñuel's latest, *That Obscure Object of Desire,* is the sixth movie version of Pierre Louÿs's novel *Woman and Puppet* and, of the ones I've seen, much the worst. The book, dating from 1896, is an unprofound but dazzling study of a mature man's sexual obsession with a perverse young girl, and was a pioneer treatment in fiction of an archetypal sadomasochist relationship. Buñuel has turned this weird but impassioned and compelling tale into his brand of doddering, self-indulgent piling up of non sequiturs. To begin with, he has double-cast Conchita, the temptress, with two actresses of whom neither is talented and only one is remotely attractive. The reason may be that one dances flamenco, the other doesn't; but since the dancing one is often cast in nondance scenes, the effect is one of sheer irrationality.

364

With his usual ungifted coscenarist, Jean-Claude Carrière, Buñuel defuses the tale of passion by reducing much of the relationship between hero and dual heroine to out-and-out farce, complete with Laurel-and-Hardyish dousings, and, further, by obtruding a series of wholly irrelevant terrorist activities as a nonsense refrain running through the movie. (To pretend that both the destructive love story and those kidnappings, assassinations, and explosions contribute to the portraying of a world gone mad is, I am afraid, too facile an explanation for the unintegrated jumbling of disparate fragments.) On top of all that, we get the characteristic bits of epigonous surrealism as when what seems to be a swaddled infant at a woman's breast is revealed as a suckling pig.

The gratuitousness of such farce and shock effects can be neither explained nor explained away, and Fernando Rey performs the protagonist with his usual suave urbanity, further undercutting the theme of desperate obsession. Yet by sabotaging, indeed excising, this theme, the director leaves his film with a gaping void at the center and pointless curlicues around the periphery. I don't know which is sadder: this last decade of disintegration in Buñuel (whose films, to be sure, always tended toward a certain lack of discipline), or the mindless adulation that heaps hosannas on such vagaries.

December 23, 1977

The Engineer of Fluid Mechanics

FRANÇOIS TRUFFAUT has had a career not untypical of some of our most gifted filmmakers: a brilliant start followed by considerable floundering. No cinematic oeuvre could have begun more felicitously than his, with that remarkable trio of films: *The 400 Blows, Shoot the Piano Player,* and *Jules and Jim.* These pictures combined vitality with poignancy; they were informed by a nervous rhythm that could nevertheless linger over lyrical incidents, and a hard-bitten humor one could almost as easily cry over as laugh at. Each of these films, for all the director's very pronounced personality, retained its own particular flavor: there were no repetitions, no transposable parts.

But already with his fourth feature, *The Soft Skin,* Truffaut was in trouble, and though there were many good sequences in *Stolen Kisses* and *The Wild Child,* and some good ideas unsteadily blinking in *The Story of Adèle H.,* there were other movies with little to recommend them. The main problem seems to be a certain sentimentality, an ingratiating bittersweetness that apportions the bitter and the sweet with almost culinary calculation. The sentimentality is not quite your standard sort, with people gallantly muddling through to a comforting conclusion; but failure and sadness have a way of becoming badges of achievement, permitting their bearers access to a world   365 of bizarre, melancholy grace—perhaps free admission to the Cinémathèque Française.

No previous film of Truffaut's, however—not the preposterous *The Bride Wore Black,* not the desperately self-plagiarizing *Two English Girls,* not even the glamorized gossip column that was *Day for Night*—can surpass *The Man Who Loved Women* in non-risk-taking triviality. The hero, Bertrand Morane, is an engineer at the Institute for the Study of Fluid Mechanics in amiably provincial Montpellier, where he also plies his avocation: the insatiable yet ingenuous pursuit of women, with countless, though often troublesome, successes, as well as an occasional picturesque failure.

To dispense with traditional suspensefulness, the film begins with Bertrand's funeral, and also ends with it, as seen from the point of view of Geneviève, his literary editor and most enlightened girl friend. For Bertrand is also the author of an amorous autobiography entitled *The Man Who Loved Women,* and the film moves along three planes: the plane of events, that of recording them in a book, and that of memory being transformed by art. Compared to what a Pirandello—to say nothing of a Proust—could do with this sort of material, Truffaut remains a piker: let us say an engineer of mechanical fluidity. At best he becomes impish, as when the same actress plays Bertrand's mother and the prostitute who initiates the hero as a boy, but even this conceit remains undeveloped.

On however many planes, though, the film is basically a retelling of the Don Juan story, and the artist who broaches one of our great myths or legends is duty bound to enrich it with his personal vision and interpretation. Truffaut, however, not only adds nothing to it, but actually detracts from the great tale by trivializing it. Morane is in love mostly with women's legs; it is by following one pair that he gets run over by a car, and by craning excessively to see another, that of a nurse, that he falls out of his hospital bed, fatally unplugging the tubes that were restoring him to life. Even that leg fixation is artistically suspect—perhaps merely an excuse for piquant camera angles: much of the film is shot from the eye level of a hunting dog.

If there is any genuine feeling in this movie, it is less for women than for literature. Truffaut recently took time off for some bookwriting, which seems to have become a passion with him equal to his passion for making films. Accordingly, Bertrand is at least as obsessed with getting his book out as with getting into women; and it is, of course, Geneviève, his editor, who is the most interesting and desirable of all his women. Indeed, the camera embraces Bertrand's typewriter as lovingly as if it had found in it a long-lost, beloved elder brother.

Otherwise, it's all the usual twists: the attractive older woman who, while Bertrand thinks he is doing her a favor, rejects him for the sake of young boys; the jolly waitress with whom one can actually have a platonic friendship (though this had something to do with the fact that the actress playing the part had to leave Montpellier after a couple of days' shooting); the old flame, bumped into without much pleasure, with whom one ends up arguing about who walked out on whom. This last part, by the way, is played by that once winsome gamine Leslie Caron, now grown into a remarkably inept middle-aged actress.

I have my doubts about a Don Juan played by Charles Denner, a swarthy little hawk-nosed fellow, but I assume that, like Jean-Pierre Léaud, he serves as a visual alter ego for Truffaut. Denner is a striking actor in the right part; here he contributes no more than a wounded-animal look and that extraordinary deep voice of his, part softness, part asperity, like velvet rubbed in the wrong direction. Among the women, Brigitte Fossey, as the brainy yet gentle Geneviève, and Geneviève Fontanel, as the aging youth-lover, pathetic but also proud, are outstanding, with the German actress Sabine Gläser also likable as a rent-a-car hostess only slightly less fast than her cars.

Nestor Almendros's photography is less exciting than usual, and Maurice Jaubert's music is even less appropriate here than in *Adèle H.* It is lovely of Truffaut to dip into the *Nachlass* of this great French film composer who fell in World War II, but the way he misapplies these heirlooms merely attests to his lack of feeling for music. What he is still splendid at is pacing, and the film moves forward with the springiness of a stalking feline. This time, unfortunately, not a leopard, only a domestic tabby, bringing home a rather measly mouse.

If, on the other hand, you want European filmmaking at its worst, consider the *Iphigenia* of Michael Cacoyannis. This arrogant coxcomb presumes to rewrite Euripides' tragedy—a very modern, almost cynical, tragedy at that— as an old-fashioned tearjerker complete with De Millean crowd scenes, hammy cinematography, much meaningless running around, and a crude score by Mikis Theodorakis. The acting, too, is quite indifferent, ranging from a rather lethargic Iphigenia, played by an adolescent who might as easily be a boy as a girl, to Irene Papas, who continues her career as Europe's leading all-purpose *mater dolorosa*, equally adaptable to tragic whores and to whorishly misadapted tragedies.

January 6, 1978

Delicate Lacework

CLAUDE GORETTA'S *The Lacemaker* addresses itself to little things—greatly. The movie is simple enough; the script, by Goretta and Pascal Lainé, is based on the latter's novel. Béatrice, nicknamed Pomme, is an eighteen-year-old apprentice in a Paris beauty parlor. She is a shy girl, friendly yet passive, not unlike her mother, whose husband took off when Pomme was a child. A credit sequence, with the camera tracking and panning, shows the shop's activities as sufficient for this unassuming innocent. Her best friend, Marilyn, is a rather too experienced young woman about to be dumped by her married lover. The scene in which she is on the phone with him for the last time is a triumph of psychological observation translated into movement even more than dialogue, with camera placement and editing superlatively conveying Pomme's quiet bewilderment at a world whose harmfulness she cannot comprehend, let alone mitigate.

Marilyn and Pomme go off to Cabourg late in the season, somewhere in between the smart set and the desolation. The weather is bad, the place and people disconcerting. Still, Pomme perks up until Marilyn leaves to move in with an American. Pomme is enveloped in a seamless loneliness. The boredom of a miscarried vacation has never been better rendered than in a series of very short scenes here that suggest, against diverse backgrounds, the same stunned isolation. Then François, a literature student from the Sorbonne, who comes here only because his parents live nearby, talks to Pomme briefly at a café. They part. There is a montage of elegiac scenes in which each of them—he consciously, she unconsciously—searches for the other in vain. They meet again, and very slowly become friends and eventually lovers. With masterly skill, Goretta embeds the seeds of their incompatibility in the very scenes of courtship. They move into a Paris garret apartment together: she continues to work, he to study.

François's typically French bourgeois family, in a brief but agonizing meeting, freeze into genteel disapproval of a beautician. The youth's friends find Pomme likable, but talk over her head. Timorously, she tries to learn; he would teach her, but there is so much she doesn't know, and his time and patience are limited. He is embarrassed by her ignorance, exasperated by her passivity, and made to feel guilty by his curtness with someone so kind, gentle, and loving. Her uneagerness to go to school and improve herself (she wants to help him finish *his* studies first) unsettles him; soon he finds even her bites into an apple jarring.

The Lacemaker is a film without much action; it deals mostly in reactions. The dialogue is sparse, but pungent and poignant. Much of it is spoken by eyes rather than mouths. Silences tingle with affection, puzzlement, anxiety, goodwill, and bad blood. In fact, the story unfurls not so much in the events, which are small, as in the spaces between them, which are vast and filled with living. Expectant, contented, boring, and anguished living, its ordinariness perceived so sharply and tenderly as to loom no less miraculous than a human hair under a microscope. Goretta's compassionate comprehension of the human condition is the most powerful of all microscopes, with the camera for its compliant lens, trustily recording the minutest changes.

Take a night scene toward the end of the affair. François is looking out of the window at nothing. Pomme undresses confidently, sweetly approaches him, and puts a bare arm around his sweatshirted waist; his sleeve, perfunctorily brushing her nakedness, is almost a gauntlet. From the way her head is tilted upward, though the entire shot is from the back, we know the pleading expression on her unseen face; from the mere closeness of his head to the window, we can gauge his unresponsiveness. She slinks off to bed: a naked, vulnerable figure, defeated by his rigid back, his silence, his clothes.

Béatrice returns to her mother, and the film records with infinite solicitude the stages of her decline. Running away from a phone booth that has finally become available is followed by being able to negotiate all the steps of a stairway except the last. One day she collapses at a busy street crossing; Goretta films most of it in a long shot, distance making it more inexorable, awful. Finally, she is in a mental hospital up north somewhere, and François comes to visit her. The colors are pale yellow and blue-gray: cold. Sere foliage crackles underfoot as they pace the hospital gardens; a doctor whom Pomme proudly describes as an acquaintance walks by ignoring her; she pathetically invents amorous adventures in Greece (she never got closer to it than posters in the recreation room) to let François off the hook, and he instead takes it badly. These and the many other details of the visit are etched in pure pain. Take the paired, blank-voiced *oui, oui*'s with which she answers his insistent questioning: a dying person might so agree with someone complaining about the weather.

Goretta can pull off elaborate crane shots such as the circular pan around Cabourg that ends with a zoom-in on Pomme walking forlornly, but that is not what the young Swiss director (making his first movie in France) is interested in. Like his superb cinematographer, Jean Boffety, he is not out to impress with his technique, only to evoke particulars with the ultimate accuracy that comes as much from self-effacement as from talent. Take the emblematic moment when Pomme deposits a sea shell she has been carrying about in her pocket on the cross of an American soldier who fell on D-day: a frail girl pays a tiny tribute to one out of so monstrously many crosses. No closeup; only a medium-long shot, scrupulously laconic. Or consider the treatment of a character as secondary as the insubstantial Marilyn: she is accorded a number of scenes in which she can reveal her frivolous yet desperately frightened nature—without prettification and, therefore, with true pathos. Florence Giorgetti plays her wrenchingly.

But all the performances, from leads to walk-ons, are carved out of truth. Yves Bereyton's François is a perfect insecure, nervous young intellectual, trying hard for magnanimity but managing only correctness. Even more remarkable is the twenty-two-year-old Isabelle Huppert's Béatrice; a heart-rendingly vivid presence fashioned out of timidity and inarticulateness, whom the author's epilogue compares to the humble artisans of yesteryear finding fulfillment in work as seamstresses, water carriers, lacemakers (an allusion, surely, to Vermeer's great painting in the Louvre)—people whose worth we pass by unnoticing in our present rush.

No more than in his two previous gems, *The Invitation* and the here stupidly mistitled *The Wonderful Crook*, does Goretta sentimentalize; even the score he gets from the excellent Pierre Jansen is lovely but spare—mostly a cello-piano duo situated somewhere between Satie and late Debussy. *The Lacemaker* is a film we go to not to judge but to be judged by; it makes the much abused "masterpiece" a clean word once again.

Grade AA Extra-Large

ONE OF THE indispensable rights of the artist is the right to fail. The creative mind needs to grow, and such growth may not be possible without convulsions or occasional false starts. Most great creators who went from one style to another had to pay for it with transitional works that remained relatively or totally unsuccessful. Even Shakespeare's problem plays are problematic in part because they are a problem to mount. Before Ingmar Bergman could make *Winter Light*, he had to stumble with *Through a Glass Darkly;* the relationship between kindred yet antagonistic women did not come off in *The Silence*, but did in *Persona*. In the former transitional phase, Bergman was evolving the chamber film; in the latter, a method of delving into psychic action under comparatively uneventful surface goings-on.

With *The Serpent's Egg*, Bergman is again striking out in a new direction, and though his failure of achievement cannot be excused by worthiness of intentions, it behooves us to understand what is at stake here. That Bergman is one of the supreme masters of the film about personal relationships, about the neuroses and psychoses men and women fall prey to both in seeking out and in trying to avoid involvements, no one in his right mind can deny. But Bergman has not been much concerned with politics, and some of the younger Swedish filmmakers have duly attacked him for his alleged elitist solipsism, his lack of social awareness. Now, Bergman has occasionally made more political films: e.g., the early *This Can't Happen Here* (1950), of which he says that he did it only for the money; that he was dead tired and ill at the time, and turned it all "into a lot of crap." A more recent political film, *Shame* (1967), likewise failed to satisfy its maker, though many of us consider it one of his finest.

The reason that *Shame* works, though it is about civil war, collaboration, betrayal of ideals, and other "public" issues, is that at its core there is still Bergman's favorite compound hero: the couple, a man and woman with, for, and against each other. Jan and Eva Rosenberg were a typical Bergmanian husband and wife, and their problems carried the film—although it seems to me that the raging war in the background was handled with equal brilliance. (The Rosenbergs were Jewish, something that was not evident to us foreign viewers.) As Bergman told me in the interview affixed to my book *Ingmar Bergman Directs*, he made *Shame* because he considers himself uncourageous, and wanted to visualize how he would have behaved under totalitarian blandishments and threats. In the new film, he pushes the investigation further.

The Serpent's Egg surveys the rise of Nazi ideology both among an underground group of scientists experimenting with ways to impose Fascism on the human organism and psyche, and among ordinary people and their victims. The hero and heroine are again called Rosenberg: Abel and his sister-in-law, Manuela, whose husband, Max, has just committed suicide. It is November 1923, Germany is in the grip of inflation and destitution, and

Hitler is preparing his abortive Munich *Putsch*. Manuela, who works nights in a tawdry cabaret and days in a brothel, and Abel, who mostly drinks and sulks, were until recently, along with Max, part of a trapeze act. Now they have set up housekeeping together in Berlin lodgings provided by Dr. Hans Vergérus, a sinister scientist whom Abel met years ago on holiday in Italy (unlikely business!), and who is an admirer and occasional client of Manuela's.

The shabby apartment is part of St. Anna's Clinic; Vergérus, who runs the clinic, has also found a job there for Manuela in the laundry, and for Abel in the rather peculiar archives. Altogether the clinic is weird, and, with the encouragement of Bauer, a tough but decent police inspector, Abel discovers that Vergérus is conducting vicious clandestine experiments on starving Berliners whom he can lure with the promise of a square meal and a bit of money. These human guinea pigs end up demented or dead; the archives document their hideous deterioration.

Abel gets to the bottom of things, but the price is overwhelming. By the time he has finished, Manuela is dead, and he himself is a wreck. As Bauer is about to apprehend Vergérus, the doctor commits suicide, but not before announcing that he and his colleagues are hatching the serpent's egg from which world dictatorship will be born. Bauer tells Abel proudly that Hitler's *Putsch* failed, and offers him safe conduct to Switzerland, there to rejoin the circus. A title tells us that, on the way to the station, Abel jumped out of the police car, and was never seen again.

I give you all this plot to make clearer the confusions of the film. There are bits of old Bergman themes clogging up the works. Thus Berlin during the inflation reminds us of wartime Timoka in *The Silence;* the uneasy, hounded Rosenbergs come, of course, from *Shame.* The intensely yet indistinctly haunted Jewish hero has much in common with David from *The Touch.* The films of his evil experiments that Vergérus shows Abel are an extension of the ominous photographic collection that the faintly unsavory architect Vergérus (that name again!) displays to the hero of *The Passion of Anna.* (This Vergérus, in turn, harks back to the similarly named doctor in *The Magician.*). The minister who has lost faith in God and from whom Manuela vainly seeks solace is descended from the similar clergyman in *Cries and Whispers,* and their common ancestor is the hero of *Winter Light.* There are also jarring—because obvious—external derivations. The archives and their keepers are straight out of Kafka; the nightclub sequences, out of *The Blue Angel,* with a possible assist from *Cabaret.* The film is simply too eclectic for its own good.

Bergman's self-imposed exile in Germany may also be part of the problem. Though he still has his trusted and tremendous cinematographer, Sven Nykvist, and his radiant star, Liv Ullmann (here, in a shadowy and unsuitable role, less than impressive), the rest of the team is new. Working in a foreign language hampers most artists, and Bergman is no exception—witness *The Touch.* With American and German actors he hasn't the same creative give-and-take that he evolved with his Swedish ones. But the main obstacle is, surely, the subject. Although smaller scenes of specific nastiness are expertly executed—the self-hating Rosenberg hurling a stone through the shop window of a manifestly Jewish namesake, and thus alter ego; Nazi hoodlums torturing a Jewish nightclub owner; starving people feasting off, then selling, the remnants of a dead horse in the streets—the overarching political drama eludes Bergman. He can touch it only in terms of science fiction, better handled by other directors from Fritz Lang to Stanley Kubrick; as for scenes of pursuit and hand-to-hand combat, they simply aren't his métier.

There is decent work from Gert Froebe as Bauer and Heinz Bennent as Vergérus, but David Carradine's Abel remains oversimplified and inexpressive, the role and the performer sharing the guilt. Even Rolf Wilhelm's songs are only self-conscious imitations of Friedrich Holländer's marvelous ones for *The Blue Angel.* Decadence is not Bergman's specialty (perhaps because of his strict Lutheran background): the homosexual orgy in *Face to Face* was a failure, and so is a scene here with Abel, a disturbed black man, and two Berlin whores, in which even the language (presumably Englished by Alan Blair, Bergman's usual subtitulist) becomes embarrassing. But there is good production design by Rolf Zehetbauer and acceptable costuming by Charlotte Flemming, photographed to moody perfection by Sven Nykvist.

The published screenplay, which, as customary with Bergman, is more prolix and ineffectual than the film, sports an epigraph from Georg Büchner's *Woyzeck:* "Man is an abyss. I get dizzy looking down into it." It may be the best thing about *The Serpent's Egg.*

March 3, 1978

Through Babel to the Flood

LAST TIME AROUND, apropos of Bergman's latest, I wrote about an artist's right to fail; this time it is Lina Wertmüller's turn to claim that privilege. The first important female fiction film director in Western cinema (there have been some major women directors in Iron Curtain countries; Leni Riefenstahl matters only as a documentarist), Miss Wertmüller has made four films on which a reputation can rest as firmly as any table on four well-measured legs. *The Seduction of Mimi* (the American titles are poorer, albeit shorter, than the Italian ones), *Love and Anarchy, Swept Away,* and *Seven Beauties* constitute a corpus that only the most rabid and purblind feminist or the most lily-white purist could find without merit, and that I consider satisfying on both the cerebral and the gut level.

In fact, this is Wertmüller's particular strength: a combination of shrewdly perceptive intelligence (not necessarily intellectuality, but what of that?) and an uncanny sense of how the human animal behaves both in its rare, exalted moments and in its numerous absurd and farcical ones. What

372

may bother some viewers of Wertmüller's films is her odd attitude toward people. Though she is fond of them, she also laughs at them relentlessly; though, save the few she admires, she kicks them in their behinds, the kicks are delivered with jovial laughter. Truly, if kicks in the pants can be affectionate, these are.

Another problem for Wertmüller, especially in Italy, is that she is a socialist-anarchist rather than a Marxist, Catholic, Zen Buddhist, or whatever the currently accepted orthodoxies and fashionable heresies may be. She believes in creative disorder: a state of absolute freedom in which long periods of hard work alternate with generous spurts of intense play. Clearly, this is a platform suited more to a person of genius (or at least considerable talent) and a self-employed artist than to the average mortal with a typical middle-class job. Wertmüller's philosophy—perhaps no more than inspired self-indulgence, but just as appealing by any name—is a kind of elitism for everybody who wants it, a democratized aristocracy. It is, most likely, an impossibility, but only a trifle more so than most political systems and ideologies, and immeasurably more attractive.

That Wertmüller's new film, *The End of the World in Our Usual Bed in a Night Full of Rain*, is an almost total failure should, on reflection, not be surprising. This is the story of the courtship and marriage of a young American woman photographer and an Italian journalist—she a bourgeoise turned feminist, he a Communist ensconced in his aunt's lavish apartment—which has to carry several bone-crushing burdens.

To begin with, it was filmed (partly in San Francisco) in English, a language that the writer-director at that time knew but very imperfectly. Rudimentary, too, was her knowledge of America. Though the film is adequately Englished, it has clearly been thought and felt in Italian, and thinking and feeling are much harder to translate than words. The result is a certain crude oversimplification of plot and character—to say nothing of dialogue—that is very different from Wertmüller's usual healthy vulgarity studded with flashes of poetry.

Then, for only the second time in her filmmaking career, the director was creating something intended to be serious drama; yet her background in comedy obtruded comic timing, comic situations, vaguely comic turns of phrase on what was meant to express a sad reality: the realization that love grows tyrannical and onerous; that sex turns mechanical; that spouses become each other's jailers and victims, with the captive as much a tormentor as the turnkey. The Fellinian verbal and visual language proved simply inadequate to the Bergmanian theme—Fellini himself had a similar problem in *Juliet of the Spirits,* which *A Night Full of Rain* resembles in spirit, if not in the letter.

Furthermore, the project was too ambitious. The husband and wife are distinctly meant to assume symbolic dimensions. He is the Old World, she the New; their inability to thrive with each other brings about that preternatural rain that keeps falling throughout, until it becomes another Noah's Flood, from which no ark may sail forth. The couple is surrounded, more-

373

over, not by identifiable secondary characters, but by a quasi-Greek chorus of friends—some charming, some grotesque—who comment on the principals' values, behavior, situation. This is probably no longer practicable even on stage; on screen, where this chorus pops up perched on interior balconies, reflected in mirrors, and in other unlikely places, the effect is particularly obtrusive, offensive, and essentially anticinematic. No wonder that, trying to do so much, the film first appeared in a four-and-a-half-hour version that was gradually whittled down to under two hours, at the cost of its rather tenuous continuity. Since Wertmüller refused to relinquish some of her beloved scenes entirely, we get shots of the hero's father suffering a heart attack or of the hero seeking advice from a prominent Catholic mentor that are so foreshortened as to be incomprehensible to anyone lacking privileged information.

Finally, there is the problem of the actors' speech. Except for Candice Bergen, who under Wertmüller's despotically demanding direction gives the best performance of her career (which still isn't saying very much), and for one or two Americans in minor roles, we have here Italians whose English sounds at best like what is misguidedly dubbed into the so-called English-language versions of Italian comedies; at worst, impenetrable. Thus Giancarlo Giannini, that delightful actor, suffers as much from his English as from an unfortunate scraggly beard that reinforces his status as the comic Italian. The film proves that a Babel of accents can be as bad as one of tongues.

Even some of Wertmüller's virtues work against this film. The director is fond of casting her friends in small parts, and of including texts by writers she knows and admires. Here some of her cronies let her down histrionically—for example, Lucio Amelio, who was wonderful as the lawyer in *Seven Beauties* but is top-heavy and incomprehensible now as one of the more vocal chorus members. Similarly, a text by the writer Guido Ceronetti, put into the mouth of another writer, Paola Ojetti (who plays the aunt unconvincingly), though much cut from the film's original version, still sticks out like a sixth finger, which I take to be worse than a sore thumb. And the score by Roberto de Simone, a new Wertmüller discovery, is disappointing—even more so when it drags in Pergolesi to overpower the rest.

Another hurtful virtue here is that visual excellence Wertmüller's films consistently display. The splendid cinematography of Giuseppe Rotunno; the impressive locations (in particular, the austerely beautiful medieval abbey at Padula, although Wertmüller can coax some extraordinary shots even from the by now vastly overphotographed city of San Francisco); and the superb interiors designed by Enrico Job, the director's husband: all these merely dwarf what goes on in front of them, making it appear even more strident and trivial.

Does this leave anything of value? Well, the first encounter of the future spouses at a religious procession in Padula has a few good moments; a scene in a San Francisco night spot in which Giannini jealously watches Bergen torment him as she clingingly dances with another man is effective, although it was even more so before it was pared down in the final cut. Such rare good moments can, like the visual riches, contribute only sadness about what might have been—and what may again be in this gifted and undauntable woman's next picture.

March 31, 1978

Partly Palatable

THE ONLY PREVIOUS FILM by Franco Brusati that I have seen is *Disorder,* which, despite some good moments and brilliant editing by Ruggero Mastroianni, left me cold. Since then, Brusati, a successful screenwriter and playwright, has made a couple of films that were not seen here—or at least not by me; *Bread and Chocolate,* his fifth film, has won scads of prizes all over Europe, and is now here to enliven our cinematically dismal summer. *Bread and Chocolate* is an interesting film—parts of it have that nice blend of humor and pathos at which the Italians are past masters—but it is not all milk and honey, I'm afraid, or even piss and vinegar.

It starts well enough with an Italian, neither young nor old, in his dark, workingman's Sunday-best; he is in a park, surrounded by prosperous, mostly white-clad people playing chamber music, promenading, having fun with their children. The Italian, Nino, tries to be friendly, but he does not speak German—for this is Switzerland—and even small children spurn him when he tries to play handball with them. When, smoking under a No Smoking sign, he bites into his bread and chocolate sandwich, that little crunch stops a string quartet in its tracks: reproachfulness is in the air, for this man is a guest worker, one of those hordes of swarthy, dark-haired creatures that invade Switzerland, which feels about them as Byron said he felt about women—unable to live either with or without them.

Nino gets into all kinds of trouble even—or especially—when he is trying to be helpful. He is competing bitterly with a Turk for the one permanent position as a waiter at a posh restaurant where they are both temporary help. Their contest is positively Homeric, though less like the *Iliad* than like *The Battle of the Frogs and Mice.* The Turk is repulsive but good at everything through sheer insane determination worthy of a bashi-bazuk; Nino, on the other hand, is charming and imposingly ineffectual. He enters into a curious business relationship with a crooked Italian millionaire, and loses his small savings. He also loses his heart, briefly, to Elena, a Greek schoolteacher in exile with her little boy, whom he befriends by teaching him Italian swear words. Funny-sad and outrageous episodes multiply, but the various threads are only very loosely held together: we lose sight of Elena, for example, far too often. There is something not merely episodic about the film but downright sporadic, and it is only Nino himself who is allowed to become a fully fleshed-out character.

Still, the bittersweet humor, the occasional artfully done bit of slapstick, 375 the sudden moments of seriousness, all testify to a much better handling of mood than of plot or even character. And yet, thanks to the marvelous acting of Nino Manfredi, Anna Karina, and a fine supporting cast mostly unknown to me, and Brusati's pleasantly slapdash direction in which things are allowed to look as sloppy as life, much of it works. Certainly, the comic coming together of Manfredi and Karina is particularly moving: after his attempts at debonair seductiveness have failed, he wins her through his ludicrousness. However, he is married already—we see one of his imaginary dialogues with the hungry mouths back home—and she, for the sake of convenience, marries a decent Swiss official who can help them all to stay in Switzerland.

So long as the film is comedy, or even *comédie larmoyante,* its footing is sure; but soon the serious and the grotesque take over. The transition occurs in a much too long-drawn-out scene reminiscent of Buñuel, Hieronymus Bosch, and even Thomas Mann, in which gnomelike Italians working as illegal poultry butchers become transformed into human chickens and watch with a mixture of obscene longing and abject veneration as the blond and blue-eyed children of their bosses disport themselves naked on the banks of a sylvan pond. Horror-struck, Nino flees to the other extreme and tries to forswear his Italianness by dying his hair blond, but a televised soccer game at which he cannot help rooting for his fellow countrymen betrays him. These and other final episodes verge on the maudlin, and the ending is ambiguous without being particularly suggestive.

Nino Manfredi, that superb comedian, who also collaborated with Brusati on the script, gets more out of it, I'm sure, than he put in. His mixture of swagger and subservience, hopefulness in the face of imminent deportation and other disasters, is nicely balanced by his growing disgust with fellow immigrant workers who still cherish the myth of the homeland. But, finally, Nino does not stand for any course of action, and even his indecisiveness is less graphic than that of, say, some Wertmüller characters.

To the sketchy role of Elena, Anna Karina brings a compassionate femininity that never postures or goes sickly-sweet, and shows talents that were completely wasted in her Godard films and only adumbrated since. In the supporting cast, Johnny Dorelli and Gianfranco Barra excel as, respectively, the devious industrialist and the dedicated Turk. Renato Berta's cinematography is, as always, a joy, and Brusati, though unable to overcome the general fragmentation, has directed individual scenes cogently.

September 1, 1978

Interiörs

IT IS SAD to have to report that with *Autumn Sonata* Bergman has made his third unsuccessful film in a row. Although it was again shot away from his homeland, the exteriors were done in neighboring Norway, the film's language is Swedish, and the cast comprises several Bergman regulars. Moreover, the plot, unlike that of *The Serpent's Egg*, returns us to familiar Bergman territory: love and hate within an intimate family group.

But this time it is the love-hate between a mother and daughter. Charlotte, a fairly important concert pianist, has always neglected or thwarted her two daughters; one of them, Eva, who has not seen her mother for seven years, and has now invited her to her house. Eva, who has achieved a minuscule reputation as a writer, is married passionlessly but peacefully to a clergyman, Viktor; they have lost a beloved child, and so Eva sympathizes with her mother, whose lover and companion of many years, Leonardo, has just died. To the arriving Charlotte's horror, Eva is also sheltering in her house her sister Helena, slowly dying of some dreadful, unspecified disease that is causing her to lose her faculties one by one.

The ingredients of a television melodrama are clearly present, and though Bergman avoids the Scylla of sensationalism, he plummets into the Charybdis of talk, talk, talk unrelieved by power, poetry, or wit. The mother-daughter duologues are interrupted by occasional flashbacks, but these too are monumentally static and rather stagily directed; for once, Bergman's remarkable sense for making film out of potentially anticinematic material forsakes the director almost entirely. In such magnificent films as, say, *Winter Light*, *Persona*, and *The Passion of Anna*, Bergman could make emotional confrontations between a few closely related people—often no more than two—come as dramatically alive as anything ever put on screen. Here, somehow, words fail him; and, watching the film, I prayed fervently for Charlotte's often reiterated wish to take a walk to come true, and for scenery to come to the rescue. No such luck; the film remains trapped in unrelieved rooms and untranscended palaver.

Perhaps the problem is that Bergman's two great themes, on which he can play endless, brilliant variations—sex and faith—are almost wholly absent from this film. Leonardo is merely a shadowy background figure; Viktor only a shadowy foreground one. Poor Helena adds little beyond some gratuitous shock value, and the all-consuming struggle between mother and daughter is perforce sexless. Religion makes a pallid appearance in Viktor, who, for all his religious contribution to the film, might as well be a furniture salesman. Near the end, Eva does soliloquize about her belief in her dead child's life beyond death, but even though the scene is set in a graveyard, its emotional impact is nil.

There are two scenes that work tidily. One has Charlotte ask Eva, a trifle patronizingly, to play some Chopin for her, which Eva timidly does; whereupon Charlotte sits down beside her, helpfully critizes the rendition, and proceeds to demonstrate how the piece should have been played—only to shatter, without the slightest bad intention, Eva's self-confidence all over again. Another quite brief scene has Charlotte, unable to sleep without Leonardo's comforting closeness, go over the notebook in which her lover kept his accounts, and discover to her delight how much he has left her. It would have been easy to make Charlotte utterly unsympathetic in this scene, 377 but the filmmaker, with exquisite artistry, keeps her pleasure human and likable.

A third, even briefer, sequence may be included among the picture's assets. It is a montage of shots of Charlotte's vigil by her dying lover's bedside in an Italian hospital. Through the mediation of Sven Nykvist's masterly camera, the changing light and colors express with reticent, wordless eloquence the pathos of mortality. For the rest, the film is so much tedious verbalizing barely stirred up by occasional outbursts of verbal violence that bring no more relief than a short thunderstorm does to a dry, hot summer. The words lack depth and impact. It has been said in Sweden that Bergman's language is outmoded and even somewhat stilted; having no Swedish, I can only say that, in translation, the dialogue of the better Bergman films has always struck me as being among the best to be had on screen.

Perhaps an added problem is the lack of significant background: the emotionally charged island scenery of so many Bergman films, the war-torn land- and cityscapes of *Shame* and *The Silence,* the austere settings and disquieting northern climate of *Winter Light.* The four walls of *Autumn Sonata,* despite the musical title, do not supply the much-needed contrapuntal elements or harmonic development. To cap it all, the film does not know how to end; there are some four or five final scenes each of which is a coda, and each of which is only to be followed by another and yet another conflicting coda.

The acting is not without its surprises. Liv Ullmann, who even in such inferior Bergman works as *The Hour of the Wolf, Cries and Whispers,* and *Face to Face* could perform miracles with her marvelous performances, is downright unsubtle in portraying Eva's regressive awkwardnesses in the early encounters with Charlotte. Though it gets better as it goes along, the performance remains shadowed by the inauspicious beginnings. Conversely and unexpectedly, Ingrid Bergman (over whose performance Ingmar reportedly sweated blood, and with which he is said to remain deeply dissatisfied) gives a splendid enactment of the neart-artist as a total bourgeoise full of characteristic middle-class strengths and failings that nevertheless catch us unawares. Only in the two scenes she plays in English is the actress, meant to be theatrical there, excessive in her disingenuous cheerfulness.

Lena Nyman, known to us only from *I Am Curious (Yellow* and *Blue),* is astonishingly controlled and effective in the role of the crippled, atrophying Helena, which might easily have become an embarrassment. To the thankless role of Viktor, Halvar Björk lends a kindly face and presence. Erland Josephson appears in an almost subliminal part, and Gunnar Björnstrand's cameo contribution as Charlotte's nonspeaking American agent (does he not speak for lack of English or because of some disease of the throat?) is scarcely more extensive. This may be an in-joke, for the *Variety*-reading agent is named Paul, and may be modeled on Bergman's American agent, Paul Kohner.

There may also be other motifs here with special autobiographical significance for Bergman. The director's father was a Lutheran minister like Viktor; a former Mrs. Bergman, Käbi Laretei, is a near-major concert pianist, who, as on previous occasions, supplies the piano music on the soundtrack. Eva's difficulties with her famous and often unavailable mother may resemble those of some of Ingmar's many children with their celebrated and otherwise occupied father. But, for once, the autobiography does not spread outward; the film remains acutely and aridly centripetal.

As others besides me have remarked, *Autumn Sonata*, with its ceaseless, undramatized exposition, displays embarrassing parallels to Woody Allen's unfortunate *Interiors*, even down to a glaring red dress that in both movies scores a facile effect. But red dress notwithstanding, when Viktor refers to the "gray film" that has settled on his and Eva's marriage, the reference might as well be to *Autumn Sonata* itself.

November 24, 1978

Tampering With Emotions

FINALLY WE HAVE Luchino Visconti's *The Innocent*, posthumously edited by other hands. I say "finally" not because I have been waiting with bated breath, but because I am glad to see the last of a director whom others may have considered a major artist, but who, to me, was no more than a clever poseur exuding a certain type of homosexual sensibility—all gorgeous costuming, lush décor, melodramatic attitudinizing, and very little substance or depth. Although he was one of the several begetters of neorealism, his early, and supposedly earthy, films strike me as mostly self-indulgent and dull. Self-indulgence, for him, had to become a baroque, operatic excess (as in *Bellissima, Senso*, parts of *Rocco and His Brothers*, and *The Leopard*) to achieve any real originality, which, however, promptly turned overbearing and outrageous. Whenever he adapted serious fiction to the screen (Dostoyevsky, Camus, Mann), he fairly consistently managed to reduce it to a kind of kitsch indistinguishable from some of his fruitier nonadaptations—*Sandra, The Damned, Ludwig*.

I am not certain whether Gabriele d'Annunzio's *L'innocente* (1892) qualifies as serious fiction, but, as written, it is not without serious psychological and stylistic interest. The high-born Tullio Hermil, a "superman" concocted from Nietzsche and Dostoyevsky, with a little French-symbolist veneer for high gloss, is meant as a demonstration in action of the following bit of the protagonist's interior monologue: "Why has man in his nature this horrible faculty of rejoicing more keenly when he is conscious of doing harm to the being from whom he desires his happiness? Why is there the germ of the most execrable sadistic perversion in every man who loves and desires?" It is, however, not only Tullio who feels and acts out these impulses, but also the *femme fatale*, Countess Teresa, who becomes his mistress: while with his lovely and gentle wife, Giuliana, he maintains a brother-sister relationship, and encourages her to have affairs of her own.

379

When Giuliana does indulge in a little sauce for the goose with the chivalrous novelist Filippo d'Arborio, she becomes pregnant, and her lover goes off to Africa. Jealousy makes Tullio ardent toward his wife, and she, reluctantly, submits. But it is not so much Catholicism that makes her refuse the abortion her atheistic husband urges upon her, as secret love for the by now dead Filippo, whose child she would protect from Tullio's vengeance. Tullio does indeed cause the baby's death, and, in the film, makes love to Teresa once more, then shoots himself.

That ending is utterly out of key: in the novel, the hero and alter ego of d'Annunzio goes on *Übermensch*-ing it up, but the paralyzed, moribund Visconti obviously wanted a grand gesture of final stoicism to be performed by *his* hero and alter ego. This battle of alter egos helps do in the film, but other flaws are equally fatal. Once again, the décor and costumes overshadow all the other components: the considerably defused screenplay that turns a superman into a mere philanderer, the infelicitously idiosyncratic direction, the mediocre performances. Visconti seems to encourage staginess in the acting; he never tires (though we do) of persons stalking one another in circles across the wide screen as the camera pans or dollies around with them; and he loves to come in for extreme closeups of heads, or even mere parts of heads.

Giancarlo Giannini, a racy portrayer of the lecherous delights and jealous outbursts of lower-class Italian males, is miscast as a demonic aristocrat: he comes across as a cocky parvenu. Laura Antonelli does better as Giuliana, although you can see that the director's heart is not in heterosexual eroticism, and the sex scenes, for all their heaving nudity, fail to ignite. Jennifer O'Neill, as Teresa, comes off best, because Visconti's extravagant costuming and an Italian actress's dubbed-in voice perform far better than Miss O'Neill ever could.

The single scene that has genuine force is the one in the shower room, where Tullio observes with raging envy the superior physical endowments of his rival. Among richly homoerotic overtones, Visconti's slender talent registers for the last time with a lurid, evanescent flicker. Benedetto Croce's dismissal of much of d'Annunzio as "lushly sensual amateurism" can stand for most of Visconti.

The National Society of Film Critics has picked as best film of the past year Bertrand Blier's *Get Out Your Handkerchiefs*. Now, I realize that 1978 was a disaster year for movies, and that the Blier film made it as a compromise to keep some other films, which various reviewers found even more hateful, from winning. Under the circumstances no film should have been proclaimed worthy, but, perhaps by analogy with politics, some candidate always gets elected, be he ever so questionable.

Blier's first film, *Going Places*, was an offensive piece of misogynistic claptrap, celebrating the alliance of two thoroughly worthless petty criminals at the expense of the bourgeois world, particularly its females. Blier's next, evidently, was so appalling that it sank *before* it could cross the ocean. *Handkerchiefs,* his third, is less overtly woman-hating and antisocial, but the basic stance of *Going Places* is present in a somewhat disguised or diluted form.

The film brings back, in similar roles, the louts from *Going Places*, Gérard Depardieu and Patrick Dewaere. Depardieu is married to pretty Carole Laure, who is bored with existence and, more particularly, with her marital bed. So Depardieu picks up a likely stranger (Dewaere), in hopes that the latter will be able to arouse his spouse's dormant sexuality; but these piquantly extramarital efforts prove equally soporific to Miss Laure. Another chap fails no less egregiously. Only a thirteen-year-old boy of genius IQ is capable of arousing Miss Laure's desire, and she sets up housekeeping with him. Depardieu and Dewaere, whom thwarted passion has briefly landed in jail, can merely look in wistfully through the window at Miss Laure's infantile bliss. Then, cursing, they depart.

Never mind the homosexual implications in the Depardieu-Dewaere relationship; never mind the film's general misanthropy; never mind even the paucity of genuine laughs in an alleged comedy. What is truly worrisome is that Blier makes not the slightest attempt to explain, even in farcical terms, what caused Miss Laure's frigidity and ennui, or why it dissolves at the touch of an adolescent. The boy's alleged genius is not conveyed by Blier's script or direction, and still less by the boy's acting, personality, or looks. And nothing is more absurd than the intelligence test by which Miss Laure demonstrates the boy's superior IQ to her adult lovers: he can draw a tree, whereas they can't. This has no humorous, satirical, psychological, or any other kind of value; yet it is a key incident in the movie and characteristic of *its* general IQ.

What emerges from *Get Out Your Handkerchiefs* is that (a) women are capricious, weird, utterly inscrutable creatures whom men cannot even begin to satisfy; (b) what can truly fulfill a woman is a crunchy thirteen-year-old boy virgin—in fact, a typical pederastic taste; and (c) men are finally safer going off into the night together, sans female encumbrances. Of scarcely lesser interest is the theme of a man sharing his woman with a male friend—according to psychoanalysis, a *locus classicus* of covert homosexuality. When I asked Blier whether he considered it fair to interpret his films in clinical terms, he answered, with engaging candor, that such an interpretation most likely is relevant. Which raises the question of why a film that is not particularly funny, that flagrantly falsifies heterosexual relations, and that is ultimately insulting to women should win rave reviews, prizes, and an Oscar nomination.

March 16–April 13, 1979

The Soil and the Soiled

ERMANNO OLMI, the Italian filmmaker, has made at least three pictures I rate among the finest I know: *Il posto* (*The Job*, but distributed under the asinine title *The Sound of Trumpets*), *The Fiancés,* and *One Fine Day.* I have not seen his first film, *Time Stood Still,* about which I hear good things; his later work ranges from interesting to disappointing, including one whopping fiasco about Pope John. Olmi is something of an anomaly among Italian directors, almost all of whom are more or less left-oriented urban nonbelievers, and all of whom are based in Rome. Olmi, however, lives in Milan, has remained true to his peasant origins, and is a good Catholic.

Paradoxically, Olmi's films have been most honored in the Iron Curtain countries. In the West, he is relatively little known; in Italy, where his films make no money, even informed moviegoers know his work only spottily, and then mostly from television. But Olmi goes on pursuing his own teleological vision, his personal muse; he writes his own scripts, works with amateur actors, and is his own cinematographer and editor. Even when his films miscarry, there is an infectious honesty and commitment in them; his respect for people and life remains unshakable, without lapsing into sentimentality or preachment. So, at least, it was until now.

I was overjoyed to learn that his 185-minute work *The Tree of Wooden Clogs* won the grand prize at Cannes last year; finally, I thought, Olmi will have the commercial success that will make him bankable. (I also thought, incidentally, that the redundant and clumsy English translation of the film's title was a pity—it should be simply *The Clog Tree,* although, in English, that, too, lacks evocativeness and euphony.) Upon seeing the film, however, I must regretfully pronounce it an earnest, well-meaning failure.

This is the story of a year in the lives of some four or five turn-of-the-century families of sharecroppers on a rich man's estate near Bergamo. Two thirds of what they earn with hard, long labor goes to the landlord. The film records their victories and defeats, work and leisure, fights and mutual support. A woman gives birth to yet another child to feed; a timid courtship ends in marriage and the (somewhat incredible) adoption of an orphan; a bright son is sent off to school despite his father's doubts about its seemliness for a peasant boy, and despite the boy's having to walk several miles to school and back every day. The two main events are the boy's breaking one of his clogs, which necessitates his father's chopping down one of the landlord's willows to carve a new pair of wooden shoes; and the discovery of this act, which leads to the family's expulsion from the farmstead while the other families, watching glumly from their windows, do not even dare to come out and offer a parting gift of sympathy.

There are some nice vignettes: the shrewd but sympathetic parish priest dispensing a widowed washerwoman, the overworked mother of six, from regular attendance at mass; a canny grandfather teaching his granddaughter how to grow early tomatoes and beat out the competition; a father and son getting into absurd fights over the former's stinginess; a wedding trip by boat to Milan, where the young couple, amazed but unmoved, watches the quashing of an uprising. But although such things are respectfully observed and conscientiously depicted, they are not enough to relieve the mounting tedium. There is something seriously wrong with a three-hour movie whose most dramatic moments record the slaughter of a pig. To be sure, the killing

382

and dismembering of so intelligent, so human an animal as a pig briefly endows the film with the unholy fascination of a snuff movie; still, in more than three hours there ought to be something to equal or surpass the impact of this scene.

Well, the only other spectacular event is the curing of the widow's cow, one of the very few beasts that do not belong to the beastly landlord. After the veterinarian has pronounced the cow incurable and suggested immediate slaughter to recover at least a few coppers, the desperate widow makes a hymn-singing pilgrimage to the local shrine, prays heart-rendingly to a horrendous statue of the tortured Jesus, and fetches back holy water which she pours down the throat of the moribund animal. Sure enough, the cow revives. I am not sold on the miraculous in life or art, and I am particularly doubtful about so bovine a miracle.

Speaking of which, the cast itself is not a little bovine. In previous films, Olmi's amateurs were city-dwellers, for whom histrionics were part of everyday urban life. But to this cast of authentic Bergamasque peasants, stolidity is what comes naturally. Hence even as pretty a girl as Lucia Pezzoli—the fiancée and, later, bride—becomes boring well before her limited screen time runs out. The fact that the language spoken is the harsh Lombard dialect rather than the *dolce stil nuovo* of Tuscany adds aural insult to visual injury. Moreover, there are just too many insufficiently developed or even differentiated characters for us to get them straight, let alone become and remain involved with them. And the Catholicism is laid on so thick throughout that, whether or not a historically accurate portrayal, it left me identifying myself with that force-fed cow. Surviving the three hours of *The Tree of Wooden Clogs* is a bit of a miracle in its own right.

The most revelatory thing about the film is the fact that political events are barely noticed and not at all understood by the characters. In this respect, as well as in its avoidance of any kind of attitudinizing, *Tree* is obviously an answer to Bertolucci's odious *1900*. But falling into Charybdis is not the way to avoid Scylla. For all its beautifully understated color photography (was Millet the model?), its solemn but inappropriate Bach organ music on the soundtrack, its occasional *trouvailles* (such as revolution seen only as puffs of gunfire clouding the crest of hillocks), and its solicitous editing, Olmi's film strikes me as a devoted, devout dud. But let me hope that its acclaim will enable its maker to turn out more films along the lines of his marvelous early work.

August 3, 1979

Tremendous Trivia

THIS SUMMER'S FILMS are at least as foolish as estival films usually are. *La Cage aux Folles (Birds of a Feather)* is typical: a young man is introducing his fiancée's proper family to his father and "stepmother," who happen to be, respectively, the homosexual owner of a transvestite nightclub and his lover, the drag star of the establishment. We are treated to equal numbers of antihomosexual and antiheterosexual jokes, so that there is something cathartic in the film for everybody.

On a somewhat higher plane, there is *Moonraker,* the eleventh in the 007 series, in which Bondmanship—after stopovers in California, Venice, and Rio—takes our hero and his intrepid mistress from the CIA to outer space (I told you this was on a higher plane), there to battle it out with the evil Drax, about to destroy the Earth and repeople it with the progeny of his chosen blond young men and women; quite a few of the latter he has earmarked for himself, even though he is distinctly dark-haired—but, then, so was Hitler.

There is still a little fun left in the stenciled nastinesses and double entendres, e.g., Drax to his Oriental manservant, "Look after Mr. Bond—see that some harm comes to him"; or Bond, upon raiding a mortal enemy's champagne: "Bollinger! If it's '69, they were expecting me." And at times there is still that vintage comic excitement, as when Bond, in free fall from a plane he has been heaved out of, wrests a parachute from one of his enemies in midair and floats to a happy landing; or when, pursued by gunmen in motorboats down the canals of Venice, his gondola reveals its true identity as an amphibious speedboat, and races onto the Piazza San Marco to the stupefaction of everyone, pigeons included.

But, under Lewis Gilbert's lackluster direction, things become progressively more mechanical as well as mechanized, and by the time we are confronted by yet another routinely spectacular Ken Adam set—outer-space hardware ostentatious enough to make the *Star Wars* crowd blink with disbelief—and after we have had our fill of Roger Moore's and Lois Chiles's less than stellar glamour, we have ample time to reflect on how much more fun the lines, gimmicks, and plot twists used to be in the days of Sean Connery. Why, even the girls were prettier then. And I don't recall, in those more literate days, hearing from the lips of a sexy blonde "exquisite" boorishly accented on the second syllable.

With the new *Dracula,* an Anglo-American coproduction, we are once again down to earth, and not only in the daytime, when the protagonist seeks the comforts of a Transylvanian-soil-filled crate, but even after dark, when, despite an unusually strong contingent of bats taking to the air, the movie itself remains earthbound. Probably the biggest problem was the uncertainty in the minds (I am speaking loosely) of the filmmakers whether to make a traditional chiller or a comic send-up in the manner of some recent stage productions of the work, from one of which Frank Langella, the current Dracula, was recruited. Moreover, the screenwriter, W. D. Richter, was obviously influenced by the new Dracula literature (a minor industry in recent years), which approaches the material with a Freudian trowel, and turns a grain of analytical insight into a silo of silliness. The women in this *Dracula* drool almost visibly at the first glimpse of the protagonist, under which circumstances the casting is particularly unfortunate, for Langella portrays a Dracula not so much from Transylvania as from Transvestitia.

384

Nor is the rest of the cast well chosen: Kate Nelligan comes across as too intelligent and not beautiful enough for Lucy, the quintessential damsel in distress; Trevor Eve turns Jonathan Harker into a graceless bumpkin; the part of Renfield is so confusedly written that even a better actor than Tony Haygart could have done little with it; Donald Pleasence is compelled to play Dr. Seward as a gluttonous imbecile, but he does so with an alacrity above the call of duty; and Jan Francis is a Mina whose reduction to a ghastly blood-sucking ghoul seems less a transmogrification than an apotheosis. That leaves only Lord Olivier, who is a delightful Van Helsing, with a Dutch accent vastly more fun than his fractured French one in *A Little Romance.*

John Badham has directed with an almost infinite variety of bad directorial choices, of which the grossest is the turning of the climactic—what shall I call it?—*Liebes*suck scene not into anything scary, sexy, or even funny, but into a montage of now-recumbent, now-upright silhouettes against a fanatically red background, looking like a set of particularly distressing examples of Soviet poster art. There is an Ossa of loopholes piled on a Pelion of self-contradictions throughout, most notably in the final scene. Here, in a cutesy reversal, it is Dracula who drives a stake through Van Helsing, who, however, without exactly becoming one of the undead, manages to impale his killer on a hook; by the rope attached to it, Harker then hoists the vampire into the sunlight where he shrivels, first into a mummy, then into something halfway between a bat and an old rag flapping in the wind. This object flies away into the distance, spelling ambiguously either Dracula's doom, if the film makes no money, or the promise of a sequel, if it does. Praiseworthy, though, is the subtly various color cinematography of Gilbert Taylor; John Williams's score, too, has a certain trashy fascination.

Peppermint Soda is the story of the maturing of two French-Jewish sisters, thirteen and fifteen, in a year filled with political unrest—Algeria, the assassination of JFK, and so on. Written and directed by Diane Kurys—obviously the younger, introverted sister, both jealous and proud of her prettier but more superficial elder—the film follows the well-worn path of such works: life-and-death struggle with eccentric teachers, bringing up Mother (their parents are divorced, and Father is merely a friendly, ineffectual revenant), the school play, quick flirtation with a classmate's dad, and so on. Yet it is, on the whole, skillful and sensible in its rapid, unsentimental forward thrust combined with good humor, just observation, and engaging dialogue, especially when the youngsters speculate about sex. The teachers are not caricatured excessively, and though neither sister is enacted brilliantly, some of the supporting performances display charm, insight, or vigor. A nice film, except in its moments of high seriousness, which have a way of falling flat.

Confusion prevails in *Why Not! (Pourquoi pas!)*—even unto the punctuation of the title, where an exclamation point usurps the place of a question mark. The film, written and directed by young Coline Serreau (the daughter of Jean-Marie Serreau, the well-known avant-garde stage director), concerns   385 the ups and downs of a *ménage à trois* as it evolves into a *ménage à quatre*. Fernand, a dropout from the business world, is a good housekeeper whom his wife seems to have left because of his bisexuality; Louis, in whose family madness rampages, plays in a band more for pleasure, it seems, than money; Alexa, a divorcée, seems to earn enough for the household just by reading the same novel over and over to a bedridden crone.

Unlikely, but you've heard nothing yet. Everyone beds everyone else in perfect serenity. An investigating police inspector is drawn ineluctably to this magically happy threesome. He also seems to be an idiot, which may explain his affinity for the heroic trio. All would be well if Fernand, smarting from his ex-wife's refusal to let him see his children, did not get involved with Sylvie, a flighty young woman. He absents himself for too long from the house he kept together; pretty soon Louis dismantles the malfunctioning vacuum cleaner into useless fragments, and Alexa starts going off on her own. The little suburban house has become a pigsty, though it did not have very far to go.

The landlady threatens eviction, but, the invalided crone having died, Alexa gets a job reading the same novel endlessly to the landlady. Fernand brings Sylvie back to the pad, and, for a while, a semblance of equilibrium returns. Sylvie's visiting mother even has a liberating fling with the police inspector. But everything threatens to fall apart when Sylvie discovers the other three enjoying a happy postcoital nap in the same bed, and realizes with a shock what a blind man or a cretin would have guessed long ago. Whereupon, to quote the publicity handout, she "packs her bags but at the last moment is unable to leave this home and relationships so filled with love and acceptance." This despite the fact that the landlady has irrevocably decided to sell the house, after all; that Louis has had an outburst of violent insanity; and that money, by now, is not forthcoming from anywhere.

Well, *pourquoi pas?* Because the whole thing is tommyrot. To begin with, an absurdist plot is being peddled as reality: absurdism on the screen, unlike on the stage, always fails because it clashes with the basic realism of the medium, the naturalistic scenery and objects. In this case, there is no way in which these people's untidy economics, to say nothing of their disheveled psychology, could keep them together and functioning for more than a few days. Further, though Mlle Serreau obviously views them as honest, charming, superior beings, the lunatic shenanigans of these creatures are most likely to elicit from us an antipathy verging on apathy.

I am willing to be convinced that unorthodox living arrangements can make us fulfilled if I am shown how they work, how they improve on traditional modes of being, and what makes them endure. But here all is arbitrariness and anomie, unbridledness and inconsistency—a pervasive emotional and spiritual slovenliness, that, even on the film's own idealizing terms, does not obviate violent friction. And never has so much putative wit proved so profoundly witless.

Moreover, this supposedly daring film lacks ultimate nerve. The homosexual lovemaking is represented by no more than a motionless tableau of male figures embracing in bed, whereas the heterosexual couplings are allowed to churn and thrash away. There is something sad about a film that wants to provoke and startle without having the courage to offend anyone—particularly when, like Mlle Serreau's immature claptrap, it still manages to be offensive.

August 17–September 14, 1979

Cut-Rate Maturity

AND THEN THERE IS the pseudo-adult film—the film that looks reality in the face, only doesn't know two things: which way is reality and where is its face. Take, for example. Franco Brusati's foolish *To Forget Venice.* Nicky, an aging but still youthful homosexual, comes from Milan to the country house of his beloved sister Marta with his young lover, Picchio. Marta, a retired operatic diva, has brought up Anna as her daughter, and Anna, in turn, has taken in her underprivileged friend Claudia, who, eventually, became her mistress. The household revolves around the theatrical, gravely ill, drug-taking, but still energetic Marta, whom everyone calls "aunt," though she is actually nobody's aunt.

The group goes to dinner at an outdoor inn; Marta is persuaded to sing for the clients, and she and Nicky even perform a dance. Nicky is accosted by the childhood chum he adored, now, depressingly, a petit-bourgeois paterfamilias. A proposed trip to Venice does not materialize, as Marta's illness worsens and she succumbs. The household becomes hysterical, but a senile maid regains her senses and keeps things going. Picchio, who quarrels with Nicky, finds Anna seminude in the attic and tries to have sex with her; even 'hough she decks him out in female frippery, she can't go through with it. The ancient retainer reverts to senility and is packed off to her native village. Ostensibly to start a new life, Anna and Claudia go to Milan with Picchio, Nicky having decided, at the last moment, to stay at the country house to bury his youth, which he has finally outgrown.

In the closing sequence, he eats his simple, hearty meal in the garden and discovers the crystal ball he long ago gave Marta as a birthday present: half buried in the ground, it has weathered many a buffeting. He lets it roll down a gentle slope; coming up against a tree, it smashes to smithereens. No crystal ball, veteran of years of exposure to the elements, would shatter at this unvehement encounter with a tree trunk. But Brusati wants a symbol, and a symbol does what it is told to do—though obedience hardly makes it good.

The same sort of arbitrariness, founded in stupidity, prevails throughout. We are to understand that homosexuality is a form of narcissism and refusal to grow up. How is this demonstrated? Anna and Claudia look somewhat alike, they frequently expose similarly copious breasts to each other, and they have become united in Anna's hatred for the parents who abandoned 387 her. In a flashback, Anna gets the timid Claudia to join her in throwing eggs and darts at a picture of Anna's delinquent parents. In another flashback, Anna's mother disgusts her daughter with a mock suicide intended to induce the child to persuade her runaway father to return to his slatternly wife. This is presumed to explain how Anna and Claudia became lesbians.

Nicky's worshiping of Marta is meant to be yet another example of arrested development. To explain Nicky's homosexuality further, there is a flashback of Nicky and his closest chum (the future paterfamilias) as choirboys, in a barn, looking at reproductions of famous nudes the chum has clandestinely acquired. Through a window, they spy on peasant girls bathing naked; the chum strips and chases after them with a huge erection only to be mocked and beaten, while Nicky is left behind to fondle his friend's cast-off robe. Obviously, such explanations explain nothing. Neither do such titillating episodes as the stab at sex between Picchio and Anna. And when the senile servant decides to liberate her canary, and the bird, unused to freedom, plummets to death on the courtyard's cobblestones, we have another symbol as preposterous as the smashed crystal ball. What points are being made?

The shattering ball means, I assume, that we must relinquish our immature clinging to childhood ways. But the caged bird's inability to fly must mean we cannot change our habits. Similarly, the old servant's relapse into dotage implies that there are remissions in life, but no cures. Yet Nicky's communion with nature and himself, and the serenity it brings to his expression, are meant to indicate the opposite. So much for the scenario Franco Brusati wrote with Jaja Fiastri, in which the dialogue is no better than the plotting. *To Forget Venice* is so bad that it even makes Brusati's previous, considerably better, *Bread and Chocolate,* look worse in retrospect. Fine actors like Erland Josephson and Mariangela Melato are here either miscast or wasted, or both. The film attitudinizes incessantly: even its title tries to be symbolic and portentous. Instead, like the film, it is meaningless. Indeed, the very names of the main women, Anna and Claudia, are (perhaps unconsciously) lifted from *L'Avventura.* Yet this stumbling affair has walked off with most Italian cinematic awards, and is Italy's submission for the Oscar.

The latest French contribution to pseudoseriousness is Claude Sautet's *A Simple Story,* which is not so much simple as simple-minded. Marie, a fortyish industrial designer, is the divorced mother of a sixteen-year-old boy, to whom Sautet and his scenarist, the ubiquitous Jean-Loup Dabadie, give the mentality of a six-year-old. Marie is pregnant by Serge, her boisterous but insecure lover, whom, for no clear reason, she is about to drop even as she is aborting their unborn child. The film shows her getting reinvolved with her ex-husband, Georges, high up in the company for which Marie works. Georges is now living with a very young woman who adores him; he enjoys, for a change, having an affair with his more mature ex-wife. Marie becomes pregnant by Georges just as one of his fellow executives, Jérôme, the husband of her best friend, Gabrielle, is let go by the firm. Jérôme proceeds to go to pieces and, though Georges tries to help him, commits suicide; Marie decides to break off forever with Georges, whom she unjustly blames for Jérôme's death; yet she decides to have his baby, which she and Gabrielle, who moves in with her, will bring up together.

Everything here, despite minute attention to physical details, is psychologically absurd. Why did the intelligent Marie and capable Georges get divorced? Why did she get involved with that odious pipsqueak Serge in the first place? (That he is played by Claude Brasseur, one of France's most unappetizing actors, does not help, either.) Why does she abort one baby and keep the other, even though she breaks off with both fathers? Why does Jérôme become, at one fell swoop, an utter loser, unable to avail himself of two perfectly good substitute jobs offered him? And why does Marie think that Georges, or anyone else, could help a person unarrestably sliding into suicide?

The minor characters make similarly little sense. There is, for instance, Anna, a colleague of Marie's, who had a seemingly very likable husband she divorced for no compelling reason. A scene in which she goes to pick up a child-support check from him is by far the most convincing and touching part of the movie. But Anna, we learn, is now sleeping with strangers for money. How does she manage this, and, above all, why? Presently she starts dating the ridiculous Serge, and we are given to understand that they are embarking on a happy, good relationship. How come?

It's no use that Sautet is able to show us office politics at work, meals in a company restaurant, people in large groups dining, arguing, and playing together, if he cannot convey basic human relationships without arbitrariness and absurdity. You might say that reality in his films decreases in direct ratio to the number of people in a sequence. And the grandiose and bathetic score by Philippe Sarde proceeds to undo even what good the cinematography of the incomparable Jean Boffety and the authoritative acting by Romy Schneider and several others contribute to the film. One final specimen of factitiousness: on a grim morning after, Serge looks in the mirror and declaims: *"Le jour se lève: il faut tenter de vivre."* This ignoramus rephrasing (or even misquoting) Paul Valéry? Forget it—like Venice. And this film is the official French submission to our Academy Awards!

March 21, 1980

Interior Exiles

No GREAT, or very good, novel should be turned into a movie. High quality in any genre is so intimately wedded to form that divorce spells certain disaster. But there is a kind of novel that no one, not even the biggest fool, should even consider transposing to the screen—yet that is precisely the kind of enterprise that tempts the biggest fools. I mean the novel that is preeminently a word construct, that lives first and last by its linguistic wits, by

389

its verbal architectonics and pyrotechnics. The extreme examples of this are, of course, *Finnegans Wake,* which has been foolishly pecked at by some avant-garde filmmakers, and *Ulysses,* from which Joseph Strick made a dismal little genre film with flat-footed fantasy sequences.

Volker Schlöndorff is a pedestrian German filmmaker who turns out pretentious middle-of-the-road films with or without the collaboration of his equally talented wife, the actress-writer-director Margarethe von Trotta. Schlöndorff made an atrocious oversimplification of Robert Musil's difficult novella *Young Törless,* ditto with Kleist's marvelous *Michael Kolhaas,* which perfectly qualified him to undertake the undoing of Günter Grass's splendid, unfilmable novel, *The Tin Drum* (1959). Readers of this book in Ralph Manheim's translation can get only a rather pale notion of its power in German, a power that, though dependent on its narrative and pictorial imagination, is even more a function of its daring, witty, lyrical, epic, outrageous style, which might prove untranslatable by anyone east of Manheim and west of the moon. Moreover, there are serious cuts in the English edition; the film carries this cautionary approach even further—for instance, by eliding the Virgin Mary episode.

The novel jeers, tickles, rages, guffaws, puns, rhapsodizes across hundreds of pages; it is cajoling and offensive, moving and absurd, earthy and totally fantastic almost simultaneously. What Schlöndorff has made of it—this time without his wife, but with Franz Seitz and Buñuel's mediocre scenarist, Jean-Claude Carrière—is a sublime specimen of Classic Comix. Granted that Günter Grass advised and supervised the filmmakers; yet a father who sells his daughter to a brothel is not going to be much more help to her than your average pimp.

The first problem, obviously, was the magnitude of the novel, the restlessness with which it keeps jumping from scandalous naturalism to sovereignly feckless phantasmagoria. Schlöndorff & Co.'s solution was, first, to lop off the postwar third of the novel; then, to strip most of the rest to the bare bones. This is rather like performing every theme of a symphony, but skipping all the repeats, variations, thematic development. Worse yet, the very meaning often becomes obscured. Thus the nausea Oskar's mother experiences at the sight of eels—her initial refusal to eat them and subsequent suicide by overeating—becomes in the film so much arbitrary, capricious, Buñuelesque surrealizing. In the novel, however, both the nausea and the counternausea are made verbally, poetically, metaphysically stomach-turning and heart-rending—in short, believable. (One might compare this to the central theme of Sartre's *La Nausée,* though I'd hate to put ideas into Schlöndorff's head.)

The novel is, among many other things, and elusively rather than rigidly, an allegory. The amoral innocence of the hero, Oskar—who, aged three, refuses to grow and grow up, and remains a marvelously imaginative yet genuinely repellent child-adult for the rest of his life—is partly an allegorical representation of the artist under Hitler: siding not so much against the Nazis as against all humanity, which made this horror possible. But to convey Oskar's monstrous excess of selfhood (which he proclaims by banging his tin drum) and intransigence (which he asserts by shrieking whatever displeases him to smithereens), to achieve for him the barely possible blend of revulsion and sympathy, you need the mediation of Grass's style—the iridescently lulling and simultaneously scorching words for which Igor Luther's accomplished camera is still only a partial counterpart. What is Bosch and Bruegel in the book becomes merely Miró and Calder on the screen.

To play Oskar, the dwarf of diabolic stature and almost no size, the director engaged David Bennent, whose father, Heinz, plays a supporting part. Much has been made by Schlöndorff of his wanting not a midget but an inspired child for the role. Yet, aged twelve and gifted with only two or three expressions, and with the height of, at best, a six-year-old, David Bennent is both a midget and an uninspired child—unless his misproportioned, spooky features are taken for inspiration. Actually, Oskar Matzerath should be deceptively engaging on the surface; like the artist's, his anarchic, destructive essence should emerge only gradually, often still mistakable for childish pranks. Bennent, looking like the imp of the perverse, could deceive no one.

There are a half dozen nice performances—notably by Angela Winkler, as Oskar's confused mother, and by Daniel Olbrychski, as his gentle, Polish father. As the hard German father, the usually apt Mario Adorf disappoints; as a decent Jewish toy merchant, Charles Aznavour is insipid. Once more, then: oversimplification and decimation, as well as transposition from a medium that makes you see with the mind's eye into one that, basically, rubs your eyes in the sights, severely dent this *Tin Drum*—except, perhaps, for people ignorant of this major twentieth-century novel, for whom the film may hold minor titillations. It is fitting that the little (and diminished) Oskar should have won Hollywood's Oscar. Midget to midget: an Oskar who won't grow up and has shrunk further on film, and an Oscar that dependably rewards the puny and immature.

A vastly more successful venture is the movie version of Carlo Levi's decent but modest autobiographical novel *Christ Stopped at Eboli* (1946), in which the leftist intellectual Levi tells of eight months' Fascist-imposed exile during the Ethiopian war in the most godforsaken part of Italy: the village of Gagliano in Lucania south of the Abruzzi, well beyond the railway stop of Eboli, where Christ Himself may be presumed to have stopped and turned back.

Francesco Rosi is a director I have always esteemed but not, until now, enjoyed. *Eboli* (as the American title has it, Christ being considered a downer at the box office) was originally an Italian TV miniseries of four hours, and would to Christ it were so still. For theatrical distribution, however, it has been whittled down to some 140 minutes, a Lucania that sometimes feels like Lacunia. Yet, even with all the gaps, the film is, nevertheless, uplifting: this is achieved by its wise, dignified, respectful view of the proud, aloof, illogical, and bitterly poor peasants of Gagliano (many of whom, in despair, have emigrated to America, whence some, in even greater despair, have returned), and by its thoughtful examination of the relationship between them and Levi who, forced by his humanity to start practicing medicine (he had his degree but had shied away from practice), finds himself as both a 391 human being and an artist. It is a film charged with understatement as it contemplates people whom politics, social and economic amenities, history itself have passed by, and it forces you to re-examine your own humanity.

Rosi has directed with empathy, restraint, and none of his often distracting intellectualizing, from a faithful screenplay by the dependable Tonino Guerra (*L'Avventura,* among many others), the fine novelist Raffaele La Capria, and himself. Pasqualino de Santis, whose cinematography can be dazzling, has wisely held back, allowing the barren brightness of the landscape and the shrouded blackness of the figures in it to find for their dialogue a self-effacing interpreter in his camera. There is sterling authenticity from the locals, who simply lived for the director; their work is worthily supplemented by that of a few fine professionals, notably François Simon as a priest crazed by the obtuseness of his parishioners. The greatest glory of *Eboli,* though, is the Levi of Gian Maria Volontè, one of the finest film actors of our time. Pity for the peasants, irony for petty Fascist officials, and patience for the absurdities of life pass across his face like magnificent cloud formations across a sky, but with infinitely deeper meaning.

May 30, 1980

Up From Down Under

JUST WHEN you think that there are no more good movies being made, along comes something to shatter your loss of faith. Now it is *The Chant of Jimmie Blacksmith,* by Fred Schepisi (pronounced Skepsee), a forty-one-year-old Australian who made his name in TV commercials and short subjects; this epic film is only his second feature. Based on a short novel by Thomas Kennealy, who appears in it as a cook, the film does not capitalize on the novel's Irish wit. Though not devoid of gritty humor, Schepisi, who is of Sicilian extraction, emphasizes in his screenplay and direction the contrast between the magnitude and majesty of the land and the mean or pitiful puniness of its inhabitants. The insistent use of the telephoto lens, which flattens people out against a background brought closer while they seem only specks against it, makes the point; again and again, crucial events seen in long shot or extreme long shot confirm the great tragedy of man's tragic smallness.

It is 1900 and Australia is on the verge of Federation, but relations with England and the world are of no importance compared to the greed for property: over and over we see fences going up whereby the whites appropriate the natives' land; beyond that, there are legal, social, economic fences that keep the aborigines out and down. Based on real events, this is the story of an intelligent and decent half-caste boy, brought up by the righteous Methodist missionary, Mr. Neville, and his self-righteous wife, who tells Jimmie that if he marries a white farm girl, their children would be only a quarter black, and *their* children hardly black at all. Neville gives Jimmie a written recommendation that is supposed to get him fair employment. But the only job he can get is building fences, which pays next to nothing; and the white wife he gets brings him ultimate grief.

Whenever he returns to his black kinfolk, whether, in a pretitle sequence, to be initiated in the rites of manhood or, later in the film, to drink or get free sex from the native wives, he finds reentry into the white world more difficult and painful. Nothing works for Jimmie, yet the short or very short scenes with which Schepisi puts together his movie, the distance between the camera and the nasty events, the very indistinctness of the sound in certain scenes (I do not mean the hard-to-understand accents, white and black, which are a bit of a drawback), the confusion in and around Jimmie, all this militates against sentimentality in the film, and creates instead a sense of pervasive injustice in almost impersonal terms.

Then, again, there is Jimmie, against the sumptuous landscape, building endless fences for various stingy employers. He builds them cheerfully and well, in fair weather or foul, in good health or with an accidental injury sustained on the job. And always he gets shortchanged by the former riffraff of Britain, who see the half-white youth as all black, and all black workers as fools who share their wages with idle relatives—as Jimmie does with his uncle, Tabidji—and fit only to be rightfully exploited. The staccato style— even more so since Schepisi cut fourteen minutes from the film because potential exhibitors deemed it overlong (I preferred the uncut version)—is used with masterly assurance. Whether Jimmie is shoveling manure on a sheep farm or assisting a sadistic constable as an auxiliary policeman (now, on horseback, he must club innocent aborigines; now, at the police station, he must stand by while the drunken constable brutally kills a black prisoner), circumstances soon force him back to building fences again. The brief, nervous scenes function as nearly self-sufficient vignettes etched in bitterness or grimy irony; cumulatively, they achieve an aura of helplessness and unavoidable doom.

Jimmie is eventually joined by Mort, his carefree, laughing, wholly black half brother, who helps him with guileless equanimity. And finally Jimmie gets a seemingly humane employer in Mr. Newby, who actually lets him build a shack at the far end of his lands. Here Jimmie will live with his white bride, a silly but well-meaning half servant-girl, half slut (thus being herself a metaphoric half-caste) who likes him and thinks she is going to bear his child. Now two or three further blows descend on Jimmie's head. The child, born with the help of Mrs. Newby in her parlor, is all white, and the Newbys, angered by the fact that Mort, Tabidji, and another black have come to stay with Jimmie (the great fear of these farmers is the forming of "a blacks' camp" on their land), refuse him the credit he needs to buy food. Moreover, Miss Graf, the schoolmistress who has been living with the Newbys, is getting married, and is trying to lure Jimmie's wife away from her black husband to become a servant to whites again.

The whites have their reasons, which seem good to them. But Jimmie, let down even by the Newbys, who had shown him some kindness, goes berserk, and starts killing them and other whites who have done him wrong—women

393

and children included, though he spares a baby. I cannot and must not go on with the plot, but must say that seldom has the downward path to predictable doom been depicted with greater suspense, or unbearable pain portrayed with chaster avoidance of easy tears though there certainly are hard-earned ones. Jimmie's war with the whites, into which he draws his reluctant uncle and half brother, is terrible yet also just, and the powerfully staged murders that are recorded in some detail (faintly reminiscent of the equally brilliant, though heavily censored, murders in Jan Troell's *The New Land,* where the killers are exploited American Indians) fill us with something approaching a sense of divine vengeance. At the opposite pole from those by a nonartist such as Brian De Palma, they have an Old Testament awesomeness like the deaths of the firstborn.

Although the murders, I repeat, are grisly, they are shot so as to convey the hypnotic manner in which frenzied blacks are drawn into committing them, as well as the pathetic incomprehension of the dying whites who thought themselves so decent and even kindly. And we realize that only when they bleed do these excessively white, pink, blond, and obtuse beings acquire full humanity, and that only through killing them can Jimmie in any sense, however misguided and horrible, reach them. Neither Tabidji nor Mort is a fully conscious, willing participant in Jimmie's war, and the three men's contrasting but connected attitudes and different but related ends are sovereignly delineated in swift, telling strokes—as in one fleeting shot of Tabidji sitting by a campfire and uncontrollably shivering.

Or consider the scene where Jimmie awaits the birth of his child outside the Newby's nocturnal porch. Boots are the symbol of white rule—aborigines don't wear them, and even as an auxiliary policeman Jimmie wasn't issued any; he had to scrimp to buy them from his meager earnings. Now, waiting, he takes them off and starts tapping out a ritual dance of, I presume, paternity. He does this with a shy pride, almost involuntarily; under an atavistic compulsion rather than from ancestral faith. Yet the way he handles the boots he divests is also ambivalent: as if he were strangling them while also revering them. Close to his bare, dancing feet, the boots stand in strict, self-assertive order, ready to take over again. We feel that Jimmie is torn not only *between* two worlds, but also *within* each of his worlds.

Even the white characters, however briefly they appear, are not without their complexities; their gruffness is countered by grudging bits of fairness, just as their decency is shot through with arrogance, stupidity, greed. We can see how these former pariahs and their descendants need to assert themselves at the expense of someone else—the aborigines. There are subtle differences among these whites, and Schepisi carefully—or, better yet, instinctively—avoids oversimplification. Thus the asthmatic schoolmaster, taken hostage by Jimmie, is a pungent mixture of contradictory strengths and weaknesses, Jimmie's wife has a wonderful repertoire of incommensurate characteristics—even her homely face and voluptuous body constitute one of the film's many deliberate and provocative contradictions. Thus when we first see her and Jimmie's white and black skins come together, it is groin to groin, while we hear giggles and pantings of lust. But the next time, it is in the miserable hut and pitifully narrow and rickety conjugal bed: the young wife's disconsolately weeping, very pale face is comforted by the caress of a black hand that envelops it in a dark hood of benediction. There are two sides to everything: what seemed like miscegenation emerges as compatibility. Also there are correspondences: a black auxiliary policeman helps the white posse trail Jimmie and Mort just as Jimmie was once a turncoat. What makes *The Chant of Jimmie Blacksmith* so extraordinary is the straightforward way in which it achieves its enormous poignancy. Even the reptiles, birds, and insects we glimpse at intervals do more than provide the obligatory nature refrain in wilderness movies. With the exception of a shot of fledglings fed by a parent bird, followed rather too obviously by a shot of a kindly schoolmaster waving goodbye to his pupils, the giant lizards, snakes, and the rest have a way of looking anxious rather than picturesque, as innocent and threatened as the aborigines. But they are also beautiful even if ghostly, like those white birds behind the final titles that drift aimlessly above an emerald landscape.

There are flaws in this wonderful film. I have already mentioned the difficulty of understanding some of the talk, black or white. The scenes in the native shantytowns are especially hard to follow, partly because of the opaque speech and partly because of the elliptical cutting. And occasionally the film does get a trifle tendentious, as in the scene in which Jimmie, Mort, and their hostage, the schoolmaster McCreadie, seek out a native initiation ground. That the sacred spot should be defaced by garbage and graffiti I can believe, but that there should be obscenities writ large by turn-of-the-century Australians all over it seems to me exaggerated, straining. And our not learning what happens to Jimmie's innocent wife after she is pronounced guilty by the court may constitute an unnecessary lacuna.

Yet how restrainedly Schepisi makes his most impassioned points! For example, Jimmie's "declaration of war" against the whites is based on what he overhears much earlier about the British having declared war on the Boers. When Jimmie asks what "declaring war" means, a skeptic answers, "It means you can officially go in and shoot the buggers . . . till they agree with you or leave you alone." That is what Jimmie wants, but the parallel is not belabored by the film. Thus, too, the political machinations surrounding Jimmie's execution—which must not cloud the joy of Federation—are evoked with curt irony, concisely and without undue underlining.

The whites, though treated severely by the film—as they seem amply to deserve—are not turned into obvious monsters. Well, the policeman Farrell is a fairly complete beast, and Stead, the fiancé of the slain schoolmistress Miss Graf, is an unmitigated fanatic. But over against them there is the decent though confused Pastor Neville, who dimly comprehends the whites' responsibility for Jimmie's furor and fall. And a companion keeps sensibly urging Stead to give up the useless pursuit: somewhere, somehow, fate will catch up with Jimmie. Yes, the attitude of the men who kill poor Mort is disgusting: they have themselves photographed grinning and with their feet on the corpse as on a hunting trophy. Contrariwise, the local butcher and executioner, Hyberry, is scrupulously noncommittal; to a fool gushing about what a thrill it must be to face Jimmie as one hangs him, Hyberry coldly replies: "I don't face them. I don't say a word to them. I'm just part of the apparatus." Yet this, too, in its cold abstractness, contrasts unfavorably with the unpremeditated passion with which Jimmie carries out his massacres—initially merely wounding Mrs. Newby, and becoming uncontrollably lethal only when reminded of Miss Graf's provocations.

The most complex characterization of a white is that of McCreadie, the teacher and counterpart to Miss Graf. He is a provocative mixture of bravery and hypochondria, common sense and self-pity, practicalness and absurdity. And this ambivalence that can exist within an individual characterizes also the society at large; thus Mrs. Neville has nothing but hate for the murderous youth she helped rear, whereas her husband despondently comments, "These are violent times. . . . Look at all the wars." Particularly effective is the closing scene, in which Mr. Neville visits Jimmie in the death cell, prays with him, and distraught, mumbles: "I feel very responsible. . . . We don't feel it's entirely your . . ." while, through the peephole, Hyberry scrutinizes the youth he will hang. Noting Jimmie's unusually developed neck muscles, he nevertheless concludes—a butcher calmly assessing methods of slaughter—"There should be no problems." Neville and Jimmie are shot in compassionate closeup; Hyberry evaluates the neck muscles in a medium-long shot to which the peephole supplies a natural iris effect—obviously an uninvolved, indeed unfeeling, way of shooting the scene. This juxtaposition of shots recapitulates the film's theme: the maddening inconsistency—kindness from some, injustice from most—that drives the aborigine to distraction and destruction.

Repeatedly, Schepisi gives us food for thought without cramming it down our throats. Mrs. Blacksmith, condemned, is led away by nuns; Jimmie, wounded and exhausted, falls asleep in the guest room of a convent he has sneaked into and is, on discovery, handed over to the police by the nuns. No antimonastic propaganda here, yet a nagging question about what is charity inevitably invades us. And consider the very whiteness of the convent bed in which Jimmie succumbs to sleep—so uncannily, ominously, terribly white as can bode no good to a fugitive black.

Perhaps the most painful and moving aspect of the film is the relationship between Jimmie and Mort: half brothers who love yet do not understand each other and who, unwittingly, prove each other's undoing. Mort's visit to his just-married kinsman causes Newby to put the fatal screws on Jimmie; Jimmie drags Mort into his suicidal race war. Yet each in his own way makes sacrifices for the other, and when they fight between themselves it is a further symbol of the native world's disintegration. Christianity, as McCreadie says, has only buggered up Jimmie; indirectly, it also buggers up Mort and Tabidji.

The powerfulness of Schepisi's technique is revealed in the strongly visual way in which he communicates the horror of Jimmie's wounding and its consequences. The youth is swimming across a river when three members of the posse open fire on him, and one shot carries off half his lower jaw. As Jimmie swims submerged, we see only blood bubbling up in the water and the dreadful joy of the hunter who has wounded his quarry. But the whites with their horses cannot cross the river, from which Jimmie emerges with his jaw hideously halved and bleeding. For the rest of the movie we see him (the make-up job is brilliant) made profoundly pitiful by disfigurement and pain. He is like one of those wounded animals that escape from a trap by forfeiting a paw; he runs and vainly presses native remedies to a wound that will not heal. As the hungry Jimmie robs a wild bees' hive of its honey, and as he can barely open the truncated jaw with the blood blackly congealed on it to swallow the honey, we experience an ache of commiseration few films have elicited from us.

Schepisi, assisted by his wife, has cast the picture superbly. Not only are the performances by both white professionals and black amateurs exquisite in themselves, but they also blend flawlessly with one another. And everyone looks right: the Australian farmers, laborers, petty officials exude benightedness, even stupidity, which at first seems to excuse their harshness to blacks, yet ultimately makes them appear even more inhuman and guilty. It may be that Tommy Lewis, then a nineteen-year-old college student, was not entirely up to the complex demands of playing Jimmie, but Schepisi knows how to create a mood through positioning of his actors, use of light, framing of a shot, which relieves the young amateur of excessive histrionic burdens. Bruce Smeaton's discreet musical score helps; even more so does Ian Baker's cinematography that seems to paint on milk glass, and achieves both translucency and a matte finish, as if a pastel were smoldering.

Past Australian films—even the better ones, such as *My Brilliant Career*—have tended to bog down in parochialism. *The Chant of Jimmie Blacksmith* is universal, and not just because of obvious parallels with other nations' treatment of their colored minorities. No, what makes the film so ecumenical and moving is the pathetic incomprehension that thickens its air. There is hardly a scene involving more than one character that does not convey a sense of cross-purposes—of stated or unstated, conscious or unconscious, misunderstanding or inability to understand. This is a deeper sadness than that caused by reversal and loss; it is the sadness of not even being able to find, to share, to begin living in earnest.

October 17–31, 1980

Heartbreaker

EASILY THE MOST distinguished film of the year just past—except for the equally Australian but somewhat deeper and more original *Chant of Jimmie Blacksmith*—is Bruce Beresford's *Breaker Morant*. This is a far finer work than most of the other specimens of the current Australian renaissance (or, rather, *naissance*), and one that greatly transcends its shopworn genre, the court-martial picture.

Breaker Morant is based on historical events, adhered to closely down to some of the pepperiest bits of its always pungent dialogue. At the ragged, dying end of the Boer War, Lieutenant Harry "Breaker" Morant (an Englishman, but an adoptive Australian) finds himself in command of the Bushveldt Carbineers, a commando unit entangled in guerrilla fighting, "a new kind of war for a new century." Captain Hunt, the previous commander, has been captured in a Boer ambush, and killed only after being brutally mutilated. Morant, his friend and intended brother-in-law, proceeds to execute Boer prisoners who surrender. Of course, he is only following Lord Kitchener's directive—carefully not committed to paper—to take no more prisoners. But he goes farther: he orders the shooting of a German minister friendly to the Boers and instrumental in the aforementioned ambush.

Germany, which has been threatening to make joint cause with the Boers, demands retribution; a peace treaty is in sight, but a propitiatory sacrifice is called for. A court-martial in Pietersburg must bring a guilty verdict against Morant and his two Australian aides: jolly, uneducated, womanizing but decent Lieutenant Handcock, and naïve, goody-goody, hero-worshiping young Lieutenant Witton. The three are assigned as their defender an inexperienced Australian back-country lawyer, Major Thomas, who, moreover, has only one day to prepare his defense. The prosecutor is dashing, experienced Major Bolton. (Incisive performances by Jack Thompson and Rod Mullinar, respectively.) The chief judge is a fine old blunted martinet, determined to see justice done in. The four other judges are not so predictable. Most of those who might testify for the defendants have been transferred to India ("Recall them," says Morant, "I am willing to wait"); several men whom Morant has justly punished for misdemeanors are spoiling to testify for the prosecution.

Australia has just become a Commonwealth nation; to prove its decolonialized gratitude to the Crown it is only too willing to wash its hands of three troublemakers. Morant, Handcock, and Witton are now totally at the mercy of British *Realpolitik,* and, despite a brilliant defense by Major Thomas and supportive testimony from the intelligence officer, Captain Taylor (John Waters, and very good)—who, however, will himself have to stand trial, and who is *merely* Anglo-Irish—they are clearly doomed. Yet even in this rigged trial, two of the judges are for acquittal—particularly because, in the middle of the proceedings, the Boers attack the British camp in Pietersburg and the three defendants, armed for the occasion, help defend it with signal bravery—but, on the chief judge's tie-breaking vote, they are found guilty. Witton, because of his youth, gets his death sentence commuted to life imprisonment (of which, in the event, he served only three years); the other two get the firing squad, which they face with magnificent courage and humor; Morant has even turned down a chance to escape.

I cannot begin to convey the many and various excellences of this film. At no point, for instance, does it try to play on our sentiments; its biting, moving, or devastating statements are made with brief, matter-of-fact, even funny remarks, or with mere looks. Beresford is especially astute in his use of reaction shots (which, however, he is just as likely to omit, reducing the other person to a sufficient voice): of angry, sardonic, or malevolent glances exchanged; of quick gushes of feeling squelched even more swiftly; of bleeding logic strangled with a juridical tourniquet.

Camera placement, camera movement, and editing are so resourceful that they can put drama into the mere routine of the prisoners being led into the dingy courtroom. But when the three officers are brought, one by one, before the chief judge to hear the verdict, the camera movements and angles manage to play variations that project the event into higher dramatic reaches: the takes are shorter, the point of view more quickly shifting, contrasts in light and dark more suggestive. Note the way the older officers communicate their death sentences to the reeling Witton, quickly and flatly, as they are being marched past his cell; or the sudden, somehow different, use of extreme closeup as each prisoner faces the judge. Such sequences could be done justice to only through frame-by-frame analysis.

Beresford has taken a mediocre play by Kenneth Ross and turned it, with Jonathan Hardy and David Stevens, into a first-rate script. This is by far the best adaptation from stage to screen I have ever encountered. The play has been "opened up," with both flashbacks to guerrilla fighting in the veldt and current events taking place elsewhere around Pietersburg, or in Kitchener's headquarters, or even (in dreams) in England and Australia. These scenes are fitted seamlessly, at just the right moments, into the trial scenes, without diminishing the claustrophobia, the tension, the cumulative buildup that the latter require. One can only marvel at such a wedding of force and finesse.

There is masterly understatement throughout. When Handcock (superbly played by Bryan Brown) writes a farewell letter to his wife, we see him only from the back: the clumsy tenderness of the letter speaks for itself. When Morant (a complex fellow—poet, scholar, journalist, as well as a horse breaker and soldier—captured in all his manifoldness by Edward Woodward) is given a chance to escape and "see the world," a whole world is compressed into his laconic answer, "I've seen it." When the condemned officers leave the presence of the unjust judge, they are reflected in his spectacles in duplicate, quietly symbolizing his corrupt double vision. When Morant and Handcock go to their deaths hand in hand, Morant's shirt is neatly cuff-linked, Handcock's unbuttoned: different personalities, worn on their sleeves, but united in friendship and death.

The shooting of the German minister is shown in extreme long shot, which, against the endless landscape, makes the event seem small and impersonal. But it is there. In the original play, the Australians were whitewashed; Beresford shows them in their full fallibility, but still human; the failure of the tribunal and the powers behind it, however, is inhuman. The shot on which the court-martial ends is splendid: the camera pulls back slightly, losing both the judges and the defendants; an overhanging beam makes the image discomfitingly trapezoidal, and leaves us with the prosecutor staring vacantly ahead, the defense counsel dejectedly down at his papers. Even at the end, the opposing points of view do not connect. Morant's ironic rejection of religion before dying, and Handcock's sweet espousal of this "paganism" after the meaning of the word is explained to him, are tremendously moving; so is Morant's calmly sarcastic request for his epitaph: "Matthew X:36." When Thomas asks the minister what this is, he is told: "And a man's foes shall be those of his own household."

I could have done without Major Thomas's excessive bumbling when he begins his defense, and without the British patriotic song heard ironically at the end. Otherwise, in a kind of movie fraught with pitfalls, Beresford makes no false moves. The film, so full of wit to the very end, wrings the heart and stirs up the mind without ever raising its voice. The terrible story is merely, as someone says, "a sideshow of the war."

March 20, 1981

Illustrated Lectures

THERE IS SOMETHING disturbing about Roman Polanski's on-screen dedication of *Tess,* his film version of *Tess of the d'Urbervilles,* to Sharon, his brutally murdered wife. On the one hand, it looks like aggrandizement, as if Sharon Tate were now to take her rightful place in the pantheon of slain beauties next to Hardy's greatest heroine. On the other hand, it is an invitation to admire the restraint with which Polanski handles this piously dedicated material, his neo-Victorian toning down of sex and violence to be taken as an earnest of his repentance for the real-life seduction of a twelve-year-old, proof of a new-found tactfulness. Thus, the genteel near-dullness of this adaptation, and the fact that any adaptation of a classic novel to the screen is an ipso-facto betrayal, are to be excused by Polanski's discretion and taste, his devotion to his beautiful, butchered wife.

To be sure, the circumstance that, during the filming, Polanski was cohabiting with his leading lady, Nastassia Kinski, then between the ages of fifteen and seventeen, and so reiterating the offense for which he had to flee America, and the further fact that the most persuasive way of remembering Sharon Tate is not likely to take place in Nastassia Kinski's bed, may subtract somewhat from the piety of that dedication, and make the movie's gentility (such as the relegation of Tess's trial and execution to a mere title card) seen rather less compelling.

I mention these facts from Polanski's personal history because they may help explain why the film's understatement feels less like cogent suggestiveness than a sort of reverse attitudinizing, as if the finest kind of chastity were self-castration. Yet it is precisely some of what Victorian mores obliged Hardy to omit that the movie could have restored, by way of partial compensation, to the novel it plundered.

400   I say "plundered," because every artist knows, or ought to know, that

whereas a poor or mediocre novel can sometimes be successfully translated to the screen, and even improved in the hands of a superior film artist, a good or great novel can only get lost in transit. For, as even bright school-children have learned by now, form is content, and whoever, by trying to adapt it into another form, fiddles with it, must also, inevitably, damage or destroy the content. One might, of course, assume that Hardy's fictions are partially suitable to filmization, seeing that they possess elaborately dramatic, indeed melodramatic, plots, and that they are suffused with colorful nature descriptions and evocations of local color for which a keen camera eye should be able to provide suitable cinematic equivalents.

It doesn't work that way. Aside from the aforementioned edulcorations, the film, though just under three hours long, leaves out a good many poignant story elements; as for the camera eye, even the best cinematographer (the film was shot by the excellent Geoffrey Unsworth and finished, upon his death, by the almost equally fine Ghislain Cloquet) cannot quite do what Hardy did. For one thing, *Tess* was made in France, and though the production designer, Pierre Guffroy, and art director, Jack Stephens, achieved some good semblances of English villages and landscapes, France is not England, and even a clever replica of Stonehenge pales beside the real thing.

But the problem goes deeper. For instance, when Tess and her friend are harvesting the lower parts of turnips uneaten by the livestock, we read in Hardy: "Every leaf of the vegetable having already been consumed, the whole field was in color a desolate drab; it was a complexion without features, as if a face, from chin to brow, should be only an expanse of skin. The sky wore, in another color, the same likeness; a white vacuity of countenance with the lineaments gone." In such a passage, Hardy's atheism is subtly (as it is, at other times, less subtly) embodied; what can the cameraman, however skillfully he may use a palette of noncolor, do to convey these two faceless faces on earth as it is in heaven? The scenarists—Polanski, Gérard Brach, and John Brownjohn—even supposing that they comprehended the atheism and dared to try to communicate it, would still be defeated by the boundaries of their particular medium, film.

Nastassia Kinski looks attractive, sexy, sometimes even striking, as Tess (although the upswept hairdo she sports as a kept woman does not flatter her sharp features), but she is not Tess; instead of a burstingly sunny creature, she is a darkling, moonlight beauty, moody almost to the point of sullenness. And though her acting is inoffensive and occasionally even touching, that is not quite enough even for Tess Durbeyfield, let alone Tess of the d'Urbervilles. Most of the other performances (many of them by French actors dubbed into English) are at least acceptable, but Peter Firth is no Angel Clare. Though Angel, God knows, is not a very physical creature, he does arouse Tess and the other farm girls to fever pitch; Firth, however, has no visible heterosexual appeal, and is not the actor to overcome such a disadvantage.

Polanski has directed the film competently, but with an essentially cold academicism that cannot, or will not, make even the final idyl in the empty house come to full, passionate life. *Tess* is not a bad film, and certainly not unwatchable (Anthony Powell's costumes are often as seductive as the landscapes), but it is a transient affair, not a Hardy perennial.

Let me now give the extremely short shrift they deserve to the latest films by three former standard-bearers of the New Wave: François Truffaut, Alain Resnais, and Jean-Luc Godard. Truffaut's *The Last Metro* is a triangle story set in the German Occupation, centering on the lovely and noble wife (Catherine Deneuve) of a German Jewish theater director, who carries on the management of his Paris theater while he, ostensibly safe abroad, is in precarious hiding in the theater's basement. That is not, however, the only carrying on; the gallant wife also drifts into a dalliance with her young leading man (Gérard Depardieu), who is, naturally, also a hero of the Resistance. The entire film is part sentimental twaddle, part illustrated lecture about life in Paris under the Occupation, with any number of all-too-well-known anecdotes about Occupational hazards and how spirited Parisians defied them. *The Last Metro* ranges from the cute to the stilted, from the obvious to the excogitated, and there is preciosity even in getting that superb cinematographer Nestor Almendros to recreate the yellowish tones of 1940s color cinematography.

Resnais's *Mon Oncle d'Amérique* is a quantum leap downward: a set of illustrated vignettes meant to dramatize the interspersed little lectures by Dr. Henri Laborit, touted as France's answer to Freud, but in truth only a Skinner-deep behaviorist at best. His simplistic pronouncements about human conditioning are then couched in foolish little interconnecting tales about a handful of dullish and clumsily manipulated characters, and sprinkled with jokes to delight the young in brain, as when these characters turn into giant laboratory rats, or when, because they used to identify themselves with certain movie stars, we get intercut sequences from Jean Gabin or Jean Marais pictures. Despite the collaboration of the sometimes effective screenwriter Jean Gruault, Resnais, who lacks a comedic sense, has come up with a fundamentally humorless, pretentious, finally quite pointless film, and his not ungifted cast (except for Dr. Laborit, who is untalented even as an actor) is misdirected into oafishness.

As for Godard, he is, in *Sauve qui peut* (*Every Man for Himself*), down to his old tricks. An alleged anticapitalist fable, the film, bursting with impotent sexuality and impotent violence, tells several confused nonstories that unconvincingly impinge on one another, are supposed to prove that everyone is some kind of prostitute, and are not even worth summarizing here. I have never considered Godard fully *compos mentis,* and there are scenes in this film that, if there were loony bins for movies, would surely be certifiable. One example: Godard has declared that repeated freezings of the frame within a sequence showing the human face reveal psychic depths. As one of the film's two leading ladies rides a bicycle, the film repeatedly freezes—and tells us nothing whatsoever about her. The device keeps reappearing, and is used also for a nocturnal traffic jam in the streets of Geneva. What do freeze-frames on the grilles and headlights reveal about the automotive psyche? Not much, but they tell us something about Godard's.

May 1, 1981

Diplomatic Immunity

THERE ALWAYS WILL BE dishonest movies around, but Federico Fellini's latest, *City of Women,* carries dishonesty to the point of contemptibility. It purports to be a tongue-in-cheek commentary on women in the age of ascendant feminism, and on the state of men under this dispensation. Good enough, but Fellini (with his two coscenarists, Bernardino Zapponi and Brunello Rondi) immediately adopts two separate strategies for evading responsibility. One is to show only the extreme positions in the sociosexual cold war, and then ridicule all of them equally. Everyone gets it in the neck: furibund feminists, lesbians, rapacious older women, autistic young swingers; men who knuckle under (like the six subservient husbands of an aging virago), male chauvinist pigs, homosexuals. Everyone is equally ludicrous, equally in error—or equally exculpated by his or her opposite's follies. The other device is to make all but a few of the film's 140 minutes the dream of its hero, Snaporaz (Marcello Mastroianni), napping on a train. Accuse the old fox Federico of foolishness, self-contradiction, absurd wrong-headedness, and he can retort complacently, "But, of course. It's only a dream, after all."

Yet does one, as an artist or a mere concerned human being, poke cruel and tasteless fun at everybody, only to hotfoot it back into diplomatic immunity the moment one's bluff is called? And there is more hocus-pocus. Although the *homme moyen sensual* portrayed by Mastroianni is at first called Snaporaz (a circus clown's name), he gradually becomes known as Marcello—to establish him either as the Fellini-surrogate from *La Dolce Vita* twenty years later or, quite contradictorily, as the actor Marcello Mastroianni himself, in no need to adopt another persona for what is only a charade, improvisation, horseplay.

Such cheating, double-bottomed filmmaking extends throughout this dishonorable enterprise and is not to be confused with creative ambiguity. Here we do not have conflicting possibilities subtly enriching one another, but schematically antithetical positions preposterously slapped together for mutual cancellation.

We begin as Snaporaz follows a sexy, fur-hatted woman to the toilet of what seems to be a third-class railroad car, has coitus interruptus with her, and, when she gets off the train, pursues her through a lyrical countryside. She makes a fool of him, eludes him, and lures him into a hotel in the middle of nowhere, where an enormous conference of feminists is in full swing. The women—some seductive, some grotesque—are shown in a Babel of activities: 403

testimonials, harangues, lecture-demonstrations with slides, movies, theatrical and consciousness-raising sessions. The camera and soundtrack simultaneously drool over them and mock them, as their behavior ranges from the rabid to the ridiculous.

Loudly denounced by the fur-hatted woman, Snaporaz becomes an endangered specimen, but is led to seeming safety in a gymnasium by Donatella, a buxom, toothsome, laughing lass who gets him to roller-skate with her, while a nearby gym session teaching women how to kick a man in his privates is in fearsome progress. Donatella helps Snaporaz escape some threateningly converging Furies on skates, but the door she points him to merely opens onto a steep staircase, which he tumbles down, whereupon a huge, ludicrous yet menacing female scoops him up and takes him, ostensibly, to the station on her motorbike. Instead, however, she maneuvers him into a hothouse on her farm, where she begins to rape him, and is put to flight only by the arrival of her ancient but embattled mother. The crone entrusts Snaporaz to her granddaughter for safe conduct to the station, but she dumps him into a car full of very young female punk rockers, one of several such vehicles that, radios blaring, rattle through the night.

Snaporaz jumps out of the car, is chased by the girls but rescued by a macho type on guard outside his mansion with gun and mighty dogs; the stalwart fellow hurls curses at the girls and shoots blanks at them. This is Kazzone (i.e., *cazzone*, large cock, rendered in the subtitles as Dr. Züberkock), whose house is a museum of male supremacist madness, complementary to the ravings of the feminist convention. Here we get things like a floor lamp in the shape of a giant phallus and a whole gallery of color transparencies of Kazzone's conquests; press a button and the suggestive portraits light up, while the voice of the woman in the picture endlessly reiterates her particular brand of talk during sexual surrender, sometimes complete with orgasmic moans.

Kazzone is throwing a party to celebrate his ten-thousandth conquest, where Snaporaz, by now usually referred to as Marcello, meets his wife, Elena, who is getting drunk and accusing him of numerous conjugal failings. Fellini lets her mount a convincing case, only to undercut it a while later when feminist police break up the party and Elena goes off, embracing one of the women officers, toward what looks like lesbian dalliance. Still later, after her husband has been ceremoniously put to bed, she will return, singing a travestied aria from *Carmen,* and demanding sexual satisfaction from him while riding him like a tyrannical jockey. When he fails to satisfy her, she rolls off him in the most ludicrous and ugly way, and drops off to sleep. In the film's final sequence, back on the train and in reality, we shall meet her again, reading a comic book.

Meanwhile what are the two highlights at Kazzone's party? His new—and last—conquest puts on an exhibition of Zen sex, which consists of standing on a couple of stools and sucking up into her vagina coins and pearls thrown toward her feet. Kazzone himself is extinguishing, by way of the other higher point, the ten thousand candles on a gigantic cake; when his breath gives out, he resorts to what appears to be a stream of his urine. A maid declares that it is really a bottle of champagne that does the dousing; later, a by-stander reasserts the urine theory. The party ends with Kazzone kissing—indeed, making love to—a smirking marble bust of his late mother. The supermale is being punctured and revealed as a pitiful mamma's boy; but mamma's boys are more likely to turn into homosexuals than into Cas-anovas wielding guns and spouting D'Annunzio and urine (or champagne).

I have summarized only about half the plot, but it should suffice to indi-cate what a tasteless, self-contradictory, uncommitted, and irresponsible af-fair *City of Women* is. It becomes even more extravagant and tiresomely surreal in its latter parts, full of threadbare allusions to $8^1/_2$, Juliet of the Spirits, Satyricon, Amarcord, and *Casanova*. Yet these are not even auto-*hommages* so much as self-plagiarism: ineffectually gesticulating cries for help in the direction of past endeavors. In one typically unappetizing sequence, entitled "The Cinema," an audience of boys and men of all ages is watching great female stars on the screen. The screening room is a wall-to-wall bed whose top sheet billows like the sea from the motion of the penises being ma-nipulated underneath. This may indeed be the aging Fellini's notion of cinema, and certainly characterizes much, if not most, of his later work.

There is nothing the director will not steal from. In a bordello scene, the whore Marcello goes upstairs with is a replica of Anouk Aimée in $8^1/_2$, who there represented the autobiographical hero's wife. Another gratuitous con-jugal insult? When she rides our hero in bed, the whore has the elephantine posterior (via trick photography) of Wertmüller's fat woman in *The Seduction of Mimi*, with the added repulsiveness that here others are watching the act. Even the continuity is utterly sloppy: Mastroianni's socks change color from one scene to the next; the same woman telephoning her psychiatrist is played by two different extras in two nearly consecutive shots. As for the postsyncing, it is so cynical as to make for minimal correspondence between dialogue and lip movement.

What cannot the film confuse and confound? When Marcello is hauled before a feminist tribunal prior to being sent out into a Roman-style arena to confront the Ideal Woman (and be, presumably, destroyed like the other dying gladiators who are periodically removed on stretchers), his guards are homosexuals ridiculed as the ultimate screaming queens. But when he is asked to say the first feminine name that pops into his head, he produces a male nickname, Pippo, and promptly waxes awkwardly defensive. Could our very masculine hero be latently homosexual and homosexuality a "nor-mal" condition?

But the height of tergiversation and equivocation is reached in the se-quence wherein Marcello goes up in a balloon made in the image of a huge Donatella, a Donatella with the halo of the Madonna, the bridal veil of the wife, and the lewd smile of the prostitute. This, in fact, is the Ideal Woman whom he went to meet in the arena; a rubber version of *das Ewig-Weibliche* that drew Goethe's Faust onward and upward. On the ground below stands, even worse than this travesty of a Superwoman, the real-life Donatella in terrorist's garb; smiling sweetly, she shoots down her ballooning alter ego with a murderous machine gun, causing Marcello to plummet to earth. 405

Three primitive old images of women shot to hell by the new deadly image, while man is, coincidentally, consigned to perdition.

Well, does this mean utter despair, then? No, we get a cheap, tacked-on, fake happy ending. As our hero wakes up in his train compartment, there are his wife, the woman in the fur hat, and Donatella (now a student) all graciously smiling; the pouring rain outside yields to sunshine (photographed as meltingly as only Giuseppe Rotunno can do it, to the accompaniment of Luis Bacalov's Rotaesque score), and the landscape around the railroad track blooms into a picture postcard. True, the train goes into a tunnel, but there is a glint of light at the end of it. Whence this unearned hope? What meaning in all this derivativeness and vulgarity? Dream on, Snaporaz-Marcello-Federico, but spare us your crude and empty dreams.

June 26, 1981

Fancy Footwork

THERE IS A GENTEEL, well-crafted, eminently worthy sort of film that used to come to us in bundles from Britain until, suddenly, the supply was gone. Now, with equal suddenness, we have a brace of such films. Yet the second, on closer inspection, fails to pass muster; and even the first is rather more jolly decent than truly good.

Chariots of Fire was directed by Hugh Hudson, a graduate of television, which has become the training ground of some our best and worst directors. The screenplay is by Colin Welland, a former actor and now an English regional writer most familiar to me as the scenarist of *Yanks*, which was a dud. The film concerns two fine young runners, both of whom feel that they are running for a cause. Harold Abrahams, an undergraduate at Caius College, Cambridge, is the son of a now wealthy Jewish immigrant and believes that, by becoming unbeatable, he will improve the post-World War I status of Jews in England, where anti-Semitism still thrives high and low, as represented in the film by the Senior Common Room and the porter's lodge, respectively. Harold is a fanatic, with a clenched jaw you could use as a carpenter's vise.

The other athlete, up in Scotland, is Eric Liddell, a glittery-eyed Presbyterian missionary to China when not running for God, whom he feels watching him when he runs. Eric has a sister who tries to dissuade him from such secular activities, and, indeed, he strictly observes the Sabbath by merely walking on it. But when, on weekdays, he runs, God's inspiration blows him invincibly forward. Clearly, the film, which alternates between Harold and Eric, is building toward their mighty clash: Harold's jaw versus Eric's glint. This does come, about midway in the film, in a race of no particular importance that Eric wins unclimactically to Harold's utter despair. But now Harold is taken on by Sam Mussabini, a great coach of partly Arab descent, himself a bit of an outcast in England. And so everything points toward a final supreme contest between these master sprinters at the 1924 Olympics in Paris, but the showdown never happens.

Instead, the drama focuses on Liddell's refusal to run, as scheduled, on a Sunday, and the panic into which this throws the Prince of Wales, Lord Birkenhead, and the other British Olympians, and on how this is resolved by the generosity of a teammate, the charming Lord Andrew Lindsay, another Cantab, and on how, in the end, both Abrahams and Liddell win in separate events and bring two gold medals to a Britain not exactly on the gold standard in international track. So the film is robbed of the climax we, like its main characters, have been spoiling for. But there are compensations.

·Chariots of Fire functions nicely as a social document. Cambridge in the early twenties, the Gilbert & Sullivan Society of which Harold is an ardent member, the snobbish masters with their jocular condescension, the spirit of fair play that consolidates the students, the world of the theater as Harold becomes involved with a popular prima donna, Scottish landscapes that provide lofty settings for Scots-sentiment-riddled sports events, the austere life of the kirk—these and more get cursory but sympathetic and evocative treatment. Aubrey Montague, another amiable undergraduate athlete, writing gently Georgian letters to his mater; Lord Lindsay practicing on the lawn in front of the ancestral manor with a brimful champagne glass on each hurdle; supper at the Savoy, with Harold and his ladylove catered to by a deliciously obsequious headwaiter—such vintage vignettes abound. A vanished England that yet seems accessible to living memory, a graciousness that extends even to harbor masters and sleeping-car attendants, a sense of the social fabric without rips or snags—except for a bit of religious intolerance and closed-shop snobbery (the masters upbraid Abrahams for hiring an outside trainer), which, in retrospect, seem almost anodyne—these things make the film as lullingly tranquil as the music of Elgar, the poetry of Edward Thomas, the early painting of Paul Nash. (Apropos music, the synthesizer-enriched score by Vangelis has greatly contributed to the film's success; I find it gimcrack, anachronistic, and blaringly monotonous.)

And, of course, there is the running. It is portrayed here in every conceivable way: lyrical, epic, comic, and dramatic. At times lacerating and disheartening, it is, at others, uplifting, imbued with an almost superhuman majesty. Some of this we owe to Hudson's directorial versatility, some to the superb acting of many young actors sufficiently unknown to seem to be authentic athletes, and very much to the camera of David Watkin, who captures both the documentary and the poetic aspects of the footrace. He can view the runners, in the opening sequence, running along a beach on an overcast day in foot-deep water, as if in an obsessive dream: an anonymous phalanx propelled through an abstract landscape in a patch of timelessness that just might be eternity. Or Watkin's camera can glue itself so tightly to a runner that it becomes a *catalogue raisonné* of what every muscle, sinew, and lump of earth underfoot contributes to exhaustion and endurance. Or the camera can lurch, swivel, hurtle with the runner around a college quadrangle so subjectively that we fear our own brains might, any moment, bespatter the Gothic architecture.

Otherwise, though, there is no violence, no explicit sex, no modern psychologizing or artiness. The film is old-fashioned in both the good and the bad senses, with an innocuousness that predisposes us to forgive its superficiality. But superficial it is: we never see deep into the characters, and even religion—so important, in different ways, to both heroes—is never much more than an extra gleam in Liddell's eyes, a heightened clenching of Abraham's jaw. Yet all performances are unfussy and fine, paced by Ben Cross's Harold, Ian Charleson's Eric, and Ian Holm's Mussabini. I was taken no less, however, by the understated grace of Nigel Havers's Lord Lindsay and Nicholas Farrell's Aubrey Montague, and many others. Altogether, craft at its most careful—only not a work of art.

I could never decide whether John Fowles was the most exalted of trashy novelists or the lowest of serious fiction writers. What is unquestionable is his pretentiousness—whether he writes *The Collector* from two points of view where one would be quite sufficient; brings out, as a young pup of a successful first novelist, a pompous collection of moral apophthegms entitled *The Aristos;* republishes *The Magus* in a slightly revised form, obliging his readers (if they are foolish enough) to remasticate that huge agglutination; presents *The French Lieutenant's Woman* simultaneously from nineteenth- and twentieth-century perspectives and with two contradictory endings; or just generally exudes smugness from every stylistic pore. But he does have a narrative gift, which, alas, is only fitfully served by the film of *The French Lieutenant's Woman,* as directed by Karel Reisz from a screenplay by Harold Pinter, himself no piker when it comes to pretentiousness.

Pinter and Reisz tried to solve the problem of the dual point of view and the antithetical twin endings by inventing another story: that of the actors performing the hero and heroine. While Sarah, the semihysterical and semi-avant-garde feminist, and Charles, the gentlemanly Darwinist dilettante, muddle through to a happy ending, they are crosscut with the story of their cinematic interpreters, Anna and Mike, who, married but not to each other, conduct a liaison that ends abruptly after the completion of shooting. The modern story suffers both from being an accumulation of arrant clichés and from butting in like the person from Porlock whenever the Victorian romance, such as it is, begins to absorb us on the visceral level.

Yet even the romance suffers greatly in the movie version. In order to accommodate the modern story, it had to be pared down even more drastically than the usual screen adaptation of a lengthy novel. It has also been made to talk down to movie audiences, as, for instance, by the omission of all references to Rossetti, in whose circle Sarah finds her spiritual self-fulfillment. Then there are the main actors. Jeremy Irons lacks the requisite charm for Charles. Meant to be somewhat weak but engaging, Irons displays a basic expression that clumsily caves in on itself, and is generally short on upper-class refinement. As for Meryl Streep, she has neither the Englishness nor the looks and period sense needed for Sarah. As Charles first beholds her on the pier at Lyme on a near-stormy, tenebrous day when her cloaked head reveals a viridescent face in the turquoise light—the moment when he is fatally smitten—she actually looks like a sickly, unpleasantly sharp-featured, homely boy.

On the credit side, there is efficient direction by Karel Reisz, impeccably moody cinematography by Freddie Francis, compelling production design by Assheton Gorton, pungent acting by the supporting cast, and breathtaking scenery by the shire of Dorset. And a grand neoromantic score by Carl Davis, worthy of Erich Wolfgang Korngold at his goldenly corniest. On the debit side, there is the awkward circumstance that we don't give a damn.

If you want to know what enjoying a cup of tea or a glass of sherry and other aspects of ordinary living are really about, I passionately recommend *Stevie*, Robert Enders's film, written by Hugh Whitemore from his own play. Stevie Smith was a London poet who died in 1971, aged sixty-nine. She lived a small life in the suburb of Palmers Green, most of it with an aunt to whom she was devoted. She also wrote small poetry midway between doggerel and genius, yet one of her poems, "Not Waving But Drowning," is a lasting contribution to English verse, and some others are not far behind. Stevie Smith was a classic British eccentric who saw the ordinary from a fiercely offbeat but spontaneous and unattitudinizing vantage point, and her life was full of small, sad, funny, provocative contradictions. The movie uses many of her poems and prose writings, and is at least two-thirds monologue in the flat shared by the sweetly unintellectual aunt and the bizarre but shrewd poet. It is minimally cinematic and maximally humane, warm, and touching, so that you care about nothing but Stevie and her Lion aunt, as she called the leonine-looking but lamblike and foxy old lady.

Glenda Jackson, though visually and temperamentally wrong for Stevie, does a powerful piece of acting and poetry reciting, and sustains interest where monotony might have obtruded. As the aunt, Mona Washbourne is sensational: no one has ever portrayed the simple pleasures and displeasures of living with greater raciness, plasticity—indeed profundity—and yet so modestly and unhistrionically. It is a great embodiment, way beyond mere performing. There is excellent supporting work from Trevor Howard and less good from Alex McCowen, also superb cinematography from Freddie Young, the old master. *Stevie* is about nothing more or less than living and dying; it cuts close to the bone (often the funny one) and goes straight for the viewer's heart. It is also, almost coincidentally, genuine art.

August 7–November 13, 1981

Eros or Agape?

IN A LETTER to Edward Garnett (July 3, 1912), D. H. Lawrence describes Frieda's torments caused by the "storms of letters" from her abandoned   409 husband begging her to sacrifice her love for Lawrence and return to her children: "She lies on the floor in misery—and then is fearfully angry with me because I won't say 'Stay for my sake.' I say 'decide what you want most, to live with me and share my rotten chances, or go back to your children— decide for *yourself*...' And then she almost hates me, because I won't say 'I love you—stay with me whatever happens.' I *do* love her. If she left me, I do not think I should be alive six months hence." There is more drama—marital and sheerly human—in that brief passage than in the entire movie *Priest of Love,* which Alan Plater adapted and Christopher Miles directed from Harry T. Moore's Lawrence biography and some of Lawrence's own writings.

The biography itself is conscientious and readable, but it is not ready-made cinematic material—as, indeed, few if any artists' biographies are. A writer (or other artist) lives largely in his work; it is the work that sanctions the idiosyncrasies, bizarrenesses, and terrible doldrums of his life; if the film cannot convey this relationship—this hallowing of the humdrum or perverse by the pursuit of the ideal (and what film can?)—the thrashings about and even the clevernesses of the writer must remain comparatively mundane and disappointing.

The Lawrence-Frieda relationship was complex, weird, glorious, and horrible enough to make a movie sufficiently absorbing for all sexual tastes, if only Plater and Miles had opted for depth instead of breadth, and treated their tragicomic lovers as human beings rather than celebrities. Graham Hough, one of the better Lawrence scholars, once remarked to a friend that he would have given anything to have spent one night hidden under the Lawrences' bed; although, given these demon lovers' proclivity for rolling onto the floor, that might not have been the right and adequate hiding place. On the other hand, the Lawrences might have welcomed Professor Hough's presence, given their need for acolytes and accomplices, to some of whom—notably to Dorothy Brett—the film does fair justice. It is the central lovers-conspirators-antagonists that are shortchanged by it.

There is a distressing superficiality to *Priest of Love,* as new people and incidents keep being rushed on and off the screen—like flipping through one of those pictorial biographies that are all photographs and minuscule captions. But in such a book you get, at least, the real faces. Ian McKellen, though a competent actor, is not a suitable Lawrence: too tall, gangly, fidgety, sulky—precious even—and definitely not virile enough. Although Lawrence may have had a hidden homosexual streak, to which the film may allude with the naked-bathing scene for him and Middleton Murry, it remained well enough hidden in life; what seems to have been most striking about Lawrence was a faunlike quality exuded by even the most grave-looking snapshots. McKellen tries for the faunishness, but it comes out cutely puppy-doggish; in fact, both in looks and in personality, what McKellen seems to be doing is not so much Lawrence as Lytton Strachey.

As for the Frieda of Janet Suzman, a good actress, she fluctuates between compelling and wildly overacted moments. Though Miss Suzman spares us Frieda's obesity and slovenliness, she also bypasses much of the earth-motherliness that must have been Frieda's chief attraction, and her German accent is extremely labile. Ava Gardner is rather too glamorous for Mabel Dodge Luhan, but otherwise not bad, and Penelope Keith is marvelously naïve and maladroit as the deaf, horse-faced, dopey but lovable Dorothy Brett. James Faulkner does not begin to convey the hypersensitivity of Aldous Huxley, and Mike Gwilym makes Murry rather more crude than devious. However, the three Italian actors portraying the main Italian members of the Lawrence entourage provide appealing vignettes. John Gielgud appears as the grotesquely spiteful Herbert G. Muskett, whom Moore describes as a minor "critic without credentials" who testified against Lawrence, but whom the film turns into a government censor and Lawerence's perennial hypocritical nemesis. Gielgud squeezes a fair amount of amusement out of this running gag of a figure, yet Muskett remains a typical example of the film's method of conflation, oversimplification, and exaggeration.

Miles, who with Plater made a good movie out of Lawrence's last, undistinguished novella, *The Virgin and the Gypsy,* has directed quite routinely here. Ted Moore, a cameraman who is best at understatement, seems an odd choice to impart the exotic stops along the Lawrences' perennial, restless peregrinations: the film has a self-effacing, almost bleached, look that makes even Mexico appear slightly anemic. There is, moreover, an aura of parsimony throughout, as if, given the various far-flung locations, half the funds were used up in the getting there, with not enough left over even for hiring the requisite extras. A curiously uninvolving movie, this, on a subject that could have legitimately inspired any number of contradictory emotions—only not emotionlessness.

December 11, 1981

Chile con Carnage

Missing is Costa-Gavras's latest political thriller, based on Thomas Hauser's book about the assassination in Chile of Charlie Horman, a young American writer and journalist. It tells mostly about how Beth, Charlie's wife, and Ed, his father, search for Charlie after his disappearance shortly after the military coup in Chile. Ed Horman is a prosperous businessman, a Christian Scientist, and a conservative; Charlie and Beth's mildly leftist views are weird, indeed incomprehensible, to him. As he and Beth get the runaround from the American authorities in Chile (the country is never named, but easily identifiable), Ed witnesses more and more killings and other horrors, and as American involvement in local politics becomes clearer and unholier, Ed and Beth get touchingly closer to each other. Charlie's death is finally confirmed, and Ed and Beth return to the States, where he initiates a lawsuit against eleven Americans including Kissinger, who, apparently, contributed to Charlie's demise. The suit gets nowhere.

The film begins with the announcement that it is a true story. I would assume that a lot of it is, though there are some concessions to cinematic thriller-making. Not one of the American officials we meet in the film is anything but smarmy, hypocritical, cowardly, or outright sinister; only one female foreign correspondent and one economic advisor to the Ford Foundation prove at all decent or trustworthy, though even they are far too scared to deploy their humanity beyond a reasonably safe point. Of the Chileans, one sees only subordinate figures, but they are sufficient to inspire fear and loathing. Yet Costa-Gavras and his coscenarist, Donald Stewart, are shrewd enough to stop generally a little short of showing the worst. Dead bodies lie about plentifully, and torture is hinted at abundantly; but what we see is mostly minor acts of brutality and a pervasive state of terror.

There is welcome restraint in the speechifying, too. Though the bad guys, from the American ambassador down, are allowed their share of dubious disclaimers, palpable evasions, and fake analogies, the good guys are not permitted to utter more than an absolute minimum of righteous indignation. Costa-Gavras concentrates on the bureaucratization of evil: for every image of actual bestiality and murder there are scores of examples of lies, official sleight-of-hand, and subtle intimidation. Some things are very effective: the soldiery cutting the pants off women caught not wearing skirts, the open brazenness with which a telephone is bugged in a luxury hotel, the terror of Beth caught in the streets after curfew, the cynicism of some people and the helplessness of others. The film was shot in Mexico, which to my inexperienced eyes looks Chilean, or chilling, enough.

Some aspects of *Missing* work simultaneously for and against it. Since most of what happened to Charlie is conjectural, the film must shroud it in darkness. This is frustrating for the viewer, but also, in its way, more frightening; moreover, it conveys perfectly the agonizing perplexity of those who search for Charlie. A lot of the film is told in flashbacks, and there is even one scene that keeps changing as two disagreeing eyewitnesses relate it differently. Such devices make for a little suspense in a story whose outcome is never in doubt, and introduce a measure of technical bravura; however, they are also gimmicky. Certain major questions, such as just how politically committed or involved Charlie really was, are left unanswered, which may provide our imagination with too much of a playpen.

There are also some outright errors. A crucial diary in which Charlie recorded some of the evidence of American military involvement he stumbled on at a seaside resort was somehow not confiscated when his arresters ransacked his and Beth's apartment. Yet nothing is made of it for several reels until Beth casually produces it and reads aloud from it. On the trip to that resort, Charlie was accompanied by a young woman photographer, Terry, a friend of his and Beth's. She saw and heard just as much as Charlie did, yet she is not liquidated, and is allowed to leave the country. Two young Americans who seem to be involved in publishing an anti-Pinochet newspaper are arrested; one is released after some torture, the other is killed.

The latter is the cockier of the two, but I would still like to know more about the reasons for the disparity in their fates.

There are also two serious moral difficulties. One is the very strong implication that no American citizen could have been executed without the tacit, or not so tacit, approval of our embassy or consular staff. This is an exceedingly serious charge, and the case the film makes for it is not compelling enough. The other is the emphasis of the plot, which, for sound enough dramatic reasons, is forced into an ethical embarrassment: it must make the survival of one American seem infinitely more important than that of countless Chileans. Oh, and one more minor complaint: a top villain is referred to as Admiral Huidobro. Now, Vicente Huidobro was one of Chile's—the world's—great lyric poets; couldn't another name have served for this unsavory purpose?

Still, the film is, I repeat, impressive in its controlled but efficacious use of grimness and violence. In the writing, there are a few minor lapses, however. There is a coy passage drooling over Saint-Exupéry's overrated fable, *The Little Prince* (it could be meant ironically, to show the naïveté of Charlie and Beth, but I doubt if it is so intended); there is an obviously and derivatively symbolic white horse escaping along the postcurfew streets of nocturnal Santiago and being machine-gunned down for purely allegorical reasons; and there is the following brief but overloaded exchange during one of the searchers' weary collapses: "ED: What kind of world is this? BETH: You sound just like Charlie." In the son's horrible end, father and son are finally reconciled; yet death as the leveler of the generation gap is just a mite precious.

On the other hand, the growing understanding between Ed and Beth is developed with quiet simplicity, avoiding all stickiness. This is helped immeasurably by the understated yet potent performances of Jack Lemmon and Sissy Spacek in the leads, surrounded by an extremely effective supporting cast. There is first-rate, unattitudinizing cinematography by Ricardo Aronovich, and Françoise Bonnot's editing has hairline perfection. Whether or not you agree with its politics or historiography, *Missing* is not to be missed.

Another political film, Volker Schlöndorff's *Circle of Deceit*, is much smaller potatoes. Though it was shot in and around Beirut and has the authenticity of viciously ravaged locales, it manages to throw no light whatever on the Lebanese conflict. Slaughter and destruction become a mere framework for the trendily political, sexual, and existential agonizing of its boring foreign-correspondent protagonist. You seldom fathom just who is currently shooting at or executing whom, and for what precise reason, or how the German correspondent-hero's troubled marriage back home and quirky love affair in Beirut reflect or are influenced by the civil war.

The film, written by Schlöndorff and his equally pretentious and untalented wife, Margarethe von Trotta, along with Kai Hermann and the overrated Jean-Claude Carrière (from a novel by the late Nicolas Born), is sheer preposterous posturing, with hardly a shred of credibility in the story and characterizations. But Beirut is there, genuinely devastated and well   413 photographed by Igor Luther. Unlike *Missing, Circle of Deceit* insists on its being a work of fiction; yet it is its incidental, documentary aspects that give it a measure of harrowing memorableness.

March 19, 1982

The Start and End of the Road

BY FAR the most interesting French filmmakers today are Jean-Jacques Annaud and Bertrand Tavernier, both represented by current films. After his stunning debut with *Black and White in Color,* Annaud, who also made the pleasant but minor *Coup de tête,* now gives us *Quest for Fire,* a monumental recreation of prehistoric man, which, though loosely based on a novel by J. H. Rosny Sr. that Annaud and, as it happens, I relished as children, is largely his own idea as developed by his scenarist, Gérard Brach (*Repulsion, Tess*). Someday Annaud will write the story of the filming in Africa, Scotland, Canada, and, very nearly but finally not, Iceland. From what he told me, this would make a fabulous book; meanwhile, the film is no slouch, either.

Annaud did extensive research into various theories about early man, as well as into the life of modern aborigines; he also hired Anthony Burgess to reinvent an *ur*-Indo-European tongue, and Desmond Morris to provide a body language for the cavemen. Some of this yields amusing results, but the film is to be enjoyed principally not for the scientific or quasi-scientific baggage it carries, but for its scope and gusto.

It is the story of how a group of Ulam (primitive *Homo sapiens*), in a fight with the yet more primitive Wagabou, lose their precious fire, which they don't know how to make, and three Ulam warriors are sent out to seek new fire. There is Naoh, the sturdy and relatively sapient leader; there is Amoukar, the crude tough guy; and there is Gaw, the comic cut-up. Their hairy adventures with other tribes (the still simian, cannibalistic Kzamm; further fierce Wagabou; and the more advanced Ivaka—hut-dwellers, fire-makers, budding artisans) and encounters with ferocious animals (saber-toothed tigers, wolves, bears, mammoths) constitute the main story. And Naoh meets the Ivaka maiden Ika, loses Ika, wins Ika. She teaches him and his fellows how to laugh and make love, and, when the new, hard-won fire is lost too, how to make that. The Ulam are well on their way to true sapience.

There are faintly preposterous things here that are nevertheless droll, such as Ika teaching Naoh, who hitherto had sex only in the Ulam doggy fashion, the joys of the missionary position. And at the end, when Naoh and Ika, now a couple, sit outside the cave and watch alternately the full moon and Ika's swelling belly, one wonders: are they about to discover the principle of menstruation or of the wheel? But other discoveries are made more plausible, for

414

example the way the Ulam learn about laughter in two separate but cleverly connected sequences. And when the questers, at journey's end, become as loquacious as travel lecturers, this can at least be accepted as a symbolic adumbration of the birth of narrative.

On the whole, Annaud strikes a fine balance between ferocity—prehistory red in tooth and claw—and comic, romantic, or just visually spectacular episodes. The story progresses nicely across three seamlessly blended continents, across some eye-teasing and mouth-watering landscapes. The camera zooms, tracks, pans, and literally soars, enhanced by Claude Agostini's subtle cinematography, and only slightly impeded by Philippe Sarde's elephantine (or mammothlike) music, which does, however, have better moments, scored mostly for amplified recorder. Annaud's camera explores an earth that indeed hasn't changed in a mere eighty millennia; somehow he manages to convey the astonishment of eyes deciphering sights hitherto unseen, and even, as it were, the amazement of places and things at being unveiled for the first time. Yet this pristine loveliness is not a riot of colors: it tends to be misty, subdued; in some of the most striking shots, almost monochrome. The scenery has not yet learned to wear make-up.

But the make-up of men and animals—especially the prehistoric faces with their cantilevered brows—is magnificent, although the mammoths do look a bit like elephants clad in scatter rugs. What acting is called for is handled capably by Everett McGill, Rae Dawn Chong, Ron Perlman, and Nameer El Kadi; others, in lesser roles, gibber, menace, or maul appropriately. *Quest for Fire* may not be a work of art, but its thorough artistry should give children and adults pleasure and something to think about as they find themselves on the same elusive road to discovery as their distant forebears.

Bertrand Tavernier's *A Week's Vacation* is not up to his best earlier films—*The Clockmaker, Let Joy Reign Supreme, The Judge and the Murderer*—but it has most of the director's characteristic virtues in, if anything, overabundance. Tavernier makes "personal films," which is to say he lets things happen in them more or less as they did in life to him or his friends; more important, he responds to and evaluates these relatively humdrum events according to a very specific Tavernier sensibility, which always perceives the droll and the heartbreaking, the sensible and the absurd as inevitably inextricable. In these films, moreover, the spoken word is as brilliant and important as the visual imagery, and speaking (whether to communicate or to fail to do so) becomes as necessary and sacred as eating and making love. But the marvelous dialogue is also used cinematically: as cascades or clusters of sound, as a kind of spoken background music, as cries for help; or it turns, abruptly or insidiously, into silences that extend speech farther inward.

A Week's Vacation, written by Tavernier, his ex-wife, Colo, and Marie-Françoise Hans, has virtually no plot. Laurence, a young Lyons schoolteacher, lives with Pierre, a real-estate agent and amateur photographer, who is a compulsive jokester but also a charming lover and friend. One day she suffers a kindergarten version of a nervous breakdown and decides to 415 play hooky for a week, during which she sees her doctor about sedatives; talks to colleagues and pupils; frequents Mancheron, the restaurateur-father of her most troublesome student; returns to Beaujolais to visit her parents (her dad is not very well); sometimes makes love to Pierre, sometimes refuses to; and, generally, tries to understand the purpose of her work and life. Though there are small surprises scattered throughout, there are no major revelations; if there is one, it concerns Anne, Laurence's fellow teacher and friend, rather than Laurence herself.

Take two examples of how the film works. Across the street from our heroine lives an unknown old woman; periodically, most often when depressed, Laurence looks through the two windows that separate them and sees the crone knitting, reading, or just staring into space. The old woman seems to be totally alone yet also resigned; she seems to convey to Laurence that life can be worse than hers and still endurable. When this visual refrain returns once more at the end of the film, the woman's window is shuttered, and sadness floods Laurence and us. To Anne, she remarks that she never noticed the woman until this week, and doesn't know what happened to her. "One day she was gone. Perhaps she moved. She never had any visitors." The camera discreetly cuts away, but both Laurence and we know where people who never have visitors move to.

Or Laurence goes for a brief stay with her parents. Pierre William Glenn's canny photography now changes from the mostly cool, misty Lyons palette to a country glow that is warm and almost overripe—as if someone had spilled some Beaujolais over the lens or the world. The entire episode is quietly moving, but especially so the farewell from the by now bedridden and taciturn father. As Laurence presses her head against him, the old man (a lovely performance by Jean Dasté) mutters—more to himself than to her, and still more to the universe: "I know so many things . . . So many things . . ." The scene, as written, acted, directed, and edited, is one of the rare moments of perfection in world cinema.

The film makes some highly pertinent visual and verbal observations on the teacher-student conflict, and ingeniously brings in commentaries from before and after. There are excerpts on the soundtrack from the first papers of very young children, and there are school reminiscences of older people— notably from the wonderful Philippe Noiret, who appears briefly as the character he played in *The Clockmaker*. Thus Laurence's quandary, although somewhat vague and never fully resolved, gains illumination from the context: a world with too many possibilities, phenomena, choices for most people to pick from with any confidence.

One other sequence. Pierre has prepared a nice dinner for Laurence and himself, with candlelight and champagne, but she returns so late that he has fallen asleep in his armchair. She squats by the coffee table and eats voraciously while gazing at him with gratitude but also compassion and guilt: if she doesn't wake him up, it is mostly to avoid having sex with him. It is a tiny scene: sweet, sad, beautiful. *A Week's Vacation*, in which the excellent Nathalie Baye, Gérard Lanvin, Michel Galabru, and Flore Fitzgerald head a fine cast, is whimsical, touching, and quite unpredictable—like life when it is

416

nost like itself. Thus it lacks a certain structure and narrative propulsion, out certainly not wisdom and charm.

April 30, 1982

Crime With Discrimination

CAN SELDOM follow the intricacies of a complicated gangster movie, and if much of the language is, as here, Cockney, I am doubly lost. Nevertheless, *The Long Good Friday*—a British gangster picture that in some ways espouses and in others transcends its genre—is so clearly a superior piece of craftsmanhip as to make complaints about its less than total comprehensibility (or, indeed, credibility) seem almost petty cavils. There is so much authenticity of atmosphere, authority of direction, and veracity of acting as to satisfy something more primeval than the craving for pellucid logic.

The initial sequences, to be sure, make wildly inordinate demands on us. Not only do we begin *in medias res* with a vengeance, we begin in several *res* simultaneously through crosscutting, and I defy any viewer, especially a non-British one, to fathom what is happening, or even remember enough of it to make sense of it retroactively. But once past this hurdle, and despite occasional others, we can race along with the film's visual, verbal, and histrionic pyrotechnics and revel in the basic intelligence and technical prowess.

Harold Shand has become London's almost benevolent criminal overlord, and is about to go respectable. Besides owning all manner of clubs, casinos, restaurants, and such, he is about to build, along a slum-lined stretch of the Thames, a huge marina, Olympic stadium, hotel, and shopping complex; a Mafia boss and his lawyer have come from New York to underwrite part of he project. A marvelous party on Harold's yacht at the proposed site is presided over by Victoria, Harold's spunky mistress, but bad news erupts on his Good Friday. A homosexual lieutenant of Harold's has been stabbed to death at a public swimming pool, Harold's Rolls and chauffeur were blown to bits moments before his mother came out of church to get into the car, another explosion guts a fancy pub Harold owns just as he and his American guests are arriving for dinner, and nobody—not his men, not the crooked cop who protects him, not various lesser gangsters whom he hangs upside down from meathooks in an abbatoir among the sides of beef—can tell Harold who is doing this to him.

Harold's hegemony is at stake; so is the deal with the progressively more estive American mobsters. A ten years' gangland peace has been broken, with no new mob powerful enough to be the possible cause. Alas, I cannot ell you more of the plot, which, in turn, makes cogent comments impossible. I can say, however, that the film turns—almost imperceptibly, which is to its credit—into a provocative moral and political allegory, as grim as it is amus-   417 ing. And, though brutal, the violence is managed with artistry, almost with taste.

John Mackenzie, a director fresh out of television, handles some standard devices such as zooms, matching shots, and racked focus with great finesse and has a splendid eye for grotesque, macabre, or merely picturesque details. The script by Barry Keeffe, one of England's better young playwrights, is literate as well as cunning and earthy. The acting is impeccable down to the tiniest role, with Helen Mirren remarkable as the tough and clever yet not invulnerable Victoria, and Bob Hoskins spectacular as Harold, managing to be at once flamboyant and understated, ruthlessly intelligent and believably purblind. A criminal Everyman, his downfall has something epic, if not eschatological, about it.

Garde à Vue, translated as *Under Suspicion* though it means preventive detention, is a curiously, maddeningly mixed bag. Based on a British crime novel but transposed into a French port city, it takes place on a heavily rainy New Year's Eve on which a wealthy, middle-aged lawyer, Maître Martinaud, until now a witness, is rapidly becoming the prime suspect in two related cases of child rape and murder. While the police commissioner and his guests make merry in another wing of the headquarters building, and as rain beats down on the windows, Martinaud is being questioned by the clever, tough, cynical Inspector Gallien, whose obtuse and sadistic colleague, Belmont, ineptly takes down the proceedings on a typewriter and often stops to interject his own brutish sarcasms. Although Martinaud is being worn down by Gallien's cunning strategy—and, in Gallien's temporary absence, by Belmont's punches and kicks—he is a man of intelligence, courage, and spiritual strength, although clearly undermined by a sense of guilt. But guilt (and I am hardly giving away anything herewith) of a rather different sort from the one for which he is being tormented.

The plot is contrived and unconvincing, and though there is much alluding to various perversions—some guessable, some not—mostly by Martinaud's hate-filled wife, the characters are not honestly examined or authentically individualized. But there is extremely snappy dialogue by Michel Audiard, bravura editing by Albert Jurgenson, solid cinematography by Bruno Nuytten, and clever but untricky direction by Claude Miller. Even if most of the action (but not, procrusteanly, all) is confined to one depersonalized office, Miller manages to keep the story moving in unstagy, unostentatious fashion. And although Romy Schneider gives a routine performance as the wife, the three main actors are superb. As Gallien, Lino Ventura conveys a world of conflicting emotions from behind a nearmarmoreal countenance; Guy Marchand makes Belmont's beastliness comic and self-righteous, and thus infinitely more horrible; and Michel Serrault is a miraculous Martinaud. A Gordian knot of the good and bad, strong and weak, tragic and ridiculous, he wittily, touchingly, overwhelmingly builds a characterization that reeks of tangled, tortured, yet ultimately transcendent humanity.

Undivine Diva, Nondelving Devil

In "An Essay on Fashionable Literature" (1818), Thomas Love Peacock observed: "The moral and political character of the age or nation may be read by an attentive observer even in its lightest literature, how remote soever *prima facie* from morals and politics." And how much more about the moral and political tenor of our time is revealed when an absurd, campy, laughable film such as *Diva*, by Jean-Jacques Beineix, wins numerous awards in France and is hailed in the U.S.A. by the enthusiastic nod of Pauline Kael, which activates the domino theory: from coast to coast, her critical acolytes fall over backward in admiration.

Diva concerns a messenger boy and opera buff, Jules, who covertly tapes a recital by his adored Cynthia Hawkins, a black American soprano, by means of a Nagra he has sneaked into the dilapidated theater in which she is appearing. Behind him sit two sharkish Taiwanese entrepreneurs who want that tape: by threatening her to distribute it illegally, they could coerce Miss Hawkins into signing a recording contract with them.

Let's stop right here. Miss Hawkins is backed up by an orchestra at her recital, which is unlikely; the hall in which she sings seems to be crumbling before our very eyes, which is unlikelier yet. (It is Peter Brook's Bouffes du Nord Theater in Paris; but no musicians would brook such theatrical reverse snobbery.) And how does a poor messenger boy get to own a Nagra, a gadget so expensive that many a lesser radio station cannot afford one? And what about all the other goodies we see in Jules's digs later on? How does he smuggle this large object into the concert? And how come no one but the Taiwanese notices his taping—is this the fall of the house ushers?

Furthermore, has there ever been an opera diva averse to having her income supplemented and her voice extended into posterity by signing a recording contract? No so, it seems, the purist Cynthia, whose perfectionism boggles at disks. Yet singers tend to sound better on recordings, just as Wilhelmenia Wiggins Fernandez sounds better as Cynthia in the film than she did as Musetta recently at the New York City Opera. And what about those crooks from Taiwan? If Jules could sneak in his Nagra, couldn't they have done likewise? Couldn't they be turned over to the police for attempted blackmail? Could they actually market a pirated recording, especially from Taiwan? And couldn't they have stripped Jules of his tape right outside the concert hall, instead of having to pursue him with difficulty later?

Yet this is only the beginning of the subplot of *Diva;* the main plot concerns another tape, which could blow the lid off a narcotics and vice ring headed by a top Paris police inspector. This tape is tossed into Jules's motorbike bag without his knowing it by a call girl just before she is killed by the inspector's henchmen. So Jules will presently be chased by two very different batches of villains, but he will also be watched over by Gorodish, an eccentric millionaire, and Alba, his teenaged Vietnamese girl friend. Gorodish lives in a sumptuous, modernistic loft, where he mostly works on a giant jigsaw puzzle when not rescuing Jules from sticky wickets; Alba roller-skates in the loft when not shoplifting pop records.

The plot, besides treating serious matters with offensive campiness, makes no sense at all, but allows Beineix to stage a variety of preposterous sequences such as the one in which a policeman on foot chases Jules up and down the stairs and along the corridors of the Métro, without anyone's noticing or interfering—scenes "so ravishing," according to Pauline Kael, "that they're funny, intentionally." (Analyze that, if you will and can.) Even higher peaks of absurdity are extolled by her as "dreamy-disco fun in the detritus of tech commercialism"; "every shot," she says, "seems designed to delight the audience," which is to equate stinking to please the unwashed with artistic virtue. "The entire movie," Miss Kael raves on, "demonstrates the richness you can get only from movies," which is the kind of perspective-less chauvinism that even today should not be allowed to pass for thought.

The characters, it seems, "charm us because they arrange their reality to suit their whims," which describes the vicious police inspector to perfection; "they're un-self-conscious about being self-conscious," which, if it is indeed feasible, must mean carrying chichi chic to the point of nausea. Sure enough, the fourteen-year-old Thuy An Luu, an ex-ice-cream-parlor waitress, who plays Alba, is praised for her "fundamental indifference" in front of a camera; as for Miss Fernandez, her "American-accented French and her amateurishness as an actress are ingratiating." Actually, the singer looks bovine, expresses little or nothing, and acts in a way for which "amateurish" is a term of unearned praise. But none of this fazes Miss Kael: "Beineix might be Carol Reed reborn with a Mohawk haircut"; the metempsychosis continues: he is also "Welles romanticized, gift-wrapped."

As supreme praise, Beineix is pronounced to be one who "thinks with his eyes," leaving in doubt what part of the anatomy Miss Kael uses for that purpose. When criticism, here and abroad, sinks to this level, it tells us a good deal about our age, "how remote soever," in Peacock's eloquent tmesis, its subject may be from matters of importance.

I am sad to be unable to affirm that István Szabó's *Mephisto* is very much better—not because it won the Oscar for best foreign film, not because it is freely derived from a novel by Thomas Mann's son, and not because some of Szabó's earlier films struck me as deserving. Rather, I deplore the missed chance in this film, based as it is (however loosely) on the life of the great German actor-director Gustaf Gründgens, to provide insight into why and how artists collaborate with totalitarian regimes. Szabó and his coscenarist, Péter Dobai, trot out the usual reasons—egocentric self-absorption, indifference to other people's needs, dependence on one's own language and consequent handicaps abroad—without examining them very closely. They advert more to the protagonist's, Hendrik Höfgen's, lust for fame and power, and to his being entrusted by the Nazis with the management of the Berlin Staatstheater. But they do not answer the master question: Why would a man of Höfgen's virtues—which, though lesser than his vices, are not negligible—put up with the frustrations and humiliations, the severe limitations accompanying this power?

I haven't read Klaus Mann's *roman à clef,* but can, from what I know of it and Gründgens's life, deduce a relation between Gründgens-Höfgen's homosexuality and the Fascist cult of the superman, which the film bypasses. Szabó has stated that so many such connections having already been made, he aimed instead for greater things, such as universality. But Höfgen is shown in a sadomasochist love relationship with Juliette, a half-German, half-black dancer (in the book, a depraved prostitute), whose entire persona, down to her style of dancing and leotards, is an anachronism. Through such improbable specifics, we do not reach the universal.

Szabó hints around about all kinds of unspecified kinkinesses, including suggestions of Höfgen's inversion, and even stronger ones about the lesbianism of both his wives. This vagueness swaths the film in a floating salaciousness that obstructs the shedding of light. And this Höfgen is merely a slapped-together *mélange* of bad, good, and bizarre traits that finally spell nothing. Moreover, Klaus Maria Brandauer, who plays him, overracts without much distinction, and, especially in the interpolated excerpts from Gründgens's stage roles, falls far short of the master as I remember him.

The film leaves us cold. None of the characters, victims or victimizers, elicits genuine compassion, fear, or involvement—with the exception of the Göring figure, played with subtle menace and considerable complexity by Rolf Hoppe. He at least conveys a network of not entirely simplistic thoughts and feelings under the glossy surface that is all we get from the others. And the film groans under an excess of second-rate dialogue—and monologue—often accompanied by extreme closeups of inert or, in the case of Brandauer, twitchy faces. The dubbing of the largely Hungarian cast into German is awkward, the costuming lackluster, and there are oodles of unattractive women not helped by poor hairstyling. Lajos Koltai's cinematography lacks definition, and *Mephisto* has been cut for American release by at least twenty minutes, which harms the continuity. A couple of good, strong scenes remain, but they only underscore the mediocrity of the rest.

June 25, 1982

Comedy of Bad Manners

THERE IS REJOICING in heaven—and certainly on earth—when a new cinema takes off, as the Australian one has been doing for the last few years. Where, for a long time, there was next to nothing, suddenly there are movies with wings to circle the earth, directors to hearken to and gape at. Though the most popular of the new filmmakers, Peter Weir (*Picnic at Hanging Rock, The Last Wave, Gallipoli*), is also the most absurdly overrated, there are Fred

421

Schepisi and Bruce Beresford, each with at least one masterwork to his name, and several others who bear pleasurable watching and waiting for. Now we have an earlier Beresford film, *Don's Party* (1976), finally reaching us, and although it is not quite a *Breaker Morant,* it is a damned absorbing piece of work.

The time is October 25, 1969, in a suburb in Sydney, on the night of the general election. Gough Whitlam's Labor party has an excellent chance of upsetting the long-incumbent Liberal party (actually the conservatives) through a coalition of labor, the intelligentsia, and the radical fringe of the bourgeoisie. Nevertheless, as we see on a television screen in Don's house early on, John Grey Gorton, the leader of the Liberal party, is confident of victory almost to the point of cockiness. Don, an easygoing teacher and would-be novelist, and Kath, his put-upon but coping wife, are giving a party to watch their party—Labor—win the election. In the event, Labor loses, and Don's party is a fiasco: marriages, relationships, even the house and surrounding garden are wrecked, or nearly; in a strange, funny-sad way it is as if Australia were reaffirming its bumbling, crassly subaltern status on both political and social levels, its postcolonial and postcoital lassitude.

At the party, liquor and lechery overflow their banks; but the sex is un-fulfilled or unfulfilling, and the verities the booze flushes out of their hiding are anything but comforting. No one is what he pretends to be, nothing is as it seems: every marriage or other nexus is worse than it appears, though each appears pretty bad. The relationships—like that between Cooley, the lawyer and lecher, and his date, the nineteen-year-old vaguely bisexual nymphomaniac Susan—are all equally precarious. The marriage between the bright but fatuous Mal, a psychologist who has flunked out of academe into business, and his smart but plain wife, Jenny, is sustained only by the money they can make or borrow and spend. Even the great galumphing bonding among the men friends is merely a spurious chumminess glossing over envy, vindictiveness, and radiant gloating over every setback your buddy incurs.

It is hard to convey the remarkable quality of *Don's Party:* call it a steady laughter out of the wrong side of the mouth. Based on a play by David Williamson, Australia's premier playwright—who, in turn, based it on the breakup of his own marriage—the film is kindred in spirit to our own *Who's Afraid of Virginia Woolf?* But despite a few lesbian overtones, it is a raucously heterosexual world, in a cannily crafted microcosmic shape, that is here going to the dogs—relatively harmless dogs, if you like, their bite almost totally superseded by their bark. But the displaced bite, lodged in the en-vious, rancorous, and (in most cases) benighted brain, wreaks its devastation inward. And its food—its soul food—is failure.

How these characters chomp, suck, feast on failure! Not, to be sure, their own failures—as when Evan, the scowling dentist, discovers Cooley humping Kerry, his artsy, provoking wife, or when Mal finds himself coolly rejected by this same Kerry—but the failures of others: spouses or lovers, best friends or even someone barely met and known just well enough to feel superior to. Even Kath, the hard-working, sensible wife and manifestly caring mother

422

(to a baby saturninely oblivious to the chaos around it), derives a perverse thrill from watching Cooley get a beating from Evan—well deserved, but still quite barbarous. And how all the rest lap up spats between other couples, how they gobble up alien misery as if it were finger sandwiches.

Not that there are finger sandwiches at Don's party. There are unsubtle pizzas, bulky sausages that get burned while Don, the cook, dallies with Susan, the teenaged cookie, and lots of junk food that is spilled on the floor along with dashed sexual hopes. The wit is funny, very funny, but it is administered with a bludgeon or, in rare moments of refinement, with a broadsword. The rapier and stiletto are reserved for Williamson's ironies and Beresford's direction. It isn't easy to make a movie out of a play, a movie almost wholly confined to a small house and garden, but Beresford and his gifted cameraman, Don McAlpine, make the constricted area into a mighty, multifarious battleground; if necessary, they use even the pictures on the wall to extend and comment on the infighting.

They picked a real house and coaxed the available space to create oddly dislocating perspectives through cunning camera angles, dizzyingly varied atmosphere through jaunty changes of décor from room to room. Thus pipe-smoking Simon, the plodding political neutralist who works in plastics, often watches his blond, blandly Liberal party wife, Jody, being drawn into more interesting conversations with other men; here racked focus and an occasional zoom shot work wonders in positing distances and differences between people in physical proximity. And the way Simon keeps popping up suddenly in camera range, or the way he is maneuvered into corners, and how he is once even wedged through a gauntlet of hanging lamps—these are marvelously graphic ways of establishing his fifth-wheelishness. When forced to leave without his wife, he rouses himself to whatever dignity and contempt he can muster in his ghastly safari outfit, and hurls this impotent Parthian shot: "I must say I didn't realize that university-educated people could be so bloody uncouth!" Though the others laugh derisively, there is a wistful, bottom-line truth to the remark.

Yet it is this very uncouthness that drives his oh-so-refined Jody into attempted sex with the vulgarian Mack, who wears a metal mug on a chain around his neck—a latter-day Prometheus chained to the thing that eats his liver—and who, at one point, enacts a particularly Rabelaisian pantomime. But Mack passes out when expected to perform; it is as if Labor could never hit it off with the Liberal party, let alone get on top of it. Says Jody: "There is nothing wrong with a discussion, but I don't think people should argue with people they don't agree with." *There* is true genteelness for you, and there, if you will, is the end of the two-party system. And, true enough, the eleven partyers discuss very little; they chiefly needle, insult, and jocundly humiliate one another. When Kerry, the languorously sensual, provokingly supercilious wife of the teeth-on-edge dentist, decides (having icily turned down the smug and horny Mal) to bed down with Cooley, she does so virtually in a spirit of condescension, ironically challenging him to prove his virility—if he can.

Beresford's direction abounds in splendidly assured touches. Thus when

Cooley and Kerry are about to hit the sack, he crosscuts between them, undressing. At a frantic pace and in extreme closeup, a male and female garment are alternately torn off, the man and woman each stripping him or herself. Appropriately, this creates frenzy without eroticism. Or when Susan and all the men except Simon end up skinnydipping in the neighbors' pool, Don, even more sanguine than the others, has jumped in with his untoward tuxedo and brown shoes on. Beresford shoots from below water level, and by mixing the nude bodies with the one ludicrously attired one, and by showing only headless bodies, conveys magisterially the farce of sex without its force. And what flawlessly foolish, dazzlingly piteous performances he has obtained from all.

As the film progresses toward its sobering conclusion, Don, the teacher whose novel never got finished, and Mal, the academician who lapsed into capitalist commerce despite his vociferous socialism—two best friends—taunt each other ever more drunkenly and destructively, though always in the guise of friendly kidding: "Now, don't take this as an insult, fellow, but you're a stupid turd." Crapulously, they offer each other their respective wives, right under the latters' indignant noses. When the wives angrily refuse, the men, lacking even the courage of their swinishness, pretend it was all a joke. By this time, the camera has long since given up switching periodically to the TV screen for election news; Labor has lost, love's (and lust's) labor's lost, and the world is well lost. When, at dawn, Kath, holding the baby, summons Don, who is inspecting the ravaged garden, to bed, the image does not promise. After such knowledge, what forgiveness? On the soundtrack, we hear a melancholy piano entoning Janáček's lovely "In the Mist."

Yes, Australia lies befogged. When Susan, nineteen, could calmly walk up to Kath, working in the kitchen, and ask permission to go to bed with her husband—there was such a wonderful feeling between them—Kath only stared back in wordless bewilderment until the camera mercifully cut away. It has come to that at the antipodes, where pioneer decencies might still have been supposed to hold sway. What hope, then, for the rest of us? Australia has become the world; the world is Australia.

August 6, 1982

Index

427

432

433

437

439

LEARNING RESOURCES
CENTER

ILLINOIS CENTRAL COLLEGE
MCMLXVI

East Peoria, Illinois